Language, Logic, and Concepts

John Macnamara

Language, Logic, and Concepts

Essays in Memory of John Macnamara

edited by Ray Jackendoff,
Paul Bloom, and
Karen Wynn

A Bradford Book
The MIT Press
Cambridge, Massachusetts
London, England

First MIT Press paperback edition, 2002
© 1999 Massachusetts Institute of Technology

This book was set in Times New Roman by Asco Typesetters, Hong Kong and was printed and bound in the United States of America.

Library of Congress Cataloging-in-Publication Data

Language, logic, and concepts : essays in memory of John Macnamara
 / edited by Ray Jackendoff, Paul Bloom, and Karen Wynn.
    p.   cm.
  Includes bibliographical references and index.
  ISBN 0-262-10078-9 (hc : alk. paper), 0-262-60046-3 (pb)
   1. Cognitive psychology. 2. Psycholinguistics. 3. Logic.
I. Macnamara, John Theodore. II. Jackendoff, Ray. III. Bloom, Paul,
1963– IV. Wynn, Karen.
BF201.L36   1999
153—dc21   98-47084
                                                                CIP

Contents

Contributors   vii

Introduction   ix
Ray Jackendoff, Paul Bloom, and
Karen Wynn

Publications of John Macnamara   xix

Chapter 1

Language and Nationalism   1   Richard Kearney

Chapter 2

Meaning and Misconceptions   15   Anil Gupta

Chapter 3

On Structuralism in Mathematics   43   Michael Makkai

Chapter 4

**The Natural Logic of Rights and
Obligations**   67   Ray Jackendoff

Chapter 5

**Deliberation Reasons and Explanation
Reasons**   97   Storrs McCall

Chapter 6

**Truth and Its Negation: Macnamara's
Analysis of the Place of Logic in a
Cognitive Psychology**   109   David R. Olson

Chapter 7

**Names of Things and Stuff: An
Aristotelian Perspective**   119   Sandeep Prasada

Chapter 8

The Unity of Science and the   Steven Davis
Distinction among Syntax, Semantics,
and Pragmatics   147

Chapter 9

Scientific Theories That Unconceal   Leslie Margaret Perrin McPherson
Being: Intentions and Conceptions in
Their Genesis   161

Chapter 10

The Nature of Human Concepts: Steven Pinker and Alan Prince
Evidence from an Unusual
Source   221

Chapter 11

Some Evidence for Impaired   Myrna Gopnik
Grammars   263

Chapter 12

The Role of Semantics in Solving the   Paul Bloom
Bootstrapping Problem   285

Chapter 13

Sortals and Kinds: An Appreciation of   Susan Carey and Fei Xu
John Macnamara   311

Chapter 14

Semantics and the Acquisition of   D. Geoffrey Hall
Proper Names   337

Chapter 15

The Learning of First and Second   Yuriko Oshima-Takane
Person Pronouns in English   373

Chapter 16

Kinship and Mathematical   F. William Lawvere
Categories   411

Chapter 17

Count Nouns, Mass Nouns, and Their   Marie La Palme Reyes, John
Transformations: A Unified Category-   Macnamara, Gonzalo E. Reyes, and
Theoretic Semantics   427   Houman Zolfaghari

Index   453

Contributors

Paul Bloom
Department of Psychology
University of Arizona
bloom@u.arizona.edu

Susan Carey
Department of Psychology
New York University
sc50@is6.nyu.edu

Steven Davis
Department of Philosophy
Simon Fraser University
sdavis@sfu.ca

Myrna Gopnik
Department of Linguistics
McGill University
inmg@musicb.mcgill.ca

Anil Gupta
Department of Philosophy
Indiana University
agupta@indiana.edu

D. Geoffrey Hall
Department of Psychology
University of British Columbia
geoff@cortex.psych.ubc.ca

Ray Jackendoff
Program in Linguistics and
Cognitive Science
Brandeis University
jackendoff@binah.cc.brandeis.edu

Richard Kearney
Department of Philosophy
University College Dublin
rkearney@ollamh.ucd.ie

F. William Lawvere
Department of Mathematics
State University of New York at
Buffalo
wlawvere@acsu.buffalo.edu

Michael Makkai
Department of Mathematics
McGill University
makkai@triples.math.mcgill.ca

Storrs McCall
Department of Philosophy
McGill University
mccall@dep.philo.mcgill.ca

Leslie Margaret Perrin McPherson
Cripple Creek, Colorado
lmpm@oldcolo.com

David Olson
Ontario Institute for Studies in
Education
University of Toronto
dolson@oise.utoronto.ca

Yuriko Oshima-Takane
Department of Psychology
McGill University
yuriko@hebb.psych.mcgill.ca

Steven Pinker
Department of Brain and
Cognitive Sciences
Massachusetts Institute of
Technology
steve@psyche.mit.edu

Sandeep Prasada
Department of Psychology
Dartmouth College
prasada@dartmouth.edu

Alan Prince
Department of Linguistics
Rutgers University
prince@ruccs.rutgers.edu

Gonzalo E. Reyes
Department of Mathematics and
Statistics
University of Montreal
reyes@mathcn.umontreal.ca

Marie La Palme Reyes
Montreal, Quebec
reyes@mathcn.umontreal.ca

Karen Wynn
Department of Psychology
University of Arizona
wynn@u.arizona.edu

Fei Xu
Department of Psychology
Northeastern University
fxu@neu.edu

Houman Zolfaghari
Montreal, Quebec
hzolfaghari@micro-intel.com

Introduction

Ray Jackendoff, Paul Bloom, and Karen Wynn

It is with a deep sense of gratitude and humility that we offer this collection of essays in memory of John Macnamara by his students, colleagues, and friends. The essays speak eloquently to the intellectual influence he had on all of us, but it is seemly that we begin with John himself.

John grew up in County Limerick, Ireland, and spent the early part of his adult life as a member of the Vincentian community. He taught at Castleknock and at St. Patrick's College, Drumcondra. In 1963 he gained a doctorate from the University of Edinburgh. His controversial research findings cast doubt on the value of some of the educational priorities of postindependence Ireland; they were published in a book entitled *Bilingualism and Primary Education*. In 1966 John moved to Canada, where he became Professor of Psychology at McGill University, a post he held till the end of his life in 1996.

John's intellectual impact in the period after he came to McGill was as a scholar in the study of the mind and how it develops. Before reviewing some of the contributions he made in different areas of psychology, it is important to understand his broader intellectual commitments. These pervade his work and are themselves interesting and important.

There is a tendency for psychologists to conclude that the human mind is really quite simple. Psychologists influenced by the ideas of Watson and Skinner have long argued that thinking and learning can be explained through a few basic laws. Some reductionists believe that psychological phenomena can be entirely accounted for in terms of principles of biology

We are grateful to John's wife Joyce for her assistance in writing this introduction. Some paragraphs are adapted from a previously published essay by Paul Bloom. We also wish to thank Albert Bregman for his assistance and encouragement in the initial stages of developing this volume.

and chemistry. Many contemporary scholars are entranced with the idea that the mind works like a computer (according to some, a rather uncomplicated computer). And surely, it is often said, we only need a simple theory to account for the inner workings of a child—who is, after all, a quite simple creature!

In John's writings, one finds the sometimes unfashionable conviction that the mind of the child is extraordinarily rich and complex. He begins his 1982 book *Names for Things* by noting that psychologists typically ignore the complexity of language learning—at the cost of not being able to explain it. His favorite example, as will be seen throughout this volume, was that something as apparently simple as learning the name of a dog requires considerable mental resources. For instance, children must be able to appreciate the intentions of others. The 2-year-old must realize that when an adult uses the name "Freddie" in certain contexts, he or she intends it to refer to the dog and nothing else. Children must also possess certain logical resources. The child has to understand how this new word "Freddie" relates to other parts of speech, such as the common noun "dog" and the adjective "brown," and how it contributes to the meanings of the sentences that it appears in. Perhaps most importantly, children can use words to refer: to a real animal for a proper name like "Freddie," to an abstract kind for a common noun like "dog," and to different kinds of entities altogether when it comes to words like "two" and "Santa Claus." John argued that explaining the child's learning and understanding of language requires a psychology that includes notions such as intentionality, reference, and truth. This means that psychology and philosophy are more related than many would have thought. It also means that a complete theory of the mind cannot be found in the fields of biology and computer science, as such sciences cannot capture these essential properties of our mental life.

The implications of this perspective can be pursued through three related aspects of John's research: his studies of language learning, his contributions to the debate over the nature of child development, and his work on a psychology of ideals—only a minority of his writings. In all the best ways, John had the style of a nineteenth-century intellectual. He wrote about an extraordinary variety of topics, from the nature of free will to the demise of Freudian psychoanalysis to what formal logic has to say about the Holy Trinity. He also did not shy away from disagreement, and he was involved in productive and civil debate with scholars such as the philosopher Mario Bunge and the linguist Noam Chomsky.

Finally, he was one of the very few psychologists who isn't a chore to read. He wrote with style and wit, and most of his work was directed to the educated public; it was not crafted for a small group of fellow scholars.

In 1972 John published a classic article with the title "The Cognitive Basis of Language Learning in Infants." This article presented a proposal that has grown to be highly influential. John suggested that although there are important regards in which language learning is special, distinct from other sorts of learning that children succeed at, it also relies crucially on the child's general understanding of the situations in which sentences are used. He proposed that the child's learning of basic grammar (what is a noun and what is a verb, how words are ordered within a sentence, and so on) requires knowing what words and sentences mean, and how they correspond to the external world. In support of this perspective, John and two colleagues, Nancy Katz and Erika Baker, wrote their 1974 article, "What's in a Name? A Study of How Children Learn Common and Proper Names," which reported an amazing finding. Their experiments found that even 18-month-olds can use subtle linguistic cues, such as the grammatical difference between "This is wug" and "This is a wug," to learn proper names and common nouns. These two articles have had a substantial influence on the study of language, motivating considerable research seeking to better clarify the relationship between children's understanding of meaning and their learning of basic grammar.

After the publication of these articles, most of John's research into language focused on the learning of words. This work was first discussed at length in *Names for Things* and was subsequently elaborated in many articles and in two further books, *A Border Dispute: The Place of Logic in Psychology* (1986) and *The Logical Foundations of Cognition* (1994, edited in collaboration with Gonzalo Reyes). This research, some in collaboration with Gonzalo Reyes and Marie La Palme Reyes, focused on the logical foundation of the learning of proper names and common nouns. Consider again what a child must know in order to understand a proper name. One aspect of this knowledge is that this word follows a single object over time. Even if Freddie were to change color or lose a leg, he would still be Freddie. On the other hand, if he were to have a twin brother that looked just like him, this brother would not be Freddie. The name "Freddie" does not pick out all objects with a certain appearance; it picks out a unique dog, regardless of his appearance. The child must also have some understanding of what changes dogs can go through and still remain dogs, as well as what events would cause something to cease being a dog. More generally, John and his colleagues argued that understanding a proper name requires an appreciation of the kind that the named object belongs to.

At some level, this is all common sense. Who would doubt that Freddie would still be Freddie if he lost a leg, or that the word "Freddie" refers to the whole dog and not just to the head or the tail? This appreciation of the logic of names comes so naturally to us that it is easy to underestimate the richness of the logical resources required for this understanding. John and his colleagues developed an extensive theory of these resources and argued further that much of the knowledge that underlies the learning of proper names and common nouns cannot itself be learned. Children must be born with it.

This research has implications for a broader debate within developmental psychology. Jean Piaget and his followers argued that the minds of children are very different from those of adults. Whereas adults are capable of complicated logical thought, children are limited to thinking about specific events; they are incapable of abstraction. Adults can take the perspective of others, but children are egocentric and believe that their own perspective on the world is all there is. An adult is a moral being, but a child is a little Attila the Hun, lacking any real understanding of fairness or morality.

John was a central figure in this debate, arguing that this conception of development is mistaken. This is not to deny that children know a great deal less than adults or that they need nurturing and care in order for their moral and intellectual capacities to thrive. But John argued that children possess considerable resources to start with. To see this, one must explore (through logical analysis, supplemented with careful experiments) the sorts of things children are very good at. The learning of proper names has been discussed above; other examples include children's knowledge of logical terms like "some," their ability to understand and manipulate small numbers, their understanding of mental notions like pretending and forgetting, and the rich moral knowledge that is demonstrated in their everyday interactions with their parents and siblings.

For each of these domains, John's research poses the same challenge to developmental psychology. If children are so limited in their capacities, how is it that they know so much? If they have no logic, how can they successfully learn expressions of language that depend so crucially on logical notions? If they are egocentric, how is it that they learn the meanings of pronouns like "I" and "me," since learning these pronouns requires taking the perspectives of others? If they have no conception of fairness or morality, how is it that they understand a fairy tale like "Cinderella," which is impossible to appreciate without understanding that the stepmother is acting unfairly? All the evidence, John argued, leads to the conclusion that children possess a rich set of cognitive, logical, and moral capacities from the very start.

John also presented more general arguments against the view that children lack an appreciation of logic and morality. He noted that psychologists fond of this view have never explained how children come to acquire such capacities. Followers of Jean Piaget have appealed to "assimilation" and "accommodation," processes through which the child's primitive knowledge becomes more abstract through interaction with the environment. But in a 1976 article entitled "Stomachs Assimilate and Accommodate, Don't They?", John argued that these notions are empty metaphors that explain nothing. Along with the work of Jerry Fodor and Noam Chomsky, John's empirical and theoretical defense of the notion of innate ideas and capacities caused a major shift in the way psychologists think about the mind and its development.

The final aspect of John's work that we wish to mention is his proposal, first outlined in a 1990 article entitled "Ideals and Psychology," that an adequate psychology must explain the human capacity to understand ideals. A good example of this, discussed first by Descartes, lies in the domain of geometry. We all possess the notion of perfect geometric forms, such as a perfect triangle or a perfect point, but no such forms exist in nature and none ever will. Scientific progress is also based on ideals; physics would be nowhere without its frictionless plane and its perfect vacuum. Similarly, we have personal ideals that we aspire to, notions such as humility, friendship, and courage. As John put it, "Idealization is as natural to the mind as breathing to the body." But how is it that we come to appreciate such ideals, given that, by their very nature, they are not to be found in our experience?

In a 1991 article called "The Development of Moral Reasoning and the Foundations of Geometry," John provided a hint of what a psychology of ideals would look like. The article begins with a critical discussion of a well-known stage theory of moral development proposed by Jean Piaget and extended by Lawrence Kohlberg. John argued that this theory seriously underestimates children's knowledge, fails to describe adult moral competence, and does not explain how notions of morality actually develop and how supposedly amoral children grow into moral adults. John then proposed an alternative theory of moral development, based on an intriguing analogy between systems of morality and systems of geometry. In both domains, there exist ideal elements (in geometry, elements such as point and line; in morality, elements such as fair and good) that are related to one another through a system of axioms. John suggested that there are extensive unlearned elements within both geometry and morality. Children start off with an understanding of certain ideals in both domains, and these are the notions that all people share. But psychologists must also explain how new geometric and moral knowledge emerges in adults and children. New geometries have been developed by mathematicians, such as the non-Euclidean geometry proposed by Riemann in the nineteenth century, and new moral ideals have been introduced in the course of history, such as the ideal of chastity introduced by the Christians. How are these learned and understood? The parallel between geometry and morality places the study of moral development in a striking new light. It might be that the child who is coming to grasp a novel moral system is actually acquiring a coherent formal structure, complete with ideals and axioms, in much the same way he or she would learn a new system of geometry, or mathematics, or physics.

This article is not as well known as many of John's other works discussed above. (Perhaps the title scares people away!) But it is hard to think of a better work in developmental psychology. Although it is entirely accessible in style and content, it does not shy away from the hard questions. It is a significant intellectual accomplishment, but also something more, as it displays several properties typical of John's work. There is creativity, intellectual courage, and a strong curiosity about the workings of the world. Most of all, there is respect for its subject matter: the minds of young children and how they develop. It is more than an article about morality; it is itself a highly moral work.

For a closer look into John as a person, we quote from the eulogy by John's friend and collaborator Gonzalo Reyes. The essence that Gonzalo so beautifully evokes here strikes a familiar chord for anyone who knew John.

I first met John ten years ago when he gave a talk in the Mathematics Department at McGill in October 1985. He raised the question of giving a logical account of the phrase "Freddie is a dog" that children learn by the age of 18 months, claiming that logical theories were unable to account for it. To tell you the truth, I thought that he was mad: how can there be problems with that? But I found his talk so intriguing that I went to discuss it with him at the end. This was the beginning of a collaboration that developed into a close friendship and resulted in one of the most beautiful and rich periods of my life.

This talk at McGill was my first encounter with John's approach to intellectual matters: to ask basic simple questions to test theories or viewpoints and to demand straightforward answers. Of course this Socratic method enraged some people, but it delighted others, especially when he used it masterfully in his talks. He had a robust, realistic, no-nonsense attitude and no patience for idealistic views that he felt did not go to the heart of things. In this respect, he was like a brick, giving a sense of security to all of us. In fact, John was a man of profound convictions: he was deeply religious and deeply realist. Probably the thinker that was closest to his heart was Aristotle. At the beginning of our collaboration, I asked what I should read in psychology, and his answer was "Only *De Anima*."

Another aspect of John's approach to intellectual problems was the unity of his thought. I discovered with bewilderment that behind the dog Freddie stood none other than Plato, and behind the questions that looked so trivial at the beginning stood in fact a formidable problem, Plato's paradox of learning, which still haunts the venerable house of philosophy. And the answer to these questions appeared to John as a first step in creating a cognitive psychology that would be, as he put it, "worthy of its name." His talks were fascinating, with flashes that allowed us to catch a glimpse of this rich web of connections.

John died in a period that burst with creativity. He thought that the time was ripe to study the relations between perception and cognition, and he had started to work on this subject: his last talk was on "The Language of Vision." It is a tragedy (for us) that he did not live to complete at least part of this work. On the other hand, I do not believe that this is necessarily a tragedy for John: he died with lots of projects to realize and with a conviction of the importance of what he had done. He worked until his mind could no longer accompany him. On one occasion, shortly before his illness was discovered, he told me that people had asked him what he would do if he knew that he had only a month to live, and his answer was, "What I have always done." One day before the operation, we had a working session in the hospital. And only one and a half months before his death, John asked Marie Reyes to give him courses in logic, since he had missed so much of what was going on during his long illness.

It is impossible to talk about John without mentioning the importance that friendship had in his life. On one occasion I quoted a phrase of the great physicist James Clerk Maxwell: "Work is good and reading is good, but friends are better." John approved wholeheartedly. He had a large number of friends, as anybody who walked with him from the Faculty Club to the Psychology Department trying desperately not to miss a lecture can witness. Everybody in the street would stop and say, "Hi, John," and some chat would result. But we would always arrive on time: punctuality was a must with John.

If we ask why he attracted so many friends, part of the answer seems clear: he would welcome anybody who needed a reference or some advice on an academic subject or on a deep human problem. No subject was considered taboo or improper. I cannot forget his words when receiving somebody, either in his office or in his home, where he and Joyce would exert their generous hospitality: "You are most welcome." This renewed reception made us feel wholly accepted once again and we could open our hearts and laugh or cry according to the circumstances.

John was also a great entertainer. An amusing and compulsive talker, he would insert jokes of his own creation, some rather elaborate, about Descartes and other historical figures. He was very proud of them and would celebrate them with gusto, getting mad at the people who didn't laugh with him. He had a talent for reating limericks and he could play the flute and the banjo. He had other talents as well, some quite unexpected. I remember that some friends in Belgium invited us for dinner after John had given a beautiful lecture on Brentano and intentionality. After the dinner our friends' children asked John to play with them. John proposed a game of catching pieces of bread in the mouth, the pieces being thrown by a designated person. John's ability was extraordinary. Afterwards, he told us that he had once beaten a dog at this game (John was rather competitive).

But I believe that part of the explanation for the love he inspired lies also in the richness of his personality, which allowed different people to find different Johns, to find "their John." There was the religious man who shared his faith with Joyce through common readings and travels and by helping those in need. There was, most visibly, the academic John: the university man, sometimes the Herr Professor. On occasions he would take on a very solemn voice and finish off some suggestion of a student or an alternative theory with the words "This simply cannot be done..." But at the same time, this man who was a Fellow of the Royal Society of Canada would sit down with undergraduates in my course of elementary logic, and would bring his homework to my teaching assistant to fight with him for a better grade. Nothing is so touching for me as the sight of this distinguished man of over sixty going back to school to study logic and category theory because he believed that these were tools that a cognitive psychologist should know. "My" John is also John the student. In this context, I cannot forget his son Kieran's role as John's teacher: John told me how he could appreciate films that were at first foreign to his sensibility thanks to his son's efforts.

But I feel that I cannot enumerate, let alone do justice to, all the Johns that so many people loved and found so fascinating.... John: we will miss you ...

The essays in this volume are grouped roughly along thematic lines. We begin with Richard Kearney's remarks expanding on John's early work on language and ethnicity. This is followed by a series of chapters on the foundations of logic and concepts by Anil Gupta, Michael Makkai, Ray Jackendoff, Storrs McCall, David Olson, and Sandeep Prasada. Then comes an interlude of chapters on more philosophical topics by Steven Davis and Leslie McPherson, after which we turn more directly to the relation between language and conceptualization in chapters by Steven Pinker and Alan Prince, Myrna Gopnik, Paul Bloom, Susan Carey and Fei Xu, Geoffrey Hall, and Yuriko Oshima-Takane. We end with two chapters on mathematical approaches to cognition, one by William Lawvere and the other by John himself and his three dear colleagues Marie La Palme Reyes, Gonzalo Reyes, and Houman Zolfaghari.

This grouping, however, does not bring out the rich interconnections among the chapters and their relation to John's work. We leave the appreciation of these details to the reader.

Publications of
John Macnamara

Books

Macnamara, J. *Bilingualism and primary education: A study of Irish experience*. Edinburgh: Edinburgh University Press, 1966.

Macnamara, J. (Ed.). *Problems in bilingualism*. April issue of the *Journal of Social Issues,* 1967, *23*.

Madaus, G. F., and Macnamara, J. *Public examinations: A study of the Irish Leaving Certificate*. Dublin: St. Patrick's College, Educational Research Centre, 1970.

Macnamara, J. (Ed.). *Language learning and thought*. New York: Academic Press, 1977.

Macnamara, J. *Names for things: A study of human learning*. Cambridge, MA: MIT Press, 1982.

Macnamara, J. *A border dispute: The place of logic in psychology*. Cambridge, MA: MIT Press, 1986. Polish translation by Michal Zagrodzki. Warsaw: Wydawnictwo Nankowe PWN, 1993.

Macnamara, J., and Reyes, G. E. (Eds.). *The logical foundations of cognition*. New York: Oxford University Press, 1994.

Articles

Macnamara, J. The use of reason at the age of seven: Two contrasting views. *Irish Ecclesiastical Record,* 1961, *98,* 92–103.

Macnamara, J. The report of the Commission on Irish: Psychological aspects. *Studies,* 1964, *53,* 164–173.

Macnamara, J. Zero error and practice effects in Moray House English Quotients. *British Journal of Educational Psychology,* 1964, *34,* 315–320.

Macnamara, J. The problem solving difficulties of bilingual children.

Paper read at A.G.M. of Northern Ireland Branch of the British Psychological Society, January 1965. *Bulletin B.P.S.*, 1965, *18*, 60, 58–59 (Abstract).

Macnamara, J. The bilingual's linguistic performance: A psychological overview. *Journal of Social Issues*, 1967, *23*, 58–77.

Macnamara, J. The effects of instruction in a weaker language. *Journal of Social Issues*, 1967, *23*, 121–135.

Macnamara, J. The linguistic independence of bilinguals. *Journal of Verbal Learning and Verbal Behavior*, 1967, *6*, 729–736.

Kellaghan, T., and Macnamara, J. Reading in a second language. In M. D. Jenkinson (Ed.), *Reading instruction: An international forum* (pp. 231–240). Newark, DE: International Reading Association, 1967.

Macnamara, J., Feltin, M., Hew, M., and Klein, M. Analysis of difficulties of reading in a weaker language. *Irish Journal of Education*, 1968, *2*, 41–53.

Macnamara, J., Krauthammer, M., and Bolgar, M. Language switching in bilinguals as a function of stimulus and response uncertainty. *Journal of Experimental Psychology*, 1968, *78*, 208–215.

Lambert, W. E., and Macnamara, J. Some cognitive consequences of following a first-grade curriculum in a second language. *Journal of Educational Psychology*, 1969, *60*, 86–96.

Macnamara, J., and Madaus, G. F. Marker reliability in the Irish Leaving Certificate. *Irish Journal of Education*, 1969, *3*, 5–21.

Macnamara, J. How can one measure the extent of a person's bilingual capacity? In L. G. Kelly (Ed.), *Description and measurement of bilingualism* (pp. 80–97). Toronto: University of Toronto Press, 1969.

Kellaghan, T., Neuman, E., and Macnamara, J. Teachers' assessments of the scholastic progress of pupils. *Irish Journal of Education*, 1969, *3*, 95–104.

Macnamara, J., and Madaus, G. F. The quality of the Irish Leaving Certificate Examination. *Irish Journal of Education*, 1970, *4*, 5–18.

Macnamara, J. Bilingualism and thought. In J. E. Alatis (Ed.), Georgetown University. *21st Annual Round Table*, 1970, *23*, 25–40.

Macnamara, J. Comparative studies of reading and problem solving in two languages. *Tesol-Quarterly*, 1970, *4*(1–2), 107–116.

Macnamara, J. Parsimony and the lexicon. *Language*, 1971, *47*, 359–374.

Macnamara, J., and Kushnir, S. The linguistic independence of bilinguals: The input switch. *Journal of Verbal Learning and Verbal Behavior*, 1971, *10*, 480–487.

Macnamara, J. Successes and failures in the movement for the restoration of Irish. In J. Rubin and B. Jernudd (Eds.), *Can language be planned?* (pp. 65–94). Honolulu: University of Hawaii Press, 1971.

Macnamara, J. The cognitive basis of language learning in infants. *Psychological Review,* 1972, *79,* 1–13.

Macnamara, J. Perspectives on bilingual education in Canada. *Canadian Psychologist,* 1972, *13,* 341–349.

Macnamara, J., Kellaghan, T., and O'Cleirigh, A. The structure of the English lexicon: The simplest hypothesis. *Language and Speech,* 1972, *15,* 141–148.

Kellaghan, T., and Macnamara, J. Family correlates of verbal reasoning ability. *Developmental Psychology,* 1972, *7,* 49–53.

Macnamara, J. The objectives of bilingual education in Canada from an English-speaking perspective. In M. Swain (Ed.), *Bilingual schooling; some experiences in Canada and the United States. A report on the Bilingual Education Conference, Toronto, March 11–13, 1971* (pp. 7–10). Toronto: The Ontario Institute for Studies in Education, 1972.

Macnamara, J. On learning each other's languages. In P. Watson (Ed.), *Psychology and race* (pp. 393–402). London: Penguin, 1973.

Macnamara, J. Nurseries, streets and classrooms: Some comparisons and deductions. *Modern Language Journal,* 1973, *57,* 250–254.

Schwartz, J. A., Singer, J., and Macnamara, J. An analytic comparison of listening in two languages. *Irish Journal of Education,* 1973, *7,* 40–52.

Macnamara, J. Attitudes and learning a second language. In R. Shuy and R. W. Fasold (Eds.), *Language attitudes: Current trends and prospects* (pp. 36–40). Washington, DC: Georgetown University Press, 1973.

Katz, N., Baker, E., and Macnamara, J. What's in a name? A study of how children learn common and proper names. *Child Development,* 1974, *45,* 469–473.

Macnamara, J. Nurseries as models for language classrooms. In S. T. Carey (Ed.), *Bilingualism, biculturalism and education* (pp. 91–93). Edmonton: University of Alberta, 1974.

Macnamara, J. The generalizability of results of studies of bilingual education. In S. T. Carey (Ed.), *Bilingualism, biculturalism and education* (pp. 95–98). Edmonton: University of Alberta, 1974.

Macnamara, J. A note on Watt's economy criteria. *Glossa,* 1975, *9,* 107–113.

Macnamara, J. A note on Piaget and number. *Child Development,* 1975, *46,* 424–429.

Mougeon, R., and Macnamara, J. Language maintenance, bilingualism and religion in Gaspé East. *Cahier de Linguistique,* 1975, *6,* 171–178.

Macnamara, J. A reply to Brainerd. *Child Development,* 1976, *47,* 897–898.

Macnamara, J. First and second language learning: Same or different? *Journal of Education,* 1976, *158,* 39–54.

Macnamara, J. Comparison between first and second language learning. *Die Neueren Sprachen,* 1976, *75,* 175–188.

Macnamara, J., Baker, E., and Olson, C. L. Four-year-olds' understanding of *pretend, forget* and *know*: Evidence for propositional operations. *Child Development,* 1976, *47,* 62–70.

Macnamara, J. Stomachs assimilate and accommodate, don't they? *Canadian Psychological Review,* 1976, *17,* 167–173.

Macnamara, J., Svarc, J., and Horner, S. Attending a primary school of the other language in Montreal. In A. Simoes (Ed.), *The bilingual child* (pp. 113–131). New York: Academic Press, 1976.

Macnamara, J. On the relation between language learning and thought. In J. Macnamara (Ed.), *Language learning and thought,* (pp. 9–11). New York: Academic Press, 1977.

Macnamara, J. From sign to language. In J. Macnamara (Ed.), *Language learning and thought* (pp. 11–35). New York: Academic Press, 1977.

Macnamara, J. Problems with concepts. In J. Macnamara (Ed.), *Language learning and thought* (pp. 141–145). New York: Academic Press, 1977.

Macnamara, J. Children's command of the logic of conversation. In J. Macnamara (Ed.), *Language learning and thought* (pp. 261–288). New York: Academic Press, 1977.

Macnamara, J. Cognitive strategies of language learning. In W. F. Mackey and T. Andersson (Eds.), *Bilingualism in early childhood* (pp. 19–27). Rowley, MA: Newbury House, 1977.

Macnamara, J. How do babies learn grammatical categories? In D. Sankoff (Ed.), *Linguistic variation: Models and methods* (pp. 197–210). New York: Academic Press, 1978.

Macnamara, J. Another unaccommodating look at Piaget. *Canadian Psychological Review,* 1978, *19,* 78–81.

Macnamara, J. What happens to children whose home language is not that of the school? In G. K. Verma and C. Bagley (Eds.), *Race, education and identity* (pp. 95–104). London: Macmillan, 1979.

Macnamara, J. Let's see. *Journal of Child Language,* 1979, *6,* 581–584.

Macnamara, J. Doubts about the form of development. *Behavioral and Brain Sciences*, 1979, *2*, 393–394.

Macnamara, J. Physical objects: The relationship between psychology and philosophy. *Canadian Psychologist*, 1981, *22*, 271–281.

Macnamara, J. Meaning. In W. B. Weimer and D. S. Palermo (Eds.), *Cognition and the symbolic process* (Vol. 2, pp. 35–61). Hillsdale, NJ: Erlbaum, 1982.

Macnamara, J. Not the talk: It's what the talk is about. *Alberta Modern Language Journal*, 1983, *22*, 3–9.

Macnamara, J. A New Testament. Review article on J. Barwise and J. Perry, *Situations and attitudes*. *Journal of Applied Psycholinguistics*, 1985, *5*, 254–265.

Macnamara, J. Citation classic: Cognitive basis of language learning in children. *Psychological Review*, 1972, *79*, 1–13. *Current Contents, Social and Behavioral Sciences*, March 1985, *17*(11), 18.

Macnamara, J. But what is belief itself? *Annals of Theoretical Psychology*, 1986, *4*, 357–364.

Macnamara, J. O nazywaniu rzeczy: Uwagi na temat zwiazku miedzy logika a psychologia (Naming things: Remarks on the connection between logic and psychology). In I. Kurcz, J. Bobryk, and D. Kadzielawa (Eds.), *Wiedza a jezyk:* Tom 1. *Ogolna psychologia jezyka i neurolingwistyka* (*Knowledge and language:* Vol. 1. *General psychology of language and neurolinguistics*). Wroclaw: Ossolineum, 1986.

Macnamara, J. Principles and parameters: A response to Chomsky. *New Ideas in Psychology*, 1986, *4*, 215–222.

Macnamara, J. On naming things: Remarks on the relation between logic and psychology. In I. Kurcz, G. W. Shugar, and J. H. Danks (Eds.), *Knowledge and language* (pp. 3–20). Amsterdam: North-Holland, 1986.

Macnamara, J., Govitrikar, V. P., and Doan, B. Actions, laws and scientific psychology. *Cognition*, 1988, *29*, 1–27.

Niall, K., and Macnamara, J. Projective invariance and visual shape constancy. *Acta Psychologica*, 1989, *72*, 65–79.

Macnamara, J. More about principles and parameters: A reply to Chomsky. *New Ideas in Psychology*, 1989, *7*, 33–40.

Macnamara, J. Ideals and psychology. *Canadian Psychology*, 1990, *31*, 14–25.

Niall, K. K., and Macnamara, J. Projective invariance and picture perception. *Perception*, 1990, *19*, 637–660.

Macnamara, J. Small numbers: A dialogue. *Canadian Psychology*, 1991, *32*, 111–115.

Macnamara, J. Understanding induction. *Journal for the Philosophy of Science,* 1991, *42,* 21–48.

Macnamara, J. The development of moral reasoning and the foundations of geometry. *Journal for the Theory of Social Behaviour,* 1991, *21,* 125–150.

Macnamara, J. Linguistic relativity revisited. In R. L. Cooper and B. Spolsky (Eds.), *The influence of language on culture and thought* (pp. 35–147). Berlin and New York: Mouton de Gruyter, 1991.

Macnamara, J. The takeover of psychology by biology or the devaluation of reference in psychology. In M. Pütz (Ed.), *Thirty years of linguistic evolution: Studies in honour of René Dirven on the occasion of his sixtieth birthday* (pp. 545–570). Amsterdam: John Benjamins, 1992.

Macnamara, J., and Austin, G. Physics and plasticine. *Canadian Psychology,* 1993, *34,* 225–232.

Macnamara, J., and Austin, G. Response to critics. *Canadian Psychology,* 1993, *34,* 245–248.

Macnamara, J. Cognitive psychology and the rejection of Brentano. *Journal for the Theory of Social Behaviour,* 1993, *23,* 117–137.

La Palme Reyes, M., Macnamara, J., Reyes, G. E., and Zolfaghari, H. Proper names and how they are learned. *Memory,* 1994, *1,* 433–455.

Macnamara, J. Father Sheehy's flashlight. *Canadian Psychology,* 1994, *35,* 124–128.

La Palme Reyes, M., Macnamara, J., Reyes, G. E., and Zolfaghari, H. The non-Boolean logic of natural language negation. *Philosophia Mathematica,* 1994, *3,* 45–68.

La Palme Reyes, M., Macnamara, J., and Reyes, G. E. Functoriality and grammatical role in syllogisms. *Notre Dame Journal of Formal Logic,* 1994, *35,* 41–66.

Macnamara, J. The foundations of logic and the foundations of cognition. In W. F. Overton and D. S. Palermo (Eds.), *The nature and ontogenesis of meaning* (pp. 145–166). Hillsdale, NJ: Erlbaum, 1994.

Macnamara, J. The mind-body problem and contemporary psychology. In R. Szubka (Ed.), *The mind-body problem: A guide to the current debate* (pp. 165–170). Oxford: Blackwell, 1994.

Macnamara, J. The Gestalt spirit in language and cognition: A critical review of *Language: A theory of structure and use* by Per Saugstad. *New Ideas in Psychology,* 1994, *12,* 183–191.

Macnamara, J., La Palme Reyes, M., and Reyes, G. E. Logic and the Trinity. *Faith and Philosophy,* 1994, *11,* 3–18.

Macnamara, J., and Reyes, G. E. Introduction. In J. Macnamara and G. E. Reyes (Eds.), *The logical foundations of cognition* (pp. 1–8). New York: Oxford University Press, 1994.

Macnamara, J. Logic and cognition. In J. Macnamara and G. E. Reyes (Eds.), *The logical foundations of cognition* (pp. 11–34). New York: Oxford University Press, 1994.

La Palme Reyes, M., Macnamara, J., and Reyes, G. E. Reference, kinds and predicates. In J. Macnamara and G. E. Reyes (Eds.), *The logical foundations of cognition* (pp. 90–143). New York: Oxford University Press, 1994.

Macnamara, J., and Reyes, G. E. Foundational issues in the learning of proper names, count nouns and mass nouns. In J. Macnamara and G. E. Reyes (Eds.), *The logical foundations of cognition* (pp. 144–176). New York: Oxford University Press, 1994.

Occasional Pieces

Macnamara, J. Tuirse sa scoil. *Dochas,* 1965, *3,* 106–107.

Macnamara, J., and Edwards, J. *Attitudes to learning French in the English-speaking schools of Quebec.* Study E8 prepared for the Commission of Inquiry on the Position of the French Language and on Language Rights in Quebec. Quebec Official Publisher, 1973.

Macnamara, J. The Irish language and nationalism. *The Crane Bag,* 1977, *1,* 40–44.

Macnamara, J. La philosophie du Livre Blanc. *Le Devoir,* 1977, jeudi 5 mai, 5.

Macnamara, J. Race and intelligence. *Irish Review,* 1988, *3,* 55–60.

Macnamara, J. Cinderella and the soul. *New Oxford Review,* 1990, Nov., 7–11.

Macnamara, J. (1994). Where Freud went wrong. Review article on Paul Roazen: *Meeting Freud's family. Literary Review of Canada, 3,* No. 11, 15–16.

Reviews

Fletcher, B. A.: *A philosophy for the teacher.* In *Philosophical Studies,* 1963, *12,* 308.

Young, M.: *Innovation and research in education.* In *Irish Journal of Education,* 1967, *1,* 150–152.

Morrison, D. F.: *Multivariate statistical methods*. In *Irish Journal of Education*, 1969, *3*, 71–73.

Chomsky, C.: *The acquisition of syntax in children from 5 to 10*. In *General Linguistics*, 1970, *10*, 164–172.

Blumenthal, A. L.: *Language and psychology* (Review title: Discovering respectable ancestors). In *Contemporary Psychology*, 1971, *16*, 497–498.

Painchaud, L.: *Le bilinguisme à l'université*. In *International Review of Applied Linguistics*, 1971, *9*, 72.

Balkan, L.: *Les effets du bilinguisme français-anglais sur les aptitudes intellectuelles*. In *Lingua*, 1972, *28*, 159–162.

Herriott, P.: *An introduction to the psychology of language*. In *Irish Journal of Education*, 1972, *5*, 116–118.

Steinberg, D. D., and Jakobovits, L. A. (Eds.): *Semantics: An interdisciplinary reader in philosophy, linguistics and psychology* (Review title: Family reunion). In *Contemporary Psychology*, 1972, *17*, 428–429.

Pearce, J.: *School examinations*. In *Irish Times, Educational Supplement*, 1973, April.

Beilin, H.: *Studies in the cognitive basis of language development* (Review title: A general theory of cognitive and linguistic development). In *Contemporary Psychology*, 1976, *21*, 649–650.

Bates, E.: *Language and context: The acquisition of pragmatics* (Review title: More talk about baby talk). In *Contemporary Psychology*, 1977, *22*, 494–495.

Maratsos, M. P.: *The use of definite and indefinite reference in young children: An experimental study in semantic acquisition*. In *Child Development Abstracts and Bibliography*, 1977, *51*, 156.

Moerk, E. L.: *Pragmatic and semantic aspects of early language development*. In *Child Development Abstracts and Bibliography*, 1978, *52*, 85–86.

Gelman, R., and Gallistel, C. R.: *The child's understanding of number*. In *Canadian Journal of Psychology*, 1978, *32*, 270–271.

McLaughlin, B.: *Second language acquisition in childhood*. In *Child Development Abstracts and Bibliography*, 1979, *53*, 76–77.

Oléron, P.: *L'enfant et l'acquisition du langage* (Review title: Cognition in language learning). In *Contemporary Psychology*, 1980, *25*, 497–498.

Lock, A.: *The guided reinvention of language* (Review title: Anthropology in the nursery). In *Contemporary Psychology*, 1981, *26*, 542–543.

Ginsburgh, H. P. (Ed.): *The development of mathematical thinking* (Review title: All about sums). In *Contemporary Psychology*, 1984, *29*, 136–137.

Johnson-Laird, P. N.: Mental models: Towards a cognitive science of language, inference, and consciousness (Review title: Faithful account of a stewardship). In *Journal of Mathematical Psychology,* 1984, *28,* 496–503.

Lycan, W. G.: *Logical form in natural language.* In *Journal of Applied Psycholinguistics,* 1986, *3,* 182–185.

Waldron, T. P.: *Principles of language and mind.* In *Journal of Language and Social Psychology,* 1986, *5,* 76–80.

Wells, G. *Language development in the preschool years.* In *Canadian Psychology,* 1987, *28,* 304–305.

Morgan, J. L. *From simple input to complex grammar.* In *McGill Journal of Education,* 1987, *22,* 165–167.

Fine, K.: *Reasoning with arbitrary objects.* In *Journal of Symbolic Logic,* 1987, *2,* 305–306.

Pateman, T.: *Language in mind and language in society.* In *Mind and Language,* 1988, *3,* 71–74.

Fodor, J. A.: *Psychosemantics* (Review title: Cognitive science in peril). In *Contemporary Psychology,* 1989, *33,* 1040–1041.

Astington, J. W., Harris, P. L., and Olson, D. R. (Eds.): *Developing theories of mind* (Review title: Children as commonsense psychologists). In *Canadian Journal of Psychology,* 1989, *43,* 426–429.

Aitchinson, J.: *Words in the mind: An introduction to the mental lexicon.* In *Journal of Language and Social Psychology,* 1989, *8,* 355–357.

Eco, U., Santambrogio, M., and Violi, P. (Eds.): *Meaning and mental representations.* In *Journal of Language and Social Psychology,* 1989, *8,* 349–353.

Pinker, S.: *The language instinct;* and Jackendoff, R.: *Patterns in the mind.* In *Boston Globe,* 13 March 1994.

Chapter 1

Language and Nationalism   Richard Kearney

John Macnamara's writings on the psychology of language are internationally recognized. Less well known perhaps is his work on the politics of language. His research on the relationship between nationality and language—ranging from his doctoral thesis on bilingualism in Irish education (1966) to his later essays in the Irish journal, *The Crane Bag*, in the 1970s—had a considerable impact on the cultural identity debates in his native country. Macnamara's interventions were controversial. His first book on bilingualism earned him the public censure of the then Minister for Education in the Republic, who called for his resignation as President of St. Patrick's Teacher Training College in Dublin. His spirited argument for the separation of racial identity and language—that is, of Irish ethnicity and Gaelic speech—in an essay entitled "The Irish Language and Nationalism" (1977) provoked equally vehement responses.

John Macnamara challenged the race-language equation, especially when narrowly applied to the politics of nationhood. He disputed, not the fact that countries that speak different languages are often different culturally, but the belief that difference in language necessarily implies difference in culture. In linguistic theory, Macnamara showed, this equation of language and national identity derived largely from German theorists like Herder and Fichte in the nineteenth century and from Benjamin Lee Whorf in the twentieth. In political history, the equation was identified with a wide variety of nationalist movements from Russia and Germany to Hungary and Ireland. In his 1977 essay, he concluded that although the Irish language played a central role in establishing the difference between the Irish Free State and the rest of the British Empire in the early part of this century, postindependence Ireland was in a position to acknowledge that one could be equally Irish speaking Gaelic or English.

With political independence and a securely based tradition of Irish literature in English, a large part of the programme that motivated the setting up of the Free State has been realized, though not in the form that the founders foresaw. We no longer need arguments to prove we are a distinct race, not because we have satisfied the world that we are, but because to us the notion of race is irrelevant. The rest of the English-speaking world is not trying to annex us politically. . . . Everyone today sees Ireland and Irish people as having a flavour and style all their own. In any case, to my mind it is just as false to aim at being distinctive as it is to imitate. (Macnamara 1977, 40–41)

In this chapter I would like to respond to Macnamara's questioning of the criteria of nationalism and national identity by extending and supplementing his argument in some critical directions. So doing, I wish to pay homage to his timely and salutary intervention.

In current usage, a nation is often assumed to be a *state*, or a group of people aspiring in common toward the condition of a state. As a state, the modern nation is generally, in fact or in aspiration, a sovereign entity with significant control over its government and identity, and recognized as such by those resident within the nation and by other nations in the world (the assembly of nation-states known as the United Nations). As a *legal* entity, the nation-state usually endorses what might be called "civic" nationalism: the claim that the nation is composed of all those—regardless of color, language, creed, or race—who subscribe to the nation's political principles or constitution. The nation is thus defined as "civic" to the extent that it is recognized as a community of "equal, rights-bearing citizens, united in patriotic attachment to a shared set of political practices and values" (Ignatieff 1993, 6–7). Britain is frequently cited as an example of civic nationalism in its efforts, from the mid–eighteenth century onward, to forge a nation-state composed of four different nations (Irish, Scots, Welsh, and English), under a civic rather than ethnic definition—that is, a shared allegiance to a common Parliament, Crown, rule of law. Whether Britain actually succeeded in this, or simply masked "English nationalism" behind the four-nation-state, is a moot point to which I will return below. Less controversial examples of the "civic" nation-state are to be found in the American and French republics after their respective revolutions of 1776 and 1789, though it must be remembered that even here citizenship was still largely confined, for many decades, to the enfranchised elite of white, propertied males and did not always include women, slaves, or aboriginal peoples.[1]

A second common way of understanding nation is as *territory*. This definition need not always involve a state as such, but it does, minimally, lay claim to a specific place or land that comprises the so-called *national territory*. To fully exist, the nation thus geographically defined must cover or occupy the national territory—"the land which the nationalists believe to be the nation's by right and (which) embraces all the members of the putative nation therein domiciled" (Fennell 1989, 13).[2] In the case of Ireland, geography has been one of the most commonly invoked criteria for justifying the aspiration to unity within the island and separation from the neighboring island of Britain. The fact that Ireland is an integral island, "surrounded by water," has been one of the mainstays of separatist nationalism.[3] The problem here is, of course, that *both* the Irish Republic and Great Britain have considered Northern Ireland to be part of their respective "national territories," though it has been reconfirmed as British *de jure* since the 1920 Government of Ireland Act. Many nations have, of course, existed *without* a land (e.g., the Jews for centuries, the Kurds, the Palestinians), but there are few if any examples of nations with *no* sense of territorial identification.

A third common sense of nation, critically discussed by John Macnamara, is that of *ethnicity*. Here the definition of belonging is one of blood rather than law. The nation is defined, accordingly, in terms of a racially homogeneous "people" that seeks out a state appropriate to its unique identity. In contrast to most Western nation-states, which today define their nationhood in terms of common citizenship (by birth, residence, or allegiance), Germany is an example of a nation that still defines itself ethnically. For the ethnic nation, a person's deepest identity is inherited rather than chosen; what unifies a society is common *roots* rather than laws. "Regardless of the real nature of the state-society, the nation-state treats it as a mass of ethnically uniform individuals who exist to serve its welfare and convenience. It *is*, after all, the nation" (Fennell 1989, 13). In such a scenario, it is the national community—the *Volk*—that defines the individual citizens rather than the other way around. The People before persons. We thus find several German Romantics of the nineteenth century repudiating the Enlightenment idea that the state created the nation, and mobilizing German patriotic resistance to Napoleon's invasion of the German principalities around a specifically German—as opposed to French revolutionary—understanding of the nation-state. The extraordinary appeal of this ethnic model of nationalism for emergent nations in the nineteenth century is described by Michael Ignatieff as follows:

What gave unity to the nation, what made it a home, a place of passionate attachment, was not the cold contrivance of shared rights but the people's preexist-
ing ethnic characteristics: their language, religion, customs and traditions. The
nation as Volk had begun its long and troubling career in European thought. All
the peoples of nineteenth-century Europe under imperial subjection—the Poles
and Baltic peoples under the Russian yoke, the Serbs under Turkish rule, the
Croats under the Hapsburgs—looked to the German ideal of ethnic nationalism
when articulating their right to self-determination. (1993, 7)

As a result, when Germany was finally unified under Bismarck in 1871
and assumed world-power status, it served as exemplar of the success of
ethnic nationalism for the "captive nations" of imperial Europe—and
beyond.[4]

As Macnamara pointed out, certain instances of Irish nationalism also
display an ethnic feature based on alleged differences between Gaelic and
non-Gaelic. This is, admittedly, uncharacteristic from a historic point of
view. Ideological geneticism or Darwinian biology were rarely invoked
in the Irish separatist cause. Probably the closest that one gets to some
kind of racist inference was Douglas Hyde's odd, and largely innocuous,
theory about natural selection and language. "As President of the linguistic revivalist Gaelic League, [Hyde] actually argued in the mid-1890s
that Irish people had been speaking Gaelic for so long that their mouths
were unfitted physically for English" (Garvin 1994, 84).[5] Even the most
zealous nationalists of the time took little heed. Less impervious, alas,
were certain members of the Irish Ministry of Justice in the 1940s who
refused to shelter Jews fleeing from Nazi persecution on the grounds that
"they do not assimilate with our own people but remain a sort of colony
of a worldwide Jewish community. This makes them a potential irritant in
the body politic and has led to disastrous results from time to time in
other countries."[6] Racism may have been rare in Ireland; it was not
nonexistent.

A fourth, more generous, understanding of the nation came under the
rubric of the "*migrant* nation"—or the nation as "extended family." Here
the definition of the nation remained at least partially ethnic but was
enlarged to embrace all those emigrants and exiles who live beyond the
territory of the nation-state per se. The most celebrated example of this is
no doubt the Jewish diaspora; but it also pertains to many other emigrant
nationalities, not least the Irish. If over 70 million people in the world
today claim to be of Irish descent, it is evident that this definition of
nationality, or at least of national genealogy, extends far beyond the
borders of a state or territory. Irish Americans or Irish Australians or

Irish Britons, for example, can affirm a strong sense of national allegiance to their "land of origin" even though they may be three or four generations away from that land and frequently of mixed ethnicity. With the formulation of a "new nationalism" in the Forum for a New Ireland (1984–85), the then Foreign Minister, Peter Barry, included the Irish emigrant population in his definition of the nation (appealing, for example, to "Irish nationalists North and South and everywhere else in the world"), as did President Mary Robinson when she came to office in 1990. Similar appeals are heard whenever the international community is solicited to support peace in Northern Ireland (the international Ireland Funds, etc.), or when it is a question of debating emigrant voting rights in national elections and selecting national football teams.

In short, although the "migrant nation" is still largely ethnically based, it is far more inclusive than the ethnic nation model in that it embraces the exiled along with the indigenous.[7] By implication, this means accepting that the Irish diaspora comprises not only different Irish peoples ("Ulster Scots" as well as "native Gaels") but, through intermarriage in the melting pots of overseas continents, different racial confections as well. One wonders how many of the Irish Irelanders—who sought to confine the nation to those of Gaelic extraction—would have believed that by the 1994 World Cup the Irish team would be over half British-born with a center forward named Cascarino.[8]

A fifth, and final, variable that merits attention here is what might broadly be called the "nation as *culture*." This is not unrelated to the two preceding definitions but differs in this crucial respect: the cultural paradigm of national identity is not reducible to any specific race. National culture can include many things besides ethnicity: for example, religion, language, art, sport, dance, music, cuisine, clothes, literature, philosophy, even (some believe) economics. As such, it is by nature far more pluralist than any strictly racial understanding of nationhood. For its part, the Irish nation includes several different religions (as Wolfe Tone's reference to "Catholic, Protestant, and Dissenter" recognized), two different languages (Gaelic and English), and a rich variety of philosophical traditions. Indeed, even when cultural nationalism does refer to ethnicity, it is obliged—if it is to be consistent—to invoke several different ethnic legacies. In the case of the Irish cultural nation this requires acknowledgment of the Viking, Norman, Scots, and Anglo-Saxon contributions alongside those of the "ancient Celtic race." Thus, we might say that the exclusivist equation of "Irish Irish" with Gaelic and Catholic, by D. P. Moran and other fundamentalists in the first decades of this century, was in fact a betrayal of the full complexity of Irish culture.

Although Gaelic is the official "first language" of the Republic, and an invaluable resource to the nation, it is not the first tongue spoken by the vast majority of the population. Nor is it the tongue, as Macnamara reminds us without revisionist rancor, responsible for making Irish writing one of the world's great modern literatures. Joyce, Yeats, Wilde, Kavanagh, Heaney may well be haunted by Gaelic as their souls "fret in the shadow of the (English) language"—but it is English that they speak and write, albeit in a singularly Irish way. The language question is even more vexed, of course, when it comes to politics. Elements in the Gaelic League did, for a time, pursue the quasi-Herderian thesis that the collective genius of the race found its true expression in the Irish tongue. Hence the view that Gaelic equaled rurality, purity, and authenticity whereas English equaled urbanity, decadence, and vice. The implication here was, of course, that because Ireland had a unique and ancient language, it had a natural right to separate political status.

However, several recent commentators, following in the wake of John Macnamara's critical intervention, argue differently. Historian Tom Garvin notes the irony that the more the Irish embraced *English*, the more nationalist they became!

English has always been the language of Irish political separatism, in an extraordinary succession from Jonathan Swift and Clement Molyneux in the early eighteenth century, through Theobald Wolfe Tone and William Drennan in the 1790s, to John Mitchel, Arthur Griffith, James Connolly and Patrick Pearse in the nineteenth and twentieth centuries. Political sentiment in the Irish Gaelic language tended to be rather pre-political, rarely getting further than a sentimental and rather rhetorical Jacobitism. (1994, 86)

It certainly seems the case that it was through English that the republican principles of the French and American revolutions spread through Ireland in the 1790s, leading eventually to the United Irishmen rebellion in 1798. Thus, it has been remarked that the acquisition of English, "far from making the Irish assimilate to English attitudes and loyalties, rather gave the weapons of European Enlightenment to a previously impotent tradition" (Garvin 1994, 88).[9] By such accounts, the historical relationship between language and Irish nationality is far from evident.

The same could be said about *religion* and Irish nationalism. Although Catholicism is the majority creed of Ireland, it is by no means the only one, and besides carries a strong "internationalist" component that contrasts with the notion of a closed insular *Volk* (e.g., the missionary tradition of diaspora throughout Europe, Africa, Asia, and the Americas). That said, one should not underestimate the powerful role religion has played in Irish nationalism, and nationalism worldwide. The fact that nationalism, particularly in its modern republican guises, is an offspring of Enlightenment secularism has not prevented its more popular manifestations from being fueled by the collectivist, and often atavistic, energies of traditional religions. Though this connection has been greatly underrated in much academic literature, recent research by Marianne Elliott (1996) shows the pivotal symbiosis between Irish nationalism and Catholicism in our own century and argues that the Ulster Protestants' rejection of Catholicism dominates their rejection of nationalism.[10] Tom Garvin makes a similar point: although he concedes that the founders of the separatist Irish tradition were Protestant rather than Catholic (largely due to the Protestants' near-monopoly of higher education in Ireland up to the twentieth century), he observes that the nationalist rank and file have been overwhelmingly Catholic since the 1790s and the nationalist leadership so since the 1900s. "Irish nationalism," he concludes, "has always been rhetorically anti-sectarian, but is tempted into sectarianism because of its anthropological rooting in the Catholic majority and in the ideology of dispossession and repossession" (1994, 89).[11] The fact that Protestantism was the religion of the dominant Ascendancy class, which disenfranchised the Catholic majority, was an additional factor in the equation.

Here once again, history is vexed. One of the main reasons the Catholic hierarchy was not officially allied to Irish nationalism during the eighteenth and nineteenth centuries was that it feared that the nationalist-republican ideas being imported into Ireland from the French Revolution were anti-Catholic. The fact that these ideas were also anti-British meant, logically, that a tacit alliance of interests bound the Catholic hierarchy and Westminster together: the Catholic hierarchy actually approved the abolition of the Irish parliament and union with Britain in 1800, and the English government financed the establishment of the Catholic seminary Maynooth in 1795. After the fall of Parnell and 1916, however, it became clear to the Church that the soul of the Irish nation was up for grabs and that the need for a unifying collective identity for the newly emerging state could best be provided by a form of Catholic nationalism that allowed (in Joyce's words) "Christ and Caesar go hand in hand." Indeed, the 1937 Constitution of Dail Eireann came close, at times, to ratifying the equation of Catholic, Gaelic, and Irish.

The Irish Republic was not, of course, unique in its early tendency to accommodate religion as a badge of national identity. North of the border, one found a "Protestant Parliament for a Protestant People" emerging, while on the neighboring island the Church of England was still a primary means of asserting English national identity. And those who consider the link between nation and religion to be now no more than an anachronism need look not only to the continuing sectarianism on both sides in Ulster, but also to the more global fate of Yugoslavia and the former Soviet Union.

Finally, although some cultural nationalists of the Sinn Fein school argued for an "economic nationalism" in the 1930s and 1940s, this ultimately came to grief. Independent Ireland's original policy of national capitalism—economic self-sufficiency—foundered because Ireland (1) lacked a sufficient body of industrial entrepreneurs, (2) inherited a bureaucratic and centralized state apparatus from the British, and (3) continued to look to Britain for ultimate solutions. As Desmond Fennell remarks in his analysis of economic nationalism, "The state was changed only to make it more what it was—more centralized, interventionist, uncoordinated, and uncontrolled by citizens' decisions" (1989, 67).[12] Economic nationalism also failed, of course, because the world economy was becoming such that nation-states were no longer the determining units in the regulation of wealth but were increasingly subject to a transnational network of global banks, markets, and industries. The notion of a quintessentially Gaelic-Catholic-nationalist economy was never more than an ideological illusion.

Whether it was predicated upon religious, linguistic, or economic grounds, Irish cultural nationalism has always displayed an unusual capacity, *pace* the stereotypes, to change its mind about itself. This is largely due to the fact that the tradition is extremely complex and its legacies multifaceted. As testified in the old quip (Garvin 1993, 63): whenever the English thought they'd found the answer, the Irish changed the question![13]

The one aspect of Irish cultural nationality that I believe John Macnamara would have approved is precisely this *multiple* nature of identity: a wonderfully confused kaleidoscope of possibilities that, at best, kept Irish people at home or abroad always on their toes and always open to others.

Notes

1. On this tension between civic universalism and state nationalism, see Ingram 1995, Garvin 1993, and Ricoeur 1995b. As Ricoeur observes, one of the main dangers of equating nation with state is the eclipse of society behind the state. Thus we see, for example, how the French Revolution apportioned political sovereignty to all levels of the community, from the government at the top to the individuals at the bottom, but allowed the state to become omnipresent in the process, reducing the citizen to a mere fragment of the state.

2. Fennell develops his analysis of territorial nationalism as follows:

The definition of the nation as a community determined by a territory—the so-called national territory—was typical of much European nationalism.... As a matter of history, most European nation-states were constructed by using force, administrative pressures, and schooling to convert this theory into fact.... The primary aim of Irish nationalism, a united, self-governing Ireland, was also typically nationalist: the nation inhabiting the national territory, so the theory ran, had the right to political autonomy under a single government. (1989, 20–21)

3. For example:

The image of the Emerald Isle alone and inviolate in the ocean has itself become a cultural symbol, a mute argument for the unity of Ireland and its necessary separation from Britain. This argument from geography has commonly impressed not only Irish separatists themselves, but also many British observers and perhaps most third-country observers of the tortured and tortuous relationship, one of mutual love and mutual hatred, between the two islands. Anti-partitionists in particular commonly justify the Republic's constitutional claim to Northern Ireland by claiming that what God and History have united, no man, and certainly no Englishman, can sunder. (Garvin 1994, 84)

This debate has direct relevance to current discussions of a revised Irish constitution. De Valera's constitution of 1937 described the "Nation" in terms of three articles. The Irish nation is asserted (axiomatically) rather than defined in Article 1. It is described in terms of national territory encompassing the entire island in Article 2; and the divided condition of the island is referred to as a temporary matter, "pending the re-integration of the national territory," in Article 3. The subsequent descriptions of the "State" that follow—Articles 4 to 9—are equally nebulous and ambiguous. Hence the need for a revised constitution setting out a clear definition of citizenship and nationality, and taking into consideration the new status of Northern Ireland as a region relating concentrically to the island of Ireland, the British archipelago, the European Union, and the United Nations. I am indebted to Philip McGuinness for several of the above comments.

4. See Sluga 1993, 60, 91, 103–108, on the Romantic philosophy of Germany as an ethnic nation. In his *Addresses to the German Nation* (1807), Fichte called on the spirit of the German people to remember "its own true nature" and to realize that the battle against other nations cannot be "fought without one's household gods, one's mythic roots, without a true 'recovery' of all things German" (sec. 23). It was not a huge leap from these musings of the German Romantics to the argument of a Nazi idealogue like Rosenberg, who, in his speech "The Crisis and Construction of Europe" (1934), called for a rejection of the Enlightenment universalism that had dominated European thought and politics, concluding, "The

point, the idea, the fact from which we must start today is the fact of the nation" (cited in Sluga 1993, 60). For further discussion of German nationalism, particularly in the contemporary context where the traditional equation of "people," "nation," and "state" is becoming increasingly confused and questioned, see Hobsbawm 1990, 180–181.

The antisemitism, racism, social Darwinism, and antipathy to all forms of internationalism that typified National Socialism were not, it is fair to say, qualities shared by Irish, British, or French nationalists in any general sense. Although British and French nationalisms are in principle civic rather than ethnic, recent responses to the "immigration problem" have revived some concept of the latter, albeit frequently at a cultural level—for example, the British Heritage Industry or the French neoconservative revivalism.

On this vexed distinction between civic and ethnic nationalism, see Ricoeur's pertinent remarks:

The notion of 'people' according to the French Constitution is not ethnic. Its citizenship is defined by the fact that somebody is born on the territory of France. For example, the son or daughter of an immigrant is French because he or she was born on this territory. So the rule of membership has nothing to do with ethnic origin. This is why it was impossible to define the Corsican people, because we had to rely on criteria other than citizenship, on ethnic criteria.... The Corsican people are also members of the French people. Here we have two meanings of the term 'people'. On the one hand, people means to be a citizen in a state, so it's not an ethnic concept. But on the other hand, Corsica *is* a people in an ethnic sense— within the French people which is not an ethnic concept. I think it's an example of what is happening throughout Europe now. (1995b, 35–36)

A further conflict of interpretations with regard to French nationality/Francophone identity/"Frenchness" applies to de Gaulle's famous Cabinet Statement of July 1967, where he spoke of the Quebec people as a "population descended from her own (French) people and admirably faithful to their country of origin." This effectively contravened the traditional civic, nonlinguistic, and nonethnic notion of Frenchness as defined by the French revolutionary constitution. Hobsbawm (1990, 181) notes the emergence of similar tensions in the British definition of citizenship and national identity: "Until the 1960s 'Britishness', in terms of law and administration, was a simple matter of being born to British parents or on British soil, marrying a British citizen, or being naturalized. It is a far from simple matter today." For a more detailed discussion of the tension between ethnic and civic nationalism, see Greenfeld 1992, 6–13.

5. Garvin acknowledges that the use of race theory has been rare and untypical "on the part of both separatists and anti-separatists in the British/Irish relationship" (1994, 83).

6. See report by Andy Pollack, *Irish Times*, April 15, 1995, based on research by Professor Dermot Keogh into government papers of the prewar and war period.

7. On this question of the "migrant nation," see contributions by Liam Ryan, Maurice Hayes, Graeme Kirkham, Kirby Miller, J. J. Lee, George Quigley, and Seamus Heaney et al. in Kearney 1990. See also Benedict Anderson's lectures titled "Exodus, Exile and the Nation-State" at Dublin City University and Trinity College Dublin, December 1, 1995. The notion of a "national people" or popu-

lation is becoming increasingly porous, if not outdated, in many countries today where three-generation families are a rarity and multiculturalism, pluralism, and mass migration are eroding the old connection between people and land (as in Bossuet's seventeenth-century phrase about those who "live and die in the land of their birth"). Increasingly, nationality is becoming something people carry with them rather than a fixed attachment of a specific place of birth. When one considers, moreover, that some 17 million people crossed the Atlantic to North America between the seventeenth and nineteenth centuries, and that millions of "nonresident aliens" lived and worked temporarily in the United States in the 1980s, with no allegiances as "national citizens" (regarding defense, elections, or taxation), one begins to grasp how attenuated the notions of national population and original homeland are becoming. Understanding nationalism to be one of the greatest means of commanding the loyalty and allegiance of people, the United States has deployed various means to "renationalize" the landscape (e.g., the frontier myth of the "Western") and the emigrant "melting pot" population (e.g., through a them/us strategy of war, from the old Revolutionary and Mexican Wars to the two world wars this century and subsequent campaigns in Korea, Vietnam, the Middle East, and Latin America).

8. An additional variation on the post-nation-state model is what Benedict Anderson calls "long-distance nationalism." His basic hypothesis here is that several forms of contemporary nationalism are the products of exile and exodus—expatriate populations looking back nostalgically on the lost homeland—rather than expressions of atavistic/nativist tradition, as is commonly supposed. The cliché of the "sea-divided Gael" has more significance than one might think. In this respect, one might cite how it is often expatriate Irish-Americans (frequently second-generation or more) who cling to the most "traditionalist" forms of nationalism, as witnessed in NORAID support for the IRA and the controversies over the participation of Irish gay and lesbian groups in the New York and Boston St. Patrick's Day parades (or, one might add, expatriate funding for the 1995 Anti-Divorce Campaign). But the nostalgia neurosis that "invents" outdated models of nationality/nationalism *retrospectively* can equally be a feature of a modern nation's *internal* sense of exile. Nationalism thus also reveals itself as a response to an internal experience of loss—for example, a lost language (Gaelic) or ancient homeland (the four green fields). Indeed, the cultural critic Luke Gibbons goes so far as to argue that the ideal of authentic territorially based nationality is often a fiction of advanced, secular, urban centers. Thus, for example, the famous St. Patrick's Day speech by De Valera in 1943 was, Gibbons suggests, a traditionalist portrait of the old, pristine nation delivered from the threshold of modernity. In this sense, notions of national tradition frequently turn out to be an *invention of modernity*, as in the American fantasy of the Wild West or the Irish fiction of the West of Ireland (see Luke Gibbons and Fintan O'Toole). Or to put this paradox in another way, it is precisely when the old securities of the classic nation-state—fixed territorial boundaries, contractual citizenship, economic-political autonomy, civic allegiance, and cultural identity—are threatened, that we find the need to retrieve and revive so-called primordial nationalism, namely, the need to combine a sense of homeland with a sense of accountability. This

phenomenon of "late nationalism," or what we might call retro-nationalism, is a phenomenon that Anderson links with the dislocationary processes of late capitalism. The more people feel surrounded by a *disenchanted* universe—an alienated, simulated, mass-produced world—the greater their need for a return to a *reenchanted* universe. Neonationalism seems a response to such a need (as witnessed in the doubling of newly formed nation-states since World War I, accelerated by the breakup of the "Communist bloc"). Yet another feature of "long-distance nationalism" is the internationalization of national politics as evidenced in the growing number of expatriate or foreign citizens—usually American or Canadian—entering the presidential campaigns of post-Communist nation-states (e.g., Croatia, Poland, Estonia). Nor should we underestimate the influential role played by American-Irish politicians, especially the Kennedys and President Clinton, in the Northern Ireland peace process (1994–1996).

9. It was through the use of the English language, as Garvin points out, that "the idea of an Irish Republic, free of aristocratic privilege, monarchical trappings and religious distinctions, was transmitted to a popular culture" (1994, 86). In this respect language proved to be a far more malleable badge of national identity than, say, race or religion. "Language has the great advantage from the point of view of nation-builders, of being learnable; unlike one's religion, there is no spiritual price to pay for 'changing sides'" (Garvin 1993, 72). See also Macnamara's (1977) more psychological-philosophical-linguistic approach to this subject.

The complex relationship between language and nation extends beyond the Irish case and has many repercussions in the emerging European context. As Paul Ricoeur puts it:

There is no political distribution of borders which is adequate to the distributions of languages and cultures, so there is no political solution at the level of the nation-state. This is the real irritator of the 19th century (legacy), the dream of a perfect equation between state and nation. That has failed so we have to look for something else. But there is a political problem here. Is the project of European federalism to be a confederation of regions, or of nations? This is something without a precedent. Modern history has been made by nation-states. But there are problems of size. We have five or six nation-states in Europe of major size, but we also have micro-nations which cannot become micro-states in the same way as national states have done. (1995b, 34–35)

This problem of size relates as much to regions as to nations, as Ascherson (1995, 20ff.) points out. Regions in the European context, for example, range from a German *Land* like Bavaria to the smaller regions of Italy or Spain where, in some instances like Catalonia or the Basque region, considerable cultural-linguistic-educational autonomy and even fiscal-economic devolution is allowed.

10. See also O'Brien's (1994) trenchant critique of what he calls "sacral nationalism"; and see Kearney 1984, Murphy 1988, and Keogh 1988. The relationship between nationalism and Catholicism resurfaced during the heated debates on abortion information and divorce in the 1990s, particularly as they affected the Irish constitution. The narrow passing of the controversial Divorce Referendum in November 1995 was a particularly significant moment in this ongoing process of Irish "self-identification." The reverse side of the Catholic-nationalist equation is the Protestant-unionist; on this relationship between Protestantism and Orangeism see, for example, Moloney 1980.

11. See also Garvin 1990, Kiberd 1995. An additional reason for the reversion of Irish nationalism to confessional allegiance may have something to do with the more general issue of new nation-states' experiencing a foundational crisis of legitimation. As Paul Ricoeur points out (1995a, 201): "A la racine du politique, à son fondement, il y a l'énigme de l'origine de l'autorité. D'où vient-elle? C'est une chose qui est toujours non reglée, et qui fait que l'ombre ou le fantôme du théologique continue de rôder autour du politique" ('The enigma of the source of authority lies at the very root and foundation of politics. From what does it derive? This is something never fully resolved, which means that the political is always haunted by a theological ghost or shadow').

12. See also Neary 1984 and Daly 1988.

13. Among these contradictions and complexities, Garvin (1993) points to the tension between the Anglo-Irish and Gaelic traditions that Yeats sought to combine in a *single* narrative.

Yeats, himself a Protestant, wished to devise an Irish national myth that provided room for people of his own 'Anglo-Irish' tradition. The trouble was that the materials he wished to use were mutually incompatible, being derived from Anglo-Irish and Irish traditions, which had historically always been at loggerheads and, worse, were still known to have been so. (p. 64)

Another, more general contradiction involves the conflict between modern-secularist and tribal-traditionalist aspects of Irish nationalism.

The modern self-contradictory, attempted derivations of Irish nationality from Gaelic, Catholic, or even Anglo-Irish aristocratic identities would have horrified and bewildered Wolfe Tone and the other France-inspired Irish Jacobins of the 1790s. The Enlightenment concept of 'citizenship' independent of one's traditional identification has survived in Ireland, but it has faced very severe competition from, in particular, religion-based identities. (p. 65)

While conceding that modern *political* nationalism is a child of Enlightenment universalism, in principle, Garvin argues that nationalism as a *cultural* phenomenon (with political consequences) is far more ancient, and more atavistic, than the modern universalized version.

In Ireland, land hunger, a quasi-racist sense of common 'stock', memories of confiscation and a strong Catholicism, all disguised ineffectively in the rags of the dead Gaelic identity, lie behind the theoretically secular modern national identity of English-speaking Ireland. The inheritance is ambivalent, and has several ideological repertoires that may be drawn upon. (p. 66)

References

Ascherson, N. (1995). Nations and regions. In R. Kearney (Ed.), *States of mind: Dialogues with contemporary thinkers on the European mind.* Manchester: Manchester University Press, and New York: New York University Press.

Daly, M. (1988). The impact of economic development on national identity. In *Irishness in a changing society* (Princess Grace Irish Library 2). Totowa, NJ: Barnes and Noble.

Elliott, M. (1996). Religion and identity in Northern Ireland. In W. A. Van Horn (Ed.), *Global convulsions: Race, ethnicity and nationalism at the end of the twentieth century.* Albany, NY: SUNY Press.

Fennell, D. (1989). *The revision of Irish nationalism*. Dublin: Open Air.

Garvin, T. (1990). The return of history: Collective myths and modern nationalism. *Irish Review*, no. 9 (Autumn, 1990), 16–20.

Garvin, T. (1993). Ethnic markers, modern nationalisms, and the nightmare of history. In P. Kruger (Ed.), *Ethnicity and nationalism*. Marburg: Hitzeroth.

Garvin, T. (1994). Nationalism and separatism in Ireland, 1760–1993: A comparative perspective. In J. Bermanendi, R. Maiz, and X. Nunez (Eds.), *Nationalism in Europe past and future*. Universidade de Santiago de Compostela.

Greenfeld, L. (1992). *Nationalism: Five roads to modernity*. Cambridge, MA: Harvard University Press.

Hobsbawm, E. (1990). *Nations and nationalism since 1780*. Cambridge: Cambridge University Press.

Ignatieff, M. (1993). *Blood and belonging: Journeys into the new nationalism*. New York: Farrar, Straus & Giroux.

Ingram, A. (1995). Constitutional patriotism. Paper presented at 17th IVR World Congress, Bologna.

Kearney, R. (1984). Faith and fatherland. *The Crane Bag, 8*(1), 55–68.

Kearney, R. (Ed.). (1990). *Migrations: The Irish at home and abroad*. Dublin: Wolfhound Press.

Keogh, D. (1988). Catholicism and formation of the modern Irish society. In *Irishness in a changing society* (Princess Grace Irish Library 2). Totowa, NJ: Barnes and Noble.

Kiberd, D. (1995). *Inventing Ireland*. London: Jonathan Cape.

Macnamara, J. (1966). *Bilingualism and primary education: A survey of Irish experience*. Edinburgh: Edinburgh University Press.

Macnamara, J. (1977). The Irish language and nationalism. *The Crane Bag, 1*, 40–44. Reprinted in M.-P. Hederman and R. Kearney (Eds.), *The Crane Bag book of Irish studies: vol. I (1977–81)*. Dublin: Blackwater Press.

Moloney, E. (1980). Paisley. *The Crane Bag, 4*(2), 23–28.

Murphy, J. A. (1988). Religion and Irish identity. In *Irishness in a changing society* (Princess Grace Irish Library 2). Totowa, NJ: Barnes and Noble.

Neary, P. (1984). The failure of economic nationalism. *The Crane Bag, 8*(1), 68–81.

O'Brien, C. C. (1994). *Ancestral voices: Religion and nationalism in Ireland*. Dublin: Poolbeg Press.

Ricoeur, P. (1995a). *La critique et la conviction*. Paris: Calmann-Lévy.

Ricoeur, P. (1995b). Universality and the power of difference. In R. Kearney (Ed.), *States of mind: Dialogues with contemporary thinkers on the European mind*. Manchester: Manchester University Press, and New York: New York University Press.

Sluga, H. (1993). *Heidegger's crisis: Philosophy and politics in Nazi Germany*. Cambridge, MA: Harvard University Press.

Chapter 2

Meaning and Misconceptions   Anil Gupta

How should we think about the meaning of sentences in discourses that contain fundamental misconceptions? Reflection on this question reveals, I shall argue, some flaws in our current ideas about meaning (sections 2.2 and 2.3). And it motivates some modifications of these ideas that, I believe, are intuitively plausible and theoretically fruitful (sections 2.4–2.6).

2.1   An Example

Let us begin with an example of a discourse that embodies a fundamental misconception: discourse about "up" in a community that believes there

This chapter is dedicated to the memory of my friend John Macnamara and his love of philosophy.

I have been thinking about the problems discussed in this chapter for a long time, and over the years I have accumulated a large debt. My most significant debt is to my friend and former colleague Professor Mark Wilson. Mark and I have had numerous discussions on the problems of meaning and truth, and these conversations have been of great value to me. Also of value to me were some early discussions I had with Eric Dalton, Adam Kovach, and especially Jerry Kapus. I presented some of the ideas in this chapter in a graduate course on the philosophy of language given at Indiana University in spring 1997. I also presented these ideas in talks at MIT, National Chung Cheng University (Taiwan), and Notre Dame University. I wish to thank my auditors for the feedback they gave me. I also wish to thank the following people for their comments and suggestions: André Chapuis, William Demopoulos, Michael Friedman, James Hardy, Allen Hazen, Christopher Hill, Peter van Inwagen, Ray Jackendoff, Hans Kim, Robert Kraut, Byeong Deok Lee, Vann McGee, George Nakhnikian, Alvin Plantinga, Jerry Seligman, Robert Stalnaker, and Bosuk Yoon. Finally, I wish to thank the National Endowment for the Humanities for support. An NEH Fellowship for University Teachers enabled me to devote a part of the academic year 1995–1996 to this chapter.

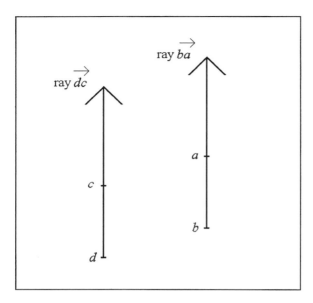

Figure 2.1

is an absolute distinguished direction in space called 'up'. It will simplify our discussion if we make the following assumptions about the community's use of 'up'. (In other respects, let the use of the term be much like ours.)

(i) Let us assume that two criteria govern the use of 'up' in the community's language. One criterion is perceptual: members of the community recognize the assertion of

(1) a is up above b

to be warranted in certain perceptually distinguishable situations. The other criterion is conceptual: members of the community recognize an assertion of (1) to be warranted when it is based on the premises

(2) c is up above d

and

(3) The direction of the ray $\overrightarrow{dc}$ is the same as that of the ray $\overrightarrow{ba}$.

(See figure 2.1.) Furthermore, they recognize the denial of (1) to be warranted when based on (2) and the denial of (3). These two criteria, let us assume, are of equal importance in the uses of 'up'. Both criteria come

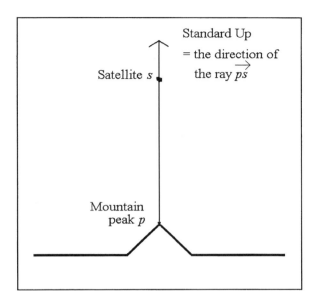

Figure 2.2

into play to an equal degree, and neither can be given priority over the other.

(ii) Let us also assume that the community uses certain objects to define the "Standard Up" direction. The community, let us assume, defines the Standard Up to be the direction of the ray $\overrightarrow{ps}$ determined by a mountain peak p and a natural satellite s located in a geostationary orbit above p. (See figure 2.2.) So, the community's conceptual criterion can also be reformulated as follows:

a is up above b iff the direction of the ray $\overrightarrow{ba}$ is the Standard Up.

This criterion, let us imagine, is so strongly embedded in the community that the two sides of the biconditional are regarded as equivalent ways of saying the same thing.

(iii) Let us assume that the community engages only in Plain Speech. There is in its discourse no subtle exploitation of conversational maxims to communicate one thing while saying another.[1] The content of, for example, an assertion made by using 'a is up above b' is precisely what the conventional meaning of the sentence would dictate it to be. The assumption of Plain Speech will enable us to focus on the main issues before us, freeing us from irrelevant distractions.

(iv) Finally, let us assume that the main conventions and facts about "up" and other related subjects are common knowledge. All members of the community are (and are recognized to be) authorities of equal standing on these subjects.[2] This assumption, like the previous one, removes merely extraneous factors from our deliberations. We lose nothing essential by making it.

The question before us is how to think about the *meaning* of sentences such as '*a* is up above *b*' in the community's language. It will be necessary to address also the parallel question about the *contents* of speech acts (e.g., assertions) and of attitudes (e.g., beliefs) that the speech acts express. The meaning of a sentence will be assumed to be fixed; it will not vary from context to context. But the content that a sentence is used to express cannot be assumed to be fixed, and I shall explore both possibilities with respect to it. In one group of theories I shall consider—namely, the *absolute* theories—content will remain fixed through all contexts. These theories will identify meaning with content. In the other group of theories I shall consider—namely, the *relativistic* theories—content will vary with context. These theories will draw a categorial distinction between meaning and content.

The concept of meaning is called upon in current philosophy of language and mind to serve many functions. These functions are so diverse that one may be excused for thinking that no concept can serve them all, that different notions of meaning are needed for different kinds of ends. The notion—or aspect—of meaning of interest here, I should stress, is one that yields a true/false distinction (or something similar such as the warranted/unwarranted distinction). The account of meaning (and content) should yield a satisfactory assessment of speech acts and of practices found in the community. The account should provide a way of separating those assertions that are true (or warranted) from those that are false (or unwarranted). And it should provide a way of separating those inferential practices that are sound (or adequate) from those that are unsound (or inadequate).

2.2   Conceptual-Role Semantics

Philosophy of language offers two broad approaches to gaining an understanding of meaning: the *representational* approach and the *conceptual-role* approach. The representational approach attempts to explain meaning by invoking language-world relations. On this approach, the meaning of a linguistic element is—or is constructed out of—what the item represents or would represent in various contexts and possible situations. Thus, on this approach, the meaning of a proper name (e.g., 'Socrates') might be identified with the referent of the name (the man Socrates)[3] and the meaning of a predicate F might be identified with the property F represents. The vocabulary this approach favors for the assessment of speech acts is that of the true and the false. An assertion of 'Socrates is F', for example, is evaluated as true if Socrates has the property represented by F; otherwise, the assertion is evaluated as false.

The second, conceptual-role, approach attempts to explain meaning via the rules governing the proper use of language. On this approach, the meaning of a linguistic element is given by the rules that specify the element's conceptual role in the linguistic system. Thus, on this approach, the meaning of a predicate F might be given by rules that state the conditions under which predications of F are warranted ("F-introduction" rules) and by rules that state the conclusions, both discursive and practical, that may be based on these predications ("F-elimination" rules).[4] The vocabulary this approach favors for the assessment of speech acts is that of the warranted and the unwarranted. An assertion of 'Socrates is F', for example, is evaluated as warranted, if the conditions under which the assertion is made are of the kind laid out in the F-introduction rules; otherwise, the assertion is evaluated as unwarranted.[5]

The two approaches to meaning rest on vastly different pictures of language. Still, the assessment of speech acts they yield are similar: the true/false distinction coincides with the warranted/unwarranted distinction over a large domain. This is not surprising, for both the language-world relations of the representational approach and the introduction-elimination rules of the conceptual-role approach have their foundations in the actual use of language. Over "decidable" assertions (i.e., assertions whose truth or falsity can be settled by the users of the language), the two approaches aim to yield the same verdicts. The debate between the two approaches centers on the "undecidable" assertions. Here the language-world relations of the representational approach may yield an assessment whereas the introduction-elimination rules of the conceptual-role approach may fail to do so.[6]

Although they illuminate much about language, the two approaches do not yield a solution to the problem of meaning before us. This is easiest to show for the conceptual-role approach. This approach takes the meaning of 'up' to be given by the rules governing its use—rules such as the per-

ceptual and conceptual criteria introduced above. The difficulty is that
these rules do not yield a satisfactory assessment of assertions. For many
pairs of objects a and b, the rules dictate that the assertion of 'a is up
above b' is warranted and also that its denial is warranted. Suppose a and
b are objects such that the direction of the ray $\overrightarrow{ba}$ is epistemically accessible to the community. The near spherical shape of the earth ensures that
objects c and d can be found (or placed) so that the direction of the ray $\overrightarrow{dc}$
is the same as that of the ray $\overrightarrow{ba}$ and, furthermore, the perceptual criterion
for 'c is up above d' is satisfied. The conceptual criterion now yields that
the assertion of 'a is up above b' is warranted. Similarly, the conceptual
criterion can be made to yield that the denial of 'a is up above b' is warranted: objects e and f can be found so that the direction of the ray $\overrightarrow{fe}$ is
not the same as that of the ray $\overrightarrow{ba}$ and, furthermore, the assertion of 'e is
up above f' is deemed warranted by the perceptual criterion (see figure
2.3).

This argument, it should be observed, reads the criteria for 'up' in a
strong way: as laying down what assertions, actual and possible, would be
warranted in various situations irrespective of the presence of a warrant-
supplying intelligence. Thus, it reads the perceptual criterion as stating

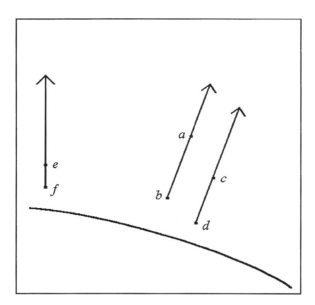

Figure 2.3

that in certain perceptually distinguish*able* situations '*a* is up above *b*' is warranted; whether someone actually experiences the situation and makes the assertion is irrelevant for the application of the criterion. This reading of the criterion is essential if the conceptual-role approach is to yield, even in unproblematic cases, a satisfactory demarcation of speech acts. On a weaker reading of the perceptual criterion (e.g., one that requires the situation to be actually experienced for '*a* is up above *b*' to be warranted), the warranted/unwarranted distinction diverges from the true/false distinction in completely unacceptable ways.

The argument assumes, I should note, that the community has the ability to determine the identity and distinctness of the directions of certain rays. This, it seems to me, is a harmless assumption and changes nothing essential in the example. In particular, it does not erase the possibility of the misconception about 'up': the community may harbor its misconception, for it may simply not have undertaken the expeditions and the experiments necessary to expose the misconception.

The conceptual-role approach, then, assesses far too many assertions of the form "*x* is up above *y*" in the same way. It attributes to them an incoherent content, a content determined by empirically incoherent conceptual rules. But, as the following examples illustrate, there can be a significant true/false distinction (or warranted/unwarranted distinction) among speech acts even in the presence of a fundamental misconception. The conceptual-role approach provides no resources for making the distinction, however.

The lamp example Suppose that two roommates A and B in our imagined community are debating which of the two lamps in their kitchen needs repair. A says that it is the one up above the stove, and B denies this. Suppose that as a matter of fact the broken lamp is the one used to illuminate the stove. Now we should assess A's assertion to be warranted (or true) and B's to be unwarranted (or false).[7]

The Vishnu example Suppose that the community has a primitive observatory that studies astronomical phenomena. The astronomers at the observatory record and predict—as far as they can—positions of astronomical objects. Their predictions are circulated in the local community and are used by the more curious members in their own study of the night sky. The astronomers, let us suppose, use their earlier observations to predict the relative positions of a bright astronomical object that the community calls 'Chandra' and another faint one the community calls 'Vishnu'. Their prediction "Vishnu will be directly up above Chandra at

9:00 p.m. today" is distributed, and is used by some astronomically inclined individuals to locate Vishnu in the night sky. Now, if the direction
of the ray from Chandra to Vishnu is in fact the same as that of the local
up direction—that is, if the astronomers' prediction is a good guide for
the community members—we should assess the astronomers' claim to be
warranted (or true).

Incoherence in conceptual rules, then, does not erase the true/false
(or the warranted/unwarranted) distinction between speech acts. The
problem before us is to find an account of meaning and content that will
enable us to draw this distinction even when the discourse contains radical
misconceptions and the resulting incoherence.

2.3   Representational Semantics

Let us now turn to the representational approach. The key question here
—one to which it is difficult to find a good answer—is what relation 'up'
represents in the community's language. Let us consider some possible
answers.

(i) Suppose it is said that 'up' represents the relation R, where

x bears R to y iff the direction of the ray $\overrightarrow{yx}$ is the Standard Up.[8]

This suggestion respects the conceptual criterion, but it neglects the perceptual criterion. As a result, it yields wrong assessments of many assertions; for instance, it yields that A's assertion in the lamp example is false
and B's assertion true.[9]

(ii) Suppose it is said instead that 'up' represents S, where

x bears S to y iff the straight line joining x and y passes through the
center of the earth o and the ray $\overrightarrow{yx}$ points away from o (equivalently,
iff the directions of the rays $\overrightarrow{yx}$ and $\overrightarrow{oy}$ are the same).

This suggestion encounters problems similar to those facing the previous
proposal. It respects some of the applications of the perceptual criterion,
but it neglects the conceptual criterion. It also yields wrong assessments of
many assertions (e.g., the astronomers' prediction in the Vishnu example).

One response to these difficulties is to insist that 'up' represents S and
that the troublesome phenomena can be explained away. But the explanatory burdens that the insistence entails are, in my view, unsustainable:
(1) An explanation has to be provided why it is S—as opposed to R and
various other relations—that constitutes the proper semantics for 'up'.

There must be something about the use of 'up' that makes S the proper interpretation, but our example provides nothing to distinguish it as proper. (2) An explanation has to be provided how certain sentences evaluated as false by the proposed semantics (e.g., the astronomers' prediction) are nonetheless good guides for action—whereas their true negations are poor guides. (3) This explanation will have to be quite different from the explanation given for those more straightforward cases in which sentences deemed true by the semantics are good guides for action. An account has to be given of this difference in the two explanations. Why are certain instances of successful linguistic behavior explained in one way and others in a completely different way?

(iii) Suppose it is said that 'up' represents the conjunctive relation R & S, where

x bears R & S to y iff x bears R to y and x bears S to y.

This suggestion lands us in an "error theory" for 'up': nearly all assertions of the form "x is up above y" are evaluated as false; only if a and b are collinear with the mountain peak p and the geostationary satellite s (see figure 2.2) can the assertion "a is up above b" be true. Thus, the theory fails in the same way that the conceptual-role approach failed: it does not yield a significant true/false distinction. (This kind of difficulty attaches, it seems to me, to all error theories. Hartry Field and J. L. Mackie are well known for their advocacy of error theories for, respectively, mathematics and ethics (see Field 1980; Mackie 1977). Field regards mathematical statements to be untrue and Mackie takes the same view of ethical claims. However, even if all the premises on which Field and Mackie base their views are granted—principally, that mathematical statements are burdened with an unacceptable Platonism and ethical statements with an unacceptable claim to objectivity—their error theories will remain unacceptable until these theories are shown to yield a significant true/false distinction.)

(iv) Suppose it is said that 'up' is ambiguous between R and S. This is also unsatisfactory. First, the postulated ambiguity is not discoverable by the community members through reflection on their language. Second, R and S are plausible candidates for the semantics of 'up' in only a few of its uses; other uses demand other relations. Hence, a manyfold ambiguity in 'up' will have to be postulated—something that is plainly unattractive.

(v) Suppose the idea of indeterminacy is tried in place of ambiguity. The suggestion now is that the semantics of 'up' is indeterminate, that 'up' is to be assigned a class of interpretations including R, S, and others. But this is not an improvement over earlier ideas. It implies that virtually all assertions of the form "x is up above y" are neither true nor false. We are landed again in an error theory.

Let us note, finally, that this and the previous difficulties are not overcome by the idea that we assign truth-conditions to 'a is up above b' directly, bypassing the specification of a relation for 'up'.

So far we have considered only absolute theories. These theories take all uses of 'a is up above b' to have the same content irrespective of the context of use. Let us now consider whether the difficulties we have encountered can be overcome if we allow content to vary with context. Perhaps the most natural way of relativizing content here is to view 'up' as being implicitly indexical—an indexical like 'I' whose interpretation varies systematically with context. We can spell out this variation as follows. Suppose we view the context as supplying the location of discourse, much as it supplies such elements as speaker and time for the interpretations of 'I' and 'now'. We can use the location to define "the standard up direction *relative to the context* c": this is the direction of the ray $\overrightarrow{ol}$ determined by the center of the earth o and the location l supplied by the context c. And we can say that, in a context c, 'up' represents the relation T_c, where

x bears T_c to y iff the direction of the ray $\overrightarrow{yx}$ is the standard up relative to c.

On this view, the relation represented by 'up' is determined by both the perceptual and the conceptual criteria governing 'up', but the application of the perceptual criterion is limited to the location of the discourse. Each location yields its own standard up direction and its own distinctive ordering of objects as constituting the relation "up above."

In contrast to the absolute theories, the relativistic theories make a categorial distinction between the contents expressed using 'a is up above b' and the meaning of 'a is up above b'. The content expressed by 'a is up above b' varies from context to context, but the meaning of 'a is up above b' does not vary. Further, the content can—but the meaning cannot—be evaluated as true or false. One can think of the content expressed by 'a is up above b' in a context c as a structured item built out of the denotations of 'a' and 'b' and the relation represented by 'up' in the context c. And, following David Kaplan, one can think of the meaning of 'a is up above b' as a rule (or function) that, given a context c, yields the content expressed by 'a is up above b' in c.

The indexical view has the virtue that it yields a nonvacuous true/false distinction for assertions. But the view faces several related—and, in my opinion, overwhelming—difficulties. First, the view does not draw the true/false distinction in the right way. In the lamp example, if the debate between A and B is conducted in the vicinity of the kitchen, then the view does yield the right truth-values for A's and B's assertions—namely, the value "true" for A's assertion that the broken lamp is up above the stove, and the value "false" for B's opposite claim. However, if the debate is conducted away from the kitchen, then the view yields assessments exactly opposite to the proper one: A's assertion is evaluated as false and B's assertion as true. For, now, the standard up relative to the debate's location differs from the standard up relative to the kitchen. And relative to the debate's location, the broken lamp does not lie in the standard up direction above the stove.

These considerations point to a second, related difficulty. The indexical view makes assessment of A's and B's assertions dependent on the location of their debate. As a consequence, the view yields a negative assessment of some practices—for example, *reassertion* and *appeal to authority* —that are fruitful and proper. It is easy to imagine that the practice of reasserting sentences such as 'The broken lamp is up above the stove', and of passing them from one mouth to another (regardless of location), can do useful work in the community. It may help, for example, in guiding a third party to repair the right lamp. According to the indexical view, however, reassertion of 'a is up above b' in a different location is always as fallacious as the reassertion of 'I am hungry' on the basis of another's assertion of the sentence. The indexical view explains the success of the practice of reassertion as due to a lucky accident: a series of fallacious moves combine to yield a happy result. Such an explanation is plainly unattractive. No fallacy is committed by A (or by B), if he reiterates his claim (possibly in a different location), or if others do so on the basis of his authority.[10] An adequate account of meaning should respect and explain this phenomenon. The success of the practice of reassertion is too ubiquitous and commonplace to warrant an imputation of error.

There is a third difficulty that highlights yet another aspect of the previous problem. Sentences of the form 'X believes that a is up above b', 'X desires that a be up above b', and the like are complete as they stand (neglecting tense as before). In this respect, they differ markedly from sentences containing genuine indexicals, such as 'X believes that *she* is not trustworthy' and 'X desires that Fred sit *over there*'. The latter sentences are incomplete: unless semantic values are specified for indexical terms in them, these sentences cannot be interpreted as making a definite claim or as expressing a proposition. The indexical view predicts that sentences such as 'A believes that the broken lamp is up above the stove' are similarly incomplete. But this plainly does not fit the facts. It is a plausible principle governing belief that the content of a belief is the content of any sincere expression (actual or potential) of it. A's belief receives sincere expression in his assertions of 'The broken lamp is up above the stove'. So the indexical view implies that the content of A's belief changes as A moves from location to location. This yields the undesirable result that the persistence of A's belief through his meanderings is as erroneous as the persistence of A's belief "Here is Mooresville" when he has long left the town behind on Route 67.[11]

The essential problem with the indexical view, then, is the same as that with the absolute views considered earlier. The indexical view finds only error where there is in fact much truth, and only fallacy where there is in fact essentially sound practice.

2.4   Conceptual Disengagement

Let us gather together what we should accept from the theories considered above. First, we should accept the absolutist idea that '*a* is up above *b*' expresses a proposition. For, as just observed, ascriptions of propositional attitudes such as '*X* believes that *a* is up above *b*' and '*X* desires that *a* be up above *b*' are complete as they stand. Their complement clauses express definite contents without needing values for any parameters. It follows that we should accept also that 'up above' expresses a binary concept (neglecting time as before). This concept takes as arguments two individual concepts—or individuals, if one prefers a Russellian semantics for names over the Fregean—and yields a proposition.[12] Second, we should concede to the absolutist that, in one sense, the proposition "*a* is up above *b*" is not true or even perhaps truth-apt.[13] That is, in one sense, all assertions of the form "*x* is up above *y*" are infected with error. Third, notwithstanding this concession, we have to recognize that there are important differences among these assertions, and we need to find a way of making sense of the differences. To do so, we shall have to accommodate relativistic ideas.

The difficulties we have had in making sense of the "up/down" discourse have their source, it seems to me, in the idea that the elements of our language have fixed interlocking conceptual connections with each other—connections that are all invoked in the uses of the elements. It is this idea, irrespective of whether we follow the lead of the absolute or of the relativistic theories, that blocks our way to making sense of the "up/ down" discourse. If we follow the absolute theories, the idea makes it impossible to see how an assertion such as "The broken lamp is up above the stove" could be true. For the assertion conceptually implies numerous claims that are plainly false—for example, "The direction of the ray that begins at the stove and goes through the broken lamp is the Standard Up."[14] The same holds of assertions of the form "x is up above y" generally. So the absolute approach lands us in an error theory for the discourse. We can avoid the error theory by shifting to the relativistic approach. But matters do not improve if we stick with the idea of rigid conceptual connections. For we are now forced to deny that sentences containing 'up' have problematic conceptual connections and, thus, that there is conceptual incoherence in "up." The indexical theory considered above goes so far in this direction as to say that the sense of 'up', like that of 'he', is not rich enough to yield assertible contents; some contextual information must be supplied before sentences containing 'up' express complete propositions. But to say this is to recoil from the phenomenon confronting us to the opposite extreme. The fact is that the sense of 'up' is not at all poor like that of the indexicals. The sense is actually far too rich—so rich that it constitutes a problem. If we stick with the idea of rigid conceptual connections, we are confined to unpalatable choices: error theory and the denial of the phenomena at hand.

Not all conceptual connections are relevant—not all are invoked, not all come into play—in every use of language. This is the lesson we should draw from the lamp example. Given the way the assertion "The broken lamp is up above the stove" is used, and is expected to be used, the relevant conceptual component is that provided by the perceptual criterion for 'up'. The normal use of the sentence might be something like this: the sentence is passed from person to person till it reaches a repairman, who then uses it to perceptually locate the lamp he will repair. Given that *this* is how the sentence is used, assertions of 'The broken lamp is up above the stove' are good and fruitful guides to action—they are true. Assertions of the negation are poor and misleading guides to action—they are false. This assessment of truth-value is one at which the community members themselves will arrive once they know the relevant facts. And the assessment would survive any unmasking of their misconception.

.

Even a god with a sweeping and eternal view of the world would concur with their assessment. In short, the assessment is neither parochial, nor fleeting, nor unstable. It is one that an account of meaning needs to respect and accommodate.

Every assertion of the form "x is up above y" contains error. The assertion of the sentence 'The broken lamp is up above the stove' can be used, it has to be conceded, in ways that conform to conceptual rules but lead to error. One, less serious, kind of error occurs in *idle* uses—when, for example, one derives from the lamp sentence the false claim that the direction of the ray that goes from the stove to the broken lamp is the Standard Up. If this derivation does not materially affect the use of the lamp sentence, then it is idle.[15] A more serious kind of error is also possible, however. Suppose, for example, that the repairman were to use the assertion in the following way: The repairman goes on an expedition to find the direction called 'the Standard Up'. Then through elaborate engineering he somehow constructs a pointer at the stove that points in this direction. Finally, he uses the pointer to locate the lamp he will repair. If he were to do all this, he might uncover a deep misconception in his community but he would not find his way to the right lamp. He would have been misled by the sign. This hypothetical way of using the sign is utterly eccentric, however.[16] And its existence should not call into question the idea that the assertion "The broken lamp is up above the stove" is, in one sense, true.

An analogy will help make this point clear. Suppose we have a flawed map of a city. The map, let us say, accurately depicts the streets in the center of the city, but is inaccurate regarding some streets that lie on the periphery. Plainly, despite the errors, the map remains a good and true instrument for navigating through the city center. This is so even though the map could mislead one if it is used to plan an eccentric roundabout route from one city-center street to another. Similarly, many conceptual paths issue from 'The broken lamp is up above the stove'; one can use this sign in many ways to guide one's actions. But some ways of using it are (in certain situations) salient and ordinary, whereas some other ways of using it are extraordinary and eccentric. The eccentric uses are valid and, indeed, important: they can expose fundamental flaws in our conceptions. Nonetheless, their possibility leaves intact the need for a distinction between truth and falsehood that respects actual practice.[17]

As noted above, not all conceptual connections come into play in all uses of language. This conceptual disengagement or isolation may occur even when we are not explicit—or even clear—about its extent or existence. Sometimes, however, conceptual disengagement results because of an explicit stipulation on our part. Consider, for example, our use of the notion of the celestial sphere—a notion that is a product of an ingenious synthesis of ages of ancient astronomical observations. We find this notion useful—even indispensable in some contexts—though we recognize it to rest on a deep error. Our use of the notion is in some ways very similar to that of the ancients: we follow them in speaking of certain parts of the sphere as constituting the constellations of the zodiac; we speak of the sun as being in Capricorn one month and Aquarius another; we infer the onset of spring when we see that the sun has a certain position in the zodiac; and so on. But we disengage all this talk from various other parts of our discourse: we no longer infer motion from variation of position; we no longer derive the true distance between stars from their (apparent) location on the sphere; we no longer think of the sphere as having a definite volume; and so on. A farmer in ancient times might have looked at the stars in the western night sky some chilly night and have said, "The sun is in Pisces; spring will be here soon." A modern child might do the same. The farmer's assertion is in one sense erroneous—the sense in which it is seen as fully engaged with the ancients' conception of the zodiac. But in another sense—one in which we are concerned with how the assertion is used in the farming community—the assertion might be as true as the child's. The child is explicit about the disengagement; the farmer is not. Nonetheless, the farmer's assertion, like the child's, can be assessed as true and can report a hard fact about the world.

Our language is not a rigid system. Its terms do not stand in fixed interlocking conceptual connections with each other. Engagement of our concepts is important for both theoretical and practical purposes. But so also, I want to stress, is disengagement. Only if we keep these dual possibilities—the possibility of engagement *and* of disengagement—firmly in mind can we make sense of how our language can function even when it is infected with deep misconceptions.

2.5   Frames

A familiar and good way of thinking about meaning is this. A declarative sentence, understood as a linguistic *type*, has meaning. When the sentence is used (e.g., to make an assertion), the speech act has a particular content—a content that is fixed by the meaning of the sentence and by certain features of context. The content, in turn, fixes, in light of the facts, the truth-value of the assertion. Thus, for example, the sentence 'She is in Indianapolis' has a certain meaning. Suppose I use the sentence to make an assertion and that the context of use supplies a person—say, MJ—as the denotation of 'she' and 24 January 1997 as the time reference for the present tense. This contextual information together with the meaning of 'She is in Indianapolis' fixes the content of my assertion to be that MJ is in Indianapolis on 24 January 1997. In view of the fact that MJ is actually in Bloomington on 24 January 1997, the content fixes the truth-value of my assertion to be the False. We can schematize this familiar way of thinking about meaning thus:

(*Meaning + Context*) Fixes $\Rightarrow$ *Content*;
(*Content + The World*) Fixes $\Rightarrow$ *Assessment of truth-value*.

Theories of meaning often use these schemata in reverse to "solve" for meaning. Thus, the second schema is used to derive the idea that content is a function that maps worlds to truth-values. And the first schema is used to derive the idea that meaning is a function that maps (relevant) contextual information to content.

This familiar way of thinking about meaning needs a little fine-tuning if it is to fit the phenomena highlighted above. We need to distinguish first of all two types of assessment, which we shall call 'assessment of *absolute* truth-value' and 'assessment of *effective* truth-value'. We encountered instances of these types in the previous section. The assessment of A's assertion, "The broken lamp is up above the stove," as erroneous is an assessment of its absolute truth-value. The other assessment, namely, that A's assertion is true, is an assessment of its effective truth-value. We need to distinguish also two types of content that are correlated with these assessments: *absolute* content and *effective* content. Absolute content is simply the old and familiar content under a new name. This content takes into account all the conceptual connections of an assertion and provides the basis for the assessment of absolute truth-value. Effective content, on the other hand, takes into account the conceptual engagements and dis-engagements that are in effect and provides the basis for an assessment of effective truth-value.[18] Absolute content captures what an act of assertion is *committed to*; effective content captures the content that is *in play*.

The two types of assessment have their own distinctive meaning-truth schemata. The version for absolute assessment parallels the original version closely:

(*Meaning + Context*) Fixes ⇒ *Absolute content*;
(*Absolute content + The World*) Fixes ⇒ *Assessment of absolute truth-value*.

The version of the schemata for effective assessment has to be a little more complicated because content that determines effective truth-value (i.e., effective content) is not fixed by meaning and context—at least, not if context is understood in the traditional way. Something else is needed; and this something else I shall call 'frame'. Under this terminology, the schemata for effective assessment are as follows:

(*Meaning + Context + Frame*) Fixes ⇒ *Effective content*;
(*Effective content + The World*) Fixes ⇒ *Assessment of effective truth-value*.

Let us clarify the notion of frame by reflecting on how contexts and frames differ.

First, let us note that contexts are local but frames are not. Contexts carry information such as denotations of personal pronouns and demonstratives, senses in which ambiguous words are to be understood, and degrees of vagueness to be tolerated in certain predicates—information that is provided by the local speech situation.[19] But this local sort of information will not suffice to fix effective content. For this we need, in addition, information about normal or standard uses of sentences—information that is not localized to any particular speech situation but is spread across uses of language. Frames, then, are not local in that they carry this nonlocal sort of information. There is another respect in which frames fail to be local: frames stay constant through a substantial range of speech situations. Contexts, on the other hand, tend to be highly variable, for the denotations, say, of the personal pronouns are liable to shift from speech situation to speech situation. Frames thus occupy a place intermediate between context and language. Language can remain fixed through variation in frame, and frame through variation in context. Context is highly local, language is global, and frame lies in between the two.

Second, contexts and frames have different functions in the fixing of content. Context often serves, as remarked earlier, to fill holes in content. Without contextual information, an assertion of, say, 'He is hungry' is incomplete. The function of frame is altogether different. Frame helps determine the content that is in play. So, although context often adds to content, frame often subtracts from it. This difference in function is reflected in a difference in relationship to the rules of language. Rules of language make reference to, and partly determine, what constitutes context. The rules governing 'I', for example, determine that the identity of the speaker is relevant contextual information, and the rules refer to this information in specifying the proper use of sentences containing 'I'. Frames, on the other hand, do not figure in the statement of the rules of language. Nor do these rules fix the character of frames. Frames concern *how* the rules of language are applied or implemented. Perhaps this contrast can usefully be put as follows: contexts are in part internal to the rules of language, but frames are wholly external.

Third, context and frame have different connections with understanding. Information carried by the context is necessary for understanding what a speaker has said; not so for information carried by the frame. If one does not know the intended denotations of indexicals used in an assertion, then one does not understand what has been said. But lack of information carried by the frame does not imply lack of understanding.[20] Frames contain information that accounts for effective uses of language, and this information is not always necessary for *using* language. The point here is general: knowledge needed for using an instrument effectively is not necessarily the knowledge needed for understanding the effectiveness of the instrument.[21]

Fourth, frames do not always exist. Successful communication implies the existence of a sufficiently rich context, but it does not imply the existence of a frame. Existence of a frame requires not only successful communication but also successful practice. Let a speaker in the community imagined earlier say, 'Up above every star there is another star'. The speaker expresses a definite thought that can be grasped, and debated, by her neighbors. But there may well not be systematic and successful practice connected with her assertion (and related assertions) to allow a separation of absolute content from effective content; there may be no frame associated with her assertion. Existence of requisite frames is a feature that separates the ordinary and the practical from the theoretical and the speculative in the use of language.

Let these observations suffice for now as an explanation of frame. Much more can be said—and needs to be said—on the subject. But let us postpone this to another occasion and turn to some philosophical consequences and applications.

2.6   Realism and Antirealism

Metaphysical debates about the reality of objects and properties (e.g., numbers, theoretical posits, everyday objects, and goodness) typically transform into debates about the nature of the discourses about the respective objects and properties (arithmetic, science, ordinary discourse, and normative discourse).[22] Two contrasting pictures dominate the latter debates. One picture, favored by those who espouse *realism*, presents the discourse as *representational*: the elements of the discourse "hook up with the world"; the names and predicates in the discourse refer to objects and properties (including relations) in the world.[23] On this picture, the discourse *engages with the world*: our use of the discourse is seen as guided and constrained by, and as being responsible to, how things are. The other picture, favored by those who espouse *antirealism*, presents the discourse as nonrepresentational, as not hooking up with the world. This picture builds on the idea that not all our discourses serve one and the same function: reporting how things are. Different discourses—for example, mathematics, physics, and everyday discourse—serve, it is suggested, different functions: the point of mathematical discourse is not to report on how things are in some otherworldly mathematical reality, but a more practical one of enabling shorter deductions; the point of physical discourse is not to report on some mysterious invisible universe, but to enable us to cope with everyday needs and problems in an efficient way; and even everyday discourse, it has been suggested, does not aim to report on an inaccessible external world, but to bring order and manageability into our chaotic sense impressions. On the antirealist picture, discourse does not engage with the world; it is not constrained by how things are. But this does not mean that the discourse is completely unconstrained and freewheeling. According to the antirealist, the distinctive function of the discourse provides a strong constraint on it.

This is, I should stress, a bare sketch of the dominant pictures underlying the current debate. The debate itself provides a wealth of alternative ways of developing, modifying, and defending the pictures. I will not enter into the details here, for my aim is to point out a problem in the dominant pictures. This problem in turn suggests a synthesis that may be useful for understanding some (not all!) of our conceptual activity.[24]

The realist picture, we have seen, subscribes to the ideas of representationalism (R) and engagement-with-the-world (E); the antirealist picture subscribes to the ideas of antirepresentationalism (not-R) and disengagement-from-the-world (not-E). The typical realist argument (e.g., for physics) is based on success: if the objects physics speaks about (gravitational action at a distance, curved space-time, and such) do not exist, then—in the words of Hilary Putnam—

it is a *miracle* that a theory which speaks of gravitational action at a distance successfully predicts phenomena; it is a *miracle* that a theory which speaks of curved space-time successfully predicts phenomena. (1978, 19)

The strength of this argument lies in the transition from success to engagement-with-the-world (E)—it would indeed be a miracle if physics yielded helpful predictions and were at the same time disengaged from the world. The rest of the realist argument consists of a move from engagement-with-the-world (E) to representationalism (R). The typical antirealist argument, on the other hand, rests on the "queerness" (to use an expression of J. L. Mackie's) of the objects, and of the "referring" or "picturing" relation, required by representationalism. The antirealist thus rejects representationalism and moves from there to embrace disengagement (not-E).

The realist argument moves from engagement (E) to representationalism (R); the antirealist argument from antirepresentationalism (not-R) to disengagement (not-E). The two arguments share an important assumption (namely, if E then R)—and one that is problematic. The fact that a discourse genuinely engages with the world does not imply that it "pictures" the world. Contrapositively, the fact that a discourse fails to picture the world does not imply that it is disengaged from the world. The problem with the realist and antirealist pictures is that they contain an illegitimate link between engagement and representationalism.

A useful synthesis of the realist and antirealist pictures is possible. This synthesis views the discourse as engaging with the world and as serving the function of informing us how things are—in this respect it follows realism—but it adopts the antirealist idea that the discourse is not representational. This possibility is illustrated by our imagined community and its talk about "up." A representational semantics for 'up', we have seen, is not acceptable. But the community's discourse is fully engaged with the world. The primary point of the "up" talk is to help community members navigate their way around the world by making them sensitive to how things are (or are desired to be).

The gap between representationalism and engagement can be made intelligible through the notion of "frame" (section 2.5). Consider again the example of the repairman and how he locates the broken lamp. Roommate A determines the position of the broken lamp perceptually and arrives at the judgment that the broken lamp is up above the stove. He utters the words 'The broken lamp is up above the stove' to inform others of the location of the lamp. These words (or their variants) are passed from mouth to mouth till they reach the repairman, who uses them to perceptually locate the lamp to be repaired. The sentence 'The broken lamp is up above the stove', we have seen, cannot be assigned determinate truth-conditions. However, relative to the pattern of use exemplified, relative to the frame of use, we may be able to assign 'up above' a definite relation—perhaps the relation S defined in section 2.3—and the sentence determinate truth-conditions. Once we keep the frame fixed, we can reasonably view A's perceptual interaction with the world as providing A with information about the relative positions of the lamp and the stove, information that he passes to the repairman via the various intermediaries. Absolutely speaking, 'up' does not represent any relation, but relative to a frame, when the use of 'up' is disengaged from some of the conceptual elements, it may well represent a definite relation. Disengagement within the conceptual system can help bring about engagement with the world.

The success of our linguistic and conceptual practices proves at most that our assertions have true effective contents. That is, it proves at most that within their respective frames our assertions hook on to the world. But from this we cannot conclude that our assertions have true absolute contents and that our discourse pictures the world. Such a conclusion would follow only if our linguistic and conceptual practices constituted a monolithic whole, unfragmented into multiple frames. Mere success of our practices does not establish the requisite unity in our thought.

The proposal, then, is to combine nonrepresentationalism and engagement in the following way. We allow a discourse to be nonrepresentational in that the absolute contents expressed by its statements are problematic—perhaps they all contain error; perhaps they are ill defined. But we allow the discourse to engage with the world in that much (perhaps most) of the discourse is viewed as separable under several frames. Relative to these frames, the statements of the discourse have (effective) contents that can be assessed for truth and falsehood.

This combination of nonrepresentationalism and engagement avoids some of the weaknesses of both realism and antirealism. Antirealism is prone to view our theory construction as being so much storytelling;

realism, on the other hand, is prone to view it as so much revealed truth. Neither tendency is acceptable—except insofar as it provides a counter to the other. Realists are correct to insist that there is a vast difference between fictional discourse and theoretical discourse. Fictional discourse does not—but theoretical discourse does—engage with the world.[25] Unlike fictional discourse, a discarded scientific theory—even one that proves to be deeply erroneous, and one for which we are unable to provide a representational semantics—generates useful frames and true effective contents. (Example: "Don't touch that. It has high caloric content.")[26] Indeed, sometimes a discarded theory proves such a convenience within certain frames that we allow its continued use, with the proviso that the use shall not extend beyond those frames (as in the celestial sphere example given above). I suspect that this kind of fragmented use is more prevalent in our language than we realize.

Antirealists, on the other hand, are correct to insist that our present theoretical terms do not have a special status over those of the earlier scientists, prophets, and myth-makers: there is little reason to count as representational our present-day theoretical terms while denying this status to the terms of the earlier, discarded theories. Our evidence and our situation in the world are not essentially different from those of our ancestors. Our evidence is not so comprehensive, nor our understanding so deep and clear, that we can rule out the possibility that we ourselves suffer from deep misconceptions. The perennial problems of philosophy and the irresistible force of the skeptical arguments stand witness to the fragmentation in our understanding and the narrowness of our evidence.[27]

Conceptual disengagement and fragmentation of thought are essential for creatures such as we are. Had God (or evolution) equipped us with the right set of concepts once and for all, had the overall structure of the world been somehow revealed to us (as Plato and Descartes thought), had our inquiries only the simple goal of filling in the mere details in a given, a priori, picture of the world—had our epistemic position been so fortunate, disengagement and fragmentation might have had no place in the workings of our language and thought. But, unfortunately, our epistemic position is a precarious one. We do not approach the task of understanding the world with perfect ready-made tools in our hands. We approach the task bare-handed; we need to *make* the tools, including the tools needed to make the tools themselves. We need to make (or discover) the system of concepts needed to conceptualize the detailed facts about the world, facts that are essential to our well-being. However, we cannot arrive at the right system of concepts without an adequate fund of facts, and we cannot arrive at an adequate fund of facts without the right system of concepts. If we had the right system of concepts, we could securely go about collecting and cataloging facts. If we had a fund of solid facts, we could securely go about improving our system of concepts. However, we begin our inquiry into the world having neither—neither the right system of concepts nor a fund of solid facts. We need somehow, through our inquiry, to work our way to both. It is inevitable that in the process we need to work with imperfect systems of concepts—systems that embody deep misconceptions—and with the resultant distortions of fact. It is this epistemic environment that makes conceptual disengagement and fragmentation of thought inevitable and important.

Notes

1. The importance of conversational maxims for the study of language was first observed by Paul Grice (see Grice 1989).

2. So I wish to set aside what Hilary Putnam calls 'the division of linguistic labor' (see Putnam 1975).

3. And it is so identified by a currently popular theory.

4. The version of conceptual-role semantics I shall be working with is due to Wilfrid Sellars and Robert Brandom (see Sellars 1953, 1974; Brandom 1994). Two distinctive features of the Sellars-Brandom semantics are worth noting. First, it explains meaning and content in terms of inferential role, as opposed to, say, functional role in the user's psychology (cf. Harman 1982). Second, it understands inferential role to include role in substantive, material inferences, not merely formal inferences.

5. Note that the conceptual-role approach uses an absolute notion of "warrant." This notion is connected to, but it is *not* identical with, the notion "warranted given that the language user is in such-and-such epistemic situation." The connection between the two notions is roughly as follows: P is warranted in the absolute sense if and only if P would be warranted by the rules of language under idealized epistemic conditions.

6. I follow Michael Dummett jn seeing the primary disagreement between the representational approach and its rivals to be over undecidable sentences (see Dummett 1978, 1993).

7. Let me stress that the sense in which 'warrant' is used here is not that of personal warrant. It does not mean "being warranted given one's epistemic situation." In this latter sense, it could well be that both the assertions of A and B are warranted—or that neither of them is.

8. Here and below, I make several simplifying assumptions—for example, that objects can be treated as if they were points and that 'up' is not vague. Further, I

suppress the relativity of 'up' to time. (Some of the complexities of our actual uses of 'up' are detailed in Jackendoff 1996.)

9. Assuming, as I shall, that A's and B's kitchen is not on the mountain peak p (figure 2.2).

10. I am assuming, of course, that there are no other reasons to call into question A's authority on this matter.

11. Another way of putting the difficulty is this: the wish of a person, X, that a be up above b can be fulfilled only by adjusting the positions of a and b, not by moving X to a place where the standard up is the direction of $\vec{ba}$!

12. The idea that 'a is up above b' expresses a proposition and 'up above' a binary concept will meet resistance from the Platonist and from the Nominalist. These new entities will seem to the Platonist to be unworthy of a place in the realm of Platonic Heaven; to the Nominalist they will seem unworthy of a place even in the realm of ordinary existence. In response, it may be observed to the Platonist that the new entities exemplify an important virtue: they do real work in our conceptual scheme. Furthermore, whatever flaws may be found in these entities, the same flaws (and many more) are found reflected in Truth, whose place in Platonic Heaven is unquestioned. To the Nominalist it may be observed that the new entities are not going to make their programs any more difficult to execute. Any scheme they devise that succeeds in eliminating the familiar abstract entities will succeed in eliminating the new, unfamiliar ones as well.

13. Propositions are defined in the literature in two nonequivalent ways. Sometimes they are defined as the objects of attitudes such as belief and desire; sometimes they are defined as objects that are truth-apt. The first definition puts propositions closer to the represent*ings*; the second puts them closer to the represent*eds*. I have chosen above to follow the first definition, but the choice is purely terminological. The important point is that the two definitions define distinct notions. Which notion ends up winning the label 'proposition' is not at all important.

14. Recall we are assuming that the kitchen is not located on the mountain peak p (see figure 2.2).

15. Another sort of idle use is worth noting. Suppose roommate A informs the repairman of the location of the lamp by saying,

(i) The direction of the ray that goes from the stove to the broken lamp is the Standard Up.

The repairman naturally uses (i) to infer that

(ii) The broken lamp is up above the stove,

and proceeds in his usual way to locate the lamp to be repaired. The use of (i) is not now idle, for it informs the repairman of the lamp's location. But the detour via directions contained in (i) *is* idle. For A arrives at (i) through (ii), and he relies on the repairman to return to (ii) from the assertion of (i). (This sort of idle detour via the theoretical is also witnessed in a college cafeteria when a student employee marks the water container 'H_2O'.)

16. More eccentric than if at a dinner party a guest should pull out a microscope to examine the contents of her plate before declaring that the host had served peas. Deep errors in our botanical theories might be revealed by this chance examination, but a dinner party is not the time and place to explore the possibility.

17. This conclusion is bolstered by the fact that *we*, who are aware of the misconception, are willing to ascribe *knowledge that* the broken lamp is up above the stove. We would explain some of the successes of the community members in terms of their possession, and some of their failures in terms of their lack, of this knowledge. Since knowledge implies truth, it follows that we recognize that there is a sense in which the assertion that the broken lamp is up above the stove is true.

18. I use the word 'effective' here to indicate that the notions of truth-value and content under discussion serve to explain the practical effectiveness of language.

This is not the place to develop a precise account of effective contents. For the purposes of this chapter, effective contents can be thought of as being of the same general type as absolute contents. Whether one favors the idea that absolute contents are conceptual roles, or the idea that they are sets of possible worlds, or that they are Russellian structured entities, one can take a parallel view of effective contents. Note that absolute and effective contents, though they can formally be similar, are, in general, materially different. For example, if content is understood as conceptual role, effective content will be restricted conceptual role. For another example, if content is understood as a set of possible worlds, the effective and absolute contents of an assertion will often be given by different sets of possible worlds.

19. For a good account of information that might be supplied by context, and how it might evolve in the course of conversation, see Lewis 1979.

20. Hence, the meaning-truth schemata for effective truth should not be used to "solve" for meaning, if we wish to preserve a connection between meaning and understanding.

21. The importance of separating factors that help explain understanding from those that help explain the workings of language has been stressed by Mark Wilson (see Wilson 1994, forthcoming a,b).

22. The literature generated by these debates is vast (see Field 1980; Mackie 1977; Leplin 1984; Sayre-McCord 1988; Devitt 1991 and the works cited there). Jackendoff 1991 is a valuable contribution to the realism debate for intentional discourse. Maddy 1990 and Wright 1992 contain illuminating discussions of several aspects of the debates.

23. This claim needs qualification. First, it should be understood to be restricted to names and predicates that are essential to the discourse. A realism with respect to physics may be willing to allow that some of the names and predicates found in physical discourse (e.g., arithmetical ones) fail to refer. Second, the names and predicates that are essential may not be discernible simply from the surface grammar of the discourse; it may be necessary to reveal the deeper logical form of the discourse. Third, on some varieties of realism, language-world relations count as representational if statements are correlated with states of affairs, bypassing

worldly assignments for names and predicates. For example, if a statement such as "The United States government has reduced all tariffs on imports" is correlated with a complicated worldly state of affairs (including the actions of the president and the various members of Congress), the correlation will count as representational, even though the terms and predicates in the sentence (and in its logical analysis) are not correlated with worldly items.

I will continue to use the simpler formulations of "representationalism" given in the text, leaving the qualifications implicit.

24. In contemporary philosophy, one finds the dialectic of thesis and antithesis followed often, not by a useful synthesis, but by a sterile super-antithesis, one which asserts that the earlier dialectic is meaningless. This super-antithesis invites, of course, a super-thesis that the dialectic is indeed meaningful. And the focus shifts to a new debate at a higher level—"higher" not in the sense of nobler or better but in the sense of being more detached from down-to-earth concerns that really matter. The entire foundation for the super-antithesis (with respect to the realism/antirealism debate) rests, in my opinion, on misconceptions about the concepts of truth and meaning. In essential respects, the super-antithesis mirrors, in content and in the ways it goes wrong, the logical positivist rejection of metaphysics on the basis of the verification theory of meaning. (The proponents of the super-antithesis are some of the most vehement critics of logical positivism. But they seem to me to exemplify many of the intellectual vices of the positivists, and few of their virtues. In philosophy wrong attitudes are often more pernicious than wrong doctrines.)

25. I am setting aside figurative uses of fictional terms.

26. A distinction is worth noting here: a complete rejection of the vocabulary of the theory and a complete rejection of the statements of the theory. The former does not imply the latter. We reject the use of 'caloric' and 'witches' in our descriptions of the world, but this does not require us to reject completely all earlier statements containing these terms. We can, and should, attribute true effective contents to many of these statements.

27. I do not mean to suggest that nonrepresentationalism is plausible for all theoretical terms. I do think that it is attractive to treat all of our theories, both the earlier rejected ones and the currently accepted ones, as semantically pretty much on a par. All engage with the world, though some more fruitfully than others. All fail to be representational, though again some more than others.

References

Brandom, R. (1994). *Making it explicit: Reasoning, representing, and discursive commitment*. Cambridge, MA: Harvard University Press.

Devitt, M. (1991). *Realism and truth* (2nd ed.). Oxford: Blackwell.

Dummett, M. (1978). *Truth and other enigmas*. London: Duckworth.

Dummett, M. (1993). *The seas of language*. Oxford: Clarendon Press.

Field, H. H. (1980). *Science without numbers: A defense of nominalism*. Princeton, NJ: Princeton University Press.

Grice, P. (1989). *Studies in the way of words*. Cambridge, MA: Harvard University Press.

Harman, G. (1982). Conceptual role semantics. *Notre Dame Journal of Formal Logic, 23,* 242–256.

Jackendoff, R. (1991). The problem of reality. *Noûs, 25,* 411–433.

Jackendoff, R. (1996). The architecture of the linguistic-spatial interface. In P. Bloom, M. Peterson, L. Nadel, and M. Garrett (Eds.), *Language and space* (pp. 1–30). Cambridge, MA: MIT Press.

Leplin, J. (Ed.). (1984). *Scientific realism*. Berkeley and Los Angeles: University of California Press.

Lewis, D. (1979). Scorekeeping in a language game. *Journal of Philosophical Logic, 8,* 339–359.

Mackie, J. L. (1977). *Ethics: Inventing right and wrong*. London: Penguin.

Maddy, P. (1990). *Realism in mathematics*. Oxford: Clarendon Press.

Putnam, H. (1975). *Mind, language, and reality: Philosophical papers, vol. 2*. Cambridge: Cambridge University Press.

Putnam, H. (1978). *Meaning and the moral sciences*. London: Routledge & Kegan Paul.

Sayre-McCord, G. (Ed.). (1988). *Essays on moral realism*. Ithaca, NY: Cornell University Press.

Sellars, W. (1953). Inference and meaning. *Mind, 62,* 313–338.

Sellars, W. (1974). Meaning and functional classification. *Synthese, 27,* 417–437.

Wilson, M. (1994). Can we trust logical form? *Journal of Philosophy, 91,* 519–544.

Wilson, M. (Forthcoming a). Inference and correlational truth.

Wilson, M. (Forthcoming b). Physica sunt, non leguntur.

Wright, C. (1992). *Truth and objectivity*. Cambridge, MA: Harvard University Press.

Chapter 3

On Structuralism in Mathematics

Michael Makkai

For some years, I have been pursuing a program I call the structuralist foundation of mathematics (SFM) (Makkai 1996, 1997, 1998, to appear). SFM is based on category theory, a branch of mathematics founded by Samuel Eilenberg and Saunders Mac Lane about fifty years ago (Eilenberg and Mac Lane 1945). William Lawvere's work (e.g., Lawvere 1969) has made category theory the basis of a new foundational approach to mathematics and logic. Lawvere's categorical logic (e.g., Lawvere 1970) and Lawvere's and Myles Tierney's topos theory (Lawvere 1971), subjects that have been extensively developed, are integral parts of SFM.

In relation to other approaches to foundations within category theory, the distinguishing features of SFM are, first, that its aims are global, encompassing the totality of mathematics, and, second, that it is committed to a total linguistic articulation in the spirit of Gottlob Frege. Today, we express the latter commitment by saying that a foundational proposal has to be presented in the form of a formal theory. At the same time, SFM intends to articulate, intuitively and philosophically, a universe of

The author's research is supported by Canada's Natural Sciences and Engineering Research Council and Quebec's Fonds pour la formation de chercheurs et l'aide à la recherche.

I want to thank Bill Boshuck, Michael Hallett, Dusko Pavlovic, Gonzalo Reyes, and Marek Zawadowski for the conversations they had with me about the subject of this chapter. The chapter is based on a talk that I gave in the Department of Philosophy at McGill University in the fall of 1994. I also thank Ray Jackendoff for reading the chapter and for valuable suggestions.

John Macnamara was, for many years, a constant source of inspiration and encouragement for me. His interests and insights in philosophy have influenced my thinking profoundly. This chapter is dedicated to his memory.

discourse behind the formal theory. It turns out that the latter articulation involves a fairly novel mathematical metatheory.

There is a structuralist philosophy of mathematics behind the program of SFM. In this chapter, my aim is to make an initial contribution to the statement of this philosophy. This structuralism, it seems to me, is quite different from the structuralism found in the literature of the philosophy of mathematics. The basis of this difference is, of course, the almost total lack of attention paid by the philosophical literature to category theory. Charles Parsons has argued, somewhat tentatively, that structuralism may be used as a philosophical justification of the classical Cantorian iterative set theory (Parsons 1990). The structuralism I have in mind involves a radically different "set theory," a new conception of mathematical totalities, the formal explication of which involves concepts of category theory, (some of which—higher dimensional categories—are being developed at present). I see mathematical structuralism as *identical to a specific conception concerning mathematical totalities*—not something that can exist independently of any such conception and can then be applied to deal with already given such conceptions. According to a pervasive complaint (see Parsons 1990) about structuralism, it cannot be an independent foundation, since it relies on the concept of structure, which, in the final analysis, is a set-theoretical concept. This complaint also assumes that the nature of set theory is given before we can discuss what structuralism is.

In this chapter, I will argue for the desirability of a comprehensive language of mathematics in which *only* structural properties of mathematical objects can be expressed. The discussion intends to lead to the conclusion that "structural properties" are identical to "mathematically meaningful properties." Paul Benacerraf's classic paper, "What Numbers Could Not Be" (Benacerraf 1965), is in fact a sustained argument to the same end: it is a plea for a language in which one talks about numbers *only as* numbers. Section 3.1 of the present chapter is a commentary on the first two sections of Benacerraf's paper. What separates my views from Benacerraf's is that I believe that the articulation of the desired structural language is possible. As a matter of fact, what Benacerraf says in his third section entitled "Way Out," especially the subsection "Identity," points importantly to what I consider to be the solution (compare the references to my work). However, in his subsequent paper "Mathematical Truth" (Benacerraf 1973), Benacerraf seems to have lost faith in a structuralist program, at least in the radical form I am advocating. In section 3.3 of the present chapter, I will try to show that the "standard semantical picture of the world," to which Benaceraff is (essentially) committed in his 1973 paper, is in fact fictitious. This conclusion will involve the thesis that the nature of mathematical objects is not fundamentally different from the nature of myriad nonmathematical everyday abstract objects. The reality of abstract objects is grounded in a *structural* language that, although referring ostensibly to concrete, representing carriers of the abstractions, manages to unambiguously refer to the abstract objects, by the discipline of staying within the framework of concepts that are meaningful for the abstract objects *as* abstract objects. In this case, *reality is grounded in language*.

Makkai 1998 is a semitechnical introduction to the mathematical work; it also contributes to explaining the philosophy of structuralism as I understand this term. However, there is much more to be said about this subject, to which I hope to return another time.

3.1 Reality through Language

In his famous 1965 paper, "What Numbers Could Not Be," Paul Benaceraff describes two children, Ernie and Johnny, "sons of militant logicists," who, before learning about numbers, how to count, and so on, had been instructed in set theory in the standard Zermelo-Fraenkel formulation. After that instruction, the parents "needed only to point out what aspect or part of what the children already knew, under other names, was what ordinary people called numbers" (p. 48). Benaceraff goes on to describe *how* this pointing out took place in the case of Ernie; but he temporarily and cleverly conceals *what* actually took place in the process. The story *looks like* the familiar one, the one of defining the natural numbers as the finite von Neumann ordinals, and defining zero and the successor operation in the familiar ways—the one we teach nowadays in set theory courses. As Benaceraff puts it:

To recapitulate: It was necessary [for a proper education in arithmetic] (1) to give definitions of "1", "number", and "successor", and "+", "×", and so forth, on the basis of which the laws of arithmetic could be derived; (2) explain the "extramathematical" uses of numbers, the principal one being counting—thereby introducing the concept of *cardinality* and cardinal number. I trust that both were done satisfactorily, that the preceding [description of Ernie's education] contains all the elements of a correct account, albeit somewhat incompletely. (p. 54)

Then we learn that Johnny underwent a similar education.

Delighted with what they had learned, they started proving theorems about numbers. Comparing notes, they soon became aware that something was wrong, for a dispute immediately ensued about whether or not 3 belonged to 17. Ernie said that it did, Johnny that it did not. Attempts to settle this by asking ordinary folk (who had been dealing with numbers *as* numbers for a long time) understandably brought only blank stares. (p. 54)

At this point in the story, we learn *what* exactly happened in the respective educations. Indeed, as we thought, Ernie was taught that the natural numbers are (Johnny) von Neumann ordinals. Johnny, on the other hand, was told that they are the (Ernie) Zermelo numerals; that is, zero is the empty set, and the successor of n is $\{n\}$, the singleton whose unique element is n.

After reflecting on the dilemma, Benaceraff arrives at the conclusion that

3 and its fellow numbers could not be sets at all. (p. 62)

Along the way, he says:

But if, as I think we agreed, the account of the previous section [in which the set-theoretic reconstruction of the concept of number was related, albeit with *what* the numbers and their operations actually were left unspecified] was correct—not only as far as it went but correct in that it contained conditions which were both necessary and *sufficient* for any correct account of the phenomena under discussion, then the fact that they disagree which particular sets the numbers are is fatal to the view that each number is some particular set. (pp. 55, 56)

Later:

Furthermore, in Fregean terminology, each [of the two] account[s] fixes the *sense* of the words whose analysis it provides. Each account must also, therefore, fix the reference of these expressions. Yet, as we have seen, one way in which these accounts differ is in the referents assigned to the terms under analysis. (p. 56)

And:

Therefore, exactly one is correct, or none is. But then the correct one must be the one that picks out which set of sets is *in fact* the numbers. We are faced with a crucial problem: if there exists such a "correct" account, do there also exist arguments which will show it to be the correct one? (p. 57)

Casting his net wider, he then probes the Fregean account according to which numbers are predicates or classes, and finds it wanting, for expected reasons related to the paradoxes, but also because there is *no grammatical evidence that seventeen is a predicate of classes* ("has seventeen members" is obviously such a predicate, but that is something else than to say that seventeen is such a predicate). He then summarizes:

> If numbers are sets, then they must be *particular sets*, for each set is some particular set. But if the number 3 is really one set rather than another, it must be possible to give some cogent reason for thinking so; for the position that this is an unknowable truth is hardly tenable.... There is no way connected with the reference of number words which will allow us to choose among them, *for the accounts differ at places where there is no connection whatever between features of the accounts and our uses of the words in question.... [A]ny feature of an account that identifies 3 with a set is a superfluous one*, and therefore, 3 and its fellow numbers could not be sets at all. (p. 62)

Benaceraff emphasizes that for the purposes of *explication*, one may very well wish to temporarily *identify* numbers with particular sets and show that we can do with the sets what we now do with numbers. However, as he says:

> It is ... obvious that to discover that a system of objects will do cannot be to discover which objects the numbers are. (p. 68)

Benaceraff mentions a result due to G. Takeuti according to which set theory is in a strong sense reducible to the theory of ordinal numbers.

> No wonder numbers are sets; sets are really (ordinal) numbers, after all. *But now, which is really which?* (p. 68)

What are we to make of Benaceraff's argument?

The first reaction may be to say that the argument invalidates the usual set-theoretic treatment of numbers. I want to argue that this is not so—that in fact, the set-theoretic Platonist engaged in the foundations of mathematics and Benaceraff can agree without compromising their positions in any essential way. A perfectly satisfactory position the standard Platonist may adopt seems to be that, indeed, set theory is incapable of telling us *what* the numbers are; but in fact, it does not aim at doing that in the first place. What set theory wants to do, and does, is explain *what we mean when we talk about numbers*. It gives us a systematic way of translating "ordinary" mathematical statements involving numbers into set-theoretic statements, and it provides reliable methods for proving and refuting such statements. Indeed, and this is an important additional fact contributing to the explanatory power of set theory, it does its work in a remarkably simple particular manner, by *identifying* numbers and other mathematical objects as certain sets, such that the original statement— say, about numbers—is translated into its set-theoretical version by simply replacing reference to the mathematician's numbers by reference to their set-theoretical surrogates. But note, set theory does this without creating any prejudice concerning the issue of *what the numbers really are*, or, for that matter, *whether they exist at all*! Further, standard set theory can do more than that: it can give a *theory* of *what* constitutes a satisfactory surrogate for the notion of number. This exemplifies a very important point about a good foundation: namely, the requirement that it should have the tools to reflect about itself to the largest extent possible. How set theory does this in relation to the concept of natural number will be discussed below, although the facts are familiar; I have in mind the (second-order) Peano axioms for the natural numbers, and their categoricity.

I conclude that from the set-theoretic point of view, Benaceraff's argument is not a problem. In fact, it may be interpreted as a support of the standard foundations, arguing that set theory is needed precisely to provide the right (because *true*) *paraphrase* of the pretheoretical language concerning numbers, and other dubious entities like them, a paraphrase that ensures the correctness of the language globally, without committing its user to any ontology—in fact, freeing the user from all commitment to any ontology!—concerning the "ordinary mathematical objects" such as numbers. Of course, it does this at the obvious price of exacting the ontological commitment to *sets themselves*; but who is unwilling to submit to such a discipline when the resulting advantages are as great as they in fact are? The set theorist treats numbers as second-class existents, the first-class existents being the sets; numbers are the results of conventions, which, by their being conventions, are arbitrary.

Incidentally, I find that the response to "Benaceraff's challenge" in Penelope Maddy's book *Realism in Mathematics* (Maddy 1992), pressing as it does the interpretation that numbers are properties (see p. 86), is on the wrong track. If set theory does anything well, then that is the job of interpreting mathematical entities as *objects* of the theory, that is, *sets*. Interpreting entities as *metatheoretical* ones such as *properties* is inherently inferior to interpretation-as-objects. Also, I do not think that Maddy is answering Benaceraff's arguments against precisely this move.

What, then, is the force of Benaceraff's argument?

As I said, the set theorist and Benaceraff may agree on the status of numbers to the effect that numbers as first-class objects either do not exist at all, or they do, and they are not sets; in short, they may agree on Benaceraff's main conclusion that numbers are not sets. But it is equally clear that they do not agree with respect to their overall positions. The difference is Benaceraff's implicit commitment to the thesis that *there must be an account of numbers that treats them as first-class entities, that treats numbers as numbers.*

Admittedly, this thesis is to a large extent normative; it may be ignored by those who do not care for the underlying imperative. The set theorist may just say, "Go ahead, try to find your precious account of numbers, but I think you are wasting your time; I personally do not care a bit for it, even if it can be found, because my account of number-talk is perfectly sufficient." Is there anything more compelling here than a possibly interesting, but ultimately unnecessary, philosophical suggestion? I believe the answer is yes; it is the reality of the language of mathematics as we find it in practice.

There is a conflict between the language of mathematical practice (the coarse talk) and the language of set theory as it applies to numbers (the refined talk). Interestingly enough, this conflict is not that set theory is unable to express things that the practitioners want to, and can, express, which would be the natural thing to expect in a relationship between an existing practice and an a posteriori foundational reconstruction of that practice. The conflict is of an opposite nature: the practitioners, after acknowledging that the refined talk handles nicely what the coarse talk did maybe not so nicely, complain that the refined talk also introduces nonsense, phrases like "3 belongs to 17," "3 equals the set whose elements are the empty set, the singleton of the empty set, and the set whose elements are the latter two sets," and the like, which clutters up the language. The practitioner immediately recognizes what is and what is not meaningful talk about numbers; there cannot be any doubt about the objective reality of the distinction. And the practitioner demands, or at least desires, that a foundation be provided that observes this distinction.

Benaceraff does not say what I just said; maybe he finds it unnecessary and/or unjustifiable to say it. But I find places in his narrative where he touches the ground of mathematical practice. In one of the quotations above, the ordinary folk are said to be dealing with numbers *as* numbers. This place in Benaceraff's text indicates the acceptance of the practice of mathematics, the locus of numbers *as such*, to be the final arbiter concerning the issue when a proposed language of mathematics is right. The little word "*as*" is the Archimedean fixed point on which the argument pivots. Another of the quotations contains the reference to "our uses of the [number] words"; these are clearly the established uses in the practice that excludes the "nonsense" I mentioned above. I feel that these instances of reliance on mathematical practice are the source of the strength of Benaceraff's argument.

It should be clear by now that I want to turn the issue at hand into one concerning *language*, from the ostensible one that is about *ontology*. True; I think the issue is not *what* numbers are, but *what the nature of numbers is*, nature that can only be revealed in the *language* of the practice dealing with numbers. The question "What are numbers?" is inherently defective. It accepts only a certain kind of answer, one that may be impossible to provide; it presumes that we can point out a domain of things that are already familiar and can proceed to narrow down that domain to arrive at the precise domain of the numbers. The question "What are numbers?" has a reductionist bias. We will not likely get to know the numbers by coming to see that they are just like some other things that we already know; it is quite possible that they are unique in their essential nature. What that nature is, is the good question. And, we then must realize, that nature is to be found in the only tangible reality that contains the numbers, the language of the practice dealing with numbers.

There is natural language as it is found in practice; and then there is formal language that is the result of philosophical reflection on natural language and of a subsequent deliberate act of articulation.

Our problem, then, is this: is it possible to articulate a language of mathematics in which we talk about numbers as numbers?

3.2 Structures

Let us get closer to the way mathematicians talk about, and use, numbers; in this instance, by "number" I mean "natural number" (any of 0, 1, 2, 3, etc.). I will invoke the "Ideal Mathematician" (I. M.), a creation of Philip J. Davis and Reuben Hersh (1980) (a delightful concept indeed!); I will construct the "ideal belief" (not necessarily the *best* belief; see Davis and Hersh 1980), I. M.'s belief, concerning numbers. I. M. says:

I. M.   All I need is a system (set) N of entities called henceforth the (*natural*) *numbers*, with a distinguished element called *zero* (0), a distinguished unary operation giving the *successor* $S(n)$ of any number n, such that 0 is not the successor of anything, S is a one-to-one function, and the Principle of Mathematical Induction is valid: given any property $P(\ )$ of numbers (equivalently, any subset P of N), if $P(0)$ holds ($0 \in P$), and $\forall n \in N. \ (P(n) \to P(S(n)))$, then all numbers have the property P ($\forall n \in N. \ P(n)$).

I. M. is familiar with logical notation. Our undergraduate students make mistakes with the quantifiers, but they know them! Frege's reform of the language of mathematics has percolated thoroughly through everyday usage in mathematics. To continue the imagined quotation from I. M.:

I. M.   There is an axiom of set theory asserting that such a system exists. Given such a system, I can do everything you have ever thought of or will ever think of doing with numbers. One such thing is defining by recursion a function one (or more) of whose variables is ranging over numbers. I mentally fix such a system, and will always refer to this one when I think of numbers. That's all there is to natural numbers.

Above, I. M. described a more or less typical *kind of structure*; in this case, an entity of the kind, a structure of the given kind, is a set with a distinguished element and a distinguished unary operation, satisfying certain definite conditions. I. M. claims that all he needs is a *Peano system*, as the structures of the described kind are called (although it was Richard Dedekind who invented them).

Let me say something that may be partly new for I. M. The definition of "Peano system" may be given equivalently in the following way. $(N, 0, S)$, where N is a set, $0 \in N$, and $S : N \to N$ ($f : A \to B$ means that f is a function with domain equal to the set A, and range contained in the set B; I. M. is familiar with this notation), is a Peano system if and only if a certain condition holds. Before I give it, for the uniformity of notation, instead of $0 \in N$, I will write $0 : t \to N$. Here t is any fixed one-element set, (say, $t = \{\varnothing\}$, but it does not have to be that); note that a mapping from t to any set A is really the same as an element of that set, the element which is the value at the unique element of t. The condition for $(N, 0, S)$ to be a Peano system is this: given any $(A, a : t \to A, f : A \to A)$ (thus, so far, we have something that is "like" our system $(N, 0, S)$),

there is a unique function $g : N \to A$ such that the diagram

$$
\begin{array}{ccccc}
t & \xrightarrow{\ 0\ } & N & \xrightarrow{\ S\ } & N \\
\Big\| {\scriptstyle i} & \circ & \Big\downarrow {\scriptstyle g} & \circ & \Big\downarrow {\scriptstyle g} \\
t & \xrightarrow[\ a\ ]{} & A & \xrightarrow[\ f\ ]{} & A
\end{array}
$$

commutes.

For example, when we first apply S, and then g (on the right), the effect is the same as when we first apply g, and then f (this is the commutativity of the right-hand square); also, the left vertical i denotes the one possible function from t to t, the identity function. When we rewrite this in "algebraic notation," we get this:

$g(0) = a$ (here, I revert to $0 \in N$, $a \in A$ from $0 : t \to N$, $a : t \to A$)
$g(S(n)) = f(g(n))$ $(n \in N)$.

We realize that, in case $(N, 0, S)$ is the Peano system that I. M. fixed in his mind, $g(n)$ is equal to

$$f(f(f(\ldots f(a) \ldots))) = f^n(a),$$

$$\underset{\underset{n-1}{\uparrow}}{\overset{\uparrow}{n}} \qquad \overset{\uparrow}{1}$$

the result of applying f to a n-times. Really, g is defined by a very special recursion, *iteration*. The fact that we thus have an equivalent definition is to say that the Principle of Iteration is equivalent to the Principle of Induction when the latter is bolstered by the first two Peano axioms.

This alternative definition of "Peano system" is due to F. W. Lawvere. I. M. should now sit down and prove to his satisfaction that indeed, we have an equivalent definition. Of course, he is allowed to use set theory; it is unlikely that he is unfamiliar with the needed tools.

This definition is nice for instance because it is more compact than the traditional one. There is no talk about S being one-to-one and missing 0 in its range; also, it is uniform in the sense of being "diagrammatic," using sets and functions, but not properties (subsets). But really, the nicest thing about it is that it has a *pattern*. It looks like we can talk about a *morphism* between any two "such things," $(B, b : t \to B, h : B \to B)$ and $(A, a : t \to A, f : A \to A)$ (let us call "such things" *pre-Peano systems*), as being a map $g : B \to A$ making the diagram

$$
\begin{array}{ccccc}
t & \overset{b}{\longrightarrow} & B & \overset{h}{\longrightarrow} & B \\
{\scriptstyle i}\big\| & \circ & {\scriptstyle g}\big\downarrow & \circ & {\scriptstyle g}\big\downarrow \\
t & \underset{a}{\longrightarrow} & A & \underset{f}{\longrightarrow} & A
\end{array}
$$

commute; and then we can say that a Peano system is distinguished among pre-Peano systems by the fact that it has *exactly one morphism* to any pre-Peano system. (An "impredicative" definition if there ever was one!)

Let us probe I. M.'s convictions about the notion of number.

Q. You said that you fixed any Peano system for the purposes of "number." Does it not matter which one you have chosen? To put it differently, suppose you are probing some property $P(n)$ of the natural numbers, and you are not sure whether the property is universally true or not of numbers. You discover that it is indeed true in your chosen system. How do you know that it would have turned out to be true if you had picked another Peano system as your numbers?

I. M. Aha! Good question. Well, the answer is simple. If I have discovered that the natural numbers have that property you have in mind, then I must have inferred this on the basis of the general principles of mathematics (set theory if you wish), and *on the basis of the definition of "Peano system"*; as I say, I make a point when I reason about numbers of not using anything else than the defining properties of "Peano system."

Q. But wait; does everybody make such a commitment? Maybe I explicitly refuse to make such a commitment; I simply take my system of natural numbers, a Peano system, and by direct examination, mixed with ingenuity, I see that in my system $P(n)$ in fact holds for all n. I tell you about this; I describe to you how I directly examined my Peano system. You said that you can do anything that I can do with numbers. Are you sure that you can now also show that all n satisfy $P(n)$, given that in effect you have committed yourself to using only methods of proof that apply to *all* Peano systems?

I. M. How clever—that is a good question indeed. But there is an important fact here: actually, any property that is verified in one Peano system is going to be true in any other. More than that: *any property of any Peano system as a whole will also be shared by any other Peano system.* Take the example that the underlying set of a Peano system (the set of natural numbers, in any one interpretation) can be mapped in one-to-one fashion into any infinite set. This is a fact; but even if I did not know that, but knew that it was true for one Peano system, I would know that it was true for any other. The reason is that any two Peano systems are *isomorphic*; there is a one-to-one and onto mapping from one to the other taking the zero of one to the zero of the other, and taking a pair that is in the relation of one term's being a successor of the other term into a pair in the same relation in the other. Isomorphic structures share all conceivable properties.

Q. That is indeed interesting. I can actually see why any two Peano systems are isomorphic; this is quite easy using Lawvere's definition. We have a morphism from one to the other, and from the other to the one; moreover, their composites are self-morphisms of the systems, and thus they must be identities; I really have an isomorphism, because I have an invertible morphism; great! But how do you know that isomorphic structures share all properties? I can see this holds for the one you just quoted; this is quite obvious. But why so in case of any conceivable property? Anyway, you cannot be quite right. Look: suppose you take the property that the empty set $\varnothing$ is an element of the Peano system. This is clearly not going to be shared by all Peano systems; I can willfully make this both true and false by simply exchanging elements, clearly not disturbing the fact that I have a Peano system! Something is wrong.

I. M. No, no! Of course, when I said "all conceivable properties," I meant "all meaningful properties," "all properties of Peano systems *as* Peano systems." $\varnothing$, being an element of the Peano system, is not a meaningful property of Peano systems at all; no sane person would contemplate such a property.

It is clear that communication is breaking down at this stage. I. M. cannot really say what he means by a meaningful property of Peano systems, although he can unerringly say of any particular proposed property whether it is meaningful or not. Of course, he could say that a meaningful property is, by definition, one that is invariant under isomorphism: if it holds of one structure, it holds of any other that is isomorphic to the first. But that begs the question; how is he so sure, and so quickly, when he is presented with a particular property? It is important to see that he can make the judgment in the cases when he has no idea whether the property in question does in fact hold in Peano systems. There is, in fact, a more basic problem. Defining "meaningful" by referring to the condition of invariance under isomorphism, one would be making an inadmissible move. The meaningfulness of a phrase should be a matter of grammar, not of a question of a possibly difficult-to-verify mathematical fact. In fact, it is demonstrably undecidable whether a property formulated in set theory of Peano systems is invariant under isomorphism.

I. M.'s colleague, I. L., a student of Alfred Tarski, overhears the discussion and joins in.

I. L. This is a question of logic. The meaningful properties of structures are the logical properties. You have in fact several precisely and explicitly defined logical languages in which you can formulate properties of structures, and you can rigorously show that these properties are invariant under isomorphism. The most basic of these languages is first-order logic. As Tarski has shown, we have a precise notion of truth for sentences of first-order logic in structures of the right kind (interpreting all the symbols in the sentence in question), defined globally for the whole language of first-order logic at once. When for instance we were asking whether $P(n)$ held for all n, we were asking whether the Peano system $(N, 0, S)$ satisfied a sentence $\forall n \hat{P}(n)$, where $\hat{P}(n)$ is a first-order formula expressing the property $P(\_)$, of course provided that such a formula is available. As a matter of fact, in most cases of interesting Ps it is *not* available; in most cases, it would become available if we added new operations such as addition and multiplication to the primitives of the structure $(N, 0, S)$.

Now, the important point is that, with the help of the Tarski truth-definition, there is a rigorous proof of the fact that properties given by first-order sentences are invariant under isomorphism; it is a proof by induction on the complexity of the sentence in question. Thus, there is a partial answer to the question "What are I. M.'s meaningful properties?"; they include the first-order properties. It is true, however, that most mathematically interesting properties of structures—and now I am talking about not just Peano systems but all the various structures mathematicians use: groups, rings, topological spaces, and so on—are in fact not expressible in first-order logic. The way out is that there are other, more expressive languages for which the Tarskian way of defining truth is also available; now the truth-definition may be more conspicuously dependent on set theory, but in fact, it was so dependent already in the case of first-order logic. These languages include second-order logic, higher-order logic, infinitary logics, logics with generalized quantifiers. It turns out that the proof that a property expressible in any of these languages is isomorphism invariant is a very straightforward structural induction on the complexity of the expression involved.

Q. May we then say that the idea of a "meaningful property of a structure" is ultimately an open-ended one; there is no uniform syntactical criterion that describes all the meaningful properties that mathematicians contemplate?

I. L. Yes, this is correct; there are large classes of explicitly described properties that are meaningful, for which we indeed have a proof in advance that they are isomorphism invariant, but it seems rather impossible to give such a class that would be all-encompassing.

I. M.   Mind you, this is not a problem in practice. I am working in group theory, and I have never yet asked myself whether something somebody proposed or asked about groups *made sense*; it simply always did when the person was mathematically competent, even on a minimal level. And when somebody proposes something like "Is the monster-group equal to the first prime number greater than 10^{100}?", then I know that this is meaningless, you are comparing apples and oranges. Mind you, when you ask "Is the monster-group the same as the largest sporadic simple group?", you are not asking about a literal equality of two objects; you are asking whether those two things are *isomorphic*. You see, provided you have identified the monster-group as a specific set, the set-theoretic statement "The monster-group is equal to the first prime number greater than 10^{100}" is meaningful as a set-theoretic statement, but not as a *mathematical* statement.

I will summarize by saying that we have a tantalizing two-faced situation within the set-theoretical foundation. On the one hand, through the process of self-reflection it provides glimpses, collectively called "logic," of large connected parts of a language of mathematics that treats numbers as numbers, and in general, structures as structures inasmuch as it allows only meaningful propositions about those things. On the other hand, it does not give an articulated and complete statement of what such a language, Logic, is; rather, it makes it look likely that such Logic does not exist. I would like to obtain a foundational language in which all well-formed propositions are meaningful.

3.3   The Nature of Things

I. M. was urging the view that one does not have to assume that terms like 3, 17, 10^{10} have absolutely fixed denotations; the latter can be made dependent on a free choice of a structure of natural numbers, a Peano system, in which the denotations then become determined. It also seems that this attitude toward denotation is the prevailing one in mathematics, dealing as it does with definite descriptions of various entities—"the monster-group," "the field of the real numbers," and so on—in a systematically ambiguous manner. This may be so in mathematical practice, but it is entirely possible that this way of behaving is necessarily a metaphorical one, and when it comes to the crunch of articulating a foundation for mathematics, this ambiguity has to be given up. This would not necessarily mean that one would have to adopt the precise foundations of Zermelo-Fraenkel set theory, but it would show that something like that system, with a single domain of well-individuated objects at its base, is necessary, after all; and in particular, it seems to me, it would answer our question "Is it possible to articulate a language of mathematics in which we talk about numbers as numbers?" in the negative.

And indeed, there are many signs in mathematical practice suggesting that ultimately it may be necessary to fix reference of terms unambiguously.

In "Complete Functors in Homology I" Max Kelly writes:

(The objects of a category have but a tenuous individuality; 'the group $\mathbb{Z}$ of integers' is not the same set of elements to different writers, or even to the same writer in different contexts. In a sense it is only the isomorphism class that counts; and yet we must at any instant be considering a definite set of elements, in order that we may sensibly talk of homomorphisms: a group is not the same thing as a group type, because there are non-identical automorphisms. . . .) (1964, 722)

This partially quoted parenthetical remark is in a section called "Generalities on Functors." It confirms the view that the systematic ambiguity of mathematical objects discussed above *reigns within a category*. However, when it comes to a functor $F : X \rightarrow A$, that is, a mapping connecting two categories, it seems that the very notion denies systematic ambiguity; it assigns a definite object $F(X)$ as value to any argument object X in the domain category X. In other words, when we step out of the context of a single category, where the precise identity of objects did not matter (see Kelly's "tenuous individuality"), and want to bridge the worlds of two categories in a global context, we seem to be forced to use tools (the functor, for instance) that do refer definitely (to the object $F(X)$ in this case), and not systematically ambiguously.

And indeed, there is an entrenched view in philosophy that truth in mathematics must be explained by a standardly referential semantical theory. Benaceraff (1973) argues to this effect, and further that this circumstance leads to an inevitable conflict between the demands of ontology and epistemology of mathematics. Without committing myself on Benaceraff's conclusions, I want to call into question the part of his basic position that concerns the necessity of a standardly referential semantical theory of mathematical truth. Along the way, I want to open up the possibility of a nonstandardly referential theory of truth, in which a systematic ambiguity of terms reigns, and thus to make it plausible that it is possible to deal with numbers as numbers in an articulate manner. Incidentally, there is a specific parallel technical issue, in the context of functors; one needs to show that "functors are not necessary," and I have made an effort to this effect in Makkai 1996. It is interesting to point out that two parenthetical paragraphs in Kelly 1964 contain a partial formulation of the notion that should replace that of functor (the concept of "anafunctor," as I call it; Kelly's description is partial since the necessary condition of "saturation" is not mentioned), though without a firm suggestion that this notion could be used to systematically reintroduce ambiguity of objects in categories.

I want to challenge Benaceraff's (1973) basic commitment to

(1) the concern for having a homogeneous semantical theory in which semantics for the propositions of mathematics parallel the semantics for the rest of the language ... (p. 661)

The quotation is footnoted as follows:

I am indulging here in the fiction that we *have* a semantics for "the rest of the language", or more precisely, that the proponents of the views that take their impetus from this concern often think of themselves as having such semantics, at least for philosophically important segments of the language. (p. 661)

The footnote shows that Benaceraff is trying to leave the door open for himself to abandon the commitment to the above concern. Even if he did not himself have this concern, his overall argument to the effect that

almost all accounts of the concept of mathematical truth can be identified with serving one or another of these masters [the other master is "(2) the concern that the concept of mathematical truth mesh with a reasonable epistemology"] *at the expense of the other* (p. 661)

would stand up. On the other hand, the rest of the paper shows that he is, after all, committed to the stated concern. For instance, he writes:

Some (including one of my past and present selves [and here he refers to Benaceraff 1965]), reluctant to face the consequences of combining what I shall dub such a "standard" semantical account with a platonistic view of the nature of numbers, have shied away from supposing that numerals are names... (p. 664)

Thus, to repeat, I am not really arguing with Benaceraff's main thesis. What I am arguing is on a more basic level. I am going to deny that one *can* maintain (1); I will assert that *one cannot have a homogeneous semantical theory of the world as we know it, even if we disregard mathematics proper*; I will assert that the "fiction" Benaceraff refers to is a fiction properly, and it is to be discarded.

To fix ideas, let us look further at Benaceraff 1973:

Consider the following two sentences:

(1) There are at least three large cities older than New York.

(2) There are at least three perfect numbers greater than 17.

Do they have the same logicogrammatical form? More specifically, are they both of the form

(3) There are at least three *FG*'s that bear *R* to *a*.

...? What are the truth-conditions for (1) and (2)? Are they relevantly parallel?...
[I]t seems clear that (3) accurately reflects the form of (1) and thus that (1) will be true if and only if the thing named by the expression replacing '*a*' ('New York') bears the relation designated by the expression replacing '*R*' (① is older than ②) to at least three elements (of the domain of discourse of the quantifiers), which satisfy the predicates replacing '*F*' and '*G*' ('large' and 'city', respectively).... But what of (2)? May we use (3) in the same way as a matrix in spelling out the conditions of *its* truth? That sounds like a silly question to which the obvious answer is "Of course". (p. 663)

Thus, for Benaceraff the homogeneity of our semantical theory means that it is like the account of (1) given above via (3). I claim that we do not have this kind of account of our reference, and truth-determination, even in discourse about certain entities that we habitually encounter in real life.

To clarify the respective positions further, before I get to the claim itself, let me point out that we see here the causal theory of reference at work. "I believe in addition in a causal theory of *reference*....," writes Benaceraff (1973, 671). The causal theory of reference is described, for example, by Maddy (1992, 38–41), who attributes it mainly to Saul Kripke in *Naming and Necessity* (Kripke 1972). According to this, the naming that Benaceraff refers to when he talks about the "thing named by the expression 'New York'" involves a causal chain of events that starts with an act of "initial baptism," the dubbing of the thing New York with the name 'New York,' an event in which New York and the dubber had to be both physically present.

I believe in a fundamental *inhomogeneity* in the kinds of things that make up the world. On the one hand, we have the "*medium-sized physical objects*" to which the causal theory of reference and of knowledge applies; but we also have, in a way parasitically living on those objects, things that I call *representational objects*: things that exist only in ambiguous representation by physical objects, but nevertheless have an irreducible presence in our world. We do not refer to representational objects directly; we refer to them *through* representations of them. Before I say what these representational objects are, I want to emphasize that I do not claim to have classified all things into the two groups I mentioned; in fact, I think, there are further kinds of things that are neither "medium-sized physical objects" nor representational objects. However, I also believe that mathematical objects have much to do with representational objects, even if I am not prepared to fully identify the former with some of the latter. Thus, my case for representational objects is but a preparation of a case for mathematical objects *as such*.

Representational objects are the ones that are symbolically represented; they are invariably artificial, human artifacts. Take William Blake's poem "The Chimney Sweeper." You probably know this poem; if you don't, I will tell you how you may find it, although this will not be the only possible way. The reference is *Blake's Poems and Prophecies*, edited by Max Plowman, in Everyman's Library (London: Dent, New York: Dutton), 1972 reprint. The poem is found on page 11. Actually, I did not in this way give you a unique way of finding the poem. In referring to *Blake's Poems and Prophecies*, I gave you only a type, not a token; here, in my hand, I have a particular copy of the book, and I can show you the poem on the 11th page. Thus, the book I described is another example of a representational object! This immediately tells you something about the hierarchical interrelatedness of representational objects.

Can I *doubt* the existence of Blake's poem "The Chimney Sweeper"? Does Blake's poem "The Chimney Sweeper" exist? Is this question a meaningful one? It seems that the question may have two different meanings. The "nonphilosophical" meaning is the question asked by someone having a possibly superficial but referentially still firm idea about Blake to the effect of whether Blake has indeed written such a poem (we hope he did not write two with this same title. . .). This is an unproblematic question from the point of view of the theory of truth and reference; the ways of answering it are, in principle, satisfactorily circumscribed by the "causal theory of reference and knowledge." But there is also the "philosophical" meaning of the same question; it is in force when we ask, "Does Blake's 'The Chimney Sweeper' exist *as a poem?*"

You may maintain, "No, there are no poems as such; what there are, are the ordered sets of inscriptions that run as follows:

"The Chimney Sweeper"
When my mother died I was very young,
(etc.)

Well, what about an electronically stored copy of Blake's poem? You say, "Of course, I meant that also in an extended sense of 'ordered set of inscriptions.'" Can you be more explicit? You may resort to the formula on the inside covers of books ("No part of this book shall be reproduced, stored in a retrieval system, or transmitted by any means, electronic, mechanical, photocopying, recording, *or otherwise.* . ."), in order to exhaust all the possible representations of the poem. But note the indefiniteness in the italicized phrase *"or otherwise"*; the practical people know that it is impossible to foresee all possible ways one may represent the poem, and they want to forestall *all* (lucrative) representations. Trying to say that the poem's essence is somehow synonymous with the totality of its representations is wrong-headed, for two reasons, at least. One is that we know perfectly *now* what the poem is, but we cannot know *now* all its representations, not even the possible types of its representations. The other is that *one* representation is perfectly enough for knowing what the poem is!

Then again, you will now say that referring to Blake's poem is just a *façon de parler*; you can eliminate it from any context, in exchange for references to first-class objects. I doubt that; how do you do that when I say, "I like Blake's poem 'The Chimney Sweeper'"? Here we enter an infinite, and familiar, controversy, involving behaviorism and the like. Suffice it to say that the corresponding question that we really care about, the one concerning objects in mathematics, is answered definitively: we know that, for instance, the presence or absence of the notion of natural number does make a difference in our ability to prove theorems (a form of Gödel's incompleteness). In other words, we cannot eliminate the notion of natural number from contexts.

In the last two paragraphs I tried to show a bit what it would be like to deny the existence of "The Chimney Sweeper" *as a poem*. I think, however, the best reaction to the "philosophical question" of the existence of "The Chimney Sweeper" *as a poem* is that it is *meaningless*. There is no mystery, we have everything in front of us; the question cannot seriously imply a search for something temporarily unknown answering a description, and it seems that how we answer the question is largely arbitrary.

Before we probe matters along these lines a bit more, I want to suggest that the question of the *existence* of the system of the natural numbers may be to a large extent similar and, as a consequence, *meaningless*. Here you will quickly object, "No; whereas in the case of 'The Chimney Sweeper' the question of the *existence of a representation* is not in question, now, with the system of the natural numbers, this is precisely the important question." To which I will reply, "Certainly, if by a representation of the system of the natural numbers we mean something involving an actual aggregate (set) of elements; but I do not think we have to, or even should, do so." Note also that the existence of a Peano system *within* a formal system of set theory, say, is of course meaningful; in fact, it is expressed by a proposition of the theory, which may or may not be provable in the theory.

The being of the poem "The Chimney Sweeper" as a poem is exhausted by our ability to talk about it as a poem. Talking about it as a poem is to be referring to its representations, possibly simultaneously more than one (for instance, the ones that you and I have in our minds), and *to make sense* while doing so. For instance, "in the second line of the poem" makes sense as talk about the poem, even though, strictly speaking, it is each of the representations that has a second line. On the other hand, "the typeface of the poem" does not make sense as talk about the poem as such; rather, with that talk we immediately know that we are talking, not about the poem as such, but about one of its representations. In natural language, we do not want to rigidly separate the higher-level talk about the poem as such and the lower-level talk about its representations; it is the very spirit of natural language that we want to be able to jump from one context to the other instantaneously. On the other hand, the legendary *purity* of mathematics is rooted in an opposite kind of requirement; in mathematics, we want to be able to talk about structures as structures, and more generally about mathematical objects as such, in a permanent manner. It is this requirement that compels us to articulate formal languages for mathematics.

We should add that talk about the poem as such grows out of talk about its representations. Continuing the work of the poet, we bring the poem into existence as a poem by articulating our talk about it as such. This is another reason why the two types of talk are not, and cannot be, rigidly separated. In fact, the process of creating the poem is an ongoing one; it has not been quite completed. In mathematics, we have completed our talk about our abstract objects to a greater extent, although the difference is only a matter of degree.

One might think that talking about poems is inappropriate in connection with mathematics. Of course, there are many other types of representational objects, and none is more important than the ones that arise in the world of computers: computer programs, pieces of software. It is in the domain of computer software that we see the characteristics of representational objects most clearly. The talk about the software becomes sharply separated from the representation, which is a particular implementation of the software. The existence of the software as such becomes more pronounced; we are now more ready to accept the existence of the software as something separate and independent from any implementation, more ready than in the case of the poem (perhaps). Another element in favor of the existence of the software as such is its potency. One may doubt whether poems *do* anything; but we do not doubt that pieces of software do things. They have very specific and occasionally large effects—of course, never in themselves, always in an implementation. Discussing, describing, planning around the effect of the software takes place mostly in talk that is independent of any particular implementation. I am inclined to the view that mathematical objects are like software, more specifically, like the *datatypes* of software.

But let us return to poetry once again. Maybe our brave talk about poems as genuine representational objects can be shown up as hot air, after all. It is very well to talk about the many representations of "The Chimney Sweeper" in books, in people's minds, and so on; but there is a distinguished, an authentic, an original representation: the one that Blake himself put to paper. When we talk about the poem "The Chimney Sweeper," we talk about this original copy; we talk about a first-class object pure and simple. When we use ostension and point to the copy on page 11 of my book, what we do is deferred ostension, to use Quine's expression. We mean referring to the Original; we *refer* to the Original. This is what Benaceraff meant by the "homogeneous semantical theory of the rest of the language," that is, the language that refers to reality as opposed to mathematics.

Before we try to answer this devastating argument, we have to acknowledge its force. In this we can see why we want the Platonistic, uniquely referring, standard semantical theory: we want authenticity, an objective point of reference, to which we can return when in doubt. There may always be a question whether a particular printing of the poem is correct; ultimately, the only way to answer this question is to go to the original and verify whether the copy in question and the original can be mapped to each other perfectly.

The attempt to answer the argument is this. Assume you discover that in fact, there is no original "The Chimney Sweeper." In fact, worse than that, you discover that there is something entitled "The Chimney Sweeper" in a manuscript of Blake's, but it differs substantially from the "standard version," the version *that has been most frequently reprinted*; moreover, no trace of a version of the poem *as we know it* can be found in Blake's manuscripts. You counter: This does not matter; the poem *as we know it* was composed by someone at some definite time and place, and when we talk about the "The Chimney Sweeper" *as we know it*, we talk about *that* original, even though it may differ from anything attributable to Blake himself. To which I say that now the original of "The Chimney Sweeper" *as we know it* is a purely fictive entity; it has lost its role as the grounding of authenticity. However, in fact still there is no problem about what "The Chimney Sweeper" *as we know it* is; it simply is what it is, and no one will try to authenticate it, especially now (we are still within the assumption that we have lost the good connection to Blake) that we know that it cannot be authenticated. To which you say: There is no way of stopping people from fixing the first, or most visible, or whatever, but in some definite way *unique* source where the "The Chimney Sweeper" can be found, a source which becomes the *standard reference* to "The Chimney Sweeper" *as we know it*. And then I reply: Oh, but now you cannot say that "The Chimney Sweeper" *as we know it* is, by definition, that given by the standard reference, since in fact there was something entirely clearly defined before we had located that standard reference; the location of the standard reference was an *a posteriori act* of mock authentication, an act entirely dependent on the clear and prior idea of "The Chimney Sweeper" *as we know it*.[1]

Maintaining "the fiction of the homogeneous semantical theory for the language of the nonmathematical world" (Benaceraff's words, essentially) is hard work. I am suggesting that it is too hard, what with all those gadgets that come flooding into our lives, each having little or large pieces of structure, defined in terms of some abstract functionality or what have you. To make sense of all this, we resort to representational objects, rather than trying to find unique authentic originals to which we would have to run in case of doubt. Certainly, these representational objects are abstractions (I do not mean to imply that the term I just used *explains* them; rather, its use puts them in their place as inferior in some sense to concrete things) and thus decidedly second-class objects that cannot live without being rooted in medium-sized physical objects. But still, we cannot do without them.

Is this a *pragmatic* argument? Yes, it is; but remember, the argument is not about the existence or nonexistence of representational objects, but about the fact or nonfact of the homogeneity of the semantics for the language of the nonmathematical world. The conclusion may be that the idea of the homogeneous, uniquely referential semantics vis-à-vis the world is in fact *incoherent*; if so, it is even worse for the fiction that Benacerraf admits to be indulging in. It now seems to me that we do mathematics precisely to get away from all this compulsion of authentication, and deal with what we call mathematical objects as we know them.

At this point, I feel optimistic that a foundational stance in mathematics that lacks the standard feature of unique reference to objects may be viable. However, the real test of it still remains a Fregean full articulation. Before we have built the whole language, we cannot be sure whether we do not, ultimately, smuggle in the "originally baptized," authentic entities that the Platonists want.

Note

1. Ray Jackendoff has suggested to me a real example paralleling the hypothetical case described above of being unable to find an authentic original. I describe it essentially in his words.

There is a piece of music that has been in the repertoire at least since the early nineteenth century, which is called "Sinfonia Concertante for oboe, clarinet, horn, bassoon, and orchestra by Mozart." Only there is no known manuscript for this piece. In a letter, Mozart himself referred to having written a sinfonia concertante for flute, oboe, horn, and bassoon—which is totally unknown—and people generally assume that the piece we know is a later reorchestration of that. The trouble is that all attempts to "reconstruct" the original have been awkward at best; basically, the clarinet part in the piece we know cannot easily be transferred to idiomatic writing for any of the instruments mentioned in Mozart's letter. Moreover, the last movement of the piece we know has some parts that Mozart never would have written. So no one knows where this piece came from, prior to its first publication some years after Mozart's death.

Jackendoff also pointed out to me that he has had to deal with representational objects in his work on music, which involves an additional layer of performance, making the semantics of, say, "Beethoven's Fifth Symphony" even stranger.

References

Benacerraf, P. (1965). What numbers could not be. *Philosophical Review, 74,* 47–73.

Benacerraf, P. (1973). Mathematical truth. *The Journal of Philosophy, 70,* 661–675.

Davis, P. J., and Hersh, R. (1980). *The mathematical experience.* Birkhauser Verlag.

Eilenberg, S., and Mac Lane, S. (1945). General theory of natural equivalences. *Transactions of the American Mathematical Society, 58,* 231–294.

Kelly, G. M. (1964). Complete functors in homology I. *Proceedings of the Cambridge Philosophical Society, 60,* 721–735.

Kripke, S. (1972). *Naming and necessity.* Oxford: Blackwell.

Lawvere, F. W. (1969). Adjoints in foundations. *Dialectica, 23,* 281–296.

Lawvere, F. W. (1970). Equality in hyperdoctrines and the comprehension schema as an adjoint functor. In A. Heller (Ed.), *Proceedings of the New York Symposium on Applications of Categorial Logic* (pp. 1–14). Providence, RI: American Mathematical Society.

Lawvere, F. W. (1971). Quantifiers and sheaves. In *Actes du Congrès International des Mathématiciens Nice 1970* (Vol. 1, pp. 329–334). Paris: Gauthier-Villars.

Maddy, P. (1992). *Realism in mathematics.* New York: Oxford University Press.

Makkai, M. (1996). Avoiding the axiom of choice in general category theory. *Journal of Pure and Applied Algebra, 108,* 109–173.

Makkai, M. (1997). Generalized sketches as a framework for completeness theorems. *Journal of Pure and Applied Algebra, 115,* 49–79 (part I), 179–212 (part II), and 241–274 (part III).

Makkai, M. (1998). Towards a categorical foundation of mathematics. In J. A. Makowski and E. V. Ravve (Eds.), *Logic colloquium '95* (Lecture Notes in Logic 11, pp. 153–190). New York: Springer-Verlag.

Makkai, M. (to appear). *First-order logic with dependent sorts* (Lecture Notes in Logic). New York: Springer-Verlag.

Parsons, C. (1990). The structuralist view of mathematical objects. *Synthese, 84,* 303–346.

Chapter 4

The Natural Logic of Rights and Obligations   Ray Jackendoff

4.1 Introduction

The focus of John Macnamara's work over three decades was an in-depth inquiry into the fundamental structure of human knowledge. Though less publicly spectacular than Chomsky's results on the nature of syntactic knowledge, John's research went beyond linguistic expression to delve into the character of meaning, thought, and reason themselves. Like Chomsky, John was asking what it is possible for a child to learn on the basis of the input in the environment—and what parts of the child's knowledge cannot be learned, but must serve as the basis for learning. Some of his results were absolutely startling, at least in the context of the sort of empiricist philosophy of meaning that prevailed at the beginning of his career and that has enjoyed a strong resurgence in these connectionist times. For those of us of a more rationalist cast, his way of chewing over issues of epistemology has been a continual inspiration.

Anyone acquainted with John sensed that he was a man of deep moral convictions. Occasionally the nature of these convictions became for him a topic of study as well, for instance in his paper "The Development of Moral Reasoning and the Foundations of Geometry." Here he argued that a sense of morality has to be as much a part of our inborn character

I am grateful to my late father Nathaniel Jackendoff, my brother Sparky Jackendoff, Larry Solan, Carlos Otero, Storrs McCall, Al Bregman, Paul Bloom, Jay Conison, Gordon Bower, and members of the audience at the 1996 Piaget Centennial in Geneva for discussion and comments on this material. I was given the honor of presenting this work as the first John Macnamara Memorial Lecture at McGill in April 1997, and I benefited a great deal from the discussion there as well. This research was supported in part by National Science Foundation grant 92-13849 to Brandeis University.

as our understanding of physical space—that moral ideals come to us as naturally as geometric ideals. The present chapter is an exercise in the same spirit, if not so ambitious, investigating a pair of notions closely related to moral reasoning: rights and obligations. I will be concerned especially with what might be called "social/legal/contractual" rights and obligations. Parts of the analysis will apply as well to "moral obligations," "moral justifications," and "human rights"; other parts will not. Some of the differences will be mentioned in section 4.6.

Rights and obligations are fundamental to the fabric of human social organization. For example, ownership of an object confers on the owner (or consists of) rights to use the object and rights to prevent others' using it (Miller and Johnson-Laird 1976, following Snare 1972). Giving someone a promise places one under obligation to fulfill the promise. Conferring on someone a social status (e.g., an official title, a professional degree, or membership in an organization) grants this person certain rights and places him or her under certain obligations. Any sort of contract— including not only financial/legal contracts but also marriage in many societies—places the participants under obligation to perform certain acts. Inasmuch as the main issues addressed by a society's legal system (written or unwritten) include the privileges of ownership, the making and enforcing of contracts, and the rights and duties of officials and of citizens, it is clear that rights and obligations play a central role in understanding concepts of law.

The notions of rights and obligations appear to be universal in human societies. A great deal of anthropological description is devoted to how societies differ in what rights and obligations pertain to their members, how such rights and obligations are obtained and lost, and how they are taken to be grounded in religion or government. But such descriptions invariably take the notions of right and obligation themselves for granted, not subject to discussion.[1] Yet, as I will show, these notions are remarkably complex and subtle. Thus, these concepts raise interesting questions about learning and the evolution of cognition—just the sort of questions with which John Macnamara was so deeply concerned. I will turn to these questions briefly at the end.

I will be investigating rights and obligations in the context of a theory of linguistic meaning—of the contextually integrated interpretations of utterances—that in my view forms the bridge between linguistic semantics and a larger psychological theory of how humans understand the world. This theory investigates *conceptual structure*, a form of mental representation over which principles of inference (including invited inference and heuristics) can be defined and in terms of which planning of actions takes place. Conceptual structure is mapped into the strictly linguistic levels of syntactic and phonological structure by sets of *correspondence rules* (Jackendoff 1990).

This approach to meaning contrasts with many standard philosophical approaches in the Frege-Tarski tradition, in that I do not take conceptual structure to map directly into the real world; rather, it maps into the world *as human beings understand it*, quite a different notion (Jackendoff 1983). I am trying to study human concepts, not "ultimate reality." However, conceptual structure is still connected to and constrained by the external world, but indirectly, via the complex mappings between sensation and cognition that are established by the perceptual systems of the brain. Here I think I am basically in agreement with John Macnamara's approach, though we did disagree deeply, in some way I still fail to understand, about how a theory of concepts should relate to the "real real world."

Like any theory of meaning, the theory of conceptual structure should be supported by linguistic (including crosslinguistic) evidence and by its ability to formally support reasoning. However, because it is supposed to be embedded in a larger psychological theory, it should also interact with evidence from perception, child development, and potentially neuroscience. And since conceptual structure is meant to be to a degree independent of the language capacity per se, we should in principle be able to test the theory against evidence from the cognition of animals, especially primates, both in the laboratory and in natural settings.

The domain of concepts investigated most intensively by myself and many others (see, e.g., Talmy 1983; Herskovits 1986; Vandeloise 1986; Bloom et al. 1996) is *spatial cognition*, the position and movement of physical objects and substances in space, the forces they exert on each other, and the temporal structure of the states and events that result. This domain is especially fruitful because there is a vast range of lexical items expressing spatial concepts and because these correspond to a rich and precise set of perceptually based intuitions. This line of research is now well established within linguistic semantics. In addition, it has long been recognized that language expressing spatial concepts is mirrored to a considerable extent by language expressing concepts in other domains (Gruber 1965; Jackendoff 1976; Lakoff and Johnson 1980; among many others). So understanding the organization of spatial concepts helps set a foundation for investigating other domains.

The domain in which the study of rights and obligations is situated is that of *social cognition*. Evidence from animal societies, especially primates (e.g., Cheney and Seyfarth 1990), suggests that a substantial component of our conception of the world is devoted to the understanding of the social context in which individuals find themselves (Jackendoff 1992, chap. 4; Searle 1995). The fundamental unit of this domain is not the physical object but the *person*, a seat of intention and volition. People (and to some degree animals) have representations in both this domain and the physical; trees, rocks, streets, and buses are represented only physically.[2] Within this framework, I will be asking how people conceptualize situations in which someone can be said to have a right or an obligation. It makes little sense to ask what rights and obligations *really* are, outside of people's understanding of their social context. In other words, I am interested in a theory of the "folk theory" of social relations. Like the theory of the conceptualization of objects, space, and force in the physical domain, this forms part of the theory of human conceptualization—but one far less directly tied to perception.

In the course of my exposition, I will make use of the formal framework of conceptual semantics developed in my previous work (e.g., Jackendoff 1983, 1990). Any alternative notation that makes similar distinctions is adequate for my purposes. However, it is important that the notation be construed as encoding regularities in the mind, not some general set-theoretic construct (involving, say, possible worlds) as in most varieties of formal semantics.

4.2   The Argument Structure of Rights and Obligations

An important aspect of my approach to conceptual structure is that the grammatical structure of the language used to express concepts can help reveal the organization of the concepts themselves. So let us start by looking at some of the ways that rights and obligations can be expressed. We see immediately that they form a closely related pair.

About the simplest way to express a right in English is with the modal verb *may*; an obligation can be expressed with the modal verb *must*.

(1) a. One may use one's possessions as one likes. (Right)
    b. One must pay sales tax in Pennsylvania. (Obligation)

One immediate impulse for formalizing these meanings might be to take the modals to express operators (notated as *RT* and *OB*) over a proposition, as in (2). This is essentially the formalization found in von Wright's (1963) foundational work on deontic logic.

(2) a. Sue may (i.e., has a right to) leave when she wants to.
       = RT (Sue leaves when she wants to)
    b. Sue must (i.e., has an obligation to) leave before noon.
       = OB (Sue leaves before noon)

Such a treatment, however, misses the basic point that a right or an obligation is a relation between a person and his or her action. The readings of *may* and *must* that do express propositional operators for possibility and necessity lend themselves to paraphrases like (3a), whose syntactic structure reflects the semantic structure rather well. Such paraphrases are impossible with rights and obligations (3b).

(3) a. It is possible/necessary that Sue will leave.
    b. *It is a right/obligation $\left\{ \begin{array}{l} \text{that Sue (will) leave} \\ \text{for Sue to leave} \end{array} \right\}$ [3]

Rather, as recognized by some more recent writers on deontic logic such as Forrester (1996), the proper treatment recognizes two separate arguments of these operators: the holder of the right/obligation and the situation with respect to which this person is entitled or obligated. The first argument of these operators must be a *person*. Rocks, clouds, and computers do not have rights and obligations. Animals are sometimes asserted to have rights, by construing them as semipersons; they never have obligations.[4] In modern capitalist legal thought, corporations are construed as susceptible to rights and obligations and therefore can enter into contracts; the language used to effect this construal is that corporations count as "legal persons."

In English, the second argument of these operators must syntactically be a verb phrase (VP) whose understood subject is the holder of the obligation or right. Thus, the arguments in (4a) are acceptable but those in (4b) are not.

(4) a. Sue has $\left\{ \begin{array}{l} \text{a right} \\ \text{an obligation} \end{array} \right\}$ $\left\{ \begin{array}{l} \text{to attend the party} \\ \text{to talk to Harold} \end{array} \right\}$.
    b. *Sue has $\left\{ \begin{array}{l} \text{a right} \\ \text{an obligation} \end{array} \right\}$ for $\left\{ \begin{array}{l} \text{the sky to be blue} \\ \text{Bill to leave} \end{array} \right\}$.

This VP is subject to semantic constraints. Both *right* and *obligation* require the situation to be nonpast with respect to the time of the obligation: the VP may be present, future, or generic time.

(5) Sue has $\left\{ \begin{array}{l} \text{a right} \\ \text{an obligation} \end{array} \right\}$ to leave $\left\{ \begin{array}{l} \text{right now} \\ \text{tomorrow} \\ \text{whenever she gets annoyed} \\ \text{*yesterday}^5 \end{array} \right\}$.

The VP of an obligation must express an action that the holder of the obligation can carry out volitionally (6).

(6) Sue has an obligation to $\left\{ \begin{array}{l} \text{leave} \\ \text{scratch her nose} \\ \text{*be tall} \\ \text{*be descended from royalty} \\ \text{*be paid for her work} \end{array} \right\}$.

The VP of a right can express either an action carried out by its understood subject (7a,b) or a situation in which its understood subject receives a benefit (7e).

(7) Sue has a right to $\left\{ \begin{array}{ll} \text{a.} & \text{leave} \\ \text{b.} & \text{scratch her nose} \\ \text{c.} & \text{*be descended from royalty} \\ \text{d.} & \text{*be tall} \\ \text{e.} & \text{be paid for her work} \end{array} \right\}$.

(8) illustrates the difference between *right* and *obligation* in this respect. The verb *receive* does not denote a voluntary action on the part of the recipient, but the verb *accept* does. Only the latter is possible as an argument of *obligation.*

(8) a. Sue has a right to accept/receive pay for her work.

  b. Sue has an obligation to accept/*receive pay for her work.

I will call the kind of right illustrated in (7e) a "passive" right, that in (7a,b) an "active" right; obligations can only be active.

For convenience, I will call the person having the right or obligation the *Actor*, and the situation to which the right or obligation pertains the *Action*, with the understanding that this includes as a special case passive rights, which do not involve an Action in the standard sense. Given this much, we can formalize rights and obligations as in (9), where *RT* and *OB* are one-place operators applying to the Action. As shown in (10), we then say the Actor "has" the right or obligation (the use of *HAVE* will be further justified shortly).[6]

(9) a. RT (ACT (α)) = 'the right to do Action'
    b. OB (ACT (α)) = 'the obligation to do Action'

(10) a. HAVE (X^α, RT (ACT (α))) = 'X has a right to do Action'
     b. HAVE (X^α, OB (ACT (α))) = 'X has an obligation to do Action'

In these formulas, the Action is notated as a function of one variable, its Actor (it may have further variables, irrelevant in the present context). In (10), this Actor position is bound to the holder of the right or obligation by the bound variable α, where the superscript α on X indicates that X binds the variable in the argument position of ACT.

The fact that rights and obligations have an Action rather than a proposition as their argument places them in the general domain of *deontic logic*, which deals with such notions as permissions and prohibitions and with the logic of *may*, *must*, *should*, and *ought*, and which contains moral reasoning as a particular subcase (von Wright 1963).

However, passive rights do not fall altogether comfortably into the standard deontic domain, since their arguments are not volitional actions. It is interesting therefore that the modal *may* cannot be used comfortably to express passive rights: *Sue may be paid for her work* does not paraphrase (7e). (*Deserve to VP*, which has a related meaning, has constraints on its VP argument similar to those of *right*.)

A further constraint on the Action argument is deeply rooted in the notions of right and obligation. Essentially, a right normally concerns something one *wants* to do, whereas an obligation normally concerns something one does *not* want to do.

(11) a. Sue has a right/??an obligation to eat her ice-cream sundae.
     b. Sue has an obligation/??a right to scrub the toilets.

The interpretations marked *??* are sensible just in case we assume Sue doesn't like the ice-cream sundae and does like scrubbing toilets. (There are exceptions, however, in which one has a right to do something odious or an obligation to do something pleasurable.)

I will state this intuition in terms of the *value* of the Action to the Actor—positive for a right, negative for an obligation. I will notate it as a function *VALUE* that maps two arguments, a Stimulus and an Experiencer, into a Value.

(12) VALUE $(Y, X) = +/-$
      'the value of Y (Stimulus) to X (Experiencer) is positive/negative'

The opposition between positive and negative value here is a primitive affective distinction that may also be paraphrased by 'in vs. not in X's interest'. (This seems to bear a relation to Freud's notion of Pleasure vs. Unpleasure (*Lust* vs. *Unlust*).) Using this notion, we can state the constraint on rights and obligations as (13). The principles are stipulated to be defeasible ('defeatable') to allow for cases in which other pragmatic factors intervene to create exceptions.

(13) a. HAVE $(X^{\alpha}$, RT (ACT $(\alpha)))$ *defeasibly presupposes*
          VALUE (ACT $(X), X) = +$
      b. HAVE $(X^{\alpha}$, OB (ACT $(\alpha)))$ *defeasibly presupposes*
          VALUE (ACT $(X), X) = -$

There are cases, such as *the right/obligation to vote*, that one may construe with either value. In *the right to vote*, we take voting as a desirable action; in *the obligation to vote*, as somewhat burdensome. This confirms the intuitions expressed by (13). Similar effects can be discerned with the choice between *right* and *obligation* in (4a) and (5).

In addition, rights and obligations have their own values: a right is generally a good thing to have, an obligation a bad thing to have. We can state this as (14).

(14) a. VALUE ([HAVE $(X^{\alpha}$, RT (ACT $(\alpha)))], X) = +$
      b. VALUE ([HAVE $(X^{\alpha}$, OB (ACT $(\alpha)))], X) = -$

There is an indirect connection between (13) and (14), to which I will return in section 4.8.

4.3   What One Can Do with Rights and Obligations

Next let us explore the range of things one can do with rights and obligations beyond having them.

First, one can perform the action to which the right or obligation pertains. We speak of so doing as *exercising* the right or *fulfilling* the obligation. Notice that the collocations for *right* and *obligation* involve different verbs for what (at this level of description at least) appear to be parallel actions. We will see that such differences pervade the whole range of verbs used with rights and obligations.

Second, a right or obligation can be created. Sometimes the creator of an obligation is the Actor him- or herself. For example, *promising* is (in part) creating and declaring an obligation upon oneself to perform the promised action. We speak in this case of *undertaking* the obligation. By contrast, though one can *declare* or *claim* one's own rights, one cannot thereby create them without the assent of other relevant parties. A person's rights and obligations can also be created by an outside party, whom I will call the *Authority*. We speak of the Authority's *giving*, *granting*, or *conferring* rights on the Actor, and of *imposing* obligations. (I return to the status of the Authority in section 4.9.)

For a slightly more complex case where rights and obligations are created, consider X's *making an offer to* Y to do such and such. This can be construed as X's conferring the right on Y to demand (i.e., impose an obligation on) X to do such and such—an embedding of an obligation within a right.

Third, a right or obligation can go out of existence. In certain cases, performing the Action has this effect. For instance, handing the usher one's ticket confers on one the right to attend a performance, after which point the right ceases to exist. Similarly, when a debt is paid, the obligation to pay it ceases to exist. (Not all rights and obligations have this property; see section 4.5.)

An Actor can also cause a right to go out of existence by *renouncing* it. The counterpart for an obligation would be for the Actor to *reject* or possibly *renounce* it. However, renunciation of an obligation does not automatically make it go out of existence, even if the obligation is self-imposed: we do not think well of someone who revokes promises.

Under certain conditions, an Authority who has imposed an obligation on an Actor can *release* the Actor from the obligation, or *remove* the obligation from the Actor, in which case the Actor is *free* of it. In the case of rights granted by an Authority, we speak of the Authority's *revoking* or *taking away* these rights—in which case the Actor *loses* them.

Fourth, one can *transfer* rights from one person to another, the first party relinquishing them and the second acquiring them. The parallel case might be one person's *taking on* someone else's obligations.

Fifth, in a situation of conflict between the Actor and the Authority, the Actor may *insist on* a right, which the Authority is supposed to *acknowledge* or *recognize*. Alternatively, the Actor may try to *get out of* an obligation, and the Authority may try to *hold* him or her *to* it.

These situations are summarized in table 4.1.

Table 4.1
What one can do with rights and obligations (# indicates 'not necessarily felicitous')

	Right	Obligation
Performing Action	exercise	fulfill
Creating		
by Actor	# declare, claim	undertake
by Authority	give, grant	impose
Voiding		
by Actor	renounce	# reject
by Authority	revoke, take away	release, remove
(effect on Actor)	lose	be free of
Transfer	transfer	take on
Conflict		
Actor	insist on	get out of
Authority	acknowledge	hold to

The use of *give, transfer*, and *take away* alongside *have* suggests that a right might be conceptualized along the lines of a possession, that is, as an independent entity that one may have, give, or take away. On this analysis, the verb *have* in *have a right*, notated as *HAVE* in (10), is essentially the ordinary *have* of alienable possession.[7] This leads to analyses as in (15). (*INCH* is inchoative, or 'coming to pass'.)

(15) a. CAUSE (Y, [INCH HAVE (X^α, (RT (ACT (α))))])
         = 'Y gives X the right to do Action'
     b. CAUSE (Y, [INCH NOT HAVE (X^α, (RT (ACT (α))))])
         = 'Y takes away the right to do Action from X'

The language associated with obligations in table 4.1 has more inconsistent and opaque associations. *Undertake, impose, remove*, and *take on* seem to image the obligation as a burden to be borne, as does the phrase *under (the weight of) obligation(s)*. On the other hand, *release, get out of*, and possibly *hold to* suggest the obligation is imaged as a constraining force. In particular, the notion of an obligation as a constraint relates it to force-dynamic expressions (Talmy 1988): it is a social force that affects one's course of action. The expression *fulfilling an obligation*, through its association with *fill*, might suggest an image of the obligation as a container. The almost synonymous phrase *meeting an obligation* carries overtones of yet another image, one whose character is difficult to pinpoint. In the face of all these distinct associations, none of them coincident with those for rights, I will adopt a formalization for obligation exactly like (15), only substituting *OB* for *RT*.

4.4   The Ontological Status of Rights and Obligations

Consider more closely the "images" associated with rights and obligations. A theorist in the vein of Lakoff and Johnson (1980) would claim that rights and obligations are understood "metaphorically" and that they derive their conceptual properties from another domain, called the "source domain." According to Lakoff and Johnson's methodology, the evidence for identifying the source domain comes precisely from the collocations in which the words in question appear. In this particular case, we would be inclined to claim that rights and obligations are understood metaphorically in terms of *different* source domains—rights as possessions, obligations as burdens or constraints. Yet, as we have already seen to some extent, and as I will continue to document, rights and obligations are near-twin concepts, with altogether parallel logic. So there is something a bit suspicious about the metaphor view.

An alternative view is that rights and obligations have their *own* logic. This logic is shared superficially with possessions and burdens, but it is close enough to draw an associative connection. In choosing verbs to express what one can do with rights, the language is swayed toward verbs of possession because rights, like possessions, generally are of positive value; verbs relating to obligations are swayed toward verbs of physical burden and constraint because obligations, like burdens and constraints, generally are of negative value. On this view, one does not understand rights and obligations metaphorically in terms of possessions and burdens/constraints. Rather, because of what one understands about rights and obligations, one chooses verbal collocations in a motivated fashion. While acknowledging the insights that Lakoff and Johnson seek to express, this view turns the notion of metaphorical understanding on its head: it is because rights and obligations are understood as they are that the metaphorical connection is possible—not the other way about. (For more detailed discussion of Lakoff and Johnson's approach, see Murphy 1996; Jackendoff 1992, chap. 3; Jackendoff and Aaron 1991.)

Looking a little more deeply, what sort of conceptual entities might rights and obligations be? In the formalization in (9), (10), and (15), the right is an independent entity, which someone may have, may be given, or may have taken away, and toward which someone may express attitudes such as insistence or acknowledgment. A more or less standard philosophical approach to rights and obligations, observing that they involve clausal complements, might suggest that they are propositional attitudes, like beliefs and desires. However, we have seen that their arguments are not propositions, but Actions (except for passive rights). More importantly, rights and obligations are emphatically not attitudes. Beliefs and desires are conceptualized as being "in an individual's mind"; having a belief or desire is being in a subjective mental state. By contrast, rights and obligations are abstract entities, and having a right or obligation is being in a certain objective social situation. To see this contrast more clearly, notice that *Bill's belief/desire is in his mind* is a sort of tautology, but *Bill's right/obligation is in his mind* attributes to Bill some kind of delusion about his social relations. In fact, understanding someone's rights and obligations requires no understanding of that person's mind. Here rights and obligations differ sharply from the more standardly studied species of deontic concept, moral/ethical understanding, which depends heavily on empathy, that is, one's understanding of others' minds and others' values (Goldman 1993; Hoffman 1987).

Beyond this observation I have little to offer about what sort of abstract objects these are. They are perhaps a bit like facts—objectively determinable persistent entities—a bit like responsibilities and opportunities, a little less like credit and blame (both mass terms). More unexpected parallels, pointed out by Searle (1995), are to the value of money and to points in a game, which are again abstract but objective entities within a social context. But since the ontology of such abstract objects in all their variety has not been explored (to my knowledge), for the moment the matter has to be left hanging.

4.5   "Existentially" versus "Universally Quantified" Rights and Obligations

Section 4.3 spoke of rights and obligations that go out of existence by virtue of exercising or fulfilling them. To repeat, handing the usher a ticket gives one the right to attend the performance—once; one has the right no longer. Paying a debt erases one's obligation to pay it; returning a borrowed item erases one's obligation to return it. On the other hand, not all rights and obligations are like this. Showing the usher one's year-long pass to the theater gives one the right to enter the theater, but one retains the right for future occasions. Similarly, one's obligation to obey a police officer does not go out of existence when one obeys an officer once: this obligation persists.

We must distinguish, then, between rights and obligations that pertain to exactly one action and those that pertain to all actions of a given type. The former are exercised or fulfilled by an appropriate action's taking place, at which point they go out of existence. We could think of these as "existential," in the sense that if there comes to exist an Action that satisfies the argument of the right or obligation, the right or obligation ceases to exist. The latter, by contrast, are "universal": they pertain to every Action of the appropriate type. (Von Wright calls these varieties *particular* and *general*, respectively; the legal tradition uses the terms *in personam* and *in rem*, respectively.)

This distinction could be encoded by a subscript on the operators *RT* and *OB*: for example, RT_{Ex} and OB_{Ex} versus RT_{Un} and OB_{Un}. Inference rule (16) then pertains only to the "existential" variety.

(16) HAVE $(X^\alpha, RT_{Ex}/OB_{Ex} (ACT (\alpha)))$ at time t_1, and
      ACT (X) at time t_2, where $t_2 > t_1$,
          entails
      NOT HAVE $(X^\alpha, RT_{Ex}/OB_{Ex} (ACT (\alpha)))$ at time t_3, where $t_3 > t_2$

It is important to our story that this inference rule involves a succession of times—that is, the principles of rights and obligations require a dynamic logic. (This temporal dependency is not present in the formalism of von Wright and his successors, even if they acknowledge it informally.)

It is worth observing that various other concepts have this curious property. For instance, an *intention* to perform an action is fulfilled—and thereby goes out of existence—when the action is performed. Parallel effects obtain with bodily sensations such as hunger, thirst, and some itches. So this odd metaphysical property of rights and obligations is actually more broadly attested among our concepts.

The situation is actually still more complex. One has the right to vote in every election; that is, exercising the right does not eliminate it. On the other hand, one has the right to vote only once in each election; having voted eliminates the right *till the next election*. So this right has a mixed flavor, partly "universal" and partly "existential." This suggests that the simple subscripts *Ex* and *Un* are not subtle enough to capture the range of possibilities; there is more internal structure to be teased out.

4.6   Consequences of Noncompliance

So far, I have not done much to distinguish social/legal/contractual rights and obligations from other kinds of deontic operators expressed by modals such as *may, should, ought to,* and *must*—in particular, from "moral obligations" and "human rights," which turn out to be a bit different in character. Now I turn to what gives social/legal/contractual rights and obligations their distinctive flavor: the consequences of noncompliance.

What happens if one fails to fulfill an obligation? Very simply, one runs the risk of getting in trouble. Suppose I have undertaken an obligation—say, by promising to wash the dishes. Making a promise involves another individual to whom one has made the promise, who typically will benefit from having the promise fulfilled. Let us call this individual the *Beneficiary* of the obligation.

Now suppose I do not wash the dishes within a reasonable amount of time. (What counts as a reasonable amount of time is a delicate matter.) Then the Beneficiary has the (Existential) right to impose some sort of punishment on me. The Beneficiary does not necessarily exercise this right, but we clearly understand that this right exists.

What does it mean to impose punishment? Roughly, if Z punishes X, Z performs some action with negative value to X, *in return for* some previous action on the part of X with negative value to Z. (*Reward* is the same, except with positive values.)

This is enough information to enable us to state a preliminary version of the inference rule for nonfulfillment of obligations. First, we must add to the predicate *OB* an argument position for the Beneficiary, as in (17). (This character is not recognized, even implicitly, in the work on deontic logic with which I am familiar.)

(17) OB (ACT (α), TO Z) = 'the obligation to Z to do Action'

We may further add that the Beneficiary normally benefits from the Action.

(18) OB (ACT (α), TO Z) (*defeasibly*) *entails* VALUE (ACT (α), Z) = +

The inference rule for noncompliance now comes out as (19); again it is stated dynamically.

(19) HAVE $(X^\alpha, \mathrm{OB} (\mathrm{ACT}_1 (\alpha), \mathrm{TO}\ Z))$ at t_1 and
     NOT $\mathrm{ACT}_1 (X)$ in period from t_1 to t_2

    entails

$$\mathrm{HAVE} \left(Z^\beta, \mathrm{RT}_{\mathrm{Ex}} \left(\left[\begin{array}{l} \mathrm{ACT}_2(\beta) \\ \lambda a(\mathrm{VALUE}(a, X) = -) \\ \mathrm{EXCH}(\mathrm{NOT}\ \mathrm{ACT}_1(X)) \end{array} \right] \right) \right) \text{ at } t_2$$

In the bottom line of (19), ACT_2 is the action that Z has the right to carry out; the lambda expression says that this action has a negative value for X; the EXCH operator says that this action is in exchange for X's nonperformance.

Rule (19) says nothing about the appropriate time interval to wait for compliance. More important, (19) says nothing about what kind of retaliatory act is appropriate—only that it should be something that the Actor won't like. Many such actions, especially for culturally loaded obligations, are prescribed in a culture's stock of customs and oral or written law.[8] In particular, there are large classes of obligations, including such things as debts, for which the appropriate action in the face of noncompliance is to call in the authorities to determine the appropriate punishment. In turn, social norms may dictate that the authorities have an obligation to the Beneficiary to mete out the appropriate punishment— one of the foundations of legal theory (Stone 1968). I return to the notion of "the authorities" in section 4.9.

In addition to (19), the nonfulfillment of an obligation has a broader consequence. Roughly speaking, *everyone*—not just the Beneficiary—is justified in criticizing the Actor (or thinking less of the Actor) for failing to fulfill the obligation. The threat of such criticism seems to me to constitute the *moral* dimension of an obligation. Here I would be reluctant to use the term *has a right* to describe what everyone may do to the Actor; something like *is morally justified* seems more appropriate. I will not attempt to formalize this inference, in part because an appropriately general form is beyond the scope of this chapter.

These two inferences, the one social/contractual, the other moral, seem both to be involved in social/contractual obligations such as promises and debts. The kinds of things we might call "moral obligations," such as the obligation to preserve the environment, seem to me to invoke only the latter inference rule.[9] It is interesting how the two rules are somewhat parallel in structure, but not entirely. In particular, only the Beneficiary has a *right* of retribution, whereas *everyone* is morally justified in sanctioning the offender.

Turning to rights, we find a related situation. Suppose I have given the usher my ticket. This gives me a right to enter the theater to see the performance. Now suppose someone tries to prevent me from going in, saying, "You have no right to go in!" I am thereby entitled to take action against this person: my right has been violated. Notice, by contrast, if I have tried to go in without presenting a ticket, I'm not entitled to express disapproval, since it's the rights of the theater (as corporate body), not mine, that are being violated.

This scenario leads us to the counterpart of rule (19) for rights. If I have a right, I may choose or not choose to exercise it. But if I attempt to exercise it, and some other party tries to prevent me, I then have the (Existential) right to exact punishment on that person. (20) formalizes this intuition.

(20) $\text{HAVE } (X^\alpha, \text{RT } (\text{ACT}_1 \ (\alpha))) \text{ at } t_1$ and
$\quad\quad \text{CAUSE } (Z, \text{NOT ACT}_1, (X)) \text{ at } t_1$

$\quad\quad$ *entails*

$$\text{HAVE}\left(X^\beta, \text{RT}_{\text{Ex}}\left(\begin{bmatrix} \text{ACT}_2(\beta) \\ \lambda a(\text{VALUE}(a, Z)) = - \\ \text{EXCH(CAUSE}(Z, \text{NOT ACT}_1(X))) \text{ at } t_1 \end{bmatrix}\right)\right)$$

$\quad\quad$ at $t_2 > t_1$

Again, there are many cultural customs and norms concerning what kind of retaliatory Action$_2$ is appropriate to what kind of Action$_1$, and under what sort of relationship between X (the Actor) and Z (the Right-Violator). In particular, just as in the case of unfulfilled obligations, X's right in many cases will consist of a right to go to the authorities to demand retaliation. For instance, if the usher doesn't let me into the theater despite my having presented my ticket, the appropriate action, after due remonstration, is to go to the manager, and if that doesn't work, to the police.

As in the case of obligations, there is also a moral dimension to violation of a right: everyone is morally justified in criticizing (or thinking less of) the person who violates someone's rights. Again, only the Actor has the *right* of retribution, but everyone is morally justified in criticizing the offender.

Rules (19) and (20), though nearly symmetrical, have one important difference. In the case of obligations, there is a specific Beneficiary of the obligation. As seen in (19), this is the individual who acquires the right of retaliation if the obligation is not met. In the case of rights, there seems to be no such specifically identified individual. *Anybody* who tries to prevent one from exercising a right is a potential target for justified retaliation.

This difference, however, conceals a deeper similarity: the individual entitled to retaliation is always the one for whom the potential Action is of positive value. In the case of a right, the Actor is the potential Beneficiary and therefore receives the right of retaliation for interference with receiving the benefit. In the case of an obligation, the Action is of negative value to the Actor; the reason the Action is to be performed is to benefit someone else. It is that someone else, then, who receives the right of retaliation.

Notice too that this parallelism extends to the moral dimension. Everyone is morally justified in criticizing the person who exacts the cost from the intended Beneficiary: the Actor in the case of an obligation, the person who interferes with the Actor in the case of a right.

My sense is that inference rules (19) and (20) are the central principles that make rights and obligations what they are. By contrast, a moral/ethical principle takes the form "One should/should not do such and such"; that is, it is similar relation of an individual to an action. But it does not carry inferences concerning rights of retaliation. Rather, it carries only what I have called the moral dimension, the fact that everyone is morally justified in criticizing the Actor for noncompliance. It is the need to regulate modes of retaliation in response to violations of social/contractual obligations and rights that leads to the development of legal and judicial systems in a society. So these inference rules lie at the foundation of social/cultural cognition.[10]

4.7   Reciprocal Rights and Obligations

To amplify the symmetries we have been observing: It is often felt that there is a sort of reciprocity between particular rights and obligations. In particular, the Beneficiary of an obligation is felt to have a "passive right" to receive the benefit. This sense can be stated as inference rule (21).

(21) HAVE $(X^\alpha, [OB (ACT (\alpha), TO Z)])$
       entails
       HAVE $(Z, [RT (ACT (X))])$

The bottom line of (21) is a passive right because Z is not the Actor of the Action. However, by entailment (18), X's action is beneficial to Z, so this Event satisfies the conditions for the argument of a passive right, as illustrated in (7e) and (8a).

Now let us apply inference rules (19) and (20) to both lines of (21). When we apply (19) to the first line, the inference is that Z is entitled to retaliation if X does not perform the Action. When we apply (20) to the bottom line, the inference is that Z is entitled to retaliation toward anyone who prevents Z from receiving the benefit of X's acting—in particular, toward X if X does not perform the Action. So the two lines lead to related inferences just in case X does not comply.

A right imposes a similar sort of reciprocal obligation: the obligation falls on *everyone* not to infringe on someone's rights.[11] In particular, the individual who grants the right is particularly bound to respect it. The general rule can be stated as (22). (In the interest of uncluttered typography, I use the notation *EVERYONE* instead of a standard universal quantifier with bound variable.)

(22) HAVE $(X^\alpha, \text{RT (ACT } (\alpha)))$
       entails
       HAVE $(\text{EVERYONE}^\beta,$
       $[\text{OB (NOT CAUSE } (\beta, \text{NOT ACT } (X))), \text{TO } X])$

Notice that the obligation in (22) is *not* to perform an action—a sort of counterpart of a passive right. Again, the outcome of someone's infringing on a right, as entailed by rule (20), is the same as the outcome of someone's failing to meet the obligation not to prevent exercise of a right, entailed by rule (22). So perhaps (22) is logically unnecessary. Nevertheless, something like it is often stated explicitly (e.g., in Stone 1968), so I include it for completeness.

4.8 Equality of Value Implied by *EXCH*

Next let us consider more closely the notion of exchange, symbolized by *EXCH* in (19) and (20). This notion not only appears in the entailments of rights and obligations, but is also expressed explicitly by means of a certain use of the preposition *for* in English.

(23) a. Susan praised her son Sam *for* behaving nicely.
       b. Fred cooked Lois dinner *for* fixing his computer.

(24) a. Susan insulted Sam *for* behaving badly.
       b. Lois slashed Fred's tires *for* insulting her sister.

These sentences describe situations in which someone does something "in return" for someone else's action. Those in (23) describe actions with positive values; those in (24) describe actions with negative values. Exchanges can felicitously take place only with another person, an entity that can be regarded as having values and responsibility. One cannot sanely punish one's car for getting a flat tire.

If we switch around the actions in (23) and (24), we get sentences that sound odd or perhaps ironic.

(25) a. Susan insulted Sam for behaving nicely.
     b. Lois slashed Fred's tires for fixing her computer.

This shows that we expect a positively valued action in return for a positively valued action, and a negatively valued action in return for a negatively valued one.

So far I have spoken of values as only positive or negative. But exchange situations show that values are conceived of as roughly quantitative. We find it odd if the two actions related by *for* do not match in quantity. The sentences in (26) convey some of this oddness.

(26) a. Fred cooked Lois dinner for saying hello to him.
     b. Fred cooked Lois dinner for rescuing all his relatives from certain death.
     c. Fred slashed Lois's tires for eating too little at dinner.
     d. Fred slashed Lois's tires for murdering his entire family.

In (26a) and (26c), we sense Fred as overreacting, as doing something unwarranted in return for Lois's action; in (26b) and (26d), we sense him as underreacting, as doing something that is not nearly enough to recognize the importance of Lois's action.

The intuition, then, is that an exchange situation presupposes rough equivalence of value between the two actions. For a first approximation, then, we could state a principle for the value of exchanges along the lines of (27). (The presupposition is defeasible in order to allow for exceptions —for example, merely thanking someone publicly for performing some heroic act.)

(27) $\begin{bmatrix} ACT_2(Z) \\ EXCH[ACT_1(X)] \end{bmatrix}$

    defeasibly presupposes
$$VALUE (ACT_2 (Z), X) = VALUE (ACT_1 (X), Z)$$

In practical situations, the equation is not this simple: each participant's judgment of the value of his or her own and the other's actions, both to himself or herself and to the other, may differ. In particular, there seems to be a general cognitive bias toward overestimating costs to oneself and benefits to others, and toward underestimating benefits to oneself and costs to others. Thus, it often requires negotiation to achieve a "fair" exchange, where both participants judge the exchanged acts to be of equivalent value to themselves and to the other. Here is an important point where "folk theory of mind" and Cosmides' (1989) "cheater detection" enter: one is more inclined to compromise if one believes the other's assertions of value are made in good faith.

The logic of exchange laid out here is a cognitive elaboration of a behavioral strategy well documented in the ethological literature, *reciprocal altruism*: "You scratch my back and I'll scratch yours." I leave open how much of its detail can be attributed to nonhuman primates (not to mention elephants and bats). What strikes me as particularly human, though, is the broad generality of the actions available to be entered into exchange equations.

Turning back to rights and obligations more specifically, we see in (27) a more or less formal statement of "The punishment fits the crime": this helps guide what actions are appropriate in retaliation for breaking obligations and violating rights in (19) and (20). (27) implies that the offending party should receive *retribution*: the cost of the retaliatory action to offenders should equal the cost of their offense to the injured party—that is, the two parties should end up equally badly off. An alternative to (27) is that the injured party should receive *restitution*: the benefit of the retaliatory action to the injured should equal the cost of the injury, whatever its cost to the offender—that is, the offended party should end up as well off as before.

(28) Retribution: VALUE $(ACT_2 (Z), X) = $ VALUE $(ACT_1 (X), Z)$
       Restitution: VALUE $(ACT_2 (Z), Z) = -$VALUE $(ACT_1 (X), Z)$

We know that the two are not equivalent. For one extreme case, "Nothing you can do to the murderer will bring my son back"; that is, restitution is impossible, though retribution might be. (The distinction between these two in conceptual development is noted by Piaget (1932); he claims the notion of restitution is established later than that of retribution.)

Combining (27) with (19) and (20) gives us an inferential link between (13) and (14), that is, between the value of rights and obligations and the value of the actions to which they pertain. Consider first obligation. Since the action to which one is obligated has a cost, and *not* performing the action risks a cost (just in case the Beneficiary exercises the right of retaliation), then having an obligation is basically a lose-lose situation— that is, obligation itself is of negative value. Conversely, since the act to which one has a right is of positive value, and being prevented from exercising the right grants one a right of restitution, then having a right is a win-win situation, that is, a benefit. So some of the pieces of the logic of rights and obligations begin to hang together.

4.9   Authority

Consider who can impose an obligation on you.[12] As pointed out in section 4.3, the simplest case is a self-imposed obligation such as a promise. Other things being equal, you are free to make whatever promises you wish. But no one else can impose an obligation on you unless particular conditions obtain. For example, if a random person says to you, "I hereby oblige you to wash my feet," you are justifiably offended and baffled. The felicity conditions for such a speech act are not met, just as if a random person were to declare to you, "I hereby name you Fuzzy-Wuzzy."

One felicitous condition under which an obligation *can* be imposed by someone else is if you have granted the other person the right to impose it, either by making an offer or by making an agreement or contract. You are perfectly free to grant such a right.

However, there is another situation in which someone can impose obligations on you: when that person has authority over you through position in the social hierarchy.[13] A society presents many authority relationships—for instance, parent to child, boss to worker, sergeant to private. The authority relationship entails the Authority's right to impose obligations on the subordinate. If, for a first approximation, we encode the authority relationship as (29), then (30) expresses the Authority's right to created obligations for subordinates.

(29) HAVE (Z, AUTHORITY (X))
     = 'Z has authority over X'

(30) HAVE (Z, AUTHORITY (X))
     entails
     HAVE (Z^α, RT (CAUSE (α, INCH HAVE (X^β,
     (OB (ACT (β), α))))))

The language used to express what one can do with authority is virtually identical to that for rights listed in table 4.1. We speak of the *exercise* of rights and of authority; a higher authority can *give* or *grant* rights or authority—or *revoke* them or *take* them *away*. One can *renounce* rights or authority that one currently *holds*; or one can through malfeasance *lose* rights or authority. One can *insist* on one's own rights or authority; one can *acknowledge* someone else's. On the other hand, there is more complexity in authority, since one can *resist* another's authority, but the phrase *resisting another's right* makes little sense.

Like all obligations, those imposed by an Authority must have a Beneficiary. (30) encodes the typical case in which the Beneficiary is the Authority him- or herself (this is notated by the α in the second argument posiion of OB, bound to Z). Thus, in case of noncompliance the Authority also has the right of punishment. Other Beneficiaries are possible—for instance, when a judge obliges a divorced parent to pay child support to the ex-spouse. In such a case, the ex-spouse's right of retaliation in case of noncompliance is typically determined by the judge as well. That is, if an Authority imposes an obligation on an Actor, with a third individual as Beneficiary, the Authority retains the right to punish the Actor for noncompliance, with or without appeal from the Beneficiary. So the logic becomes still more complex; I will not attempt to formalize it here.

Even with these added complexities, the account in (30) is still missing an important caveat, in that it is necessary to recognize limitations of authority. For instance, in our society, we believe that your boss does not have the right to oblige you to take your clothes off. A more adequate formalization relativizes authority to a particular class of actions, as in (31).

(31) HAVE (Z, AUTHORITY (X^{β}, ACT_a (β)))
    = 'Z has authority over X with respect to actions of type a'

The appropriately revised form of (30) is (32) (where I also add the Authority's right to confer rights).

(32) HAVE (Z, AUTHORITY (X^{β}, ACT_a (β)))
    entails
    HAVE (Z^{α}, RT (CAUSE (α, INCH HAVE (X^{β},
    (RT/OB (ACT_a (β), α))))))

(32) leaves about the right loopholes for social negotiation (and conflict): Over exactly what actions can a given Authority impose obligations? And how are those decided? These are issues with which every society must grapple.

How does one obtain authority? One way is to be granted it by a higher Authority, who is then said to be *delegating* authority. But this leaves open who grants authority at the top of the pyramid. This problem of the "apex norm" (Stone 1968, following Hans Kelsen) lies at the root of a society's conception of itself. Three possible solutions: despotism, where the ultimate authority simply asserts authority without recourse and maintains it through the exercise of power; supernatural authority such as the "divine right of kings," in which the top-ranked person is said to be granted authority by a deity whose rights in turn require no justification; and representative government, in which authority is taken to arise from the "consent of the governed." In addition, all societies recognize the "natural" authority of parents over children, which seems to need no justification. Perhaps there are other possibilities.

4.10   Where Does It Come From?

I have surely left many subtleties still untouched—and some major points as well, such as how to reason about conflicting rights and obligations, and how to characterize rights as legitimate or illegitimate.[14] Nevertheless, I will now step back a bit.

I have shown that notions of right and obligation are richly interconnected by inferences to each other and to the notion of the value of an action to an individual. The central inference rules (19) and (20) depend on the notion of linking two actions as exchanges of value, and through that on notions of fairness or justice. The notion of authority depends heavily on the notion of rights. In short, many of the conceptual foundations of social organization either depend on an understanding of rights and obligations, or else are developed in justification of the assertion of particular rights and obligations.

Like the sorts of concepts with which John Macnamara was so deeply concerned, the concepts of right and obligation are, it seems, quite abstract, not linked to perception of the physical world except very indirectly. In fact, the analysis here suggests that their content may lie entirely in the inferences that can be drawn from them. They are, as it were, part of an elaborate social accounting system for keeping track of the implications of an individual's actions with respect to others, a system rooted ultimately in the notion of value.

In order for an individual to function in a society, then, it is essential for him or her to intuitively grasp the concepts of right and obligation. Indeed, most of the discussion here has consisted of pointing out intuitions that all of us share. So the question arises of how people acquire these concepts. As Macnamara puts it (1991), how does one gain entry to a system of interrelated terms and ideas, if they cannot be defined in terms of some other system?

There is no question that people must learn the particular network of rights and obligations inculcated (or presupposed) by their society: who has an obligation to whom, who has a right to impose obligations and grant rights over what actions, what retaliation is appropriate for failure to meet what obligation, and so forth. This must by all means be a major part of cultural learning. But, returning to a point made at the outset, it is less clear that people must learn that there *are such things* as rights and obligations. As far as I know, every culture shares these concepts. They seem to be building blocks as fundamental to understanding the social world as force is to understanding the physical world. (This point is also made by Forrester (1996).)

Moreover, the inferential patterns of rights and obligations have no analogue in the physical (or sensorimotor) domain, such that there could be a progression in learning along the lines of Piaget, or a learning through metaphor along the lines of Lakoff and his colleagues. The latter possibility was rejected in section 4.4, even before approaching the complexities of retaliation and exchange, for which a physicalistic metaphor is still more far-fetched. (In fact, if anything, the tendency often goes the other way: people attempt to understand the physical world by anthropomorphizing it into a metaphorically social world full of wills and desires.)

It seems to me, therefore, that an important question for research into social cognition is how the child learns the concepts of right and obligation—or whether they are learned at all. The latter possibility, not to be discounted, is that these concepts are largely if not entirely innate, a specialized "way of thinking" wired into the brain by the human genome. Such a hypothesis would certainly account for the cultural universality of these concepts: they would form a preestablished species-wide skeleton of social understnding over which each particular culture builds its own flesh. Under this hypothesis, the child learning a culture would then come to the task predisposed to interpret the social world in terms of rights and obligations, among other things. If there is an identifiable developmental stage where such concepts become available, relatively uniform across cultures, this might well be interpreted as evidence of biological maturation of the brain. If so, the argument would be parallel to the arguments for the biologically based language capacity that makes language acquisition possible (Chomsky 1965; Lenneberg 1967).

I am not aware of any research that bears directly on the acquisition of these precise concepts. However, suggestive evidence appears in the experimental work of Piaget (1932), who discusses the development from ages 6 to 11 of the child's understanding of related deontic concepts such as the rules of games and of moral concepts such as prohibition and fairness, as well as their relation to authority. In particular, rules of games have some of the same "objective" ontological status as obligations, so should provide suggestive evidence.

Looking earlier in child development, work by Cummins (1996, to appear) and Harris and Núñez (to appear) investigates children's understanding of the deontic concepts of prohibition, permission, and reciprocal exchange at the ages of 3 and 4. These authors find a degree of understanding of these concepts more sophisticated than one might have expected from Piaget's research—in fact, an understanding more reliable than with equally complex propositional statements. For instance, Cummins compares 3- and 4-year-olds' understanding of a prohibition such as "All squeaky mice have to stay in the house" with that of a declarative statement such as "All the squeaky mice are in the house." The children's understanding is tested by asking them which (toy) mice they have to check in order to determine whether the order has been carried out or the statement is true. The question is phrased in such a way that the very same mice must be checked under both conditions. Cummins finds that the children are much more reliable with the prohibition than with the statement. (Notice also that this is not exclusively ego-centered deontic understanding, as might be acquired through a child's experience with parents' orders: the task involves checking whether other individuals have obeyed someone else's order.) Cummins concludes that this aspect of deontic understanding is in place early on in development. This is not a test of the entire logic of rights and obligations, but at least an important part.

If the logic of rights and obligations were part of the human endowment, it would have likely emerged from some evolutionary antecedent. So some precursors might be expected in the social behavior of primates. In section 4.8 I have already alluded to reciprocal altruism and aggression as a precursor of exchange. More pointedly, Hauser et al. (1995) describe a behavior in rhesus macaques that appears to present a precursor of obligation. It seems that when an individual finds a food source on his own, there is a special call he utters to signal to the troop that food has been found. If the individual does not utter the call, of course, he will benefit from a greater quantity of food for himself, so there is a payoff in not uttering the call. However, if other members of the troop discover the individual eating *and the call has not been uttered*, then they beat him up— even if he is the most dominant individual in the troop. It is striking, however, that nonmembers of the troop will not be beaten up under parallel conditions. One is highly tempted to interpret this scenario as an understanding on the part of the monkeys that one is "obligated" to the members of one's own troop to signal the finding of food. In particular, what makes this suite of behaviors look like obligation is that the right of punishment, expressed here as inference rule (19), seems to be an essential component. Although it is important not to overinterpret ethological observations, the detail of current work like that of Hauser and his colleagues bids us not to underinterpret either. I would not go so far as to call this behavior illustrative of an understanding of obligation in the full human sense, but it certainly appears to be on the way. If so, it again provides indirect evidence that the notion of obligation has a biological basis.

Three directions suggest themselves for investigating the issue further. First, crosslinguistic and crosscultural work on the language and understanding of rights and obligations would add a great deal to the analysis. Second, I have barely scratched the surface of the formal detail of rights and obligations, their dynamic functioning in social reasoning, and their relationships with other social concepts (including dominance hierarchies and moral and ethical thought). To figure out exactly what the child has to learn—and what the child *can* learn—it is crucial to pull these concepts apart further into their components and to see what external evidence could lead to the acquisition of such components. A third direction is to use formal analysis of this sort to help guide further research in anthropology, primatology, and especially child development on this topic that is so vital to our social existence. It is my hope that researchers better versed than I in these disciplines will be stimulated by the present chapter to undertake the challenge.

Notes

1. To be politically correct, one might justifiably ask whether taking these notions for granted is a cultural bias on the part of anthropologists, and whether other cultures might indeed have quite different notions underlying their social organization. I don't think so: the apparent success of anthropological description—the fact that one can make sense of cultures while taking these notions for granted— suggests that there is little danger of conceptual chauvinism on this particular point of analysis. I might be wrong, of course; but I suggest that proving me

wrong requires more than a blanket invocation of cultural relativism. See Brown 1991 for discussion.

2. Although, of course, the conceptualized *functions* of streets and buses must involve the actions and goals of persons.

3. I follow the notational convention of linguistics in marking unacceptable sentences with a *.

4. Though I gather that during the medieval period there were such things as trials of pigs for killing children, pushing pigs toward a more responsible status.

5. *Sue **had** a right/obligation to leave yesterday* is of course acceptable. In this case, the time for which the right/obligation is asserted is yesterday or earlier—not five minutes ago, for instance.

6. For readers unacquainted with this style of formalization, the point is to have a canonical and precise way of expressing claims about meaning, which permits us to state rigorous principles by which meanings may be composed and by which they may be used to draw inferences. The notation used here can be thought of as an enriched form of predicate logic. For those uncomfortable with the formalism, I will take care to explain the formulas in ordinary English as well.

In (10) and succeeding examples I use the predicate *HAVE* to express possession, following Pinker 1989. An alternative in line with the practice of Jackendoff 1983 would be (i); I leave it to the interested reader to work out the differences in the rules throughout the chapter.

(i) BE_{Poss} ([RT/OB (ACT (α))], AT_{Poss} X^{α})

7. There is however a degree of circularity in this suggestion, in that, as mentioned at the outset, possession in large part consists of rights. I will not attempt here to grapple with problems this may raise.

8. We can include among "customs" the sorts of things discussed in "Miss Manners" columns in the newspaper: what do I do if someone doesn't fulfill the customary obligation of writing a thank-you note for a wedding present?

9. What I am calling here the moral dimension is the main one considered by Conison (1997), who draws the inference that everyone is entitled to sanction someone who breaks a promise. Von Wright (1963, 12), however, says, "'By definition', one could say, promises ought to be kept. But this is only one aspect, beside others, of the obligation in question.... To try to explain the obligation to keep promises, for example, in terms of the 'normative pressure' of customs seems utterly out of place." This is the intuition I am trying to capture here.

10. In certain religious traditions, moral/ethical strictures are taken to be obligations to a deity, and the deity acquires the right of retaliation. I take this to be a cultural construct whose purpose is to sharpen ethical norms, giving them the same "objective" status as laws.

11. "Infringe": yet another thing one can do with a right. This verb has associations of treading on another's territory, a variation on possession.

12. This section is a particular area where I realize I run a risk of overly presupposing something like the Western democratic tradition, with its stress on the

rights of the individual. If the logic works out differently for different cultures, so be it.

13. Authority is a form of social dominance, but not the only one. For example, siblings often fall into a dominance hierarchy by age, but that does not necessarily make it possible for an older sibling to impose obligations on a younger.

14. In particular, I have not dealt with what many take to be the most important issue concerning rights: the notion of universal human rights. I see some difference between these and the more mundane type of rights discussed here. Unlike contractual rights, issues of human rights typically arise in the context of *claiming* rights that are not acknowledged by governmental authority. In the time of the American Revolution, such rights were asserted to be granted by higher (divine or natural) authority (as in "... endowed by their Creator with certain unalienable rights..."); in this century, they have been to some extent acknowledged through international agreements such as the United Nations Universal Declaration of Human Rights. In either case, there is to some extent a failure of mutual belief in the existence of the rights in question, as well as questionable effectiveness in enforcement on the part of the higher authority.

References

Bloom, P., Peterson, M. A., Nadel, L., and Garrett, M. F. (Eds.). (1996). *Language and space.* Cambridge, MA: MIT Press.

Brown, D. (1991). *Human universals.* New York: McGraw-Hill.

Cheney, D., and Seyfarth, R. (1990). *How monkeys see the world.* Chicago: University of Chicago Press.

Chomsky, N. (1965). *Aspects of the theory of syntax.* Cambridge, MA: MIT Press.

Conison, J. (1997). The pragmatics of promise. *Canadian Journal of Law and Jurisprudence, 10,* 273–322.

Cosmides, L. (1989). The logic of social exchange: Has natural selection shaped how humans reason? Studies with the Wason selection task. *Cognition, 31,* 187–276.

Cummins, D. D. (1996). Evidence for the innateness of deontic reasoning. *Mind and Language, 11,* 160–190.

Cummins, D. D. (to appear). Evidence of deontic reasoning in 3- and 4-year-old children. *Memory and Cognition.*

Forrester, J. W. (1996). *Being good and being logical: Philosophical groundwork for a new deontic logic.* London: M. E. Sharpe.

Goldman, A. (1993). Ethics and cognitive science. *Ethics, 103,* 337–360.

Gruber, J. S. (1965). Studies in lexical relations. Reprinted 1976 as part of *Lexical structures in syntax and semantics.* Amsterdam: North-Holland.

Harris, P., and Núñez, M. (to appear). Children's understanding of permission and obligation. In L. Smith, J. Dockrell, and P. Tomlinson (Eds.), *Piaget, Vygotsky and beyond.* London: Routledge.

Hauser, M., Clark-Schmidt, K., Davis, R., and Leeman, B. (1995). Punishment and convention in rhesus monkeys. Unpublished manuscript, Departments of Anthropology and Psychology, Harvard University, Cambridge, MA.

Herskovits, A. (1986). *Language and spatial cognition.* Cambridge: Cambridge University Press.

Hoffman, M. L. (1987). The contribution of empathy to justice and moral judgment. In N. Eisenberg and J. Strayer (Eds.), *Empathy and its development.* Cambridge: Cambridge University Press.

Jackendoff, R. (1976). Toward an explanatory semantic representation. *Linguistic Inquiry, 7,* 89–150.

Jackendoff, R. (1983). *Semantics and cognition.* Cambridge, MA: MIT Press.

Jackendoff, R. (1990). *Semantic structures.* Cambridge, MA: MIT Press.

Jackendoff, R. (1992). *Languages of the mind.* Cambridge, MA: MIT Press.

Jackendoff, R., and Aaron, D. (1991). Review of George Lakoff and Mark Turner, *More than cool reason. Language, 67,* 320–338.

Lakoff, G., and Johnson, M. (1980). *Metaphors we live by.* Chicago: University of Chicago Press.

Lenneberg, E. (1967). *Biological foundations of language.* New York: Wiley.

Macnamara, J. (1991). The development of moral reasoning and the foundations of geometry. *Journal for the Theory of Social Behaviour, 21,* 125–150.

Miller, G., and Johnson-Laird, P. (1976). *Language and perception.* Cambridge, MA: Harvard University Press.

Murphy, G. (1996). On metaphoric representation. *Cognition, 60,* 173–204.

Piaget, J. (1932). *The moral judgment of the child* (trans. M. Gabain). New York: Free Press.

Pinker, S. (1989). *Learnability and cognition: The acquisition of argument structure.* Cambridge, MA: MIT Press.

Searle, J. (1995). *The construction of social reality.* New York: Free Press.

Snare, F. (1972). The concept of property. *American Philosophical Quarterly, 9,* 200–206.

Stone, J. (1968). *Human law and human justice.* Stanford, CA: Stanford University Press.

Talmy, L. (1983). How language structures space. In H. Pick and L. Acredolo (Eds.), *Spatial orientation: Theory, research, and application.* New York: Plenum.

Talmy, L. (1988). Force dynamics in language and thought. *Cognitive Science, 12,* 49–100.

Vandeloise, C. (1986). *L'espace en français.* Paris: Editions du Seuil. Trans. as *Spatial prepositions.* Chicago: University of Chicago Press (1991).

Wright, G. H. von (1963). *Norm and action: A logical enquiry.* London: Routledge & Kegan Paul.

Chapter 5

Deliberation Reasons and Explanation Reasons

Storrs McCall

Practical deliberation—*bouleusis*—is discussed by Aristotle in books 3 and 6 of the *Nicomachean Ethics*. Although Aristotle doesn't mention this, it is necessary to distinguish practical deliberation from what may be called "cognitive deliberation." Cognitive deliberation is deliberation over whether something is true or false, whereas practical deliberation is over what to do. In jury trials, for example, the jury is asked to decide the cognitive question, is the accused guilty as charged? Its deliberations concern this matter exclusively. If the judgment is "guilty," the judge must deliberate about something quite different, namely, what sentence to impose. The jury's deliberations are cognitive, the judge's practical.[1] In this chapter, I shall be concerned with practical deliberation.

Aristotle makes two remarks about deliberation that are familiar to every philosopher: first, that we deliberate about means not ends; second, that we deliberate about things that are in our power and can be done (*Nichomachean Ethics* 1112^{a}30, 1112^{b}11–16, 1139^{b}6, 1140^{a}32). I need a table; to make a table requires a hammer and saw; I have a hammer but no saw; so let me go out and buy a saw. Again a doctor, qua doctor, does not deliberate about whether a patient should be healed, but *how to heal him*. No one will disagree with this. To be sure, one can imagine circumstances in which a doctor might deliberate over whether a patient should be healed—say, if there were 1,000 patients and drugs for only 500. But in this case the doctor isn't really deliberating about ends, but about the practical problem of how to treat as many people as possible with the

John Macnamara and I talked about many things, over many years, in the area of practical deliberation and intention. As I write this chapter I imagine his voice, objecting, sometimes chiding, but always encouraging, and I dedicate these pages to the memory of a true friend.

means available. If a doctor were truly to deliberate about ends and ask, for example, "Is healing worthwhile?", the question would fall under cognitive rather than practical deliberation.

What exactly is deliberation? In what follows, I try to give a philosophically adequate account of it and to answer some difficult questions. I finish up by speculating about what sorts of structures and neurophysiological functioning in the brain would make possible in real life the philosophical description of the deliberative process that I have given.

Let's start off with a concrete example. Marsha has to decide whether to accept an offer of graduate study in philosophy at UBC, Western Ontario, or McGill. Call these alternatives A, B, and C. Each one has its advantages and its disadvantages, and it is important to make the right decision. Marsha deliberates.

The first step in the deliberative process is to be clear about the alternatives, to represent them accurately and keep them in focus. Is the list exhaustive? Should she make a last-minute application to McMaster, where her sister is studying? Should she simply do nothing, and not accept any of the offers? Call this last option D, the do-nothing alternative. Let's suppose that A, B, C, and D exhaust the alternatives facing her and that each one is a "live" alternative in the sense that (a) she can choose it, and (b) if she chooses it, her choice determines what happens subsequently. Thus, if she chooses UBC, she goes to UBC. We may imagine that Marsha has lined up three envelopes on her desk, addressed to UBC, Western, and McGill. All she has to do is to put a stamp on one of them and mail it, or alternatively forget about graduate study. The first requirement for deliberation, then, is the existence of a "choice set," a set of two or more alternative courses of action $\{A, B, C, D, \ldots\}$ each of which it is physically possible for the deliberator to perform or implement, and which together exhaust the available options.

Once the choice set has been established, the process of deliberation begins in earnest. Each option has its advantages, which constitute the reasons for choosing it, and its disadvantages, which constitute the reasons for not choosing it. I shall call these *deliberation reasons*. For example, UBC has made a generous scholarship offer, but on the other hand has no staff member who works directly in Marsha's area of interest. These facts constitute positive and negative deliberation reasons for A, and there will be other positive and negative deliberation reasons for B, C, and D. In deliberation, we weigh deliberation reasons. We compare their relative strength with the aim of arriving at an overall comparative evaluation.

The process of evaluation is normally but not invariably the most time-consuming part of deliberation and ideally should result in a list of the options ordered by preference.

Once evaluation is completed, it might seem that the deliberative process is at an end. But this is not so. There is one more step, frequently ignored in studies of rational choice and decision but still essential: the element of choice or decision itself. It may seem difficult to imagine, once an ordered evaluation of the options has been made, what more a deliberator could need. But suppose the first two alternatives are very close in the ordering? Suppose they come out equal? What if the deliberator is faced with a difficult decision? Even in the case where an evaluation is unambiguous, with a clear-cut winner, something else besides evaluation is needed for action. The missing element is what Aristotle calls *prohairesis*, deliberative choice.

More needs to be said about *prohairesis*, but I should first sum up what has been established so far. The philosophical account of deliberation given above has distinguished three separate components of the deliberative process, ordered in strict temporal sequence:

1. Representation of the alternatives
2. Evaluation
3. Choice

With decision, which is choice of one of the alternatives, the deliberative process ends. I turn now to decisions and the reasons for them, the latter being distinct from the deliberation reasons for the different options.

In deliberation we weigh and assess deliberation reasons, each being a reason for or against one of the alternatives. When eventually we decide, and choose one of the options, there is normally also a reason why that option was selected over the others. I shall call the latter an *explanation reason*, or, occasionally, a *decision reason*. In the deliberative process there are deliberation reasons, which are the reasons for or against the different options, but there are also explanation reasons, which are the reasons why, after examination of the deliberation reasons, one of the options is chosen.

A principal objective of this chapter is to be clear about the exact difference between deliberation reasons and explanation reasons. Without a good understanding of the difference, I don't think we can know what deliberation is. Therefore, I shall spend some time discussing the relationship between them.

First, is it certain that a sharp line can be drawn between deliberation reasons and explanation reasons? On the face of it, yes. Deliberation reasons, in the deliberative process, have a relatively long life. Some may be present from the start, as when a diner at a restaurant perceives an excellent reason for choosing a chocolate mousse dessert at the very moment he becomes aware that it is on the menu. Others may emerge later, when the calorie count of the mousse is compared with that of the fruit salad. The explanation reason, on the other hand, comes into existence only at the end of the deliberation, when the choice has been made. As long as there is not yet a choice or decision, there cannot as a matter of logic be any explanation of it. Deliberation reasons are reasons *for* deciding this way or that; explanation reasons are reasons *that* or *why* a certain decision was made. A typical explanation reason might be of the form "X chose A rather than B because in the end X attached more weight to the deliberation reasons for A than to the deliberation reasons for B." If it exists at all, the explanation reason comes into existence only when the decision comes into existence. This isn't the case with deliberation reasons. Hence, the two are quite different.

That being said, we still want to know more about explanation reasons. Could they perhaps be associated, or identified, with comparisons among deliberation reasons, or more strictly perhaps with *comparative rankings* of alternatives based on deliberation reasons? If Marsha for example were to conclude that the program and the second language opportunities at McGill were more important than the funding and the friends she has in Vancouver, would this not be a perfectly good explanation reason for the decision to go to McGill? We must proceed carefully here. A reason *for* going to McGill, even though it results from a comparative weighing of all the deliberation reasons, is still a deliberation reason. One can, if Aristotle is right in maintaining there is such a thing as *akrasia*, conclude that overall the reasons for doing X outweigh the reasons for doing Y, and still do Y. In Davidson's memorable example (1980, 4), someone may conclude that there is nothing to gain and everything to lose from drinking a can of paint, and still one day drink it. No matter how strong it is, and how much it dominates all other deliberation reasons, a deliberation reason is not an explanation reason. Not until the decision has been taken, and the choice made, does the explanation reason come into existence.

Second, must every decision have an explanation reason? Or are there some totally irrational decisions, for which there is no explanation at all? Is the difference between a decision that is made lightly, casually, or thoughtlessly, and a decision that is made carefully and deliberately, the difference between a decision that lacks, and a decision that has, an explanation reason? These questions are not easy to answer. Let us start with Buridan-type situations, in which a choice must or should be made, but in which there is absolutely no reason for choosing one thing rather than another.

Buridan's ass starved to death halfway between two piles of hay because there was nothing to incline his choice toward *A* rather than *B*.[2] Here the deliberation reasons for *A* and *B* are equally balanced, and as a result no decision is taken. A similar problem, based on fear rather than desire, is the "railroad dilemma."[3] What fascinates us in these examples is not just the specter of decisional paralysis, but the feeling that the outcome— death by indecision—is in a genuine sense an affront to reason. If the ass had been rational, or more rational than he was, he would not have starved. He would have drawn straws and said, "Long left, short right." Failing this, if he had been clever enough, he could simply have made an arbitrary or criterionless choice (Ofstad 1961; McAdam 1965). If you believe this is impossible, reflect on how you manage to choose one of a hundred identical tins of tomato soup in a supermarket. The example of the soup tins was a favorite of Macnamara's, and he used it with great effect in discussion. If you made the mistake of saying that an arbitrary choice in these circumstances was difficult or impossible, that would indicate that you, like Buridan's ass, were not very intelligent.

Moving from Buridan-type examples to cases where there is a significant difference between the alternatives, but where the deliberation reasons are still equally balanced, the same question arises: can a choice be made for which there is no explanation or decision reason? If Marsha finds it difficult or impossible to decide between UBC and McGill because between them there is "nothing to choose," can she use some tie-breaking mechanism like a coin and in so doing make a choice that lacks an explanation reason? Not really. Although in this case the explanation is different from what it would have been if the evaluation process had produced a winner, an explanation reason still exists. If Marsha is asked why she chose UBC rather than McGill, she may answer that she flipped a coin. The reason why she chose UBC is that the coin fell heads. There need be nothing irrational about this. Compared to the paralysis of the Buridan example, and bearing in mind the approaching deadline for mailing the letter of acceptance, it is a supremely rational procedure. Sometimes we just have to stop deliberating and decide. It's a sign of rationality that we're able to do this.

Although the conclusion toward which we're moving seems to be that decisions always have explanation reasons, even if the reason in question may be something like "Because the coin fell heads," there still remain other cases to be examined. All our examples have been decisions that were made carefully, thoughtfully, deliberately. Even if a coin had to be used to break ties, its use was deliberate and rational. But what of decisions that are taken carelessly, without adequate thought? What if we are inebriated, and our deliberative powers impaired? Such cases may provide examples of decisions without explanation reasons.

The making of a decision, like the activity of evaluation, is a rational process. In fact, deliberation as a whole is a rational process, and each of the components that make it up is subject to norms by which it can be judged.

First, in the formation of the choice set, the alternatives should be realizable, and each option should be such that the decision of the deliberator alone is sufficient to implement it, or to initiate its implementation. The alternatives should also be exhaustive: no important or significant alternative should be excluded from the choice set.

Second, for the process of evaluation, different norms apply. Have all the deliberation reasons for all the alternatives been recognized and collected? Has each deliberation reason been appropriately weighted? If there are several deliberation reasons for the same alternative, has the total weighting of all of them, including possible negative reasons, been reasonably assessed? Finally, given appropriate total weighting for each alternative, has the comparison between them been carried out honestly and without bias? Or if there is bias, is the deliberator conscious of it, rather than having it work behind the scenes and affect the evaluation without the deliberator's being aware of it? These are the questions to be considered if an evaluation is to be judged rational. It is true that frequently we lack sufficient insight and self-knowledge to be sure whether in a particular case we are giving due and appropriate weight to a set of deliberation reasons, particularly if the decision is one that touches us emotionally. In many cases, the degree of objectivity and detachment required may be beyond us. Nevertheless, if the deliberative process is to be a rational one, a certain level of objectivity and self-knowledge is needed.

Finally, in addition to the above requirements, there are norms for rational choice. The first requirement is that to be considered rational, a choice or decision must have an explanation reason. If, for example, a choice is made for no reason at all, not even with the aid of a randomizing device like a coin as part of the decision-making process, then the decision cannot be considered rational. Furthermore, even in cases where an explanation reason is provided by the deliberator, norms of rationality still apply to it, and the rational assessment of a decision must take them into account. For example, if Marsha were to explain her decision to go to UBC by saying, "Because I'm a Libra," the relevance and consequently the rationality of this supposed explanation could be questioned. Decision, therefore, like choice set formation and evaluation, is a procedure that it is appropriate to subject to rational norms, and to judge rational only if it satisfies these norms. The same applies, mutatis mutandis, to the whole deliberative process.

An important question that should be addressed is whether an explanation reason for a decision is a cause of that decision. The immediate answer would seem to be no. An explanation reason for a decision comes into existence only once the decision is made, whereas a cause should antedate the thing it causes. The whole question of causality and its role in the deliberative process is nevertheless of great interest and must be looked at carefully.

First, our discussion from the start has taken us outside the framework of causal determinism, since the very existence of a choice set with two or more physically realizable alternatives is not consistent with determinism. One might attempt to remove the inconsistency by requiring that in any choice set one and only one alternative was causally possible, the deliberator necessarily being ignorant of which one that was. As long as the deliberator believed (falsely) that each alternative in the choice set was realizable, deliberation could proceed as usual, the eventual decision being taken in favor of the one option that was in fact open. This is deliberation according to the script that would be written for it by a determinist. The rewriting does indeed remove the inconsistency, but at the price of (a) abandoning choice sets with two or more real alternatives and (b) drawing a veil of ignorance over the eyes of deliberators about which is the sole choosable option. Behind the veil, "deliberation" can proceed. But rewriting the script in this way is unnecessary, if it can be shown that it is simpler and more elegant to abandon determinism.

Since the 1920s, quantum mechanics has provided the example of a science that is probabilistic rather than deterministic. As a result, replacing deterministic models of deliberation by indeterministic ones is not such a daunting or unthinkable project today as it would have been for

Hume, or Mill, or Brentano, or any philosopher working within the paradigm of Newtonian science. This is not the place to speculate exactly how or in what respect the overall neuronal functioning of the brain could be regarded as probabilistic rather than strictly deterministic, but at least the hypothesis that the brain is a complex indeterministic mechanism makes sense, is testable, and may one day be confirmed or falsified.

What is important for present purposes is the fact that if the central nervous system functions probabilistically rather than deterministically, then this functioning permits the formation of choice sets in deliberation. At the neurophysiological level, a choice set requires different physically possible neural states $n(A), n(B), n(C), \dots$ corresponding to the different actions $A, B, C, \dots$, the states being such that if $n(A)$ obtains then A is performed, if $n(B)$ obtains B is performed, and so on. Just as each of $A, B, C, \dots$ excludes the others, so each of $n(A), n(B), n(C), \dots$ excludes the others. These states are "missing" states of the brain that neuroscientists should one day be able to specify and describe, but that during deliberation are not actual existents. What is essential, however, for the existence of a choice set is that throughout the deliberative process each one of the neural states $n(A), n(B), n(C), \dots$ should be physically possible, that is, capable of becoming actual at the end of the process. Since each state is incompatible with the others, the only way this could be the case would be if the brain functioned indeterministically. Indeterministic neural functioning consequently underpins choice set formation in the sense that it makes it possible, that it is a necessary condition for its existence. If we believe in choice sets, with each option separately realizable, I don't see how we can avoid regarding the operations of the brain as in some yet-to-be-discovered way indeterministic.

The next step is to consider probabilities. If each of the outcome neural states $n(A), n(B), \dots$ is physically possible, it will have a probability value, and the probability values of all the members of a given choice set will sum to one. Needless to say, in keeping with the idea of the brain as a complex indeterministic mechanism, we are talking of objective probability values, not epistemic ones. With the introduction of probability comes the possibility of saying something about causality and perhaps ultimately being able to conclude whether deliberation can be considered a causal process.

At the beginning of the deliberative process, once the choice set is formed, the existence of the underpinning neurological mechanism, with the different target neural states, gives each alternative of the choice set a precise probability value. An interesting and important question is whether these probabilities change during deliberation.

If the probabilities change during the deliberative process, considerations of probabilistic causality may apply. For example, if J is some factor that enters consciousness during deliberation—a thought, a desire, a fact, a memory, a goal—and if A is one of the options of the deliberator's choice set, then if

$$p(A|J) > p(A|\text{not-}J),$$

we may say that J is a (prima facie) *probabilistic cause* of A (Suppes 1970, 12; Fetzer 1988, 118; Cartwright 1989, 55; Eells 1991, 56; DeVito 1997).[4] This is not equivalent to saying that J causes the alternative A to be chosen, since together with the above inequality we may also have

$$p(B|J) > p(B|\text{not-}J),$$

and J could not be the cause of A's being chosen and also B's being chosen. Hence, probabilistic causality is of limited interest in connection with deliberation.

Again, the factor J may increase the probability of option A's being realized, but can it increase it to unity? Can any deliberation reason, or deliberative factor, be of such strength that it makes it physically or causally impossible for any alternative other than A to be selected? Might it, before the choice is made, reduce the choice set to a single choosable option? This takes us back once more to determinism. One cannot rule out the possibility that during deliberation something should occur (e.g., paralysis or a violent fit) that restricts the alternatives to one option only. But such cases are so far removed from the norm as not to qualify as instances of deliberation at all. At the end of a deliberation, we are left either with the choice set with which we began, or with a reduced choice set, or an enlarged one, but in any case a set consisting of at least two members. The probabilities of these options can change, but if any of them reaches the value one, deliberation ceases.

A final question concerning probabilities, which reintroduces the subject of explanation or decision reasons, is this. At the end of the deliberative process, before a decision is made, the deliberator is faced with a choice set of different alternatives $A, B, C, \ldots$, each with a corresponding neural state $n(A), n(B), n(C), \ldots$. The objective probabilities of realizing these different options, and hence of the different target neural states' becoming actualized, will not in normal circumstances be known to the deliberator. Each probability will in fact be nonzero and some may be exceedingly small. Is it possible for a deliberator to choose, deliberately and intentionally, an alternative of very low objective probability?

From the point of view of probabilistic science, the occurrence of an event of low probability is not impossible, but would not be expected. If it happened, the only explanation that could be given would be something like "By the laws of chance, improbable events do occasionally occur. By pure chance, a bridge player may be dealt a hand of 13 spades." There exists no better causal/probabilistic explanation than this of why an improbable event occurs. But this isn't true of a choice made by a deliberator. No matter how objectively improbable the chosen option may be, a perfectly good explanation reason for the choice may be forthcoming. The deliberator who has for years drunk nothing but whiskey may say that this time he chose a Tia Maria, no matter how objectively unlikely his choice may have been, because he felt like it.

The lesson here, I think, is that in the realm of deliberation and choice there may occur events for which there is no causal/probabilistic explanation, but for which there is an intentional explanation. Some intentional explanations may be of the form "Ivan chose the Tia Maria because he felt like it"; others may be of the form "Unbelievably, Sally isn't here today because she deliberately and intentionally chose to go to jail." Perhaps the clearest examples of intentional explanations are those given in circumstances where nonintentional explanations (i.e., causal/probabilistic ones) don't exist. But detailed examination of the difference between intentional and causal/probabilistic explanation is a lengthy matter and must await another occasion.

Summing up, I began by listing the three essential components of a deliberation. These are, in strict temporal order, (1) choice set formation, (2) evaluation, (3) decision. In evaluation the reasons for and against the different options (deliberation reasons) are both appropriately weighted and weighed by the deliberator. Eventually, one option is chosen. Each element of the deliberative process is subject to rational norms by which it may be judged, a common but nonmandatory norm of element (3), choice or decision, being the existence of an explanation reason for the choice once it is made. If choice set formation is underpinned by an indeterministic neural mechanism, with a specific neural state $n(A_i)$ and a specific probability corresponding to each alternative A_i of the set, then the explanation of why the deliberator chooses one of the alternatives will not in general be a causal/probabilistic explanation based on those probabilities. Instead, it will be an intentional explanation. The precise relationship between intentional and causal/probabilistic explanations in deliberation remains to be investigated.

Notes

1. The distinction between practical and cognitive deliberation is discussed in McCall 1987 and McCall 1994, 254.

2. The dilemma antedates Buridan. See Rescher 1959 for why the problem of "Buridan's ass" should more justly be known as "al-Farabi's dates." Buridan's problem is discussed in Bratman 1987.

3. You are hiking with your partner through mountainous wooded country and come to a horseshoe-shaped valley with a railway track at the bottom. While you are crossing the track, a heavy branch falls on your partner's leg, pinning him or her to the rails; and while trying vainly to move the branch, you hear the whistle of an approaching train. Unfortunately, the echoes in the valley make in impossible to tell which direction the train is coming from. Game theory tells us you have a 50% chance of saving your partner's life if you pick a direction arbitrarily and run as fast as possible down the track to stop the train, but how many of us would have the strength of mind to do this as the whistle grows louder and the uncertainty becomes more agonizing?

4. This definition of probabilistic cause is normally supplemented by requiring that $p(A|J) > p(A|\text{not-}J)$ in all partitions of A's causal factor-space, meaning in all circumstances in which other combinations of other causal factors of A are held fixed and only J is allowed to vary. In the case of deliberation, however, we are concerned with a single unique process, not in general repeatable, and so this supplemental requirement cannot be met. Nor would it be appropriate to require, in addition to $p(A|J) > p(A|\text{not-}J)$, that the anticipated probabilistic effect A actually occurs, since if A occurs then in the probability calculus $p(A) = 1$, and hence $p(A|C) = 1$ for any C, provided $p(C) \neq 0$.

References

Bratman, M. (1987). *Intention, plans, and practical reason.* Cambridge, MA: Harvard University Press.

Cartwright, N. (1989). *Nature's capacities and their measurement.* Oxford: Clarendon Press.

Davidson, D. (1980). *Essays on actions and events.* Oxford: Clarendon Press.

DeVito, S. (1997). Probabilistic causality without propensities. Unpublished manuscript, University of Pittsburgh.

Eells, E. (1991). *Probabilistic causality.* Cambridge: Cambridge University Press.

Fetzer, J. H. (1988). Probabilistic metaphysics. In J. Fetzer (Ed.), *Probability and causality.* Dordrecht: Reidel.

McAdam, J. (1965). Choosing flippantly or non-rational choice. *Analysis, 25,* 132–136.

McCall, S. (1987). Decision. *Canadian Journal of Philosophy, 17,* 261–287.

McCall, S. (1994). *A model of the universe.* Oxford: Clarendon Press.

Ofstad, H. (1961). *An inquiry into the freedom of decision.* Oslo: Norwegian Universities Press.

Rescher, N. (1959). Choice without preference. *Kant-Studien, 51,* 142–175.

Suppes, P. (1970). *A probabilistic theory of causality.* Amsterdam: North-Holland.

Chapter 6

Truth and Its Negation: David R. Olson
Macnamara's Analysis of the
Place of Logic in a Cognitive
Psychology

Logicians, I gather, toil away at specifying the relations between symbols and the things the symbols represent. Thus, they concern themselves with how names can refer to things, how propositions can be true, how the logical particles *and*, *or*, *not*, and *if-then* work, and generally with issues of reference, truth, and validity. They formulate the results of their inquiry in terms of logical schemata such as

$$\frac{p \supset q, \ \sim q}{\sim p},$$

which reads something like: if *p* implies *q*, and *q* is not the case, then *p* is not the case either. The question is, what is the status of such a logical schema? Is it, for example, a law of thought? Is thinking achieved by applying rules of logic, or is logic merely a description of how thinking proceeds, or, yet again, is logic a set of "regulative" or normative principles quite independent of the way people ordinarily think?

The question has a venerable history, as John Macnamara informs us in his daunting book *A Border Dispute* (1986). The idea that logic constitutes the laws of thinking is known as psychologism and it is well expressed in J. S. Mill's *System of Logic*, in which the author claims that the necessary truths of logic are simply those things that we find it impossible to doubt. That is, Mill identified necessity with certainty. Frege in his *Begriffsschrift* distinguished the two, arguing that certainty is based on the facts of experience whereas necessity is connected "with the inner nature of the proposition considered" (1879/1967, 5). As Macnamara points out,

Parts of this chapter were first published as a review of Macnamara 1986 (see Olson 1987).

Frege claimed that logic is a "normative" law, a law that states how thinkers ought to judge, not a description of how they do judge.

Macnamara wants to add a third stage to this history by showing that logic is not something different and apart from thought but, rather, that "logic supplies a competence theory for the psychology of human reasoning" (p. 185). In so doing, he echoes the views of George Boole, his more famous Irish predecessor, who claimed that the laws of logic "possess an authority inherent and just, but not always commanding obedience" (1958, 409).

Macnamara's line of attack is borrowed from the grammarians rather than the mathematicians. The work of the logician is somewhat similar to the work of the grammarian who attempts to spell out the internal relations within linguistic structures. Since Saussure and especially since Chomsky, it has been common to think of linguistic structures as constituting the competence of native speakers. Grammars do not just describe products or sentences; they specify the implicit knowledge of speakers, knowledge that figures both in the generation of sentences and in intuitions of grammaticality.

Those developments in linguistics have given us a new respect for the rich structure of the linguistic system and, consequently, a new respect for the complexity of structure of the human mind. Rules, representations, constituent structure, meaning, propositional structures are all part of current discourse about mind. There is no longer any talk of tabula rasa.

Why not approach logic this way? Why not indeed, says Macnamara. Rather than leave logic to the logicians, he argues that logical competence is part of the endowment of rational creatures just as linguistic competence is part of the endowment of verbal ones. And then he sets out to explicate that competence.

Macnamara spent several of the last few years of his life with logicians learning about logic and then trying to specify what is logically implied in children's learning to do such apparently simple things as refer to objects by proper names and to make assertions. In the course of this study he examined the logic of proper names, common names or sortals, kinds, existential predicates, truth predicates, and sentential connectives including negations. Needless to say, children's acquisition of these structures is no small achievement!

Consider Macnamara's analysis of the child's learning of a proper name. To call a particular dog "Freddie" requires, Macnamara points out, that the child have the notion that this particular dog, Freddie, is a member of a category, dog, that the child recognize that dog is a kind of thing, that the particular individual in front of the child is what is being named, and that there is some equative relation between the thing pointed at and the proper name. He convincingly shows how much more a child brings to the learning of a proper name than Saint Augustine or anyone else had noticed. And he provides interesting evidence that very young children distinguish names, expressed by proper nouns, from sortals, expressed by common nouns, by the presence or absence of the articles *a* and *the*. Remarkable!

But Macnamara goes much further to insist, in addition, that all of these things must be represented in a language of thought in the form of a full proposition that the child judges to be true. For those of us who believe in genuine development—that knowledge is in some sense constructed—this goes much too far. Is there some way to escape Macnamara's claim that such elaborate representation is presupposed in the learning of a proper name? As truth and its negation, falsity, are the fundamental logical notions and as they play the central role in Macnamara's analysis and because truth is one of those axes that it does no harm to grind, I shall consider it in some detail.

Utterances express propositions that are, in fact, true or false. "To say of what is that it is, is true," said Aristotle. Moreover, truth is the criterion for agreement that parents use in talking to their children. If a child says "Freddie" while pointing at Muffin, they say "No, Muffin." So truth and falsity, expressed by the negation, are implicated in talk. But Macnamara is digging deeper. He is not examining truth and falsity in discourse. He is examining how truth and its negation function in the internal language of thought. Specifically, Macnamara claims that the 1-year-old, in saying "Freddie," is asserting a proposition, "That is Freddie," which, fully expressed in the language of thought, has some form equivalent to "That [which is a member of the kind dog, which refers to a kind] is Freddie is true" (p. 62). In saying "Freddie," the child is not only asserting a proposition that we adults may characterize as expressing a truth judgment. The child, Macnamara claims, understands that the expression asserts that particular proposition and in so doing has judged that proposition to be true. Lest you think I am putting words in Macnamara's mouth (as I am implying he has put them into the child's), let us allow Macnamara to speak for himself:

Assertion presupposes a grasp of the notion of truth; it presupposes a judgment of truth.... The learner does not need the concept of judgment because he can perform the act of judging without knowing that he is judging. But the learner must have the concept of truth; there is no action that can stand in its place. (pp. 106–107)

So Macnamara claims that the predicate *is true* (in the language of thought) must be used in judging the sentence true any time the child names an object. Its use implies the presence of the concept true and its opposite, not true, that is, false. "Children are endowed by nature with an understanding of both" (p. 108). Finally, "the conclusion that forces itself on us is that neither the concepts of truth and falsity nor the fundamental principles of logic are learned" (p. 109).

Thus, Macnamara has concluded that children have concepts of truth and falsity represented in an innate language of thought that permits them to learn, among other things, proper names. But are we compelled by logical argument to grant that young children not only produce utterances that are, in fact, true or false, but also that 1-year-old children have concepts of truth and falsity and know the principle of contradiction? Macnamara claims that we are, the primary reason being that it seems impossible to him that "logic-free activities can ever yield logical resources" (p. 30). This, of course, is a denial of the Piagetian hypothesis that representational structures can develop from sensorimotor ones, a central plank of Piaget's epigenetic theory.

Even after several careful readings of Macnamara's arguments, I can see no reason why the predicates *true* and *false* could not be acquired (rather than being presupposed). Children do encounter utterances that are objectively true and others that are objectively false, and they do encounter adults' judgments of utterances as being true or false. Why could not these objective facts be sufficient grounds for children's acquisition of these predicates? I see no reason that these predicates are preconditions for naming any more than that the predicates *say* and *mean* are preconditions for saying and meaning things. Admittedly, all predicates presuppose some mechanism for representing predicates, but that is not the issue here. The issue here is whether it is a necessary truth that children must have predicates for truth and falsity represented in a language of thought in order for them to learn proper names.

Concepts of truth and falsity (false being not true) do presuppose a concept of negation, and it is worth asking whether, as Macnamara insists, the concept of negation is also innate. Negation is fascinating in that it is clear that negation does not exist in nature. Russell (1948, 520) pointed out that "the world can be described without the use of the word *not*."

Geach (1957, 23), too, wrote that "nowhere in the sensible world could you find anything, nor could you draw any picture, that would suitably be labeled *or* or *not.*" Yet a mind that could represent only what is the case would be a mind without logic, hypotheses, or language (Harrison 1972).

Although negations are absent from nature, they are central to language. Comparativists have argued that negation is conspicuously absent from the communication systems of other animals (Sebeok 1962), and although nonhuman animals can issue warnings and register disappointment, they cannot mark in their communication that some expected event has not occurred. Visalberghi and Fragaszy (1996, 294) write, "We can think of no impediment to the use of these forms of negation in nonhumans; but they simply do not use them." Indeed, it is possible that an animal cannot mentally represent negation and that the ability to represent a cat as "not a dog" is peculiar to language-using humans. Could, contrary to Macnamara, the concept of negation (and hence falsity) be acquired as a child acquires a natural language?

There is a rich literature on children's acquisition of negation in language (for a summary, see Horn 1989) that indicates a clear progression in understanding and use of negatives beginning with expressions of rejection, disappearance, and finally denial, so-called truth-functional negation. Although rejections, refusals, and prohibitions are not necessarily linguistic—even dogs can reject food or refuse to come—denials constitute the "linguistic category of negation par excellence" (Tottie 1982, 96). As we shall see, only when children are approximately school-aged do negation and falsity come apart in such a way that they can judge a sentence containing a negation to be true. They come to agree with Aristotle in the second part of the definition mentioned earlier: "To say of what is not that it is not, is true." Thus, to judge a proposition as true or false is a late and sophisticated achievement entirely dependent upon the acquisition of negation.

Macnamara could say of such a counterargument that it confuses logical performance with logical competence. It is easy to design tasks that make it difficult for children to display their underlying logical ability. The tasks I discuss examine complex judgments about English sentences, whereas he discusses the logical competence that must be present to account for children's acquisition of names, assertions, and inferences. So, he may claim, I misunderstand. That, and worse, is what he said about Piaget. In a comment that is as close as one gets to a call to arms,

Macnamara says, "It is in fact doubtful that Piaget had any sharable insights into the fundamental processes of cognitive growth" (p. 114).

Piaget's subjects, he claims, are "faced with a complicated induction problem and simply become muddled" (p. 116). Piaget's tasks, he suggests, test only subjects' ability with an algebra for possible combinations of propositions (he'd say the same of Wason and Johnson-Laird's "four-card" task), whereas he is interested in only "the most basic logical connectives themselves" (p. 115). Of those basic notions he says, "There is nothing in [Piaget's] evidence to even suggest that [the child] was so totally lacking in logical intuitions as to knowingly assent to both a proposition and its negation" (p. 116).

However, consider the evidence provided by Alison Dewsbury and later explored in some detail by Janet Astington and myself (Astington and Olson 1984; Olson 1997). Four- and five-year-old children are shown a picture of a man with a hat, accompanied by a series of sentences. They are asked to put a check mark by the ones that are true, right, correct, or OK and to put an X by the ones that are false, wrong, or in error. Here is what children reliably do:

The man has a hat.   √

The man has no hat.   √

As if that was not enough, they go on thus. Shown a picture of a cat, and asked to mark the following sentences, they do thus:

This is a dog.   X

This is not a dog.   X

Such judgments would seem to contradict Macnamara's claim directly; children do seem to knowingly assent to both a proposition and its negation. In fact, the explanation is not that simple. I have argued that rather than judging truth or falsity as requested, children are either agreeing or disagreeing with the assertion of a speaker and not judgments of the truth or falsity of the proposition. Thus, in response to "The man has no hat," children are using a check mark to express "Yes, he does [have a hat]," and in response to "This is not a dog," they are using an X to express "No, it's not [a dog]." Thus, both supposedly wrong responses are in fact appropriate. Only after children are of school age (and perhaps even then only in a literate society) do they master the more specialized predicates, *true* and *false*. Judging a proposition as true or false, far from being a presupposition for naming and saying things, is a consequence of treating utterances in a certain way—namely, as propositional objects that exist independently of the sentences that express them and the situations they represent and, hence, as objects that can be judged as true or false of those situations. Admittedly, children are sensitive to the fact that something has gone wrong if they disagree, but the nature of this "going wrong" may be pragmatic rather than truth-functional (Volterra and Antinucci 1979).

Rather than treating logic as a competence theory for thought, I would prefer to see logic as a metalanguage for expressing certain properties of statements in situations. As Macnamara acknowledges, logic is a device for characterizing arguments, not a device for making them. However, there is something deeply counterintuitive in arguing that the predicates represented in the metalanguage are presupposed in learning the language in the first place. As mentioned, Macnamara borrows this assumption from grammatical theory, where the abstract properties of a grammar are attributed to a learner as an explanation of what makes the learning of language possible.

Extending this approach to logic leads Macnamara to claim that calling one's dog "Freddie" is an exemplar of the class of assigning proper names. Proper names have a number of logical properties including that they assert the truth of a proposition "This particular individual dog is Freddie." Macnamara next argues that if this abstract characterization of the logical structure of proper names is correct, then this logical structure must be known by learners if they are to learn a proper name. Indeed, Macnamara claims, it is presupposed in the acquisition of a proper name. What is required, he argues, is that children possess an unlearned language of thought that has all the logical resources that the natural language will come to have when it is acquired. It is seen as the unlearned competence that makes the learning of logical particles in natural language possible. Is such attribution inescapable?

In my judgment, the argument is analogous to the following. When children learn the word *fish*, they learn a word, a one-syllable word, a four-letter word, and a number of other things. These are all properties of the stimulus that can be characterized by means of a metalanguage. Why couldn't the same be true of logic? Children learn to make utterances in contexts. Utterances constitute new objects in the world, *objets trouvés*. A metalanguage is evolved to talk about the properties of those newly created objects, propositions and truth being the most important of these. Truth is, in this view, an emergent property of a created object. Concepts of proposition and of truth are not presupposed in learning a language; they do not characterize a language of thought that makes learning of language possible. Rather, they are the properties of symbolic objects that the metalanguage brings into reflective consciousness (to use a term that is not to be found in Macnamara's index).

Now there is a sense of competence that this metalanguage reflects. The metalanguage, like the language, is a human invention, and human inventions do reflect, however indirectly, the structures of the human mind. Thus, as the late Robin Gandy, a friend of Alan Turing, claimed, exploration of mathematical structures is essentially an exploration of the properties of the human mind. That notion of competence is more appealing to me than Macnamara's notion of competence, which sees any acquired logical or linguistic structure as an explicit representation of the structures already present in a language of thought. Needless to say, it was not more appealing to Macnamara.

In developing his own views, Macnamara does justice to a complex body of knowledge and at the same time engages the reader in a complex but important debate. Just as language and thought came to be seen in a new light when psychologists finally began to pay some attention to linguistic structure, so thinking and reasoning may come to be seen in a new light when psychologists begin to pay attention to the issues Macnamara set out. There can be no doubt that Macnamara is a Moses leading a reluctant people out of bondage to an oversimplified view of mind. I would be much happier if I could be sure that this wilderness was, in fact, a route to the promised land.

References

Astington, J. W., and Olson, D. R. (1984, May). Children's comprehension of true negation. Paper presented at the University of Waterloo Conference on Child Development. Waterloo, Canada.

Boole, G. (1958). *An investigation of the laws of thought*. New York: Dover.

Frege, G. (1879/1967). Begriffsschrift. In J. v. Heijenoort (Ed.), *Frege and Gödel: Two fundamental texts in mathematical logic*. Cambridge, MA: Harvard University Press.

Geach, P. T. (1957). *Mental acts, their content and their objects*. London: Routledge & Kegan Paul.

Harrison, B. (1972). *Meaning and structure: An essay in the philosophy of language*. New York: Harper & Row.

Horn, L. R. (1989). *A natural history of negation*. Chicago: University of Chicago Press.

Macnamara, J. (1986). *A border dispute: The place of logic in psychology.* Cambridge, MA: MIT Press.

Olson, D. R. (1987). Thinking about logic (Review of J. Macnamara, *A border dispute*). *Canadian Journal of Psychology, 41,* 392–398.

Olson, D. R. (1997). The written representation of negation. *Pragmatics & Cognition, 5*(2), 239–256.

Russell, B. (1948). *Human knowledge, its scope and limits.* New York: Simon & Schuster.

Sebeok, T. A. (1962). Coding in the evolution of signaling behavior. *Behavioral Science, 7,* 430–432.

Tottie, G. (1982). Where do negatives come from? *Studia Linguistica, 34,* 101–123.

Visalberghi, E., and Fragaszy, D. (1996). Pedagogy and imitation in monkeys. In D. R. Olson and N. Torrance (Eds.), *Handbook of education and human development.* Oxford: Blackwell.

Volterra, V., and Antinucci, F. (1979). Negation in child language: A pragmatic study. In E. Ochs and B. Schieffelin (Eds.), *Developmental pragmatics.* New York: Academic Press.

Chapter 7

Names for Things and Stuff: An Aristotelian Perspective

Sandeep Prasada

Freddie is a dog. As an undergraduate in one of John Macnamara's courses, I spent the better part of a semester studying what knowledge must be attributed to someone who understands that sentence. I intend to borrow a page from John and will spend much of this chapter discussing what knowledge must be attributed to the person who understands the sentences (1)–(4). In doing so, I will be addressing an aspect of the question posed by Macnamara (1978): How do we talk about what we see? Given that we can use any of the sentences (1)–(4) to talk about the same entity in the world, we need some kind of account of how it is that these sentences differ in how they are related to our visual representations of the entity. As we will see, the simple fact that we can use any of these sentences to talk about the same entity in the world, if taken seriously, leads to interesting conclusions concerning the nature of our perceptual and conceptual systems. Recent work by Landau and Jackendoff (1992) has addressed the question of how we talk about objects and locations. In this chapter, I will be focusing on what is involved in talking about objects and materials.

It is impossible for me to adequately express the intellectual debt I owe John Macnamara. In addition to the vast amount of knowledge he imparted, he has, through example, shown me the virtues of taking problems in cognitive psychology seriously and trying to make progress on the problems by using a wide array of methods and insights from different disciplines. I am grateful to have had the opportunity to have him as a teacher, a colleague, and a friend. I thank John Kim for helping me clarify my thinking on all of the issues discussed in this chapter; he is, however, in no way responsible for any confusion or mistakes that remain. Finally, I'd like to thank Paul Bloom and Ray Jackendoff for helpful comments on an earlier version of this chapter. Preparation of this chapter was supported in part by National Science Foundation grant SBR-9618712.

(1) That is a table.

(2) That is wood.

(3) That is a piece of furniture.

(4) I have no idea what that is, but it is brown, hard, and weighs 10 pounds.

In each of the sentences (1)–(4), the demonstrative *that* directs our attention to a particular part of our environment. Typically, this is a spatiotemporally bounded solid entity, though this does not have to be the case (e.g., *That is a shadow, That is coffee, That is a forest, That is a somersault*). Clearly, there are principles of perception that operate to organize the information available in ways such that particular spatiotemporally bounded entities are segregated from others. These entities serve as the natural objects of our attention, action, and understanding. Exactly what types of information are used and how they are used to define these entities, which are the natural objects of our attention, is what a theory of perception should give us.

Crucially, that which is being attended to can be distinguished from that which is not being attended to in purely spatiotemporal terms. This is what allows for the possibility of a given entity (described in purely spatiotemporal terms) being understood (in nonspatiotemporal terms) in more than one way by a given person (e.g., as a table or as some wood), or in different ways by different people. The fact that we can disagree about what something is, or think about it in more than one way, requires that we be able to attend to the thing in a manner that is independent of our understanding of that thing. That is, the perception of an entity has to be autonomous of its conception (Macnamara and Reyes 1994a). Note that this claim does not rule out the possibility of top-down influences in perception; rather, it claims only that it is possible to perceive entities in a manner that is independent of any particular way of understanding the nature of the thing—how often this happens, or how easy this is to do, is another matter. In fact, sentences such as (4), which are noncommittal with respect to the nature of an entity, are rare except perhaps in archaeological contexts. The claim of autonomy also does not imply that the perceptual properties of an entity are not related to how it is conceived; it only means that there are principles of conception that are distinct from, and are not solely determined by, principles of perception and/or perceptual properties.

Given that we can perceive an entity without having committed ourselves to what it is, it is necessary to provide answers to the following
questions: (1) what is the nature of the conceptual representations that
underlie different construals of the entity (e.g., table/wood)?, and (2) what
are the factors that determine which construal is made? The answer to the
first question should have implications for the answer to the second one.
In approaching these issues, I have taken to heart Macnamara's observation that whereas modern-day physicists and biologists may safely ignore
Aristotle's writings, modern-day psychologists have much to gain from
Aristotle. In the next section, I will briefly describe Aristotle's account of
the nature of things and stuff because, although it is lacking as a scientific
account, I think it accurately captures our natural ways of understanding
and talking about the world and is implicit in our conceptual structures.
Furthermore, such an account will help us formulate answers to the
questions raised above. The account of Aristotle's thought on the nature
of objects, essence, and the four causes is based largely, though not
exclusively, on the interpretations of Lear (1988), Scaltsas (1994a,b), Witt
(1989), Bolton (1976), Cohen (1996), and Moravcsik (1975).

7.1   An Aristotelian Account of the Nature of Things and Stuff

According to Aristotle, an appropriate answer to the question "What is
it?" requires citing the essence of the entity in question or the cause of its
being what it is. Furthermore, he proposes that there are four ways in
which we cite cause. The four types of causes we cite are the *material*, the
formal, the *final*, and the *efficient*. It is important to note, however, that
even though these are often presented as four distinct causes, there really
are only two basic kinds of causes, the material and the formal, the final
and efficient causes being aspects of the formal cause. Aristotle felt that
we can adequately characterize the essence or nature of both things and
stuff in terms of these causes.

Let us unpack these claims. Aristotle called things like dogs and tables
(what we would call basic-level objects) *substances* and things like wood
and sand *matter*. Because we now use *substance* and *material* synony-
mously, much confusion arises. To try to minimize confusion, I will use
basic-level object, *object*, and *thing* to refer to what Aristotle would have
called substances and *matter*, *material*, and *stuff* to refer to what Aristotle
would have called matter. It is important to remember, however, that in
calling entities objects or things I do not mean simply spatiotemporally

bounded solids, as these could be understood either as being an object of some kind or as being a piece of matter of some kind. Aristotle claims that basic-level objects are a composite of matter and form. What he means by this is that certain aspects of an object's being are caused by its matter, whereas others are caused by its form. For example, certain aspects of a table's being, such as its being hard or burnable, are caused by its matter. This is why it is appropriate to cite the material of which the table is made when we are seeking to explain why it is hard and why it burns. The properties of being hard and burnable are not caused by the structure of the table, its function, the process by which it was created, its color, its size, or any property other than the material of which it is made. Thus, there is a subset of properties of objects, which includes properties such as hardness and burnability, that are caused by, and thus explainable by reference to, the kind of matter of which the object is constituted.

Other aspects of an object's being are caused by its form. For example, a ball's ability to roll, a dog's ability to walk, a bird's ability to fly, or a car's ability to transport us are all caused by, and are explainable in terms of, the structure of these objects. Aristotle noted, however, that the structure of an object does not arise spontaneously, nor could it, because having a particular structure is not a property of matter. In fact, matter is indeterminate with respect to structure. Thus, the structure itself must be caused by and explainable in terms of a process of growth or construction, what Aristotle called the *principle of growth and maintenance* (or sometimes the *principle of change and rest*). Furthermore, this process, which causes changes in structure, does not simply change the structure of the matter in random ways but is *directed at* producing a particular structure (or a particular range of structures). Thus, the principle of growth and maintenance cannot be defined independently of the structures that it is aimed at producing, and the presence of a particular structure in matter cannot be explained without reference to a process of growth or creation.

Finally, we are led to ask why the process of growth or creation is directed at producing the structures it does, and not others. Once again, the explanation for this cannot be found in the material constitution of the object, because matter, in and of itself, lacks both determinate form and any principle of growth or creation. However, we might expect that some aspect of the form may provide the relevant explanation. This is what Aristotle proposes. For example, he would argue that if we are to explain why a carpenter engages in the activity of building that culminates in the creation of this particular structure and not some other structure, we must cite certain functional properties of the created structure as being the reason why the carpenter created this structure and not some other structure.[1] In the case of natural kinds such as plants or animals, the fact that they have the particular structures they have can be explained by citing the fact that these structures allow the organisms to function in various ways that allow them to grow, maintain, and reproduce themselves.

To summarize, the principle of growth and maintenance (often called the efficient cause) is responsible for changes in the structure of matter and is the cause of a determinate structure. This structure (often called the formal cause), in turn, is the cause of certain functional properties' being present. These functional properties (often called the final cause), in turn, are the cause of the existence or continued existence of the process of growth and maintenance. Thus, there is a single formal cause that has three aspects or components, rather than three independent causes. This cause is called the *substantial form* or sometimes just *form* or *formal cause*; but it should be understood that this term does not refer to shape but to the complex cause discussed above.

The introduction of the formal cause into matter causes it to cease being matter and become the *matter of the object* that results. This is not simply a terminological distinction, but a metaphysical distinction. It involves a change from something that is essentially matter to something that is essentially an object. Recall that matter lacks any determinate structure, and any structure that is present in an amount of matter is accidental and is not due to its material nature. It follows that any unity that is found in an amount of matter (e.g., a piece of wood) is also accidental and not due to its material nature. The unity is merely spatiotemporal and is not due to its material essence. This is the reason why the matter would survive as the same matter even if it lost its spatiotemporal unity (e.g., by being broken into separate pieces). The introduction of the formal cause into matter changes all this. The structure of the matter found in an object is not accidental but is due to the substantial form. Furthermore, the unity found in the matter of an object is not accidental or merely spatiotemporal but is due to its substantial nature. It is essentially a unitary object. The unity is due to the fact that it is the product of a process directed at creating a structure of a particular kind that is essential for its functioning in ways that are responsible for the existence and/or continued existence of the process and the object itself.

We are now in a position to provide an account of what is involved in offering (1) and (2) as responses to the question "What is it?" In responding with (2), we are saying that the entity in question is (essentially) wood. In giving this answer, we are citing only the material cause. That is, we are claiming that various aspects of its being, such as its being hard, brown, and burnable, are caused by, and thus explainable in terms of, the kind of material it is. The nature of the material does not, however, account for the structure of the entity. Therefore, we are also claiming that the particular structure the entity has is not the result of any process that was directed at creating that structure (because in this answer we do not cite the presence of the formal cause); instead, the structure is the result of a process that was not directed at creating that structure (e.g., erosion, breaking, tearing). It follows also that any functional properties of the entity that depend on its structure must be considered accidental (i.e., they are not caused by the entity's material nature). Finally, in stating that the entity is simply wood, we are claiming that the unity that is present in the entity is accidental and not due to what it is essentially (in this case, wood).[2]

Conversely, in responding to the question "What is it?" with (1), we are saying that the entity is (essentially) a table. This means that it is essentially a composite of matter and form, which in turn means that the structure of the entity is the result of a process that is directed at creating that structure. Furthermore, we are claiming that at least some of the functional properties that are dependent on the structure are not accidental, but are the reason why the structure was created in the first place and will govern modifications and repairs that may be made (see Bloom 1996a).[3] Finally, the unity that is found is not merely accidental or spatiotemporal but is the result of the directed process that creates the structure that is essential to the entity's being what it is.

I submit that these Aristotelian responses to the question "What is it?" are implicit in our conception of entities as kinds of objects and stuff. In the next section, I present some evidence for this claim.

7.2 Some Evidence for the Aristotelian Nature of Our Conception of Things and Stuff

A spatiotemporally contiguous amount of matter is distinguished from an object by the presence of the formal cause in the object. Given this understanding of the nature of things and stuff, we predict that subjects should be more likely to construe a solid entity as an object if they are presented with evidence that the entity has a definite form that is the product of a process directed at creating that structure and that it possesses functional properties that depend on that structure than if they are led to believe that the structure is the product of an undirected process and are not presented with any evidence of structure-dependent functions of the entity. Furthermore, entities construed as objects should be referred to through the use of count nouns (as in (1)) because the unity of the entity is essential to its construal as an object, whereas entities that are construed as amounts of material should be referred to through the use of mass nouns (as in (2)) because the unity present in an amount of matter is not essential to its construal as some stuff. Data from a recent series of experiments by Prasada, Ferenz, and Haskell (in preparation) bear out these predictions.

In a first experiment, subjects were presented with either "regularly" shaped entities or "irregularly" shaped entities and asked to choose a count noun description (*There is a blicket in the tray*) or a mass noun description (*There is a piece of blicket in the tray* or *There is blicket in the tray*) of the entities. Not surprisingly, subjects chose the count noun description significantly more often when describing regularly shaped entities than when describing irregularly shaped entities.[4] Crucially, the regularly shaped entities had been judged, in a pilot experiment, to have structures that were likely to be the product of a process that was directed at creating that particular structure, whereas the irregularly shaped items were rated as having structures that were unlikely to be the product of a process that was directed at creating that particular structure. Although these data are consistent with the prediction that entities that are seen as having structures that are the result of a directed process should be construed as objects and spoken about through the use of count nouns more often than entities that are seen as having structures that are the result of an undirected process, it is possible that some other difference between the regularly and irregularly shaped entities was responsible for the results. A third condition in the experiment ruled out this possibility.

In the third condition, subjects were initially shown three identical instances of an irregularly shaped entity. Then one of the instances was moved into a tray of its own and, as in the previous conditions, the subjects were asked to choose either a count or mass noun description of just a single instance. The irregularly shaped entities used in this condition were the same as in the previous single-instance condition, and the conditions under which subjects chose the description were identical to the conditions in the single-instance condition (i.e., with a single entity in the tray). The only difference between this condition and the previous one was that before subjects were asked to pick a description for the target entity, they saw it in another tray with two other identical entities. Subjects in this condition chose the count noun description significantly more often than the subjects who had not initially seen multiple identical instances of the entity. Furthermore, subjects in the multiple-identical-instances condition rated the structure of a single irregularly shaped entity as more likely to be the product of a process that was directed at creating that particular structure than subjects who saw only a single instance of the irregularly shaped entity. These results show that if subjects are given evidence that a particular structure is unlikely to have arisen through an undirected process (e.g., because there exist multiple identical instances), they are more likely to construe the entity as an object and refer to it through the use of a count noun than if they are not provided with such evidence.

Finally, there was a fourth condition in which subjects were initially presented with three nonidentical irregularly shaped entities before being asked to choose a description for the single irregularly shaped item. As predicted, simply seeing multiple instances that were not similar in structure to the target entity did not lead subjects to choose a count noun description any more often than they did when they saw only the single instance. Also, as predicted, seeing multiple nonidentical instances did not affect subjects' intuitions concerning the likelihood that the structure of the target item was the result of a directed process.

A second experiment investigated whether providing subjects with evidence of a structure-dependent function would lead them to be more likely to construe an irregularly shaped entity as an object and refer to it through the use of a count noun than if they were not provided with evidence of a structure-dependent function and were instead only provided with evidence of a structure-independent function. Half of the subjects were shown a series of videotaped trials in which an irregularly shaped entity was used to perform a structure-dependent function (e.g., as when a key is used to open a lock); the other half were shown a presentation in which the irregularly shaped entity was used to perform a structure-independent function (e.g., as when a key is used to ring a bell). At the end of each trial, the entity appeared on the screen and, as in the previous experiment, subjects had to indicate whether they preferred a count noun or a mass noun description of the entity. As expected, subjects chose the count noun description more often in the structure-dependent condition than in the structure-independent condition.

Finally, a large body of research shows that even very young children construe names for regularly shaped solid entities as names for objects, whereas they interpret names for regularly shaped nonsolid entities as names for the kind of material (Dickinson 1988; Hall 1996; Hall, Waxman, and Hurwitz 1993; Imai and Gentner, in press; Landau, Smith, and Jones 1988; Markman and Wachtel 1988; Soja, Carey, and Spelke 1991; Soja 1992). These results are predicted if in our conception of matter and objects, matter lacks definite form, but objects have a definite form. Nonsolid entities clearly do not have a definite form (as is evident from their lack of cohesiveness); thus, according to the present proposal, labels for them should be interpreted as names for the kind of material. Conversely, regularly shaped solid entities have a definite form (as is evident from their cohesiveness), and furthermore, the forms are regular and thus unlikely to have arisen by accident, but instead are likely to be the result of directed processes; thus, according to the present proposal, labels for them should be interpreted as names for the kind of object rather than as names for the kind of solid material.

The experiments discussed above suggest that we expect objects to have a definite form that is the result of a directed process and that they possess functional properties that depend on that structure, whereas we do not have the same expectations of amounts of matter.[5] These data show that our conceptions of what constitutes an object as compared to an amount of matter is in important ways Aristotelian. The hypothesis that our conceptual representations of things are Aristotelian in nature is developed further in the next few sections.

7.3   Aristotelian Essences

Given that, according to Aristotle, it is essences that are the cause of things' being what they are, it is important to get a better understanding of the nature of Aristotelian essences and how they may be represented. Aristotelian essentialism differs from many contemporary essentialist theories in important ways. For example, most contemporary theories would not consider having two feet an essential property of humans; however, Aristotle claims that humans are essentially two-footed. How are we to reconcile these positions? Does Aristotle think that when a person loses a foot, he or she stops being human? Clearly not. Aristotle would agree with our intuitions that a person who loses a foot continues to be a person. However, he would not conclude that having two feet is merely a stereotypical but nonessential property of humans. Instead, he would argue that humans are essentially two-footed, though certain individual humans may be accidentally one-footed. Thus, the person who has lost a foot may be said to be essentially two-footed but accidentally one-footed.

The difference between these two conclusions is best understood by considering how essential and nonessential properties are determined by the two types of theories. Many contemporary approaches determine essential and nonessential properties on the basis of whether something continues to exist as the kind of thing it is even when the property in question is no longer true of it, or by considering whether things that lack the property in question may nevertheless belong to the kind in question. This is the view of essentialism expressed in the following quotations from Kripke and Lakoff:[6]

Another example one might give relates to the problem of essentialism. Here is a lectern. A question which has often been raised in philosophy is: What are its essential properties? What properties, aside from trivial ones like self-identity, are such that this object has to have them if it exists at all, are such that if an object did not have it, it would not be this object? (Kripke 1971, 178–179)

Essentialism: Among the properties that things have, some are essential: that is, they are those properties that make the thing what it is, and without which it would not be that *kind* of thing. (Lakoff 1987, 161; original emphasis)

To see why Aristotle does not pursue this strategy in determining essence, we must recognize first that the essence, for Aristotle, is not a set of necessary and sufficient properties or a probabilistic cluster of properties. Instead, an Aristotelian essence is the cause that defines what something is. This is why it provides an adequate response to the question "What is it?" In this respect, the Aristotelian view of essences is similar to "psychological essentialism" (e.g., Medin and Ortony 1989; Keil 1989; Gelman, Coley, and Gottfried 1994). Although the exact relation between the present proposal and psychological essentialism is unclear, one way to think about the former is as an explicit proposal concerning what constitutes an essence for us and the basis upon which we distinguish essential and nonessential properties.

In the case of an object such as a human being, the essence is the substantial form that, by informing the appropriate kind of matter, gives rise to a human being. Recall that the substantial form is the process of growth and maintenance that is directed at creating a particular kind of structure that allows the entity to function in ways that are responsible for its process of growth and maintenance. In the case of human beings, the process of growth and maintenance is directed at creating an entity that has two feet. In some cases, however, because of causes other than the essence, such as the environment in which the growth occurs, or an accident, the resulting body will have only one foot. Thus, the contrast between essential and nonessential properties, for Aristotle, lies in the *kind of cause* that is responsible for the property in question, rather than in whether the property is required for membership in the relevant kind.

If a property is part of the "blueprint" that the process of growth or creation is trying to implement, and thus in normal circumstances caused by it, then the property is considered to be essential. If, on the other hand, the property is the result of other processes (causes), or due to errors in the "implementation" (growth/construction) process, then the property is considered accidental. Therefore, particular objects (e.g., dogs) are *what they are* by virtue of their (dog) essence, but they are *the way they are* by virtue of their essence and other causes. For example, some dogs are wet because they are outside and it is raining; other dogs may have three legs because of an accident, or have fleas because of where they live; others may be skinny and weak because they don't get enough, or nutritious, food; still others may be overweight because they eat too much fatty food; and so on.

It should now be clear that Aristotle does *not* require that all members of a given kind actually possess a specific set of properties, even essential properties, because actual members of the kind are subject to other causes that might introduce other properties, fix parameters left open by the essence, and even remove essential properties. In fact, the Aristotelian conception of essences and objects *predicts* that, in general, not all members of a kind will have all their essential properties because different members will be subject to different causes and some of those causes will destroy various essential properties. In general, it will also be the case that those properties that are shared by most members of the kind are more likely to be essential than those that are shared by only a few members. Finally, essential properties should, in general, be found to be present in most members because, in most cases, there should not be any systematic cause that interferes with the expression of essential properties. It is important to note, however, that these statistical generalizations are only heuristic and are neither necessary, nor constitutive of, essences.

7.4   Representation of Essences: Evidence for the Aristotelian Conception

The manner in which we interpret sentences such as (5) and (6) provides evidence concerning the manner in which we think and talk about essences and how they are related to essential and nonessential properties (Chomsky 1975a; Moravcsik 1994).[7]

(5) a. Chickens live to be x years of age.
     b. Chickens live to be x years of age, by virtue of what they are.
     c. All chickens live to be x years of age.

(6) a. Chickens live in chicken coops.
     b. Chickens live in chicken coops, by virtue of what they are.
     c. All chickens live in chicken coops.

Notice first that although we feel that (5a) and (5b) are almost identical in meaning and may be considered to be paraphrases of each other, the same is not true of (6a) and (6b). This shows that although we feel that the property of living for x years is caused by the essence or nature of chickens, the property of living in a chicken coop is not caused by their essence. As has often been noted, the bare plural is not equivalent to universal quantification, and thus neither (5a) nor (6a) is interpreted as a statement about all chickens, and both (5c) and (6c) are judged to be false. Instead, both (5a) and (6a) can be interpreted as making statements about what is generally, though not always, true of chickens. Thus, either statement could be made as long as the predicates are true of a suitably large percentage of chickens. Crucially, though this statistical interpretation is possible for both (5a) and (6a), it is *necessary* for (6a), but not (5a). Therefore, it would be false to say (6a) if a suitably large number of chickens did not live in chicken coops—for example, if tomorrow we let all chickens out of chicken coops. However, we continue to judge (5a) to be a valid statement even though it is the case that the vast majority of chickens are raised on poultry farms and are killed long before they reach the age of x. Finally, notice that even though no particular percentage of chickens need to live to be x years of age in order for (5a) to be true, we tend to assume that the predicate is true of most chickens and only become aware of the contingency of this fact when a systematic reason why the essential property is not expressed is pointed out to us. Unless such a cause is made explicit, we assume that there is no systematic cause for chickens' lacking an essential property and thus assume that the property is true of the majority of chickens.

These data show that (1) we distinguish essential and nonessential properties in terms of their causes, not on the basis of whether all instances of the kind have the property, or need the property to belong to the kind, (2) essential properties need not be true of the majority of instances of the kind, and (3) it is assumed that most members of the kind will have essential properties, unless there is an explicit reason why a cause other than the substantial cause is systematically present and responsible for destroying an essential property. Thus, the interpretation of generic sentences such as (5a) provides evidence for the Aristotelian notion of what an essence is and how essential and nonessential properties of things are to be distinguished.

It should also be noted that these data are not explained by essentialist theories that assume that essential and nonessential properties are to be distinguished on the basis of whether a property is necessary for existence as a particular kind of thing. The qualitative difference in the interpretation of sentences such as (5a) and (6a) also poses serious problems for theories that do not posit a distinction between essential and nonessential properties in our conceptual representations and instead assume that properties are to be distinguished simply in terms of strength of belief, frequency, or centrality. Note that this does not mean that we cannot revise our beliefs about which properties are essential—we can, and sometimes do. The point is that the properties we deem essential play a qualitatively different role in our thought and speech than the properties we deem nonessential.

7.5 Acquiring Names for Things and Stuff

The foregoing discussion suggests that we have at least two ways in which we naturally understand the entities that populate our world. These two ways of understanding explain different aspects of the spatiotemporally defined entities. To construe an entity as an object (an object of some kind) is to understand the structure of the entity as being the product of a process directed at creating that structure (out of a suitable kind of matter), such that the functional properties that the structured matter affords are responsible for the growth and maintenance of the object. Furthermore, this entails that the unity present in the entity is caused by the substantial form and thus is essential to its being that object. Finally, this also leads us to consider certain structure-related properties including parts and structure-dependent functions to be essential properties of the entity because they are caused by its essence. Alternatively, to construe the entity as an amount of matter is to say that the structure of the entity is not the product of a directed process; thus, we do not consider any of the structure-dependent properties to be essential. Instead, we consider some of the structure-independent properties (e.g., burnability, hardness, texture) to be essential (i.e., due to the material cause). Furthermore, the unity present in the entity is not considered to be the result of the material cause (and thus the unity is not essential).

This account allows us to fill in an essential component of what is involved in the acquisition of names for things and stuff. Putnam (1975) and Kripke (1982) have made a strong argument that there is an indexical component to the representation of natural kind terms such as *gold* and *tiger* as well as artifact kind terms such as *table*.[8] The key idea is that the reference of a term such as *tiger* is not determined by a description, a set of descriptions, or beliefs we may have about tigers, but is determined by the real-world essence of tigers. Within this type of theory, there is an "introduction" or "baptism" event in which the word *tiger* is first used to talk about a particular tiger. After this, the word is taken to refer to all things that have the same essence—that is, all the things that are tigers (i.e., things that are of the same kind as the thing that was baptized *tiger*). We may, of course, mistakenly call things tigers that are not tigers; however, the mere fact that we recognize this possibility shows that we distinguish the information on the basis of which we choose to call something a tiger from the information that determines which things actually are tigers.

Although the part of the theory that is concerned with the roles of indexicality and descriptions in a theory of reference has been discussed in considerable detail, a crucial aspect of the introduction event has not received much attention. Putnam (1975) describes what is involved in introducing a natural kind term as follows:

> There are two obvious ways of telling someone what one means by a natural-kind term such as 'water' or 'tiger'. One can give him a so-called ostensive definition— 'this (liquid) is water'; 'this (animal) is a tiger'; 'this (fruit) is a lemon'; where the parentheses are meant to indicate that the 'markers' *liquid, animal, fruit,* may be either explicit or implicit. . . . (p. 229)

Clearly, the markers have a central role to play in the introduction of a novel word. Without a theory of what markers are, the type of theory of reference proposed by Putnam and Kripke cannot be exploited. It is the (implicit) markers that help distinguish the reference of the words *table* and *wood* in (1) and (2). I propose that the account of objects and matter developed in this chapter constitutes a plausible theory of the semantic markers 'object' and 'material' and that an adequate account of the reference of terms such as *table* and *wood* requires these markers.

Given this account, we can characterize what is involved in the acquisition of the words *table* and *wood* in an ostensive context as follows. A demonstrative directs the learner's attention to a spatiotemporally defined entity. Next, the learner must decide (unconsciously) whether the entity is an object of some sort or simply an amount of matter. Actually, what the learner really has to decide is whether the speaker, in using the word to refer to the entity in question, does so with the intention of referring to it as an object or as some matter. Insofar as the learner makes the wrong guess, the learner will have interpreted the word "incorrectly." This, of course, is the reason why as pragmatically competent users of a language we would never choose to teach the word *wood* through an ostensive definition such as (2) in which the entity in question is a table if we knew that the learner did not know that the name for that kind of object is *table*. If we were to teach *wood* in this context, we would probably do so by first teaching the object name and then making the relation of the material name to the object explicit (e.g., "This is a table. The table is made of wood"). In general, we would choose to introduce a material name such as *wood* through a sentence such as (2) only if the entity in question was unlikely to be construed as an object, as when the entity is irregularly shaped and has no obvious structure-dependent properties. Pragmatic competence may minimize the probability of miscommunication but does not, in and of itself, provide us with an analysis of what is involved in learning a word like *table*, and how (or if) this differs from what is involved in learning a word like *wood*. In fact, the type of pragmatic competence described here probably makes crucial use of this information.

In deciding that the entity is essentially an object, the learner interprets the novel word as referring to all objects of that kind. In doing so, the learner has posited that the entity is essentially a unit and that the structure that is present in the entity is (for the most part) the product of a process directed at creating that structure, which, in turn, functions in ways that are the reason for the (continued) existence of the process itself.[9] The decision about whether to think of the entity as an object or an amount of matter is made upon the evidence available to the learner. In addition to the perceptual cues discussed in section 7.2, adult learners can use the form class of the entity to determine whether the entity should be thought of as an object or as matter; however, as Macnamara (1982) has pointed out, this evidence cannot be used in the earliest stages of word learning because the surface cues that signal count and mass nouns vary from language to language. Soja, Carey, and Spelke (1991) have provided empirical evidence that children can in fact exploit perceptual cues about how to construe novel entities when learning names for the entities before they have mastered the count noun/mass noun distinction.

Importantly, to construe the entity as an object, and to fix the reference of the novel term as referring to objects of that kind, the learner need not know (and usually does not know) what the directed process is, or even the nature of the directed process (biological/intentional), or which functions that are afforded by the structure are the essential ones, only that such processes and functions exist and are responsible for the structure of the object. In fact, it is even logically possible, though unlikely, that the learner could find out that tables are not the result of intentional processes but are the result of a biological process and thus organisms of some sort rather than artifacts (see Putnam 1975 for a more detailed discussion of this kind of possibility). In this case, it is perfectly natural to say something like (7). However, it does not make sense to say something like (8a,b).

(7) It turns out that tables are organisms.

(8) a. It turns out that tables are (just) wood./ It turns out tables are (simply) matter.
     b. It turns out that hunks of wood are organisms.

This is because the form of the understanding associated with an object term such as *table* is incompatible with the form of the understanding associated with a material term such as *wood*. In the baptism, *table* was used to refer to something that is essentially a unit, whereas *wood* was used to refer to something that is not essentially a unit.[10] Thus, the logic of the terms, which derives from the nature of the things referred to, is incompatible. That a term that is stipulated to refer to things that are understood to be units essentially (objects) cannot refer to things that are understood not to be units essentially (amounts of matter) is a logical fact that is unrevisable. We can, of course, revise what we believe the entities in question to be. The change in belief can be expressed through the use of sentences such as (9a,b) in which the entities in question are referred to through the use of *thing*, which, like *entity*, is noncommittal with respect to whether the entity is essentially a unit or not (Macnamara 1994).

(9) a. Those things we thought were tables are simply hunks of wood.

    b. Those things we thought were simply hunks of wood are tables.

Note that we may appeal to experts to decide when we should make this type of revision (Putnam 1975); however, nothing experts could tell us would allow us to meaningfully make statements such as those expressed in (8a,b). The distinct logic of the terms *table* and *wood* derives from their status as names for objects and matter that are essentially units and non-units. Thus, learning words like *table* and *wood* requires the ability to construe entities as essentially being units or nonunits. The Aristotelian conception of objects and matter allows us to formulate what this ability consists in, and provides a characterization of what the form of the essences in the two cases is, such that whether the entity is thought of as a unit or not follows as a consequence.[11]

7.6 Abstract Definitions and the Representation of Superordinate Concepts

Finally, I want to briefly consider how the Aristotelian conception of an object also allows us to develop Macnamara's (1982) suggestion, based on the ideas of Cassirer (1953), that we regard the representation of super-ordinate categories such as ANIMAL and VEHICLE as being related to the representation of more specific categories such as DOG and CAR in a way that is analogous to the way that mathematicians regard the relation of an expression such as $y = mx + b$ to the expression $y = 2x + b$.

There are two standard ways in which psychologists think of the relation of a category to a superordinate category. The first is to think in extensional terms, in which case the superordinate category is simply a superset of the extension of the lower-level category. Alternatively, thinking intensionally, superordinate categories are seen as being represented by a subset of the features used to represent the more specific, lower-level categories. This is a perfectly reasonable way of proceeding if one's representation of concepts consists of sets of features. If, on the other hand, our representation of what something is, is not represented as a set of features, but is instead a representation of the essence that causes something to be what it is, then an alternative way of representing super-ordinate categories must exist. Furthermore, we should expect the form of the superordinate representation to be constrained by the representation of the basic-level category.

It is in this connection that it is helpful to consider the way in which the formula that defines a particular kind of line (e.g., all lines of slope 2) is represented (in a Cartesian coordinate system), and how this representation is related to the representation of the general class of lines of which the first class is a subset. A line is a single thing that is generated by a formula that is defined in terms of two components: a slope and a y-intercept. The slope and the y-intercept are not independently existing features that are combined to produce a line, but they are components of a line that represent and explain different aspects of the line (*slope:* the rate of change of y with respect to x; and *y-intercept:* its position within the coordinate system, specified by where the line crosses the y-axis). Both the slope and the y-intercept are aspects *of* lines. The formula for the line is represented in terms of these components. The parallelism between the definition of a line and its components and the definition of an Aristotelian object and its components is, I hope, evident. An Aristotelian object is a single thing that is generated by an essence whose formula is represented in terms of four components. The four causes are not independently existing features that are combined to produce the object, but components of an object that explain different aspects of the object. The matter, form, function, and principle of rest and change are aspects *of* objects. Thus, we can expect that the formula that represents an object will be stated in terms of these components.

Given this parallelism, we can turn to the representation of lines of a specific kind (e.g., lines of slope 2) and the relation of this representation to a representation of a more general class of lines (e.g., all lines) for insight into how one might represent the relation between a specific kind of object (e.g., dogs) and a more general class of objects (e.g., animals). Lines of slope 2 are represented by the formula $y = 2x + b$, the class of all lines by $y = mx + b$. The more general formula is arrived at by replacing the constant that defines the slope with a variable. Note, specifically, that the more general formula is not arrived at by looking at lines of slope 2, 3.5, 7.1, 4, . . . and finding all the features that are common to them. There are no independent features that are common to all lines or classes of lines. The only thing that the different classes of lines have in common is the *form* of their definition, which captures the relevant relations between the distinct components of lines. Generalization is achieved by replacing the constants associated with the components that define a given class of lines (slope and y-intercept) with variables that can take on a range of values.

This notion of generalization by replacing constants with variables can be applied to derive the representation of substantial concepts at varying levels of generality. Recall that objects are defined as essentially being a composite of matter and form. Furthermore, because the substantial form is itself defined in terms of the structure, process of growth and mainte- nance, and structure-dependent functions, the essence, or definition, of an object may be represented as in (10), where m = matter, s = structure, p = process, and f = function.

(10) $Object = G\ (m, s, p, f)$

Although we do not know the exact form of substantial form (and there- fore G), we do know the constraints that must hold between the different components that define an object. The constraints are as follows: (1) the process must lead to the structure in the matter, (2) the structure must afford essential functions, (3) the functions are responsible for the process, and (4) the matter must be of the appropriate sort (such that the process is able to form the required structure out of the matter and that it allows the structure to have the function(s) required by the process of growth and maintenance). It is important to note that the representation in (10) is meant to be simply a general way of stating the formula that generates an object and should not be taken to be a mathematical function.[12] Given this formulation, categories such as DOG can be represented by constants for each of the components that define the object, whereas categories such as TABLE can be represented as having constants for each of the compo- nents except for the material component, which will have, in place of a constant, a variable that can be filled in by any constant that satisfies the relevant constraints on the nature of the matter of the object. Thus, the representation provides a straightforward way for us to represent intu- itions concerning the possibility of different ways of realizing an essence through the use of a variable, and specific realizations through the use of specific constants. The constants in the case of objects are not numbers as is the case with lines, but instead are representations of the essential shape, the essential activities, the nature of the principle of change and rest (biological/intentional), and the type of matter.

It should now be clear how we can derive the representation for the category ANIMAL from the representation of the category DOG. This is achieved by simply substituting the variables for constants for structure and matter. Dogs, by virtue of having a certain structure and being com- posed of a certain kind of matter, are capable of moving in order to get food, to avoid danger, and generally to engage in activities that allow them to maintain themselves, grow, and reproduce. These functions, which are responsible for (continued) existence, can be instantiated by a variety of objects, each possessing its distinctive form and matter (and thus satisfying these functions in its own characteristic manner) while being the product of the same type of process of growth and maintenance. Thus, when we think of a dog as an animal, we are thinking of the entity from a perspective in which we consider the particular form and matter it has as one of several composites of form and matter that are capable of functioning in ways that allow them, just as they allow the dog, to grow, maintain, and reproduce itself. An advantage of this approach to forming representations of general categories is that it is possible to do so on the basis of very limited information. In principle, this can be done on the basis of the representation of a single basic-level category. It is important to note that the present account is concerned with the representation of types of things and the relation between types of varying generality (e.g., DOG/ANIMAL; CAR/VEHICLE) rather than the representation that is required for concepts such as those represented by *laundry*, *livestock*, or *groceries* in which only particular tokens of various types are grouped together to form categories.

The type of relation that is found between the representation of categories such as DOG and ANIMAL or CAR and VEHICLE is one in which the representations of the former, more specific categories are a special case of the representation of the latter, more general categories. A different type of relation is found between the representations of categories such as TABLE and FURNITURE or SHIRT and CLOTHING in English. In these cases, the more specific representations are not a special case of the more general representation. Instead, the more specific representations provide only a partial representation of the more general representations, which are only fully represented through the combination of multiple specific representations. Thus, we may think of the representations for FURNITURE or CLOTHING as piecewise-defined representations whose pieces are given by the representations that are derived by substituting variables for specific values for structure and matter. Furthermore, because the piecewise-defined representations do not directly refer to anything that is essentially a unit, they are lexicalized as mass nouns rather than as count nouns.

This account of the representation of superordinate categories suggests that there are two ways in which we can think about functions: as being discrete or nondiscrete. Discrete functions are those that are either satisfied or not, and cannot be satisfied only partially or to varying extents. Consider, for example, the ability to transport: either something is capable of transporting (e.g., cars, buses) or it is not (e.g., chairs, necklaces), and thus multiple items of different kinds do not help satisfy this function any more than a single item of the relevant kind does. On the other hand, a function such as furnishing or clothing is one that can be satisfied to varying degrees. We even have expressions such as *partially furnished* and *partially clothed*. Single items within the category are unable to fully satisfy the category function—a single chair does not furnish a room, nor does a shirt clothe a person. Furthermore, simply putting on multiple shirts or putting multiple chairs in a room does not allow one to be fully clothed or a room to be fully furnished. What is required is that multiple items of different kinds, each of which is capable of partially clothing or furnishing, be used.[13]

A straightforward prediction of the proposed account of superordinate representation is that instances of superordinate categories that are referred to by mass nouns should be more likely to be used together to perform some function than instances of superordinate categories that are referred to by count nouns. This is, in fact, what Wisniewski, Imai, and Casey (1996) and Prasada, Kim, and Eschemeyer (1997) have found. These data provide some initial support for the representation of superordinate categories proposed above, which is based on the nature of the representation of basic-level categories that follows from the Aristotelian conception of the essence of things. Importantly, the current proposal demonstrates how the relation between basic-level and superordinate categories may be represented, if it is the case that basic-level categories are to be represented in terms of an essence rather than as a set of properties as many theories of conceptual structure now maintain. There are, of course, many questions that this approach to superordinate representation raises that cannot be addressed here and must be the subject of future research.

7.7 Summary and Conclusion

In this chapter, I have argued that the Aristotelian distinction between object and matter plays a crucial role in the way that we think and talk about things and stuff. The distinction is required for explaining the referential properties of words like *table* and *wood*. These words enter our lexicons as names for a particular kind of object or as a name for a particular kind of matter. Although we generally do not know the nature (essence) of the object or the matter in question, we do know the distinct types of essence that enter into the reference of the terms. Furthermore, because objects are essentially units whereas matter is not, the two types of words must be represented by logically different types. The modes of understanding and talking about what we see that are represented by these two types of words are simply incompatible.

Given the Aristotelian characterization of the essences of objects and matter, and thus the mode of understanding that is required to grasp something as an object or as matter, it was possible to formulate, in a principled manner, the types of perceptual evidence we might use to trigger a particular mode of understanding. Evidence concerning the definiteness of structure comes from cohesiveness; evidence that the structure is the product of a directed process comes from the regularity of the shape as well as the repeatability of the structure; finally, evidence for the presence of a final cause can be indicated by the presence of a structure-dependent function. Each of these types of evidence was shown to influence whether experimental subjects thought and spoke about entities as objects or as matter.

Although the focus of this chapter has been on names for things and stuff and trying to explicate what is involved in understanding an entity as some one thing rather than an amount of stuff, the factors that account for our thinking of objects as units are likely to be at work in determining what is involved in understanding multiple objects as some one thing (e.g., as one forest) rather than as many objects (e.g., as many trees). The work of Paul Bloom and colleagues suggests that this is in fact the case (Bloom 1996a,b; Bloom and Kelemen 1995; Bloom et al. 1995).

Finally, the representations of objects in Aristotelian terms provide us with a natural way of constructing a theory of how it is that we are able to generate representations of categories of varying generality, as well as an explanation for the levels of generalization that are most natural. Pustejovsky (1995) provides extensive evidence that various linguistic phenomena can be accounted for if we assume that the nature of the understanding provided by various lexical items is represented in Aristotelian terms. The findings in this chapter complement Pustejovsky's findings and suggest that much progress may be made concerning the manner in which we naturally understand and talk about the world, if we approach the issues from the perspective provided by Aristotelian metaphysics.

Notes

1. Here, as elsewhere, a range of putative counterexamples can be formulated. To keep the exposition clear and concise, I will address only the most obvious ones. For more detailed discussion, see Prasada 1998. One might argue that the carpenter built the table simply because of an urge to build. Note, however, that in making this argument, one is conceding that the fact that a table was built is a complete accident (the carpenter could just as well have built a chair or a house or a random conglomeration of boards) and thus there is no explanation for why the structure is what it is and not some other structure. But this is not the kind of case Aristotle is interested in. He is interested in what explains the regularity with which certain processes culminate in the creation of a particular structure and not others. That is, in the cases where there *is* an explanation, what is the nature of the explanation? His answer is that the explanation lies in functional properties of the created structure. It is important to note that within the present approach, intentional and functional explanations are not independent or opposed to one another. A functional property of the intended structure provides the reason for the intention to create the structure in question. A different class of putative counterexamples can be created by pointing out that the table may have been built simply because the carpenter was paid to do so, was told to do so, was threatened into doing so, and so on. Note, however, that these kinds of cases raise questions of the sort, "Why would someone pay the carpenter to build this structure and not some other structure?"; and these questions are ultimately to be answered by citing some functional property of the structure. This is where explanation ends. Once we have a reason for why the process is directed at creating the structure it does, we feel we have a complete explanation. If, on the other hand, we are asked just to accept as a brute fact that there exist processes that are directed at creating a structure and there is no explanation for why they create the structures they do, we feel that an important regularity has gone unexplained. Finally, note that teleological explanation is not necessarily intentional and thus is also applicable to nonartifacts (on this point see Asma 1996; Broadie 1987).

2. What I have described is the case in which the entity is believed to be simply a hunk of wood and not a table. If the entity in question is believed to be a table, then a statement such as (2) does not imply that no directed process gave rise to the structure. Instead, it means that in thinking of the table as wood, the fact that it has the structure it does as the result of a directed process is not considered to be relevant.

3. The present account of our conception of artifacts accords a central role to functional properties. This seems to conflict with arguments put forth by Malt and Johnson (1992) and Bloom (1996a) that seem to suggest that functional properties are not a necessary component of our conception of artifacts. It is unclear, however, the extent to which Malt and Johnson's and Bloom's criticisms apply to the current way of thinking about essences (see text below) and how various aspects of the essence, including the final cause, are related to each other. Space limitations prevent a more detailed discussion of these issues; however, I take them up in Prasada, in preparation.

4. In this and all other conditions in this and the next experiment, there was no difference in subjects' preference for either of the two mass noun locutions (*There is a piece of blicket in the tray*/*There is blicket in the tray*).

5. It is important to quality this claim. There are entities such as those things that we call clouds, rocks, pebbles, and boulders that we tend to think of as objects rather than pieces of stuff, and yet we do not believe that these entities are the result of processes that are directed at creating the structure that the entities have. Why is it, then, that we treat these entities as objects rather than as pieces of stuff? There are three possibilities. First, it is possible that the above account of what it means to conceive of an entity as an object of some kind rather than as an amount of solid material is sufficient but not necessary and thus there are other ways in which we can conceive of entities as objects of some kind rather than as an amount of solid material of some kind. Second, it is possible that these counter-examples show that the account is wrong and there is a single alternative account of what is involved in conceiving of entities as objects of some kind rather than as amounts of material of some kind. Third, it is possible that the account accurately represents what is involved in our conceiving of entities as objects of some kind and as amounts of matter; however, the world presents us with cases that seem to fall between these two conceptual schemes that are given by our ontology, and we assimilate them as best we can. The intermediate cases betray their problems in being variable from language to language, in the existence of ambidextrous lexical items within a single language (e.g., *a stone*/*made of stone*), and in the largely arbitrary bases on which these things in the world are thought of as objects and as stuff (e.g., *pebbles*/**gravels*). Although it remains an open question which of these possibilities is right, the third has the advantage of providing a natural explanation of various "problematic" aspects associated with the conceptualization of these entities, whereas the first two would render rocks and stones equally good objects as dogs and tables and thus would require some other way of accounting for their "problematic" aspects.

6. Lakoff does not endorse this or any other view of essentialism; however, the quotation provides a concise expression of the common view of essentialism.

7. The interpretation of generic statements involves many complexities. Here, I am concerned only with using it as a tool to illustrate the manner in which our conceptual systems distinguish essential and nonessential properties. For a discussion of some of the complexities involved in the interpretation of generic sentences, see Chomsky 1975a and the references cited therein.

8. For an application of this insight to artifact kind terms from a psychological perspective, see Bloom 1996a.

9. The qualification on the characterization of the structure is necessary because particular substances have the structure they do by virtue of their essence as well as other causes. Therefore, one of the tasks that faces the learner is to determine which aspects of the structure are caused essentially and which are due to other causes.

10. Sentences such as *This ring is jewelry* do not constitute counterexamples to this claim because, as will be seen in section 7.6, mass superordinates of basic-level count nouns do not require thinking of the entities in question as not being units essentially. In fact, mass superordinates such as *jewelry* require that the entity be thought of as essentially a unit (e.g., a ring) rather than as essentially not a unit (e.g., some gold).

11. It might be suggested that what is crucial here is the "standard" distinction between concepts of objects and substance (which presumably are conceived of as units and nonunits, respectively) rather than the Aristotelian conception of objects and substances. The question, of course, is just how this "standard" distinction between our concept of an object of some kind and a material of some kind is represented and how the representation entails, rather than stipulates, viewing the entity as a unit or nonunit. The Aristotelian conception of things and stuff does just this.

12. It is assumed that an appropriate formalism could be developed for the representation of objects; however, the details of such a formalism are not important to the nature of the solution concerning the relation of the representation of specific categories and more general categories. Category theory, concerned as it is with models of becoming and the realization of plans, may be a promising direction in which to search for the right type of formalism (see Lawvere 1994 and other papers in Macnamara and Reyes 1994b).

13. The general idea that the difference between the representation of count and mass nouns for superordinate categories is related to whether multiple instances of a category are used for some common function is also found in McCawley 1975/1979, Wierzbicka 1985, and Wisniewski, Imai, and Casey 1996; however, the present account differs from these proposals in degree of explicitness as well as substance. Space limitations prevent an adequate discussion of the similarities and differences.

References

Asma, S. T. (1996). *Following form and function: A philosophical archaeology of life science*. Evanston, IL: Northwestern University Press.

Bloom, P. (1996a). Intention, history, and artifact concepts. *Cognition, 60*, 1–29.

Bloom, P. (1996b). Possible individuals in language and cognition. *Current Directions in Psychological Science, 5*, 90–94.

Bloom, P., and Kelemen, D. (1995). Syntactic cues in the acquisition of collective nouns. *Cognition, 56*, 1–30.

Bloom, P., Kelemen, D., Fountain, A., and Courtney, E. (1995). The acquisition of collective nouns. In D. MacLaughlin and S. McEwen (Eds.), *Proceedings of the 19th Boston University Conference on Language Development*. Somerville, MA: Cascadilla Press.

Bolton, R. (1976). Essentialism and semantic theory in Aristotle. *Philosophical Review, 85*, 514–544.

Broadie, S. (1987). Nature, craft and *phronesis* in Aristotle. *Philosophical Topics, 15*, 35–50.

Cassirer, E. (1953). *Substance and function*. New York: Dover.

Chomsky, N. (1975a). Questions of form and interpretation. *Linguistic Analysis, 1*, 75–109.

Chomsky, N. (1975b). *Reflections on language*. New York: Pantheon.

Cohen, S. M. (1996). *Aristotle on nature and incomplete substance*. New York: Cambridge University Press.

Dickinson, D. G. (1988). Learning names for materials: Factors constraining and limiting hypotheses about word meaning. *Cognitive Development, 3*, 15–35.

Gelman, S. A., Coley, J. D., and Gottfried, G. M. (1994). Essentialist beliefs in children: The acquisition of concepts and theories. In L. A. Hirshfeld and S. A. Gelman (Eds.), *Mapping the mind: Domain specificity in cognition and culture*. New York: Cambridge University Press.

Hall, D. G. (1996). Naming solids and nonsolids: Children's default construals. *Cognitive Development, 11*, 229–264.

Hall, D. G., Waxman, S. R., and Hurwitz, W. M. (1993). How 2- and 4-year-olds interpret adjectives and count nouns. *Child Development, 64*, 1651–1664.

Imai, M., and Gentner, D. (in press). Linguistic relativity vs. universal ontology: Cross-linguistic studies of the object/substance distinction. *Cognition*.

Jackendoff, R., and Landau, B. (1992). Spatial language and spatial cognition. In R. Jackendoff, *Languages of the mind*. Cambridge, MA: MIT Press.

Keil, F. C. (1989). *Concepts, kinds, and cognitive development*. Cambridge, MA: MIT Press.

Kripke, S. (1971). Identity and necessity. In M. K. Munitz (Ed.), *Identity and individuation*. New York: New York University Press. Reprinted in Moore, A. W. (Ed.), (1993). *Meaning and reference*. Oxford: Oxford University Press.

Kripke, S. (1982). *Naming and necessity*. Oxford: Blackwell.

Lakoff, G. (1987). *Women, fire, and dangerous things: What categories reveal about the mind*. Chicago: University of Chicago Press.

Landau, B., Smith, L. B., and Jones, S. (1988). The importance of shape in early lexical learning. *Cognitive Development, 3*, 299–321.

Lawvere, F. W. (1994). Tools for the advancement of objective logic: Closed categories and toposes. In J. Macnamara and G. E. Reyes (Eds.), *The logical foundations of cognition*. New York: Oxford University Press.

Lear, J. (1988). *Aristotle: The desire to understand*. New York: Cambridge University Press.

Macnamara, J. (1978). How do we talk about what we see? Unpublished manuscript, McGill University.

Macnamara, J. (1982). *Names for things: A study of human learning*. Cambridge, MA: MIT Press.

Macnamara, J. (1994). Logic and cognition. In J. Macnamara and G. E. Reyes (Eds.), *The logical foundations of cognition*. New York: Oxford University Press.

Macnamara, J., and Reyes, G. E. (1994a). Foundational issues in the learning of proper names, count nouns, and mass nouns. In J. Macnamara and G. E. Reyes (Eds.), *The logical foundations of cognition*. New York: Oxford University Press.

Macnamara, J., and Reyes, G. E. (Eds.). (1994b). *The logical foundations of cognition*. New York: Oxford University Press.

Malt, B. C., and Johnson, E. C. (1992). Do artifact concepts have cores? *Journal of Memory and Language, 31*, 195–217.

Markman, E. M., and Wachtel, G. F. (1988). Children's use of mutual exclusivity to constrain the meanings of words. *Cognitive Psychology, 20*, 121–157.

McCawley, J. D. (1975/1979). Lexicography and the count-mass distinction. In J. D. McCawley (Ed.), *Adverbs, vowels and other objects of wonder*. Chicago: University of Chicago Press.

Medin, D., and Ortony, A. (1989). Psychological essentialism. In S. Vosniadou and A. Ortony (Eds.), *Similarity and analogical reasoning*. New York: Cambridge University Press.

Moravcsik, J. M. E. (1975). *Aitia* as generative factor in Aristotle's philosophy. *Dialogue, 14*, 622–638.

Moravcsik, J. M. E. (1994). Essences, powers, and generic propositions. In T. Scaltsas, D. Charles, and M. C. Gill (Eds.), *Unity, identity, and explanation in Aristotle's Metaphysics*. Oxford: Clarendon Press.

Prasada, S. (1998). Conceptual representation of artifact kinds. Manuscript submitted for publication, Dartmouth College.

Prasada, S., Ferenz, K., and Haskell, T. (in preparation). Speaking of things and stuff: The role of perceived arbitrariness of structure. Unpublished manuscript, Dartmouth College and University of Southern California.

Prasada, S., Kim, J., and Eschemeyer, L. (1997). [Ratings of frequency with which exemplars of superordinate categories are used together]. Unpublished raw data, Dartmouth College and University of Southern California.

Pustejovsky, J. (1995). *The generative lexicon*. Cambridge, MA: MIT Press.

Putnam, H. (1975). The meaning of "meaning." In *Philosophical papers: Vol. 2. Mind, language, and reality*. New York: Cambridge University Press.

Scaltsas, T. (1994a). *Substances and universals in Aristotle's Metaphysics*. Ithaca, NY: Cornell University Press.

Scaltsas, T. (1994b). Substantial holism. In T. Scaltsas, D. Charles, and M. C. Gill (Eds.), *Unity, identity, and explanation in Aristotle's Metaphysics*. Oxford: Clarendon Press.

Soja, N. N. (1992). Inferences about the meanings of nouns: The relationship between perception and syntax. *Cognitive Development, 7*, 29–45.

Soja, N. N., Carey, S., and Spelke, E. (1991). Ontological categories guide young children's inductions of word meaning: Object terms and substance terms. *Cognition, 38,* 179–211.

Wierzbicka, A. (1985). *Lexicography and conceptual analysis.* Ann Arbor, MI: Karoma.

Wisniewski, E., Imai, M., and Casey, L. (1996). On the equivalence of super-ordinate concepts. *Cognition, 60,* 269–298.

Witt, C. (1989). *Substance and essence in Aristotle: An interpretation of Metaphysics VII–IX.* Ithaca, NY: Cornell University Press.

Chapter 8

The Unity of Science and the Distinction among Syntax, Semantics, and Pragmatics

Steven Davis

One of the outstanding issues in the philosophy of linguistics is how to draw the distinction among syntax, semantics, and pragmatics. A related issue is what falls within these different domains. On the one hand, there are those who see theories of syntax, semantics, and pragmatics as theories of human linguistic capacities that are supposed to account for the properties of human languages and of communication involving natural languages. This view has it that human languages and communication are sui generis. Because of this, theories of human languages and linguistic communication are not to be assimilated to a general theory of signs, but are theories about particular human capacities that differ in fundamental nonreducible ways from the phenomena involving systems of signs that are supposedly found in myths, art, clothing, films, and so on. This view is found in the syntactic work of Noam Chomsky, the psychological work of John Macnamara, and the pragmatic theory of Dan Sperber and Deirdre Wilson. Let us call this view the *narrow* view of human languages and natural language communication.

On the other hand, there are those who see theories of syntax, semantics, and pragmatics very broadly to include all phenomena related to systems of signs, including cultural, social, and cognitive features, where the system of signs can include such things as literary works, scientific theories, paintings, dance, cinema, clothes, gestures, facial expressions, and human languages. There are two approaches to what I shall call the *broad* view of syntax, semantics, and pragmatics. First, there are theorists who take human languages to be systems of signs no different in kind from any other system of signs. The theories that account for the properties of systems of signs can be applied to any domain in which signs are used, including human language. Such theorists consider all systems of signs to have an underlying unity and to fall within the same sorts of theories. This approach finds its expression in various forms of what is called semiotic—that is, in the work of such people as Roland Barthes, Claude Lévi-Strauss, Ferdinand de Saussure, and Charles Morris.[1] Second, there are theorists who take the broad view of syntax, semantics, and pragmatics, but leave it open whether all systems of signs can be accounted for within the same theoretical framework. This is the view of pragmatics adopted by the International Pragmatics Association, for which "pragmatics is interpreted very broadly as a cognitive, social and cultural perspective on language" (5th IPrA Conference Brochure), a view that is called *perspectivalism*. Pragmatics is viewed, then, as a perspective on language, rather than as a component of a grammar, a discipline, or even a field of study. Perspectivalism, as I hope to show, is the direct descendant of Charles Morris's views about pragmatics.

In this chapter I shall concentrate on the work of Charles Morris, one of the founders of the current movement in semiotic, and try to show how the semiotic program has its roots in logical positivism and in particular the project of logical positivism to provide a unified science. I shall try to show why Morris took the broad view of syntax, semantics, and pragmatics and the relationship that this view has to the project of a unified science. In closing, I shall make some critical comments about this project and try to show what consequence it has for semiotic and also for the study of natural language.

Logical positivism can trace its beginnings in 1923 in Vienna to a seminar led by Moritz Schlick. The members of the seminar came from diverse academic and intellectual backgrounds. Many of them, including Schlick, who did his doctorate in physics with Max Planck, had training in science or mathematics. It is these two domains that gave the central characteristics to the logical positivists' movement. One way of viewing this fusion is to consider it, as does Morris (1955, 64), as the union of empiricism and rationalism. The rationalists, like Descartes, thought that it was possible to construct a pure theory of the physical universe without any appeal to empirical observations to justify the theory. All that was necessary was the supposed a priori truth that space was Euclidean and that it and any events in it could be described by Euclidean mathematical models. The empiricists, on the other hand, looked to observation for the justification of theories. Locke thought that there could not be any a priori theories of nature, but that any theory of nature would have to arise from observation. What was lacking from his view about theories of the world, however, was any appreciation of the role that mathematics plays in science. Modern science, especially the physical sciences, borrows from both the empiricist and rationalist traditions. The empiricist appeal to experience appears in the scientist's controlled experiments, and the rationalist appeal to mathematics appears in the use to which scientists put mathematical models in formulating their theories of the universe.

Morris draws our attention to another dimension of science that he adds to the mix of empiricism and rationalism, namely, pragmatism. A scientific theory, according to Morris, can be thought of as a set of sentences, constituting for Morris a language, the formal structure of which can be modeled by the apparatus of logical theories and which can be justified by its relationship to the world of objects. But formal structure and relationship to the world do not exhaust the nature of scientific theories and thus of science. As Morris points out, scientific theories also are related to the users of the theory. On his view, the particular "rules," "procedures," and "conventions" that are operative in science "involve reference to users of signs..." (1955, 67). Appealing to the underlying behaviorism of pragmatism, Morris regards such rules, procedures, and conventions as "habits actually found in operation or set up by deliberative convention" (1955, 67). Moreover, pragmatism emphasizes the fact that scientific theories are created by people who are actors within various sorts of social institutions, and thus, in order to have a fuller understanding of the connection between scientific theories and their users, we must have an understanding of the social context of science.

On Morris's view, then, science includes three elements: first, its formal structure embodied in the mathematical models that science employs in constructing its theories and in the logical structure that the resulting theories have; second, its empirical character in its relationship to the world, namely, in the confirmation relationship between observational consequences of scientific theories and the experiences that either validate or invalidate these observational consequences, thereby confirming or disconfirming the theories; and third, the relationship that scientific theories have to the social institutions in which they are created and used and to the people who think up the theories, confirm or disconfirm them, and use them in understanding and controlling the world in which they find themselves. Thus, science, Morris claims, can be characterized as an admixture of traditional empiricist, rationalist, and pragmatist elements.

The logical positivists, however, did not see themselves as merely continuing the past empiricist, rationalist, and pragmatist traditions. They wished to break with past philosophy and viewed their activity as a rejection of what they regarded as traditional philosophical practice issuing in the construction of various metaphysical theories that were supposed to give a total account of the world. The logical positivists took as their goal the laying bare of the foundations and meaning of human knowledge, which they regarded as obtainable only through scientific practice. In fact, they held that traditional metaphysical theories are not only of no value for human knowledge, but, given the verificationist theory of meaning that many of them subscribed to, literally meaningless. One consequence of this total rejection of metaphysics and with it traditional philosophy is that the logical positivists did not think of themselves as doing philosophy, since they regarded most of the statements of philosophy, not only those of metaphysics, as not being open to verification and therefore as meaningless.

What then was left for the logical positivists to do? One of the central tasks they took for themselves was the understanding of the nature, meaning, and logical structure of science, since it was science that was supposed to provide whatever understanding could be obtained about the world. The initial problem that the logical positivists faced was that there are a number of sciences, including not only the physical sciences but also the human sciences, such as psychology, sociology, and economics. To solve this problem, the logical positivists took as one of their central goals

to form an *Einheitswissenschaft*, i.e., a unified science comprising all knowledge of reality accessible to man without dividing it into separate, unconnected special disciplines, ... (Joergensen 1951, 4)

The logical positivists thought that this goal could be achieved by "clarifying the notions and statements of science" (Carnap 1934, 33). Philosophy is thus transformed into a discipline about the language of science, including its logical structure, its empirical connection with the world, and the use to which scientists put science in explaining and controlling the world. Unification would be achieved by showing, despite the differences in the subject matter of the diverse sciences, that they share a common logical structure, the same methods of verification, and similar uses. Gone then from philosophy are the overarching metaphysical theories that are supposed to tell us what there is and the nature of what there is. The answers to these questions are left to the special sciences, and philosophy becomes the study of the language of science. Morris calls this approach to reaching the goals of unified science "the science of science" or "metascience" (1955, 69). Hence the explosion of interest in the nature of language among the logical positivists and their descendants in the analytical philosophical tradition.

As we have seen, logical positivism had its beginning in Vienna between the wars, but its influence quickly spread beyond Vienna. Soon it counted important groups in Berlin, Warsaw, and the United States; groups in Paris, Uppsala, Münster, Finland, and Great Britain; and individual proponents in Denmark, Argentina, Peking, and Norway. It was, in other words, a worldwide movement, with a journal, *Erkenntnis*, which began publishing in 1930; a project for an *International Encyclopedia of Unified Science*, which grew to two volumes, with 19 monographs; and congresses that were held from 1929 to 1939. Morris was an important member of the American group. He was a professor at the University of Chicago, where Carnap moved in 1936, and an associate editor with Carnap of the *International Encyclopedia of Unified Science*.

Morris's *Foundations of the Theory of Signs* was published in 1938 as the second monograph in the *International Encyclopedia of Unified Science*. His work in semiotic has to be viewed, then, as a part of the logical positivist movement and in particular as part of the goal of achieving a unified science. Morris is quite explicit that semiotic theory should be seen as part of the project of a unified science. He claims that

[s]emiotic holds a unique place among the sciences. It may be possible to say that every empirical science is engaged in finding data which can serve as reliable signs; it is certainly true that every science must embody its results in linguistic signs.... The sciences must look to semiotic for the concepts and general principles relevant to their own problems of sign analysis. Semiotic is not merely a science among sciences but an organon or instrument of all sciences. (1938, 56)

Semiotic, then, can be viewed as metascience, that is, the science of science.

According to Morris, semiotic, the theory of semiosis, is not just a theory about scientific language. It is, he maintains, applicable "to all signs, however simple or complex" (1938, 10). He holds that the following disciplines can be absorbed into semiotic in whole or in part: logic, mathematics, linguistics, aesthetics, epistemology, the sociology of knowledge, rhetoric, psychology, and the human social sciences. This is on the surface a heterogeneous list, but what brings the disciplines together, Morris claims, is that they study in whole or in part systems of signs with common elements that can be captured by his semiotic theory. Thus, Morris is led to give a wide and loose account of the central notions in semiotic. As well, his taking semiotic to be the science of science pulls him in this direction.

According to Morris, as a metascience semiotic has three aspects that correspond to the three philosophical positions, rationalism, empiricism, and pragmatism, that are incorporated into logical positivism. The first is the "rationalist" feature of science.

> Science exists as a body of written characters and spoken words. It is possible to investigate this linguistic residue of the scientists' activity purely formally.... This type of investigation may, in one sense of the term, be called logical analysis; because of the ambiguity of the term 'logical', it maybe preferable to call it ... the syntactical investigation of the language of science. (1955, 69)

Hence, syntax is part of the semiotic theory of the language of science. The second feature has its origin in empiricism.

> The signs which constitute scientific treatises have, to some extent at least, a correlation with objects, and the investigation of all aspects of this relation constitutes a second task of metascience.... This may be called ... the semantical investigation of the language of science. (1955, 69)

Thus, semantics becomes part of semiotic. Third, there is the element that has its source in pragmatism.

> [T]he signs which constitute the language of science are parts and products of the activities of scientists. The study of the relation of signs to scientists may be called ... the pragmatical investigation of the language of science. (1955, 70)

Consequently, pragmatics is part of semiotic.

Let us look more closely at Morris's views about what should be included in syntax, semantics, and pragmatics. According to Morris, "Syntactics ... is the study of the syntactical relations of signs to one another" (1938, 13). But syntax, on Morris's view, not only encompasses what linguistics takes to fall within syntax, but also includes logic and mathematics. The reason for this is Morris's concern to construct a theory that is adequate for an account of the formal structure of scientific theories. And both logic and mathematics play a role in giving science its formal structure. But Morris's "syntax" goes beyond even this wide sweep. As well, he includes within its scope an account of analytic, contradictory, and synthetic properties of sentences. In addition, he claims that "syntax" is to account for synonymy, deal with the logical paradoxes, and "clarify the modal expressions of necessity, possibility and impossibility" (1938, 15). Thus, Morris's syntax encompasses not only logical theory, including modal logic, but also phenomena that fall within what theorists such as Jerry Katz regard to be in the domain of semantics.

For Morris, "[s]emantics deals with the relation of signs to their designata and so the objects which they may or do denote" (1938, 21). A word must be said about 'designatum' and 'denotation'. According to Morris, "The designatum of a sign is the kind of object which the sign applies to . . ." (1938, 5). Morris assimilates 'kind' to 'class of objects'. Every sign must have a designatum, he claims; that is, it must designate a class of objects. However, it is not necessary that every sign denote an object. Consider 'Santa Claus'. This sign, on Morris's view, designates the Santa Claus unit class, but the class is empty. Hence, 'Santa Claus' does not denote anything. (In a later work, Morris replaces 'designatum' with 'significatum' and gives it a behavioristic analysis, but it is not necessary for our purpose to follow him into this dead end.) For every sign, Morris holds, there is a semantical rule that "determines under which conditions a sign is applicable to an object or situation" (1938, 23). The form such rules take is "The sign vehicle 'x' designates the conditions $a, b, c \ldots \ldots$ under which it is applicable" (1938, 24). If an object or situation, y, meets the conditions, $a, b, c, \ldots$, then 'x' denotes y. Morris's view of semantics is quite close in many respects to Carnap's. In recent years, a number of decisive criticisms have been raised against this conception of semantics by Kripke, Putnam, Quine, and others, but I want to pass over these problems and turn to Morris's views about pragmatics.

Pragmatics, Morris claims, is "the study [of] the relation of signs to interpreters" (1938, 6). To have an understanding of Morris's view of pragmatics, we must understand his use of 'interpreter' and 'interpretant'. Semiosis, according to Morris, involves four factors: "that which acts as a sign, that which the sign refers to, and that effect on some interpreter in virtue of which the thing in question is a sign to that interpreter" (1938, 3). This gives us the *sign vehicle*, the *designatum*, the *interpretant*, and the *interpreter*. Interpreters are agents that "take account" of the designatum of signs. "Taking account" is a central notion in Morris's semiotic, to which he attaches the technical term 'interpretant'. Morris gives a behavioristic account of this notion. The interpretant of a sign is "the habit of the organism to respond, because of the sign vehicle, to absent objects which are relevant to a present problematic situation as if they were present" (1938, 31). This gives rise in pragmatics to a pragmatic rule that is, Morris says, "the habit of the interpreter to use the sign vehicle under certain circumstances and, conversely, to expect such and such to be the case when the sign is used" (1938, 32). Here we see the tight connection between Morris's views about semiotic and behaviorism. He takes it that "from the point of view of pragmatics, a linguistic structure is a system of behavior" (1938, 33).

Morris's turn to behaviorism arises because of his concern with the unification of science. Since semiotic is supposedly the science of science, it is itself a science and can be studied in the same way that other sciences are studied. A question then arises for semiotic as a science. How can it be unified with the other sciences? Morris's solution is to try to show how the various aspects of semiosis (i.e., syntax, semantics, and pragmatics) can be accounted for by behaviorism. He argues that his account of the process involving signs, that is, semiosis, "lends itself to treatment from the point of view of behaviorists, . . ." (1938, 5). Hence, semiotic becomes part of psychology. Consequently, there is no independent problem, apart from the unification of psychology, about unifying semiotic with the rest of science.

Morris claims that the behavioristic account that he gives of the basic notions of semiotic is not necessary (1938, 6). Well that it is not, since behaviorism is inadequate for the purpose. Sentences, for Morris, are signs that are supposed to be connected with interpretants, that is, a habit of the interpreter to respond. For there to be a habit, there must be conditioning. And for there to be conditioning with respect to a particular stimulus, there must have been past exposure of the subject to the stimulus. But there can be no such conditioning and thus no such habit, as Chomsky has taught us, connected with sentences. The reason is that most of the sentences we hear and use are novel. We have never heard or uttered them before; hence, there can be no habit connected to their comprehension or use.

It might be thought that Morris's behaviorism can be sustained for subsentential units. We can imagine that there are habits connected to all or some of the morphemes in a language. Syntax, then, would be a system that operates over these habits and composes them into habits connected to sentences. There are many objections to this compositional behaviorism. First, there are many morphemes for which it makes no sense to connect them with a habit. What, after all, would be the habit connected with the syncategoric expressions 'the', 'and', or 'but'? Second, the minimum unit of use is a sentence. Therefore, for a morpheme to be connected with a habit, it must be possible to use it as a one-word sentence. Some nouns and verbs, like 'red', 'chair', 'run', and 'horse', pass the test, but other morphemes do not—for example, 'prudentially', 'possible', and 'rather'. Third, in some cases a morpheme can be used as a one-word sentence, but it is difficult to see what the stimulus patterns could be for establishing a habit for the morpheme behind the sentence. What stimulus patterns are connected with 'love', 'quark', or 'contract'? Understanding these terms comes with understanding theories or sets of laws in which they are embedded or complicated forms of life that give them their meaning. Even if these words were used as one-word sentences, there is no possibility of connecting them with stimulus patterns. It seems, then, that there is no hope for saving behaviorism, even in its more sophisticated compositional version.

So Morris's behaviorism must be dropped, and we must return to his "taking account of." The problem with 'interpretant' is that it is a very broad notion. It includes, for Morris, "all the psychological, biological and sociological phenomena which occur in the functioning of signs" (1938, 30)—that is, any response by an interpreter or effect on an interpreter that arises from the use of signs. Given the very broad notion of sign, this definition of pragmatics includes many of the phenomena studied in psychology and the social sciences. Hence, we see how Morris is able to bring much of human behavior within the purview of semiotic; it falls within pragmatics.

Let me summarize the argument to this point. We have seen that Morris's notion of semiotic is very wide, encompassing all of science, including the physical and the human sciences. The sciences fall within its range, because on Morris's view scientific theories are languages—thus, systems of signs. As such, they are to be studied by semiotic, which Morris considers to be metascience. As we have seen, Morris holds that

[s]cience, as a body of signs with certain specific relations to one another, to objects and to practice, is at once a language, a knowledge of objects and a type of activity; the interrelated study of syntax, semantics and pragmatics of the language science in turn constitutes metascience—the science of science. (1955, 70)

It does not follow from the inclusion of the study of science within semiotic that the phenomena that the scientist studies are themselves signs, in Morris's sense of 'sign'. For example, the solar system itself is not a system of signs; rather, the theory that describes it is supposed to be such a system and thus, open to study by semiotic. There is another sense in which certain theories in the human sciences fall within semiotic. Morris claims that many of the actual phenomena studied by the human sciences are themselves systems of signs; for example, various sorts of ritual behavior that anthropologists and sociologists study fall within Morris's view of semiotic. In fact, Morris thinks that the reach of semiotic is very broad: "Psychology and the human social sciences may find part (if not the entire) basis of their distinction from biological and social sciences in the fact that they deal with responses mediated by signs" (1938, 56). Hence, the range of semiotic for Morris is wide in two ways. First, it includes all the sciences, since they themselves are systems of signs. Second, it includes the human sciences and psychology, since supposedly what they study is human behavior mediated by a system of signs.

I now turn to some criticisms of Morris's wide view of semiotic. First, attempts at achieving a linguistic unification of the sciences have been completely abandoned. One of the main doctrines underpinning this supposed unification, the verificationist theory of meaning, and its correlate, the verificationist theory of meaningfulness, have been shown to face insurmountable problems (Hempel 1965, 101–120). Moreover, it is now thought that there is no common logical and semantic structure to scientific theories in the physical and human sciences that can throw any light on the epistemological questions that motivated the logical positivists. One of the central issues for the logical positivists was the problem of demarcating science from nonscience. On one side of the line was what humans can know; what was on the other side of the line was not only beyond human knowledge, but was literally nonsense (Ayer 1946, 5–15, 35–44). The collapse of the verificationist projects showed that there was no such demarcation to be made. In addition, recent work in the philosophy of the human sciences has shown that its theories are shot through with normativity. The normativity arises because of the ineliminable necessity for theories within the human sciences to attribute to human activity meaning that involves the construction of theories of interpretation that assign meanings to human activities. As a result, there is no possibility of unity with the physical sciences, the theories of which are devoid of theories of interpretation that assign meaning to their objects of study (Davidson 1984, 125–141). Any attempt to bridge the gap—currently fashionable connectionist theories, for example (Churchland 1984, 43–51)—ends up removing meaning from the range of phenomena for which it must account and, with that, removing from explanatory reach what the human sciences wished to explain in the first place. Even if we restrict our domain of unification to the physical sciences, the current view is that if such unification is to come about at all, it will come about by providing a theoretical unification of different domains of inquiry.

Thus, to unify, say, some branch of biology (e.g., genetics) and chemistry it must be shown that genetic phenomena in biology can be explained by chemical theory. This sort of unification is not linguistic; instead, it requires well-worked-out theories in microbiology and corresponding experimental results. An example of such unification is the discovery of the chemical structure of DNA. Hence, semiotic cannot provide a unification of the sciences by showing that scientific theories share common formal, semantic, and pragmatic properties. Second, there is no evidence that the various phenomena that Morris describes as involving semiosis have very much in common that is of theoretical interest. Morris holds that scientific theories, natural languages, dance, rituals, gestures, body language, facial expressions, and the like, can be accounted for by semiotic. He claims that they all involve the relations among signs, designatum, interpretant, and interpreters. Work in linguistics in the last 30 years shows—conclusively, I believe—that natural human languages are not sets of signs, in Morris's sense of 'sign'. For Morris, as we have seen if a morpheme is to function as a sign, it must be connected to some object or other. But there are many morphemes, like syncategorematic expressions, for which no such connection is possible; and there are expressions, like speech act verbs, that are connected not to objects but to sets of rules. There might be some extended use of 'sign', other than Morris's, so that we could count human languages as sets of signs, but this use would be so broad that it would be of little theoretical interest (Sperber and Wilson 1995, 3–9). Last, and most important, Morris includes too much within semiosis, especially within pragmatics; as a result, it is impossible to have a coherent theory that could give a theoretically unified account of the disparate phenomena that he claims fall within the domain of semiotic. This is one of the reasons that some pragmaticians who have followed Morris's lead now claim that pragmatics, which is only a subdomain of semiotic, is not a theory on a par with syntax, but a discipline, or even more widely yet, a perspective on language. I would like to suggest that Morris's wide view of semiotic, and especially of pragmatics, be abandoned, since the underlying reason for it, the desire to have a unified science, no longer can be sustained.[2]

Let me close by saying something about the way I think research should proceed in pragmatics. Theories, perspectives, or disciplines that cover everything explain nothing; unconstrained theories that attempt to account for everything will not tell us anything interesting about natural languages and human communication. What is needed are theories that give explanations for a restricted range of data and that are constrained in various ways by the data they are supposed to explain and by the ordinary norms that govern scientific theorizing, including simplicity, relevance, explicitness, and preciseness.

Notes

1. There is some variation in the term used for the study of signs. Morris uses *semiotic*, following Locke and Pierce; Margaret Mead uses *semiotics*; and Roland Barth, following Saussure, uses *sémiologie*, which is translated into English as *semiology*. (For a discussion of these variants, see Morris's quotation from Sebeok in Morris 1971, 9.)

2. It might seem that I am beating a dead horse and that Morris's wide view of pragmatics is only of historical interest. I began the chapter by citing the underlying perspectivalism that informs the organizing principles of the International Pragmatics Association. It is shared by a number of researchers who work on pragmatics, including Mey, Östman, and Verschueren (see Mey 1993; Östman 1988; Verschueren 1987).

References

Ayer, A. J. (1946). *Language, truth, and logic*. London: V. Gollancz.

Carnap, R. (1934). *The unity of science*. London: Kegan Paul, Trench, Trubner.

Churchland, P. (1984) *Matter and consciousness*. Cambridge, MA: MIT Press.

Davidson, D. (1984). *Inquiries into truth and interpretation*. New York: Oxford University Press.

Hempel, C. (1965). Empiricist criteria of cognitive significance: Problems and changes. In *Aspects of scientific explanation and other essays in the philosophy of science*. New York: Free Press.

Joergensen, J. (1951). *The development of logical positivism* (*The international encyclopedia of unified science*, vol. 2, no. 9). Chicago: University of Chicago Press.

Mey, J. L. 1993. *Pragmatics*. Cambridge, MA: Blackwell.

Morris, C. W. (1936). Remarks on the proposed encyclopedia. In *Actes du Congrès International de Philosophie Scientifique II Unité de la Science*. Paris: Hermann.

Morris, C. W. (1937). *Logical positivism, pragmatism and scientific empiricism*. Paris: Hermann.

Morris, C. W. (1938). *Foundations of the theory of signs*. (*The international encyclopedia of unified science*, vol. 1, no. 2.) Chicago: University of Chicago Press.

Morris, C. W. (1955). Scientific empiricism. In *Encyclopedia and unified science* (*The international encyclopedia of unified science*, vol. 1, no. 1). Chicago: University of Chicago Press.

Morris, C. W. (1971). *Writings on the general theory of signs*. The Hague: Mouton.

Östman, J.-O. (1988). Implicit involvement in interactive writing. In J. Verschueren and M. Bertucelli-Papi (Eds.), *The pragmatic perspective: Selective papers from the 1985 International Pragmatics Conference*. Amsterdam: John Benjamins.

Sperber, D., and Wilson, D. (1995). *Relevance: Communication and cognition*. Cambridge, MA: Blackwell.

Verschueren, J. (1987). Pragmatics as a theory of linguistic adaptation. In *Working documents #1*. Antwerp: International Pragmatics Association.

Chapter 9

Scientific Theories That Unconceal Being: Intentions and Conceptions in Their Genesis

Leslie Margaret Perrin McPherson

You must inquire into all, both the untrembling heart of well-rounded unconcealment and the opinions of mortals, in which there is no unconcealing assur-
ance. Yet nonetheless these too you shall learn, as the seeming things one must
intend to prove to be (though, through it all, all of them transgress all assurances),
because all are pervading everything.

The Goddess of Day to Parmenides

When John Macnamara agreed to be my doctoral supervisor, I had no
idea what a joyful graduate experience awaited me, for I had never met
him. But I had two good reasons for wanting him to supervise my graduate work. First, out of all the psychological theories on language and
cognition, his were the only ones that really made good sense to me. His
theories mirrored my own experience of my own mind—something few
other theories did. Second, when I asked around to find out what his
former graduate students thought of him, I was told, "They adore him."
I was intrigued.

When I began my studies at McGill, I quickly learned why John's
students adored him. I discovered that he had a brilliant mind that

This work was inspired to an immeasurable degree by Robert H. Schmidt, who
always seems to point me in the right direction. Many of the insights are taken
wholly from him, including some of the insights regarding the original senses of
scientific concepts, which he earned through years of contemplation and research.
I acknowledge also his help in pointing me to certain important passages, in various old works, relevant to changes in these concepts. Further, his comments and
insights regarding the ideas in this chapter proved invaluable. I am extremely
grateful to him. This chapter benefited also from useful comments from David
Alexandre Nicolas, Ray Jackendoff, and Keith Niall. And I thank my dear
departed friend and mentor John Macnamara for creating such beautiful theories
that I could not help but ask myself how he did it.

instinctively aimed at only the most fundamental questions and pene-
trated straight into the core of them. He had a profound understanding of
critical philosophical and psychological problems, and he shared his
knowledge and insights with his students generously. To listen to him
speak was as entertaining as reading his wonderfully elegant prose. But
besides all this, he was sweet, loving, kind, wise, charming, playful, and
funny—a delightful gentleman. I quickly came to count myself among the
students who adored him.

It took me considerably longer to discover why his ideas and theories
make so much sense. I believe I can now explain why. This chapter is
devoted to this effort. I hope to show why the approach John took to
theorizing results in superior theories, and why the usual approaches do
not. Though I focus on theories of natural language semantics early in the
discussion, the insights should apply to theory in any domain of inquiry.[1]

9.1 Theory

The word *theory* derives from the Greek *theōria*, 'a viewing' or 'a
beholding'. Ideally, a theory should result from a theorist's viewing or
beholding (or noetic perception) of being,[2] and it should permit others
to behold that being. At a minimum, this implies that any concept guiding
a theorist's thinking and transmitted to others along with a theory must
originate in an authentic and relatively complete conception of being of
some sort, and that the theory must be compatible with each such concept. What a theorist must do (and avoid doing) to ensure these outcomes
will become clear.

9.2 Intentions in Theories

In the context of theories or, more generally, declarative statements in
some language, an "intention" (from the Latin *intentio*, 'tension' or 'aim')
is a noetic tensing or aiming of the mind toward being of some sort, an
aiming concomitant with speaking or writing, and brought about by
hearing or reading, a string of signs for which one knows the conventional
(or theorist-defined) interpretations.[3] I take this to be the original sense of
intention in the context of signification; be warned that it bears little
resemblance to modern senses of the term (e.g., Bertrand Russell's "propositional attitude" understood as a relation of a person to a proposition,
such as the "relation" of belief, where no relation of the person to being is

necessarily implied; for instance, those who advocate "methodological solipsism," such as Fodor (1980), conclude, from the fact that false beliefs can affect a person's actions, that a propositional attitude enters into the explanation of behavior under an opaque construal, which is considered to be the only construal relevant to psychological theories because the explanation of behavior is now typically said to be *the* goal of psychology—a naturalistic pretense of the behaviorist and postbehaviorist eras). The original sense of *intention* is more similar, in some respects, to the modern sense of *attention*.

In describing the object of an intention as "being," I do not mean to imply that its object must be "objective reality," or being as it is carved up by a god or nature, independently of our characterization of it (e.g., a "natural kind"); I am not presupposing the correctness of what Putnam (1981) calls the "externalist" perspective, according to which being and beings are necessarily defined or individuated objectively, and reference to anything extrapsychic is necessarily a connection of some sort to objectively defined being or beings. Theories—especially in psychology, the social sciences, mathematics, and semantics—often require that being be carved up or defined in other ways (e.g., the firms, consumption, and income of economic theory). Being that is carved out mentally by us is not imaginary or unreal just because its definition has no "objective" (i.e., nonsocial and nonpersonal) source; as Field (1982) argues, "what we have carved out existed independent of our carving it out, despite its non-salience from the God's-eye perspective" (p. 561).[4]

9.3   A Defense of Intentions

The theses of this chapter presuppose the existence of intentions qua intentions. But the supposition of their existence is surprisingly controversial these days. So, with the aim of reducing the appeal of modern skepticism about them, and to show why scientific theorizing would be impossible without them, I will examine some claims that have been made about their nonexistence as well as some of the attempts to reduce them to something else.

The physicalist philosopher Daniel C. Dennett and his many followers would have us regard the intentions we ascribe to ourselves and others as "idealized fictions in an action-predicting, action-explaining calculus" (Dennett 1978, 30), and our ascription of them as a "stance" we take in relation to an organism or a machine when that stance seems useful in explaining or predicting actions or behavior, but one irrelevant to scientific theorizing; talk of reference, thoughts, beliefs, perceptions, desires, fears, aims, and so on, is "a sham and ... mere word play" (Haugeland 1982, 616; Dennett claims that "intentional theory is vacuous as psychology" (p. 15)). But Dennett owes us an answer to this question: how can one adopt the intentional stance, or any explanatory stance, toward something's actions without coming into any (genuine) intentional states such as *perceiving* actions, *desiring* or *trying* to explain them, and *believing* or *asserting* that their explanation lies in, say, beliefs and desires? (See also Slors 1996.) As Putnam (1989) observes, "*Explanation* is a flagrantly intentional notion" (p. 217).

Some physicalists (e.g., Churchland (1981)) would have us embrace the goal of eliminating all talk of intentions—deemed unreal—from a science of the mind. But it seems to me foolish to deny the reality of that which one experiences directly in every waking moment just because averting one's eyes eases ontological queasiness. As Silvers (1991) remarks, "Eliminativism with respect to intentional phenomena is a way out but it is much like the way of the ostrich" (p. 68). If that which manifests itself to us does not accord with what we know about nature, then our knowledge of nature must be less than complete! The fact that intentional notions such as reference resist naturalistic explanation merely shows, as Putnam (1992b) explains, "the limitations of a certain notion of 'nature' and a certain notion of 'explanation'" (p. 384). Instead of denying the manifest, one might fruitfully aspire to what James Clerk Maxwell (1877) called "that state of thoroughly conscious ignorance which is the prelude to every real advance in knowledge" (p. 245).

It is easy to show that eliminativism is untenable. The eliminativist cannot even state his or her thesis without making covert use of intentions. When Churchland (1984) claims that the commonsense (or "folk psychology") conception of the mind as intentional "is a *false* and radically misleading *conception* of the causes of human behavior and the nature of cognitive activity" (p. 43; emphasis added), he uses the essentially intentional notions of falsity and a conception. When he says of folk psychology, considered as "an empirical theory," that "its *ontology* is an *illusion*" (1981, 72; emphasis added), he implies that theories are *about* (illusory or real) being and therefore intentional; and since an illusion is a type of intentional state (i.e., *perceiving something* as other than what it is), one cannot sensibly dismiss the intentional states in the ontology of the folk theory as illusions. Eliminativists cannot even maintain, without inconsistency, that their goal is to eliminate all mention of intentions from scientific discourse because they are fictions, for goals are intentional. Garfield (1988) sums up the problem:

> The eliminativist enterprise is, in a straightforward sense, self-refuting. It commits, as Baker [(1987)] has put it, "cognitive suicide" by denying what is necessary in order to give it sense, viz., that those who assert it believe its truth (or, for that matter, anything at all) or mean anything by asserting it. (p. 123)

The whole of the scientific enterprise involves goals (e.g., the goal of generating hypotheses from a theory, and the goal of obtaining evidence in support of those hypotheses) and intentions of other kinds (e.g., desires for procedural rigor in experiments, perception and a belief in the veracity of one's senses during observation, and assertions about experimental results); as Baker (1987) argues, "Without intentionality science would be impossible" (p. 173; see also Garfield 1988, 112–116). Moreover, I cannot see how a scientific theory could be meaningful—something other than a word game or a kind of dream—unless it permitted the mind to intend being.

To make sense of what follows, the reader would do well to resist another (even stronger) modernistic temptation, namely, to try to understand signification, not in terms of intentionality, but in terms of the popular modern concept of a "mental representation." Having changed radically from the "representation" of German philosophers such as Kant and Brentano (i.e., their *Vorstellung*, the act of presentation to or placement in front of the conscious mind), a representation is now understood as a mental being (e.g., a mental symbol) to be operated upon, one unavailable to consciousness, in the context of the computational (or "information-processing") view of the mind. As Searle (1980) has demonstrated with his "Chinese room" argument, operating upon symbols in conformity with formal rules (i.e., rules that depend upon the shapes of the symbols) does not lead to any *understanding* of the symbols. Fodor (1986) puts it this way: "You can't get semantical properties out of symbols just by piling up their syntactical ones" (p. 13). More to the point, no existing theories of mental representations succeed in reducing intentionality to something else, I will argue, or allow for the mind to make the kind of contact with being necessary for scientific theorizing to proceed.

Sometimes mental representations of linguistic meaning are imagined to be symbols or symbolic formulae (in a mental dictionary, lexicon, or encyclopedia, or in some representational "space") in some partially or entirely unlearned language (e.g., "Mentalese" or "the language of thought"). This view leads to a problem that Harnad (1990) calls the "symbol-grounding problem" and that Johnson-Laird (1988) calls the "symbolic fallacy": the interpretations of symbols cannot be just more symbols.

Some theorists seem to be blissfully unaware of the problem or unwilling to recognize it (e.g., Eco (1988); Schank and Kass (1988); Wilks (1988)), or seem to think it can be solved by some sort of "encoding" of semantic content by symbols in a formal system, but leave in shadow the mysteries of the encoding and decoding (e.g., Pylyshyn (1984, 258)).

Among those who recognize the problem and make a serious attempt to find a solution to it, some grasp at the slender hope that the interpretation of a sign or symbol is a causal connection of some sort (e.g., Dretske (1981); Stampe (1979)). Fodor (e.g., 1987), for instance, tries to explain semantic content in terms of the reliable causation of tokenings of a certain symbol by percepts of a certain kind, which are in turn caused by observable properties of beings of a certain kind; the covariation of tokens of a symbol and the referents that cause them is supposed to determine the interpretation or content of the symbol—presumably even when a referent is not present to cause its tokening. This seems to be not so much an explanation of interpretation as a change of topic; it seems plausible only as a partial account of why we tend to think "There's something red there" when a red surface fills the visual field (but a full account of that would require more, including accounts of how the English word *red* came to be associated with red things, how one takes one's perception of redness as evidence for something red—cf. Silvers 1991—and how one then interprets "something red" into it; all of these accounts would surely involve intentions). Moreover, the causes of tokenings of a sign (and of beliefs about its referents) need not be referents of the sign (or of any phrase headed by it), as when one learns about electrons from textbooks; and though *some* causal chain may link electrons to tokenings of *electron* immediately "caused" by textbooks, that causal chain could not be specified unless one already knew the referents of *electrons* and could refer to them by some other means (Putnam 1981). Contrary to the assumptions of those who espouse causal theories of semantic content, causes and causal chains are not purely objective and unique things. A cause or a causal chain leading to some event is not determined independently of observers; an observer must decide, out of the entirety of being—all of which somehow influences the event—which things are the most important to mention in giving an explanation in line with his or her current purposes (Putnam 1984). Causal accounts of meaning also leave mysterious the way in which the expression *causal chain* comes to have *its* content (Putnam 1984). And attempting to explain the content of individual words in terms of causal connections does nothing to explain the content of complex referring expressions such as *the first baby born after the year 2500* that have referents with which one cannot possibly now interact causally (Putnam 1992a, 163). But perhaps the most serious problem with causal theories like Fodor's is that, *even when the referent is present*, the being that causes the sensory stimulation that is supposed to lead to the tokening of a symbol is rarely being that the symbol can be used to signify. The being that stimulates the retina so as to lead to a tokening of *person*, namely, parts of the exposed surfaces of a person's clothing and of the body of matter currently coincident with the person, is not equivalent to the referent of any noun phrase headed by the noun *person*. Causal accounts of reference will only seem plausible to those who unwittingly presuppose the intentionality such accounts are supposed to explain (cf. Searle 1980, 454).

Others hope that symbols can be grounded by nonsymbolic representations—icons or images (e.g., Harnad (1990); McGinn (1989)) or mental models (e.g., Johnson-Laird (1988)) that are supposed to represent by means of similarities, (natural, not assigned) correspondences, or isomorphisms with the being represented, and to intrinsically preserve information about it.

Sometimes such representations—or even symbolic representations— are imagined to give signs meaning in and of themselves. But this would imply that all statements, including theoretical statements in science, are about mental representations rather than being—which would make psychology the basic science (as in Tlön, the imaginary world invented by Jorge Luis Borges, one populated entirely by idealists); as Macnamara once remarked, "Flattering to a psychologist, but dubious!" (Macnamara 1989, 350). Moreover, the idea simply makes no sense. The fact that we can discuss whether or not statements put the mind in contact with something outside the mind presupposes our ability to refer to the extrapsychic. Macnamara (1989) made the point this way:

One might ask: Does the expression 'extramental reality' put us in contact with something outside the mental models? If it does, why do other words not? If not, what might the expression mean? And how could any of us conceive the existence of an extramental reality, let alone wallow in its exuberant presence? (p. 352)

An inability to refer to the external would also make obscure the meaning of an indexical or demonstrative such as *this, that, here,* or *there* (especially in discourse contexts in which it had no antecedent) and would leave us with no way to account for its obvious kinship with (and frequent concomitance with) an indexical gesture such as pointing, nodding, or gazing toward something so as to indicate to another person an object of thought; one does not (and cannot) point, nod, or gaze in the direction of one's own mental representations. It is apparent that, as Putnam (1973) says, "'meanings' just ain't in the *head*" (p. 704).[5]

Sometimes some relation of a nonsymbolic representation to being is imagined to ground or give meaning to a symbol or formula. But theorists fail to characterize this relation in any way that could explain reference or interpretation, or that would permit scientists to theorize about the being represented.

This relation to being is most popularly described as a map or function from the representations to states of affairs in the extrapsychic world (e.g., Millikan 1984). But no such function could *explain* reference because it *presupposes* reference. Unless the mind already had the capacity to refer, such a function could not be computed in the mind because, though the arguments of the function (representations) could be in the mind, its values (extrapsychic states of affairs) could not.

Some (e.g., Palmer (1978)) seem to think that the mere (objective) existence of a similarity, correspondence, or isomorphism will, by itself, do the trick—that such a correspondence with being is what we really mean by *reference* or *intention* (or at least *representation*). But that is not enough. Mental images or models could not, just by means of correspondences, determine what signs signify. For one thing, they would leave the signified indeterminate because a given one is similar to, corresponds to, or is isomorphic to many beings or states of affairs, and is similar to, corresponds to, or is isomorphic to a given being or state of affairs in many different ways, "representing" the truth-conditions of many different sentences and the referents of many different signs (see Cummins 1996; Fodor 1990; Putnam 1981). The correspondence to the signified being that is relevant to reference and truth-conditions would have to be singled out somehow. It could not be singled out by stipulation (cf. Morris 1991), since stipulating that the correspondence between *this* and *this* or stipulating that *this* correspondence between a representation and being of a given kind is the *relevant* correspondence *presupposes reference* (to the representation, the represented being, and, perhaps, the correspondence), which is the very thing that correspondence is supposed to explain (see Putnam 1981). Nor could any causal connection fix the relevant correspondence (see Fodor 1990; Putnam 1984). But even if one correspondence could somehow be singled out by some nonintentional means, still more would be needed to give rise to representation of, reference to, or an intention toward being. A given correspondence (or similarity, or isomorphism) does not a representation make (see, e.g., Pylyshyn 1984, 40–41). One thing can represent another only by virtue of an *intention* to represent (see Fodor 1990; Putnam 1981; and so it is foolhardy to try to reduce intentions to representations). The moon may happen to look like a man's face, but it would be odd indeed to say that it is a *representation* of a man's face; as far as we know, nobody shaped the surface of the moon so as to create the likeness of a man's face (or, for that matter, the likeness of a rabbit, which some people see in the moon). As Putnam (1981) points out, "Thought words and mental pictures do not *intrinsically* represent what they are about" (p. 5); "believing that some correspondence intrinsically just *is* reference (... as an *ultimate* metaphysical fact) amounts to a magical theory of reference" (p. 47)— that is, "a theory on which certain mental representations necessarily refer to certain external things and kinds of things" (p. 15).

A thinking subject must *do* something with, say, a mental icon if it is to bring the mind into contact with being. Three possibilities occur to me (but all of them presuppose intentionality). The subject could interpret the icon as (1) a linguistic sign of a special sort, one that happens to look like the being it signifies (comparable to early Sumerian cuneiform ideograms and early Egyptian hieroglyphs), in which case it is redundant; (2) an image of the being pictured; or (3) a representative, proxy, or counterpart for the being represented (see also Cummins 1996), something that stands in for it in mental activities, just as a map can stand in for a region in planning a route of travel. The latter possibility is pertinent to mental *activities* such as planning actions in the imagination, but it could not provide a plausible general account of interpreting signs or strings of signs in sentences. An icon (one available to consciousness) interpreted in the third way *may* play a role in signification when there is no particular or definite referent for a word or phrase embedded in a sentence so that the mind cannot fall upon extrapsychic being in interpreting it, as when one is interpreting an indefinite noun phrase in the predicate of a denial (e.g., *a ball* in *Rick did not hit a ball*, which obviously does not refer to any particular ball, since it makes no sense to ask, "Which ball?"; see Geach 1962; McPherson 1995, app. B) or in the predicate of a sentence such as

You will need an umbrella today (where the lack of a definite referent of *an umbrella* is evident, again, in the inappropriateness of the question "Which umbrella?"); in such cases, the mind may aim at an icon understood as a representative, proxy, or counterpart for any individual whatsoever of the kind. If a representation is interpreted in accordance with one of the first two possibilities, as an imagelike sign or an image, it may play a mnemonic role, helping the subject to remember the sort of being the associated linguistic sign conventionally signifies. But in any of these cases, we would not want to say that the icon *determines* what is signified so that the associated sign (or a referring expression headed by it) signifies just those aspects of being that are represented. That would determine the being signified too narrowly. Representation by means of an icon or model is always partial (see also Cummins 1996), and to think that only what is represented is signified would be, in the case of theoretical terms, to miss the whole point of scientific investigation: to discover or unconceal the *unknown* aspects of the nature of being. Moreover, the history of science demonstrates that a word can be used to refer to something even when it has been conceived *wrongly*. Science could not proceed if scientists could not use a scientific term such as *electron*, *gene*, or *gold* to refer to being of the same kind while they entertained different concepts of it and different theories about it (see also Putnam 1988). (Of course, the current concept cannot be *completely* mistaken. One could not use *electrons* to refer to electrons if one's concept of their nature were so far off that one did not even know that they are subatomic constituents of matter, for instance. And though one can *refer* to something not correctly conceived, its nature cannot yet be fully revealed to and beheld by one's mind; full unconcealment would lead to the conception of a new, correct concept.) The potential referents of a sign are fixed by a *convention* according to which the sign is used to refer to, or aim the mind at, being of a particular sort. The being toward which a linguistic sign can direct the mind is determined, not by a similarity, a natural correspondence, or an isomorphism between any associated mental representation and the being, but by a convention of a speech community (see also Aristotle, *On Interpretation* 2, 16[a]19).

9.4   Intentional Objects and Semantic Theory: Macnamara's Contemplation of Being

The nature of thinking can be seen only by looking away from thinking.
Martin Heidegger, *Discourse on Thinking*

If we take the interpretation of signs or combinations of signs in sentences to be the objects of the intentions to which the signs give rise, then a theory of the interpretation of sentences—a theory of semantics—must characterize or define the objects of the intentions that arise upon hearing or reading sentences (where *object* is to be understood, here and elsewhere, as that toward which the mind is aimed, which is not necessarily an object in the sense of a sensible thing). A semanticist must characterize or define the being signified; to do so is to define what is meant. This is just what John Macnamara did. He did not merely *name* the objects of intentions (e.g., the word *John* is interpreted into John), for to do so is to leave their definition implicit; he characterized or defined the being toward which the mind aims. In his theory of the semantics of proper names, for instance, he identified the referent of a proper noun as an individual individuated or informed by a kind (or form or species), some psychologically (and perhaps ontologically) privileged kind such as PERSON—as opposed to an individual individuated by some other kind (e.g., WOMAN, FRIEND, DANCER, or PASSENGER), and as opposed to, say, a particular collection of molecules (which would not permit the application of a proper name both to a given woman and to the infant she once was), or a set of predicates or properties (for the properties of the bearer of a proper name change), or something that gives rise to a certain appearance (for that which bears a proper name—say, a person—can change radically in appearance—for example, from infancy to old age, through changes in hair color and hairstyle, and through changes in clothing, which alter the appearance radically but do not change a part of the person proper), or that appearance itself (for that which bears a proper name may well be largely hidden, as a person beneath his or her own skin, and usually under clothing as well; an appearance does not itself bear a proper name, but announces the presence of that which does). The identity of the named individual across factual and counterfactual situations is traced through the individuating kind (or form). (See La Palme Reyes, Macnamara, and Reyes 1994; La Palme Reyes et al. 1993; Macnamara and Reyes 1994.)

John arrived at definitions of intentional objects by "carefully sifting through" his own intuitions, as he put it. He would find meaningful utterances that seemed to reveal something about the interpretation of a sign or phrase and contemplate the nature of the being into which it is interpreted. He once described the process to me by comparing himself to a worm turning over the same piece of earth again and again. The analogy is apt. To turn over earth, a worm must make direct contact with the earth. In his contemplation, John seems to have kept his mind in direct intentional contact with the objects of linguistic intentions. Those who knew John will know that the earth he turned over most frequently was the being intended in interpreting the sentence *Freddie is a dog*. The late Freddie was a large black poodle who shared his life with John and his family. The fact that the sign *Freddie* can still be used to pick out a certain dog, who is no longer with us, as well as a certain pup who was born in Montréal, that it can be used to pick out the same dog even in counter-factual situations (such as one in which Freddie was adopted by other humans), and other such facts led John to his theory about the nature of the being into which a proper name is interpreted. The theory accounts well for the facts of interpretation for proper nouns, and reveals or unconceals or brings to light the nature of the being implicitly and sponta-neously understood to bear a proper name in every instance of the inter-pretation of a proper name.

John's choice of a declarative sentence (*Freddie is a dog*) as the focus of his contemplation may have facilitated his discovery of the nature of that being. A declarative sentence is the only type of utterance that can be judged true or false, and, when true, it unconceals being of some sort to the mind (which is why the Greeks used the word *alētheia*, 'unconceal-ment', for truth; see Aristotle, *On Interpretation* 1, 16^a9–18; 4, 16^b33–17^a4); and so a true declarative sentence can bring the mind into direct intentional or noetic contact with being. Contemplation of an isolated word may not permit such contact, for a word by itself may not actually signify; a word uttered or written in isolation, such as "person" or "green," does not seem to aim the mind at any definite or particular being or beings; it may only *potentially* signify (i.e., have the potential to signify) by virtue of one's having conceived a concept of, or formulated a defini-tion of, the kind of being it would *actually* signify in a referring expression in accordance with a convention of a speech community. (And this may explain the Greeks' use of the word *dunamis*, 'power' or 'potentiality', for the force of an individual word.)[6] When a word is out of context, one cannot even determine on which side of the use/mention distinction it falls, that is, whether it is to be interpreted in its signifying function or as a string of sounds or letters (La Palme Reyes et al. 1993).

9.5   Inner Perception and Psychological Method

John came to understand his sifting of intuitions largely in terms of Franz Brentano's "inner perception" (*innere Wahrnehmung*; see, e.g., Macnamara

1994). Brentano (1838–1917) was, along with Wilhelm Wundt, one of the first empirically minded psychologists. Neither Wundt nor Brentano advocated the use of the methods of the natural sciences in psychology (see Macnamara 1992, 1993). Brentano advocated the use of inner perception as the proper empirical technique for a genuine science of psychology (see Brentano 1924).

Brentano maintained—and quite rightly, I believe—that all and only psychological phenomena are intentional; in any psychological phenomenon, the mind is turned toward—the attention is focused on—something as its object. Psychology, then, is the science of the intentional. Brentano argued that one can study intentions *directly* only by means of inner perception, which he described thus: 'Only while one's attention is turned toward another object, it happens that one also incidentally arrives at the perception of psychical events that are referred toward it [i.e., the other object]' (1924, 41).[7] In the context of semantics, this means that when a sign or combination of signs makes one's mind intend something as its object, one can perceive or notice or become aware of aspects of the intention such as the conditions under which it arises, its character, and the nature of its object.

Brentano took great pains to distinguish inner perception from introspection or inner *observation*, which he regarded as impossible (see Macnamara 1992, 1993). One cannot *observe* one's own intentions, for to do so would require a redirecting of one's attention—of one's mind's firm or taut aiming or tensing—away from the objects of intentions and toward the intentions themselves, which would abate or relax in one's so doing, ceasing to be; but one can notice characteristics of one's intentions incidentally as they occur (or, as Aristotle put it, *en parergōi*, 'in by-work', or 'in a deed done on the side'; *Metaphysics* Λ.9, 1074[b]36). One can in some sense observe one's intentions only when they have passed out of existence, through contemplating memories of them.

The science of psychology that Brentano envisioned, though founded on inner perception, was not fettered by the fact that one can perceive directly only one's own intentions. Brentano recognized that we can learn about the intentions of others through their reports about them or evidence of them in actions or in facial expressions or other involuntary behaviors. Such indirect means of learning about intentions can be the basis of psychological experimentation. But a theory that generates experimental hypotheses can only be a genuine theory of, or permit a genuine *beholding* of, intentions of some sort if the theorist uses inner perception to gain direct evidence of the nature of those intentions—for no other direct means of discovering their nature exists. It is the discovery of their nature by this direct means that permits an interpretation of indirect evidence of intentions such as facial expressions and actions; no knowledge about intentions could be acquired on the basis of the indirect evidence by itself, for, as Brentano (1924) pointed out, 'what is a perception, what a judgment, what joy and sorrow, desire and aversion, hope and fear, courage and despair, what a decision and an aim of the will, we would never come to know if the inner perception of our own phenomena did not bring this knowledge to us' (p. 40). Psychologists cannot escape the need for inner perception.

I turn now to an examination of intentions and conceptions that will reveal some of the reasons a theory can fail to permit a beholding of being when the theoretical work behind it is done without the theorist's keeping his or her mind firmly aimed at the being of interest.

9.6   First Intentions and Second Intentions

Following the Scholastics, philosophers distinguish "first intentions" and "second intentions," or concepts conceived by direct intentional contact with being and concepts conceived by reflection upon concepts already conceived. But the distinction seems originally to have been between two types of intention rather than two types of concept. First intentions seem to have been understood originally as aimings of the mind toward 'real beings' (*entia realis*) directly, and second intentions as aimings of the mind first toward concepts (conceived either first-intentionally or through reflection upon concepts; concepts conceived in the latter way were called 'beings of reason',[8] *entia rationis*) before the mind may be redirected toward real beings. The distinction has consequences for theoretical work. Theories are usually about being of which our concepts are second-intentional (i.e., beings of reason—concepts originally conceived by reflection upon concepts), but theoretical reasoning that proceeds without the mind's aiming directly at any extrapsychic being can result in theories that fail to reveal the nature of any such being (partly because of the tendency of second-intentional concepts to change in sense and become depleted in sense—a problem addressed in the next section).

The original senses of *first intention* and *second intention* are evident in expositions of some of the Renaissance Scholastics.

Jacopo Zabarella (1533–1589) described the original, etymologically discovered sense of (*first*) *intention* as that action in which 'the soul aims [or stretches; *tendit*] toward an object with which it is to become acquainted [*in objectum cognoscendum*]' (1590–1605/1966, 870). The notion of an aiming (or stretching) of the soul toward something (some extrapsychic being) as its object was central to the understanding of a first intention even when the word *intentio* was being used by medieval Scholastics just for aims of the will. Aquinas, for instance, said that 'an intention, as the very name implies, means *to aim* [or *stretch*; *tendere*] *toward another*' (1266/1970, 111–112).

Eustachius a Sancto Paulo (1573–1640) pointed out that the name of a second intention reveals the original sense to be an aiming of the mind at real being secondarily rather than directly as in a first intention:

A second intention, if you look at the force of the name, is that very operation of the mind by which it secondarily aims in the direction of a real thing already known previously, insofar as it is known. (*Summa Philosophiae Quadripartita* 4; see Gilson 1979, 107)

Francisco Suárez (1548–1617) gave a more detailed treatment of second intentions (in *De Entibus Rationis*, 'On Beings of Reason'):

Second intentions [i.e., second-intentional *concepts*] ... [result] from a second intention or attention or consideration of the intellect, by which name is properly called a reflexive intellection [i.e., one turned back upon the intellect itself], because it supposes another [intellection] with which it is occupied [*circa quam versatur*].... Properly that operation is reflex, and (if I may put it this way) is in accordance with itself [*per se*] second, which falls upon another cognition, or upon an object according as it is denominated by a prior cognition, and is from that participating in some properties. Therefore because those logical relations are always based on reflex cognition of this kind, for that reason they in particular are called second intentions, or second objective notions, because they are objects for a second notion [i.e., acquaintance] or formal intention.... These relations of reason are usually called things of second intention ... because ... [they have their] being only objectively in [i.e., as the object of] a second or reflexive cognition of the intellect.

From this moreover, it further arises that the intellect could be reflexed [i.e., bent back] again upon second intentions themselves, and consider agreements or differences among them, and define these, or reason discursively from these, and then after that base similar relations on these; as from genus and species it abstracts the relation of universal, and denominates that a genus, similarly also with regard to others; then those are relations of reason now not only by reason of the other deficiencies [e.g., not having any being except as objects of second intentions], but because they are not occupied [*non versantur*] proximately with real things, or existing [things], and for that reason when these relations are said to be in some way based on things, it must be understood to be because of the first relations of this series.... These relations can be multiplied nearly to infinity by fictions [i.e., formations or inventions] or reflexions of the intellect. (1597/1965, 1041)

A first intention, then, in the original sense, is an aiming of the mind directly at real being. A second intention is reflex (*reflexus*, 'bent back', directed toward itself), with the mind turning toward or intending some of its own contents, namely, concepts; if it turns toward the real being of which they are concepts, it does so only secondarily. Second intentions toward or reflection upon concepts can give rise to a new concept, which was also called a second intention. As Suárez noted, the being of reason so conceived can then be taken up as the object of further reflexive intellection to conceive further concepts, as when one conceives a relation through reflecting upon the concept of a ratio and concepts of comparative being such as being greater than and being less than, where some of these concepts have themselves been conceived by second intentions (e.g., the concept of a ratio is conceived through reflection upon the concepts of double, triple, etc.).

How is this distinction between first and second intentions relevant to theorizing? If a being of reason can be the object of an intention in the reflection that permits new conceptions, then surely it can be the same in theoretical reflection. Now when a theorist makes use of a second-intentional concept such as that of a relation, the theorist's mind aims at this being of reason. If the theorist's mind is to fall upon any real being, it must then aim toward one of the concepts that gave rise to the second-intentional concept, a concept such as that of being greater than, and it can only then aim at any being that is an instance of a relation (just as the mind, when thinking of the genus ANIMAL, can only fall upon a particular animal after aiming toward a concept of some particular species of animal). But the theorist's mind need never be redirected toward any real being; the theorist may think about a relation without ever thinking about specific instances of it in being, such as the ratio of the magnitude of one of the long sides of a certain rectangle to the magnitude of one of its short sides. Suppose, though, that in some instances at least the theorist's mind does continue to be redirected until it comes into intentional contact with real being. A concept is, by necessity, the result of a partial conception (or a partial taking into the mind) of the real being that gave rise to it, and especially so when the concept is conceived by second intentions. When some real being is viewed "through" a being of reason or concept (i.e., as an instance of the being of which it is a concept), the concept serves as a kind of filter, focusing the attention so as to limit the experience of the being to a reexperiencing of that which is already known about it—that which has already been conceived. Second intentions thereby hamper any new revelations about being; they deny being any real opportunity to unconceal or reveal itself. And any such opportunity is most certainly denied whenever the theorist's mind fails to aim toward any real being at all, standing firm in an intention toward a concept or being of reason. This purely reflexive aiming is most likely to occur when the concept that is its object is second-intentional, since such a concept is further removed from being than a first-intentional concept.

If a theorist has only second intentions while theorizing, and especially if second-intentional concepts are the sole objects of the theorist's intentions (which is not unlikely, because the being a theory is supposed to describe or explain is often conceived second-intentionally), any real intentional contact with being is wanting, and so any real opportunity for genuine discovery is passed over. If being is to unconceal itself and thereby guide the formation of theories about it, a theorist's mind must aim at it directly. This is not to say that second-intentional concepts should be avoided (for many theories require the introduction of signs tied to such concepts in order to achieve the appropriate level of generality), but just that they should be grounded in first intentions. Such concepts may even facilitate a revelation of being if they are compared to the first-intentional concepts upon which they are based, and to the being that gave rise to those concepts, to see if they "fit" the being of which they are supposed to be (secondary) concepts; whether or not they fit, the exercise of comparing them to being may lead the theorist to look at the being in a new way such that something about it is revealed.

Theorizing solely by means of second intentions toward second-intentional concepts is especially dangerous because such concepts can change so that, in addition to impeding the unconcealment of aspects of being not previously conceived, they actually come to *conceal* the nature of being. This kind of change is addressed next.

9.7 Conceptual Sedimentation and Sense Depletion

["The disciplines," said I,] "which we said did lay hold of being to some extent, geometry and also those [disciplines] attending it, are, as we see, dreaming about being, but a waking vision of it is impossible for them to behold so long as they leave unstirred the suppositions being used, not being able to offer an account of them. For when the origin is not examined, and the conclusion as well as the intervening steps are interwoven out of that which is not examined, what means can ever transform taken-for-grantedness such as this into understanding?" "None," said he.

Plato, *The Republic*

A scientific or philosophical concept, when originally conceived, may well reflect the being of which it is a concept—to the degree to which it is true to intuitions arising from first-intentional contemplation of the being conceived. But over the course of its use in theoretical and philosophical reasoning, and especially through its transmission to new generations of thinkers, a concept can diverge from and come to conceal its original sense.

Edmund Husserl (1859–1938) described such conceptual change as "sedimentation." If we regard a concept as it was originally conceived (ideally in a contemplation or noetic beholding of being) as the original "deposit," sedimentation can be understood as a process by which layers of sense are imposed upon the concept, usually with the effect of bringing it into line with contemporary philosophical views and contemporary methods, techniques, and tools (e.g., symbolic logic). It occurs when a concept is used without the being that originally gave rise to it ever getting contemplated anew. The additional layers of sense alter the way we regard that being, the perception of which is filtered through the concept; the mind falls upon the changed concept before it falls upon the being (if it falls upon it at all). As Husserl (1925/1977) put it, "Our opinions which stem from our theoretical or practical activities clothe our experience over, or clothe its sense with new layers of sense" (p. 41). The superimposed layers of sense conceal the original sense, the sense most likely to reflect the nature of the being that originally gave rise to the concept.

To uncover the original sense of a concept (which implies uncovering its ontic or first-intentional root or source, if it was conceived through first intentions), and to distinguish this sense from the acquired senses that cover it up, one must engage in what Husserl called "genetic analysis." Harvey (1989) describes it as follows:

Genetic analysis is the investigation backwards (*Zurückuntersuchung*) from the given, into the layers of accumulated sense that constitute the given. Or, more colorfully stated, it is the archaeological dig into the sense-chains of understanding. By uncovering these sense-chains, genetic phenomenology can restore meaning to knowledge domains that have become severed from their intuitive, intentional, and semantic roots. (pp. 52–53)

For a theory to be truly meaningful, the theorist must conduct such a dig through the layers of sense in any concept that guides the interpretation of a sign used in stating the theory and, having uncovered the original sense, examine that sense to make sure it is true to carefully sifted intuitions arising from first intentions—for even the original sense may carry conceptual baggage inherited from earlier thought. And so Husserl (1954/ 1970) said,

A theoretical task and achievement ... can only be and remain meaningful in a true and original sense *if* the scientist has developed in himself the ability to *inquire back* into the *original meaning* of all his meaning-structures and methods, i.e., into the *historical meaning of their primal establishment*, and especially into the meaning of all the *inherited meanings* taken over unnoticed in this primal establishment, as well as those taken over later on. (p. 56)

Few theorists currently see the need to inquire back into the original sense and the acquired senses of any given concept. A concept's contemporary sense is typically regarded as evident and not in need of examination, and it is imagined to have been immutable across generations. The concept gives the impression of what Husserl called *Selbstverständlichkeit*, literally 'self-understandability' or 'self-intelligibility'. Harvey (1989) describes this "obviousness" as the "taken-for-grantedness" of inherited ideas. Husserl argued that taking a concept for granted leads to 'sense depletion' (*Sinnentleerung*); the concept comes to reflect less and less the being from which it originated.

To the degree to which a concept is sedimented and depleted of sense, theories that make use of a sign interpreted in keeping with that concept fail to reveal the nature of being, and the science that permits itself to be guided by those theories is not sound, for it is not anchored to being. For this reason, Husserl cautioned scientists against adopting and using scientific concepts and terms in a thoughtless way:

It is easy to see that even in [ordinary] human life, and first of all in every individual life from childhood up to maturity, the originally intuitive life which creates its originally self-evident structures through activities on the basis of sense-experience very quickly and in increasing measure falls victim to the *seduction of language*. Greater and greater segments of this life lapse into a kind of talking and reading that is dominated purely by association; and often enough, in respect to the validities arrived at in this way, it is disappointed by subsequent experience.

Now one will say that in the sphere that interests us here—that of science, of thinking directed toward the attainment of truths and the avoidance of falsehood —one is obviously greatly concerned from the start to put a stop to the free play of associative constructions. In view of the unavoidable sedimentation of mental products in the form of persisting linguistic acquisitions, which can be taken up again at first merely passively and be taken over by anyone else, such constructions remain a constant danger. (1954/1970, app. 6, 362)

Husserl pointed out that the incorporation of a concept into mathematized theories, or into mathematics itself, and the facile manipulation, in formal operations, logical or otherwise, of a symbol for the being of which it is a concept increases the likelihood that it will become sedimented and sense-depleted. There is a tension between mathematics as a *technē* (i.e., a practical art) and mathematics as a science; proficiency at calculation and innovations that facilitate calculation may obstruct the unconcealment of being.

When the original sense of a concept that was conceived through first-intentional contemplation of being is discovered (e.g., through a careful and unprejudiced examination of ancient texts in the original languages, or through an etymological study of the roots of the word for the being of which it is a concept), it should seem natural and authentic, and, in my experience, it is readily intelligible—perhaps because it arises naturally from a contemplation of being that is entered into at will, or perhaps because, as Jacob Klein (1940) claimed, it somehow exists within the current sense and is understood semiconsciously or latently:

No science, in its actual progress, can escape the "seduction" emanating from the spoken and written word. For the signifying function of a word has, by its very nature, the tendency to lose its revealing character. The more we become accustomed to words, the less we perceive their original and precise "significance": a kind of superficial and "passive" understanding is the necessary result of the increasing familiarity with spoken and written words. The original mental activity, and production of significance, embodied in sounds and signs, is not reproduced in the course of actual communication. Yet it is there, in every word, somehow "forgotten" but still at the bottom of our speaking and our understanding, however vague the meaning conveyed by our speech might be. The original "evidence" has faded away but has not disappeared completely. It need not be "awakened" even, it actually underlies our mutual understanding in a "sedimented" form. "Sedimentation is always somehow forgetfulness" [(Husserl 1939, 212)]. And this kind of forgetfulness accompanies, of necessity, the development and growth of a science.

He added,

The "sedimentation of significance" can reach such a degree that a particular science, and science in general, appear almost devoid of "significance." (pp. 155–156)

These critical problems of sedimentation and sense depletion can be truly understood only through an examination of instances of them. And so I devote most of the remainder of this chapter to genetic analyses of three concepts: that of a number, that of a relation, and that of a predicate. An "archaeological dig" into the layers of sense in these concepts will, moreover, be of benefit to theorists because of their wide use in scientific theories. These three concepts are examined together because sedimentation in the number concept was accompanied by sedimentation in the concept of a relation, and the latter contributed to sedimentation in the concept of a predicate.

I will not attempt to give a complete or fully documented history of changes in each concept. (See McPherson 1995, apps. A and B, for somewhat fuller treatments.) I aim only to give the reader a feel for the ways in which scientific concepts can change and what sorts of forces can drive the changes. I begin, in each case, with a description of the concept as it was understood in classical Greece, for I have concluded (on the basis of my studies of relevant Greek texts) that when these concepts were conceived by Greek scholars (some of the first thinkers to treat of them thoughtfully), they arose from these thinkers' own reflections upon concepts arising from first intentions. In each case, the original sense of the concept will be seen to come from conceptions of things present in or somehow depending upon real being, whereas the current sense of the concept is such as to lead to the conclusion that its conception did not involve any real being; it is, rather, an *ens rationis* in the most literal sense, something that can reside only in the mind.

9.7.1 Numbers

Natural numbers were made by God; the rest is the work of man.

Leopold Kronecker

In ancient Greek thought, numbers were distinct from the continuous magnitudes of geometry; what we would call positive whole numbers were the whole of number. Moreover, numbers were always tied to collections of individuals of some kind (see Klein 1934–1936/1968). As Aristotle revealed, a number, in the Greek way of thinking, is always a number *of* particular things (*Metaphysics* N.5, 1092^b19–20), whether apples or fingers or coins; it is the number of individuals of one species or genus in a definite collection (*Metaphysics* N.1, 1088^a8–14).

In the Greek science of numbers (i.e., arithmetic), the concept of a monad figured prominently. Some modern scholars claim that monads were understood as abstract units to be counted, which may be taken to imply that numbers were not always tied to real individuals. But there is evidence that a monad was understood as a boundary or partition *between* items being counted, where the items are individual beings of one species; a monad may have been understood to separate or partition off one individual as it was added to a collection of individuals already separated out in counting (as Robert H. Schmidt has argued, in conversation; alternatively, a monad may have been understood as a resting-place or stopping-place, *monē*, for the movements (say, of a finger or hand) making up the act of separating out an individual as items are counted in succession—as the *telos* or end of one cycle of movements during counting). This thesis is compatible with Aristotle's description of counting as 'by parts' or 'by portions' (*kata meridas*), which implies separating something out and setting it apart or allotting it, and as 'takings in [or additions]' (*proslambanontes*; *Metaphysics* M.7, 1082^{b}34–36), as well as his description of a count (i.e., a number;[9] *arithmos*) as 'a delimited multitude' (*plēthos peperasmenon*; *Metaphysics* Δ.13, 1020^{a}13) and Eudoxus's definition of a count as 'a multitude marked [or separated] out by boundaries' (*plēthos hōrismenon*; see Klein 1934–1936/1968, 51). It is also compatible with Aristotle's characterization of monads as being one after another or in succession (*ephexēs*; *Physics* E.3, 227^{a}29–30), his description of a monad (along with a point, a line, and a plane) as something by which a body gets marked (or separated) out by boundaries (or bounded, defined, or delimited; *[toutōi] hōristai to sōma*; *Metaphysics* B.5, 1002^{a}4–6), and his description of a count or counting (*arithmos*) as that which marks (or separates) out by boundaries (or bounds, defines, or delimits) all things (*horizein panta*; *Metaphysics* Δ.8, 1017^{b}20–21). The thesis accords as well with a statement of Nicomachus: 'By means of the monad, all the counts having begun from the dyad, being separated out together one after another, generate the orderly species of that which is multiple in the proper sequence' (see Klein 1934–1936/1968, 52, for the Greek).

If monads were, in addition or instead, understood by some mathematicians to be the items of counting themselves, they nonetheless seem not to have been regarded as separate from real beings, but rather as *present in* real beings.[10] A monad (*monas*, 'aloneness', derived from *monos*, 'alone' or 'solitary') seems sometimes to have been understood as the *oneness* in an atomic being as isolated by abstraction in the Greek sense, that is, what is left over in an atom (e.g., a cat) when all its particular properties other than its oneness—a oneness concomitant with its indivisibility as something informed by its *eidos* or species (or "basic-level kind"; see Aristotle, *Metaphysics* B.3, 999^{a}1–6; Δ.6, 1016^{b}3–6; M.3, 1078^{a}23–25)—are mentally stripped away from it. (See *Metaphysics* K.3, 1061^{a}29–35, and *Categories* 7, 7ª31–7ᵇ9, for examples of abstraction as the Greeks understood it—*aphairesis*, 'taking away from', 'carrying off', or 'removal', or *periairesis*, 'taking away that which surrounds' or 'stripping off'.) This thesis (and the partition thesis as well) is in line with Euclid's definition of a monad: 'A monad is that because of which [or in accordance with which] each of the beings gets called one' (*Elements*, bk. 7, def. 1; see Heath 1956). Also compatible with the abstraction thesis are Aristotle's arguments that mathematical entities (presumably including the monad) do not exist separately from beings (*Metaphysics* M.2), even though they are sometimes considered separately by arithmeticians and geometricians (*Metaphysics* M.2; M.3, 1078ª21–23; *On the Soul* Γ.7, 431ᵇ15–17), and that *arithmoi* in particular, which are counts of monads, do not exist separately (*Metaphysics* M.8).[11] The understanding of a monad as the oneness in an atom that is concomitant with the indivisibility deriving from its species is complemented by the understanding as a partition, for to delimit or define the items of counting by means of a partition is to reveal which species is the source of oneness for each of them. Counting individuals delimited in this way may even, in some sense, effect the abstraction that leaves only the oneness in a being, for to separate out an individual and count it as one is to ignore everything about the individual except its being an atom or monad; in being counted (and in having been counted), an individual is understood as one—as a monad.

It seems, then, that a number (or count) was normally understood to exist only by virtue of a collection of beings of the same kind, as the count of individuals in that collection. For the ancients, numbers could not exist independently of collections of beings.

This view was preserved by Roman mathematicians, but they created a numeric notation that allowed them to use collections of strokes on papyrus as the objects of their calculations (much as the Babylonians had used collections of slim wedge-shaped impressions in clay in their calculations). These exemplars of collections could take the place of other collections to facilitate reckoning. In the Roman numeral system (as in the Babylonian numeral system), the symbols for the numbers one through three are *I*, *II*, and *III*. A manipulation of these symbols is a manipulation of collections—collections of strokes. These collections can stand for, or stand in for, collections of individuals of any kind whatsoever (Schmidt 1986). Schmidt calls them "counterparts," and I will use this term here. A counterpart is not a *sign* for a collection, but an *example* of one that can stand in for another so that operations on it stand in for operations on the collection for which it is a counterpart. Schmidt gives as another example of a counterpart a nautical chart. A course is planned on the chart, whereupon the planned movements are executed in the place that the chart represents. In a comparable way, manipulations of numeric counterparts lead to results that can be transferred to any other collections having the same numbers of individuals: if two strokes counted together with three strokes gives a collection of five strokes, then two coins counted together with three coins will give a collection of five coins. The Roman numeral for the number five, V, is not itself a collection of strokes, but it was understood to be a sign for, or rather shorthand for or a proxy for, five strokes; it meant IIIII. And so some Roman numerals (e.g., V, X, L) were not themselves counterparts, but stood in the place of counterparts and were operated upon just as if they were the counterparts they stood for.

When the Hindu-Arabic numeric notation became popular in the West, late in the twelfth century, the symbols seem initially to have been understood in just the same way as the Roman numeral V, namely, as shorthand marks or proxies for collections of strokes on paper that were counterparts for collections of individuals of any kind whatsoever. (Leonardo of Pisa—now known as Leonardo Fibonacci—called his book of 1202 on Hindu-Arabic numeric symbols and algebra *Liber Abbaci*, 'Book of the Abacus'. The new numeric symbols would have brought to mind an abacus because both the counters on an abacus and the digits of a Hindu-Arabic numeral were understood as counterparts in a place-value system.) Alternatively, the symbols may have been understood as proxies for Roman numerals, which were either counterparts for collections of individuals or shorthand or proxies for such counterparts (Schmidt 1986).

Over time, this understanding of the symbols was lost; mathematicians began to forget that their symbols were originally intended to be proxies for counterparts. As a result, the symbols began to lose their conceptual tie with collections of individuals, and the number concept began to change correspondingly, losing its basis in multitude.

With collections of individuals no longer consciously guiding the conception of number, the concept became more inclusive. Proper fractions were reinterpreted as numbers; ratios (newly interpreted as quotients) of whole numbers and of commensurable magnitudes were reinterpreted as (rational) numbers; and ratios of incommensurable magnitudes were reinterpreted as (irrational) numbers (or at least this seems to be the way in which irrational numbers were originally understood; in modern times, irrationals are understood as "real" numbers invented so as to fill in gaps in the "real number line," where the filling of gaps is accomplished by means of Dedekind cuts or Cauchy sequences). For the number concept to include fractions of units, quotients of any two numbers, and quotients of any two magnitudes, whether commensurable or not, a number had to have been newly conceived as something similar in nature to a continuous magnitude; and so it had, as John Dee (1527–1608) explained:

Practice has led *Numbers* farther, and has framed them, to take upon them, the show of *Magnitudes'* property: Which is *Incommensurability* and *Irrationality*. (For in pure *Arithmetic*, a *Unit*, is the common Measure of all Numbers.) And, here, Numbers are become, as Lines, Planes and Solids: sometimes *Rational*, sometimes *Irrational*. (1570/1975, 5)

The change in the concept likely came about because mathematicians thoughtlessly began to perform operations that the syntaxes of their mathematical languages permitted (such as multiplying and dividing, not just numbers, but also ratios) but that were not meaningful until the concept of number changed. This may be what Dee meant by "practice" framing numbers to take on a property of magnitudes.

Though the new concept of number as continuous like magnitude seems implicit in mathematical writings of the late Middle Ages and the early Renaissance, the first mathematician to whom an explicit espousal of it is attributed is Simon Stevin (1548–1620). He viewed number as a property of magnitude comparable to the wetness of water:

Number is something in magnitude comparable to wetness in water, for as this extends everywhere and in each part of the water, so number tied to some magnitude extends everywhere and in each part of its magnitude: Just as to a water continuum there corresponds a wetness continuum, so to a magnitude continuum there corresponds a number continuum. Just as the wetness continuum of the entirety of the water undergoes the same division and separation as its water, so the number continuum undergoes the same division and separation as its magnitude, so that these two quantities cannot be distinguished by continuity and discontinuity. (1585/1958a, 502)

Stevin may have been influenced by his own adoption of decimal notation for fractions (see Stevin 1585/1958b). He was one of the first mathematicians in the West to use decimal fractions, and the first to successfully promote their use. Acceptance of this notation could lead one to believe that there is a number for every possible decimal expansion, so that the numbers can fill up a continuum.

Stevin even went so far as to argue that the notion of discontinuous (or whole) numbers is merely a product of the imagination:

All that is just a quantity is not at all a disjunct quantity. Sixty, according as it is number, is a quantity (that is to say a number). Sixty, then, according as it is number, is not at all a disjunct quantity. As for that which you divide by your imagination, this proposed unique and whole quantity, into sixty *unities* [or *units*] (which you could divide, by equal reason, into thirty dualities, or twenty trinities, etc.), and which then you next define [to be] the divided up, that is not definition of the proposed of which there is some question: you could similarly divide the proposed magnitude, by the imagination, into sixty *parts*, and then by equal reason define it to be discontinuous quantity, which is absurd. (1585/1958a, 501–502; emphasis added)

So for Stevin, at least, numbers had become completely divorced from collections of beings and multitude. But this means that numbers had (ironically) moved completely into the realm of imagination, as *entia rationis* alone (despite the reality Stevin attributed to the "number" he imagined to be inhering in magnitudes).

Stevin's view of number as continuous found easy acceptance, perhaps because of its practical utility, or the utility of the associated decimal fractions, and perhaps also because it had been implicit in mathematical reasoning for some time (despite explicit rejections of the irrational numbers it permitted; e.g., Frater Fredericus said, c. 1460, 'An irrational number is not a number. For a number is that which a unit measures'; in 1544, Michael Stifel said that 'an irrational number is not a true number'; see Klein 1934–1936/1968, 251, n. 176; in 1560, Jacques Peletier argued that irrational numbers are not numbers in the absolute sense, but that they are nonetheless necessary in practice, even though unintelligible; he said that what they truly represent 'conceals itself in perpetual darkness'; see Klein 1934–1936/1968, 290, n. 302). The new number concept may also have been welcomed because it facilitated contemporaneous attempts to submit both numbers and magnitudes to algebraic treatment; doing so presupposed either interpreting geometric objects as special cases of numbers (as John Wallis seems to have done[12]) or interpreting arithmetic objects (i.e., numbers) as special cases of geometric magnitudes (as Descartes may have done[13]). But not all mathematicians understood the new, continuous number in the same way as Stevin. John Wallis (1616–1703) assimilated his concept of number to the concept of a ratio of continuous magnitudes. In Greek geometry, continuous magnitudes acquired something comparable to values only through comparison with other (commensurable) continuous magnitudes; for instance, the magnitude of one side of a triangle was understood quantitatively in terms of its magnitude *relative to* the magnitude of another side of the triangle—that is, the ratio that magnitude had to the magnitude chosen as a standard. (For the Greeks, this ratio was always understood in relational, not numeric, terms; as will be seen in the next section, it was only much later understood to be a number.) For Wallis, any number was a ratio of some quantity to a unit quantity, or rather the quotient of the antecedent and consequent of that ratio (which he called an 'index' or 'exponent'):

The whole of arithmetic itself, if looked at more closely, seems scarcely other than a doctrine of ratios. And numbers themselves [are] indices of just so many ratios whose common consequent is I, unity [i.e., the unit]. For when I, or unity, is regarded as [the] quantity set forth [as the reference unit], all the rest of the numbers (whether whole, or broken, or even irrational) are indices or exponents of just so many ratios of other [quantities] to [the] quantity set forth [i.e., to unity]. (*Mathesis Universalis*; for the Latin, see Wallis 1657/1695, *Opera*, vol. 1, as cited in Klein 1934–1936/1968, 220–221)

In this interpretation of numbers, Wallis attempts to understand the strange new continuous numbers in terms of the more familiar geometric concept of a ratio of magnitudes.

When even quotients of incommensurable magnitudes came to be understood as numbers, mathematicians could imagine that to every point along a continuous magnitude there corresponds a number.[14] To facilitate calculation, they even came to include negative numbers among the so-called real numbers. With no possible tie to multitude or even geometric magnitude, numbers were now fully divorced from any *entia realis* (making ironic the appellation "real numbers"). In the modern view, numbers correspond to points on the "number line," an imaginary entity that allows number to be understood to be continuous and extending to infinity in two directions from an origin.

With numbers divorced from *entia realis*, mathematicians got into great muddles trying to describe the interpretation of a numeral. Gottlob Frege (1813–1890), for instance, took a numeral to be a proper name for a number, which is, according to him, an invisible and locationless but self-subsistent individual of some mysterious sort defined in terms of one-to-one correspondence (see Frege 1884/1980). This odd view may again reveal an effect of notation. The interpretation of a numeral as a proper name for an individual of some sort follows naturally from the notation that mathematicians had come to use. In natural language, numerals enter mostly as quantifiers with count nouns for individuals (e.g., *three cats*), in keeping with the Greek (and presumably our first-intentional) understanding of numbers; but in modern mathematical notation, numerals appear in isolation, just as proper names do in noun phrases. (The Greeks always placed a count noun next to a numeral, because a number was always a number *of something*; in arithmetic, the noun was *monas*— 'monad'. The disappearance from mathematics of count nouns is a consequence of number moving into the realm of the purely imaginary, where numbers are no longer counts of beings; instead, they are points on the number line.)

Some mathematicians steered clear of the muddles by abandoning attempts to interpret a numeral. Mathematicians in the formalist camp came to view the written or typed marks on paper that are instances of numerals as the objects of mathematics, and operating on symbols, or syntactic manipulation, as the whole of number science. The symbols are not interpreted at all, in this way of thinking.

The concept of number seems to have become one of what Husserl (1954/1970) called "ideas emptied [of sense] which have been obscured and have become mere word-concepts; ideas burdened, through attempts at exposition, with false interpretations" (p. 74). The concept has become so weirdly distant from anything involving real being that numeric symbols have become little more than tokens—in the sense of vestiges of the numeric proxies for counterparts that mathematicians used into the Renaissance (for a numeral is no longer understood as shorthand for or a proxy for a counterpart for a collection of beings), as well as in the sense of formal marks that signal the permissibility of certain operations upon them. The original sense of the concept survives in only the vaguest forms, namely, in the fact that definitions of number begin with the definition of the natural numbers (though these include zero and one; the former is not a count, and the latter was originally the *measure* for counting) and in the fact that these numbers are defined in terms of succession, which is understood (if not initially defined) in terms of successive additions of one (but not of one *thing*) as an imperfect reflection of counting in the Greek mode. But as soon as the integers (which include negative numbers), the rationals, and the reals enter the picture, the original sense is tossed aside. This is not to deny the utility of the modern number concept in practical applications, but that utility depends upon interpreting a positive number that is the result of calculations as the measure of the multitude of the beings in a collection, or as a multiple of unit magnitudes (such as inches or centimeters).

Changes in the concept of number appear to be attributable, in a great measure, to changes in notation that set up conditions for forgetfulness about the original sense (see also Schmidt 1986). The Hindu-Arabic numeric notation made the counterpart function of numerals invisible, opening the door to the imposition of a new layer of sense upon the number concept (with the new sense apparently seeping into mathematics through initially meaningless extensions of mathematical operations that were permitted by the syntaxes of mathematical languages). The modern sense of the number concept, with number regarded as continuous like magnitude, fully covered over the original sense after the introduction into widespread use of decimal fractions.

9.7.2 Relations

A new interpretation of the ratio accompanied the new interpretation of number as continuous. The ratio was the prototypical relation for mathematicians, and so the new understanding of it may be responsible for observable change in the concept of a relation in general.

Greek mathematicians understood a ratio to be an aspect of the being of one magnitude or number as considered relative to another. So a magnitude—say, one side of a given triangle (understood as a magnitude, i.e., as a length)—having a ratio of 2:1 to another magnitude—say, one of the other sides of the triangle (understood as a magnitude)—was seen to have as a part of its being doubleness in relation to the other; the greater magnitude was understood to be the subject or substrate for the doubleness, which was determined or defined by reference to the lesser magnitude, the object of the relation. A relation of any sort was understood in this way, as an aspect of the being of one individual, its subject, defined with reference to another individual, its object.

Oddly enough, ratios came to be interpreted as *numbers*. The ratio 6:3 is now interpreted as the common fraction 6/3, which is equal to the number 2, the result of dividing the numerator by the denominator (i.e., the quotient). We call the numbers that are identified with the new "ratios" *rational numbers*.

The reinterpretation of ratios as numbers seems to have been tied to the new concept of number as something along a continuum. When numbers were no longer understood as measured multitudes, but as exponents or indices of ratios of magnitudes (for Wallis), properties of magnitudes (Stevin), or multiples of unit magnitudes (Descartes), the result of the division of the antecedent of a ratio by the consequent could be interpreted as a number whether or not the result was a whole number. Even before numbers were *explicitly* interpreted as continuous, the potential reinterpretation of ratios as numbers may have been at least partially actualized through forgetfulness concerning the use of what were called "denominations." In use from the late Middle Ages, denominations are names given to ratios, taken from their "base" ratios. A ratio—say, $6:3$—is denominated by the ratio of the smallest numbers for which the antecedent is in the same relation to the consequent—or $2:1$ in this case. But how did denominations contribute to a reinterpretation of ratios as numbers? It seems that denominations themselves came to be understood as numbers. Probably the first to be so understood were denominations of the prototypical ratios, "multiples" such as double ($2:1$) and triple ($3:1$), which are ratios to the unit; such denominations were especially likely to come to be understood as numbers because they were given as the antecedent alone (e.g., 2 for $2:1$, 3 for $3:1$). But it seems that the denomination for any ratio of commensurables came to be understood as a number; Thomas of Bradwardine (1290–1349) said that any ratio of commensurables 'is immediately denominated by some *number*, just as in the case of the ratio double, and triple, even so in the cases of the others' (1328/1955, 66; emphasis added). Moreover, from the thirteenth century onward, denominations were used in mathematical computations just as if they were numbers.

When ratios came to be interpreted as numbers, mathematicians' understanding of relations seems to have changed concomitantly. The number to which a ratio is reduced—say, the quotient 2 as the reduction of the ratio $6:3$—is not an aspect of the being of the antecedent defined by reference to the consequent; it is, rather, *a separate individual number.* (The 2 is a measure of parts of the antecedent, where each part is equal to the consequent; but unlike the *ratio* of that measure to unity, or $2:1$, it is not *relational.*) A relation in general likewise came to be viewed as separate from the two individuals involved, not present in either individual—a third "thing" of some sort. For this reason, scholars ceased speaking of the relation *of* one thing *to* another (where the *of* implies that the relation *belongs to* the first thing, and the *to* implies that the relation is defined with reference *to* the second thing). They began to speak instead of the relation *between* two things. This way of talking seems to imply that a relation came to be viewed as something that exists in neither individual, but that exists between them somehow, connecting them with one another. With a relation newly conceived as a connection of some sort, it can involve more than two individuals, in which case it is sometimes spoken of as a relation *among* individuals.

Gottfried Wilhelm Leibniz (1646–1716) wrote what is perhaps the first and maybe even the only explicit description of the modern "relation." He characterized it as a type of relation distinct from the usual and described it as an 'ideal thing', which meant, for him, an idea in the mind of God (e.g., 1714/1902, 262). His description of the new "relation" appears in a letter written to Isaac Newton's disciple Samuel Clarke:

> The ratio or proportion *between* two lines L and M can be conceived in three ways: as a ratio *of* the greater L *to* the lesser M, as a ratio *of* the lesser M *to* the greater L, and finally as *something abstracted from the two*, that is to say as the ratio *between* L and M, without considering which is the antecedent or the consequent, the subject or the object.... In the first consideration, L the greater is the subject; in the second, M the lesser is the subject of that accident, that the philosophers call relation or rapport. But which of them will be the subject in the third sense? One could not say that both of them, L and M together, are the subject of such an accident, for that way we would have one accident in two subjects, which would have one leg in the one, and the other [leg] in the other, which is contrary to the notion of accidents. Therefore one must say, that this rapport [or relation] in this third sense is really *outside of the subjects*; but that being neither substance nor accident, it must be *a purely ideal thing*, the consideration of which is nonetheless useful. (1717/1965b, 401; emphasis added)

By the "ideal" relation "abstracted" from the two lines, Leibniz likely meant the *order* of the magnitudes of the two lines, for elsewhere he described time and space as orders that he called "relations" (see Leibniz 1717/1965b), and, in the following passage, he again describes orders, as well as various other arrangements of interrelated entities, as individual relations:

> There are ... examples of a relation among several things at once, as that of order or that of a genealogical tree, which expresses the rank and the connection of all the terms or members; and even a figure like that of a polygon contains the relation of all the sides. (1765/1965a, 211)

A "relation" in the new sense (which was, for Leibniz, an idea in the mind of God) cannot be present in any *ens realis*, and so it can be nothing more than an *ens rationis* in the minds of modern thinkers.

In mathematics, a relation (or what is called a "binary relation") has come to be defined and understood as a *set of ordered pairs*. The order is such that the first coordinate in a pair is always in the relation to the second coordinate in the pair. The set of all the first coordinates and the set of all the second coordinates are called the "domain" and the "range" of the relation, respectively. A relation defined as a set of ordered pairs of individuals resembles Leibniz's favorite "ideal" relation, namely, an *order* of individuals; but it is not the order itself; it is, rather, ordered *individuals*. It is a poor reflection of a relation in the original sense, for both coordinates are *individuals*—say, the numbers 6 and 3 (or delimited multitudes of 6 and 3 individuals, if numbers are interpreted more traditionally)— whereas a relation—say, *double*—is just one aspect of the being of an individual (or of a delimited multitude of individuals), which is defined with reference to another individual (or to another delimited multitude of individuals)—say, of 6 (defined with reference to 3); the doubleness of 6 as compared to 3 is not equivalent to 6 or to 3, or to 6 and 3 considered together, or to their order. The order of two individuals in an ordered pair is a conventional way of signaling which individual bears the relation and which individual it is related to, which reveals the stamp of the original sense of the concept. But since the *inverse* of a relation, or the set of ordered pairs with the order reversed, is usually *identified* with the relation, and since sets of ordered triples, ordered quadruples, and so on, are also considered to be relations, the modern sense of a relation as something separate from and somehow connecting the individuals involved has evidently been laid over the original sense. And since a relation is *defined* as a set of ordered pairs, as opposed to an aspect of the being of the first coordinate as considered relative to the second coordinate, the original sense is covered over with yet another layer of sense. The original sense nonetheless peeks through the formalization in the ordering of the individuals in a pair (with the bearer of the relation first in the order). The original sense of *relation* somehow lies at the bottom of the mathematical concept, but the Leibnizian notion and another idea, that of individuals in a certain order, are laid over the original sense.

The concept of a relation had its original sense covered over, it seems, primarily because of a new conception of the prototypical relation, the ratio—a new conception tied to change in the concept of number. An additional layer of sense that conceals further the original sense came to be laid upon the concept as a result of its being incorporated into set-theoretical mathematics, which deals only with individuals—individuals qua individuals—so that relational being can be accommodated only through placing individuals possessing it and the individuals to which they are referred into sets. Set theory provides no means for dealing with relational being in a way true to its nature as an aspect of the being of some substrate, dependent for its existence upon that individual and some other individual to which the former is referred so as to define the relation.

9.7.3 Predicates and Predication

Aristotle's teachings on *logos* in the *Organon* reveal a highly developed understanding of predicates and predication. Though his view was probably unique to him, his concepts of predicates and predication appear to be based on first intentions, so they are worthy of careful consideration—especially because they are so well hidden in modern translations and treatments of his works.

The words Aristotle used for a predicate and predication are clues to his concepts of them. The noun he used for a predicate is *katēgoria*, which is derived from the verb he used for predication, *katēgoreō*. This verb means 'accuse', or literally 'speak out against publicly'; it is formed from the prepositional prefix *kata*, 'against', and the verb *agoreuō*, 'speak in the agora (i.e., the assembly of the people)'. In common language, the noun *katēgoria* was used for the speech for the prosecutor in front of a tribunal (and it was opposed to *apologia*, the speech for the defendant). Aristotle sometimes used another expression for predication, one synonymous with *katēgoreō*: *legō kata tinos*, 'speak against someone/something'. Aristotle's choice of expressions for a predicate and predication[15] suggests that he regarded predication as an attribution of responsibility to the subject for whatever the predicate signifies (cf. Heidegger 1927/1962). In accusing someone of some deed, we hold that person responsible for it; we claim that the person gave rise to it. (In Athenian law, an accusation could be made against an animal or something inanimate if, say, it had played a part in a death by unnatural causes (see McPherson 1995). So the use of accusation as a metaphor for predication would not carry the implication that predication is restricted to predications about persons.)

Aristotle seems to have based his ascription of responsibility to the subject on its being the origin or *archē* of that which the predicate signifies. He used the verb *huparchō* to describe what a predicate does in relation to a subject. This word contains, as a prefix, the preposition *hupo*, 'under', and the verb *archō*, 'originate'. It means to originate *under* in the sense of being dependent upon or under the power of.[16] So Aristotle seems to have understood the being a predicate signifies to originate in dependency upon a subject. (In *On Interpretation* 5, 17ᵃ23–24, he said that 'the simple declarative sentence [*apophansis*] is significant spoken sound about whether something [in the case of an affirmation] originates in dependency [*huparchei*] or [in the case of a denial] does not originate in dependency'. In *Prior Analytics* A.37, 49ª6–8, he explained that this dependent origination is to be apprehended differently for each of the 10 schemata of predication, or *katēgoriai*.) Much the same idea is implied by the word chosen for a subject: *hupokeimenon*, the present (middle) participle of the verb *hupokeimai*, 'underlie', here used as a nominal, means 'that which is underlying'. The subject is the being that supports the being signified by the predicate; it is its substrate and its source.

Laying an accusation against someone also brings something about that person to light; it reveals something brought into being by that person (say, an unlawful deed), something that was hidden. Aristotle seems also to have understood predication to reveal, or make noetically manifest, something about the subject.[17] This view is revealed, again, in his terminology. His word for a declarative sentence, which combines a predicate with a subject and a copula, is *apophansis*; the preposition *apo* that appears as a prefix means 'away from' or 'forth', and *phansis* is equivalent to *phasis*, a noun derived from the verb *phainō*, this verb meaning 'bring to light', 'cause to appear', 'show', 'uncover', or 'reveal', but also 'denounce' or 'inform against'. The primary meaning of the word *apophansis* seems to have been 'showing forth'. In contrasting the effect of an apophantic utterance with the effect of an isolated word, Aristotle said, 'Now the noun as well as the *rhēma* [i.e., verb or adjective], let it be [called] only an utterance, for one is not, in speaking in this way, making something [noetically] manifest with that spoken sound so as [for it] to show itself forth [*apophainesthai*]' (*On Interpretation* 5, 17ª17–19). His use of the middle-voice form of the infinitive of the verb *apophainō* reveals that the subject is showing *itself* forth, from itself (see Heidegger 1927/ 1962); for much the same reason, Aristotle described the sorts of being signified in the different schemata of predication—the *katēgoriai*—as *kath' hauta*, or 'because of (or in accordance with) themselves' (*Metaphysics* Δ.7, 1017ª22–23).[18] The nature of the showing can be discerned through a consideration of the word *phasis* that is a part of the word *apophansis*, and that is also a part of the words for an affirmation and a denial, that is, a positive and a negative declarative statement, namely, *kataphasis* and *apophasis*.[19] *Phasis* (as derived from *phainō*; *phasis* was derived from *phēmi* as well) had one meaning that seems to be particularly enlightening in this context: it was used for the appearance of a (fixed or wandering) star as it rose above the horizon, and especially for its first such appearance after a period of concealment under the sun's beams (i.e., for its heliacal rising). So the word strongly suggests something that was hidden coming to light or becoming manifest. The same suggestion comes from another source. As Aristotle pointed out, *apophansis* is the only kind of utterance that can be judged true or false; neither an individual word or phrase nor a sentence of any other type (e.g., a question, a prayer, a request, or a command) can be said to be true or false (see *On Interpretation* 1, 16^a9–18; 4, 16^b33–17^a4). But the Greek word translated as 'true' is *alēthēs* (*a-lēth-ēs*), 'taking out of hiding' or 'unconcealing' (or 'unconcealed'). The privative or negative prefix *a-* expresses want or absence, loss, or forcible removal, and the verbal stem contained in this adjective is that of the verb *lēthō* or *lanthanō*, which means 'escape notice', 'be unseen', 'be unnoticed', or 'be unknown'; in the middle and passive voices, this verb means 'forget'. So the word usually translated as 'true' suggests something failing or ceasing to escape one's notice or remain unseen; it suggests something that was hidden or forgotten—or something unknown—being brought to light or revealed. (The Greek word for *false* is *pseudēs*, 'deceitful' or 'lying'; it means giving the impression of unconcealing something without doing so.)

That which predication brings to light is *being*. This is evident in the fact that the copula, in any language that has it, is the verb meaning 'be'. In declarative statements, the copula (whether or not it is explicit)—which is conjugated to agree with the subject (in person and number)—indicates that being is unconcealed from the subject.[20] (When a predicate and the copula combine with a subject, the being that is shown forth or unconcealed from the subject—the being that the predicate signifies—is being that depends for its existence upon the subject, its support and its origin. When the copula combines with a subject alone, as in *Socrates was*, the being unconcealed is that of the subject as a whole.) And so Aristotle said that the 'is' in an affirmation signifies that it is true or unconcealing (*Metaphysics* Δ.7, 1017^a31–34), that being is the true or the unconcealed, and that a true affirmation is unconcealing because the being signified by the predicate is lying together with the being signified by the subject (*Metaphysics* Θ.10, 1051^a34–1051^b13).

The nature of the experience of an unconcealment of being is revealed in the use of the word *epistēmē* for the understanding that comes from hearing a true apophantic utterance or a syllogism or dialectical argument in which such utterances are properly combined. This noun is derived from the verb *epistamai*, which is believed to be an old middle-voice form of *ephistēmi*; the latter is composed of the prepositional prefix *epi*, mean-

ing 'upon', and the verb *histēmi*, which has among its intransitive meanings 'stand', 'stand still', and 'stand firm'. And so the most literal meaning
of the nominal *epistēmē* (formed with the suffix *-mē*) would seem to be
'standing upon', 'standing still upon', or 'standing firm upon'; what we
call *understanding* (or standing under) was called *overstanding* (or standing over or upon). The standing would seem to be the mind's standing
upon unconcealed being. Aristotle regarded this standing as a stillness or
resting of the mind—resting not in the sense of being slack, but in the
sense of being arrested by a tension in one direction: 'Mental perception
[*noēsis*] is more like a sort of rest [or stillness] and stopping than motion'
(*On the Soul* A.3, 407ª32–33); 'When the discursive thought [*dianoia*] has
come to rest and has come to a standstill, we are said to stand upon [or
understand; *epistasthai*] and to intend [or attend; *phronein*]' (*Physics* H.3,
247ᵇ11–12). The experience Aristotle described is likely the aiming of the
mind that is concomitant with an unconcealment of being; in intending or
aiming toward being, the mind is necessarily standing firm for so long as
the being is unconcealed—for when it ceases to stand still, it will turn in
other directions, and the being toward which it was aimed will slip out of
awareness, entering into or returning to a state of escaping one's notice or
being hidden or forgotten.

The Aristotelian account of predication and of the *apophansis* or
showing forth that results from it implies that hearing or reading or
saying to oneself "Cats are furry" makes the being of cats' furriness—
being that originates in and depends upon cats—appear noetically to
the mind as it aims toward that being, which was escaping one's notice,
hidden from consciousness or forgotten, and which now comes to light
(and remains in the light until the mind ceases to stand firm, aimed
toward it, and turns elsewhere).

After the Aristotelian theory of predication was forgotten, concepts of
predication were swept every which way with the currents of philosophical movements, like shifting sediment. For a partial history of the various
views that arose, see McPherson 1995. Briefly, here are a few of those
views: According to nominalists such as William of Ockham, the subject
and the predicate are names for the same thing (and Geach (1962) has
thoroughly trounced this view). In the opinion of Thomas Hobbes, they
are marks that bring to mind thoughts of the same thing. James Mill,
influenced by Hume's and Hartley's associationism, asserted that they are
names for ideas experienced in succession or concurrently. The theories of
Hobbes and Mill are examples of one general trend. Under the influence

of materialism—a tenet that precludes any serious consideration of first intentions—many thinkers came to deny that linguistic signs can bring the mind into any relation to being. The force of the copula 'be' was forgotten, and predication came to be seen as a relation of one mental entity (e.g., a concept or an idea) to another. As such, it could not involve any attribution of responsibility for the origination of being, or any unconcealment of being.

A view revealing another trend had become the "established opinion" by the mid-nineteenth century (Mill 1851, 103) and still prevails: the idea that the subject is included in a class of things that the predicate is supposed to signify; *Cats are furry* is supposed to mean that cats are included in the class of furry things. John Stuart Mill (1851) described this theory as "a signal example of a logical error very often committed in logic, that of ... explaining a thing by something which presupposes it" (p. 104); predication in the original sense is presupposed in the class-inclusion approach because the class of furry things cannot be defined unless one can determine which things are furry—that is, of which things the predicate *furry* can be truly predicated. This class-inclusion approach is in keeping with a trend toward extensional versus intensional thinking. As modern times approached, the extensional (e.g., spatial dimensions of bodies) came to be deemed more and more real as compared to the intensional (i.e., that which intensifies and remits, such as a form or a quality; more and more qualities came to be considered "secondary," or primarily subjective). This trend is evident in Descartes's assertions that only extension and its concomitants (e.g., figure and motion) can be deemed real with any certainty, the reality of qualities being questionable (e.g., *Meditations on First Philosophy* 3), and that extension is the essence of bodily substance (e.g., *Principles of Philosophy* 3). (Robert H. Schmidt has argued, in conversation, that this extensional bias arose because of a desire to follow Galileo in seeking a mathematical reality behind the appearances combined with a continuing failure to adequately measure intensive magnitudes so that intensions could be mathematized—a failure that led to the abandonment of this measurement problem.) With the reality of intensional being (such as a quality) qua intensional widely denied, such being came to be reinterpreted as a collection, a class or a set, so that it could be imagined to be extensional rather than intensional.

As modern symbolic logic developed, the class-inclusion interpretation of predication underwent a change so as to include classes or sets of ordered couples, triples, and so on. In symbolic logic, a "predicate" is understood to signify, in the case of a monadic or one-place predicate, a *property*, or, in the case of a polyadic or many-place predicate, a *relation* in the modern sense (i.e., an order or other "connection" of any number of interrelated individuals), and the usual interpretation is extensional rather than intensional, with a property identified with the class or set of individuals possessing that property, and with a relation identified with the class or set of ordered pairs (or ordered triples, etc.—ordered *n*-tuples) for which the relation holds. The idea has its origin in Frege's many-place function (even though Frege did not understand predication in terms of class inclusion). In a Fregean function, variables symbolized by letters are substituted for some or all of the noun phrases that are the arguments of a verb heading the predicate of a declarative sentence. This historical source alone suggests that the concept of a predicate in symbolic logic is irrelevant to a theory of predication, for Frege did not design his symbolic language to take account of the distinction between a subject and a predicate, and so predicates did not find their way into his language:

> A distinction of *subject* and *predicate* finds *no place* in my way of representing a judgment.... [Take] the two propositions 'the Greeks defeated the Persians at Plataea' and 'the Persians were defeated by the Greeks at Plataea'.... Even if a slight difference of sense is discernible, the agreement in sense is preponderant. Now I call the part of the content that is the same in both the *conceptual content*. *Only this* has significance for our symbolic language; we need therefore make no distinction between propositions that have the same conceptual content. (1879/1952a, 2–3)

Frege found that retaining the distinction between a subject and a predicate in a formalized language was "obstructive of [his] special purpose" (p. 4), namely, to model a language of thought on the formalized language of mathematics (in which, he said, "subject and predicate can be distinguished only by doing violence to the thought" (p. 3))—a language to be used for drawing valid inferences. He therefore dismissed as "slight" the difference in the sense of an active and a passive statement—a difference he seems not to have understood, for he thought that the subject is merely that which occupies the place in the word order that the speaker wants the hearer "to attend to specially" (p. 3). Frege failed to see the real difference in sense: an active predicate signifies action, and a passive one signifies an undergoing of action. Aristotle characterized these as distinct types of *katēgoria*, and distinct types of being—and so they are, for to hit and to be hit, or to defeat and to be defeated, are surely different things. Unfortunately, Frege's view that active and passive utterances have (more or less, for his purposes) the same conceptual (or semantic) content came to be shared by many later thinkers (who saw no difference at all in sense, irrespective of any purpose). This erroneous way of thinking likely came to prevail when the modern concept of a relation was incorporated into the concept of a predicate. Since a relation, in the modern sense (which includes transitive actions), is not an aspect of the being of any particular one of the individuals involved (but something outside all of them and somehow connecting them), any given relation is often assumed to be unchanging in nature regardless of which individual involved in it is chosen as the subject of a sentence (though the unchanging nature attributed to it always comes from choosing—sometimes unconsciously or tacitly —one individual as the subject; with verbs for actions, that individual is the one acting, so that the nature attributed to the "relation" or "predicate" is active, even when the associated verb is in its passive form). And so the sense of *defeated* can be imagined to be the same in the two sentences *The Greeks defeated the Persians* and *The Persians were defeated by the Greeks*; the second sentence, like the first, can be taken to be about an action rather than an undergoing of action. The following consideration may help highlight the distinct sense of the passive. The passive voice developed out of the middle voice in ancient languages; the distinct meaning of a passive utterance can thus be seen more clearly through considering an utterance with a meaning comparable to that of an utterance in the middle voice: *The Persians let themselves be* (*or got themselves*) *defeated by the Greeks* clearly has a different meaning than *The Greeks defeated the Persians*.

The concept of a predicate came to subsume the modern concept of a relation through David Hilbert (1862–1943) and his collaborators, who were the first mathematicians to use the term *predicate* (*Prädikat*) for polyadic relations and Fregean polyadic functions (see Hilbert and Bernays 1934; Frege (1891/1952b) called grammatical predicates "functions," but he did not call polyadic functions "predicates"). Hilbert and Ackermann (1938/1950) described such "relations" as "predicates having several subjects" (p. 45), revealing a confusion of subjects with arguments and a failure to see that the predicate must change with the subject (e.g., from *defeated the Persians* to *defeated by the Greeks*). They attempted to justify the new concept of a predicate as follows:

The Aristotelian formalism [based on the structure of a declarative sentence, i.e., a predicate attributed to a subject] turns out to be inadequate even in quite simple logical situations. It is basically insufficient for dealing with the logical foundations of mathematics. It fails, specifically, whenever a *relation among several objects* is to be represented symbolically.

This may be clarified by a simple example. Consider the statement: "If *B* lies between *A* and *C*, then *B* also lies between *C* and *A*." ... In the ... [monadic predicate calculus, the statement] may in fact be formulated thus: "If an ordered triple of points has the property that the second point lies between the first and third, then it also has the property that the second point lies between the third and first." This formulation, however, fails to express the logical essence of the statement, namely, the symmetry with respect to *A* and *C* of the relation "between." Therefore, it cannot be employed to derive the mathematical consequences of the statement under consideration....

... Since the foregoing calculus has turned out to be inadequate, we are forced to seek a new kind of logical symbolism. For this purpose we return to that point in our discussion at which we first went beyond the sentential calculus. The decisive step there was the division of sentences into subject and predicate.... [We now] separate in the rendering of a sentence the *objects* (*individuals*) from the *properties* (*predicates*) attributed to them and ... symbolize both explicitly.

This is done by employing *functional symbols with argument places* (*n*-adic functional symbols where *n* is the number of argument places) for the symbolic rendering of predicates, in which symbols representing objects are to be substituted in the argument places.... If the relation of the smaller to the greater is expressed by the two-place functional symbol $<(\ ,\ )$, then $<(2, 3)$ is the symbolic rendering of the sentence "2 is less than 3." Likewise, the sentence "*B* lies between *A* and *C*" may be rendered by $Z(A, B, C)$.

All mathematical formulas represent such relations among two or more quantities. For example, to the formula $x + y = z$ there corresponds a triadic predicate $S(x, y, z)$. The truth of $S(x, y, z)$ means that $x, y,$ and z are connected by the relation $x + y = z$. (1938/1950, 55–57)

They pointed out the novelty in their use of the word *predicate* for the modern "relation" in a footnote and without explanation:

Hitherto it has been customary in logic to call only functions with one argument place predicates, while functions with more than one place were called relations. Here we use the word "predicate" in a quite general sense. (1938/1950, 57, fn. 1)

Hilbert and Bernays first introduced the new usage of the term as follows:

We understand "predicate," here and in what follows as well, always in a wider sense [than the usual], so that even predicates with two or several subjects are included. Depending on the number of subjects, we speak of "one-place," "two-place" ... predicates. (1934, 7)

This extension of the term *predicate*, so casually introduced, was unfortunately accepted by later mathematical logicians, apparently without question, and it has even influenced views on predicates and predication outside of mathematics (e.g., in philosophy of language, linguistics, and psychology). As a result, many modern scholars think a predicate is predicated of all the arguments of a verb heading an actual (i.e., a grammatical) predicate. And so we find Rispoli (1995) saying that in the sentence *I took a spoon from the drawer*, "*took from* is a predicate predicated of three arguments: I, spoon, and drawer" (p. 333). In reality, a different predicate is predicable of each of the three noun phrases, for the type of being that can be shown forth from each of the individuals involved in the event is different in each case; the predicate *took a spoon from the drawer* is predicable of *I*, *taken from the drawer by me* is predicable of *a spoon*, and *the place from which I took a spoon* is predicable of *the drawer*.

Modern linguists have a number of different opinions about the nature of predication. Some describe it simply as "saying something" about the subject, and others claim that "the speaker announces a topic and then says something about it" (Hockett 1958, 201), a view sometimes understood in terms of the subject's or topic's expression of *given* information (i.e., information already given in the discourse context) and the predicate's introduction of *new* information. The idea that a predicate "says something about" a subject is far too vague to qualify as a theory. The reduction of the subject and the predicate to a topic and a comment upon it seems misguided, for in the sentence *That idiot wrecked my car*, the subject noun phrase seems to comment on the character of the subject, not just to point to an individual about whom something will be said. But perhaps the most serious problem with this view, as well as with the view that a subject provides information given in the discourse context and a predicate provides new information, is that it does not account for the facts of predication, such as the fact that subjects tend to be *ousiai*, that is, 'beingnesses' or substances, that primary beingnesses or individuals cannot be predicated of anything other than themselves, that genera are predicated of species but species are not predicated of genera, and that being that is dependent upon a substrate for its existence, such as a quality, a relation, or an action, can be predicated of beingnesses but beingnesses cannot be predicated of any such dependent being.

The modern concepts of a predicate and predication are so sense-depleted that modern linguists rarely find any place for them in their theories, and when predicates *do* find a place in linguistic theories, they are typically treated as purely syntactic entities.

In postclassical times, new conceptions of predicates and predication seem to have been shaped largely by philosophical trends rather than the nature of the being a predicate signifies or its relation to the being a subject signifies. The concept acquired a new layer of sediment when it was incorporated into symbolic logic. The aim of modeling a logical language after a mathematical language, such as the language of arithmetic or algebra (Boole and Frege) or the calculus of sets (Peano), and the aim of creating a language for the deduction of mathematical consequences (e.g., Whitehead and Russell, Hilbert) blurred the distinction between a declarative sentence and a mathematical formula; and a rash, ill-considered decision to use the term *predicate* for a Fregean function followed by the almost universal, unquestioning adoption of this use of the term led to widespread forgetting of the distinction between a predicate and both a Fregean function and a relation in the modern, sedimented sense and of the distinction between a subject and an argument. Contemplation of predicates has been conspicuously absent in the creation and adoption of new concepts of a predicate. Geach (1962), regarding a class-inclusion interpretation of predicates in statements of a certain kind, commented that "writers hurry over the topic, as over a thin patch of ice" (p. 15); the same can be said about discussions of predication in general.

9.8   Some Consequences of Sedimentation for Scientific Theories

It is one thing for people who do no scientific work to let sedimented concepts guide their thinking; it is another thing for a theoretical scientist to use words or signs tied to sedimented concepts in the construction of theoretical statements. When a concept becomes sedimented so that it no longer reflects the nature of the being that originally gave rise to it, any theory shaped by that concept will fail to permit a beholding or unconcealment of that being and will actively conceal it. The theory may reflect well the thinking of the theorist, but it will be of little value if the being it reveals is only that of *entia rationis* in the minds of the theorist and his or her followers.

A consideration of some specific consequences of using the sedimented concepts analyzed above will help to show how sedimented concepts can impede the formation of true theories—that is, theories that unconceal being.

Psychologists and philosophers of mind often aim to distinguish unlearned from learned concepts (or mental representations). But discussions about whether a concept is unlearned or learned can only be meaningful if the original sense of the concept is known—for this is the only sense that could be unlearned. Consider, for instance, the concept of number. The modern concept of number as continuous emerged in human thought only within the last few centuries. It is highly unlikely that it is unlearned, or that we have some special unlearned capacity just for understanding or using this sedimented concept. For this reason, arguments in favor of unlearned mental representations of numbers that are continuous, with any whole number represented as an extent or magnitude that is a multiple of a unit magnitude (e.g., Meck and Church 1983), would seem to require careful examination.

Because sedimentation hides the original sense of a concept, or the sense most likely to have been conceived through first intentions and to reflect the nature of being, doors that would be open to a theorist familiar with the original sense are closed. But removing sedimented layers from one's concept to reveal the original sense can open those doors. For example: if numbers are understood first-intentionally as counts of individuals of the same kind, then unlearned representations of numbers (if there are any) may be counterparts for collections of individuals (much like Roman numerals), with collections of like symbols representing collections of individuals of any kind whatsoever with the same cardinalities. (Wynn (1992) presents evidence consistent with the existence of unlearned representations of numbers that are counterparts of this sort.)[21]

Sedimented concepts can lead theorists down blind alleys. Take, for instance, the sedimented concept of a predicate adopted by modern mathematicians and those influenced by them, which subsumes the sedimented concept of a relation. This concept led some linguists down a path that is now fairly widely recognized as a dead end. The mathematician's (polyadic) "predicate" is a relation in the modern sense, so that it is imagined to apply equally and simultaneously to all the arguments of a verb that heads a grammatical predicate (i.e., to be something that connects them together somehow, with a nature that remains the same regardless of which argument is chosen as the subject of a sentence). Linguists who adopted this sedimented concept were blinded to the difference in sense of an active and a passive sentence containing the same verb and the same noun phrases but with a different noun phrase in subject position and possibly a different verb form. They thought that *any* sentence with a predicate headed by the verb *defeat* (even when it is in its passive participial form) must be about the action of defeating (and so they made a distinction between the "grammatical" or actual subject of a sentence and the "logical" subject, which is the noun phrase for the indi-

vidual carrying out an action—but this reveals an inconsistent vestige of
the Aristotelian view according to which a predicate signifies being that
originates in the subject). They failed to see that a passive utterance is
about the undergoing or suffering of an action, which is being of a distinct
type. For this reason, they regarded a passive sentence as an active sentence that has undergone a "transformation" in which the words were
rearranged, the verb may have changed form, and a few elements were
added (e.g., *is* or *was* and *by* in English) without any accompanying
change in meaning. This way of thinking is tied to the invention of two
notions: (1) transformations in language processing (and so Chomsky
(1965) said that sentences containing passive participles, or sentences in
which the "logical" subject and object differ, in this way of thinking, from
the "grammatical" subject and object, "provide the primary motivation
and empirical justification for the theory of transformational grammar"
(p. 70)), and (2) a "deep structure" (later "D-structure"), which contains
the untransformed version of a sentence—a notion supplemented by the
"Katz-Postal principle," or the idea that the meaning of the sentence in
deep structure is unaffected by the transformation that produces the
"surface-structure" sentence. Though the notion of deep structure was
rejected by some linguists not long after its emergence in Chomsky's
(1965) theories (e.g., in some papers first circulated in 1967: Lakoff and
Ross 1976; McCawley 1968), and though the accompanying Katz-Postal
principle was soon rejected by Chomsky and his followers (e.g., Jackendoff
1972), deep structure (as D-structure) remained a part of Chomsky's
popular theories for many years (e.g., Chomsky 1991), albeit with progressively less prominence (see, e.g., Lakoff 1980) and a progressively
more restricted role with regard to meaning; Chomsky (e.g., 1995b) only
recently eliminated it from his theories. The notion of a transformation,
though also questioned early on (e.g., in 1967 by Postal; see Postal 1976),
still survives in Chomsky's theories (e.g., Chomsky 1995b), even though it
has a greatly diminished role in the grammar (and has largely fallen out of
favor with other linguists as proposed alternatives to a transformational
grammar have come into favor). Much ink will have been spilled in vain
over this notion and the notion of deep structure before they are both
finally abandoned.

9.9 Generating Theories That Unconceal Being

Let us not fool ourselves. All of us, including those who think professionally, as
it were, are often enough thought-poor; we all are far too easily thought-less.

Thoughtlessness is an uncanny visitor who comes and goes everywhere in today's world. For nowadays we take in everything in the quickest and cheapest way, only to forget it just as quickly, instantly....

... Man today is in *flight from thinking*. This flight-from-thought is the ground of thoughtlessness.

Martin Heidegger, *Discourse on Thinking*

If theoretical statements are to be genuinely apophantic, unconcealing being and permitting a noetic beholding (*theōria*) of being, theorists must adopt and use scientific concepts and terms much more consciously and deliberately than is usual nowadays. They must not allow themselves to fall an easy prey to the pervasive forgetfulness of sense depletion and sedimentation—to that which only *seems* to be—but must pursue its opposite, the unforgetting of well-rounded unconcealment or full understanding.

Concepts should not be adopted passively. Rather than trusting other scholars to have properly conceived a second-intentional concept through reflection upon first-intentional concepts, and rather than having faith that the concept remains unsedimented, a theorist should compare any second-intentional concept used with the first-intentional concepts that originally gave rise to it to see whether the former adequately reflects the latter, and should compare the first-intentional concepts with the being that gave rise to them. If a theorist is using the second-intentional concept of a relation, for instance, concepts of individual types of relation (e.g., the ratio *double*, the relation *taller than*) can be examined to see if the theorist's concept of a relation reflects something in the nature of a relation of each type as it is conceived—and, more importantly, as it resides in being.

In addition to this sort of reflection, a theorist can attempt to unearth, through historical or etymological investigation, the original sense of any concept guiding the thought behind a theory, and to dig up whatever layers of sense have been deposited over it to conceal it. But the theorist should also determine whether the original sense reflects authentic conceptions of being originating in first intentions, and this determination can be made only through a contemplation of being.

Contemplation of being serves a purpose other than restoring meaning to sedimented and sense-depleted concepts: it can also lead to new conceptions so that theories are freed from the limitations of concepts that happen to be ready to hand.

Because apophantic (or declarative) sentences can unconceal being, a theorist attempting to conceive being anew through first-intentional contemplation might benefit from embedding a word for the being of interest in true declarative sentences. And since apophantic sentences are the *only* linguistic entities that can unconceal being, semanticists trying to discover the meaning of a word or the schema of meaning for a class of words (e.g., a class of words belonging to one part of speech) should always embed the word (or an exemplar of the part of speech) in declarative sentences that they judge to be meaningful (such as *Freddie is a dog*) and try to become aware of the nature of the being signified.

Because statements in standard modern mathematical notation (whether algebraic or logical or of another sort) are not (or are not properly) modeled after apophantic utterances, theoretical work should begin with nonmathematical statements and reasoning. When the being under investigation has been conceived, properly speaking, and a theory developed, mathematical formulations can then be introduced—but they should be introduced only with great caution, with the theorist making sure that in formalizing a theory, he or she is not importing sedimented concepts into the theory by virtue of the formalization. Further, if contemplations of being reveal inadequacies in existing mathematical concepts and notation, mathematical languages can be revised or constructed so as to provide adequate formal tools for theorists (as Macnamara (1994) argued).

All of these recommendations point in the same direction. Because the mind is only in direct (noetic) contact with being in first intentions, these must be the foundation of theoretical work. If theories are not anchored to being by first intentions, they will drift in whatever directions the imagination and philosophical currents take them. The result is usually a series of theoretical fads (especially in psychology and the social sciences—in the *Geisteswissenschaften*—where the being under investigation—intentions, as well as the actions that follow from them—is not, strictly speaking, sensible, and so it does not force one's mind to turn toward it; it even resists its own unconcealment because intentions are directed away from themselves, and, being the very stuff of consciousness, their constant presence in one's waking psyche leads one to take them for granted so that they typically escape one's notice).[22] Faddish theoretical frameworks often stimulate fruitless debates about issues irrelevant to actual phenomena, which retreat into concealment to the degree to which the positions taken in the debates are accepted as guides to one's thinking. A genuine resolution of such debates is rarely found (even though one position may come into favor by virtue of the strength of the personalities supporting it); far more frequently, the debated issues are forgotten as it becomes fashionable to follow new currents.

If theories are to be about anything other than human imaginings, theorists must develop their capacity for first intentions and make a habit of them. Having done so, they will be far more likely to adopt theoretical terms, and concepts of the being they signify, that permit being to be unconcealed; moreover, they will be far more likely to combine those terms in structures that reflect the constitution of the unconcealed being.

Notes

1. Edmund Husserl and Jacob Klein made use of many of these insights, either explicitly or implicitly, in evaluating theories in modern physics and mathematics (see Husserl 1954/1970; Klein 1934–1936/1968, 1932/1985).

2. I use *being* as a general term for that which is, including existent and substantial beings (where *beings* is comparable to the Greeks' *ta onta*; it does not necessarily refer to living things) as well as matter and the being that inheres in, originates in, or otherwise depends upon beings or matter, such as qualities, quantities, relations, actions and passions, locations in space and time, and so on (and *being* is here understood as a mass noun, comparable to the Greeks' *to on*). What I refer to as *being* is not identical with the "Being" of Heidegger and the Greek philosophers who inspired him. *That* Being is the proper subject of philosophy (see Aristotle, *Metaphysics* Γ.1, 1003ᵃ21–22; Heidegger 1927/1962; theories in the special sciences deal only with parts of Being (*Metaphysics* Γ.1, 1003ᵃ22–26). Wherever I use *being* as a count noun, it implies an individual informed or individuated atomically by some form (or species), and where I use *being* as a mass noun, the context should make clear whether I mean matter or dependent being alone or whether I mean beings, matter, and dependent being together.

3. For other mental phenomena, an intention arises under different conditions, and it is a qualitatively different kind of aiming at something as an object, originating not through activation of the noetic faculty, but of some other faculty of the psyche. In a state of desire, for instance, a person intends something or aims his or her mind at something by longing for it. In an instance of the perception of sensible things, he or she intends something by perceiving it sensibly.

The notion of an intention entered into Scholasticism through the Islamic philosophy of Al-Farabi and Avicenna. Like *intentio*, the word these philosophers used for it, *ma'na* (or sometimes *ma'qul*; see Engelhardt 1976), means concretely the drawing or stretching back of a bow (which brings it into a state of tension) in aiming an arrow at a target. This word brings together in one concept the ideas of aiming and tensing. The tensing that accompanies the aiming might best be understood as the mind's standing firm in its aiming—its tensing in that sense. But the characterization of an intention as a tensing also brings out the fact that it can vary in intensity, intensifying and remitting; the standing firm in the aiming can be more or less firm. Desires, fears, loves, angers, and so on, can be more or less intense, and thoughts too can in some sense intensify and remit, being entertained more or less intently, or, one might say, involving more or less attention.

4. Some theorists (e.g., Chomsky (1992, 1995a)) seem to think that a carving up that involves a human mind necessarily implies that what is carved up cannot be *outside* the mind. But the involvement of the mind in the carving no more implies that the stuff being carved is internal to the mind than the involvement of arms, hands, and an axe in chopping up the wood of a tree (an act that violates the tree's natural boundaries) implies that the stuff being chopped up does not exist in the world outside the instruments used in chopping—the arms, the hands, and the axe. If the members of a speech community collectively delimit, bound, or define certain beings—say, the beings called DANCERS (defined as people who dance)—this does not imply that those beings exist in our minds rather than in the extrapsychic world; dancers, like the dancing that makes them dancers, and like the people who underlie them, exist outside our minds (and, unlike mental beings, may be found performing on a stage). The fact that dancers (as well as firms, consumption, and income) are not beings with metaphysical primacy (in the sense of Aristotle's *prōtē ousia*, 'primary beingness' or primary substance)—that is, beings that underlie all other being—does not mean that they are not extrapsychic beings. The example of dancers serves to highlight another point. In comparing the carving up of being to chopping wood, I do not mean to imply that the being to be carved up is necessarily *matter*. A dancer is carved from a person, coming into being when the person takes up dancing, and passing away when the person ceases to dance. A person is not a portion of matter (though a portion of matter coincides with a person at any given moment); the matter in a given person's body changes throughout the lifespan. Nor is a person the mereological sum of time-slices of all the matter that is, was, or will be in his or her four-dimensional (space-time) body (a view that Putnam (1994) attributes to David Lewis), for the summation of the portions of matter that happen to coincide with a given person at different times presupposes the person, the identity of whom guides the summation.

Being can also be defined relative to other being without implying that it is unreal or imaginary. If Patricia is taller than Katherine, the fact that reference to Katherine is necessary to determine Patricia's being taller than her does not mean that Patricia's relative tallness is not really an aspect of her being. And being can be defined with respect to individual observers and yet reside outside their heads. That beauty is imaginary is not implied by the fact that beauty is relative to observers ("in the eye of the beholder"). If some people judge a painting to be beautiful, then the aspects of its being that give rise to that judgment are the components of the beauty they perceive. (This idea is reminiscent of Locke's (1694) view that to say an object is red is to say it has the power, by virtue of the nature of its surface, to give rise to a certain sensation in us. But unlike Locke, I would not deem redness unreal and the physical property that makes something look red real; I would identify the two instead. As Berkeley (1710/1982) pointed out, *all* qualities—not just those that Boyle and Locke called "secondary"—are experienced the way they are because of properties of the observer. But I do not conclude, as Berkeley did, that all qualities are secondary and there is no reality outside our experiences; I conclude, rather, that most qualities are "primary" and the peculiar and mutable nature of our experiences of them is irrelevant to their reality. The fact that the appearances we experience may not *resemble* or be *simi-*

lar to the qualities that give rise to them does not means that those qualities are not bona fide qualities of being (cf. Putnam 1981).)

5. Most of the semanticists who adopt the "It's all in your head" view (or what Jerry Fodor calls "psychosemantics")—the view that all linguistic meaning arises somehow from mental representations—seem, like eliminativists, to be guided primarily by skepticism about the mind's manifest ability to intend being or beings, skepticism motivated by faith in a physicalistic ontology, which, as it is currently conceived, excludes this ability (see also Baker 1987; Morris 1991). It is skepticism of this sort that led Fodor (1987) to say, "If the semantic and the intentional are real properties of things, it must be in virtue of their identity with (or maybe of their supervenience on?) properties that are themselves *neither* intentional *nor* semantic. If aboutness is real, it must be really something else" (p. 97)—which I would answer with Joseph Butler's observation that "everything is what it is and not another thing" (see Kripke 1972, 94).

Fodor attests to the fact that many cognitive scientists and philosophers "are repulsed by the idea that intentionality is a *fundamental* property of mental states (or, indeed, of anything else—talk about your ontological dangers!)" (1990, 313). He points out that "the deepest motivation for intentional irrealism derives ... from a certain ontological intuition: that there is no place for intentional categories in a physicalistic view of the world; that the intentional can't be *naturalized*" (1987, 97).

Such ontological dogmatism seems inappropriate in science, where being comes to be understood by means of observation and evidence. Evidence from inner perception and observation of people's use and interpretation of language clearly reveals the capacity of the mind to intend being outside the mind in its thoughts, perceptions, desires, and so on. If, for instance, a girl asks a salesclerk for an ice-cream cone, both the girl and the salesclerk understand perfectly well that the girl desires an ice-cream cone, not a mental representation of one.

6. The dependence of an isolated word's potential to signify upon a concept or definition may be one source of the belief of many semanticists that utterances of all sorts get their meanings solely by virtue of mental representations (where *mental representation* seems to be understood as a general term for mental entities of various sorts, including concepts and definitions). Semanticists typically take a compositional view of sentence meaning, seeing the meanings of sentences as structured aggregations of the meanings of the words in the sentences. If words considered individually do not permit the mind to intend being, but have a "sense" or "meaning" only by virtue of a concept or definition, then a compositionalist could be led to believe that the meanings of sentences are combinations of mental representations.

But even if a theorist is only interested in the "senses" of individual words—the mental representations (or concepts or definitions) of the being they have the potential to signify—the theorist must nonetheless characterize the being the words would signify in declarative statements (or, more generally, in referring expressions), for the simple reason that mental representations are representations of being; one cannot characterize the representations until one has characterized the being or beings they represent.

7. This translation and the other translation of Brentano's German are my own, as are all the translations in this chapter from classical Greek (i.e., of Aristotle, Euclid, Eudoxus, Nicomachus, Parmenides, Plato, and Porphyry), Latin (i.e., of Aquinas, Bradwardine, Descartes, Eustachius a Sancto Paulo, Fredericus, Peletier, Stifel, Suárez, Wallis, and Zabarella), and French (i.e., of Leibniz and Stevin). Translations of German authors other than Brentano (i.e., Dedekind, Frege, Heidegger, Hilbert and Ackermann, Husserl, and Klein) are from the published English editions cited, except for the translation of the passage from Hilbert and Bernays, which is my own. Wherever a quotation that I have translated into English is incorporated into the text, I have enclosed it in single quotation marks to distinguish it from direct quotations from works published in English, which are enclosed in double quotation marks.

8. 'Being of reason' is the standard (and literal) translation of the Scholastic expression *ens rationis*. It refers to a being, such as the concept of a universal, that exists in the mind (and perhaps only in the mind).

9. The Greeks had no word meaning 'number' per se; their word *arithmos* is best translated as 'count' or 'counting' (depending on the context). The Greeks did not understand numbers to fall under a single idea corresponding to our number concept, for they did not believe that things that have an *order* can fall under a common idea, definition, or genus (see Aristotle, *Nicomachean Ethics* A.6, 1096^{a}17–19; *On the Soul* B.3, 414^{b}22–28; *Metaphysics* B.3, 999^{a}6–10). And, indeed, if numbers are understood as counts, it does not make sense to think of them as belonging to a genus, since each one contains within it, or is a successor of, all smaller ones. To count 5 beings, one must first count 2 beings, then 3 beings, then 4 beings, successively adding 1 being to the collection of beings already counted. Two is not separate from 3, or from 5, but rather a part or antecessor of it. And so even though each number is a species (with, e.g., all counts of 3 belonging to one species), the different species of number are not independent species that can be included under a common genus.

10. For Plato, monads were separate, nonsensible, noetically perceived beings, real beings in the realm of the mathematicals; but, as Klein (1934–1936/1968) pointed out, "the emphasis with which the thesis of 'pure' monads is propounded is indicative of the fact that *arithmoi* were ordinarily, and as a matter of course, understood only as definite numbers of sensible objects" (p. 70).

11. The idea that a monad is that which remains in an atom when all but its oneness is abstracted away is also consistent with Aristotle's comment that a monad, like a point, is indivisible in any dimension, but whereas a point has position, a monad has none (*Metaphysics* Δ.6, 1016^{b}24–31; and so he calls a monad a point without position, *stigmē athetos*; *Metaphysics* M.8, 1084^{b}26–27); a point is what remains in a being when its species, its sensible qualities, its matter, and its extension in every direction are mentally stripped away (*Metaphysics* K.3, 1061^{a}29–35; and so Aristotle describes the objects of geometry as physical, e.g., physical points or lines drawn on papyrus, but not qua physical; see *Physics* B.2, 194^{a}9–11).

12. Wallis said, 'Geometry is more or less subordinated to arithmetic, and to that extent it applies universal assertions of arithmetic specially to its objects' (*Mathesis*

Universalis; for the Latin, see Wallis 1657/1695, *Opera*, vol. 1, as cited in Klein 1934–1936/1968, 216).

13. Descartes (1596–1650) stated that the geometric figures used in his algebraic geometry as counterparts for magnitudes or quantities of any sort whatsoever (see Schmidt 1986) 'must exhibit at one time continuous magnitudes, at another time multitude or number also' (1701/1966, 452). By introducing a unit magnitude with which other magnitudes could be compared, he was able to interpret magnitudes as numbers: 'Thanks to the unit we have assumed, continuous magnitudes can in some instances be reduced in their entirety to multitude' (pp. 451–452); he also said, 'If number be the question, we imagine a particular subject [i.e., a figure] measurable by a multitude of units' (p. 445), and, 'That very division into a plurality of equal parts, whether it be real, or only intellectual, is properly a [mode of] measuring in accordance with which we count things' (pp. 447–448).

14. In a later era, Richard Dedekind (1831–1916), who regarded numbers as "free creations of the human mind" (1888/1963, 31), stated explicitly that the goal of introducing irrational numbers is to permit numbers, as points, to fill up a straight line. After comparing the fact of one rational number's being greater than another to a point's being to the right of another on a straight line, and of its being less than another to a point's being to the left of another, and similarly, he said,

To every rational number *a*, i.e., to every individual in *R* [the domain of rational numbers], corresponds one and only one point *p*, i.e., an individual in *L* [the points in a line]....
  Of the greatest importance, however, is the fact that in the straight line *L* there are infinitely many points which correspond to no rational number.... The straight line *L* is infinitely richer in point-individuals than the domain *R* of rational numbers in number-individuals.
  If now, as is our desire, we try to follow up arithmetically all phenomena in the straight line, the domain of rational numbers is insufficient and it becomes absolutely necessary that the instrument *R* constructed by the creation of the rational numbers be essentially improved by the creation of new numbers such that the domain of numbers shall gain the same completeness, or as we may say at once, the same *continuity*, as the straight line. (1888/1963, 8–9)

The use of the points on a line as a model for numbers was so customary by his time that Dedekind felt no need to justify the assumption that for every point on a straight line there must be a corresponding number.

15. Aristotle used these words as if they were standard terms, not commenting on his use of them, so he may have been borrowing from and developing an existing theory. But by the third century C.E. at the latest, the words for predicates and predication that Aristotle used were deemed to have been of his own choosing. Porphyry (232–309), in his commentary on the *Categories*, asked,

Why, since *katēgorias* in customary language is said, in respect of the forensic speeches, of the [*katēgorias*] in accusation, to which is opposed the speech for the defendant, did Aristotle, not having undertaken to instruct us about how to speak against opponents in the courts of justice, but [about] something else, which very thing is not called by this name among the Hellenes, choose to make strange [use of language] by entitling the book *katēgorias*? (265/1887, 55)

16. Modern English editions of Aristotle's logical writings often give 'belong to' as the translation of *huparchō*. Alternative and even more unrevealing translations

are 'apply to' and 'hold of', which do not correspond to any meanings the word ever had for the Greeks.

17. As Plato pointed out (*Sophist* 262d–263a), a simple declarative sentence such as *Theaetetus sits* has two aspects, which he captured in the expressions *peri hou esti* and *hotou esti*, 'whom/what it is about' and 'whosever it is': (1) Viewed as a *rhēma* (a verb or an adjective) mingled (*kekramenon*) or intertwined (*sumplekes*) with a noun (or as a predicate intertwined with a noun phrase), the simple sentence reveals something *about* something (i.e., the subject, or Theaetetus in this case)—some determination (*logos*) of the subject. (Plato said that intertwining a *rhēma* with a noun *ti perainei*, 'brings something to an end', 'limits something', or 'determines something', and that for this reason we call this combination of intertwined word a *logos* (see 262d). Robert H. Schmidt has argued, in conversation, that the original meanings of *legō* as 'lay (to rest)' and 'gather (together)' suggest that a *logos* was understood as a gathering together that lays to rest. The gathering together of words in an intertwining of a verb with a noun (through conjugation for person and number) gives a sense of completion and thus brings the mind to a rest or standstill, whereas a word or a phrase by itself does not do so. A verb intertwined with a noun determines or brings to an end in that sense. The intertwining of a verb with a noun, or of a predicate with a noun phrase, also limits or defines the being of the subject that is shown forth from the subject.) (2) Viewed as that which has laid down together (*suntheis*) a noun (or a noun phrase) with a *rhēma* (or a predicate), a *logos* (or 'determination') is seen to belong to something, or be *of* something (i.e., the subject, Theaetetus). The two aspects correspond to two roles as answers to questions of two sorts, exemplified by "What is Theaetetus doing?" (or "What *is* it about Theaetetus?") and "Who sits?" (or "Who is *it* who sits?"). Both can be answered with "Theaetetus sits"; this utterance both reveals something about Theaetetus (namely, that he sits) and lets it be known that the particular determination of the subject (namely, the sitting) is the determination of Theaetetus (the possessor of the sitting). But since predication, or affirming or denying something about a subject, is the intertwining of a predicate with a (presupposed) noun phrase, it brings into being an utterance with the former role or aspect—one that reveals something about the subject.

18. This description reveals the error in the claim of scholars, at least since Boethius (480–524), that the categories other than *ousia*—literally 'beingness' but conventionally translated as 'substance'—are supposed to be categories of "accidental" being, for Aristotle explicitly contrasted the being of the categories, or being that is *kath' hauto*, with accidental being, or being that is *kata sumbebēkos*—'because of (or in accordance with) concomitance' (see *Metaphysics* Δ.7).

19. Here, *phasis* seems to mean primarily 'denunciation' or 'a charge laid'—a bringing to light in that sense; the prepositional prefix *kata* in *kataphasis* implies a charge being laid *against* someone (or something), and *apo*, which appears also in *apologia* and *apologeomai* ('speak in one's defense'), as well as in *apopsēphizomai* ('vote a charge away from' or 'acquit'), implies a charge being removed. (Alexander of Aphrodisias, in his commentary on Aristotle's *Topics*, said that *apophasis* is *anairesis*, which means 'taking up' or 'taking away'; in legal contexts,

it means the quashing of an indictment.) Aristotle said that 'kataphasis is apophansis [i.e., showing forth] of something [laid] against something, and apophasis is apophansis of something [i.e., some charge] removed from something' (*On Interpretation* 5, 17^a25–26).

20. When sentences of other types contain the verb meaning 'be' (explicitly or implicitly), it plays some other role regarding being. In a question, it indicates that being can be unconcealed in the response the question is intended to elicit. In a command (e.g., "Be kind"; "Don't be cruel"), a request (e.g., "Please be quiet"), or a prayer (e.g., "Be merciful to him"), where there is no subject, it indicates that being of the type desired (or desired to be free of) can get brought into existence (or taken or kept out of existence) if the addressee complies, thereby becoming (or ceasing to be, or ensuring he or she is not) the subject or origin of the being (so that, in the case of desired being, the verb meaning 'be' can be conjugated to agree with that subject in an affirmative declarative statement unconcealing the being from that subject). Among clauses with the structure of a declarative sentence, in some (such as those that follow *because* after verbs such as *quit*) the copula indicates that being is unconcealed from the subject of the clause, but in others (such as those that follow *that*, *whether*, or *if* in the complements of verbs such as *hope*, *believe*, *wonder*, *say*, and *report*) the copula indicates that being would be unconcealed from the subject of the clause if it were true.

21. It is possible that we have no unlearned representations of numbers per se, but rather an unlearned ability to detect sameness and difference in the cardinalities of collections of beings, combined with an unlearned ability to understand something as a counterpart for something else (which is similar to but not identical with the ability to understand an image as an image, i.e., as transparent rather than opaque, and let one's mind fall upon that of which it is an image through assenting to the image's announcement of it, rather than being spellbound by the image so that one's mind stands firm in an intention toward the image itself; the Greeks called this ability *eikasia*). These abilities would permit us to use any image of a collection of individuals of any kind held in the imagination as a counterpart for other collections with the same cardinality, much as when we use our fingers, in counting, as counterparts for individuals in a collection of beings of some other kind.

The ability to understand something as a counterpart for something else (which permits us, for example, to use a map as a counterpart for a region) seems to be present from an early age, for young children learning common nouns (along with the adults teaching them) seem to understand pictures of, say, animals in books as counterparts for real animals, so that the children take the nouns applied to the pictures by the adults to be names for species of real animals.

As the examples of a map, pictures in books, and fingers used in counting show, representations used as counterparts need not be internal to the mind (see also Houghton 1997), as is usually supposed.

22. Perhaps some of the best examples of such fads are to be found in psychology, where the views of the mind that have dominated theories are, for the most part, metaphorical: the mind as chemical compounds (e.g., Locke's complex or compound ideas formed out of simple ideas, Wundt's and Titchener's structuralism),

the mind as a mechanical system (e.g., Hume's associationism, where "ideas" are governed by laws of "attraction" or association analogous to Newton's law of gravitation), the mind as "Poof!" (behaviorism, or the mind's retreat into complete concealment), the mind as a computer (the "information-processing" model of the mind, functionalism), and the mind as a brain ("neural-network" models). Psychology can only begin to be a genuine science when theoretical approaches based on such metaphors—crude attempts to naturalize psychology—are abandoned and we begin in earnest to study the mind *as a mind*—when the nature of the being in psychology's domain (namely, intentional being) is allowed to guide our choices in classifying phenomena, our choices of terminology, our choices of problems to address, and the ways we choose to go about solving them, including methods and theoretical approaches, as that being gradually unconceals its nature to us (as Husserl (1954/1970) urged).

References

Aquinas, St. T. (1970). *Summa theologiae* [The sum of theology]*: Vol. 17. Psychology of human acts* (T. Gilby, Ed. and Trans.). Cambridge: Blackfriars. (First published 1266)

Baker, L. R. (1987). *Saving belief: A critique of physicalism*. Princeton, NJ: Princeton University Press.

Berkeley, G. (1982). *A treatise concerning the principles of human knowledge* (K. P. Winkler, Ed.). Indianapolis, IN: Hackett. (First published 1710)

Bradwardine, T. (1955). Tractatus proportionum sue De proportionibus velocitatum in motibus [Treatise on ratios, or On the ratios of the speeds of motions]. In H. L. Crosby, Jr. (Ed. and Trans.), *Thomas of Bradwardine, his* Tractatus de proportionibus [Treatise on ratios]*: Its significance for the development of mathematical physics* (pp. 64–140). Madison, WI: University of Wisconsin Press. (Written in 1328)

Brentano, F. (1924). *Psychologie vom empirischen Standpunkt* [Psychology from an empirical standpoint] (Vol. 1, 2nd ed., O. Kraus, Ed.). Leipzig: Verlag von Felix Meiner.

Chomsky, N. (1965). *Aspects of the theory of syntax*. Cambridge, MA: MIT Press.

Chomsky, N. (1991). Linguistics and cognitive science: Problems and mysteries. In A. Kasher (Ed.), *The Chomskyan turn* (pp. 26–53). Cambridge, MA: Blackwell.

Chomsky, N. (1992). Explaining language use. *Philosophical Topics, 20,* 205–231.

Chomsky, N. (1995a). Language and nature. *Mind, 104,* 1–61.

Chomsky, N. (1995b). *The Minimalist Program*. Cambridge, MA: MIT Press.

Churchland, P. M. (1981). Eliminative materialism and the propositional attitudes. *The Journal of Philosophy, 78,* 67–90.

Churchland, P. M. (1984). *Matter and consciousness: A contemporary introduction to the philosophy of mind*. Cambridge, MA: MIT Press.

Cummins, R. (1996). *Representations, targets, and attitudes*. Cambridge, MA: MIT Press.

Dedekind, R. (1963). *Essays on the theory of numbers* (W. W. Beman, Trans.). New York: Dover. (Original work published 1888)

Dee, J. (1975). *The mathematicall praeface to the* Elements *of geometrie of Euclid of Megara*. New York: Science History Publications. (First published 1570)

Dennett, D. C. (1978). *Brainstorms: Philosophical essays on mind and psychology*. Cambridge, MA: MIT Press.

Descartes, R. (1966). Regulae ad directionem ingenii [Rules for the direction of the mind]. In C. Adam and P. Tannery (Eds.), *Oeuvres de Descartes* [Works of Descartes] (pp. 349–469). Paris: Librairie Philosophique J. Vrin. (First published posthumously in 1701)

Dretske, F. I. (1981). *Knowledge and the flow of information*. Cambridge, MA: MIT Press.

Eco, U. (1988). On truth. A fiction. In U. Eco, M. Santambrogio, and P. Violi (Eds.), *Meaning and mental representations* (pp. 41–59). Bloomington, IN: Indiana University Press.

Engelhardt, P. (1976). Intentio [Intention]. In J. Ritter and K. Gründer (Eds.), *Historisches Wörterbuch der Philosophie* [Historical dictionary of philosophy] (Vol. 4, pp. 465–474). Basel: Schwabe.

Field, H. (1982). Realism and relativism. *The Journal of Philosophy, 79*, 553–567.

Fodor, J. A. (1980). Methodological solipsism considered as a research strategy in cognitive psychology. *Behavioral and Brain Sciences, 3*, 63–109.

Fodor, J. A. (1986). Banish DisContent. In J. Butterfield (Ed.), *Language, mind and logic* (pp. 1–23). Cambridge: Cambridge University Press.

Fodor, J. A. (1987). *Psychosemantics: The problem of meaning in the philosophy of mind*. Cambridge, MA: MIT Press.

Fodor, J. A. (1990). Psychosemantics or: Where do truth conditions come from? In W. G. Lycan (Ed.) *Mind and cognition* (pp. 312–337). Cambridge, MA: Blackwell.

Frege, G. (1952a). Begriffsschrift: A formalized language of pure thought modelled upon the language of arithmetic (Chapter 1, P. T. Geach, Trans.). In *Translations from the philosophical writings of Gottlob Frege* (P. T. Geach and M. Black, Eds., pp. 1–20). Oxford: Blackwell. (Original work published 1879)

Frege, G. (1952b). Function and concept (P. T. Geach, Trans.). In *Translations from the philosophical writings of Gottlob Frege* (P. T. Geach and M. Black, Eds., pp. 21–41). Oxford: Blackwell. (Original work presented 1891)

Frege, G. (1980). *The foundations of arithmetic: A logico-mathematical enquiry into the concept of number* (rev. ed., J. L. Austin, Trans.). Oxford: Blackwell. (Original work published 1884)

Garfield, J. L. (1988). *Belief in psychology: A study in the ontology of mind*. Cambridge, MA: MIT Press.

Geach, P. T. (1962). *Reference and generality: An examination of some medieval and modern theories*. Ithaca, NY: Cornell University Press.

Gilson, E. (1979). *Index Scolastico-Cartésien* [Scholastic-Cartesian index] (2nd ed.). Paris: Librairie Philosophique J. Vrin.

Harnad, S. (1990). The symbol grounding problem. *Physica D, 42,* 335–346.

Harvey, C. W. (1989). *Husserl's phenomenology and the foundations of natural science*. Athens, OH: Ohio University Press.

Haugeland, J. (1982). The mother of intention [Review of the book *Brainstorms*]. *Noûs, 16,* 613–619.

Heath, T. L., Sir (Ed. and Trans.). (1956). *The thirteen books of Euclid's Elements: Vol. 2. Books III–IX* (2nd ed.). New York: Dover.

Heidegger, M. (1962). *Being and time* (J. Macquarrie and E. Robinson, Trans.). San Francisco: Harper & Row. (Original work published 1927)

Hilbert, D., and Ackermann, W. (1950). *Principles of mathematical logic* (R. E. Luce, Ed., L. M. Hammond, G. G. Leckie, and F. Steinhardt, Trans.). New York: Chelsea. (Original work, as a 2nd edition, published 1938)

Hilbert, D., and Bernays, P. (1934). *Grundlagen der Mathematik* [Foundations of mathematics] (Vol. 1). Berlin: J. Springer.

Hockett, C. F. (1958). *A course in modern linguistics*. New York: Macmillan.

Houghton, D. (1997). Mental content and external representations. *The Philosophical Quarterly, 47,* 159–177.

Husserl, E. (1939). Die Frage nach dem Ursprung der Geometrie als intentional-historisches Problem [The inquiry into the origin of geometry as an intentional-historic problem] (E. Fink, Ed.). *Revue Internationale de Philosophie, 1,* 203–225.

Husserl, E. (1970). *The crisis of European sciences and transcendental phenomenology: An introduction to phenomenological philosophy* (D. Carr, Trans.). Evanston, IL: Northwestern University Press. (Original work published posthumously in 1954)

Husserl, E. (1977). *Phenomenological psychology* (J. Scanlon, Trans.). The Hague: Nijhoff. (Original work presented 1925)

Jackendoff, R. S. (1972). *Semantic interpretation in generative grammar*. Cambridge, MA: MIT Press.

Johnson-Laird, P. N. (1988). How is meaning mentally represented? In U. Eco, M. Santambrogio, and P. Violi (Eds.), *Meaning and mental representations* (pp. 99–118). Bloomington, IN: Indiana University Press.

Klein, J. (1940). Phenomenology and the history of science. In M. Farber (Ed.), *Philosophical essays in memory of Edmund Husserl* (pp. 143–163). Cambridge, MA: Harvard University Press.

Klein, J. (1968). *Greek mathematical thought and the origin of algebra* (E. Brann, Trans.). Cambridge, MA: MIT Press. (Original work published 1934–1936)

Klein, J. (1985). The world of physics and the "natural" world (D. R. Lachterman, Trans.). In R. B. Williamson and E. Zuckerman (Eds.), *Jacob Klein: Lectures and essays* (pp. 1–34). Annapolis, MD: St. John's College Press. (Original work presented 1932)

Kripke, S. A. (1972). *Naming and necessity*. Cambridge, MA: Harvard University Press.

Lakoff, G. (1980). Whatever happened to deep structure? *Behavioral and Brain Sciences, 3,* 22–23.

Lakoff, G., and Ross, J. R. (1976). Is deep structure necessary? In J. D. McCawley (Ed.), *Syntax and semantics: Vol. 7. Notes from the linguistic underground* (pp. 159–164). New York: Academic Press.

La Palme Reyes, M., Macnamara, J., and Reyes, G. E. (1994). Reference, kinds and predicates. In J. Macnamara and G. E. Reyes (Eds.), *The logical foundations of cognition* (pp. 91–143). New York: Oxford University Press.

La Palme Reyes, M., Macnamara, J., Reyes, G. E., and Zolfaghari, H. (1993). Proper names and how they are learned. *Memory, 1,* 433–455.

Leibniz, G. W. (1902). The monadology. In *Discourse on metaphysics; Correspondence with Arnauld; Monadology* (G. Montgomery, Trans.). La Salle, IL: Open Court. (Original work published 1714)

Leibniz, G. W. (1965a). Nouveaux essais sur l'entendement humain [New essays on human understanding]. In C. I. Gerhardt (Ed.), *Die philosophischen Schriften von Gottfried Wilhelm Leibniz* [The philosophical works of Gottfried Wilhelm Leibniz] (Vol. 5). Hildesheim, Germany: Georg Olms Verlagsbuchhandlung. (First published posthumously in 1765)

Leibniz, G. W. (1965b). Streitschriften zwischen Leibniz und Clarke [Polemical correspondence between Leibniz and Clarke]. In C. I. Gerhardt (Ed.), *Die philosophischen Schriften von Gottfried Wilhelm Leibniz* [The philosophical works of Gottfried Wilhelm Leibniz] (Vol. 7, pp. 345–440). Hildesheim, Germany: Georg Olms Verlagsbuchhandlung. (First published 1717)

Locke, J. (1694). *An essay concerning humane understanding* (2nd ed.). London: Printed for Awnsham and John Churchil and Samuel Manship.

Macnamara, J. (1989). [Review of the book *Meaning and mental representations.*] *Journal of Language and Social Psychology, 8,* 349–353.

Macnamara, J. (1992). The takeover of psychology by biology or the devaluation of reference in psychology. In M. Pütz (Ed.), *Thirty years of linguistic evolution* (pp. 545–570). Philadelphia: John Benjamins.

Macnamara, J. (1993). Cognitive psychology and the rejection of Brentano. *Journal for the Theory of Social Behaviour, 23,* 117–137.

Macnamara, J. (1994). Logic and cognition. In J. Macnamara and G. E. Reyes (Eds.), *The logical foundations of cognition* (pp. 11–34). New York: Oxford University Press.

Macnamara, J., and Reyes, G. E. (1994). Foundational issues in the learning of proper names, count nouns and mass nouns. In J. Macnamara and G. E. Reyes (Eds.), *The logical foundations of cognition* (pp. 144–176). New York: Oxford University Press.

Maxwell, J. C. (1877). The kinetic theory of gases [Review of the book *A treatise on the kinetic theory of gases*]. *Nature, 16,* 242–246.

McCawley, J. D. (1968). Lexical insertion in a transformational grammar without deep structure. *Papers from the Regional Meeting, Chicago Linguistic Society, 4,* 71–80.

McGinn, C. (1989). *Mental content.* Oxford: Blackwell.

McPherson, L. M. P. (1995). *Identifying verbs early in language learning: The roles of action and argument structure.* Unpublished doctoral dissertation, McGill University, Montréal.

Meck, W. H., and Church, R. M. (1983). A mode control model of counting and timing processes. *Journal of Experimental Psychology: Animal Behavior Processes, 9,* 320–334.

Mill, J. S. (1851). *A system of logic, ratiocinative and inductive, being a connected view of the principles of evidence, and the methods of scientific investigation* (Vol. 1, 3rd ed.). London: John W. Parker.

Millikan, R. G. (1984). *Language, thought, and other biological categories: New foundations for realism.* Cambridge, MA: MIT Press.

Morris, M. (1991). Why there are no mental representations. *Minds and Machines, 1,* 1–30.

Palmer, S. E. (1978). Fundamental aspects of cognitive representation. In E. Rosch and B. B. Lloyd (Eds.), *Cognition and categorization* (pp. 259–303). Hillsdale, NJ: Erlbaum.

Porphyry (1887). In Aristotelis Categorias [On Aristotle's Categories]. In A. Busse (Ed.), *Commentaria in Aristotelem Graeca: Vol. IV, Pars I. Porphyrii* Isagoge *et* In Aristotelis Categorias *commentarium* [Greek commentaries on Aristotle: Vol. 4, Part 1. Porphyry's commentary, *Introduction* and *On Aristotle's Categories*] (pp. 53–142). Berolini: Typis et Impensis Georgii Reimer. (First published c. 265)

Postal, P. M. (1976). Linguistic anarchy notes. In J. D. McCawley (Ed.), *Syntax and semantics: Vol. 7. Notes from the linguistic underground* (pp. 201–225). New York: Academic Press.

Putnam, H. (1973). Meaning and reference. *The Journal of Philosophy, 70,* 699–711.

Putnam, H. (1981). *Reason, truth and history.* Cambridge: Cambridge University Press.

Putnam, H. (1984). Is the causal structure of the physical itself something physical? In P. A. French, T. E. Uehling, Jr., and H. K. Wettstein (Eds.), *Midwest studies in philosophy: Vol. 9. Causation and causal theories* (pp. 3–16). Minneapolis, MN: University of Minnesota Press.

Putnam, H. (1988). *Representation and reality*. Cambridge, MA: MIT Press.

Putnam, H. (1989). Model theory and the 'factuality' of semantics. In A. George (Ed.), *Reflections on Chomsky* (pp. 213–232). Oxford: Blackwell.

Putnam, H. (1992a). *Renewing philosophy*. Cambridge, MA: Harvard University Press.

Putnam, H. (1992b). Reply to Noam Chomsky. *Philosophical Topics, 20,* 379–385.

Putnam, H. (1994). Logic and psychology: Comment on 'Logic and cognition.' In J. Macnamara and G. E. Reyes (Eds.), *The logical foundations of cognition* (pp. 35–42). New York: Oxford University Press.

Pylyshyn, Z. W. (1984). *Computation and cognition: Toward a foundation for cognitive science*. Cambridge, MA: MIT Press.

Rispoli, M. (1995). Missing arguments and the acquisition of predicate meanings. In M. Tomasello and W. E. Merriman (Eds.), *Beyond 'Names for things': Young children's acquisition of verbs* (pp. 331–352). Hillsdale, NJ: Erlbaum.

Schank, R., and Kass, A. (1988). Knowledge representation in people and machines. In U. Eco, M. Santambrogio, and P. Violi (Eds.), *Meaning and mental representations* (pp. 181–200). Bloomington, IN: Indiana University Press.

Schmidt, R. H. (1986). *On the signification of mathematical symbols: Repairing the number/numeral breach with the restored Renaissance counterpart concept*. Annapolis, MD: Golden Hind Press.

Searle, J. R. (1980). Minds, brains, and programs. *Behavioral and Brain Sciences, 3,* 417–457.

Silvers, S. (1991). On naturalizing the semantics of mental representation. *The British Journal for the Philosophy of Science, 42,* 49–73.

Slors, M. (1996). Why Dennett cannot explain what it is to adopt the intentional stance. *The Philosophical Quarterly, 46,* 93–98.

Stampe, D. W. (1979). Toward a causal theory of linguistic representation. In P. A. French, T. E. Uehling, Jr., and H. K. Wettstein (Eds.), *Contemporary perspectives in the philosophy of language* (pp. 81–102). Minneapolis, MN: University of Minnesota Press.

Stevin, S. (1958a). L'arithmétique [Arithmetic]. In D. J. Struik (Ed.), *The principal works of Simon Stevin: Vol. IIB. Mathematics* (pp. 477–551). Amsterdam: C. V. Swets & Zeitlinger. (First published 1585)

Stevin, S. (1958b). De thiende [On the tenth]. In D. J. Struik (Ed.), *The principal works of Simon Stevin: Vol. II. Mathematics* (pp. 386–425). Amsterdam: C. V. Swets & Zeitlinger. (First published 1585)

Suárez, F. (1965). *Disputationes metaphysicae* [Metaphysical disputations] (Vol. 1). Hildesheim, Germany: Georg Olms Verlagsbuchhandlung. (First published 1597)

Wilks, Y. (1988). Reference and its role in computational models of mental representations. In U. Eco, M. Santambrogio, and P. Violi (Eds.), *Meaning and mental representations* (pp. 221–237). Bloomington, IN: Indiana University Press.

Wynn, K. (1992). Evidence against empiricist accounts of the origins of numerical knowledge. *Mind & Language, 7,* 315–332.

Zabarella, J. (1966). *De rebus naturalibus; In Aristotelis libros de anima* [On natural things; On Aristotle's books on the soul]. Frankfurt: Minerva. (Works first published posthumously in 1590 and 1605)

Chapter 10

| The Nature of Human Concepts: Evidence from an Unusual Source | Steven Pinker and Alan Prince |

10.1 Classical and Family Resemblance Categories

This chapter is about an extensive parallel we have discovered between a part of language and a part of cognition, and about the possibility that the parallel is not a coincidence. The parallel involves the difference between a *classical category* and a *prototype* or *family resemblance category*, a topic of controversy for many years in cognitive psychology, philosophy, linguistics, and artificial intelligence.

Classical categories are defined by necessary and sufficient criteria, and membership in them is all-or-none. Examples include squares, grandmothers, odd numbers, and the vertebrate class Aves. Family resemblance categories differ from classical categories in a number of ways:

• They *lack necessary and sufficient conditions* for membership. For example, the category "chair" includes objects that have legs and that lack them (e.g., beanbag chairs), and objects that can be sat upon and that cannot (e.g., delicate museum pieces).
• They have *graded degrees of membership*. A robin is a better example of the family resemblance category "bird" than an eagle is; and a penguin is a worse example.

John Macnamara was a man of extraordinary wit, wisdom, and warmth. His insights on the relations among cognition, logic, and the world greatly influenced the thinking that went into this chapter. It is an honor to contribute to a volume in his memory.

The order of authors is arbitrary. We thank Ned Block, Paul Bloom, Ray Jackendoff, and Ed Smith for comments. Preparation of this chapter was supported by National Institutes of Health grant HD 18381.

A longer version of this chapter may be found in *Communication and Cognition*, *29*, 307–361.

• The category can be summarized by an ideal member or *prototype*, sometimes but not always an actual exemplar of the category. The more similar other members are to the prototype, the better examples they are. The sparrow, which is used to illustrate the entry for "bird" in many dictionaries, might be a prototype of the bird category.

• There can be *unclear cases*—objects that may or may not be members of the category at all. One example is the fossil genus *Archaeopteryx*, characterized by one paleontologist as a "poor reptile, and not very much of a bird" (Konner 1982). Garlic is an unclear example of the category "vegetable," as is ketchup, as we saw in the famous controversy that followed the Reagan administration's proposal that ketchup be classified as a vegetable in meeting nutritional guidelines for school lunch menus.

• They often display a *family resemblance* structure (Wittgenstein 1953). The members of a family of people generally do not have a single feature in common. Instead, a pool of features such as hair color, mouth shape, or nose size is shared by various sets of family members. Similarly, the members of family resemblance categories have different features that run through different subsets: green color is shared by spinach, celery, and broccoli, but not carrots or cauliflower; stems and bunches of florets are shared by broccoli and cauliflower but not carrots.

• Good members tend to have *characteristic nondefining features*. For example, gray hair and a domestic lifestyle characterize many grandmothers, but someone can be a grandmother without possessing either property, such as Elizabeth Taylor.

10.1.1   Evidence for Family Resemblance Categories

Human concepts pick out categories of objects; what kind of category do they pick out? There is a large body of evidence (summarized in Smith and Medin 1981; Rosch 1973, 1978, 1988) that has been taken to show that human concepts correspond to family resemblance categories. First, semanticists and philosophers have generally failed in their attempts to find necessary and sufficient conditions for most natural concepts that are labeled by words (see Fodor et al. 1980). Second, psychologists have found that subjects can give ratings of the goodness of membership of a list of exemplars with respect to a category that are reliable and in close agreement with one another. Similarly, there is good agreement about prototypes and unclear cases. Third, these judgments are not unanalyzable gut feelings but can be predicted in a systematic way using a feature calculus, in which the features possessed by a given exemplar (assessed independently, for example, by asking subjects to list the attributes of the object) are compared with those possessed by the other members of the category. Fourth, judgments of goodness of membership have strong effects on performance in many psychological tasks. For example, people can verify that prototypical members belong to a category faster and more accurately than they do with peripheral members, and when asked to recall instances of a category, they name prototypical members first. Fifth, developmental psychologists have found that children often learn the names for prototypical exemplars of a category before learning the names for other exemplars, and that they apply superordinate terms such as *bird* to its prototypical members first. Sixth, linguists have found that certain adverbials called *hedges* are sensitive to prototypicality: one can say that a sparrow, but not a penguin, is a bird *par excellence*, and that a penguin, but not a sparrow, is *technically* or *strictly speaking* a bird.

10.1.2   Evidence against Family Resemblance Categories
On the other hand, there is also evidence that certain aspects of human concepts do not correspond to family resemblance categories. Some of the empirical effects that have been interpreted as demonstrating family resemblance classes also occur for categories that people clearly treat as being classical. Armstrong, Gleitman, and Gleitman (1983) have found that subjects show a great deal of agreement with one another in rating the degree of membership of exemplars of categories like "female" and "odd number." For example, they agree that a mother is a better example of a female than a comedienne is, and that 13 is a better example of an odd number than 23. Similarly, Armstrong, Gleitman, and Gleitman found that people take less time and are more accurate at deciding that 13 is an odd number than that 23 is, and that a mother is a female than that a comedienne is. Since these subjects surely knew that "female" and "odd number" in reality have sharp boundaries and all-or-none membership (and Armstrong, Gleitman, and Gleitman discovered, in an independent questionnaire, that their subjects believed as much), it calls into question whether the analogous results that Rosch and others obtained for "bird" or "tool" really tell us anything about people' representations of those concepts.

Moreover, most judgments of membership in family resemblance categories based on characteristic features are highly corrigible when people are asked to engage in careful reasoning about it. For some purposes, people are willing to consider a penguin as a full-fledged bird and Elizabeth

Taylor a full-fledged grandmother. In fact, characteristic nondefining features can be quickly abandoned, even by young children. Children say that three-legged dogs are dogs, and that raccoons with stripes painted down their backs are raccoons, not skunks (Rey 1983; Armstrong, Gleitman, and Gleitman 1983; Keil 1989; Gelman, Coley, and Gottfried 1994).

Similar demonstrations with adults have shown that inference is often not driven by the similarity criteria that define family resemblance categories (see Murphy 1993; Medin 1989; Kelly 1992; Smith, Langston, and Nisbett 1992; Rips 1989; Rey 1983). For example, when people are asked which two out of three belong together—white hair, gray hair, black hair—they say that black is the odd hair out, because aging hair turns gray then white. But when asked about a white cloud, a gray cloud, and a black cloud, they say that white is the odd cloud out, because gray and black clouds give rain. In another experiment, subjects were asked whether a three-inch disk is more similar to a quarter or a pizza, and whether it is more likely to *be* a quarter or a pizza. Most said it is more similar to a quarter but more likely to be a pizza, presumably because quarters have to be standardized but pizzas can vary. Most people, upon being presented with a centipede, a caterpillar that looks like it, and a butterfly that the caterpillar turns into, feel that the caterpillar and the butterfly are "the same animal," but that the caterpillar and the centipede are not, despite appearances to the contrary.

10.1.3 Possible Resolutions
This conflicting evidence can be resolved in several ways.

First, human concepts could basically pick out family resemblance categories. Classical categories would be special cases or artifacts resulting from explicit instruction, such as in formal schooling. Alternatively, human concepts could basically pick out classical categories. Family resemblance categories would be artifacts of experimental tasks asking subjects for graded judgments or asking them to make categorization decisions under time pressure. A third, compromise position would say that human concepts correspond to both classical and family resemblance categories. Classical categories are the "core" of the concept, used for reasoning. Family resemblance categories are "identification procedures" or "stereotypes," used for identification of category exemplars on the basis of available perceptual information, or for rapid approximate reasoning. Although most theorists have tended toward compromise positions, something close to the mainly-family-resemblance view can be found in

Lakoff 1987, Rosch 1978, and Smith, Medin, and Rips 1984; something close to the mainly-classical-category view can be found in Rey 1983, Fodor 1981, and Armstrong, Gleitman, and Gleitman 1983; and tentative proposals favoring the core-plus-identification-procedure compromise can be found in Smith and Medin 1981, Armstrong, Gleitman, and Gleitman, and Osherson and Smith 1981.

This leads to several open questions. (1) Is one type of category psychologically real, the other an artifact or special case? (2) If both are psychologically real, can they be distinguished by function (e.g., reasoning vs. categorization)? (3) If both are psychologically real, are they handled by the same kind of computational architecture? (4) If either or both are psychologically real, do they correspond to ontological categories? That is, are classical (or family resemblance) categories incorrectly imposed by people on the world because of limitations of the way the mind works, or is there some sense in which the world contains classical (or family resemblance) categories, which people can accurately represent as such, presumably because the mind evolved to grasp aspects of the world accurately?

We will attempt to shed light on these questions by examining an unusual source of evidence: English past tense forms.

10.2   An Unexpected Test Case: English Past Tense Forms

English verbs come in two types: those that have regular past tense forms, and those that have irregular past tense forms. Consider them as two categories: "regular verbs," such as *walk/walked, talk/talked, jog/jogged, pat/patted, kiss/kissed*, and *play/played*, and "irregular verbs," such as *hit/hit, go/went, sleep/slept, make/made, ring/rang, bring/brought, stink/stank*, and *fly/flew*.

In fact, the irregular verbs are not a single class but a set of subclasses, which can be subdivided according to the kind of change that the stem undergoes to form the past tense (see Pinker and Prince 1988 for a full list). Here are some examples:

- Lax the vowel: *bleed, breed, feed, lead, mislead, read, speed, plead, meet, hide, slide, bite, light, shoot*
- Lax the vowel, add a -*t: lose, deal, feel, kneel, mean, dream, creep, keep, leap, sleep, sweep, weep, leave*
- Change the rhyme to -*ought: buy, bring, catch, fight, seek, teach, think*

- Change /ɪ/ to /æ/ or /ʌ/: *ring, sing, spring, drink, shrink, sink, stink, swim, begin, cling, fling, sling, sting, string, swing, wring, stick, dig, win, spin, stink, slink, run, hang, strike, sneak*
- Change the vowel to /u/: *blow, grow, know, throw, draw, withdraw, fly, slay*

Let us consider some properties of the irregular subclasses.

10.2.1 Properties of the Irregular Subclasses

10.2.1.1 Characteristic Nondefining Features The irregular subclasses tend to be characterized by phonological properties other than those that define the change from stem to past form. Consider the subclass that changes on *o* or similar vowel to *u*: *blow, grow, know, throw, draw, withdraw, fly, slay*. In principle, any verb with an *o* or similar vowel could be included in the subclass. In fact, all the verb roots in the subclass end in a vowel, usually a diphthong, and most begin with a consonant cluster.

Similarly, the subclass that changes /ay/ to /aw/—*bind, find, grind, wind*—could include any verb with the vowel /ay/, but in fact, all the verbs happen to end in -*nd*. The subclass that changes a final *d* to *t*—*bend, send, lend, rend, build*—could include any word ending in *d*, but in fact, most of the verbs rhyme with -*end*. Finally, the subclass that changes the vowel /ey/ to /ʊ/—*take, mistake, forsake, shake*—could include any word with an /ey/, but in fact, all the verbs roots rhyme with -*ake* and begin with a coronal consonant.

Note that the characteristic nondefining features are arbitrary, not lawful, with respect to the sound pattern of English. No rule of phonology excludes *loon* as the past tense of *loan* or *choud* as the past of *chide*.

10.2.1.2 Family Resemblance Irregular subclasses display a family resemblance structure (Bybee and Slobin 1982a; Bybee and Moder 1983). Consider the subclass that changes an /ɪ/ to an /ʌ/. Most of the verbs end with a velar nasal consonant: *shrink, sink, stink, cling, fling, sling, sting, string, swing, slink*. Some end in a consonant that is velar but not nasal: *stick, dig, sneak, strike*. Others end in a vowel that is nasal but not velar: *win, spin, swim, begin*.

Similarly, within the subclass that changes a final diphthong to /u/, some begin with a ⟨consonant-sonorant⟩ cluster and contain the diphthong /ow/: *blow, grow, throw*. But one member, *know*, contains the /ow/

diphthong but does not begin with a consonant cluster. Others begin with a consonant cluster but have a different diphthong or no diphthong at all: *draw, withdraw, fly, slay.*

10.2.1.3 Prototypicality Bybee and Moder (1983) point out that for many of the subclasses, one can characterize a prototype, based on the kinds of characteristic phonological properties that define the family resemblance structure. According to Bybee and Moder, the prototype of the *ing* → *ung* subclass is

$$s \quad C \quad C \quad i \quad \begin{bmatrix} \text{velar} \\ \text{nasal} \end{bmatrix}$$

where C stands for a consonant. This prototype is maximally similar to most members of the existing subclass, but more interestingly, it predicts subjects' generalization of the $/ɪ/ \rightarrow /ʌ/$ change to novel verbs. Bybee and Moder asked subjects to rate how natural a variety of putative past tense forms sounded for each of a set of nonce stems. The independent variable was the similarity of the stem to the prototype listed above. They found that subjects were extremely likely to accept the vowel change for stems like *spling, strink,* and *skring,* which match the schema for the prototype exactly. They were only slightly less willing to accept *struck* and *skrum* as the past of *strick* and *skrim,* which differ from the prototype in one feature. Somewhat lower in acceptability were *spruv* for *spriv,* and similar past forms for *sking, smig, pling,* and *krink. Glick, krin, plim, shink* were even less likely to admit of the vowel change, and *trib, vin,* and *sid,* the forms furthest from the prototype, were the least acceptable of all. The results have been replicated by Prasada and Pinker (1993), and with analogous German forms by Marcus et al. (1995).

10.2.1.4 Graded Goodness of Membership Within most of the subclasses, there are some verbs that clearly accept the irregular past tense form, but there are others, usually of low but nonzero frequency, for which the specified past tense form is less than fully acceptable and which are felt to be unusual or stilted. In (1) we contrast some "good examples" of the past tense form with "poor examples" of the same kinds of forms; the intuitions vary from person to person, as is true for nonprototypical exemplars of conceptual categories. The judgments for these and similar forms are documented quantitatively by Ullman (1999).

(1) **Good examples**   **Poor examples**
   hit, split   spit, forbid
   bled, fed   pled, sped
   burnt, bent   learnt, lent, rent
   dealt, felt, meant   knelt, dreamt
   froze, spoke   wove, hove
   got, forgot   begot, trod
   wrote, drove, rode   dove, strove, smote, strode

10.2.1.5 Unclear Cases For some verbs associated with a subclass, the mandated past tense form is so poor in people's judgment that it is unclear whether the verb can be said to belong to the subclass at all. Sometimes these verbs are restricted to idioms, clichés, or other specialized usages. For example, the expression *forgo the pleasure of*, as in *You will excuse me if I forgo the pleasure of reading your paper until it's published*, sounds fairly natural. Because the verb has a transparent morphological decomposition as [*for* + *go*], the form *forgoed* is clearly unacceptable, but the irregular past tense form, as in *Last night I forwent the pleasure of grading student papers*, is decidedly peculiar if not outright ungrammatical (this intuition has been corroborated by ratings from subjects in Ullman 1999). Similarly, *That dress really becomes you* is a natural English sentence, but *When you were thinner, that dress really became you* is almost unintelligible.

In other cases, grammatical phenomena conspire to make the past tense form of a verb extremely rare. The transitive verb *stand* meaning 'to tolerate' is fairly common, but because it is usually used as the complement of a negated auxiliary, as in *She can't stand him*, the verb is almost always heard in its stem form. In constructions where the past is allowed to reveal itself, the verb sounds quite odd: compare *I don't know how she stands him* with *I don't know how she stood him*, and *I don't know how she bears it* with *I don't know how she bore it*.

10.2.1.6 Conclusions about the Irregular Subclasses Subclasses of irregular verbs in English have characteristic nondefining features, family resemblance structures, prototypes, gradations of goodness of membership, and unclear or fuzzy cases. Since these are exactly the properties that define family resemblance categories, we conclude, in agreement with Bybee and Moder (1983), that the irregular subclasses are family resemblance categories.

This is a surprising conclusion. Linguistic rules are traditionally thought of as a paradigm case of categorical, all-or-none operations and might be thought to correspond to classical categories if anything did. The fact that entities subject to grammatical operations can have a clear family resemblance structure thus has far-ranging implications for some theorists. For example, for Rumelhart and McClelland (1986), this phenomenon is part of an argument for a radically new approach to studying language, based on a computational architecture in which rules play no causal role. For Lakoff (1987), it is part of a call for a radically new way of understanding human cognition in general.

10.2.2 Properties of the Regular Class

Before we accept the claims of Rumelhart and McClelland and of Lakoff, we must ask, Do *all* linguistic objects fall into family resemblance categories? Indeed, does the class most associated with English irregular verbs—namely, English *regular* verbs—fall into family resemblance categories? One answer, favored by Bybee (Bybee and Moder 1983; Bybee 1991) and by Rumelhart and McClelland (1986), is yes: the regular class just has more members, and more general characteristic features. Let us examine this possibility.

The regular and irregular classes interact in a specific way, and it is necessary to take account of this interaction so that the properties of the irregular subclasses do not confound our examination of the properties of the regular class. The interaction is governed by what has been called the *Blocking Principle* (Aronoff 1976) or the *Unique Entry Principle* (Pinker 1984): if a verb has an irregular past tense form, its regular form is preempted or blocked. Thus, the fact that *go* has an irregular past *went* not only allows us to use *went*; it prevents us from using **goed*. The verb *glow*, in contrast, does not have an irregular past **glew*, so its regular past *glowed* is not blocked.

We have seen how some irregular past forms are "fuzzy" or marginal in their grammaticality. As a result of blocking, these gradations of goodness can cause the appearance of complementary gradations of goodness of the corresponding regular. Thus, because *pled* is a marginal past tense form for *plead* but one that we nonetheless recognize, the regular form *pleaded guilty* sounds fairly good but may be tinged with a bit of uncertainty for some speakers. Conversely, *wept* is a fairly good past tense form of *weep*, though not maximally natural (cf., e.g., *kept* for *keep*). As a result *weeped* does not sound terribly good, though it is not perceived as being completely ungrammatical either (cf. *keeped*). This effect has been documented by Ullman (1999; see also Pinker 1991 and Pinker and Prince 1994), who asked subjects to rate the naturalness of irregular and regularized past tense forms for verbs whose irregular pasts are somewhat fuzzy in goodness. The two sets of ratings were negatively correlated.

We now put aside this reciprocity effect due to blocking and try to determine whether the regular class has family-resemblance-category properties independent of those of the irregular subclasses with which it competes.

10.2.2.1 Independence of the Phonology of the Stem The first salient property of the regular class is that it has no sensitivity to the phonological properties of its stems. As a result, it has no phonologically characterized prototype, gradations of membership, or characteristic features.

First, the phonological conditions that govern the irregular subclasses can be entirely flouted by regular verbs. In the extreme case, homophones can have different past tense forms: *ring/rang* versus *wring/wrung*, *hang/hung* (suspend) versus *hang/hanged* (execute), *lie/lay* (recline) versus *lie/lied* (fib), *fit/fit* (what a shirt does) versus *fit/fitted* (what a tailor does). More generally, there are regular counterexamples to the membership criteria for each of the irregular subclasses.

(2) shut/shut   jut/jutted
     bleed/bled   need/needed
     bend/bent   mend/mended
     sleep/slept   seep/seeped
     sell/sold   yell/yelled
     freeze/froze   seize/seized
     grow/grew   glow/glowed
     take/took   fake/faked
     stink/stunk   blink/blinked
     ring/rang   ring/ringed

This shows that the phonologically defined fuzzy boundaries of the irregular subclasses do not create complementary phonological fuzzy boundaries of the regular classes. The effect of the Blocking Principle is that specific irregular *words* block their corresponding regulars. Though most of those words come from regions of phonological space whose neighbors are also often irregular, those regions do not define complementary fuzzy "holes" in the space from which the regulars are excluded; a regular form can occupy any point in that space whatsoever. Moreover, it is not just that there *already* exist regular verbs in the language that live in irregular phonological neighborhoods; the regular class can *add* members that violate *any* irregular membership criteria. The reason has been spelled out by Kiparsky (1982a,b), Pinker and Prince (1988, 1994), Kim et al. (1991), and Kim et al. (1994). Irregular forms are verb *roots*, not verbs. Not all verbs have verb roots: a verb that is intuitively derived from a noun (e.g., *to nail*) has a noun root. A noun or an adjective cannot be marked in the lexicon as having an "irregular past," because nouns and adjectives do not have past tense forms at all; the notion makes no sense. Therefore, a verb created out of a noun or adjective cannot have an irregular past either. All such verbs are regular, regardless of their phonological properties.

(3) He braked the car suddenly. ≠ broke
　　 He flied out to center field. ≠ flew
　　 He ringed the city with artillery. *rang
　　 Martina 2-setted Chris. *2-set
　　 He sleighed down the hill. *slew
　　 He de-flea'd his dog. *de-fled
　　 He spitted the pig. *spat
　　 He righted the boat. *rote
　　 He high-sticked the goalie. *high-stuck
　　 He grandstanded to the crowd. *grandstood

This makes it possible, in principle, for *any* sound sequence whatsoever to become a regular verb. There is a lexical rule in English that converts a name into a verb prefixed with *out*, as in *Clinton has finally out-Nixoned Nixon*. Like all verbs derived from nonverbs, it is regular. Since any linguistically possible sound can be someone's name, any linguistically possible sound can be a regular verb, allowing there to be regular homophones for any irregular. For example:

(4) a.   Mary out-Sally-Rided Sally Ride.
　　　　　　*Mary out-Sally-Rode Sally Ride.
　　 b.   In grim notoriety, Alcatraz out-Sing-Singed Sing-Sing.
　　　　　　*In grim notoriety, Alcatraz out-Sing-Sang Sing-Sing.
　　　　　　*In grim notoriety, Alcatraz out-Sing-Sung Sing-Sing.

This effect has been demonstrated experimentally in several populations. Kim et al. (1991) asked subjects to rate the regular and irregular past tense forms of a set of verbs that were either derived from nouns that were homophonous with an irregular verb or were derived directly from the irregular verbs. For verbs with noun roots, the regular form was give higher ratings; for verbs with verb roots, the irregular form was given higher ratings. Similar effects have been demonstrated in non-college-educated subjects (Kim et al. 1991), children (Kim et al. 1994), and German-speaking adults (Marcus et al. 1995).

Perfectly natural-sounding regular past tense forms exist not only when the verb root is similar to an irregular, but also when it is *dissimilar* to existing regular roots and hence lacks a prototype that would serve as the source of an analogical generalization. Prasada and Pinker (1993) replicated Bybee and Moder's (1983) study but also presented novel *regular* words of differing similarity to existing English regular words. For example, *plip* is close to one of the prototypes for regular verbs in English, because it rhymes with *slip, flip, trip, nip, sip, clip, dip, grip, strip, tip, whip,* and *zip*, whereas *smaig* rhymes with no existing verb root, and *ploamph* is not even phonologically well formed in English. Nonetheless, people rated the prototypical and peripheral forms as sounding equally natural (relative to their stems) and produced the prototypical and peripheral forms with the same probability when they had to produce them.

10.2.2.2 No Prototypes, Gradation of Membership, or Unclear Cases Caused by Low Frequency or Restricted Contexts   Unlike irregular past tense forms, regular past tense forms do not suffer in well-formedness on account of frequency, familiarity, idiomaticity, frozenness, or restricted syntactic contexts. In earlier work (Pinker and Prince 1988), we noted that though the verb *perambulate* may be of low frequency, it is no worse-sounding in its past tense form than it is in its stem form; there is no feeling that *perambulated* is a worse past tense form of *perambulate* than *walked* is of *walk*. In fact, a verb can be of essentially zero frequency and still have a regular past tense form that is judged as no worse than the verb itself. Though *fleech, fleer,* and *anastomose* are unknown to most speakers, speakers judge *fleeched, fleered,* and *anastomosed* to be perfectly good as the past tense forms of those verbs. These observations have been confirmed experimentally by Ullman (1999): subjects' ratings of regular pasts correlated highly with their ratings of the corresponding stems, but not with the frequency of the past form (partialing out stem rating). In contrast, ratings of irregular pasts correlated less strongly with their stem ratings but significantly with past frequency, partialing out stem rating.

Unlike what happens with irregular verbs, when a regular verb gets trapped in a frozen or restricted expression, putting it into the past tense makes it no worse. For example, the verb *eke* is seldom used outside contexts such as *She ekes out a living*, but *She eked out a living*, unlike *forwent the pleasure of*, does not suffer because of it. Similarly: *He crooked his finger; She stinted no effort; I broached the subjects with him; The news augured well for his chances.* The regular verb *to afford*, like the irregular verb *to stand*, usually occurs as a complement to *can't*, but when liberated from this context its past tense form is perfectly natural: *I don't know how she afforded it.* Similarly, both *She doesn't suffer fools gladly* and *She never suffered fools gladly* are acceptable.

These phenomena show why the apparent gradedness of acceptability for regular forms like *pleaded* or *weeped* can be localized to the gradedness of the corresponding irregulars because of the effects of the Blocking Principle and are not inherent to the regular verbs per se. The gradedness of certain irregulars generally comes from low frequency combined with similarity to the prototypes of their subclasses (Ullman 1993). But for regular verbs that do not compete with specific irregular roots, there is no complementary landscape of acceptability defined by phonology and frequency; all are equally good.

10.2.2.3 Default Structure As we have seen, the regular past tense alternation can apply regardless of the stem's phonological properties, verb-root versus non-verb-root status, frequency, listedness (familiarity), and range of contexts. Apparently, the regular class is the *default* class. More generally, there is a sense in which the category of regular verbs has no properties; it is an epiphenomenon of the scope of application of the regular rule.

10.2.2.4 Conclusions about the Regular Class These phenomena invite the following conclusion: the class of regular verbs in English is a classical category. Its necessary and sufficient conditions are simply the conditions of application of the regular rule within English grammar. Those conditions for membership can be stated simply: a verb, unless it has an irregular root.

10.3 Psychological Implications

We have shown that by standard criteria the irregular subclasses are prototype or family resemblance categories, and the regular class is a classical category. This conclusion has several implications.

10.3.1 Psychological Reality

First, both family resemblance categories and classical categories can be psychologically real and natural. Classical categories need not be the product of explicit instruction or formal schooling: the regular past tense alternation does not have to be taught, and indeed every English-speaking child learns it and begins to use it productively in the third year of life (Marcus et al. 1992). The fact that children apply the regular alternation even to high-frequency irregular stems such as *come* and *go*, which they also use with their correct irregular pasts much of the time, suggests that children in some way appreciate the inherently universal range of the regular rule. And like adults, they apply the regular suffix to regular verbs regardless of the degree of the verbs' similarity to other regular verbs (Marcus et al. 1992), and to irregular-sounding verbs that are derived from nouns and adjectives (Kim et al. 1994). Gordon (1985) and Stromswold (1990) have shown that children as young as 3 make qualitative distinctions between regular and irregular plural nouns related to their different formal roles within the grammar, without the benefit of implicit or explicit teaching inputs (see Marcus et al. 1992 and Kim et al. 1994 for discussion).

The regularization-through-derivation effect (*flied out, high-sticked*) provides particularly compelling evidence that classical categories do not have to be the product of rules that are explicitly formulated and deliberately transmitted. The use of the regular rule as a default operation, applying to any derived verb regardless of its phonology, is a grass-roots phenomenon whose subtleties are better appreciated at an unconscious level by the person in the street than by those charged with formulating prescriptive rules. Kim et al. (1991) found that non-college-educated subjects showed the effect strongly, and in the recent history of English and other languages there are documented cases in which the language has accommodated such regularizations in the face of explicit opposition from editors and prescriptive grammarians. For example, Mencken (1936) notes that the verb *to joyride*, first attaining popularity in the 1920s, was usually given the past tense form *joyrided*, as we would predict given its derivation from the noun *a joyride*. Prescriptive grammarians unsuccessfully tried to encourage *joyrode* in its place. Similarly, Kim et al. (1994) showed that children display the effect despite the fact that most have rarely or never heard regularized past tense forms for irregular-sounding verbs in the speech of adults.

On the other side, family resemblance categories are not necessarily artifacts of reaction time studies or rating studies, as Fodor (1981) and Armstrong, Gleitman, and Gleitman (1983) have suggested. Children generalize family resemblance patterns of irregular subclasses to inappropriate regular and irregular verbs in their spontaneous speech, as in *brang* for *brought* and *bote* for *bit*, and their generalizations appear to be sensitive to the frequency and family resemblance structure of the subclasses (Xu and Pinker 1995; Bybee and Slobin 1982a; Rumelhart and McClelland 1986; Pinker and Prince 1988). The irregular subclass structure also affects dialectal variation and historical change in adult speech (Bybee and Slobin 1982b; Mencken 1936; Prasada and Pinker 1993), with new irregular forms occasionally entering the language if their stems are sufficiently similar to existing irregular stems.

10.3.2 Psychological Function
A further corollary is that classical categories and family resemblance categories do not have to have different psychological functions such as careful versus casual reasoning, or reasoning versus categorization of exemplars. What is perhaps most striking about the contrast between the regular and irregular verbs is that two kinds of entities live side by side in people's heads, serving the same function within the grammar as a whole: regular and irregular verbs play indistinguishable roles in the syntax and semantics of tense in English. There is no construction, for example, in which a regular but not an irregular verb can be inserted or vice versa, and no systematic difference in the temporal relationships semantically encoded in the past tense forms of regular and irregular verbs.

More specifically, it is difficult to make sense of the notion that family resemblance categories are the product of a set of identification procedures used to classify exemplars as belonging to core categories with a more classical structure. The suggestion that "irregulars are used in perceptually categorizing members of the regular class" makes no sense. The irregulars are a class of words that display one kind of category structure; the regulars do not display it.

Perhaps a closer analogy would be between membership conditions for the irregular subclasses and the operation on the stem that generates the past tense form. One might say that a family resemblance structure characterizes the membership of each subclass, but once an item is a member (for whatever reason), it is transformed into a past tense form by a classical all-or-none operation such as laxing the vowel. But even here, the core/identification distinction does not easily apply, because the *changes* that the member stems of a class undergo, and not just the *properties* of the stems, have a heterogeneous structure. Within the subclass of irregulars ending in *ing/ink*, *sing* goes to *sang* while *sting* goes to *stung* and *bring* goes to *brought*. Similarly, within the subclass that adds a /d/ to the past tense form, some verbs have their vowel laxed (e.g., *hear/heard*), some have their final consonant deleted (e.g., *make/made, have/had*), some undergo the *e − o* ablaut that is frequent across the various subclasses (e.g., *sell/sold*), and one undergoes a unique vowel change (*do/did*). In sum, both the membership conditions *and* the operations of the irregular subclasses display family resemblance category effects. Later we will show that the core/identification distinction does not work well for conceptual categories either.

10.3.3 Underlying Psychological Mechanism

Though classical and family resemblance categories, in the case of the past tense, do not differ in psychological function—what they are used for—they do differ in psychological structure—what mental processes give rise to them. Our main claim is that the psychological difference between regulars and irregulars is a fundamental one, and is of a piece with the psychological difference between classical and family resemblance categories in general, including conceptual categories.

As we have seen, the classical category consisting of regular verbs is defined completely and implicitly by the nature of a rule in the context of a formal system, in this case, a rule within English grammar that applies to any word bearing the part-of-speech symbol "verb" (unless it has an irregular root). The category is not a generalization or summary over a set of exemplars; indeed, it is blind to the properties of the exemplars that fall into the category. It falls out of the combinatorial rule system that allows humans to communicate propositions (including novel, unusual, or abstract propositions) by building complex words, phrases, and sentences in which the meaning of the whole can be determined from the meanings of the parts and the way in which they are combined.

Family resemblance categories, in contrast, are generalization of patterns of property correlations within a set of memorized exemplars. Consequently, factors that affect human memory affect the composition of the irregular class. A well-known example is word frequency. Irregular verbs tend to be higher in frequency than regular verbs (Ullman 1993; Marcus et al. 1995), and if an irregular verb's frequency declines diachronically, it is liable to become regular (Hooper 1976; Bybee and Slobin 1982b; Bybee 1985). Presumably this is because irregulars are memorized. To memorize an item, one has to hear it; if opportunities for hearing an item are few, its irregular form cannot be acquired and the regular rule can apply as the default. This is also presumably the cause of the fuzziness of the past tenses of irregular verbs that are used mainly in nonpast forms, such as *forgo* or the idiomatic meanings of *stand* or *become*.

A related account could help explain the genesis of irregular verbs' family resemblance structures. Rosch and Mervis (1975) found that people find lists of letter strings that display family resemblance structures easier to remember than ones with arbitrary patterns of similarity. Just as frequency affects the memorizability, hence composition, of the irregular subclasses, so might family resemblance structure. The current subclasses may have emerged from a Darwinian process in which the irregular verbs that survived the generation-to-generation memorization cycle were those that could be grouped into easy-to-remember family resemblance clusters.

In sum, the properties of the regular and irregular classes of verbs in English show that both classical categories and family resemblance categories can be psychologically real, easily and naturally acquired, and not subject to a division of labor by function along the lines of reasoning versus identification of exemplars. Rather, they differ because they are the products of two different kinds of mental processes: a formal rule system and a memorized, partially structured list of exemplars. We now point out two less obvious implications: classical and prototype categories are suited to different kinds of computational architectures, and the mental mechanisms giving rise to the two kinds of categories are suited to representing different kinds of entities in the world.

10.3.4   Computational Architecture

The acquisition of English past tense morphology has been implemented in a widely discussed computer simulation model by Rumelhart and McClelland (1986; see also Pinker and Prince 1988, 1994; Lachter and Bever 1988; Sproat 1992; Prasada and Pinker 1993; Marcus et al. 1992, 1995). The Rumelhart–McClelland (RM) model makes use of a pattern associator architecture, which is paradigmatic of the parallel distributed processing (PDP) or connectionist approach to cognitive science (Rumelhart and McClelland 1986; McClelland and Rumelhart 1986; Pinker and Mehler 1988). Two properties of pattern associators are crucial in understanding their behavior: items are represented by their properties, and statistical contingencies between every input property and every output property across a set of items are recorded and superimposed.

Before being applied to the case of learning past tense forms, pattern associators had been studied in detail, including their ability to learn and identify members of conceptual categories (McClelland and Rumelhart 1985), and they are known to do certain things well. They can often reproduce a set of associations in a training set and generalize to new cases on the basis of their similarity to existing ones. They are sensitive to input pattern frequencies in ways similar to humans. Furthermore, they reproduce many of the effects displayed by people when dealing with family resemblance categories. McClelland and Rumelhart (1985) and Whittlesea (1989) have devised pattern associators that are fed patterns of data concerning properties of a set of nonlinguistic objects. They found that the models do fairly well at duplicating the effects of frequency, prototypicality, family resemblance, gradations of membership, and influence of particular exemplars on human classification times and error rates. Since such effects are known to be related to cooccurrence frequencies among objects' features (Smith and Medin 1981), this is not surprising.

Thanks to these abilities, the pattern associator that Rumelhart and McClelland applied to learning past tense forms handled the irregular verbs with some success. After training on a set of regular and irregular verbs, the model was able to approximate the past tense forms for all of them given only the stem as input. Furthermore, it was able to generalize to new irregular verbs by analogy to similar ones in the training set, such as *bid* for *bid*, *clung* for *cling*, and *wept* for *weep*. In addition, it showed a tendency to extend some of the subregular alternations to regular verbs on the basis of their similarity to irregulars, such as *kid* for *kid* and *slept* for *slip*, showing a sensitivity to the family resemblance structure of the irregular subclasses. Finally, its tendencies to overgeneralize the regular /d/ ending to the various irregular subclasses is in rough accord with children's tendencies to do so, which in turn is based on the frequency and consistency of the vowel changes that the verbs within each subclass undergo (Pinker and Prince 1988; Sproat 1992).[1]

However, pattern associators do not seem to perform as well for other kinds of mappings. In particular, they are deficient in handling regular verbs. For one thing, their uniform structure, in which regulars and irregulars are handled by a single associative mechanism, provides no explanation for why the regular class has such different properties from the irregular classes; it falsely predicts that the regular class should just be a larger and more general prototype subclass.

Moreover, the pattern associator fails to acquire the regulars properly. In earlier work (Pinker and Prince 1988), we pointed out that the model is prone to *blending*. Competing statistical regularities in which a stem participates do not block each other; they get superimposed. For example, the model produced erroneous forms in which an irregular vowel change was combined with the regular ending, as in *sepped* as the past of *sip* or *brawned* for *brown*. It would often blend the /t/ and /ɨd/ variants of the regular past tense form, producing *stepted* for *step* or *typted* for *type*. Sometimes the blends were quite odd, such as *membled* for *mailed* or *toureder* for *tour*.

Furthermore, we noted that in contrast to the default nature of the regular rule, the RM model failed to produce any past form at all for certain verbs, such as *jump, pump, glare*, and *trail*. Presumably this was because the model could not treat the regular ending as an operation that was capable of applying to any stem whatsoever, regardless of its properties; the ending was simply associated with the features of the regular stems encountered in the input. If a new verb happened to lie in a region of phonological space in which no verbs had previously been supplied in the training set (e.g., *jump* and *pump*, with their unusual word-final consonant cluster), no coherent set of output features was strongly enough associated with the active input features, and no response above the background noise could be made. Our diagnosis was tested by Prasada and Pinker (1993), who presented typical-sounding and unusual-sounding verbs to the trained network. For the unusual-sounding items, it produced odd blends and chimeras such as *smairf/sprurice, trilb/treelilt, smeej/leefloag*, and *frilg/freezled*.

Finally, the model is inconsistent with certain kinds of developmental evidence. Children first use many irregulars properly when they use them in a past tense form at all (e.g., *broke*), then begin to overregularize them occasionally (e.g., *broke* and *breaked*) before the overregularizations drop out years later. Since pattern associators are driven by pattern frequency, the only way the RM model could be made to duplicate this sequence was first to expose it to a small number of high-frequency verbs, most of them irregular, presented a few times each, followed by a large number of medium-frequency verbs, most of them regular, presented many times each. Only when the model was swamped with exemplars of the regular pattern did it begin to overregularize verbs it had previously handled properly. However, the onset of overregularization in children is not caused by a sudden shift in the proportion of regular verbs in the speech they hear from their parents; the proportion remains largely unchanged before, during, and after the point at which they begin to overregularize (Pinker and Prince 1988; Slobin 1971; Marcus et al. 1992). Nor is it caused by a rapid increase in the proportion of verbs in their vocabulary that is regular; the percentage of children's vocabulary that is regular increases quickly when they are *not* overregularizing, and increases more slowly when they *are* overregularizing (Marcus et al. 1992).

The results support the traditional explanation of overregularization, which appeals not to frequency but to different internal mechanisms. Children at first memorize irregular and regular pasts. Then they discover that a regularity holds between many regular stems and their past forms and create a rule that they apply across the board, including instances in which a memorized irregular form does not come to mind quickly enough. The rule is available to fill the gap, resulting in an overregularization. Consistent with this interpretation, Marcus et al. (1992) found that children begin to overregularize at the age at which they first start using *regular* forms consistently in the past tense; that, presumably, is the point at which the regular rule has been acquired. As mentioned, the fact that the regular rule is applied even to high-frequency irregular stems, which remain high in frequency in children's input throughout development, shows that children treat the regular rule as having an unlimited range.

Proponents of connectionist models of language have offered two kinds of counterarguments, but both are inadequate. One is that the RM model was a two-layer perceptron, and that three-layer models, whose hidden layer's weights are trained by error-back-propagation, perform much better (see, e.g., Plunkett and Marchman 1991, 1993; MacWhinney and Leinbach 1991). However, Sproat (1992), Prasada and Pinker (1993), and Marcus (1995) have shown that hidden-layer models have the same problems as the original RM model. The other is that the effects of regularity in English come from the fact that regular verbs are in the majority in English, fostering the broadest generalization. German presents the crucial comparison. Marcus et al. (1995) reviewed the grammar and vocabulary statistics of German in detail and documented that the participle -*t* and plural -*s* are found in a *minority* of words in the language, compared to irregular alternatives, but nonetheless apply in exactly the "default" circumstances where access to memorized verbs or their sounds fails, including novel, unusual-sounding, and derived words (i.e., the *flied out* examples have exact analogues in German). The findings were verified in two experiments eliciting ratings of novel German words from German adults. The crosslinguistic comparison suggests that default suffixation arises not because numerous regular words reinforce a pattern in associative memory but from a memory-independent, symbol-concatenating mental operation.

In sum, pattern associators handle irregular subclasses reasonably well but handle the regular class poorly, both in terms of computational ability and in terms of psychological fidelity. We suggest that this is a symptom of the relative suitability of this architecture to handle family resemblance and classical categories in general. The reasons, we suggest, are straightforward:

• Classical categories are the product of formal rules.
• Formal rules apply to objects regardless of their content—that is what "formal rule" means.
• Pattern associators soak up patterns of correlation among objects' contents—that is what they are designed to do.
• Therefore, pattern associators are not suited to handling classical categories.

We conclude that the brain contains some kind of nonassociative architecture, used in language and presumably elsewhere.

10.3.5 Epistemological Categories versus Ontological Categories
Rey (1983) has pointed out that even if people can be shown to use prototype (or classical) categories, it doesn't mean that the world contains prototype (or classical) categories—that is, that the lawful generalizations of how the world works, as captured by the best scientific description, make reference to one kind of category or the other. That raises a question: if there is a psychological distinction between the representations of prototype and classical categories, is it because these representations accurately reflect different kinds of categories in the world? Or does the human system of categorization arise from some limitation or quirk of our neurological apparatus that does not necessarily correspond to the lawful groupings in the world?

The questions of what kinds of categories are in the mind and what kinds of categories are in the world are clearly related. If the mind evolved to allow us to grasp and make predictions about the world, the mental system that forms conceptual categories should be built around implicit assumptions about the kinds of categories that the world contains, in the same way that a visual algorithm for recovering structure from motion might presuppose a world with rigid objects and might work best in situations where the assumption is satisfied.

Because the English past tense system shows classical and family resemblance categories but must have a very different ontology from that underlying concepts of tools, vegetables, animals, and other entities that ordinarily compose conceptual categories, an analysis of the source of classical and family resemblance categories in the past tense system may help us to identify the distinctive conditions in which these two kinds of categories arise.

10.3.6   Where Do the Properties of the Regular and Irregular Classes Come From?

The properties of the regular class are simply products of the regular rule. From any speaker's perspective, the class exists "in the world" in the sense that other speakers of the language possess the rule and use it in speaking and understanding. This in turn comes from the basic requirement for parity in any communicative system. Language can only function if the rule system that generates forms is shared by a community of speakers. Thus, one person's use of a past tense rule (or any rule) in production presupposes that that same rule is in the head of the listener and will be used to interpret the produced form. Similarly, use of a rule in comprehension presupposes that the speaker used it in programming his or her speech. So the answer to the question "What class of entities in the world is picked out by a rule-generated class, such as the regular verbs?" is "The class of entities that can be generated by a replica of that rule in other speakers' minds."

For the irregulars, the issue is more complex. Of course, irregulars, like regulars, are usable only because they are shared by other speakers. But unlike the case of regulars, where the rule is so simple and efficient that it naturally fits into a grammar shared by all members of a community, the composition of the irregular class is so seemingly illogical that one must ask how other speakers came to possess it to begin with.

Earlier we suggested that the family resemblance structure of the irregular past tense subclasses is related to the fact that irregulars must be memorized and human memory has an easier time with family resemblance categories (Rosch and Mervis 1975). Interestingly, the obvious

Darwinian metaphor, in which the most easily memorized verbs survive, does not apply to the psychology of the child doing the learning. Note that family resemblance structure is not a property that some individual verbs have and others lack, but a property of *an entire class* of verbs. But unlike the subjects of Rosch and Mervis's experiment, children are not given two classes to learn, one with a random organization, the other with a family resemblance structure, with the latter being better retained in memory. One might suppose that the similarity of a verb to other verbs affects how easy it is for the child to memorize that verb, and that in the aggregate, a family resemblance structure arises. But this, too, does not properly characterize the acquisition of irregular forms. There is relatively little change in the composition of the subclasses between one generation and the next; children end up pretty much learning the same irregulars that their parents learned. Moreover, if the children's memory really shaped their irregular classes, we would expect them to arrive at classical categories, not family resemblance categories. For example, a rule that said "All verbs ending in *ing* go to *ang*" would have much higher inter-item similarity than the current English *ing* class, so verbs like *bring* would be even easier to memorize. In fact, given children's ability to regularize the irregular verbs by assimilating them to the regular rule (*bringed*), they would be in a position to obliterate irregularity altogether if their memory were all that fragile.

A more accurate version of the Darwinian metaphor would point to effects of memory not in the child doing the learning in a given generation but in the children (and adults) of previous generations whose learning shaped the input to the current generation. Even though each generation reproduces the previous generation's irregulars with high accuracy, changes occasionally creep in. These can be characterized as a kind of convergent evolution toward certain forms. For example, some lower-frequency irregular verbs may be consistently regularized in a given generation, and this might be more likely for verbs that were most dissimilar from other irregulars and hence most weakly protected from forgetting. (Marcus et al. (1992) documented that irregulars that are more dissimilar from other irregulars are more prone to being overregularized by children.) In the other direction, some regulars might be attracted into an irregular class because of their high similarity to existing irregulars, as is happening with *sneak/snuck* (cf. *stick/stuck, string/strung*, etc.). If some of these occasional forgettings and analogies get fixed in a language community in a contagion-like process (see Cavalli-Sforza and Feldman

1981) and accumulate across generations, classes of verbs with a family resemblance structure can arise. The past tense forms *quit* and *knelt*, for example, are fairly recent additions to the language and are presumably irregular because of their similarity to verbs like *hit* and *feel*. This phenomenon can be seen even more clearly in the more rapid process of dialect formation in smaller communities, where forms such as *bring-brang*, *slide-slud*, and *drag-drug* are common (see Mencken 1936).

Though this convergent evolution process surely occurs, it cannot explain the entire structure of the irregulars in English. First, it does not capture the historical facts completely. The language never contained arbitrary irregular classes whose members were attracted into or drifted out of prototype classes because of fussy learners, leaving the next generation with a slightly more orderly class than they had found. Rather, as we will illustrate, the irregular subclasses are in evidence from the earliest sources. Second, the account posits a kind of harmony between properties of the memory of one generation and properties of the memory of succeeding generations: the errors of forgetting and assimilation of generation n result in a stimulus set that is easier for generation $n + 1$ to acquire without error, because the memory of both generations is biased toward remembering items that are similar along multiple dimensions to other items. But in doing so it begs the question of why memorization of categories in any generation should be biased toward partial similarities to begin with. Why does memory work that way? Why not do away with remembering patterns of irregularity altogether and give the next generation a nice regular class?

In the history of English, *divergence* has been the more prominent trend. That confronted learners in each generation with the task of learning classes whose family resemblance structure was not simply caused by the psychology of previous generation of learners. The Old English strong classes, ancestors of most of today's irregular verbs, evolved out of classes that can be traced back to Proto-Indo-European. Many scholars believe that the Proto-Indo-European classes were defined by regular rules: the number and type of segments following the vowel within the stem determined the kind of change the vowel underwent (Johnson 1986; Prokosch 1939; Campbell 1959). By the time of Old English, the patterns were more complicated, but they were still more pervasive and productive and tolerated fewer arbitrary exceptions than the alternations in the modern English irregular subclasses. That is, many stems that are now regular but fit the characteristic pattern of an irregular subclass in fact used to undergo the irregular change: *deem/dempt, lean/leant, chide/chid, seem/sempt, believe/beleft, greet/gret, heat/het, bite/bote, slide/slode, abide/abode, fare/fore, help/holp*, and many others. Furthermore, there was a moderate degree of productivity within the classes (Johnson 1986).

Beginning in the Middle English period, there was an even greater decline in the productivity and systematicity of the strong past tense subclasses. The main causes were the huge influx of new words from Latin and French that needed a general, condition-free past tense operation, and the widespread shifts in vowel pronunciation that obscured regularities in the vowel change operations. The "weak" suffixing operation was already being used for verbs derived from nouns in Old English, which did not fit the sound patterns defining the strong classes of verbs, so their extension to borrowed words was natural (see Marcus et al. 1995 for further discussion).

In sum, there has been a consistent trend in the history of English since the Proto-Indo-European period for the strong classes, originally defined by phonological properties of their stems, to become lists of items to be learned individually. This had an interesting consequence. Originally, lists would have been relatively homogeneous, owing to their once having been generated by rule-like operations. But then, a variety of unrelated processes, operating on individual items, destroyed the homogeneity of the classes. Here are three examples:

Phonological change The verbs *blow, grow, throw, know, draw, fly, slay* all begin with a ⟨consonant-sonorant⟩ cluster except for *know*. The reason that *know* is exceptional leaps from the page in the way it is spelled. As it was originally pronounced, with an initial *k*, it did fit the pattern; when syllable-initial *kn* mutated to *n* within the sound pattern of the language as a whole, *know* was left stranded as an exception within its subclass.

Morphological category collapse In Old English, past tenses were distinguished by person and number. For example, *sing* had a paradigm that we can simplify as follows:

(5)	**Singular**	**Plural**
1st	sang	sung
2nd	sung	sung
3rd	sang	sung

When the number distinctions collapsed, each verb had to pick a form for its past tense as if playing musical chairs. Different verbs made different choices; hence, we have *sing/sang/sung* alongside *sling/slung/slung*. The contrast between *freeze/froze* and *cleave/cleft* has a similar cause.

Attrition Earlier, the class in which /d/ changed to /t/ had the following members: *bend, lend, send, spend, blend, wend, rend, shend, build, geld, gild, gird* (Bybee and Slobin 1982b). The class is succinctly characterized as containing a vowel followed by a sonorant followed by *d*. In modern American English, the verbs *geld, gird, gild, wend, rend*, and *shend* are now obsolete or obscure. The residue of the class has five members, four rhyming with *end* and one with *ild*. Although logically it still can be characterized as ending in a ⟨vowel-sonorant-*d*⟩ cluster, the presence of regular verbs ending in *eld* and *ird*, and the highly specific nature of the rhyme with *end*, makes it more natural to represent the class as containing verbs that rhyme with *end* but with one exception.

We conclude that a class of items that originally is homogeneous because it is generated by a rule can acquire a family resemblance structure by divergent evolution once the rule ceases to operate and the effects of unrelated processes acting on individual members accumulate through history. Superimposed on these patterns is a convergent process in which the accumulated effects of the analogizing and forgetting tendencies of previous generations of learners cause partly similar forms to accrete onto an existing class. Thus, a learner in a single generation is confronted with family resemblance structures as products of these divergent and convergent historical processes, and these structures can be said to exist in the world independent of his or her psychology.

10.4   Implications for Conceptual Categories

Do the discoveries about classical and family resemblance categories in past tense forms offer insight into the role of classical and family resemblance categories in the domain of conceptual categories like birds and mothers? To answer this question, we must begin by considering what conceptual categories are for.

10.4.1   The Function of Conceptual Categories: Inference of Unobserved Properties

No two objects are exactly alike. So why do we use conceptual categories? Why don't we treat every objects as the unique individual that it is? And why do we form the categories we do? Why lump together salmon, minnow, and sharks, as opposed to sharks, leaves, and spaghetti? Sometimes it is suggested that people need categories to reduce memory or processing load. But given that the cortex has on the order of a trillion synapses and that long-term memory is often characterized as "infinite," the suggestion carries little force. Furthermore, for many categories (e.g., months, baseball teams, one's friends) both the category and every individual member of it are stored in memory.

Bobick (1987), Shepard (1987), and Anderson (1990) have attempted to reverse-engineer human conceptual categories in terms of their function in people's dealings with the world. They have independently proposed that categories are useful because they allow us to infer objects' unobserved properties from their observed properties (see also Rosch 1978; Quine 1969). Though we cannot know everything about an object, we can observe some things; the observed properties allow us to assign the object to a category, and the structure of the category then allows us to infer the values of the object's unobserved properties. Categories at different levels of a hierarchy (e.g., cocker spaniels, dogs, mammals, vertebrates, animals, living things) are useful because they allow a variety of trade-offs between the ease of categorization and the power of the licensed inference. For low-level, specific categories, one must know a lot about the object to know that it belongs in the category, but one can then infer many unobserved aspects of the nature of the object. For high-level, general categories, one need know only a few properties of an object to know it belongs to the category, but one can infer only a few of its unobserved properties once it is thus categorized.

To be concrete: Knowing that Peter is a cottontail, we can predict that he grows, breathes, moves, was suckled, inhabits open country or woodland clearings, spreads tularemia, and can contract myxomatosis. If we knew only that that he was a mammal, the list would include only growing, breathing, moving, and being suckled. If we knew only that he was an animal, it would shrink to growing, breathing, and moving. On the other hand, it's much harder to tag Peter as a cottontail than as a mammal or an animal. To tag him as a mammal, we need only notice that he is furry and moving, but to tag him as a cottontail, we have to notice that he is long-eared, short-tailed, and long-hind-legged, and that he has white on the underside of his tail. To identify *very* specific categories, we have to examine so many properties that there would be few left to predict. Most of our everyday categories are somewhere in the middle: "rabbit," not mammal or cottontail; "car," not vehicle or Ford Tempo; "chair," not furniture or Barcalounger. They represent a compromise between how hard it is to identify the category and how much good the category does. These compromises correspond to Rosch's (1978) notion of the "basic level" of a category.

We can get away with inductive leaps based on categories only because the world works in certain ways. Objects are not randomly distributed through the multidimensional space of properties that humans are interested in; they cluster in regions of co-occurring properties that Bobick calls "natural modes" and Shepard calls "consequential regions." These modes are the result of the laws of form and function that govern the processes that create and preserve objects. For example, the laws of physics dictate that objects denser than water will be found on lake bottoms rather than lake surfaces. Laws of physics and biology dictate that objects that move quickly through fluid media have streamlined shapes, and bigger objects tend to have thicker legs. If we know some of the coordinates of an object in property space, the existence of natural modes allows us to infer (at least probabilistically) some of its unknown coordinates.

10.4.2   Classical Categories: Inferences within Idealized Lawful Systems

All this raises the question of what kinds of regularities in the world generate natural modes that humans can exploit by forming concepts. In the most general sense, regularities in the world are the result of scientific and mathematical laws (e.g., of physics, geometry, physiology). Laws can be captured in formal systems, given a suitable idealization of the world. By "formal system" we mean a symbol manipulation scheme, consisting of a set of propositions and a set of inference rules that apply to the proposition by virtue of their form alone, so that any knowledge not explicitly stated in the proposition cannot effect the inferences made within it. Formal systems, we suggest, are the contexts in which classical categories are defined. Therefore, under whatever idealization of the world a set of scientific or mathematical laws applies, the world contains classical categories. For example, when the texture, material, thickness, and microscopically ragged edges of real-world objects are provisionally ignored, some can be idealized as plane geometry figures. Under this idealization, objects with two equal sides can be assigned to the category "isosceles triangle." Once the object is assigned to the category, one can make the inference that it also has two equal angles, among other things. Frictionless planes, ideal gases, randomly interbreeding local populations, and uniform communities of undistractable speaker-hearers are other idealizations under which regularities in the behavior of objects can be captured in formal systems. A smart organism could use formal systems as idealizations of the world to infer unknown properties from known ones. In the psychology of categorization, no less than in the history of science, idealization or selective *ignoring* of salient correlational structure is crucial to apprehending causal laws.

We suggest, then, that wherever classical categories are to be found in human cognition, they will be part of a mentally represented formal system allowing deductions to be made. Given the function of concepts, why else would one bother to assign an object to a classical category? What is unnatural, then, about traditional experiments in concept formation, such as those of Bruner, Goodnow, and Austin (1956), in which subjects learn categories like "red square with two borders," is not that the categories have sharp boundaries or necessary and sufficient conditions, but that the categories are not part of a system allowing interesting inferences to be drawn—they are unnatural because they are literally useless.

Though one tends to think of formal systems as the province of systematic education in modern societies, there are a variety of kinds of formal systems capturing inference-supporting regularities that could be accessible to people, including those in preindustrial and preagricultural societies. For example, bodies of folk science need not resemble their counterparts in modern scientific systems, but they can reproduce some of their visible predictions with alternative means. Mathematical intuitions too are incorporated into many other systems of common knowledge. Here are some examples:

• Arithmetic, with classical categories like "a set of three objects," supporting inferences like "cannot be divided into two equal parts," independent of the properties of objects that can be grouped into threes.
• Geometry, with classical categories like "circle," supporting inferences like "all points equidistant from the center" or "circumference is a constant multiple of diameter," regardless of whether previously encountered circles are sections of tree trunks or drawings in sand.
• Logic, with classical categories like "disjunctive proposition," supporting inferences like "is true if its second part is true" or "is false if the negations of both its parts are true."
• Folk biology, with classical categories like "toad of kind x," which support inferences like "extract of mouth gland when boiled and dried is poisonous," regardless of its similarities to nonpoisonous toads or its dissimilarities to other poisonous toads.
• Folk physiology, with the famous all-or-none category "pregnant," supporting the inferences "female," "nonvirgin," and "future mother," regardless of weight or body shape.

In addition, the world of humans contains other humans, and there is reason to expect mentally represented formal systems to arise that govern the conduct of humans with one another. Given the fuzziness and experience-dependent individual variation inherent to family resemblance categories, it is not surprising that conflicts of interest between individuals will often be resolved by reasoning within systems that have a classical structure, allowing all-or-none decisions whose basis can be agreed to by all parties. There is a rationale to assigning drinking privileges to people after their twenty-first birthday, arbitrary though that is, rather than attempting to ascertain the emotional maturity of each individual when he or she asks for a drink. Furthermore, Freyd (1983) and Smolensky (1988) have suggested that certain kinds of socially transmitted knowledge are likely to assume the form of discrete symbol systems because of constraints on the channels of communication with which they must be communicated between individuals and transmitted between generations. It is not hard to identify formal systems involved in social interactions that define classical categories:

• Kinship, with classical categories like "grandmother of X," supporting inferences like "may be the mother of X's uncle or aunt" or "is the daughter of one of X's great-grandparents," regardless of hair color or propensity to bake muffins.
• Sociopolitical structure, with classical categories like "president" or "chief," supporting inferences like "carries out decisions on entering wars," regardless of physical strength, height, sex, and so on.
• Law, with classical categories like "felon," supporting inferences like "cannot hold public office," regardless of presence or absence of a sinister appearance, social class, and so on.
• Language, with the category "verb," supporting the inference "has a past tense form suffixed with [d] unless it has an irregular root," regardless of its phonological properties.

It is unlikely to be a coincidence that humans uniquely and nearly universally have language, counting systems, folk science, kinship systems, music, and law. As we have discussed, classical categories deriving from formal systems require a neural architecture that is capable of ignoring the statistical microstructure of the properties of the exemplars of a category that an individual has encountered. One can speculate that the development of a nonassociative neural architecture suitable to formal systems was a critical event in the evolution of human intelligence.

10.4.3   Family Resemblance Categories: Inferences within Historically Related Similarity Clusters

In a previous section, we showed that learners of English are presented with a family resemblance structure and must cope with it if they are to speak the same language as their parents. Are there cases where learners of conceptual categories are similarly forced to cope with a family resemblance structure in nature if they are to be able to make inferences about it? Many people have noted similarities between linguistic and biological evolution (see, e.g., Cavalli-Sforza and Feldman 1981), and there is a particularly compelling analogy in the formation of family resemblance categories in the evolution of biological taxa.

It is generally believed that a novel species evolves from a small interbreeding population occupying a local, hence relatively homogeneous stable environment. Through natural selection, the organisms become adapted to the local environment, with the adaptive traits spreading through the population via sexual reproduction. As a result, the population assumes a morphology that is relatively uniform—since selection acts to reduce variation (Sober 1984; Ridley 1986)—and predictable in part from engineering considerations to the extent that the organism's niche and selection pressures can be identified (Hutchinson 1959; Williams, 1966; Dawkins 1986).

Subsequent geographic dispersal can cause the members of the ancestral population to form reproductively isolated subgroups. They are no longer homogenized by interbreeding, and no longer subject to the same set of selection pressures imposed by a local environment. In the first generation following dispersal, the species is still homogeneous. Then, a set of distinct processes destroys the homogeneity of class: genetic drift, local geographic and climatic changes imposing new selection pressures, adaptive radiations following entry into empty environments, and local extinctions. As a result, the descendants of the ancestral species form a family resemblance category—the category of "birds," for example. Robins, penguins, and ostriches share many features (e.g., feathers) because of their common ancestry from a single population adapted to flying, while differing because of independent processes applying to different members of that population through history.

This suggests that as in the cases of irregular past tense subclasses, the family resemblance structure of many biological taxa comes from the world, not just the minds of those learning about them. Note that such family resemblance structures are not always identical with classically defined categories, and they may be indispensable even in the best scientific theories. Many traditional biological taxa are somewhat arbitrary, serving as useful summaries of similar kinds of organisms. There are, to be sure, some biological categories that are well defined, including species (a population of interbreeding organisms sharing a common gene pool) and monophyletic groups or clades (all the descendants of a common ancestor also belonging to the category). But many important biological taxa are neither. For example, fish comprise thousands of species, including coelocanths and trout. But the most recent common ancestor of coelocanths and trout is also an ancestor of mammals. Therefore, no branch of the genealogical tree of organisms corresponds to all and only fish; trout and coelocanth are grouped together and distinguished from mammals by virtue of their many shared properties. To some biologists this is reason to deny the scientific significance of the category altogether, but most probably agree with the sentiment captured by Gould when he writes, "A coelocanth looks like a fish, tastes like a fish, acts like a fish, and therefore—in some legitimate sense beyond hidebound tradition—*is* a fish" (1983, 363). In other words, biologists often recognize a category that is characterized as a cluster of co-occurring properties. Indeed, some taxonomists have tried to characterize taxa with the help of clustering algorithms that use criteria similar to those thought to lead to the formation of prototype conceptual categories in humans (see Ridley 1986; Bobick 1987).

Thus, we have noted two examples of family resemblance categories that exist in the world and that have the same genesis: a law-governed process creating a relatively homogeneous class, followed by a cessation of the influence of the process and the operation of independent historical causes that heterogenize the class, though not to such an extent that the intermember similarities are obliterated entirely. Since objects can escape the direct influence of laws while retaining some of their effects, a smart organism cannot count on always being able to capture the world's regularities in formal systems. For example, no observer knowing only the United States Constitution would be able to explain why presidents are always wealthy white Christian males. Similarly, presumably no observer, not even a scientist equipped with a knowledge of physiology and ecology, would be able to explain why penguins have feathers, like robins, rather than fur, like seals. Instead, it will often be best simply to record the interpredictive contingencies among objects' properties to infer unknown properties from known ones. Thus, a smart observer can record the contingencies among feathers, wings, egg-laying, beaks, and so on, to note that the world contains a set of objects in which these properties cluster and to use the presence of one subset of properties to infer the likely presence of others.

Just as irregular subclasses were shaped by both divergent and convergent historical processes, so in the domain of conceptual categories there is a convergent process that can cause objects to cluster around natural modes even if the objects are not linked as descendants of a more homogeneous ancestral population. For example, there is no genealogical account of chairs that parallels the ones we give for languages or species. The similarities among chairs are caused solely by a convergent process, in which a set of properties repeatedly arises because it is particularly stable and adaptive in a given kind of environment, and several historically unrelated entities evolve to attain that set. Examples from biology include nonhomologous organs such as the eyes of mammals and of cephalopods, the wings of bats and of birds, and polyphyletic groups such as cactuslike plants (which have evolved succulent leaves, spines, and corrugated stems as adaptations to desert climates in several parts of the world). As in the case of divergent evolution discussed above, there is a mixture of shared and distinct properties that are respectively caused by law-governed adaptation and historical accident, though here the influences are temporally reversed. For example, although vertebrate and cephalopod eyes are strikingly similar, in vertebrates the photoreceptors point away from the light source and incoming light has to pass through the optic nerve fibers, whereas in cephalopods the photoreceptors point toward the light in a more sensible arrangement. The difference is thought to have arisen from the different evolutionary starting points defined by the ancestors to the two groups, presumably relating to differences in the embryological processes that lay down optic and neural tissue. Artifacts such as chairs develop via a similar process; for a chair to be useful, it must have a shape and material that is suited to the function of holding people up, but it is also influenced by myriad historical factors such as style, available materials, and ease of manufacture with contemporary technology. Social stereotypes, arising from the many historical accidents that cause certain kinds of people to assume certain roles, are another example.

We might expect family resemblance categories to be formed whenever there is a correlational structure in the properties that people attend to among sets of objects they care about, and that the world will contain opportunities for such clusters to form wherever there are laws that cause properties to be visibly correlated and historical contingencies that cause the correlation to be less than perfect—which is to say, almost everywhere.

10.4.4   Interactions between Classical and Family Resemblance Categories

The referents of many words, such as *bird* and *grandmother*, appear to have properties of both classical and family resemblance categories. How are these two systems to be reconciled? The distinction between cores used for reasoning and stereotypes used for identification was of no help in the case of English past tense forms, and the distinction does not do much better when applied to conceptual categories. Many classical categories have no family resemblance identification procedure associated with them, for example, the number "-3." Many family resemblance categories have no classical category serving as a core that they identify, such as "seafood" or Wittgenstein's famous example, "game." Furthermore, some classical categories can be identified by simple, easily computable, all-or-none tests. For example, odd numbers can be quickly identified by tests such as "Divide by 2 and check for remainder" or "See if last digit is 1, 3, 5, 7, or 9"; in fact, the features of the associated family resemblance class, such as "has many odd digits" (which Armstrong, Gleitman, and Gleitman (1983) found to be a feature that led subjects to judge that a given number was a better example of the "odd" class), are not even probabilistically diagnostic. On the other side, family resemblance classes can support nonperceptual reasoning, sometimes quite reliably, such as "Presidents are well-off," "Vegetables are not served for dessert," or "Tools have metal in them." We are not denying that categories may have "cores" in the sense that some kinds of knowledge are given priority over others when they conflict, but it does not seem that this distinction can be equated either with quick-identification versus reasoning or with classical versus family resemblance categories (Armstrong, Gleitman, and Gleitman (1983) and Rey (1983) mention some of these problems).

A more likely reconciliation is that people have parallel mental systems, one that records the correlational structure among sets of similar objects, and another that sets up systems of idealized laws. Often a category within one system will be linked to a counterpart within the other. In general, we might expect family resemblance categories to be more accessible to observers than classical categories. Most objects in the world are cluttered by the effects of the myriad historical processes that led to their creation and preservation, obscuring underlying laws. In the lucky cases when people are able to see these laws peeking through the clutter and try to capture them in idealized systems, the elements of these systems may be seen to apply to many of the objects belonging to the family resemblance clusters that were independently formed through simple observation of the correlational structure displayed by frequently encountered exemplars. In such cases, languages appear to assign the same verbal label to both. This is what leads to the ambiguity of *A penguin is a perfectly good bird*, one of whose readings is true, the other false. It also is what leads to such paradoxes as the behavior of Armstrong, Gleitman, and Gleitman's subjects, who could assert both that odd numbers form an all-or-none category tolerating no intermediate degrees of membership and that 13 is a better example of it than 23.

The fact that these systems are distinct is at the heart of Putnam's (1975) and Kripke's (1972) well-known argument that natural kind terms are not defined by a set of conditions that pick out the members of the category in the world. Thus, even though we think of "animal" as a necessary part of the definition of *cat*, if we were to discover that cats were in fact robots controlled from Mars, we would not conclude that *cat* no longer referred to the entities formerly called cats, or that it did refer to catlike entities on some other planet that really were animals. Rather, the label *cat* is rigidly assigned to a set of objects in the world. According to Putnam, people have a "stereotype" of such objects that helps them with tentative identification, but they will defer to an expert in establishing category membership more definitively.

Schwartz (1979) points out that such intuitions about natural kind terms are driven by a belief that their members have an "underlying trait" in common. People act as if they believe in the existence of such a trait even if they are prepared to accept that their current belief about the nature of the trait is incorrect, even if they have no idea of the nature of the trait, indeed even if *no one* knows the nature of the trait. Schwartz's analysis suggests that people's intuitions are influenced by a metatheory, a kind of essentialism, that asserts that the varying forms that an object can assume are causally related in terms of their relation to a hidden trait or essence. These essences are clearly not family resemblance categories since it is possible, indeed typical, that they are not associated with *any* properties of the relevant objects at all, let alone a cluster of frequently co-occurring properties (that is, if Putnam and Kripke are correct, there is no property associated with the concept underlying "cat" or "gold" that cannot be relinquished by a person while he or she still believes the concept to apply to that category of objects). Rather, the hidden essences must be represented as abstract symbols within internally represented formal systems, defining slots for particular traits provided by folk or formal science, and allowing inferences to be made about heredity, growth, physical structure, change, and behavior. Subsequent research by Keil (1989) and Gelman (Gelman, Coley, and Gottfried 1994) has gathered evidence for essentialist thinking in preschool children and adults in nonliterate cultures. More generally, Medin (1989), Murphy (1993), Rips (1989), and Smith, Langston, and Nisbett (1992) have emphasized the importance of intuitive rule-like theories in the organization of people's conceptual categories.

In sum, natural kind terms like *cat* or *gold* are linked both to stereotypes, or family resemblance categories acquired by observing the correlational structure in sets of similar familiar objects, and to abstract essences, or hidden traits within an intuitive theory that unite an object's varying appearances and provide the infrastructure for bits of folk science and institutionalized science. (The Putnam-Kripke puzzles arise from thought experiments in which these systems are separated.)

The human tendency to induce categories from clusters of similar objects one has encountered, to construct formal systems of rules applying to ideal objects, and to link entities of the two kinds with each other is probably the root of many apparent paradoxes in the study of concepts and often within the conceptual systems themselves. For example, exactly this duality can be found in the legal system in the distinction between reasoning by constitutionality and reasoning by precedent. Legal questions are commonly resolved by appealing to precedents, with more similar prior decisions carrying more weight. However, when the constitutionality of a current decision is at issue, only a restricted set of principles is relevant, and similarity to earlier cases must be ignored.

10.5   Conclusion

It may be surprising to see so many parallels drawn between two phenomena that seem to be in such different domains. We are not claiming that past tense forms and conceptual categories are alike in all essential respects or that they are generated by a single cognitive system. But often widespread similarities in remote domains make the case for *some* common underlying principles compelling. English past tense forms come in two versions that are identical in function and at first glance differ only in size and degree of uniformity. On closer examination, they turn out to represent two distinct systems that correspond point for point with classical and family resemblance categories, respectively. Moreover, the two systems are linked with distinct psychological faculties, developmental courses, real-world causes, and computational architectures. A fundamental distinction must lie at the heart of this duality. Specifically, we suggest, human concepts can correspond to classical categories or to family resemblance categories. Classical categories are defined by formal rules and allow us to make inferences within idealized law-governed systems. Family resemblance categories are defined by correlations among features in sets of similar memorized exemplars and allow us to make inferences about the observable products of history.

Note

1. There are also problems with the model's treatment of these phenomena (see Pinker and Prince 1988; Lachter and Bever 1988; Sproat 1992).

References

Anderson, J. R. (1990). *The adaptive character of thought*. Hillsdale, NJ: Erlbaum.

Armstrong, S. L., Gleitman, L. R., and Gleitman, H. (1983). What some concepts might not be. *Cognition, 13,* 263–308.

Aronoff, M. (1976). *Word formation in generative grammar*. Cambridge, MA: MIT Press.

Bobick, A. (1987). *Natural object categorization*. Unpublished doctoral dissertation, Department of Brain and Cognitive Sciences, MIT.

Bruner, J. S., Goodnow, J., and Austin, G. (1956). *A study of thinking*. New York: Wiley.

Bybee, J. L. (1985). *Morphology*. Philadelphia: John Benjamins.

Bybee, J. L. (1991). Natural morphology: The organization of paradigms and language acquisition. In T. Huebner and C. Ferguson (Eds.), *Crosscurrents in second language acquisition and linguistic theories*. Amsterdam: John Benjamins.

Bybee, J. L., and Moder, C. L. (1983). Morphological classes as natural categories. *Language, 59,* 251–270.

Bybee, J. L., and Slobin, D. I. (1982a). Rules and schemes in the development and use of the English past tense. *Language, 58,* 265–289.

Bybee, J. L., and Slobin, D. I. (1982b). Why small children cannot change language on their own: Suggestions from the English past tense. In A. Ahlqvist (Ed.), *Papers from the 5th International Conference on Historical Linguistics* (Current Issues in Linguistic Theory Vol. 21; Amsterdam Studies in the Theory and History of Linguistic Science IV). Philadelphia: John Benjamins.

Campbell, A. (1959). *Old English grammar*. Oxford: Oxford University Press.

Cavalli-Sforza, L. L., and Feldman, M. W. (1981). *Cultural transmission and evolution: A quantitative approach*. Princeton, NJ: Princeton University Press.

Dawkins, R. (1986). *The blind watchmaker*. New York: Norton.

Fodor, J. A. (1981). The present status of the innateness controversy. In J. A. Fodor, *Representations*. Cambridge, MA: MIT Press.

Fodor, J. A., Garrett, M. F., Walker, E. C. T., and Parkes, C. H. (1980). Against definitions. *Cognition, 8*, 263–367.

Freyd, J. J. (1983). Shareability: The social psychology of epistemology. *Cognitive Science, 7*, 191–210.

Gelman, S. A., Coley, J. D., and Gottfried, G. M. (1994). Essentialist beliefs in children: The acquisition of concepts and theories. In L. A. Hirschfeld and S. A. Gelman (Eds.), *Mapping the mind: Domain specificity in cognition and culture*. New York: Cambridge University Press.

Gordon, P. (1985). Level-ordering in lexical development. *Cognition, 21*, 73–93.

Gould, S. J. (1983). What, if anything, is a zebra? In S. J. Gould, *Hens' teeth and horses' toes*. New York: Norton.

Hooper, J. B. (1976). *Introduction to natural generative phonology*. New York: Academic Press.

Hutchinson, G. E. (1959). Homage to Santa Rosalia, or why are there so many kinds of animals. *American Naturalist, 93*, 145–159.

Johnson, K. (1986). Fragmentation of strong verb ablaut in Old English. *Ohio State University Working Papers in Linguistics, 34*, 108–122.

Keil, F. C. (1989). *Concepts, kinds, and cognitive development*. Cambridge, MA: MIT Press.

Kelly, M. H. (1992). Darwin and psychological theories of classification. *Evolution and Cognition, 2*, 79–97.

Kim, J. J., Marcus, G. F., Pinker, S., Hollander, M., and Coppola, M. (1994). Sensitivity of children's inflection to morphological structure. *Journal of Child Language, 21*, 173–209.

Kim, J. J., Pinker, S., Prince, A., and Prasada, S. (1991). Why no mere mortal has even flown out to center field. *Cognitive Science, 15*, 173–218.

Kiparsky, P. (1982a). From cyclical to lexical phonology. In H. van der Hulst and N. Smith (Eds.), *The structure of phonological representations*. Dordrecht: Foris.

Kiparsky, P. (1982b). Lexical phonology and morphology. In I. S. Yang (Ed.), *Linguistics in the morning calm*. Seoul: Hanshin.

Konner, M. (1982). *The tangled wing*. New York: Harper and Row.

Kripke, S. (1972). Naming and necessity. In D. Davidson and G. Harman (Eds.), *Semantics of natural language*. Dordrecht: Reidel.

Lachter, J., and Bever, T. G. (1988). The relation between linguistic structure and associative theories of language learning: A constructive critique of some connectionist learning models. *Cognition, 28,* 195–247.

Lakoff, G. (1987). *Women, fire, and dangerous things: What categories reveal about the mind.* Chicago: University of Chicago Press.

MacWhinney, B., and Leinbach, J. (1991). Implementations are not conceptualizations: Revising the verb learning model. *Cognition, 40,* 121–157.

Marcus, G. F. (1995). The acquisition of inflection in children and multilayered connectionist networks. *Cognition, 56,* 271–279.

Marcus, G. F., Brinkmann, U., Clahsen, H., Wiese, R., and Pinker, S. (1995). German inflection: The exception that proves the rule. *Cognitive Psychology, 29,* 189–256.

Marcus, G., Pinker, S., Ullman, M., Hollander, M., Rosen, T. J., and Xu, F. (1992). Overregularization in language acquisition. *Monographs of the Society for Research in Child Development, 57*(4), Serial No. 228.

McClelland, J. L., and Rumelhart, D. E. (1985). Distributed memory and the representation of general and specific information. *Journal of Experimental Psychology: General, 114,* 159–188.

McClelland, J. L., Rumelhart, D. E., and The PDP Research Group. (1986). *Parallel Distributed Processing: Explorations in the microstructure of cognition: Vol. 2. Psychological and biological models.* Cambridge, MA: MIT Press.

Medin, D. L. (1989). Concepts and conceptual structure. *American Psychologist, 44,* 1469–1481.

Mencken, H. (1936). *The American language.* New York: Knopf.

Murphy, G. L. (1993). A rational theory of concepts. In G. H. Bower (Ed.), *The psychology of learning and motivation: Vol. 29.* New York: Academic Press.

Osherson, D. N., and Smith, E. E. (1981). On the adequacy of prototype theory as a theory of concepts. *Cognition, 15,* 35–58.

Pinker, S. (1984). *Language learnability and language development.* Cambridge, MA: Harvard University Press.

Pinker, S. (1991). Rules of language. *Science, 253,* 530–535.

Pinker, S., and Mehler, J. (Eds.). (1988). *Connections and symbols.* Cambridge, MA: MIT Press.

Pinker, S., and Prince, A. (1988). On language and connectionism: Analysis of a Parallel Distributed Processing model of language acquisition. *Cognition, 28,* 73–193.

Pinker, S., and Prince, A. (1994). Regular and irregular morphology and the psychological status of rules of grammar. In S. D. Lima, R. L. Corrigan, and G. K. Iverson (Eds.), *The reality of linguistic rules.* Philadelphia: John Benjamins.

Plunkett, K., and Marchman, V. (1991). U-shaped learning and frequency effects in a multi-layered perceptron: Implications for child language acquisition. *Cognition, 38,* 43–102.

Plunkett, K., and Marchman, V. (1993). From rote learning to system building. *Cognition, 48,* 21–69.

Prasada, S., and Pinker, S. (1993). Generalizations of regular and irregular morphology. *Language and Cognitive Processes, 8,* 1–56.

Prokosch, E. (1939). *A comparative Germanic grammar.* Philadelphia: Linguistic Society of America.

Putnam, H. (1975). The meaning of 'meaning'. In K. Gunderson (Ed.), *Language, mind, and knowledge.* Minneapolis, MN: University of Minnesota Press.

Quine, W. V. O. (1969). Natural kinds. In W. V. O. Quine, *Natural kinds and other essays.* New York: Columbia University Press.

Rey, G. (1983). Concepts and stereotypes. *Cognition, 15,* 237–262.

Ridley, M. (1986). *The problems of evolution.* Oxford: Oxford University Press.

Rips, L. J. (1989). Similarity, typicality, and categorization. In S. Vosniadou and A. Ortony (Eds.), *Similarity and analogical reasoning.* New York: Cambridge University Press.

Rosch, E. (1973). On the internal structure of perceptual and semantic categories. In T. E. Moore (Ed.), *Cognitive development and the acquisition of language.* New York: Academic Press.

Rosch, E. (1978). Principles of categorization. In E. Rosch and B. B. Lloyd (Eds.), *Cognition and categorization.* Hillsdale, NJ: Erlbaum.

Rosch, E. (1988). Coherences and categorization: A historical view. In F. Kessel (Ed.), *The development of language and of language researchers: Papers presented to Roger Brown.* Hillsdale, NJ: Erlbaum.

Rosch, E., and Mervis, C. B. (1975). Family resemblances: Studies in the internal representation of categories. *Cognitive Psychology, 7,* 573–605.

Rumelhart, D. E., and McClelland, J. L. (1986). On learning the past tenses of English verbs. In J. L. McClelland, D. E. Rumelhart, and the PDP Research Group, *Parallel Distributed Processing: Explorations in the microstructure of cognition: Vol. 2. Psychological and biological models.* Cambridge, MA: MIT Press.

Schwartz, S. P. (1979). Natural kind terms. *Cognition, 7,* 301–315.

Shepard, R. N. (1987). Toward a universal law of generalization for psychological science. *Science, 237,* 1317–1323.

Slobin, D. I. (1971). On the learning of morphological rules: A reply to Palermo and Eberhart. In D. I. Slobin (Ed.), *The ontogenesis of grammar: A theoretical symposium.* New York: Academic Press.

Smith, E. E., Langston, C., and Nisbett, R. (1992). The case for rules in reasoning. *Cognitive Science, 16,* 1–40.

Smith, E. E., and Medin, D. L. (1981). *Categories and concepts.* Cambridge, MA: Harvard University Press.

Smith, E. E., Medin, D. L., and Rips, L. J. (1984). A psychological approach to concepts: Comments on Rey's "Concepts and Stereotypes." *Cognition, 17,* 265–274.

Smolensky, P. (1988). On the proper treatment of connectionism. *Behavioral and Brain Sciences, 11,* 1–74.

Sober, E. (1984). *The nature of selection.* Cambridge, MA: MIT Press.

Sproat, R. (1992). *Morphology and computation.* Cambridge, MA: MIT Press.

Stromswold, K. J. (1990). *Learnability and the acquisition of auxiliaries.* Unpublished doctoral dissertation, Department of Brain and Cognitive Sciences, MIT.

Ullman, M. (1999). Judgments of English past tense forms: Implications for the mental computation of English morphology. *Language and Cognitive Processes.*

Whittlesea, B. W. A. (1989). Selective attention, variable processing, and distributed representation: Preserving particular experiences of general structures. In R. G. Morris (Ed.), *Parallel distributed processing: Implications for psychology and neuroscience.* New York: Oxford University Press.

Williams, G. C. (1966). *Adaptation and natural selection: A critique of some current evolutionary thought.* Princeton, NJ: Princeton University Press.

Wittgenstein, L. (1953). *Philosophical investigations.* New York: Macmillan.

Xu, F., and Pinker, S. (1995). Weird past tense forms. *Journal of Child Language, 22,* 531–556.

Chapter 11

Some Evidence for Impaired Grammars

Myrna Gopnik

Over the last few years, specific language impairment (SLI) has become a hot topic because it may have the potential to tell us something about the biological basis of language. I am afraid that comments about this research, on both sides, have often generated more heat than light. If we are really interested in the science of it all, then it is important to get the issues out on the table and see which ones we can agree about, which ones are still outstanding, and how we could resolve them. This chapter is intended to make a stab at clarifying some of the issues.

The fact that we would even be discussing language and biology in the same breath would have been unimaginable when I was an undergraduate in 1955 (though Darwin, himself, did suggest that learning language might be an instinct). Over the last 40 years the picture has changed radically. Research has shown that all languages, despite their seeming differences, are built on the same general plan and that most children acquire their native language as easily as they learn to walk upright, without explicit teaching and with no apparent effort. Newborns can't do it, but it appears in the first year of life, and the necessary precursors for this achievement seem to be there at birth. Experiments with very young babies have shown that humans come equipped with special abilities to selectively pay attention to and process language (Kuhl 1991; Kuhl and Meltzoff 1997). These data suggest that there is a biological basis to language. It follows that if language is part of the biological endowment of humans, then humans must have some genetic properties that build the particular kinds of brain circuitry that are specialized for human language. If this is true, then it would not be surprising to find that some change in this genetic endowment can interfere with the way brain circuitry is built and thereby impair the ability to acquire or use language in the normal way. And in fact this does happen. Though most children do acquire language without any conscious effort, there are some children who have real trouble with language, and their linguistic problems persist into adulthood. What makes this population particularly interesting is that this disorder seems to be associated with some genetic factors and neurological anomalies. If this is true, then this situation provides a ready-made natural experiment to investigate various hypotheses about the biology of language.

This "ready-made" looks easier than it is, however. There are lots of pieces to the argument that have to be put together, linguistic, psycholinguistic, genetic, and neurological, before we can be sure about what we are seeing. The first problem is to show that at least some cases of this disorder are really genetic.

11.1 Genetics

Several epidemiological studies have shown that an individual with a developmental language disorder is significantly more likely to have a relative who is also affected than is an unaffected individual (Tomblin 1989, 1996). Data from the ongoing Genetic Language Impairment Project conducted at McGill University confirms this pattern of familial clustering of SLI (Palmour 1997). In this study, we looked at subjects who had a clinical history of language impairment, but no history of any other exclusionary criteria, such as impaired auditory acuity, mental retardation, or autism. Then we took detailed family histories. Of the 95 subjects in this initial study, 53 (55.8%) had at least one affected first- or second-degree relative. In 21 of the families there was a clear pattern of multigenerational impairment. Our research team has also found evidence of familial aggregation in language-impaired subjects in England (Gopnik 1990),[1] Greece (Dalalakis 1994), and Japan (Fukuda and Fukuda 1994).

So we have converging evidence from a number of independent studies that show that language impairment clusters in families. The question is, "Is this pattern the result of some genetic factors or is it the result of social or linguistic factors that prevail in this family?" The latter seems extremely unlikely because some members of the family have perfectly normal language and other individuals in the same family appear to have grammars that violate the universal properties that are found in language. Within genetics, the way to distinguish between the influence of the environment and the influence of genes is to compare the pattern of impairment in monozygotic (identical) with that in dizygotic (fraternal) twins. If the crucial factors for clustering are social, then both kinds of twins should look similar. If, on the other hand, the pattern is due to genetic factors, then the twins with the same genes should be more alike than those who are merely siblings genetically but have shared a similar social context. Several independent studies have shown that this disorder is significantly more concordant in monozygotic twins than in dizygotic twins (Bishop, North, and Donlan 1995; Tomblin 1997; Tomblin and Buckwalter 1998).

Therefore, both the epidemiological data and the twin studies strongly suggest that genetic factors are associated with this disorder. But genes do not code for behavior such as language. They code for proteins that control development that, in turn, may have consequences for the way in which language develops. To really understand what is going on, then, we have to find some likely consequences that the genetic factors could have for development; and since language happens in the brain, the most likely place to look is neurology.

11.2 Neurology

Previous studies have documented neurological anomalies in the brains of subjects with familial language impairment (Plante et al. 1991). Our team has examined magnetic resonance images (MRIs) from five of the affected adult members of the families we have been studying and has found that "compared to controls, the CSF (cerebro-spinal fluid)/grey and CSF/grey + white ratios were significantly high in FLI-adults [familial language impairment] ... whereas the grey/white ratio was significantly low.... These findings suggest that FLI in adults may be associated with cortical atrophy" (Kabani et al. 1997). Though these data are all very interesting and go in the right direction, they are far from the end of the story. The global patterns documented in these studies do not provide the kind of fine-grained picture that we need if we are to really understand the details of how the neurological anomalies interact with the linguistic problems. Our imaging team, headed by Alan Evans, is now developing procedures that can look at the MRI data in much finer detail, and this has the potential for clarifying some of these questions.

One interesting question is how these neuroanatomical anomalies arise. We are just beginning to get some hints of how this might happen. Current evidence seems to suggest that this genetic impairment interferes with normal brain development in the fetus. Gallagher and Watkin (1997) used 3D ultrasonic neuroimaging to study in utero brain development from 24 to 32 weeks of gestational age. Three of the fetuses were from families that had no history of language impairment (−FLI). The fourth fetus was from a family that did have a clear history of language impairment (+FLI). Gallagher and Watkin found that though all the fetuses had overall brain volumes within the normal range, their patterns of growth were significantly different. In particular, the +FLI fetus showed limited growth in those regions of the brain that are associated with language performance. This evidence from fetal development is consistent with the evidence from older subjects.

11.3 Neuropsychology

The data given above suggest that the genetic factors associated with this disorder have consequences for the development of the brain and that these neuroanatomical anomalies have direct consequences for the acquisition of language. Since we know that genes can have many different effects, it is to be expected that some genes that affect language may have pleiotropic effects and so not be "specific" to language. Moreover, the extensive anomalies that have been observed in brain structure would make it surprising if these subjects had no other deficits. And, indeed, clinicians report that *some* of these language-impaired subjects do have other problems including low performance IQ, dyslexia, spatial rotation difficulties, depression, and apraxias; however, none of these other specific deficits reliably occurs with the language disorder, and there are many individuals who have one of these other problems without having any language disorder. The question is whether the language impairment that we see in these individuals comes from a separate and special "language faculty" that is out of order, or whether some more general cognitive or perceptual processing system is not functioning and the purported "language" problems are merely a result of a breakdown in a much more general system.

In our own project, Dr. H. Chertkow, a neurologist, has examined 30 of our Canadian subjects and finds that some, but not all, of the individuals with this language disorder do have other nonlinguistic problems and that some of the members of these families who are not impaired on our diagnostic language test also have other problems.

For example, as shown in table 11.1, in a sample of 12 subjects from these families, 6 were clearly impaired by our diagnostic language test and 6 were not. Neurological testing revealed that 3 of the 6 language-impaired subjects had mild impairment in left and right hemisphere sen-

Table 11.1
Neurological assessment; impaired versus nonimpaired subjects

Subjects	Tests										
	Ha	RH	LH	FL	NM	Co	Pr	LP	RP	Ax	Gl
I	0	0	0	0	0	0	0	0	0	0	0
I	2	1	1	1	0	0	0	2	1	0	2
I	0	1	1	0	0	0	0	1	0	1	1
I	0	0	0	0	0	0	0	0	0	0	0
I	1	1	1	0	0	0	0	0	0	0	0
I	0	0	0	0	0	0	0	0	0	0	0
N	2	0	0	0	0	0	0	0	0	0	0
N	0	0	0	0	0	0	0	0	0	0	0
N	0	0	0	0	0	0	0	0	0	0	0
N	2	0	0	0	0	0	0	0	0	0	0
N	0	0	0	0	0	0	0	0	0	0	0
N	0	1	1	0	0	0	0	1	0	2	1

Subjects
I = impaired, N = nonimpaired

Tests
Ha   handedness (0 = right, 1 = left, 2 = ambidextrous)
RH   right hemisphere sensorimotor function
LH   left hemisphere sensorimotor function
FL   frontal lobe function
NM   nonverbal memory
Co   concentration
Pr   praxis
LP   calculation/left parietal function
RP   spatial attention/right parietal function
Ax   axial/body coordination
Gl   global assessment of nonverbal cognitive abilities

Scoring
0 = normal function, 1 = mild impairment, 2 = moderate impairment,
4 = severe impairment

sorimotor function, but then so did 1 subject who showed no language impairment by our tests. Two of the language-impaired subjects exhibited some impairment in mental calculation, as did 1 non-language-impaired subject. In general, the language-impaired subjects appear to be more vulnerable to having other disorders in addition to their language disorder, but there seems to be no necessary pattern to these other problems. And, as we have shown, it is by no means the case that these other disorders always co-occur with language problems. The fact that this disorder affects neuroanatomy makes it not surprising that other areas might also be implicated in some cases. This does not mean, however, that these other disorders *cause* the language impairment.

The evidence indicates that this linguistic disorder has some genetic foundation and that the genetic factors produce anomalous neuroanatomical structures. If we want to know how this affects language, we must have a detailed and extensive picture of precisely what goes wrong with these subjects' language.

11.4 Linguistics

Our research goals in linguistics over the years have been clear: to describe the grammatical system that produces the pattern of errors that are observed. After 10 years and almost 100 language-impaired subjects and well more than 100 controls representing four different native languages (English, French, Greek, and Japanese), the data converge to tell us that the language-impaired subjects cannot construct normal representations for grammatically complex words and they therefore cannot use rules that depend on the content of these representations. For example, though they appear to have no problems with the larger grammatical categories of language like noun and verb, they are unable to recognize that words can be composed of roots and affixes. They therefore do not construct abstract linguistic features such as tense, number, aspect, case, or gender, and they do not recognize that there are linguistic rules that operate on these features. But this does not mean that they cannot use words that, from the point of view of the normal grammar, have these features. For example, in spontaneous speech they usually use the correct forms such as "books" or "walked." They can do this because they memorize these forms as unanalyzed chunks that in their lexicon simply encode the semantic meaning of "more than one" or "in the past" rather than the sublexical features "plural" or "past." They are more accurate in using the "more than one" forms than the "in the past" forms. This is probably because in English the relationship between the form with the plural marker and the semantic context of "more than one" is very regular and direct and therefore is easy to memorize. However, the relationship between the past-marked forms and temporal past context is extremely complicated and not at all regular or direct (Shaer 1996), and therefore it is more difficult to assign a consistent meaning relationship between the inflected form and the meaning of pastness by any rote means.

How do we know that these individuals do not construct complex representations? We have two sources of evidence, linguistic and psycholinguistic. The linguistic evidence comes both from spontaneous speech and from a wide series of linguistic tests. One of the things that makes parents notice that their children have difficulties with language is that they make mistakes in spontaneous speech in forms like past tenses and pronouns long after their playmates and siblings have got the system figured out. And these problems persist into adulthood. But as these individuals get older, they do not make these errors very often. Many of them get tense right over 80% of the time. This is in contrast to the control subjects, who get tense right virtually all of the time. Marking tense in your native language is an automatic, unconscious process, not something that you get wrong. And this leads us to a very interesting problem. Is someone who gets tense right 80% of the time impaired, or simply absent-minded? Let's put it another way. Generally speaking, people get their own name right all of the time. If someone got his or her name right 80% of the time, we might begin to wonder. What our model suggests is that the language-impaired subjects, in fact, *never* get tense right. They do not have the category "tense" in their grammar. What they do 80% of the time is produce a word that has the same surface form as the marked form in the normal grammar. It looks like they get tense marking right most of the time, but they get there by a very different route—by memorization or by explicit rule (Paradis and Gopnik 1997).

The only way to figure out what these individuals really know about language is to give them linguistically significant tests. The data from these diagnostic tests converge to tell us that the pattern of what they can do and what they cannot do is strikingly similar in all of the five populations—speakers of English from Canada and England, and speakers of French, Greek, and Japanese—that we have looked at (see figure 11.1). These tests show that the language-impaired speakers have significant problems with grammaticality judgments, tense production, and deriva-

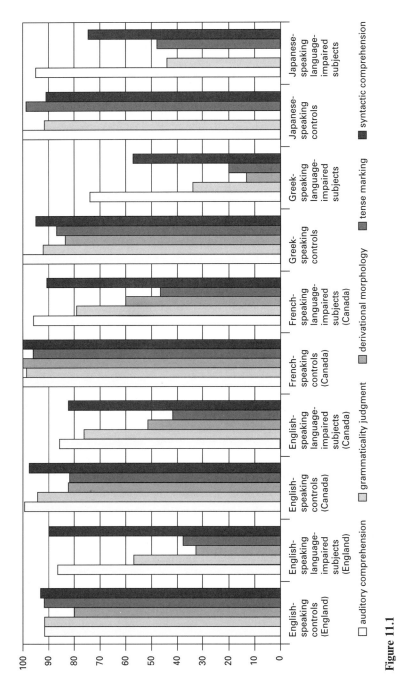

Figure 11.1
Results of five linguistic tasks given to language-impaired subjects and to controls

Table 11.2
Ability to produce tense marking (% correct). Subjects were given items like "Every day I walk to school. Just like every day, yesterday I _____." This task requires the subject to recognize that the temporal context specified in the second sentence requires a particular verb form.

	English (England)	English (Canada)	French (Canada)	Japanese	Greek
Language-impaired subjects	38.3	52.3	46.7	48.1	20.0
Controls	91.7	93.5	96.4	97.9	87.1

tional morphology.[2] They have fewer problems with a pointing task that requires them to auditorily distinguish between words like "book" and "books" or "books" and "cooks." These general diagnostic tests have been supplemented by much more detailed tests designed to test particular hypotheses. For example, we have data about tense from spontaneous speech, grammaticality judgment tasks, grammaticality rating tasks, storytelling, and tense production; and these results are consistent over a wide range of types of stimuli and responses—oral, aural, written, pointing, and so on (Gopnik 1994). We also have results that show that these speakers have problems with plurals and comparatives.

One question was whether these problems with tense in English could be accounted for by the fact that regular past tense in English is encoded by a form that has been described as "phonologically vulnerable" (Fletcher 1990) or by some special and particular problems with our first set of English-speaking subjects, who all came from one particularly interesting family. In order to resolve this question, we decided to look at more English-speaking subjects and at subjects whose native language was not English. These data show that the problem with tense is unique neither to our first subjects nor to English. It shows up in every population we have looked at (see table 11.2; see also Fukuda 1994; Dalalakis 1996; Gopnik et al. 1996; Royle 1996; Gopnik 1998; Ullman and Gopnik, to appear). All of these populations have similar problems with producing correct tense forms, no matter how tense is encoded in their native language—in a final stressed syllable as in French or in a three-syllable element like "mashita" in Japanese. Interestingly, both the Greek control and language-impaired subjects have lower scores than the other subjects; this happens because each verb in Greek has more than 60

Table 11.3
Forms of Greek "lik-os" ("wolf")

	Singular	Plural
Nominative	lik os	lik i
Genitive	lik u	lik on
Accusative	lik o	lik us
Vocative	lik e (!)	lik i

different inflected forms, as opposed to 4 in English, so there are simply many more ways to go wrong and it is harder to be right just by chance.

The next question that we had to address was whether the subjects' problem with language was confined to tense, as has been suggested (Rice, Wexler, and Cleave 1995), or whether they made similar errors in other parts of the inflectional system. Tests show that across the four languages they make errors in number, case, and gender.[3]

All of this led us to think that these individuals had a particular problem with inflectional rules, but Jenny Dalalakis's innovative work on compounds and diminutives in Greek made it clear that the language-impaired subjects have just as much difficulty with finding the root of a complex word as they have with adding an inflection (Dalalakis 1996). It is not merely that they cannot add an inflection to a root; they do not even recognize that there are roots and inflections. There is no way to check this in English because there are words in English like "walk" and "book" that do not have any overt inflectional marking. In Greek, however, all nouns and verbs are inflected. For example, the word for "wolf" has eight different forms (see table 11.3). It would seem to be child's play to figure out that "lik" is the root and all of the rest are inflectional forms. But not for these children. They make serious errors in tasks like compounding and diminutivization that depend upon the manipulation of roots. They seem to know that they are supposed to take part of the word, but they are not sensitive to the boundaries between roots and inflections so sometimes they take a part that is shorter than the root and sometimes they take a part that is longer than the root. The rule for compounding in Greek requires that the two roots be conjoined (1a), in some cases with the insertion of an "o" that marks the morpheme boundary (1b); then the inflection is added to the end of the conjoined roots.

(1) a.
lik	-anthrop	-os		→	likanthropos
wolf	man	masc.sing.			werewolf
		nom.			

b.
lik	-o	-fol	-a	→	likofola
wolf	compound	nest	fem.sing.		wolfnest
	morpheme		nom.		

(A similar rule holds for forming diminutives. For the details, see Dalalakis 1996.) The subjects were shown pictures and told (in Greek), for example, "This is a mouse (pondikos) and this is a man (anthropos) that becomes a mouse. We would call him a 'mouseman' (pondikanthropos)." They were asked to form similar compounds in response to other pictures. The language-impaired subjects had significantly more difficulty with this task than did the controls (see table 11.4). Sometimes the language-impaired subjects produced forms in which the first root was shorter than required (2a), and sometimes they produced forms in which it was longer (2b).

(2) a.
anthrop	-fagh	-os	→	*anthrofàghos
man	eater	masc.sing.		man-eater
		nom.		

b.
lot	-fagh	-os	→	*lotosfàghos
persimmon	eater	masc.sing.		persimmon-eater
		nom.		

It is clear then that these subjects' problem with inflectional rules is an epiphenomenon of their problem with knowing that there are roots and inflections at all.

Now we are back to one of the problems that we discussed at the beginning: where do the "inflected" forms that these speakers do produce come from? One of the compensatory mechanisms that we have suggested is memorization—they simply learn inflected words one at a time as

Table 11.4
Greek compounding and diminutivization (% correct)

	Language-impaired subjects	Young controls	Age-matched controls
Compounding	16	95	99
Diminutivization	38	100	100

everyone has to do for irregulars. If this is true, then they should be more successful with regularly inflected words that they have heard frequently than with those that are rare. And that is precisely what we find: frequency is a more robust predictor of problems than regular versus irregular inflection (Fukuda and Fukuda 1994; Gopnik 1994; Gopnik and Goad 1997; Ullman and Gopnik, to appear).

This is precisely the opposite from what we see with normal controls, for whom regularly inflected forms do not show any frequency effects. This strongly suggests that memory and not rules are producing the inflected forms used by language-impaired subjects. To clinch this argument, we looked at the absolute endpoint of the frequency scale, novel words that these individuals could never have seen before. If they were using a rule, they should have had no problem with this task. If they were producing actual forms from memory, then it should have been impossible for them. We tested such forms in all four languages and over a wide range of different kinds of rules (for results, see table 11.5). These data clearly and convincingly show that the language-impaired subjects perform significantly worse than non-language-impaired subjects on every grammatical task and for every language population that we have tested. One might then ask, "If these speakers do not have the rule, how do they ever get it right at all?" The answer seems to be that they do not ever get the unconscious, automatic rule for inflection right. What they can do is use an explicit rule—in the case of the English speakers, for example, a rule that tells them to add an "-s" for plurals or an "-ed" for past. And there is clear evidence that this is what they are doing. In our original scoring of these tests, we were very generous and gave the subjects credit for producing an inflected form even if it did not sound precisely like the normal form. In a very detailed phonological analysis of these subjects' attempts at producing plurals, Goad and Rebellati (1995) found that even when the English-speaking language-impaired subjects do produce a kind of sibilant at the end of the word given in the stimulus sentence, they do not obey the normal rules in English that govern the incorporation of the affix into the word. For example, they do not have voicing assimilation and say "wug-s" instead of "wug-z." The plural does not behave like an affix in the grammar of the language-impaired subjects. It is as if they were producing a kind of compound by adding a wordlike "s" that means "more than one." This careful analysis shows that only 9% of the forms that they produce phonologically resemble the "correct" form. A similar analysis of the novel verbs shows the same pattern. Apparently, then,

Table 11.5
Ability to mark novel words grammatically (% correct). In each of these tests the subjects were given a context, usually in pictures, which required that a grammatical rule be applied to a novel word: "This pencil is weff. This pencil is even _____."

	Controls	Language-impaired subjects
Past tense		
English (in England)	95.4	38.0
English (in Canada)	93.5	52.3
French (in Canada)	92.6	33.3
Greek	87.1	20.0
Japanese	89.1	37.0
Plurals		
English (in England)	95.7	57.0
English (in Canada)	99.2	58.3
Greek	79.8	42.1
Comparatives		
English (in England)	74.0	21.0
Compounds		
Greek	93.6	12.8
Japanese	80.5	20.2
Diminutives		
Greek	83.9	40.2

these speakers produce forms that look "inflected" by very different means than the normal grammar.

So far, all of our hypotheses about the way that the language-impaired subjects must be representing words in their grammar have been inferred from their performance on linguistic tests. But there is another, more direct way to look at their mental lexicon. Eva Kehayia conducted a series of on-line psycholinguistic tests to probe the way in which language-impaired subjects were processing complex words. It might be the case that these subjects have normal representations for the inflected forms, but some processing difficulties make these forms unavailable to them in spontaneous speech or elicited production tasks. Psycholinguistic research on aphasics shows that though they make errors in spontaneous speech and in linguistic tests, their mental representations appear to be intact (Kehayia and Jarema 1994; Kehayia, in press). The language-impaired subjects in these tests were 12 speakers of Canadian English, 7 speakers of French, and 4 speakers of Greek (in Greece). They were compared with 24 controls in each language. The general form of the tests required the subjects to look at a single word that appeared on a computer screen and decide whether it was a real word in their language or not. The word stayed on the screen until the subject pushed the button to register a decision. Half of the tests were simple lexical decision tasks and half were primed lexical decision tasks. The experimental model assumes that the amount of time that it takes a subject to make a decision is a measure of the way in which the subject is processing the item. Though the subjects thought that we were interested in their ability to judge whether a word was a real word or a novel word, the real experimental variables investigated inflection, compounding, and derivation. The results are consistent across all of the tests and all of the languages (see table 11.6). Both groups are above 90% accurate in judging whether a sequence is or is not a word; however, they are very different in the way that they process the words and nonwords. In the processing experiments, the English-, French-, and Greek-speaking control subjects all show a significant difference in reaction times, more than 30 milliseconds, for inflected versus uninflected words and nonwords. Affected individuals show no such difference. This indicates that the language-impaired subjects, crosslinguistically, are building mental representations that differ in nature from those of non-language-impaired individuals.

These results suggest that these subjects are insensitive to the internal structure of words. They treat all words as if they were simple unanalyzed chunks. They are good at knowing if a word is a real word or not: they simply look it up in their mental lexicon. In some cases, this takes them longer than controls because they have more items to search, but in other cases (e.g., Greek compounds), where the rules for forming the complex word are intricate, their whole-word strategy is actually more efficient. This result is illustrated in table 11.7. Notice that the language-impaired individuals process all three forms in the same way, whereas the controls process them significantly differently. The controls perform fastest on the existing compounds and slowest on the compounds that are made up of real words but that do not exist in the language. What is particularly interesting is that the language-impaired subjects' whole-word lookup strategy makes them perform significantly faster than the controls on nonword compounds and especially faster on novel compounds.

Table 11.6
Reaction time (in ms) on simple lexical decision task

	Language-impaired subjects (English)	Controls (English)	Language-impaired subjects (French)	Controls (French)	Language-impaired subjects (Greek)	Controls (Greek)
Nonwords						
Root tash (English) fousse (French) kraf (Greek)	825	661	790	731	880	638
Inflected Words tashed (English) foussait (French) krafo (Greek)	810	697	795	772	890	720
Words						
Root wash (English) pousse (French) graf (Greek)	700	555	690	595	880	760
Inflected word washed (English) poussait (French) grafo (Greek)	710	600	715	673	768	600

Table 11.7
Reaction time (in ms)

	Language-impaired subjects (Greek)	Controls (Greek)
Nonword compounds kigofàghos ("kigoeater"; like English "wugeater")	817	870
Novel compounds migofàghos ("flyeater")	820	970
Existing compounds hortofàghos ("vegetable eater" = "vegetarian")	815	760

The results of the experiments in this study clearly show that the performance pattern of the language-impaired subjects is significantly different from that of the control subjects on word and nonword targets for inflection, derivation, and compounding. The controls in this study behave just as reported elsewhere in the literature (Taft and Forster 1975; Laudanna, Badecker, and Caramazza 1989; Kehayia and Jarema 1994). They process productively formed complex words by means of decomposition, and they process simple and idiosyncratic complex words by means of whole-word access. The language-impaired subjects appear to process all of the items by means of whole-word access (Kehayia 1994, in press; Dalalakis 1996). The results of these on-line studies are consistent with what the off-line linguistic tests have shown: the language-impaired subjects do not build complex representations for words; instead, they treat both complex and simple words in the same way—as if they were unanalyzed chunks.

The question then is, "What do their representations look like?" There are two possibilities for representing words with no internal structure.

(3) a. V [+past]
        walked
        "move on foot" (+past)
     b. V
        walked
        "move on foot in the past"

The difference between these representations is that in (3a) the information that this word refers to something that happened in the past is expressed by a morphological feature (+past) and in (3b) the concept of pastness is expressed as part of the meaning of the word.

As I have argued, the data from a wide range of grammaticality judgment tasks, production tasks, novel-form tasks, and reaction time experiments indicate that these subjects show no sensitivity to the internal structure of words. These data strongly suggest there is no evidence that the lexical entries of language-impaired speakers contain sublexical (morphological) features for tense, number, and perhaps other inflectional properties. Since there is no evidence for such features from the linguistic behavior of these speakers, we have no grounds for introducing such features into their representations. Given that regular pasts end in a coronal stop in English, and given that language-impaired individuals can sometimes add a pastlike ending to novel words, we assume that these individuals store such forms in family resemblance classes and that they can thus perform "wug"-type tasks through analogy (Gopnik and Goad 1997). We therefore have a broad range of crosslinguistic evidence, both on-line and off-line, that all tells the same story: that the language-impaired subjects, though they get the same linguistic input as their siblings, do not build the same sort of grammar. The grammars that they do build appear to rely on memory and analogy and not productive rules for handling the morphological aspects of language. The spontaneous speech of the older subjects, and even their performance on some linguistic tests, demonstrates that a reasonable simulacrum of morphology can be constructed by using memory and analogy instead of productive rules. They do not perform perfectly, but they are not terrible either. It is only when the subjects are given tests that depend on productivity or when their internal processes are monitored that the full extent of their inabilities can be detected.

All of this would be interesting even if it only provided a description of the difficulties that a small group of language-impaired subjects have. But if it is all true, and if this disorder is related to some genetic factors that in turn have consequences for neurological development, then apparently there are some genetic and neurological precursors that are required for the normal course of these aspects of language development to take place. This does *not* mean that we think that there is a gene for morphology! From the point of view of linguistics, there is good evidence that though morphology is one of the striking aspects of language that seems to stump these individuals, it is by no means the only one they have trouble with. The question that is still open is whether their prosodic and syntactic difficulties are directly related to the same out-of-order linguistic system that causes their problems in morphology or whether these other language problems are an independent result of their general pattern of neurological damage. The answer to this question would shed light on the relative independence of the three levels of grammar. Though there is abundant evidence that this disorder is associated with some genetic factors, no one yet knows what these factors are. And even if the genes associated with this disorder were found, it would not follow necessarily that these same genes would be the ones that guide the normal linguistic system to develop; the factors that make a system function in the normal case might not be the same as those that can cause the system to break down. Of course, there is much more to find out. We are only at the beginning of this intellectual journey, but it does appear that it will turn out that Darwin was right that language is part of the biological nature of humans.

Notes

1. This family has been the subject of much debate (Fletcher 1990; Vargha-Khadem et al. 1995). For a detailed discussion of some of these disputes, see Gopnik and Goad 1997. From the data, it is clear that the language impairment seen in this family is not caused by oral apraxia or low performance IQ. Moreover, as I will show, the same pattern of impairment is found in English-speaking subjects in Canada as well as in French-, Greek-, and Japanese-speaking subjects.

2. Since Japanese does not have a rich, productive system of derivational morphology, we did not test the Japanese-speaking subjects on this task.

3. They also make errors in syntax and in some phonological processes such as prosody, but discussing these in detail would take us too far afield here (van der Lely and Harris 1990; van der Lely 1997; Clahsen 1992; Piggott and Kessler 1994; Rice, Wexler, and Cleave 1995; Goad, in press).

References

Bishop, D. V., North, T., and Donlan, C. (1995). Genetic basis of specific language impairment: Evidence from a twin study. *Developmental Medicine and Child Neurology, 37,* 56–71.

Clahsen, H. (1992). *Linguistic perspectives on specific language impairment* (Theorie des Lexikons Arbeitspapier 37). Düsseldorf: Heinrich Heine Universität.

Dalalakis, J. (1994). Familial language impairment in Greek. *McGill Working Papers in Linguistics, 10,* 216–227.

Dalalakis, J. (1996). *Developmental language impairment: Evidence from Greek and its implications for morphological representation.* Unpublished doctoral dissertation, McGill University.

Fletcher, P. (1990). Untitled scientific correspondence. *Nature, 346,* 226.

Fukuda, S. (1994). Lexical representation of Japanese complex verbs: A theoretical model and implication from dysphasic children. *McGill Working Papers in Linguistics, 10,* 194–205.

Fukuda, S. E., and Fukuda, S. (1994). Developmental language impairment in Japanese: A linguistic investigation. *McGill Working Papers in Linguistics, 10,* 150–177.

Gallagher, T., and Watkin, K. (1997). 3D ultrasonic fetal neuroimaging and familial language disorders: In utero brain development. *Journal of Neurolinguistics, 10,* 187–201.

Goad, H. (in press). *Plurals in SLI: Prosodic deficit or morphological deficit? Language Acquisition.*

Goad, H., and Rebellati, C. (1995). Pluralization is compounding in SLI. In P. Koshinen (Ed.), *Proceedings of the Annual Meeting of the Canadian Linguistic Association.* Toronto: University of Toronto, Department of Linguistics.

Gopnik, M. (1990). Feature-blindness: A case study. *Language Acquisition, 1,* 139–164.

Gopnik, M. (1994). Impairments of tense in a familial language disorder. *Journal of Neurolinguistics, 8,* 109–133.

Gopnik, M., Dalalakis, J., Fukuda, S. E., Fukuda, S., and Kehayia, E. (1996). Genetic language impairment: Unruly grammars. In W. G. Runciman, J. Maynard Smith, and R. I. M. Dunbar (Eds.), *Evolution of social behaviour patterns in primates and man.* Oxford: Oxford University Press.

Gopnik, M., and Goad, H. (1997). What underlies inflectional error patterns in genetic dysphasia? *Journal of Neurolinguistics, 10,* 109–137.

Gopnik, M. (1998). Familial language impairment: More English evidence. *Folia Phoniatrica et Logopaedica.*

Kabani, N., MacDonald, D., Math, M., Evans, A., and Gopnik, M. (1997). Neuroanatomical correlates of familial language impairment: A preliminary report. *Journal of Neurolinguistics, 10,* 203–214.

Kehayia, E. (1994). Whole-word access or decomposition in word recognition in familial language impairment: A psycholinguistic study. *McGill Working Papers in Linguistics, 10,* 123–128.

Kehayia, E. (in press). Morphological representation and processing of inflected and derived words in Greek-speaking individuals. In *Proceedings of the 2nd International Conference on Greek Linguistics.*

Kehayia, E., and Jarema, G. (1994). Morphological priming (or Prim#ing) on inflected verb forms: A comparative study. *Journal of Neurolinguistics, 2,* 83–94.

Kuhl, P. K. (1991). Human adults and human infants show a "perceptual magnet effect" for the prototypes of speech categories, monkeys do not. *Perception & Psychophysics, 50,* 90–107.

Kuhl, P. K., and Meltzoff, A. N. (1997). Evolution, nativism, and learning in the development of language and speech. In M. Gopnik (Ed.), *The inheritance and innateness of grammars.* New York: Oxford University Press.

Laudanna, A., Badecker, W., and Caramazza, A. (1989). Priming homographic stems. *Journal of Memory and Language, 28,* 531–546.

Palmour, R. (1997). Genetic studies in specific linguistic impairment. *Journal of Neurolinguistics, 10,* 215–230.

Paradis, M., and Gopnik, M. (1997). Compensatory strategies in genetic dysphasia: Declarative memory. *Journal of Neurolinguistics, 10,* 173–185.

Piggott, G. L., and Kessler Robb, M. (1994). Prosodic constraints in familial language impairment: A preliminary report. *McGill Working Papers in Linguistics, 10,* 16–23.

Plante, E., Swisher, L., Vance, R., and Rapcsak, S. (1991). MRI findings in boys with specific language impairment. *Brain and Language, 41,* 52–66.

Rice, M. L., Wexler, K., and Cleave, P. (1995). Specific language impairment as a period of extended optional infinitive. *Journal of Speech and Hearing Research, 38,* 850–863.

Royle, P. (1996). *Verb production in French DLI subjects.* Unpublished Master's thesis, McGill University.

Shaer, B. (1996). *Making sense of tense: Tense, time reference and linking theory.* Unpublished doctoral dissertation, McGill University.

Taft, M., and Forster, K. I. (1975). Lexical storage and retrieval of prefixed words. *Journal of Verbal Learning and Verbal Behavior, 14,* 638–647.

Tomblin, J. B. (1989). Familial concentration of developmental language impairment. *Journal of Speech and Hearing Disorders, 54,* 287–295.

Tomblin, J. B. (1996). Genetic and environmental contributions to the risk for specific language impairment. In M. L. Rice (Ed.), *Toward a genetics of language.* Mahwah, NJ: Erlbaum.

Tomblin, J. B. (1997). Epidemiology of specific language impairment. In M. Gopnik (Ed.), *The inheritance and innateness of grammars.* New York: Oxford University Press.

Tomblin, J. B., and Buckwalter, P. R. (1998). Heritability of poor language achievement among twins. *Journal of Speech, Language & Hearing Research, 41,* 188–199.

Ullman, M., and Gopnik, M. (to appear). The production of inflectional morphology in hereditary specific language impairment. *Applied Psycholinguistics, 20.*

van der Lely, H. (1997). Language and cognitive development in a grammatical SLI boy: Modularity and innateness. *Journal of Neurolinguistics, 10,* 75–107.

van der Lely, H., and Harris, M. (1990). Comprehension of reversible sentences in specifically language impaired children. *Journal of Speech and Hearing Disorders, 55,* 101–117.

Vargha-Khadem, F., Watkins, K., Alcock, K., Fletcher, P., and Passingham, R. (1995). Praxic and nonverbal cognitive deficits in a large family with a genetically transmitted speech and language disorder. *Proceedings of the National Academy of Sciences, 92,* 930–933.

Chapter 12

The Role of Semantics in Solving the Bootstrapping Problem

Paul Bloom

Some knowledge of language is expressed in terms of grammatical categories such as nouns, verbs, and adjectives. For instance, English-speaking adults know that adjectives precede nouns within NPs—we say "the big dog," not "the dog big." This chapter is about a puzzle that arises from this fact, first raised by Fodor (1966). Children must learn the linguistic categories that words and phrases belong to; they must learn that the English word "dog" is a noun and the English word "big" is an adjective. But syntactic categories do not reduce to nonsyntactic categories. Nouns, for instance, do not universally sound the same, or occur in the same position, or share the same type of meaning. Pinker (1984) has described this as "the bootstrapping problem" in language acquisition. How do children use nonsyntactic information (such as phonology, position, or meaning) to arrive at syntactic knowledge?

The proposal defended here is that children use semantic information to solve this problem. This is not a new proposal. Macnamara (1982) proposed one important semantic theory, in which children's first word combinations are the result of rules that map over semantic categories—rules such as "modifier + object word" that generate phrases such as

I have been working on different drafts of this chapter for over five years; the version presented here is a very modified version of what I presented in my doctoral dissertation (Bloom 1990a, chap. 3). I thank Susan Carey, LouAnn Gerken, Lila Gleitman, Jane Grimshaw, Lisa Menn, and Steven Pinker for discussion of these issues, and Ellen Courtney, Ray Jackendoff, and Karen Wynn for extensive comments on a previous draft. I am particularly grateful to John Macnamara, who first introduced me to the study of mind and language, and encouraged and guided me in the years that followed.

Preparation of this chapter was supported by grants from the Spencer Foundation and from the Sloan Foundation.

"good boy" and "nice hat." Since these rules cannot account for much of what children hear (e.g., "good story" and "nice smile"), they are forced to gradually expand and transform categories such as "object word" until they correspond to syntactic categories such as "noun." As Macnamara (1992, 134) put it, "The child climbs to grammar on a semantic ladder and then kicks the ladder away."

A different approach is the theory of "semantic bootstrapping" (Grimshaw 1981; Pinker 1984), which posits that children possess a language acquisition device (LAD) that leads them to categorize names for things as nouns, names for actions as verbs, and so on. Through application of these mappings, along with innate knowledge of structural universals of grammar, children parse some of the utterances they hear and thereby learn some language-particular rules of grammar. After they have acquired such rules, they can use them to categorize new words that do not fall under the syntax-semantics mappings, such as nouns that do not name things and verbs that do not name actions.

I will begin by defending the premise that children learn the syntactic categories that words belong to through use of semantic information. But I'll also argue that neither of the two approaches summarized above is adequate. I will then discuss an alternative that differs from previous proposals in certain significant ways, explore implications of this alternative for the study of word learning, and conclude with some more general remarks.

12.1   Why Semantics?

One alternative to the view that children use semantics to solve the bootstrapping problem is that they group words and phrases together according to their distributional properties, such as their absolute location in the sentence, what inflections they appear with, and what words they precede and follow. Under this view, a child comes to understand that "dog" and "door" belong to the same linguistic class because they can each follow "the," can precede the suffix "-s" and the word "is," and so on. In the strongest version of this account, semantic properties of the words and phrases are irrelevant (e.g., Maratsos and Chalkley 1981; see also Harris 1954).

This proposal is partially motivated by the widely perceived failure to find semantic definitions for syntactic categories. For instance, there are count nouns that do not name physical things (e.g., "joke") and verbs that do not name actions (e.g., "know"). Although child language does have a semantically transparent flavor, with a high proportion of nouns describing things, and verbs describing actions (Macnamara 1982), even 1- and 2-year-olds know words that do not fit this pattern (Nelson, Hampson, and Shaw 1993; Pinker 1984). The possibility that children might use prosodic information to carve up sentences into grammatically relevant units (Gleitman and Wanner 1982; Hirsh-Pasek et al. 1987) as well as phonological information to distinguish function morphemes from members of open-class categories (Gerken, Landau, and Remez 1989) introduces further sources of evidence that a nonsemantic learning procedure could use.

Nevertheless, it has long been known that an unconstrained distributional learning model has serious limitations as a solution to the bootstrapping problem (Gordon 1982, 1985; Pinker 1979, 1984, 1987). There are an enormous number of surface correlations that children could encode. A child exposed to "Look at the dog" could note that "look" is the first word of the sentence, that it appears to the immediate left of "at," two words to the left of "the," three words to the left of "dog," and so on for each of the other words in the sentence. But most of these facts are irrelevant—it does not matter from the standpoint of grammar that "look" appears in the same sentence as "the." Focusing on a specific linguistic domain, Gordon (1982) has calculated that a child who tried to distinguish count nouns from mass nouns through purely distributional differences would have to sift through about 8 billion possible contexts in order to converge on the distinction. Yet children command count/mass syntax by the age of 2 1/2 (Gordon 1982, 1988; Soja 1992).

Recent theories have responded to these concerns by positing that children are constrained in the sorts of correlations they look for. Under one proposal, they consider only immediate adjacency relations (Finch and Chater 1993); under another, they focus only on the locations of words relative to a small set of highly frequent function morphemes, such as "the" and "was" (Gerken and McIntosh 1993). Connectionist implementations of these more constrained distributional theories (e.g., Redington, Chater, and Finch 1994) have done surprisingly well when tested on their capacity to syntactically categorize caregiver speech from the CHILDES corpora (MacWhinney 1991), although the full capacities of these models are as yet unclear.[1]

There are problems, however, with the claim that this is how children actually solve the bootstrapping problem. For one thing, the proposal that children categorize words through the exercise of general inductive capacities entails that there should not exist developmental dissociations between syntax acquisition and inductive learning in other domains. But such dissociations exist. One example is the population of children and adults suffering form specific language impairment (SLI) studied by Gopnik (this volume). They are normal with regard to their nonlinguistic learning abilities, but suffer form a severe deficit in grammar and morphology. For instance, they have great difficulty with the count/mass distinction (producing errors such as "I love bicycle" and "I play musics"), number agreement ("I find a cops"), and noun-verb agreement ("The ambulance arrive"). A similar phenomenon shows up with critical period effects in first and second language learning (Newport 1990); adults are better learners than children in virtually all domains other than language. These cases are problematic for the distributional account. If the count/ mass distinction is acquired, for instance, by simply noting correlations between determiners and nouns, it is a puzzle that SLI children and non-language-impaired 30-year-olds are so *bad* at this task, while succeeding at other tasks that clearly do involve the ability to attend to and learn correlations.

Related to this, distributional mechanisms have no a priori commitments regarding the number and type of categories they can acquire. As a result, they are necessarily incompatible with the proposal that there exists innate knowledge particular to specific linguistic categories. Even if such a mechanism could succeed at categorizing the input the child is presented with, all it is going to produce is a series of distinct groups of words—one with "dog" and "door" in it, another with "kick" and "know," and so on. It has no way of telling *which* of these classes corresponds to which syntactic categories and so it does not fully solve the bootstrapping problem; it would tell you which words go together, but it would not tell you how to find the nouns (see also Pinker 1984).

The reason why this matters is that there are linguistic universals that apply to specific syntactic categories. For instance, if a language has Subject-Object-Verb order, it is likely to have postpositions; if it has Subject-Verb-Object order, it is likely to have prepositions (Greenberg 1966). At a more abstract level, conditions on grammar such as constraints on question formation or restrictions on coreference appear to hold universally, subject to constrained parametric variation (e.g., Chomsky 1986; Manzini and Wexler 1987). Most relevant to the point of this chapter, it has long been known that words with the semantic role of referring to objects universally fall into the syntactic class of nominals (Bloomfield 1933; Macnamara 1986).

To the extent that these generalizations exist because of how the human mind is structured, they pose a problem for a purely distributional theory of children's learning. A similar problem arises in cases in which children are exposed to impoverished input (input in which distributional evidence for linguistic categories is diminished or absent) but nevertheless come to possess syntactic rules and categories. Such instances show up in creolization (Bickerton 1981), first language acquisition of American Sign Language based on input from nonproficient users (Singleton and Newport 1993), and "home-sign," in which children create a signed communication system with no linguistic model at all (Goldin-Meadow and Mylander 1990). In all of these instances—and most likely in normal acquisition as well—the child is *imposing* structure on the input, not merely abstracting it away.

Finally, the premise behind distributional theories is that syntactic categorization is fundamentally holistic: the linguistic status of a word is determined relative to how all other words behave; there is no sense in which it can be classified in isolation, through the use of semantic or any other information. But there is considerable evidence that very young children possess a rich understanding of syntax-semantics mappings. For instance, in a classic acquisition experiment (Katz, Baker, and Macnamara 1974), 17-month-olds were taught a new word as either a count noun ("This is a wug") or a lexical NP ("This is wug"). When the new word was used to describe a doll, children were sensitive to this difference; they tended to interpret the count noun as naming the kind of doll, but treated the NP as a proper name for that specific doll. Two- and 3-year-olds are also sensitive to contrasts between subclasses of nouns. In particular, they can focus on the difference between count nouns and mass nouns (e.g., between "a wug" and "some wug") when inferring properties of word meaning. They will tend to construe a novel count noun as referring to a kind of individual and a novel mass noun as referring to a kind of nonindividuated entity (Bloom 1994; Brown 1957; Soja 1992). Finally, certain early categorization errors, such as treating object mass nouns like "furniture" and "toast" as count nouns (Bloom 1994), are best explained in terms of childrens using semantics as a clue to category membership.

Other linguistic domains yield similar findings. For instance, Naigles (1990) found that 24-month-olds attend to the distinction between NP-V and NP-V-NP contexts when inferring aspects of the meanings of verbs.

Although the precise nature of children's competence is a matter of considerable debate (Fisher et al. 1994; Pinker 1994), there is little doubt that they can use mappings from syntactic categories to semantic structure in the course of word learning and syntax acquisition, which militates against any theory that children are initially restricted to attending to nonsemantic properties of sentences.

12.2   Two Semantic Theories

Under the theory presented by Macnamara (1982), children begin with rules that map over semantic categories like "object word." Since such rules are inadequate to capture the patterns of adult language, children come to expand such categories and make them more abstract, gradually transforming them so that they are truly syntactic, such as "noun." In this way, the child moves from a semantic understanding of language to a syntactic one (for similar approaches, see Braine 1988, 1992; Schlesinger 1988).

One problem with this proposal was raised above. As Macnamara explicitly states, his theory is incompatible with the notion of innate knowledge about specific grammatical categories. Under his proposal, categories such as "noun" emerge only through a domain-general procedure of abstraction. The child would be just as happy to stick with "object word" since this is the natural category she forms—the shift to "noun" occurs only because the input is incompatible with this initial interpretation. Put differently, "noun" is just the name for the category that used to be "object word"; there is nothing else to be said about it. As a result, any evidence for innate syntactic knowledge about nouns poses a problem for Macnamara's theory.

Another problem is empirical. Some studies suggest that there is no stage of language development in which the child's rules map onto semantic categories such as "object word." For instance, an analysis of children's very first word combinations shows that—contrary to Macnamara's proposal—utterances like "big dog" and "nice hat" are *not* generated by a rule such as "modifier + object word." This is because children's early utterances also include expressions in which modifiers are followed by substance names ("hot water," "good milk," etc.), names for actions ("little fall," "big hug"), and names for nonmaterial entities ("big hug," "big noise"). From the very start, their knowledge seems best captured in terms of the syntactic categories "adjective" and "noun"

(Bloom 1990b). More generally, there appears to be no stage of language development in which children's rules utilize different categories than adults' rules do (Pinker 1984). It looks like syntax all the way down.

This finding favors the proposal that both semantic categories and syntactic categories are present at the very start. This brings us to "semantic bootstrapping." Grimshaw (1981) and Pinker (1984) have proposed that the form-meaning correspondences that children exploit in the bootstrapping procedure are not part of knowledge of language itself, but are instead the result of special mechanisms of language acquisition. Thus, Grimshaw (1981, 171) posits as a principle of Universal Grammar that "form and function are independent." Given this, whatever correspondences exist, do so because "the LAD ... gives priority to a grammar with a one-to-one correspondence between form and function." Similarly, Pinker (1984, 39) states, "Although grammatical entities do not have semantic definitions in adult grammars, it is possible that such entities refer to identifiable semantic classes in parent-child discourse"; and he notes later that these correspondences are only sure to hold in "basic sentences," not in passives, contextually dependent sentences, and so on (but see Pinker 1989 for a somewhat different proposal).

One problem with this view is that by stipulating that the syntax-semantics mappings are part of a separate LAD, independent from the rest of language, it cannot explain why these particular ones occur and not others. There is no principled explanation for why the mapping is from object names to nouns instead of (for instance) from object names to modals. But these mappings are unlikely to be arbitrary from the standpoint of how language works. Would it be a possible language if the LAD instead led children to categorize "dog" as a modal and "kick" as a quantifier? Probably not; other universal properties of language, such as structural constraints on coreference or conditions on quantifier interpretation, could not naturally occur. So long as the syntax-semantics mappings exploited in language acquisition are viewed as distinct from the rest of linguistic knowledge, systematic relationships between the role of semantics in language acquisition and the role of semantics as part of linguistic knowledge itself are left unexplained.

This relates to a further problem, which is that the proposed mappings associate syntactic categories with reference to concrete entities; in the case of nouns, the proposed semantic correlate is "name of person or thing" (Pinker 1984, 41). There are advantages to this. For one thing, it provides the child with a tractable entry (via perception) into the linguistic system. For another, generalizations such as "Names for kinds of discrete physical objects are nouns" are likely candidates for descriptive universals of language (Bloomfield 1933; Macnamara 1986). However, this theory leaves certain semantic aspects of syntactic categories unexplained. It is hardly an accident, for instance, that words such as "day," "nightmare," and "conference" are nouns and not prepositions or modals. Furthermore, even 3-year-olds appear to be sensitive to the semantic correlates of nominal syntax in nonmaterial domains, such as when learning names of sounds or events (Bloom 1994). At least within the nominal system, then, there exist syntax-semantics mappings that appear to go beyond the domain of names for people or things, and it would thus be preferable to view generalizations like "Names for people or things are nouns" as by-products of more abstract semantic properties of grammatical categories, not as mental principles in their own right.

A final issue has to do with how semantic bootstrapping applies. Under Pinker's (1984) theory, children learn the meanings of some words prior to learning their syntactic category. They learn the meanings of "the" and "dog," for instance, and use the mappings that are part of the boot-strapping procedure to categorize them as a determiner and a noun: determiner because "the" refers to definiteness in discourse; noun because "dog" is the name of a thing. Upon hearing a string of words like "the dog," the child parses it as determiner-noun, and then uses principles of X-bar theory to flesh out the phrase structure, so that both words are dominated by an NP and "dog" is immediately dominated by an N'. A further mechanism analyzes the resulting tree and posits a phrase structure rule of the form NP → Det – N'. Once this rule is in the child's grammar, he can use it to determine the syntactic category of words that do not fall under the initial bootstrapping procedure. If he hears "the joke," he can use this rule to infer that "joke" is a noun, even though it is not an object name. (There are syntax-semantics mappings that apply to phrases under Pinker's theory; these are used to annotate NPs with different grammatical functions, such as Subject or Topic. But they apply only once the NPs have been categorized through the procedure sketched above.)

Pinker is explicit that semantic bootstrapping is not a theory of the acquisition of word meanings; it assumes that children have learned the meaning of some words prior to syntactic development, but makes no commitments as to how. Nevertheless, the specific procedure discussed above does make one nontrivial assumption about word learning: it assumes that children can learn the meanings of nouns prior to categorizing phrases as NPs, that they can learn verbs prior to categorizing VPs, and so on. The same assumption is also made by many theories that posit that children move from semantic categories to syntactic categories, such as the theories proposed by Braine (1992) and Macnamara (1982).

But the claim that children learn lexical categories before phrasal ones may be wrong. After all, nouns and verbs do not themselves refer to objects or actions, they are not subjects or predicates, and they do not have thematic roles. It is phrasal categories that are initially "visible" to the child through a semantic analysis of sentence meaning. Furthermore, phrases—and not words—might also be identifiable on the basis of a prosodic parse (Gleitman and Wanner 1982) and frequently appear as isolated units (Peters 1983).

Consider some specific examples. How does a child learn the meaning of the word "dog"? Presumably part of the solution rests on the child's somehow figuring out that adults use the word "dog" with the intent to refer to the category (or kind) of dogs. But the word "dog" does not itself describe or refer to the category (or kind) of dogs. An adult who wishes to describe a dog is likely to point and say something like, "Look at the dog" or "That's a dog" or "There's that big dog again." The linguistic unit that refers is not "dog"; it is the NP "the dog" or "a dog" or "that big dog." This suggests that the only way children can gain access to the meaning of "dog" is through its contribution to the semantics of the NP. They must determine that a phrase like "the dog" refers to a dog, and they must figure out which of the words in this phrase refers to the kind. Determiners are a similar case. Words like "the" and "a" appear only in the context of phrases and gain their meaning through their contribution to the semantics of the NP. Such words cannot be acquired in isolation, suggesting again that children learn them after analyzing utterances like "the dog" as NPs, not before.[2] Note also that for lexical NPs—like "Fred" and "he"—the single word is itself a referring element, and there is no noun that the child must learn in order to gain access to the NP.

A related concern is that Jelinek (in press) and Kinkade (1983) argue that Straits Salish lacks a noun/verb distinction; there are no lexical elements that are uniquely associated with the maximal projections NP and VP. Put differently, those roots that would correspond to English nouns are syntactically and morphologically identical to those corresponding to English verbs, and each can appear within both NPs and VPs. Salish *does* mark a distinction between nominals and predicates but only at the phrasal level—it has NPs and VPs, just not nouns and verbs. Quechua poses a related puzzle, because verb roots cannot stand as independent morphemes and, more generally, there are many contexts in which the syntactic category of a root can only be determined through its semantic and morphological contribution to the larger syntactic constituent that it belongs to (Courtney 1994; Lefebver and Muysken 1988). These phenomena are difficult to explain in a theory that assumes a lexical category–to–phrasal category analysis in the course of syntactic development.

These considerations motivate a somewhat different conception of the role of semantics in solving the bootstrapping problem, one that I sketch below.

12.3   A Mapping Theory

The scope of the alternative is modest. It will focus mostly on the acquisition of nominals, though it will also touch on the acquisition of determiners and verbs. It has two aspects: a representational claim, concerning the nature of the syntax-semantics mappings that are used to learn the syntactic categories that words belong to, and an acquisition claim, concerning the nature of the learning process.

12.3.1   The Representational Claim
In Pinker's and Grimshaw's theory, the mappings children use are part of a separate LAD, independent from knowledge of language. The alternative proposed here is that the mappings children exploit in language learning are instead derived from syntax-semantics mappings that exist as part of knowledge of language itself. This alternative is based to a large extent on proposals made by Jackendoff (1990, 1996) and Macnamara (1986), though the specifics differ in certain regards.

In a language such as English, there is a lexical/phrasal contrast within the nominal system. Nouns are words that refer to kinds, whereas NPs are words or phrases that can refer to individuals. Thus, "dog" itself does not refer to dogs, but it can be quantified and modified to form an NP, which can refer. For instance, "that dog" picks out a particular individual that is a dog, "those big dogs" picks out a set of dogs that are big, and so on. Pronouns and proper names are lexical NPs because, unlike words such as "dog," they inherently pick out individuals, not kinds.

The notion that NPs, and not nouns, refer to individuals is familiar from work within formal semantics, where nouns are sometimes viewed as predicates, which must combine with determiners to establish reference (e.g., Barwise and Cooper 1981). More generally, the notion is that nouns are semantically incomplete (or "unsaturated"; see Higginbotham 1983); only NPs are semantically complete. As such, only NPs can participate in certain forms of semantic interaction, such as having thematic roles, participating in coreference relations, and being able to refer to entities in the world.

Although the lexical/phrasal contrast within nominals may not hold across all languages, one could posit as a universal of language the following:

NPs refer to individuals.

This is a unidirectional mapping; it does not preclude the possibility that some NPs might serve other semantic roles. This qualification is essential: some NPs do not refer at all. An expletive such as "it" as in "It is raining" exists only to satisfy a grammatical condition in English stating that tensed clauses must have subjects (Chomsky 1981; Rothstein 1983). There are also NPs that have semantic substance, but do not refer to individuals. An NP such as "a dog" has a different semantic role in a sentence such as "Fred is not a dog" than in a sentence such as "A dog walked into the room." Only the second sentence actually refers to a dog; in the first, the NP serves as a predicate and has much the same semantic role as the Adjective Phrase "happy" in "Fred is not happy" (see Williams 1983 for discussion). Finally, some NPs, such as "some water" or "much sand," refer to portions of stuff, not to individuals. In general, NPs headed by mass nouns do not refer to individuals, since mass nouns refer to kinds of nonindividuated entities, not kinds of individuals (Jackendoff 1990; Macnamara 1986).[3]

The contrast between "object" and "individual" is crucial here. This shift to "individual" follows naturally if one assumes that the mapping children apply is part of more general properties of language and cognition, and not a separate LAD. NPs in natural language are not limited to referring to objects. They can refer to parts ("a hand"), portions of substance ("a puddle"), bounded events ("a race"), abstract notions like jokes and ideas, collections of objects like flocks and families, and so on. Nominals behave identically from the standpoint of linguistic semantics regardless of what sorts of individuals or kinds of individuals they refer to. For instance, the numerical contrast between "two cookies" and "five cookies" is identical to the contrast between "two jokes" and "five jokes," and the same properties of binding theory apply regardless of whether the referring expressions refer to material ("the cookie") or nonmaterial ("the joke") entities. In general, the semantic structures of language don't care whether or not the individuals denoted by nominals are physical objects.

In light of this, it might be most parsimonious to view the child's tendency to construe phrases that describe objects as NPs as a special case of the mapping that states that NPs can refer to individuals. In particular, children might possess the following bias concerning the relationship between linguistic semantics and nonlinguistic cognition:

Physical whole objects are canonical individuals.

There is considerable support for the claim that children are biased to construe whole objects as individuals, support that is quite independent from considerations of syntactic development. When children hear a word (especially a count noun) used to describe a novel object, they show a strong bias to take the word as referring to the kind of object, not to a part, or property, or anything else (see Markman 1989). Related to this, Shipley and Shepperson (1990) asked preschoolers to count different sorts of entities. For instance, they showed children a picture of five forks, one of them broken into two pieces, and asked, "Can you count the forks?" Most of the children said, "Six," presumably because there were six discrete physical objects in front of them—although only five forks. Shipley and Shepperson call this the "discrete physical object" bias, which is equivalent to the above claim that, when it comes to quantifying over individuals, objects are highly salient. Note also that a considerable amount of knowledge about objects appears to be innate in humans (Spelke et al. 1992).

Although objects are salient individuals, even infants and young children can quantify over individuals that are not objects. In one study, infants were exposed to either two sounds or three sounds and then presented with two pictures: one with two objects and one with three objects. Even 6-month-olds tended to look longer at the picture that showed the same number of objects as there were sounds, providing some evidence that infants possess notions of "two individuals" and "three individuals," where "individual" encompasses both discrete sounds and discrete objects (Starkey, Spelke, and Gelman 1990). When there are no salient objects present, 2-year-olds have no problem counting sounds or actions; this capacity emerges at the same time that they are able to count objects (Wynn 1990).

Returning to language, even 20-month-olds know many nouns that describe nonobject kinds, such as parts ("hand"), events ("race"), and periods of time ("hour") (Nelson, Hampson, and Shaw 1993). Finally, children can use syntactic cues to learn count nouns that form NPs referring to discrete sounds (Bloom 1994), bounded portions of stuff like puddles (Soja 1992), and collections of objects (Bloom and Kelemen 1995).

These considerations support the view that the relationship between NPs and objects is not direct. Instead, even young children possess an abstract semantic notion of "individual" that maps onto NPs. Objects are salient individuals, but other entities can be individuals as well. It is likely, for instance, that children can categorize a word or phrase as an NP by hearing it used to refer to a collection, or to a bounded substance, or to a discrete sound. One factor that determines what can count as a possible individual is boundedness, either in space or in time, which is why NPs can refer to entities like puddles (Soja 1992) and discrete sounds (Bloom 1994). A more fundamental consideration might have to do with having a single causal role—if adults see a group of objects moving together and acting as a single agent (e.g., a flock or an army), they will construe the objects as a single individual, but if the objects are stationary, the individual interpretation is much less salient (Bloom 1996). For different perspectives on the category of "individual" and constraints on possible kinds of individuals (i.e., possible count nouns), see Bloom 1996, Langacker 1987, and Macnamara 1986.

12.3.2 The Acquisition Mechanism

The discussion above has focused on a putative semantic correlate of NPs—individuals—and its relationship to the notion of discrete physical object. But children must somehow use this knowledge to categorize the NPs they are exposed to. Further, they must categorize other parts of speech, such as determiners.

As discussed above, the usual proposal is that children first categorize words as lexical categories and then use grammatical information to infer further aspects of phrase structure. The problems with this view motivate an alternative, which is that children start off parsing sentences they hear into phrases, perhaps with the aid of prosodic information, and use structural principles of grammar along with further semantic information to determine which words belong to which lexical categories. In the case of nominals, the relevant procedure can be summarized as follows:

Primacy-of-NPs procedure

Categorize a word (or combination of words) that refers to an individual as an NP. Recategorize it as a noun (or as a noun and other parts of speech) only if there is semantic evidence that this initial NP-construal is mistaken.

This proposal leads to the following acquisition scenarios.

Children can categorize their first *pronouns* and *proper names* as lexical NPs by noting that they refer to discrete physical objects, categorizing them as referring to individuals (through the relationship between non-linguistic cognition and this semantic notion) and thus as NPs (through the mapping between semantics and grammar). Prior to the acquisition of other parts of speech, this is the only way in which new words can be encoded as NPs, and it might serve as the foundation for children's grasp of syntax. In other words, children's very first syntactic categories might be NPs. In support of this, pronouns and proper names are among the very first words learned by children across a variety of cultures (Gentner 1982).

The only way to acquire *determiners* and *common nouns* is through decomposition, as these words rarely appear in isolation. Through the procedure above, children initially categorize phrases such as "the dog" or "some cups" as NPs and must do further analysis in order to categorize "dog" and "cups" as nouns and "the" and "some" as determiners. In particular, only after hearing the different words used in distinct phrases (e.g., "the cat," "a cup") will they decompose the phrase into two components (the determiner "the" and the noun "cup"), by noting the different contributions that the two words make toward the meanings of the phrases in which they appear. (This process would be facilitated if children are capable of distinguishing closed-class forms like determiners from open-class forms like nouns on the basis of phonological properties, such as weak versus strong stress; Gerken, Landau, and Remez, 1989.) Note that identifying the parts of a given NP as a determiner and a noun is not sufficient to decompose it. There must be *semantic* evidence for compositionality as well—the meaning of the determiner and the meaning of the noun must combine in the expected manner to form the meaning of the referential NP. Otherwise, the phrase is stored in the lexicon as a whole, as is the case with NP idioms such as "the big cheese" (see below).

As Pinker (1984) notes, this decomposition process is similar to the one that takes place in the course of morphological acquisition. Children acquiring English must learn that the words "cups," "dogs," and "houses" are not semantic monads, but instead decompose into the aspect of meaning expressed by the noun and the notion of plurality expressed by the plural morpheme. The suggestion here is that an analogous procedure takes place when children hear a phrase like "the dog." They initially encode it as a semantically simple NP and store it in their lexicon; only later do they decompose it into two semantic units, the determiner "the" and the noun "dog." In support of this, morphemes that are semantically equivalent to words such as "the" and "some" are often affixes in other languages, just as the plural morpheme is in English.

This proposal seems to make the wrong prediction about children's spontaneous speech, however, as it suggests that they should produce phrasal NPs prior to count nouns—"a cup" before "cup," for instance. This does not occur, of course. But the reason for this may be that children are capable of extracting the noun from a determiner-noun NP early in language development, perhaps even prior to the onset of spontaneous speech. In addition, determiners are not phonologically salient; sometimes young children might simply not perceive them (Gleitman and Wanner 1982), leading them to parse a phrasal NP like "a cup" as just "cup" and then to categorize "cup" as a noun through the semantic decomposition procedure discussed below. Slightly older children do appear to have identified certain English words as determiners, distinct from nouns, and this would allow them to parse the NP in an adultlike way (Gerken, Landau, and Remez 1989; Katz, Baker, and Macnamara 1974). Note also that even if a 2-year-old did store phrases such as "a cup" or "the dog" in his lexicon as nondecomposed NPs, such phrases would likely be *produced* as just "cup" and "dog," since 2-year-olds have problems producing determiners in their spontaneous speech, because of articulatory limitations (e.g., Gerken, Landau, and Remez 1989).

To see how semantic evidence might lead to decomposition when no syntactic motivation is present, imagine being shown an inanimate entity, like a cup, and being told, "This is wug." From the standpoint of grammar alone, "wug" could be a lexical NP that refers to that *specific* individual (i.e., a proper name) or it could be a noun that refers to that *kind* of individual. Even young children assume that such words are nouns (Katz, Baker, and Macnamara 1974), possibly because they are unwilling to construe things like cups as having their own names. This semantic consideration is sufficient to motivate a decomposition of the single word into a noun preceded by a null determiner, even without any syntactic motivation for this analysis.

Idioms provide the opposite situation. Although an NP idiom like "the big cheese" appears to be syntactically decomposable (into determiner-adjective-noun), it is not semantically decomposable and thus must be acquired by the child as a lexical NP. Even once the child knows the meanings of the constituent words ("the," "big," and "cheese"), the phrase will only be syntactically decomposed to the extent that it is semantically transparent.

This claim is supported by psycholinguistic evidence. Cutler (1982) discusses the role of certain factors in determining how frozen different idioms are (i.e., how accessible they are to syntactic movement, such as passivization). She noted a strong trend that she sums up as "the colder the older." In other words, older idioms are more resistant to syntactic transformation than newer ones. One explanation is that older idioms may be harder to make sense of (especially to children) and thus may be acquired as unanalyzed elements; hence, they would be "colder." Supporting this, there is experimental evidence suggesting that degree of semantic "analyzability" is correlated with how syntactically decomposable a given idiom is (Gibbs and Nayak 1989).

Expletives belong to the class of NPs that do not refer to individuals. There are two potential explanations of how such words could be categorized, both of which are consistent with the theory proposed above.

The first proposal is that the acquisition of expletives is simply independent of the proposed mapping. Since expletives do not refer, they will not be categorized through the mapping from individuals to NPs; instead, they will be learned through syntactic inference. In particular, once children have acquired the meaning of a verb like "raining"—that it has no semantic arguments—and given that they know overt subjects are obligatory in English (knowledge present early in development; see Bloom 1993; Valian 1991), this will force them to categorize "it" as an expletive NP on the basis of a sentence such as "It is raining."

A second proposal makes a stronger assumption about the syntax-semantics mappings. It is possible that not any lexical NP can be an expletive, but only those lexical NPs *that are initially acquired through the syntax-semantics mapping*. To put it differently, there may be a sufficiently strong correspondence between the syntactic fact of being an NP and the semantic fact of referring to an individual, such that although lexical NPs can be co-opted to serve other semantic roles (as in the case of expletives), they can only enter the lexicon via the syntax-semantics mapping. If this is so, children would not be capable of learning the expletive "it" unless they had already acquired "it" as a referential prnoun.

This leads to two predictions: (1) children should use an NP as an expletive only after they have acquired its referential meaning, and (2) no language should have NPs that are solely expletive and have no referential double life, because children would never be able to acquire such words. Nishigauchi and Roeper (1987), who present a similar theory of the acquisition of expletives, argue that both predictions hold, but admittedly the evidence is relatively scanty.

What about *verbs*? The discussion above has focused on NPs and parts of NPs, but children must also acquire other parts of speech. No doubt syntax-semantics mappings can apply in these domains as well. Just as there is a mapping between individuals and NPs, so there may be similar mappings between events and VPs, propositions and sentences, and so on. The semantic bootstrapping theory also posits such mappings, although, as with nominals, these are presumed to be independent of more general linguistic knowledge.

It is also likely that once children have categorized some words or phrases as NPs, principles of grammar could lead them to categorize words belonging to other syntactic categories, even in the absence of any prior knowledge of what these words mean. Consider a child who knows (through the procedure discussed above) that "Mary" and "Joe" are NPs that refer to individuals, and then hears these NPs used with the novel word "kissed" (e.g., "Mary kissed Joe"). Assuming that children can determine whether a string of words is a sentence as opposed to a fragment, and that they expect semtences to express propositions, the utterance would be semantically encoded as follows, using a notation based on Jackendoff's (1990):

PROPOSITION
([INDIVIDUAL]   ???   [INDIVIDUAL])
    Mary   kissed   Joe

One likely candidate for a universal of language is some constraint to the effect that all NPs with semantic content must get their semantic role from some predicate, as with the Theta Criterion of Chomsky (1981), though the proper formulation of such a constraint is a matter of some debate (see Jackendoff 1987). If children possess this constraint, then they can categorize "kissed" as a predicate (since there must be something licensing these NPs and this is the only candidate) and give it the following representation:

EVENT
"KISSED": ([INDIVIDUAL], [INDIVIDUAL])

Finally, if children possess some mapping from EVENTs to verbs, this could allow children who have only acquired NPs to use syntax-semantics mappings to categorize novel words as verbs.

12.4   Mechanisms of Word Learning

In the discussion of how children learn pronouns and proper names, I assumed that children have the capacity to categorize a word or string of words as an NP by noting that it is used to refer to an individual (in many cases, a whole object)—and that they can do this even if they have no prior knowledge of the syntax of the particular language they are exposed to. Gleitman (1990), however, discusses certain issues that arise from the assumption that children can determine the reference of a word without already knowing its linguistic category, and these are worth considering here.

At first blush, it is not obvious where the problems lie. All children must do is hear a word or phrase (e.g., "Freddie"), follow an adult's gaze or point, and note that the adult is intending to refer to an object (e.g., to Freddie). Since Freddie is an object, the child will construe it as an individual, and since NPs refer to individuals, "Freddie" must be an NP. Along these lines, note that even 12- and 13-month-olds are drawn to focus on the individual when exposed to a new word that describes an object—and will do so regardless of whether the word is a noun or an adjective, suggesting that overt syntactic cues are not essential at this early stage of word learning, at least not for the acquisition of names for object kinds (Waxman 1994).

However, there are situations in which children cannot be assured of exposure to ostensive labeling. For instance, Kaluli mothers do not engage in labeling behavior with their children. Instead, they provide their children with extensive training in conversational interaction, often modeling sentences for them (Schieffelin 1985; see also Heath 1983). Despite this difference in input, Kaluli children acquire words at much the same rate as children acquiring languages such as English. To see the problem this raises, imagine such a child seeing a bird in the sky and hearing, for example, "Zav goop wicket mep." By hypothesis, the child knows no words at this point, no inflections, and nothing about the syntax. (And in fact, it is optimistic even to assume that she is capable of parsing the utterance into distinct words and phrases; if not, she will hear "Zavgoopwicketmep.") Which word or string of words (if any) does the child construe as referring to the bird? How do Kaluli children learn any word meanings?

There are two possible types of solutions. The first is that children perform a constrained distributional analysis; they store sentence-situation pairs in memory and then look for correlations between specific words or phrases and discrete aspects of meaning. For instance, if the same child hears "Blub mendle wicket mep" to refer to another bird, she might assume that "wicket mep" (which was present in both sentences) is used to refer to birds and is thus an NP. The analysis might be simplified if children only store strings of stressed phrases (instead of whole sentences) and representations of relevant individuals (instead of entire situations). But such an analysis might conceivably lead to problems. Imagine a child who sees one bird, hears the equivalent of "Isn't that pretty?", sees another bird, and hears the equivalent of "That's also pretty." Such a child, using the procedure above, would infer that "pretty" is an NP referring to the bird. Such errors hardly ever occur with real children. Nevertheless, if children only hear NPs in the context of sentences that include other phrases, some such procedure must be applying.

The alternative is to deny the premise above. Perhaps all children are exposed to *some* words in isolation, and these can be categorized as NPs. One candidate class of words is proper names, as there is evidence that these are privileged in lexical acquisition. They appear among the very first words of children learning a range of different languages (Gentner 1982)—including Kaluli children. Further, proper names might be the one class of words that all children are guaranteed of having been exposed to in isolation, or at least in some special stressed context. Regardless of a society's beliefs concerning how children learn names for kinds of entities, it is unlikely that any culture assumes children are born knowing the proper names of the people surrounding them. These must be taught, even to other adults.

This predicts that even in cultures in which adults do not standardly label objects for children, proper names will be taught to children. Looking at Kaluli children, we find this to be the case. Schieffelin (1985, 534) notes,

There are no labeling games to facilitate or encourage the learning of object names. This is primarily due to the linguistic ideology of the culture. It is only in families who are acquiring literacy that one sees any attention paid to saying the names of objects, and this activity is initiated by the child when the mother is looking at books. When extended by the child to other contexts, the mother's response is disinterest.

In contrast, because of the cultural importance placed on learning the proper names and kinterms of the individuals with whom they interact, Kaluli children are consistently encouraged to master a large number of proper names, kinterms, and other relationship terms . . .

Perhaps every culture has some class of nominals that are special with regard to interaction with children. In Western societies, this is a very broad class, including virtually all object and substance names; within the Kaluli society, it is much more narrow, restricted to proper names and relationship terms. Another distinct candidate for privileged nominals is the class of deictic pronouns, like "this" and "that." These are also universal, show up early in child language, and serve to draw children's attention to objects and other individuals in the environment.

In sum, it might be that all cultures use some NPs that refer to individuals in isolation, allowing children to bootstrap into the language system. If not, then children must be capable of somehow learning the meanings of words that are embedded in sentences, by extracting the referential NPs from such sentences through a constrained distributional analysis. Thus, an adequate theory of lexical acquisition must assume either strong extrinsic constraints (all cultures use some nominals in isolation) or a powerful learning mechanism (one that can learn words that are not presented in isolation). Either possibility would be of considerable interest.

12.5   Conclusion

Higginbotham (1989, 119) has described the question of the autonomy of syntax within linguistic theory as having "perished or been transformed" in that the initial considerations in favor of autonomy "seem to have been not refuted or vindicated but merely superseded by later developments." The same sort of transformation has not yet occurred in the field of language development, where it is often assumed that "semantic" theories of acquisition are an alternative to "syntactic" theories, and experimental data are interpreted as favoring one sort of theory over the other. Children's early understanding of semantic structure is presented as evidence against innate syntactic knowledge (Braine 1992; Lieberman 1991); conversely, early command of syntax and morphology is interpreted as showing that semantics plays little or no role in grammatical development (Levy 1988).

Some recent work rejects this dichotomy and attempts to develop a theory of language acquisition consistent with the notion of a distinct level of syntactic representation that relates systematically to nonlinguistic cognition (e.g., Gleitman 1990; Pinker 1989). The proposal here falls into this research program, as it posits that innate mappings from syntax to semantics—as well as properties of the interface between semantic categories like "individual" and cognitive notions like "discrete physical object"—are used by children to determine the syntactic categories that new words and phrases belong to. These mappings are presumed to be present prior to the onset of language acquisition, in contrast to the view that syntax is in some sense abstracted or derived from prior semantic structure, as maintained by Braine (1988), Macnamara (1982), Schlesinger (1988), and others.

The proposal here was originally developed as an alternative to semantic bootstrapping, but it accepts two fundamental insights behind that proposal: children use word meaning to determine the syntactic categorization of new words, and syntactic categories are available at the outset, distinct from nonlinguistic cognition. It differs from semantic bootstrapping by claiming that children do not need to utilize mappings from a special language acquisition device and by adopting the assumption that syntactic development runs from phrase to word, not vice versa. This provides a plausible explanation of how children solve the bootstrapping problem, one that can apply across different languages and that is consistent with how children learn the meanings of words.

Notes

1. One specific problem involves homophony (Pinker 1979). Many of the words children learn can appear as both nouns and verbs. Full grammatical knowledge of English requires knowing that "drink" is a verb when used to describe an action and a noun when used to describe a substance. To this extent at least, the syntactic categorization of some words *must* be determined relative to their meanings.

2. This is related to Pinker's (1984) own proposal, which treats the acquisition of determiners in the same way as the acquisition of nominal morphology, such as the plural morpheme. The difference is that Pinker proposes that the segmentation of "the" and "dog" is the result of initially analyzing "the-dog" as a single *noun*, not, as argued here an NP.

3. Mass nouns can be used to form NPs that establish reference to individuals when they appear with constructions that supply a principle of individuation over the kind that the mass noun refers to, as in "*a grain of* sand" or "*a glass of* water" (see Macnamara 1986).

References

Barwise, J., and Cooper, R. (1981). Generalized quantifiers and natural language. *Linguistics and Philosophy, 4,* 159–219.

Bickerton, D. (1981). *Roots of language.* Ann Arbor, MI: Karoma.

Bloom, P. (1990a). *Semantic structure and language development.* Unpublished doctoral dissertation, MIT.

Bloom, P. (1990b). Syntactic distinctions in child language. *Journal of Child Language, 17,* 343–355.

Bloom, P. (1993). Grammatical continuity in language development: The case of subjectless sentences. *Linguistic Inquiry, 24,* 721–734.

Bloom, P. (1994). Semantic competence as an explanation for some transitions in language development. In Y. Levy (Ed.), *Other children, other languages: Theoretical issues in language development.* Hillsdale, NJ: Erlbaum.

Bloom, P. (1996). Possible individuals in language and cognition. *Current Directions in Psychological Science, 5,* 90–94.

Bloom, P., and Kelemen, D. (1995). Syntactic cues in the acquisition of collective nouns. *Cognition, 56,* 1–30.

Bloomfield, L. (1933). *Language.* New York: Holt.

Braine, M. D. S. (1988). Modeling the acquisition of linguistic structure. In Y. Levy, I. M. Schlesinger, and M. D. S. Braine (Eds.), *Categories and processes in language acquisition theory.* Hillsdale, NJ: Erlbaum.

Braine, M. D. S. (1992). What sort of innate structure is needed to "bootstrap" into syntax? *Cognition, 45,* 77–100.

Brown, R. (1957). Linguistic determinism and the part of speech. *Journal of Abnormal and Social Psychology, 55,* 1–5.

Chomsky, N. (1981). *Lectures on government and binding.* Dordrecht: Foris.

Chomsky, N. (1986). *Knowledge of language: Its nature, origin, and use.* New York: Praeger.

Courtney, E. (1994). *Children's first parses and syntactic rules: A proposal.* Unpublished manuscript, University of Arizona.

Cutler, A. (1982). Idioms: The colder the older. *Linguistic Inquiry, 13,* 317–320.

Finch, S. P., and Chater, N. (1993). Learning syntactic categories: A statistical approach. In M. Oaksford and G. D. A. Brown (Eds.), *Neurodynamics and psychology.* London: Academic Press.

Fisher, C., Hall, D. G., Rakowitz, S., and Gleitman, L. (1994). When it is better to give than receive: Syntactic and conceptual constraints on vocabulary growth. *Lingua, 92,* 333–375.

Fodor, J. (1966). How to learn to talk: Some simple ways. In F. Smith and G. Miller (Eds.), *The genesis of language*. Cambridge, MA: MIT Press.

Gentner, D. (1982). Why nouns are learned before verbs: Linguistic relativity versus natural partitioning. In S. A. Kuczaj (Ed.), *Language development: Vol. II. Language, thought, and culture*. Hillsdale, NJ: Erlbaum.

Gerken, L. A., Landau, B., and Remez, R. E. (1989). Function morphemes in young children's speech perception and production. *Developmental Psychology, 27*, 204–216.

Gerken, L. A., and McIntosh, B. J. (1993). Interplay of function morphemes and prosody in early language. *Developmental Psychology, 29*, 448–457.

Gibbs, R., and Nayak, N. (1989). Psycholinguistic studies on the syntactic behavior of idioms. *Cognitive Psychology, 23*, 100–138.

Gleitman, L. R., (1990). The structural sources of word meaning. *Language Acquisition, 1*, 3–55.

Gleitman, L. R., and Wanner, E. (1982). Language acquisition: The state of the state of the art. In E. Wanner and L. Gleitman (Eds.), *Language acquisition: The state of the art*. Cambridge: Cambridge University Press.

Goldin-Meadow, S., and Mylander, C. (1990). Beyond the input given: The child's role in the acquisition of language. *Language, 66*, 323–355.

Gordon, P. (1982). *The acquisition of syntactic categories: The case of the count/mass distinction*. Unpublished doctoral dissertation, MIT.

Gordon, P. (1985). Evaluating the semantic categories hypothesis: The case of the count/mass distinction. *Cognition, 20*, 209–242.

Gordon, P. (1988). Count/mass category acquisition: Distributional distinctions in children's speech. *Journal of Child Language, 15*, 109–128.

Greenberg, J. H. (1966). Some universals of grammar with particular reference to the order of meaningful elements. In J. H. Greenberg (Ed.), *Universals of language*. Cambridge, MA: MIT Press.

Grimshaw, J. (1981). Form, function, and the language acquisition device. In C. L. Baker and J. McCarthy (Eds.), *The logical problem of language acquisition*. Cambridge, MA: MIT Press.

Harris, Z. S. (1954). Distributional structure. *Word, 10*, 140–162.

Heath, S. B. (1983). *Ways with words*. Cambridge: Cambridge University Press.

Higginbotham, J. (1983). Logical form, binding, and nominals. *Linguistic Inquiry, 14*, 395–420.

Higginbotham, J. (1989). The autonomy of syntax and semantics. In J. L. Garfield (Ed.), *Modularity in knowledge representation and natural-language understanding*. Cambridge, MA: MIT Press.

Hirsh-Pasek, K., Kemler-Nelson, D. G., Jusczyk, P. K., Wright, K., and Druss, B. (1987). Clauses are perceptual units for prelinguistic infants. *Cognition, 26*, 269–286.

Jackendoff, R. (1987). The status of thematic relations in linguistic theory. *Linguistic Inquiry, 18*, 369–411.

Jackendoff, R. (1990). *Semantic structures*. Cambridge, MA: MIT Press.

Jackendoff, R. (1996). *The architecture of the language faculty*. Cambridge, MA: MIT Press.

Jelinek, E. (in press). Quantification in Straits Salish. In E. Bach, E. Jelinek, A. Kratzer, and B. Partee (Eds.), *Quantification in natural language*. Dordrecht: Kluwer.

Katz, N., Baker, E., and Macnamara, J. (1974). What's in a name? A study of how children learn common and proper names. *Child Development, 45*, 469–473.

Kinkade, M. D. (1983). Salish evidence against the universality of "noun" and "verb". *Lingua, 60*, 25–40.

Langacker, R. W. (1987). Nouns and verbs. *Language, 63*, 53–94.

Lefebvre, C., and Muysken, P. (1988). *Mixed categories: Nominalizations in Quechua*. Dordrecht: Kluwer.

Levy, Y. (1988). On the early learning of formal grammatical systems: Evidence from studies of the acquisition of gender and countability. *Journal of Child Language, 15*, 179–186.

Lieberman, P. (1991). *Uniquely human: The evolution of speech, thought, and selfless behavior*. Cambridge, MA: Harvard University Press.

Macnamara, J. (1982). *Names for things: A study of human learning*. Cambridge, MA: MIT Press.

Macnamara, J. (1986). *A border dispute: The place of logic in psychology*. Cambridge, MA: MIT Press.

MacWhinney, B. (1991). *The CHILDES project: Tools for analyzing talk*. Hillsdale, NJ: Erlbaum.

Manzini, R., and Wexler, K. (1987). Parameters, binding theory, and learnability. *Linguistic Inquiry, 18*, 413–444.

Maratsos, M. P. and Chalkley, M. (1981). The internal language of children's syntax: The ontogenesis and representation of syntactic categories. In K. Nelson (Ed.), *Children's language, vol. 2*. New York: Gardner Press.

Markman, E. M. (1989). *Categorization and naming in children: Problems of induction*. Cambridge, MA: MIT Press.

Naigles, L. (1990). Children use syntax to learn verb meanings. *Journal of Child Language, 17*, 357–374.

Nelson, K., Hampson, J., and Shaw, L. K. (1993). Nouns in early lexicons: Evidence, explanations, and extensions. *Journal of Child Language, 20*, 61–84.

Newport, E. (1990). Maturational constraints on language learning. *Cognitive Science, 14*, 11–28.

Nishigauchi, T., and Roeper, T. (1987). Deductive parameters and the growth of empty categories, In T. Roeper and E. Williams (Eds.), *Parameter setting and language-acquisition*. Dordrecht: D. Reidel.

Peters, A. M. (1983). *The units of language acquisition.* New York: Cambridge University Press.

Pinker, S. (1979). Formal models of language learning. *Cognition, 1,* 217–283.

Pinker, S. (1984). *Language learnability and language development.* Cambridge, MA: Harvard University Press.

Pinker, S. (1987). The bootstrapping problem in language acquisition. In B. MacWhinney (Ed.), *Mechanisms of language acquisition.* Hillsdale, NJ: Erlbaum.

Pinker, S. (1989). *Learnability and cognition.* Cambridge, MA: MIT Press.

Pinker, S. (1994). How could a child use verb syntax to learn verb semantics? *Lingua, 92,* 377–410.

Redington, M., Chater, N., and Finch, S. (1994). *The potential contribution of distributional information to early syntactic category acquisition.* Unpublished manuscript, University of Edinburgh.

Rothstein, S. (1983). *The syntactic forms of predication.* Unpublished doctoral dissertation, MIT.

Schieffelin, B. (1985). The acquisition of Kaluli. In D. I. Slobin (Ed.), *The cross-linguistic study of language acquisition: Vol. 1. The data.* Hillsdale, NJ: Erlbaum.

Schlesinger, I. M. (1988). The origin of relational categories. In Y. Levy, I. M. Schlesinger, and M. D. S. Braine (Eds.), *Categories and processes in language acquisition.* Hillsdale, NJ: Erlbaum.

Shipley, E. F., and Shepperson, B. (1990). Countable entities: Developmental changes. *Cognition, 34,* 109–136.

Singleton, J., and Newport, E. (1993). *When learners surpass their models: The acquisition of sign language from impoverished input.* Unpublished manuscript, University of Rochester.

Soja, N. N. (1992). Inferences about the meanings of nouns: The relationship between perception and syntax. *Cognitive Development, 7,* 29–45.

Spelke, E. S., Breinlinger, K., Macomber, J., and Jacobson, K. (1992). Origins of knowledge. *Psychological Review, 99,* 605–632.

Starkey, P., Spelke, E. S., and Gelman, R. (1990). Numerical abstraction by human infants. *Cognition, 36,* 97–127.

Valian, V. (1991). Syntactic subjects in the early speech of American and Italian children. *Cognition, 40,* 21–81.

Waxman, S. R. (1994). The development of an appreciation of specific linkages between linguistic and conceptual organization. *Lingua, 92,* 229–257.

Williams, E. (1983). Semantic vs. syntactic categories. *Linguistics and Philosophy, 6,* 423–446.

Wynn, K. (1990). Children's understanding of counting. *Cognition, 36,* 155–193.

Chapter 13

Sortals and Kinds: Susan Carey and Fei Xu
An Appreciation of
John Macnamara

Rereading *A Border Dispute* (Macnamara 1986), we were struck by the
degree to which this work, published in 1986 and thus in progress the
years before that, anticipates our research program in 1997, and by how
illuminated we still can be by John's words. Each time we return to this
rich work, we encounter ideas missed before. The similarity between
John's concerns in that book and those that currently engage us is not an
accident, of course, for we have studied the book, read parts of it in
graduate seminars on several occasions, and assigned it to and discussed it
with our students.

What John did, first in *Names for Things* (Macnamara 1982) and then
in *A Border Dispute*, was spell out in detail what it is we learn when we
learn a name like "Freddie" or a noun like "dog."[1] As he insisted, we can
only begin to provide an account of learning after we have an adequate
account of what is learned. And what he saw more clearly than any psychologist before him was the extent of the knowledge required to master
such simple words, words that appear in children's vocabulary before the
age of 2.

13.1 What Is Learned When a Child Learns a Proper Noun

In his analysis of names like "Freddie" (the name of the new family dog),
John focused on several properties of proper nouns (PNs): They designate
individuals, which they pick out across all times, places, and counterfactual worlds. The identities of the individuals are traced by means of
sortals, which denote kinds. Finally, the references of PNs are not mediated by a Fregean sense (Kripke 1972).

A PN is often learned through ostension; the mother points out the new
puppy and says, "This is Freddie." In order to learn the PN from such

input, toddlers must have the ability to refer and to understand when others are referring. They must have some other means of identifying the bearer of the name—a demonstrative such as "this" or "that," a point, or a gaze could all do the trick. They must understand the *is* of identity, which specifies the relation between *this* and *Freddie*. And they must know a sortal concept that traces the identity of Freddie through time and counterfactual situations. Note that identity plays two roles in this account: (1) the identity of Freddie and the individual picked out by the demonstrative, point, or gaze, and (2) the identity of Freddie over time, determined by the criteria of identity supplied by the sortal *dog*.

13.2   Sortals

Sortal concepts supply principles of identity (and as we show later, they do other work as well). Freddie the puppy turns into an adult dog, changes size, coloring, location, owner, but is still the same dog. The sortal *dog* designates a kind of animal, so to represent *dog* the child must also represent the sortal *kind*. For the child to learn from ostension "That's a dog" the sortal *dog*, he or she must have been directed by something to assign to "dog" the correct referent—not an individual dog, or a group of dogs, or some property of dogs, but a kind.

As John characterized sortals, they are concepts that do the logical work of count nouns: they provide principles of individuation, numerical identity, and application. In John's terminology, "principles" are metaphysical, not psychological. John accepted the Kripke/Putnam view that meanings are not in the head. What makes a dog a dog is a property of the world, not of the mind, as is what makes one dog different from another dog, and that puppy the same as this dog. By force of representing sortal concepts, minds deploy criteria of individuation, numerical identity, and application, but these are best shots and revisable. As psychologists studying concepts, the best we can do is to study the criteria our subjects deploy.

Most psychological work on concepts concerns criteria of application: the bases of people's categorization of entities such as dogs, tables, people, and so forth. All concepts provide criteria of application—exemplars of properties such as red and predicates such as jumping must be identified in order for these concepts to be used. What differentiates sortal concepts from all others is that only they provide criteria for individuation and numerical identity.

To see the role sortals play in our conceptual life, consider these two questions: (1) How many are there in this room? (2) Is that the same as what was here before? We cannot begin to answer either question without specifying individuals—how many *what*? We can count tables, people, legs, fingers, or shirts, but we can't count the red, the sleeping, or the wood. Only sortals provide criteria of individuation. Similarly, "same," in the sense of numerical identity, means *same one*, and a sortal is needed to specify the individual being traced through time. The body we see on the floor is the same one that existed just before Freddie died, but Freddie, whose identity is traced by the sortal *dog*, not the sortal *body*, has ceased to exist. Individuals are established by sortals and different sortals provide very different criteria of identity.

The criteria of individuation that sortals provide are logically distinct from the criteria of numerical identity. To see this, consider two dogs, Freddie and George. As you conceptualize them playing on the lawn, the criteria of individuation provided by the sortal *dog* establish two individuals there, and if they go behind a wall and reemerge, the sortal *dog* again establishes two individuals. But additional criteria are needed to establish which one is Freddie and which is George, or which one reemerging from behind the wall was the first dog to disappear. Although the criteria for individuation establish two individuals each time, criteria for numerical identity are needed in order to determine which dog was which.

13.3 The Continuity Thesis

We agree with John's characterization of what is learned when one learns a PN or a count noun. But John assumed that as soon as a child produced or comprehended a word like "Freddie" or "dog," the child had mastered a PN or sortal term, respectively. Indeed, he thought that the fact that young infants are sensitive to similarity among exemplars of toy dogs and differentiate these from exemplars of toy trucks suggests that even prelinguistic infants have a sortal concept *dog* or *stuffed dog* (Cohen and Younger 1983). But as Quine (1960, 1969, 1974) forcefully argued, as Millikan (1998) has recently endorsed, and as psychologists studying the earliest stages of language acquisition (e.g., Vygotsky 1962; Dromi 1987) have repeatedly stressed, young children could establish representations of words that differ markedly, even qualitatively, from those adults establish for the same words.

Psychologists have offered many different proposals for how young children's word meanings may differ qualitatively from those of adults. Vygotsky (1962), for example, suggested that toddlers' words refer to complexes of properties, such as Dromi's (1987) son's use of "paper" to mean pens, paper, pencils, crayons, the act of writing or drawing or cutting, and so on. Words in no natural language unite such disparate entities in a single category. Landau, Smith, Jones (1988), for another example, propose that early count nouns refer to entities specified by shapes. Although there are words in natural languages that refer to shape (e.g., "round," "square," "dog-shaped"), these are not count nouns like "dog." If proposals such as these are correct, then early count nouns are not sortals and their meanings are indeed qualitatively different from those that adults assign them.

Perhaps the most articulated proposal for how the earliest meanings of early count nouns might differ from those of adults is Quine's (1960, 1969, 1974; see also Millikan 1998 for a nearly identical proposal). Quine also explicitly denied that infants' earliest nouns function as sortals; he claimed that infants lack the capacity for what he called "divided reference," which is the capacity to refer to distinct individuals of a given kind. On Quine's proposals, the first meanings of words like "Mama," "red," "water," and "table" do not differ qualitatively or systematically from each other. They all refer to "scattered portions of what goes on" when adults use the words, that is, to features of the perceptual experiences the child is having when he or she hears the words. If this is so, then "table" does not pick out a sortal concept (see Carey 1994 for a detailed exposition of Quine's speculations and a review of the empirical evidence both consistent and inconsistent with them).

We will argue below that these proposals are wrong; infants do have the capacity for divided reference, and terms like "dog" serve as sortals from the very earliest stages of language acquisition. However, proposals such as those reviewed above are serious empirical possibilities. Our point in raising them is to question a methodological tenet John articulated repeatedly during his career—a methodological commitment to strong continuity of logical and conceptual resources throughout development. For example, in *A Border Dispute*, he wrote, "I believe it is wise psychological strategy to assume that a child's mind resembles an adult's, unless there is evidence to the contrary. That is, I take seriously the obvious null hypothesis—that the two are similar. This places on research the onus of discovering differences between child and adult" (p. 56). John recognized, of course, that ultimately it is an empirical question; strong continuity could be false. Whereas John believed that there is no convincing evidence against continuity, we disagree.

13.4   Where Evidence Favors Continuity

John assumed, and we agree, that much of what is necessary to support the acquisition of sortals and PNs is innate, or at least in place before the first words are learned (the capacity for reference, some demonstratives, the *is* of identity). We will not belabor this point here, merely noting that research both before and since *A Border Dispute* supports John's assumption. As just one example of the kind of work we have in mind, consider demonstratives and reference. To understand reference and demonstratives, the infant must understand that other people can pay attention to entities in the world, that words (and other mental entities such as some emotional states) refer to things in the world, and that people can indicate in various ways what they are referring to. In a justly famous paper, Scaife and Bruner (1975) showed that infants as young as 7 months of age follow eye gaze; if an adult turns to look at something, infants will turn their head and eyes in the same direction. Hood, Willen, and Driver (in press) have recently shown that under restricted circumstances,[2] even 3-month-olds will do the same. Johnson, Slaughter, and Carey (in press) recently showed that this behavior is elicited, among 12-month-olds, by a faceless nonsense object, so long as that object reacts contingently to the child. They argue that the baby takes contingent reaction as evidence that the object is capable of intentional states, and takes a sudden turn from "facing" the baby to "facing" 45 degrees to the left or the right as a shift in attention. The babies turned to see what the object was attending to. Finally, in a series of elegant experiments, Baldwin and her collaborators (Baldwin and Moses 1994) showed that infants under a year monitor what the mother is looking at when she says, "Yuck" in a disgusted tone of voice, or "Mmm, how nice." Even if they are examining an unfamiliar object at the time of the emotional utterance, they do not assume that the mother's "Yuck" refers to it. And by 15 months of age, infants similarly monitor the gaze of the speaker when the speaker uses a novel word (e.g., "That's a blicket"), even if they themselves are attending to a novel object that is a perfectly good candidate for the referent of that word at the time of the utterance. In sum, infants and toddlers attribute to other people both intentionality and the capacity to refer, and they have at least some heuristics for figuring out what entities a person is referring to, just as John's continuity assumptions dictate.

13.5 Prelinguistic Representation of Sortal Concepts

In order for a child to learn the meaning of a sortal term like "dog" or a PN like "Freddie," more is required than an understanding of reference, intentionality, and demonstratives. The child must represent sortal concepts, specifically the sortal *dog*. When do sortal concepts become available to the child? Our focus here is the state of evidence that children possess a sortal such as *dog* that provides criteria of individuation and identity of Freddie. Even John, strong continuity theorist as he was, did not think that the sortal concepts themselves, such as *dog*, *table*, and *book*, are innate. So how and when are they acquired?

John explicitly denied that there is an unlearned expression synonymous with *dog* in the language of thought. Rather, he thought the origin of the sortal *dog* is a gestalt supplied by vision, a prototype abstracted from experience with dogs. Indeed, prototype abstraction is a powerful psychological process (Posner and Keele 1968) available to infants (Cohen and Younger 1983; Quinn 1987). John's idea was that the psychological representation of basic-level sortals such as *dog* is equivalent to *same kind as [gestalt of dog]*.

13.5.1 Prima Facie Evidence for Prelinguistic Representations of Sortals
In support of this proposal, John pointed to the experimental evidence that children are able to classify objects into categories for which they have no natural language symbols. Since *A Border Dispute*, there is now even more evidence of this type. For example, Quinn and Eimas have carried out an extensive series of studies showing that infants as young as 3 months of age perceive the similarity among photographs of exemplars of a variety of natural kinds (e.g., dogs, cats, horses). In their procedure, infants are familiarized with pairs (typically six) of photographs of a single kind of object (e.g., six pairs of cats, taken from different angles, of different breeds, coloring, and so forth). On test trials they are presented with a pair of photographs consisting of a new cat and a member of a contrasting category (e.g., a dog, a horse, a car). A looking time preference for the exemplar of the novel category is taken as evidence that infants are sensitive to the categorical similarity among the original

familiarization set (e.g., Quinn, Eimas, and Rosenkrantz 1993; Eimas and Quinn 1994). In these studies, infants as young as 3 months of age succeed in categorization at the basic level (e.g., distinguishing dogs from cats). Also, Mandler and her colleagues have carried out an extensive series of studies with older babies, using the manual habituation procedure pioneered by Ruff (1986), in which infants examine a series of toys from a single category (e.g., a bird, a turtle, a dog, a fish) and then are given either a new animal (e.g., an elephant) or a new exemplar from a novel category (e.g., a car) to play with. Again, novelty preference is a measure of categorization. With this technique, infants show evidence of categorization at the more superordinate level (what Mandler calls the "global level") by 7 months of age, and at the basic level by 9 months of age (see also Mandler, Bauer, and McDonough 1991; Oakes, Madole, and Cohen 1991; Waxman and Markow 1995).

John was aware, of course, that these data do not prove that infants represent sortals such as *dog, stuffed dog, animal, vehicle,* or *car.* He asked of a study using a manual habituation procedure (Cohen and Caputo, cited in Cohen and Younger 1983) whether one could be sure that infants had formed a concept such as *stuffed animal, animal,* or *toy animal,* as opposed to basing their response on a perceptual feature common to all 11 toys in the study, such as texture or shape. But he clearly meant his question to be rhetorical, for he answered it, evidently to his own satisfaction, with the observation that anyone familiar with 7-month-olds has the distinct impression that they already know many categories of objects—animals, bowls, cups, hands, bottles, and so forth. By that age, they behave differently toward cups and toward their contents.

John's response misses the mark in two ways. First of all, it is not clear that there are good data on this point. What data there are suggest that knowing what to do with members of kinds, at least newly encountered kinds, is not robust until 12 months and later. Baldwin, Markman, and Melartin (1993) asked when infants would project a distinctive action relevant to a kind of object (e.g., turning it a certain way to produce a sound) on the basis of kind membership, and found only shaky and weak evidence for this ability at 9 months, in the face of definitive success at ages 12 and 14 months. Second, suppose we did grant the point (that babies of this age know that to do with bottles). Babies could simply recognize examples of bottleness, bottlehood, or bottle-shape, and have associated this property with other properties such as containing milk or juice. As Quine so rightly pointed out, recognizing a shape and associating that shape with other properties is not equivalent to categorizing under a sortal.

Another way to put this second point is that John's proposal has a logical problem: *same kind as [gestalt of dog]* contains criteria neither of individuation nor of numerical identity. For this expression to serve as the representation of the earliest sortals, it must be elliptical for *same kind of individual as [gestalt of dog]*, but then what specifies the individual? Further, as indicated above, the habituation data surely show sensitivity to similarity in shape, but shape (e.g., round, square, or dog-shaped) is a property, not a sortal. At the very least, we would want to know whether representations of *[gestalt of dog]* and *[gestalt of cup]* provide criteria of individuation and numerical identity for infants. We have carried out three extensive series of studies with 10- and 12-month-old infants addressing this point and have clear and consistent evidence that for 10-month-olds the answer is probably not.

13.5.2   Sortals for Kinds of Objects Not Represented until Late in the First Year of Life

Imagine the following scenario: a duck emerges from one side of a screen and returns behind it, and then a ball emerges from the other side and then returns. How many objects are behind the screen? For adults, the answer is clear: at least two, a duck and a ball. We know there are two because we code them under different sortals: a duck and a ball must be two different individuals. We (Xu and Carey 1996) asked whether the answer is similarly clear for babies. In a series of four experiments, we showed infants scenarios as in figure 13.1. Sometimes the objects were members of contrasting kinds at the global level (e.g., a duck and a car), the level of contrast infants of this age consistently have been shown to be sensitive to in manual habituation studies. Sometimes the contrasts were of highly familiar functional kinds (e.g., a cup and a ball; a bottle and a book), the level at which exemplars elicit contrasting actions according to John's intuitions. Sometimes infants were fully habituated to each object as it emerged from each side; other times they were more briefly familiarized with a fixed number of emergences.

We infer how many objects the infants posit in this situation by removing the screen and measuring how long the infant looks at what is revealed there—either the expected outcome (for adults) of two objects or the unexpected outcome (for adults) of only one of the two objects. If infants have the same expectations as adults, they look longer at the un-

Property/Kind Condition

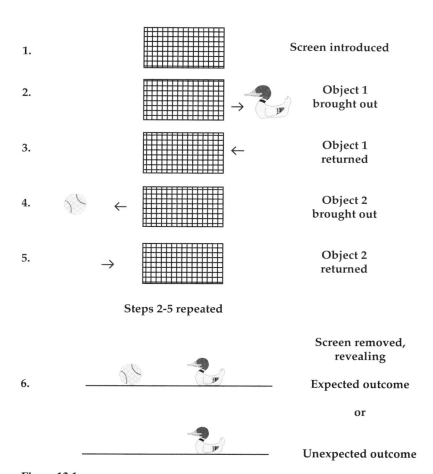

1.   **Screen introduced**

2.   **Object 1 brought out**

3.   **Object 1 returned**

4.   **Object 2 brought out**

5.   **Object 2 returned**

Steps 2-5 repeated

6.   **Screen removed, revealing**

Expected outcome

or

Unexpected outcome

Figure 13.1
Schematic representation of the property/kind condition in Xu and Carey 1996

expected outcomes in experiments such as these that exploit the violation-of-expectancy looking-time methodology (see Spelke 1990; Spelke et al. 1992; Baillargeon 1995 for reviews).

The results were the same under all the conditions: 10-month-olds failed to draw the inference that there should be two objects behind the screen, whereas 12-month-olds succeeded in doing so. Further controls established that the method was sensitive for 10-month-olds as well as older infants; if the younger babies were given *spatiotemporal* evidence that there were two numerically distinct objects in these events (e.g., if they were shown an elephant and a car *together, at the same time,* next to the screen for a few seconds before the successive emergences took place), then they too succeeded by looking longer at the unexpected (one-object) outcome than at the expected (two-object) outcome.

We do not deny the lessons from the visual and manual habituation studies. Ten-month-olds *are* sensitive to the differences between cups and cars, ducks and balls (and they are so under the conditions of our (1996) studies; they take longer to habituate to a duck and a car alternately appearing from each side of the screen than to a car repeatedly appearing from behind the screen). The conclusion to be drawn from our (1996) studies is that 10-month-olds do not yet represent sortals such as *duck, car, animal, vehicle, cup, bottle, book.* The differences that babies under 10 months of age are sensitive to are irrelevant to object individuation.

This conclusion may be premature, however. In order to arrive at a representation of two objects in our (1996) task, infants must be able to *recall* the representation of the first object, including its kind, and compare this recalled representation with that of the second object. Perhaps the failure of the 10-month-olds reflects an information-processing limitation on short-term memory, rather than the unavailability of the relevant sortal concepts. To address this possibility, we explored whether kind contrasts would help babies individuate objects under conditions of ambiguity in two very different paradigms, one of which makes no demands on short-term memory and one of which makes even greater information-processing demands than does our (1996) paradigm.

In the studies reported in Xu and Carey 1996, ambiguity regarding object individuation was introduced by occlusion; the object is not always visible, so there is no unambiguous spatiotemporal evidence about how many objects are present in a scene. Ambiguity can also be introduced by shared boundaries, as in figure 13.2 (top panel). How many objects are depicted in this figure? Adults respond that there are two, a duck and a

HABITUATION

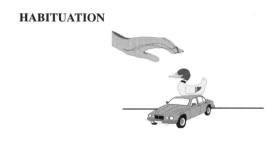

**APART
(EXPECTED)**   **TOGETHER
(UNEXPECTED)**

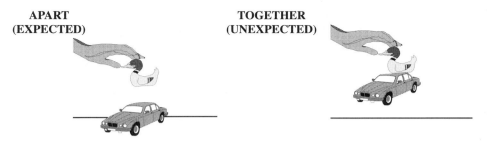

Figure 13.2
Schematic representation of the duck-car experiments in Xu, Carey, and Welch
1998

car. However, it is also possible that there is only one, the top half of
which resembles a duck and the bottom half of which resembles a car.
When adults parse the object into two, they are using their knowledge of
the sortals *duck* and *car* to do so.

We asked when infants would segment an ambiguous object such as
that in figure 13.2 into two separate objects, the duck and the car. Here
the kind distinction is at the global level (an animal and a vehicle). We
also examined a display consisting of two familiar functional kinds (a cup
on top of a shoe). We again used a violation-of-expectancy looking-time
paradigm. Infants were habituated to the ambiguous duck/car display, or
to the ambiguous cup/shoe display, with a hand poised a few centimeters
above it. After the habituation, the hand grasped the top object and lifted,
revealing either the expected outcome (for adults) of just the top object
coming up (figure 13.2, bottom left) or the unexpected outcome (for
adults) of the single duck/car or cup/shoe object being lifted as a single
piece (figure 13.2, bottom right). Notice that in this experiment, no short-
term memory demands are placed on the child. Both the duck and the car,

or the cup and the shoe, are fully visible at all times when the ambiguous display is in view. We found exactly the same age effects as we reported in Xu and Carey 1996. Ten-month-olds failed to use the kind contrasts between the duck and the car, or the cup and the shoe, to infer that there were two separate individual objects in this display; they did not look longer at the unexpected outcome of the single object being raised as a piece. Twelve-month-olds, in contrast, succeeded at the task, confirming both that 12-month-olds have constructed relevant sortals and that the task sensitively reflects such representations. The sensitivity of the task was further confirmed by the finding that if the 10-month-old infants were given *spatiotemporal* evidence concerning the number of objects in this display (if the objects were briefly moved, laterally, relative to each other at the beginning of each habituation trial), they succeeded; they looked longer if the object moved as a single piece (Xu, Carey, and Welch 1998).

Thus, data from two quite different paradigms, which place very different information-processing demands on the child, converge on the same conclusion. Even though infants can discriminate ducks from cars, cups from shoes, contrasts such as these do not provide criteria for individuation until sometime between 10 and 12 months of age.

The two studies reviewed above depend upon a rather indirect measure of how many objects infants take to be involved in these events—their pattern of looking times at outcomes of one or two objects, compared to baseline preferences for these same outcomes in the absence of any habituation of familiarization. Other, more direct measures of how many objects infants believe to be involved in some event can be imagined. One cannot *ask* the babies, for they obviously cannot talk. But we could have them reach for hidden objects and measure how often and persistently they reach as a function of how many objects are in a box and as a function of what kind of evidence they have had concerning this matter. This is the approach taken in our third line of studies in this series. In these experiments, on two object trials infants watched the experimenter pull out an object (say, a toy telephone) from a box, return it to the box, then pull out a second object (say, a duck), and return it to the box. On one-object trials, the experimenter pulled out one object (say, the telephone), twice. Infants were then allowed to reach into the box (the opening of the box was well covered with fabric so the infants could not see what was inside) to retrieve the objects. Infants at both 10 and 12 months always reached in and retrieved the first object, which they were allowed to play with for some time before it was removed from them. Unbeknownst to them, the second object had been removed from an opening at the rear of the box, so they could not have felt it when they retrieved the first object. At issue was what happened then. At 12 months, infants reached persistently for the second object on two-object trials, exploring the inside of the box, apparently trying to find it. On one-object trials they either did not reach a second time at all, or did so only cursorily (after all, there was nothing else to do; the box was left in place and the first object had been taken away). At 10 months of age, the pattern of reaching was identical on one-object and two-object trials: cursory reaching in both cases. At 10 months, however, infants succeeded in a condition in which they were given *spatiotemporal* evidence that there were two objects on two-object trials. (Twelve-month-olds succeeded in this condition as well, of course.) If both objects had been shown together before being replaced in the box, babies of both ages reached persistently for the second object, differentiating these trials from the one-object trials (Prevor 1997; Van de Walle, Prevor, and Carey 1998).

Note that this is exactly the same pattern of results as in the first two series of studies. Twelve-month-olds succeeded in establishing representations of two objects on the basis of kind differences, whereas 10-month-olds did not. At both ages babies succeeded when provided spatiotemporal evidence that there were two objects in the box.

The first lesson we draw from these widely different studies of object individuation is that John was wrong in the inference he drew from young infants' success at categorizing dogs or animals together and differentiating them from cats or vehicles, or from young infants' knowing what to do with a cup, ball, bottle, or shoe. These achievements do not mean that young infants represent the relevant sortal concepts. If we are right in our interpretation of our results, we have provided evidence against John's continuity thesis: infants 10 months of age and younger are clearly capable of seeing animals as similar to each other, but they do not represent a sortal *animal*. Coming to represent one's first sortals for kinds of objects would be a good candidate for the construction of a new representational resource.

13.6   Success Based on Sortals or Properties at 12 Months?

So far, we have drawn two conclusions from the above data: (1) 10-month-olds do not represent sortals for kinds of objects, and (2) 12-month-olds do represent sortals for kinds of objects. The inference from the 10-month-olds' failures in these tasks to the first conclusion seems warranted, but the inference from the 12-month-olds' successes to the second conclusion is not, for the following reason. Although concepts lexicalized as properties do not provide criteria for individuation (we can't count the red in this room, the big in this room, the striped in this room), in the situations we have described above the property differences among the objects certainly do provide relevant information about number. For example, if A sees B draw a black, plastic thing from a box, return it, and then draw out a red, striped, round, rubber thing, A might infer there are two objects in the box, even if A did not identify the two objects as a toy telephone and a ball. From what we have presented so far, we do not know whether the 12-month-olds are individuating the objects on the basis of kind differences or on the basis of property differences. We do not know whether their representational system marks the distinction between properties and kinds.

We have recently completed a series of studies with 12-month-olds that begins to address this question (Xu, Carey, and Quint 1997). The procedure described in Xu and Carey 1996 (see figure 13.1) was followed, except that the objects were, for the most part, objects of a single kind that differed in properties such as color or size. For instance, a pink cup emerged from the left, and an identical yellow cup then emerged from the right; or a big cup emerged from the left, and a small cup then emerged from the right; or a coffee mug emerged from the left, and a sippy cup then emerged from the right. Finally, we tried a pair that differed in many properties: a big, red, plastic cup with colored dots and a small, blue, ceramic cup. The outcome displays were similar to those described in Xu and Carey 1996: the screen was removed to reveal either two cups (one big, one small; or one pink, one yellow) or just one of the two cups. Adults certainly can use these property differences to infer two distinct objects. However, the 12-month-olds failed to individuate the cups on the basis of these property differences. In contrast, they succeeded at individuating a cup from a ball in the study reported in Xu and Carey 1996, and a duck from a car in the study reported in Xu, Carey, and Welch 1998. So far, only kind differences have been found to provide 12-month-olds with criteria for individuation and identity in these experiments.

This series of studies provides preliminary evidence that 12-month-old infants represent the distinction between kinds and properties, and that their successes in the above series of studies are indeed based on their early sortals for kinds of objects, not on their representations of properties. We tentatively conclude, then, that Quine's speculations have been shown to be false. At the very outset of language acquisition, children represent the distinction between properties and sortals, well before they have even begun to master the syntactic reflection of these distinctions in any natural language. As we will show in section 13.9, Quine may have been right in one respect; language learning may have a role to play in the construction of the first sortals for kinds of objects.

13.7 *Physical Object* as a Sortal

There is a third lesson to be drawn from the individuation studies reviewed above. Remember that the 10-month-old infants succeeded in the spatiotemporal conditions in all three series of studies. When shown both objects together at the same time separated in space, infants established representations of two objects, which they maintained throughout the event. If representations of sortal concepts are those representations that provide criteria for individuation and numerical identity, young infants *do* represent at least one sortal concept, *physical object,* itself. There is now massive evidence that infants as young as 4 months of age establish representations of bounded coherent rigid objects that move on spatiotemporally continuous paths, individuating these objects on the basis of criteria such as "one object cannot be in two places at the same time; one object cannot go out of existence at one time and place and come back into existence at another time and place" (e.g., Baillargeon and Graber 1987; Kellman 1984, 1993; Spelke et al. 1995). For example, Spelke et al. (1995) showed 5-month-old infants objects emerging from the far sides of two screens separated in space, never appearing in the middle of the two screens. That is, an object would emerge from the left side of the left screen and return behind it, followed by a physically identical object emerging from the right side of the right screen and returning behind it. The infants never saw both objects together. Nonetheless, they inferred from the fact that these two objects could not be on a single spatiotemporal trajectory that there must be two objects involved in this event, for when the screens were removed, they looked longer at the impossible outcome of only one object behind the two screens than at the possible outcome of two objects (see Xu and Carey 1996, for a replication with 10-month-olds).

We conclude from studies such as these that infants distinguish one object seen on different occasions from two numerically distinct objects.

To do so, they must have criteria for individuation and numerical identity for physical objects. Recall our argument above that *same kind as [gestalt of dog]* is not a representation of the sortal *dog*. We have now provided an answer to that might specify the individual in the expression, *same kind of individual as [gestalt of dog]*, namely, the individual picked out by the sortal *physical object*. This insight provides part of the answer to the question John posed concerning how infants learn sortals like *dog*, but it is only part of the answer. So far, we have shown that at 10 months, infants can represent both the sortal *physical object* and the perceptual *[gestalt of dog]* without having the sortal *dog*, since *[gestalt of dog]* does not provide criteria of individuation and identity.

More is needed for the infant to construct the first sortals for kinds of objects. But before we offer our speculations about what else the infant recruits for this task, we must address another issue. John would certainly not have accepted our friendly amendment of his expression *same kind as [gestalt of dog]* to *same kind of individual as [gestalt of dog]*, with *physical object* specifying the relevant individual. And that is because he, like many others, explicitly denied that *physical object* is a sortal concept. In what follows, we sketch why he and others hold this position, and we show why they need not do so.

13.8   Problems Arising from Considering *Physical Object* as a Sortal and a Possible Solution

Along with philosophers such as Geach (1957), Wiggins (1980), Gibbard (1975), Gupta (1980), and Hirsch (1982), John denied that *object* or *thing* is a sortal. Their arguments have three parts. First, they claim that people do not have clear intuitions about the criteria for judging something as *the same object* or *the same thing*. More importantly, if *object/thing* is a sortal, then questions arise concerning the relations between this general sortal and more specific ones. Perhaps there are *no* more specific sortals such as *car, cup*, or *dog*—these more specific sortals might now be construed as predicates of the general sortal *object/thing*, thus undermining the enterprise these philosophers have advocated. Finally, if *physical object* and *dog* are both sortals, paradoxes of transitivity of identity seem to arise. Here, we focus on John's particular version of these worries.

In *A Border Dispute*, John used the following example to illustrate "the weakness of our intuitions about how to trace identity under the description 'the same thing'" (p.52). Suppose that all of the atoms constituting

Ronald Reagan's body when he was the governor of California were replaced by new ones and the old ones were reassembled to form the body of Walter Mondale in 1984. According to John, if we trace identity under the sortal *thing*, we would encounter the following problem of the transitivity of identity: Governor Reagan is identical with President Reagan, Governor Reagan was identical with a set of atoms, and the same set of atoms is identical with Walter Mondale; therefore, by transitivity of identity, Governor Reagan was also identical with Mondale. Since Governor Reagan is also identical with President Reagan, we would conclude that Reagan would stand for election against himself, "which is preposterous, and not just on political but logical grounds" (p. 53). The solution, said John, is to trace the identity of Reagan under the sortal *person*, which is *not* identical with a set of atoms.

Similarly, in *The Logical Foundations of Cognition* (Macnamara and Reyes 1994), John argued that *thing/object* does not provide criteria for what to count as one instance of something; that is, it does not provide principles of individuation. If one were to count the things in the room, one could count the chair as a chair, four legs, plus one top, hence six things altogether!

It may indeed be the case that the English words, "object" or "thing," are not sortals, given people's vague intuitions about their criteria for individation and identity. However, *physical object*, or *Spelke-object*, which is any entity that is three-dimensional, is bounded, and retains its boundaries as it moves through space and time, is a sortal. It provides principles of individuation and identity, and it does not eliminate the necessity for postulating other more specific sortals such as *cup* or *dog*. Finally, in John's formalism for categories, a natural extension can be made to specify the relation between *physical object* and sortals such as *cup* and *dog*, an extension that dissolves the paradoxes of identity (see Xu 1997 for further discussion of these issues).

Let's go back to John's two examples above and see how applying this more restricted sense of object—namely, *physical object*—can help us dissolve the problems.

John's first example, involving Reagan, Mondale, and the set of atoms constituting Reagan, is a case of the general problem of the transitivity of identity. Note that because John believed that intuitions about *the same object* or *the same thing* are vague, he stipulated that thing/object is equal to the set of atoms constituting Reagan. However, the more restricted sense of object, *physical object*, is not the same as *a set of atoms*. The set of atoms constituting an object could change; the object still remains the same object. Therefore, the problem of transitivity of identity disappears when we apply the sortal *object* to Reagan, just as it disappears if we apply the sortal *person* to Reagan, as argued by John.

John's second example illustrates how our concept of thing/object is vague. Indeed, one could think of the top and the legs of a chair as objects. However, it seems unlikely that if one were asked to count the things/objects in the room, a chair would be counted as six things/objects. Instead, most people would agree that a chair is one thing or one object. Why is this so? Our intuition is that although in everyday speech, a leg (of the chair) is a thing/object, when asked to count in this fashion people spontaneously apply the more restricted sense of object/thing (namely, *physical object*), which eliminates the ambiguity, and the result is a count of one thing/object given one chair.

Clearly, if *physical object* is a sortal, one must show that it provides principles of individuation and numerical identity. From the empirical work reviewed above, we see that *physical object* does provide such criteria: (1) one object cannot be in two places at the same time (e.g., two identical cups in two distinct locations simultaneously are two numerically distinct cups); (2) objects travel on spatiotemporally connected paths (e.g., if an object appears to have "jumped" from point A to point B without traversing a continuous path in between, there must be two distinct objects); (3) objects maintain their boundaries and move as a whole (e.g., if one part of an object moves independently of the rest, there must be two distinct objects). These criteria are well specified, and both adults and infants deploy them.

What about the second, deeper worry that if *thing/object* is a sortal, all the other more specific sortals can be construed as predicates of this general sortal? The existence of such a general sortal is damaging for advocates of the sortal view since this general sortal may be the only one needed. At the same time, there are good reasons to believe that *cup*, *dog*, and *rock* are sortals since they provide principles of individuation and identity above and beyond the principles provided by the sortal *physical object*. A dog ceases to exist when it dies, but its body continues to exist and it is the same body as before. The problem is in fact a rather general one since more than one sortal can be applied to any given entity; besides being an object, that thing over there (indicating Freddie) is also a pet, a poodle, a mammal, an animal, a body, a set of atoms.

What is the relation among these sortals? Macnamara and Reyes (1994) argue that contrary to classical logic, it is not one of class inclusion and identity. For example, the set of atoms constituting a dog could change, but one would still have the same dog; in cases of metamorphoses, a dog could change into a mouse, or a frog into a prince, and one would still have the same animal or the same living thing. Macnamara and Reyes (1994) present a formalism for characterizing the relations among sortals by means of underlying maps. An underlying map is a function that maps members of a set A to members of a set B. For example, a passenger from set A is mapped onto a person from set B by an underlying map *u*: passenger → person. A member of the kind *passenger* is *identified with*, but not *identical to*, a member of the kind *person* through the mapping process. Similarly, a member of the kind *dog* is identified with a member of the kind *animal* by the same mapping process. This formalism can be extended to allow members of the kinds *dog/animal/car* to be identified with members of the kind *physical object*.

In sum, we have shown that a more restricted sense of object—namely, *physical object*—is a sortal for both infants and adults, and one can specify the relation between the sortal *physical object* and the more specific sortals such as *dog* or *chair* by underlying mapping, thus avoiding long-standing problems regarding transitivity of identity. Postulating the sortal *physical object* is part of the solution to how infants construct sortals such as *dog* or *chair*, and the hypothesis that young infants represent it is supported by empirical evidence.

13.9   Final Speculations: How Are the First Sortals for Kinds of Objects Learned?

Before infants are 10 months of age, they are able to abstract a visual prototype from a set of dogs, and they represent at least one sortal concept, *physical object,* yet they have not constructed the sortal *dog.* And, we have argued, they have constructed some sortal that individuates dogs, or at least toy dogs, from other kinds of objects by 12 months of age. How do they do so?

John posed the question in the context of word learning, asking how children learn the meaning of a sortal term like "dog." His answer was that infants bring to the word-learning task an understanding of reference, demonstratives, the *is* of identity, the sortal *kind,* and a sortal that covers dogs: *same kind as [gestalt of dog].* We have offered a crucial friendly amendment to his proposal: that the sortal that covers dogs is *same kind of physical object as [gestalt of dog]. Physical object,* in this expression, provides spatiotemporal criteria for identity and individuation, and these are not overridden by the more specific sortal *dog,* even though dogs are not identical to their bodies. It is true that no two dogs can be in the same place at the same time; one dog cannot be in two places at the same time, and dogs trace spatiotemporally continuous paths. But *physical object* does more for babies than establishing individuals in their immediate models of the world; it enables them to establish individuals in order to learn about their kinds.

We have not yet dwelt upon John's proposal that the child's ability to learn specific sortals requires a prior sortal, *kind.* When we mentioned this proposal in section 13.2, we gave only John's logical justification for it: the child must eventually distinguish concepts that cover kinds of individuals, groups of individuals, individuals themselves, and properties of individuals, and so must have some way of representing these distinctions. We certainly agree with this logical point, and we offered empirical evidence in section 13.6 that infants have distinguished kinds of objects from properties of objects by 12 months of age.

But here we wish to emphasize the importance of the prior sortal *kind* to the learning of sortals for kinds of objects. Suppose children not only know that there will be kinds of objects, but also have expectations about kinds that help them identify candidate kinds in their experience of the world. It is an open question what these antecedently represented expectations will be. We tentatively offer the following suggestions: (1) kinds are determined by deep, often hidden properties, which determine some of the surface properties of objects, (2) the deep properties that determine kinds influence many intercorrelated surface properties, (3) the deep properties that determine kinds are causal and thus interpreted in terms of whatever causal understanding the child has constructed, (4) object kinds do not change over time, whereas surface properties may, and (5) object kinds are named by adults. Notice that these are properties of substance sortals like *dog* and *animal,* not stage sortals like *pet* and *passenger.* But stage sortals are acquired late, and children's first interpretation of a count noun applied to a novel object is that it is a basic-level substance sortal (Hall 1993).

The sortal *physical object* enables infants to pick out individuals and trace them through time, so that they can observe which properties change with time and which remain stable, and so that they can observe stable intercorrelated properties. Such observation would help identify kinds, if the baby is looking for them. There is now evidence that some of these assumptions are beginning to play a role in the infant's conceptual life between ages 9 and 12 months. Baldwin, Markman, and Melartin (1993) have shown that infants 12 months of age and older expected a hidden property of a given object (e.g., the disposition to make a given sound if handled in a particular way) to also be a property of another object of the same shape and size, as if kind membership predicts nonobservable properties. Further, Sabbagh and Baldwin (1997) recently reported pre-liminary results that 10-month-old infants in our (1996) paradigm might succeed if the two objects behave in distinctive manners predicted by their form when they emerge from each side of the screen (e.g., if a round object rolls and a square object turns discretely), as if form-function correlations provide information about object individuation.

It is the fifth assumption—that words will refer to object kinds—that has recerived the most systematic study. If this connection were part of the child's language-learning apparatus, then the infant could use adult word usage as a clue about the kinds in the world. Three results are con-sistent with this possibility. First we (Xu and Carey 1996) divided the 10-month-olds in our two studies with highly familiar kinds (bottle, book, cup, ball) into two groups: those whose parents said they understood the words for at least two of these kinds (less than a third of the sample) and those whose parents said they understood zero or at most one of the words (the majority of the sample). Those who comprehended the words succeeded on the individuation task, even though the objects were never named. At the very least, it appears that infants will not learn a word that means *bottle-shaped, bottleness,* that they must construct the relevant sortal to map the word onto. But it is also possible that word learning plays a role in the construction of the sortal. In support of that possibility, Xu (1997) has preliminary findings that naming the objects as they emerge from both sides of the screens in our task (Xu and Carey 1996) promotes success at 9 months of age. And finally, in a series of studies, Waxman and her collaborators have found that naming objects during both manual habituation and visual habituation promotes categorization at both the basic and global basic levels among both 9-month-olds and 12-month-olds (Waxman and Markow 1995; Balaban and Waxman 1997; Waxman and Balaban 1996).

In sum, we offer a tentative answer to the question John raised in *Names for Things* and *A Border Dispute*: how do children construct the sortals that are the meanings of count nouns and provide the criteria of identity for proper nouns? We have argued, on both logical and empirical grounds, that John's solution will not work: *same kind as [gestalt of dog]* is not a sortal that covers dogs. Also needed are (1) an individual that provides the first criteria of individuation and identity and (2) a stronger notion of kind than can be provided by shape similarity. Regarding the first, we offer the sortal *physical object*. And regarding the second, we offer several expectations about kinds that infants might bring to the task of constructing their first sortals and some tentative evidence that these expectations may actually play a role in this achievement.

Notes

1. Throughout the chapter, mentions of words are in quotation marks and mentions of mentally represented concepts or sortals are in italics.

2. Children this young have difficulty disengaging attention. Following eye gaze requires disengaging attention from a visible face. In Hood, Willen, and Driver's procedure, 3-month-old infants succeeded when they were looking at a schematic face whose eyes moved and which then disappeared from the screen, leaving the infants free to follow the gaze.

References

Baillargeon, R. (1995). A model of physical reasoning in infancy. In C. Rovee-Collier and L. P. Lipsitt (Eds.), *Advances in infancy research* (Vol. 9, pp. 305–371). Norwood, NJ: Ablex.

Baillargeon, R., and Graber, M. (1987). Where is the rabbit? 5.5-month-old infants' representation of the height of a hidden object. *Cognitive Development, 2,* 375–392.

Balaban, M. T., and Waxman, S. R. (1997). Do words facilitate object categorization in 9-month-old infants? *Journal of Experimental Child Psychology, 64,* 3–26.

Baldwin, D. A., Markman, E. M., and Melartin, R. L. (1993). Infants' ability to draw inferences about nonobvious object properties: Evidence from exploratory play. *Child Development, 64,* 711–728.

Baldwin, D. A., and Moses, L. J. (1994). Early understanding of referential intent and attentional focus: Evidence from language and emotion. In C. Lewis and P. Mitchell (Eds.), *Children's early understanding of mind* (pp. 133–156). Hove, England: Erlbaum.

Carey, S. (1994). Does learning a language require the child to reconceptualize the world? *Lingua, 92,* 143–167.

Cohen, L. B., and Younger, B. A. (1983). Perceptual categorization in the infant. In E. K. Scholnick (Ed.), *New trends in conceptual representation* (pp. 197–200). Hillsdale, NJ: Erlbaum.

Dromi, E. (1987). *Early lexical development.* Cambridge: Cambridge University Press.

Eimas, P., and Quinn, P. (1994). Studies on the formation of perceptually-based basic-level categories in young infants. *Child Development, 65,* 903–917.

Geach, P. (1957). *Mental acts: Their content and their objects.* London: Routledge and Kegan Paul.

Gibbard, A. (1975). Contingent identity. *Journal of Philosophical Logic, 4,* 187–221.

Gupta, A. (1980). *The logic of common nouns.* New Haven, CT: Yale University Press.

Hall, G. (1993). Basic-level individuals. *Cognition, 40,* 199–221.

Hirsch, E. (1982). *The concept of identity.* New York: Oxford University Press.

Hood, B., Willen, R., and Driver, J. (in press). Gaze following by 3-month-old infants. *Psychological Science.*

Johnson, S., Slaughter, V., and Carey, S. (in press). Whose gaze will 12-month-olds follow? *Developmental Science.*

Kellman, P. (1984). Perception of three-dimensional form in infancy. *Perception and Psychophysics, 36,* 353–358.

Kellman, P. (1993). Kinematic foundations of infant visual perception. In C. Granrud (Ed.), *Visual perception and cognition and infancy.* Hillsdale, NJ: Erlbaum.

Kripke, S. (1972). *Naming and necessity.* Oxford: Blackwell.

Landau, B., Smith, L. B., and Jones, S. S. (1988). The importance of shape in early lexical learning. *Cognitive Development, 3,* 299–321.

Macnamara, J. (1982). *Names for things: A study of human learning.* Cambridge, MA: MIT Press.

Macnamara, J. (1986). *A border dispute: The place of logic in psychology.* Cambridge, MA: MIT Press.

Macnamara, J., and Reyes, G. E. (Eds.). (1994). *The logical foundations of cognition.* Oxford: Oxford University Press.

Mandler, J., Bauer, P., and McDonough, E. (1991). Separating the sheep from the goats: Differentiating global categories. *Cognitive Psychology, 23,* 263–298.

Millikan, R. (1998). A common structure for concepts of individuals, stuffs, and real kinds: More mama, more milk and more mouse. *Behavioral and Brain Sciences, 21,* 55–100.

Oakes, L. M., Madole, K., and Cohen, L. B. (1991). Infants' object examining: Habituation and categorization. *Cognitive Development, 6,* 377–392.

Posner, M. I., and Keele, S. W. (1968). On the genesis of abstract ideas. *Journal of Experimental Psychology, 77,* 353–363.

Prevor, M. (1997). A new method for studying numerical representations in infancy. Unpublished master's thesis, Department of Psychology, New York University.

Quine, W. V. O. (1960). *Word and object*. Cambridge, MA: MIT Press.

Quine, W. V. O. (1969). *Ontological relativity and other essays*. New York: Columbia University Press.

Quine, W. V. O. (1974). *The roots of reference*. New York: Columbia University Press.

Quinn, P. C. (1987). The categorical representation of visual pattern information by young infants. *Cognition, 27*, 145–179.

Quinn, P. C., Eimas, P., and Rosenkrantz, S. L. (1993). Evidence for representations of perceptually similar natural categories by 3- and 4-month-old infants. *Perception, 22*, 265–288.

Ruff, H. A. (1986). Components of attention during infants' manipulative exploration. *Child Development, 57*, 105–114.

Sabbagh, M. A., and Baldwin, D. A. (1997). Infants' ability to distinguish objects on the basis of feature information and form-function type correspondences. Poster presented at the biennial meeting of the Society for Research in Child Development, Washington, DC.

Scaife, J. F., and Bruner, J. S. (1975). The capacity for joint visual attention in the infant. *Nature, 253*, 256–257.

Spelke, E. S. (1990). Principles of object perception. *Cognitive Science, 14*, 29–56.

Spelke, E. S., Breinlinger, K., Macomber, J., and Jacobson, K. (1992). Origins of knowledge. *Psychological Review, 99*, 605–632.

Spelke, E. S., Kestenbaum, R., Simons, D. J., and Wein, D. (1995). Spatiotemporal continuity, smoothness of motion and object identity in infancy. *British Journal of Developmental Psychology, 13*, 113–142.

Van de Walle, G., Prevor, M., and Carey, S. (1998). The use of kind distinctions for object individuation: Evidence from reaching. Manuscript submitted for publication.

Vygotsky, L. S. (1962). *Thought and language*. Cambridge, MA: MIT Press.

Waxman, S. R., and Balaban, M. T. (1996). Ursines and felines: Novel words support object categorization in 9-month-old infants. Paper presented at the International Conference on Infant Studies, April, Providence, RI.

Waxman, S. R., and Markow, D. B. (1995). Words as invitations to form categories: Evidence from 12- to 13-month-old infants. *Cognitive Psychology, 29*, 257–302.

Wiggins, D. (1980). *Sameness and substance*. Oxford: Blackwell.

Xu, F. (1997). Distinct labels may provide pointers to distinct sortals in 9-month-old infants. Paper presented at the 22nd Boston University Conference on Language Development.

Xu, F. (1997). From Lot's wife to a pillar of salt: Evidence that *physical object* is a sortal concept. *Mind and Language, 12*(3/4), 365–392.

Xu, F., and Carey, S. (1996). Infants' metaphysics: The case of numerical identity. *Cognitive Psychology, 30,* 111–153.

Xu, F., Carey, S., and Quint, N. (1997). Object individuation at 12 months: Shape and other properties. Poster presented at the biennial meeting of the Society for Research in Child Development, Washington, DC.

Xu, F., Carey, S., and Welch, J. (1998). Infants' ability to use object kind information for object individuation. Manuscript submitted for publication.

Chapter 14

Semantics and the Acquisition of Proper Names

D. Geoffrey Hall

A Swedish court fined the parents of a young boy the equivalent of $925 for not giving him a first name, at which point they named him "Brfxxcxxmnpcccclllmmnprxvclmnckssqlbb1116" (pronounced "Albin"), which the court has ruled to be unacceptable.

Article in the *Georgia Straight*, Vancouver, BC, December 26, 1996

Having a proper name (e.g., "Tom," "Dick," or "Harry") is a fundamental property of being human, so basic that it has been called a universal right in a number of international declarations and covenants. For example, Article 7-1 of Convention of the Rights of the Child, adopted by the General Assembly of the United Nations in 1989, states that "[t]he child shall be registered immediately after birth and shall have the right from birth to a name" (Valentine, Brennen, and Brédart 1996). As the epigraph to this chapter reveals, countries may even impose restrictions on what counts as an acceptable proper name, indicating the seriousness with which humans treat the act of naming people.

According to ethnographers, all human societies confer proper names upon their members (Alford 1987), and linguists have noted that proper names crop up in all the world's languages (Hockett 1966). Nonetheless, there are many striking crosscultural differences in practices associated with naming people. For example, societies differ in terms of whether people receive one or more first names in addition to one or more surnames; whether names are bestowed at birth or after a period of weeks,

This chapter was written with the support of a Natural Sciences and Engineering Research Council of Canada operating grant. I thank Paul Bloom, Susan Graham, and Ray Jackendoff for their very helpful comments on previous versions. I am immensely grateful to John Macnamara for all that he taught me during the 10 years that I had the great fortune to have him as a teacher and friend.

months, or even years; whether proper names are drawn from a large and diverse set of possibilities or a small stock of conventional options; whether names given near birth are used throughout life or changed at important points (e.g., puberty); and whether proper names are used freely in public discourse or kept private (Alford 1987). In addition, the universality of proper names for humans does not mean that people are the only bearers of these labels. Among other things, humans routinely name animals (e.g., dogs), artifacts (e.g., boats), places (e.g., cities), media products (e.g., movies), events (e.g., hurricanes), and institutions and facilities (e.g., companies and schools) (Hall, Veltkamp, and Turkel 1997; Valentine, Brennen, and Brédart 1996).

This chapter examines how children learn proper names. The task of learning these expressions has at least two components. First, children must learn the mappings between individual proper names and their appropriate interpretations in the particular language they are acquiring, because the inventory of proper names differs from language to language. For example, children learning English must somehow learn that the word "Tom" should be interpreted as referring to an individual (i.e., Tom) in a specific manner. Second, children must acquire knowledge of how the syntax and morphology of their particular language treat proper names, because proper names behave as a coherent class grammatically within a language but do not accept the same affixes or appear in the same serial positions within sentences crosslinguistically. For example, English learners must somehow discover that the word "Tom" shares important grammatical features with "Mike" and "Bill" that it does not share with "bike" or "mill."

How do children learn the links between proper names and their appropriate interpretations, and how do they gain knowledge of the grammatical properties of expressions of this class? The answer proposed in this chapter is that children do so by exploiting implicit semantic knowledge that they possess when they begin to acquire language. This knowledge consists of an understanding of the semantic definition of proper names, along with an expectation that expressions used under certain conditions (related to this definition) should be interpreted as belonging to this class. Children exploit this knowledge in the following way: As they hear novel labels used by speakers to refer to things in the world, they interpret some of them as satisfying conditions that imply they should be taken to be proper names; as a result, children take them to be proper names, assigning them interpretations that are consistent with the semantic definition of expressions of this class. As children learn more and more proper names in this way, they note how their language treats these expressions morphologically and syntactically (e.g., how they combine with affixes and how they interact with other words inside sentences). As a result, children come to learn the grammatical properties of proper names in their language. In this way, semantic knowledge—knowledge about the semantics of any proper name, as well as knowledge about the conditions under which speakers should use expressions of this class—provides children with a way both to map individual proper names onto their appropriate interpretations and to master the language-specific grammatical properties of expressions belonging to this class.

Section 14.1 presents a description of the grammatical and semantic properties of proper names. Section 14.2 reviews previous research on children's early understanding of these expressions. Section 14.3 examines in detail the hypothesis that children learn proper names by exploiting knowledge of their semantic definition, along with an understanding that labels interpreted as satisfying certain conditions (related to this definition) should be taken to be members of this class. The section does two things. First, it proposes four conditions of using novel labels that learners should see as implying that the labels could be interpreted as proper names. Second, it reviews experimental evidence bearing on whether young children favor interpreting a novel label as a proper name if any one of these conditions is satisfied but not if it is violated. Section 14.4 concludes the chapter with discussion.

14.1   What's in a Proper Name?

14.1.1   Grammar
One way to identify proper names is through their morphology and syntax. Even though the class of proper names is universal, the environments in which these labels can appear within sentences vary from language to language. In English, proper names are expressions that do not normally take the plural morpheme and do not usually follow determiners, quantifiers, or adjectives. For example, we may speak of "Tom" but not "Toms" (unless we mean, for example, "people named Tom"). In addition, we do not say "a Tom" or "several Toms" without leaving something to be specified (e.g., "a person named Tom" or "several people named Tom"). Finally, we rarely use adjectives to premodify proper names (e.g., "happy Tom"), restricting this practice to a pragmatically

limited set of contexts, such as in expressions of approval or disapproval (e.g., "Bad Fido!") or in utterances where a name is used to pick out a set of objects individuated across situations (e.g., "Big Tom is over there, and little Tom is here") (Bloom 1990). Bloom (1990) has noted that the morphological and syntactic properties of proper names are the same as those of noun phrases, like "the fat dog" or "the shoe with the brown lace." For this reason, Bloom (1990) has dubbed proper names (along with pronouns, like "I" and "her") "lexical" noun phrases.

To see how an understanding of the morphological and syntactic properties of English proper names could help to identify these labels in speech, notice that these properties are distinct from those associated with words from other lexical categories, such as count nouns (e.g., "dog"). Count nouns contrast with proper names in each of the ways noted earlier. In English sentences, count nouns may appear marked with the plural morpheme (e.g., "dog" and "dogs"); they may also be preceded by determiners (e.g., "a dog"), discrete quantifiers (e.g., "several dogs"), and adjectives (e.g., "big dogs"). In sum, proper names belong to a discrete class in terms of their grammatical properties (i.e., to the class of noun phrases), and the properties of this class contrast with those of the class of count nouns (as well as with those of other grammatical classes).

14.1.2   Semantics

Another way to identify proper names is via their semantics. Unlike their morphological and syntactic properties, which differ across languages, the semantic properties of proper names appear to be universal (e.g., Kripke 1980; Macnamara 1986; Macnamara and Reyes 1994). Specifically, a proper name is an expression that refers to an individual (in a kind), in all the situations in which that individual appears, regardless of the conditions under which it is used. In this way, proper names contrast with expressions from other classes, such as count nouns (which refer to *kinds* of individuals; e.g., "person," "dog"). For example, the proper name "Bill Clinton" is a label that refers to the individual, Bill Clinton, and can be used to pick him out in all the contexts in which he figures. These might be real situations (e.g., those associated with his childhood in Arkansas or his current adulthood serving as president of the United States), or they might be counterfactual (e.g., those associated with a childhood spent in Iceland, had he moved there when he was a baby, or an adulthood working as a veterinarian, had he chosen not to become a politician). An important consequence of this fact is that proper names are not synonyms for definite descriptions. For example, the proper name "Bill Clinton" cannot be defined by the description "the president of the United States raised in Arkansas," even though that description (in fact) picks out the individual, Bill Clinton, uniquely. If a proper name were simply synonymous with such a description, then it would be impossible to account for the intuition that the individual can be picked out using that proper name in situations where the description does *not* apply (e.g., the intuition that "Bill Clinton" can be used to pick out Bill Clinton in the situation in which he had chosen to treat sick animals for a career and had lived his whole life in Reykjavik) (see Kripke 1980; for different versions of the descriptivist view of proper names, see Frege 1892; Russell 1905; Searle 1958).

"Bill Clinton" also picks out the same individual regardless of who happens to be speaking and regardless of the context in which that person happens to be situated. Of course, there may be more than one person named "Bill Clinton," and so there is a sense in which the interpretation of a proper name does depend upon the occasion of its use (see Barwise and Perry 1983). Yet the context-specificity associated with interpreting proper names seems to stem more from the fact that there are not enough of them to go around than from any feature of their semantics. To appreciate this argument, note the contrast between proper names and other noun phrases, such as pronouns (e.g., "I") or definite descriptions (e.g., "the president of the United States"). These other expressions also can be used to refer to individuals, even to Bill Clinton, but they require that the context be specified in order for their referents to be fixed. For example, the referent of the pronoun "I" varies in a systematic way with the situation (e.g., who happens to be speaking). Similarly, a definite description like "the president of the United States" depends crucially upon the context in which it is uttered for its referent to be identified (e.g., if the conversation were about the Civil War, the referent might be Lincoln; if it were about Watergate, Nixon; or if it were about Whitewater, Clinton) (see Macnamara and Reyes 1994).

Finally, a proper name refers to an individual that is typed by a kind of individual. (In languages like English, kinds of individual are named by count nouns—for example, "person," "dog.") Macnamara (1986; Macnamara and Reyes 1994) has argued that a proper name needs the support of such a kind in order to specify the individual and in order to account for the tracing of that individual's identity across situations. Consider pointing to a man who is sitting in the Oval Office in the White

House and saying, "That is Bill Clinton." What is the "that" that the proper name "Bill Clinton" is meant to name? The answer is a person. Yet without a kind (e.g., PERSON) to make this specification, it is impossible to know whether the name should pick out Bill Clinton's entire body, or just his visible surface, or the set of molecules of which he is presently constituted, or whether to include his clothing and the pen in his hand. A kind serves to tell which individual a proper name designates. In addition, in order for "Bill Clinton" to function as referring to the same person when it is used to pick out both a little boy in Arkansas and a president in the White House, there must be something to provide for the identity of the boy with the president. This something is, again, a kind like PERSON. By supporting statements in which the name "Bill Clinton" appears, a kind enables a proper name to do its job of picking out one persisting individual across these situations (e.g., the 2-year-old and 51-year-old bearers of the name "Bill Clinton"). In sum, proper names form a discrete semantic class, distinct even from other noun phrases, as expressions that refer to individuals (typed by kinds) in all the situations in which they appear, regardless of the context.

14.2   What Children Know about Proper Names: Previous Research

Children first produce proper names very early in development (e.g., Nelson 1973; Macnamara 1982). This fact raises the question of what they understand about these labels near the outset of language acquisition. Of the several studies that have addressed this question, some have focused on young children's productions of these expressions in early speech, and others have explored children's appreciation of links between the syntax and semantics of these labels.

First, children as young as about 1 1/2 years of age appear to impose appropriate restrictions on the sentence environments in which proper names can appear. For example, they seem to know that proper names cannot follow adjectives. Bloom (1990) studied the spontaneous speech of English-learning children ranging in age from 18 to 34 months. Focusing on a set of 43 adjectives (e.g., "big," "happy," "red"), Bloom found that even the youngest child's speech appeared to respect a restriction against using these words to premodify proper names. For example, children rarely said things like "big Tom." In contrast, the same children did not show this restriction when producing these adjectives in conjunction with count nouns, commonly and appropriately saying things like "big dog."

Second, 2-year-old children seem to know the relation between some of the syntactic and semantic properties of proper names. Specifically, they appear to understand that a novel word applied to an object in a proper name syntactic context (e.g., "This is X") refers to an individual. In a seminal study, Katz, Baker, and Macnamara (1974; Macnamara 1982) showed two groups of children a pair of dolls differing in hair color. One group heard a novel label presented syntactically as a proper name (e.g., "This is ZAV") for one of the dolls. The children's task was then to choose one of the two dolls to perform requested actions formulated using the novel word (e.g., "Can you give me ZAV?"; "Can you show your mother ZAV?"). The dependent measure was the percentage of actions performed with the named doll. The main finding was that children (girls as young as 17 months; boys as young as 27 months) showed a strong tendency to select the named doll in response to the requests: they chose it about three quarters of the time. This result suggests that they typically took the label to refer to an individual, consistent with their having interpreted it as a proper name.

To demonstrate that children do not believe that *all* types of words refer to individuals, Katz, Baker, and Macnamara (1974) presented the same label for the same doll to a second group of children. For this group, however, they modeled the label in a sentence context that was appropriate for a count noun (e.g., "This is *a* ZAV"). Count nouns, recall, do not refer to individuals; they refer to kinds of individuals. These children heard requests to perform actions formulated in sentences that supported a count noun interpretation of the label (e.g., "Can you give me *a* ZAV?"; "Can you show your mother *a* ZAV?"). This group showed no tendency to favor the named doll in performing the actions: they chose it only about half the time; the remainder of the time, they picked the other doll. This outcome is consistent with the possibility that these children interpreted the word as naming the kind, DOLL, or the particular kind of doll. (It is also, of course, consistent with the possibility that children were simply guessing.) Children thus seemed to expect that a word named an individual only if it was modeled in a proper name sentence context, not if it appeared in a count noun sentence environment.

In another part of the study, Katz, Baker, and Macnamara (1974) labeled one of two differently colored blocks, rather than one of two dolls, for two other groups of children. These children selected the named block only about half the time in response to the experimenter's requests, regardless of whether the experimenters modeled the novel word as a proper name (as they did for one group) or a count noun (as they did for the other group). These results are consistent with the possibility that children interpreted the label as naming the kind, BLOCK, or the specific kind of block (as well as with the possibility that they guessed). The difference between children's interpretation of an intended proper name for a doll and their interpretation of the same word for a block suggests that their willingness to treat a word as a name for an individual depended not only on the syntactic context in which the word appeared, but also on the specific kind of object (or properties of the object) being labeled.

To follow up the study by Katz, Baker, and Macnamara (1974; Macnamara 1982), Gelman and Taylor (1984) conducted a similar study but changed the method in several ways. They tested groups containing both boys and girls; children's average age was about 2 1/2 years. They used unfamiliar (previously unlabeled) toys as target stimuli, two surrogates of animate objects (animal-like stuffed toys) and two inanimate objects (blocklike plastic toys). In addition, they presented children with all four objects at once. Half the time, the animals served as target stimuli (i.e., one of them received a label modeled as a proper name or a count noun) and the blocklike toys were distractors. The remainder of the time, the blocklike toys played the role of target stimuli (i.e., one of them received the label modeled as either a proper name or a count noun) and the animals served as the distractors. Adding two distractors to the two target stimuli in the array of object choices enabled Gelman and Taylor to do something that Katz, Baker, and Macnamara could not: clearly distinguish guessing (in which case, children should have chosen randomly among all four objects) from other, more systematic interpretations, such as a kind of object (in which case, children should have selected randomly between the two target stimuli).

Gelman and Taylor's main result replicated that of Katz, Baker, and Macnamara. They observed the strongest tendency to select the named toy in the group that heard the label modeled syntactically as a proper name for an animal-like toy. This result suggests that children in that group took the word to name that individual. In addition, Gelman and Taylor found evidence that children interpreted the novel word modeled syntactically as a count noun, for either an animal-like or a blocklike object, as naming a kind of object, because children in these groups chose randomly between the two target stimuli, ignoring the two distractors. In fact, children tended to select one of the distractors only if they heard a label that was presented syntactically as a proper name and the named object was blocklike. In that group, some children appeared to forget the act of labeling and selected exclusively one of the animal-like distractors, as if they interpreted the label as referring to that individual. Other children in this group chose randomly between the two blocks, as if they took the label to refer to a kind, such a BLOCK. Like the children in Katz, Baker, and Macnamara's study, the children in Gelman and Taylor's study thus appeared to show an understanding of a link between proper name syntax (e.g., "This is X") and proper name semantics (e.g., "X" refers to an individual), but only for some kinds of objects (or objects with certain properties).

Liittschwager and Markman (1993) clarified an interpretive issue raised by the results of the preceding studies. They argued that the earlier findings do not, in fact, unambiguously show that children think that a novel word modeled in the sentence context "This is X" is a proper name when it is applied to a surrogate of an animate object. They noted that children's strong tendency to select the named doll (Katz, Baker, and Macnamara 1974) or the named animal-like toy (Gelman and Taylor 1984) after learning the word for either of these objects might, as claimed, reflect an interpretation of the label as a proper name referring to the named individual (e.g., "This is Sue"). However, they pointed out that children could also have interpreted the word as an adjective referring to a property of the named object (e.g., "This is blonde"), because the named object always had a salient property (e.g., hair color) that distinguished it from the other object of the same kind.

To address this issue, Liittschwager and Markman introduced a group of 3-year-old children to an object (an animate surrogate, such as a stuffed bear, or an inanimate, such as a shoe) with a distinctive property (e.g., the bear was wearing a bib). They labeled it with a novel word modeled inside the sentence frame used in previous research to imply a proper name interpretation (e.g., "This is DAX"). Next they moved the object to a new location, removed its distinctive property (e.g., took the bib off the bear), and brought out another identical-looking object that lacked the distinctive property (e.g., another bear without a bib). They placed this new object where the original object had been located at the beginning of the task. They now asked the children, "Where's DAX?"

The authors argued that children who thought the label named a property of the originally named object should have chosen either of the two objects with equal probability. For example, they might have thought the word named the distinctive property of the named object (e.g., bib-wearing); neither object now had that property, and so children should have chosen randomly between the objects. Alternatively, children might have taken the word to name some other property of the original object (e.g., its shape or color); both objects now had the same properties, and so again children should have chosen either object. However, if children thought that the label named the original object as an individual, then they should have picked it, despite the loss of its distinctive property, the change in its location, and the fact that it was indistinguishable from the new object.

Liittschwager and Markman found that 3-year-olds did show a strong tendency to pick the originally named object as the referent of the novel word; subsequent analyses suggested that this tendency was specific to the animate surrogates they used (i.e., bears and trolls) and did not extend to the inanimates they used (i.e., shoes and baby bottles). These results suggest that children did, as previously claimed, interpret the novel word modeled in the sentence context "This is X" for an animate surrogate as naming an individual. Confirming that children do not treat words modeled in all sentence contexts in this way, the authors also found that another group of 3-year-olds who heard the same novel word modeled in a count noun sentential context (e.g., "This is *a* DAX," followed by the test question "Where's *a* DAX?") showed no preference for the originally named object, regardless of whether it was animate or inanimate, consistent with their having interpreted the label as naming a kind of object (or, of course, with their having guessed).

To summarize: By the time children are 2 or 3 years old, they possess at least some elements of a mature understanding of proper names. Two-year-olds produce proper names in appropriate sentential contexts (i.e., not following adjectives) (Bloom 1990). In addition, 2-year-olds and 3-year-olds appear to interpret a novel word modeled in a sentential environment appropriate for proper names (i.e., "This is X") and applied to an animate surrogate object (a doll or an animal) as referring to an individual (Gelman and Taylor 1984; Katz, Baker, and Macnamara 1974; Liittschwager and Markman 1993; Macnamara 1982).

14.3   Using Semantic Knowledge to Learn Proper Names

How do young children acquire their early understanding of proper names? At least two types of account could be proposed. One is that children first isolate proper names in speech via their grammatical properties, independent of their semantics. For example, children might engage in a distributional analysis of the speech they hear. They might note which affixes can appear attached to the expressions that are proper names in the adult language and where these expressions can occur inside sentences in their language (e.g., they might note what absolute positions they can occupy, as well as what words can precede and follow them). Gradually, children might cluster these expressions into a distinct class on this basis. They might then (somehow) "abstract" a formal class out of this initially distributionally defined one. By then noting the properties of the referents of the labels assigned to this class, children might come to tie expressions from this class to the set of semantic properties that define proper names. Children might even be able to identify these labels as members of the class of proper names (noun phrases), if they also knew that it was proper names (noun phrases) that had these semantic features.

This type of account runs into problems, however. One concern stems from the fact that, as Bloom (1990) noted, proper names share their grammatical properties with other noun phrases (including pronouns). This fact complicates children's task of identifying proper names in speech solely on the basis of their morphological and syntactic features (unless there is a set of sentence contexts that are reserved for proper names and do not accept other noun phrases, at least in speech addressed to children—Oshima-Takane (this volume) suggests that the vocative may be such a context). In addition, unconstrained distributional learning procedures for acquiring lexical categories have been criticized on a number of grounds. For example, it is unclear whether such procedures can work (e.g., whether children have enough memory or computational resources), given that convergence upon the appropriate class distinctions would require children to sort through and keep track of a staggering number of contrasting sentences (e.g., Bloom 1994; Gordon 1985; Pinker 1994). Moreover, the complexity of such procedures would suggest that learners who used them would experience a protracted (and error-filled) period of learning. Yet, as already noted, very young children (i.e., 2-year-olds) already appear to know (at least some of) the syntactic properties of English proper names (Bloom 1990) and to understand links between their syntax and their semantics (Gelman and Taylor 1984; Katz, Baker, and Macnamara 1974; Macnamara 1982).

The preceding problems suggest the need for a different type of account of how children learn proper names. Perhaps, instead of first identifying proper names in speech via their grammatical properties (e.g., through a distributional learning procedure), young children learn proper names by exploiting implicit knowledge about their semantics. Where would this semantic knowledge come from? Whereas the grammatical properties of proper names vary from language to language and so would have to be learned, the semantic properties of these expressions are universal and so could be known innately. Thus, children could initially approach the task of language acquisition with an understanding of the semantic definition of proper names, along with knowledge of special conditions of using labels (related to this definition) that imply they should be interpreted as members of this class of expression. If children did so, then the burden of learning proper names would be much more manageable than the one involved in acquiring them distributionally via their grammatical properties. Equipped with such knowledge, children would, then they first begin to learn language, have a way to make mappings between individual proper names and their appropriate interpretations. For example, if children interpreted an expression as being used under certain conditions (related to the semantics of proper names), then they would simply construe it as a proper name, assigning it the semantic properties of labels belonging to this class. Learning the grammatical properties of the expressions assigned to this class would be relatively straightforward, because children would need to perform a distributional analysis on only a small subset of the expressions in their language (i.e., those picked out as proper names because speakers used them under certain conditions). No prolonged period of error-ridden learning would be expected (see Bloom 1994; Pinker 1984).

Under what conditions should speakers use a novel label in order for learners to see it as potentially being a proper name (i.e., as an expression that refers to an individual in a kind in all situations in which the individual figures, regardless of the context)? Here are four suggestions, inspired by the semantic definition of proper names: (1) it should be used to refer to only one object (rather than more than one object); (2) it should be used to refer to an object for which learners do not already know a proper name (rather than one for which they do); (3) it should be used to refer to an object seen as important as an individual rather than one not seen in this way); and (4) it should be used to refer to an object for which learners know the kind of individual (rather than one for which they do not).

The remainder of this section is devoted to two tasks: (1) explaining *why* learners should see labels used under each of the four conditions as potentially being proper names, and (2) providing evidence bearing on whether young children who hear new labels used under these conditions are inclined to interpret them as proper names (e.g., Hall 1991, 1993b, 1994a,c, 1996; Hall and Graham 1997; Liittschwager and Markman 1993). The evidence comes from experimental studies involving one of two types of design. One type involved varying the conditions under which a speaker used a novel word (modeled as a proper name) to pick out things in the world. One group of children heard the label used in a way that satisfied one of the conditions hypothesized to imply that it could be a proper name; the other group heard the same label used in a way that violated the condition. The prediction was that those who heard the label used consistently with the condition would be more likely to interpret it as a proper name than those who heard it used inconsistently. The second type of design was more indirect. It involved presenting children with a novel word (modeled as a proper name) and then asking them to *choose* one of two objects as its referent. Choosing one object satisfied one of the conditions proposed to imply that a label could be a proper name; choosing the other object violated it. The prediction was that children would select the object that was consistent with the condition.

14.3.1 Only One Object per Proper Name

One condition of using a novel label that learners should see as implying that it could be a proper name is that it serve to refer to only one object. Recall that a proper name's semantic role is to refer to an individual. Thus, learners should be more likely to view a novel word as a proper name if it is given to only one object than if it is given to two different objects. Notice that proper names contrast with words from many other lexical categories in terms of this semantic property. For example, an adjective is a word whose semantic role is to refer to a property of an object, and so it can be used to pick out any number of objects that happen to have that property (see Hall and Moore 1997; Hall, Waxman, and Hurwitz 1993; Taylor and Gelman 1988). As a result, whereas learners should view the existence of two dogs both labeled "Fido" as inconsistent with the possibility that "Fido" is a proper name, they should not find the existence of two dogs both labeled "striped" to be inconsistent with the possibility that "striped" is an adjective.

Do children assume that a label used to refer to only one object can be interpreted as a proper name, but a label used to refer to more than one object cannot? On the one hand, some evidence suggests the answer might be no. In many cultures, including our own, there are far fewer proper names than there are proper name bearers. For example, Anderson (1977, cited in Alford 1987) estimated that there are 6 million men named "John" and 4 million women named "Mary" in the United States. On the other hand, anecdotal evidence suggests that children *do* make the assumption. For example, Macnamara (1982) made the following observations about his son, Kieran:

> For a time he seemed to assume that proper names were uniquely paired with individuals. The reason for believing so is that when he met his first "doppelgänger" he refused to accept the name. He was at the time [16 months and 13 days old] and had met a cousin of his, Lisa. He was then introduced to a girl of about the same age as Lisa also called Lisa. They played for half an hour, yet, most unusual for him, he refused to say her name, no matter how often anyone said it or urged him. Shortly after he met three girls all named Aimee and he accepted the name for all three. (p. 28)

Here is another anecdote reported by the mother of a boy, Matthew, when he was 20 months and 21 days old:

> He has a friend Rebecca at the sitters' that he loves to play with very much. He calls her Becca because it's easier for him to say. I have a friend who has a three-month old daughter named Rebecca, and Matthew will not call her by her name. I introduced him to her saying that her name was Rebecca, and he said "No Becca!" He has since been calling her "baby."

The preceding anecdotes suggest that young children initially *do* expect that a proper name can have only one bearer, and thus, that in order for a novel word to be interpreted as a proper name, it should be used to refer to only one object. This anecdotal evidence suggested the need for an experiment to determine more systematically whether children have this expectation. To meet this need, I conducted a study (Hall 1996) that compared how one group of young children interpreted a potential proper name used to refer to one object with how another group interpreted the same word used to refer to two objects.

In the study, two groups of 4-year-olds heard a novel word modeled in a sentence context (e.g., "This dog is ZAVY") that supported a proper name interpretation (e.g., "ZAVY" could refer to an individual, like "Fido") but that also *permitted* an adjective interpretation (e.g., "ZAVY" could refer to a property, like "striped"). One group heard this label applied to a drawing of a single object with a salient novel property (e.g., a dog with a novel striped pattern). I expected that children in this group

"This dog is ZAVY"

"This dog is ZAVY and this dog is ZAVY"

Figure 14.1
Sample schematic target stimuli from Hall 1996

would interpret the expression as a proper name (e.g., "Fido"), given that it was applied to only one object, given that the syntax of the sentence allowed a proper name interpretation, and given that the object was an animate surrogate. The other group heard the same label applied separately to drawing of *two* different objects (e.g., two dogs with the same novel striped pattern). Here I expected that children would be more reluctant to interpret the novel word as a proper name, because it was applied to two objects. Instead, I suspected that they would take the word to be an adjective (e.g., "striped") naming a property, because the word could also be disambiguated in this way. (See figure 14.1.)

To assess the interpretation of the novel label, I showed children in both groups a set of object drawings, including (1) the labeled object or objects (e.g., the original striped dog or dogs), (2) an object of the same kind that lacked the named object's (or objects') salient property (e.g., a different stripeless dog), and (3) an object of a different kind that possessed the labeled object's (or objects') salient property (e.g., a striped umbrella). I then asked whether children would extend the novel label to each of these objects in turn (e.g., "Is this dog ZAVY?", "Is this umbrella

ZAVY?"). I intentionally phrased the questions so that the word would remain ambiguous between a proper name (e.g., "Is this dog Fido?") and an adjective (e.g., "Is this dog striped?"). I expected that children who interpreted the word as a proper name would agree that it could apply to only the labeled object or objects. However, I predicted that those who took the word to be an adjective would assent to its applying to both the labeled object(s) and the object from a different kind with the same salient property as the labeled object(s).

As predicted, children who heard the label for only one object showed a strong tendency to interpret it as a proper name. In contrast, children who heard the same label for two different objects tended to interpret it as an adjective. These results suggest that children readily interpret a novel word as a proper name if the word is applied to one object but are more reluctant to do so if it is applied to two objects.

In the study reported in Hall 1996, I also demonstrated that 4-year-olds understand that one proper name sometimes can apply to two different objects (as they must do, of course, in learning a language like English). Two different groups of children heard the same novel word applied to the same object or pair of objects, but the sentences used to introduce the label made the word unambiguously a proper name. For example, instead of introducing the word in the ambiguous sentence "This dog is ZAVY," I now modeled it in three additional sentences that called clearly for a proper name construal (e.g., "The *name* of this dog is ZAVY. This dog is *called* ZAVY. This dog's *name* is ZAVY"). In both groups, children more readily made a proper name interpretation. Taken together, these results thus suggest that children's default assumption (their interpretation given no unambiguous information to the contrary) is that a novel word should be used to refer to only one object if it is to be interpreted as a proper name. The findings also indicate that children will relinquish this assumption in the fact of unambiguous evidence (e.g., clear linguistic cues) to do so.

14.3.2 Only One Proper Name per Object

A second condition of using a novel label that learners should see as implying that it could be a proper name is that it serve to refer to an object that has not already been assigned a proper name. The semantic function of a proper name is to designate an individual "rigidly": to refer to the individual in all the situations (real or counterfactual) in which it appears, and to pick out the individual regardless of the context of use. A consequence of this fact is that two proper names for one individual would both have the same interpretation. Given independent evidence that learners do not like to acquire more than one word with the same interpretation (e.g., they tend to assume that words contrast in their interpretations; Clark 1987), they should be more likely to see a novel word as a proper name if it is used to refer to an object that does not already have one of these labels than if it is used to refer to an object that does. For example, they should view the existence of one dog labeled both "Fido" and "Rover" to be inconsistent with the possibility that both these words are proper names.

Notice that the semantic redundancy associated with two proper names for one individual would not be true in the case of multiple words from other lexical categories for the same individual. For example, the semantic function of an adjective is to refer to a property of an individual, and any individual has many properties. As a result, learners should be willing to interpret a novel label as an adjective if it is applied to an object that has already been labeled with another adjective. For example, learners should view the existence of one dog designated both "spotted" and "furry" as consistent with the possibility that both these words are adjectives. In addition, because proper names and adjectives have different semantics, learners should find the existence of two words for the same object, one from each of these classes, to be consistent with these words' belonging to these two classes. For example, they should see the existence of one dog labeled both "Fido" and "furry" to be consistent with the possibility that these words are a proper name and an adjective, respectively.

Do children assume that a label used to refer to an object can be interpreted as a proper name if the object lacks a proper name, but not if it already has one? Some evidence suggests the answer might be no. There are societies in which different people refer to the same person by using entirely different proper names (Valentine, Brennen, and Brédart 1996), and in our own culture, different people may refer to the same individual using distinct variants of the individual's name (e.g., in decreasing formality, we might use a surname alone, a surname plus first name, a first name, and some diminutive form of a first name) (Alford 1987). However, some recent experimental evidence suggests that young children *do* make the assumption. One way to test for its existence would be to compare how two groups of children interpret a novel label modeled as a proper name, using a design like that described in Hall 1996. One group would hear the new label used to refer to an object previously labeled with another proper name; the other group would hear it used to refer to the same object previously labeled *not* with a proper name but with a word from a different class. A proper name interpretation of the new label should be more likely if the referent object had no previous proper name than if it did. Susan Graham and I took another, more indirect approach (Hall and Graham, in press). We presented children with a novel label modeled as a proper name, along with a *choice* of two referents, one of which had been previously labeled either with a proper name or with a word from a different class. If children assumed that a label could be a proper name if it was applied to an object that lacked a proper name (but not if it was applied to one that had one), then we predicted that they would choose the previously labeled object only if the previous label was not a proper name.

In one of the studies, we taught one group of 4-year-old children a novel word modeled unambiguously as a proper name for a familiar object (e.g., a stuffed dog). For example, we said, "This dog is *named* ZAVY." We taught another group of 4-year-olds the same word for the same object but modeled it unambiguously as an adjective. For example, we said, "This dog is *very* ZAVY." (See the top half of figure 14.2.) We then brought out a second object that looked identical to the first (e.g., another stuffed dog). We placed it to the side of, and several inches behind, the first object, but still within the child's easy reach. Now we provided a second word modeled unambiguously as a proper name and asked children to choose its referent. For example, we said, "Show me a dog that is *named* DAXY." (See the bottom half of figure 14.2.)

If children believe that a novel word can be taken as a proper name only if it is used to refer to an object that *has not* already been labeled with a proper name (e.g., one dog *cannot* be both "Fido" and "Rover"), then we predicted that those in the group who had learned a proper name for the first object (dog A in figure 14.2) would select the second object (dog B in figure 14.2). In contrast, if children assume that a novel word can be interpreted as a proper name if it is used to refer to an object that either *has* or *has not* previously been labeled with an adjective (e.g., one dog *can* be both "spotted" and "Rover"), then we predicted that those in the group who had learned an adjective for the first object would show no strong tendency to select the second object. This is, in fact, what we found. Children strongly favored the second object as the referent of the second word (a proper name) if they had learned a proper name for the first object, but not if they had learned an adjective.

"This dog is named ZAVY"
or
"This dog is very ZAVY"

"Show me a dog that is named DAXY"

Figure 14.2
Sample schematic stimuli from Hall and Graham, in press

In addition, after children chose the referent of the second word
(the proper name), we asked them whether this label could also apply
to the object that they did not choose. On those trials where children
chose the second object, we found that they were more likely to *refuse* to
apply the second word (the proper name) to the first object if they had
already learned a proper name for it than if they had learned an adjective
for it. Thus, children not only preferred to map a proper name onto an
object that did not already have a proper name but also refused to accept
a proper name for an object that already had one.

One interpretation of the preceding results is that children dislike
assigning two proper names to one object; and so in order to interpret a
label as a proper name, they assume it should be applied to an object that
lacks one of these expressions. An alternative interpretation, however, is
that children do not like two words from any one lexical class for the
same object. Thus, they assume that in order to be interpreted as belonging to any class, a novel label should be applied to an object that lacks

an expression already assigned to that class. To rule out this alternative we gave two other groups of 4-year-olds the same task, using the same materials and procedure. As with the previous groups, we began by teaching a novel word (e.g., "ZAVY") modeled as either a proper name or an adjective for one object (e.g., a stuffed dog; dog A in figure 14.2). Again, we then introduced a second identical-looking object (e.g., another stuffed dog; dog B in figure 14.2), and we asked children to choose the referent of a second word. Now, however, we presented this second word as an *adjective*. For example, we said, "Can you show me a dog that is *very* DAXY?"

If children assume that a novel word can be interpreted as an adjective if it is applied to an object that either *has* or *has not* already been labeled with an adjective (e.g., one dog *can* be both "spotted" and "furry"), then we predicted that those who had heard an adjective for the first object (e.g., dog A) would show no strong tendency to select the second object (e.g., dog B). In addition, if children believe that a novel word can be interpreted as an adjective if it is applied to an object that either *has* or *has not* previously been labeled with a proper name (e.g., one dog *can* be both "Fido" and "furry"), then we predicted that those who heard a proper name for the first object would again have no clear bias to choose the second object. The result again supported the predictions. Children did not favor the second object as the referent of the second word (the adjective) in either group. Children were somewhat more likely to select the second object if they had heard an adjective for the first object than if they had heard a proper name, but neither group selected the second object at a level that exceeded what would be expected by chance. In addition, comparing these results with the results obtained when the second word was a proper name, we found that children were less likely to select the second object upon hearing a second adjective than upon hearing a second proper name.

After they chose a referent for the second word (the adjective), we again asked children whether the label could also apply to the object they did not choose. On those trials where children chose the second object, we found no difference in their tendency to refuse to apply the second word (the adjective) to the first object, whether they had already learned a proper name or an adjective for it. Moreover, in both groups, this tendency was lower than it was in the group where children were asked about a second proper name for the first object. Thus, children showed no strong unwillingness to map an adjective onto an object that had already been labeled with an adjective, and they also showed no clear tendency to refuse to accept an adjective for an object that already had been labeled with an adjective.

Taken together, the results of this study suggest that preschoolers reject assigning two proper names to one object. Thus, the findings are consistent with the hypothesis that children assume that a novel label for an object could be interpreted as a proper name if they lack a proper name for it, but not if they already know one. The findings are also consistent with the claim that this assumption does not extend to all word classes. Specifically, children did not reject two adjectives for one object, supporting the view that children are willing to permit a novel label to be interpreted as an adjective for an object, regardless of whether they already know another adjective for that object.

14.3.3   Objects Important as Individuals

A third condition of using a novel label that learners should see as implying that it could be a proper name is that it serve to refer to an object that belongs to a kind (or has the properties) that makes that object worthy of being referred to as an individual. The semantic function of a proper name is to refer to an individual, without any restrictions on its specific kind (or its specific properties). However, learners may (independently) construe only some individuals as being important as individuals; they may see others as more or less interchangeable members of a kind. As a result, learners should view the use of a label to refer to an individual considered significant as an individual to be more consistent with the label's being a proper name than the use of the same label to refer to an individual seen to lack such significance.

Are children more likely to interpret a label as a proper name if it is used to refer to an individual seen to be important as an individual than if it is used to refer to an individual seen to lack such importance? The answer depends upon which individuals matter to young children as individuals. In previous work, researchers have proposed that people believe that humans and other animate objects matter more as individuals than many common artifacts (e.g., Macnamara 1982). Thus, children might be more likely to interpret a novel word as a proper name for an animate or animate surrogate than for an artifact. Liittschwager and Markman (1993) recently obtained evidence consistent with this prediction, using a two-object forced-choice procedure (as in the design of Hall and Graham, in press).

Liittschwager and Markman (1993) asked a group of 3-year-olds to choose the referent of a novel word modeled as a proper name (e.g., "Where's BIF?"). Children had to choose between a novel animate surrogate object and a novel inanimate object. (The authors do not report what kinds of object these were.) Liittschwager and Markman found that children chose the animate object significantly more often than would be expected by chance. The authors asked another group of 3-year-olds to choose the referent when the novel word was modeled syntactically as a count noun (e.g., "Where's *a* BIF?"). These children chose the animate surrogate object only as often as would be expected by chance. Moreover, children's tendency to choose the animate object was (marginally) significantly higher if they heard the word modeled as a proper name than if they heard it presented as a count noun (Woodward and Markman, in press). These findings provide evidence that children prefer to map a proper name (but not a count noun) onto an animate surrogate object rather than onto an inanimate object. The results are thus consistent with the claim that children assume that a novel word could be interpreted as a proper name if it is applied to a surrogate of an animate object but not if it is given to an inanimate object. On the assumption that children tend to seen animates but not inanimates as important as individuals, the findings are also consistent with the claim that children are more likely to interpret a novel word as a proper name if it is applied to an individual seen to be important as an individual than if it is applied to an individual seen to lack such importance.

Several of the studies reviewed earlier in this chapter have also tested the prediction that children are more likely to take a novel label as a proper name if it is applied to an animate surrogate than if it is applied to an artifact, by examining children's interpretation of a novel label given directly to an object (as in the design of Hall 1996). In those studies, recall, children showed a readiness to interpret a novel word as a proper name if it was used to name a doll but not a block (Katz, Baker, and Macnamara 1974; Macnamara 1982); an animal-like monster but not a plastic block-like toy (Gelman and Taylor 1984); and a bear or a troll but not a shoe or a baby bottle (Liittschwager and Markman 1993). Thus, children have been more likely to interpret a novel label as a proper name if the referent is an animate surrogate than if it is an artifact. Again, on the assumption that people and animates matter more to young children as individuals than many artifacts, the results are consistent with the proposal that young children are more likely to take a word as a proper name if it is used to refer to an individual seen as important as an individual than if it is used to refer to an individual seen as lacking this importance.

I conducted a series of studies (Hall 1994c) to test further the hypothesis that children are more likely to take a novel word as a proper name if it is applied to an animate or animate surrogate than if it is applied to an artifact. The method was again similar to the one described in Hall 1996, in that it explored the interpretation children assigned to a novel word used to refer directly to an object. Preschoolers saw a drawing of a familiar object, an X. They then heard a novel word modeled in a sentence frame that was ambiguous between a proper name and an adjective (e.g., "This X is ZAVY"). Children heard the label applied to a drawing of either an animal or an artifact with a salient novel property (e.g., a striped pattern). The question was whether children would interpret the label as a proper name naming the individual (e.g., as a word like "Tom") or as an adjective referring to the salient property (e.g., as a word like "striped").

To assess children's interpretation of the novel label, I showed them a set of object drawings, including (1) the labeled object (e.g., a striped animal or artifact), (2) an object of the same kind that lacked the labeled object's salient property (e.g., a different nonstriped animal or artifact of the same kind), and (3) an object of a different kind that possessed the labeled object's salient property (e.g., a striped animal or artifact of a different kind). A puppet then pointed to each of the drawings, one at a time, asking children whether they thought that the object (X) could be labeled with the new word (e.g., "Is this X ZAVY?"). The question phrasing left the word ambiguous between a proper name (e.g., "Is this X Tom?") and an adjective (e.g., "Is this X striped?"). I expected that children who interpreted the word as a proper name would agree that it could apply to only the named object. However, I thought that those who construed the word as an adjective would assent to applying it to both the labeled object and the object from a different kind that shared a salient property with the labeled object.

The first two studies reported in Hall 1994c examined whether 4-year-olds (experiment 1) and 3-year-olds (experiment 2) were more likely to interpret the novel word as a proper name if the drawing was an animal that was a typical pet (a dog, a bird, a cat, or a rabbit) than if it was a simple artifact (a shoe, a balloon, a cup, or a hat). (See the top half of figure 14.3.) As predicted, the groups who learned the words for the petlike animals tended strongly to interpret them as proper names. In

"This dog is ZAVY"   "This shoe is ZAVY"

**"This caterpillar   "This boat is ZAVY"
is ZAVY"**

Figure 14.3
Sample schematic target stimuli from Hall 1994c. Top: Sample target stimuli from
experiments 1 and 2. Bottom: Sample target stimuli from experiments 3 and 4.

contrast, the groups who learned the words for the simple artifacts were
less likely to construe them as proper names; instead, they showed a
strong tendency to take them as adjectives. Thus, children were more
likely to interpret a novel label as a proper name for a petlike animal than
for a simple artifact.

Experiment 3 of Hall 1994c explored whether 4-year-olds would give
the same patterns of answers for *all* kinds of animals and *all* kinds of
artifacts. Would children have the same strong tendency to interpret novel
ambiguous words as proper names if the animals were less typical and less
petlike than they were in the previous experiments (i.e., if they were cat-
erpillars, bees, snails, and spiders)? Would they show the same weak tendency to interpret the words as proper names if the artifacts were more
complex than they were in previous experiments, and if they belonged to
kinds to whose members adults often do give proper names (i.e., if they
were boats, airplanes, cars, and trains)? (See the lower half of figure 14.3.)

Using the same procedure as in the previous experiments, I discovered that the group of children who heard the words for the nonpet animals were, in fact, less likely to interpret the labels as proper names than the group in experiment 1 who heard the words for the petlike animals. However, the group who learned the words for the complex artifacts were as unwilling to interpret the labels as proper names as the group in experiment 1 who learned the words for the simple artifacts. In addition, I found that the group of children who learned the words for nonpet animals were no more likely to make a proper name interpretation than the group who learned the words for the complex artifacts. Thus, pre-schoolers did not seem to treat all animals as being equally suitable as candidate recipients of proper names, although they appeared to see all artifacts (both simple and complex) as equally bad potential bearers of these labels.

Experiment 4 explored the basis of the difference between 4-year-olds' willingness to interpret a novel word as a proper name for a petlike animal (experiment 1) and their relative unwillingness to do so for a nonpet animal (experiment 3). One difference between pets and nonpets is that the former are usually owned by people (although some nonpets may be owned by people). I examined whether mentioning that the to-be-labeled objects were possessed by the experimenter would increase children's tendency to interpret the labels for them as proper names. I used the same drawings as in experiment 3. Now, however, before introducing the ambiguous labels, I inserted an additional sentence to indicate that I owned the object, the X: "This is *my* X."

The addition of this information about possession increased children's tendency to interpret the labels as proper names if the objects were nonpet animals, but not if they were complex artifacts. Children in experiment 4 were significantly more likely to interpret the words as proper names if they were in the group for which the labeled objects were nonpet animals than if they were in the group for which the labeled objects were complex artifacts. Taken together, the results of these experiments thus suggest that children's willingness to interpret a novel word as a proper name for an object is very strong if the object is an animal and if it is marked as possessed by a person (either by being a typical pet or by having its own-ership noted explicitly). Preschoolers do not readily construe a novel label for an artifact as being a proper name. On the assumption that animate objects (or objects with animate properties), especially those that are marked as possessed by someone, are viewed as more important as individuals than many common artifacts, the results suggest that another condition leading children to construe a novel word as a proper name is that the labeled object be viewed as significant as an individual.

The results from this series of studies (Hall 1994c) and earlier ones (e.g., Gelman and Taylor 1984; Katz, Baker, and Macnamara 1974; Liittschwager and Markman 1993) do not imply that preschool children cannot understand (or learn) a proper name in conjunction with an object that is not animate (and possessed). If children fully grasp the semantics of proper names, then they should be able to comprehend (and acquire) a proper name used in conjunction with anything that they can conceptualize as an individual, including artifacts. In fact, many young children likely do encounter (and understand) artifacts bearing proper names, such as "Thomas" the Tank Engine or "Budgie" the Helicopter, although these artifacts are often anthropomorphized (e.g., they have human facial features). In addition, Sorrentino (1997) has shown that 2-year-olds will interpret a novel word as a proper name for an artifact if it is described as possessing mental states (but not if it is described neutrally). However, the finding that children (and adults) can learn and understand the use of proper names in conjunction with a wide range of individuals, including artifacts, would not be inconsistent with the findings reported in Hall 1994c or the findings from earlier studies. When trying to identify these labels in speech, children simply may be disposed, as a default, to seek them out as the expressions used to refer to those individuals that matter as individuals, and (aside from people) these may be seen to be objects that are animate and possessed by humans.

14.3.4 Objects from Known Kinds

A final condition of using a novel label that learners should see as implying that it could be a proper name is that it serve to refer to an object for which they already know the kind of individual. Recall that, in order to carry out its semantic role of referring to an individual, a proper name needs the support of such a kind, in order to specify that individual and to trace its identity across situations. Because kinds of individuals are labeled by count nouns, learners should see a novel word (e.g., "This is ZAV") as more likely to be a proper name if it is used to label an object for which they know a count noun (e.g., a dog, for which the learner knows the word "dog") than if it is used to pick out one for which they do not know a count noun (e.g., a novel monster, for which the child knows no label and which the child has never seen before). (See figure 14.4.)

"This is ZAV"   **"This is ZAV"**

Figure 14.4
Sample schematic target stimuli from Hall 1991

How should knowledge of a count noun for an object be assessed? One index of the presence or absence of such knowledge is the ability or inability to *produce* the word for the object. However, because production lags behind comprehension in language development, learners may know (i.e., understand) count nouns for many objects before they produce the words, especially those objects with which they have had some previous encounters. Thus, simply equating children's having or lacking knowledge of a count noun with their ability or inability to produce it may be inappropriate. The ability to produce a count noun for an object does seem a reasonable index of *knowing* a count noun for it; however, a more plausible index of *not knowing* a count noun for an object would be the inability to produce a count noun for an object, along with a lack of experience with the object and its kind (e.g., no previous encounters with objects of the kind, and so no opportunities to gain any understanding of a count noun for the kind).

Is there any evidence bearing on the claim that children are more likely to interpret an expression as a proper name if it is used to refer to an object for which they know a count noun than one for which they do not? On the negative side, there is anecdotal evidence suggesting that learners will sometimes produce a proper name for an object before producing a corresponding count noun. For example, Macnamara (1982) noted that his son, Kieran, produced many proper names for people before producing a related count noun (such as "man," "person," or even "thing" or "object"). In addition, Kieran produced "Freddie" as a name for his dog six weeks before he produced the count noun "dog" (see also Nelson 1973). However, as noted earlier, simply failing to produce a count noun for an object does not necessarily imply that children lack knowledge of the word, and so this evidence is not conclusive.

On the positive side, there is other evidence suggesting that children have difficulty in learning proper names in conjunction with objects for which they do not already produce a count noun. For example, it is commonly observed that young children will extend a first word produced for a parent, like "Daddy" or "Mommy," from the labeled person to other people (see Merriman 1986; Nelson 1973). One interpretation of this phenomenon is that children misinterpret an intended proper name as referring to the kind of object (as a count noun), because they do not already know a count noun for the kind, such as "man," "woman," or "person." Again, however, this interpretation is subject to the concern that failure to produce a count noun does not indicate that children necessarily lack any knowledge of it. Another problem with the interpretation is that words like "Daddy" and "Mommy" are not unambiguous proper names. For example, in speech to children, these words may appear as either count nouns (e.g., "Wait till your daddy sees that!") or proper names (e.g., "Wait till Daddy sees that!").

To obtain clearer evidence about the relevance of knowing a count noun for an object to children's tendency to interpret a novel word as a proper name, I conducted two experiments (Hall 1991). Both studies compared how one group of children interpreted a novel word presented as a proper name for a "familiar" object (i.e., one for which they produced a count noun) with how another group interpreted the same word for an "unfamiliar" object (i.e., one for which they did not produce a count noun and with which they lacked any prior experience).

In the first study, two groups of 2-year-olds heard a novel word modeled syntactically as a proper name (e.g., "This is ZAV"). One group heard it for a familiar stuffed toy (a cat), and the other group heard it for an unfamiliar stuffed toy (a novel monster). The toys were both surrogates of animate objects, because children in previous research were less willing to learn proper names in association with other kinds of objects, regardless of their familiarity (e.g., blocks or unfamiliar blocklike toys). I assessed familiarity by asking an independent group of slightly older preschoolers to generate a count noun for the kinds of object. Children regularly produced a count noun, such as "cat," for the cat, but they generally failed to provide a count noun label for the novel monster (and it is very unlikely that they had any prior experience with it, given that it was an invented creature). After children in both groups heard the novel label, I brought out three other stuffed animals. One was from the same kind of object as the named one (either another cat or another monster of the same kind) but wore differently colored clothes. The other two were distractors from different kinds. The task was similar to the one used by Gelman and Taylor (1984): to select one of the four toys in response to a series of requests formulated using the new word (e.g., "Can you put ZAV on top of your head?"; "Can you point to ZAV?"). As in Gelman and Taylor's study, the main dependent measure was the percentage of trials on which children chose the labeled object. A higher percentage of named object choices suggested a stronger tendency to interpret the label as a proper name for that individual.

Children in both familiar and unfamiliar groups showed, overall, a strong tendency to select the named toy. This finding was not surprising, because both the familiar and unfamiliar labeled objects were animate surrogates, and both were described with a word modeled syntactically as a proper name. However, as predicted, children who learned the word for the familiar object (the cat) were significantly more likely than those who learned it for the unfamiliar object (the monster) to select the named object (i.e., to make a proper name interpretation). Those who heard the word for the unfamiliar object often selected the other object of the same kind as the labeled object in response to the requests, suggesting that they had misinterpreted the word as a name for the kind (as a count noun). In addition, children's spontaneous comments transcribed from tape recordings of the test sessions provided further evidence that those in the familiar group were more likely than those in the unfamiliar group to interpret the word as a proper name. In the familiar group, children sometimes asked the experimenter what the unlabeled cat was "named" or "called," suggesting that they had taken the word for the labeled object as a proper name. In the unfamiliar group, children did not ask these questions; instead, they often made comments revealing that they had misconstrued the intended proper name as a count noun. For example, after hearing the intended proper name (e.g., "This is ZAV") for the labeled monster, children often pointed to the other monster of the same kind and described it using the novel word, but they placed the word in sentence contexts reserved for count nouns, such as "two ZAVs" or "another ZAV."

The second study included two new groups of 2-year-olds and used a similar procedure, but different familiar (i.e., dogs) and unfamiliar (i.e., novel monsters of a different kind) animate surrogates as test stimuli. The main procedural change involved introducing the labeled object to both groups as the experimenter's pet. The hypothesis was that this change would increase children's tendency to view the unfamiliar object as worthy of being referred to as an individual (because it was marked as being possessed by someone) and so increase their willingness to learn a proper name for it. However, despite adding this information about pet-hood, I still found that children were more likely to make a proper name interpretation (i.e., to select the named object and to make proper name–appropriate spontaneous comments) if they heard the novel word applied to the familiar object than if they heard it for the unfamiliar object. Thus, in both studies reported in Hall 1991, knowledge of a count noun (and so, presumably, knowledge of a kind) for an object enhanced young children's tendency to learn a proper name for it. These results provide evidence consistent with the hypothesis that children are more likely to interpret a novel word as a proper name if it is used in conjunction with an object that has already been typed by a kind than if it is used along with an object that has not. (For an alternative interpretation of these findings, see Hall 1991; Markman 1994; Woodward and Markman, in press).

One intriguing finding from the second experiment reported in Hall 1991 was that, despite hearing that the labeled object was the experimenter's pet, children were more likely to interpret a novel word for it as a proper name if it was familiar than if it was unfamiliar. This was a puzzling result because "pet" is a count noun naming a kind of individual. Children thus should have been willing to learn a proper name for both the familiar and the unfamiliar object. Why, then, were children less likely to acquire a proper name for the unfamiliar than for the familiar animal? One possibility is that the 2-year-olds simply did not understand the word "pet." Another possibility, however, is that they understood the count noun "pet" but recognized that it is not the right type of count noun to support the interpretation of a proper name.

Philosophers distinguish between "substance" count nouns (words like "dog," "person," and "shoe") and "phase" count nouns (words like "pet," "puppy," and "passenger") (e.g., Gupta 1980; Wiggins 1980; for discussion of the acquisition of these words, see Hall 1993a; Hall and Waxman 1993; Macnamara 1986). Phase count nouns differ from substance count nouns in that they refer to kinds that pick out individuals defined in restricted terms (e.g., as existing over limited periods of time or in particular contexts). It may be that phase count nouns are not good candidates for supporting the interpretation of proper names, because people assume that proper names refer to individuals that are not tied to particular conditions. In other words, when people bestow proper names, they tend to do so on the back of substance kinds, not phase kinds. They name individual dogs and persons, not individual puppies and passengers.

Of course, it is possible to introduce a proper name for an object in conjunction with a phase count noun, as in the second experiment reported in Hall 1991 (e.g., "This is my pet. This is ZAV"). In fact, there are many situations in which a proper name can be introduced with the support of a phase kind. For example, a friend might introduce his spouse through an utterance like, "This is my wife, Susan." For adults, however, a phase count noun like "wife" does not seem to support the interpretation of a proper name like "Susan." The reason is that it is unlikely that the proper name "Susan" names a wife. Instead, "Susan" appears fundamentally to name a person (supported by a substance kind, PERSON). For example, "Susan" probably picked out Susan long before she got married and became a wife. Thus, as adults, we appear to use a substance kind to support the interpretation of a proper name, even in situations where we know a phase kind for an object and actually hear a proper name in conjunction with it. These considerations suggest that the children who participated in this experiment may have assumed that the novel label was not a proper name for the unfamiliar monster, because they required a substance kind (e.g., KIND OF MONSTER), not a phase kind (e.g., PET), in order to type the object suitably. I am currently planning an experiment to test the hypothesis that in order to interpret a novel label as a proper name, children need knowledge of not just any kind (count noun), but specifically a substance kind (count noun).

14.3.5 Summary

This section explored the idea that learners should be more likely to interpret a novel label as a proper name if certain conditions of using the word are met than if they are violated. These conditions, inspired by the semantic definition of proper names (i.e., expressions that refer to individuals in kinds in all situations in which the individuals appear, regardless of the context), are that the label be applied to only one object; that the label be applied to an object that has not already been labeled with a proper name; that the label be applied to an object that is marked as important as an individual in some way (e.g., by being animate and possessed by someone); and that the label be applied to an object for which children know a (substance) kind (e.g., a substance count noun). The results from studies using either of two types of experimental design indicated that preschool children *are* more likely to interpret a novel word as a proper name if it is used in a way that upholds any of these conditions than if it is used in a way that violates it. One type explored children's construal of a novel word used to label objects in such a way that one of the conditions was either upheld or violated; the other (more indirect) type examined children's choice of the referent of a proper name given two alternatives, one that upheld one of the conditions, but another that violated it.

These findings are consistent with the possibility that children learn proper names by relying on implicit knowledge of their semantic definition, along with knowledge that novel labels used under special conditions (related to this definition) should be construed as belonging to this class of expression. This knowledge could aid children in making mappings between proper names and their interpretations; and it could also provide a way for children to learn the grammatical properties of these expressions, if they were disposed to note the contexts in which these semantically identified labels can appear within sentences in their language.

14.4   Discussion

By about their second birthday, children appear to understand some of the syntactic properties of proper names, as well as links between the syntax and semantics of these expressions. This early knowledge presents an intriguing puzzle to researchers interested in language acquisition: how do children acquire it? One solution to the puzzle, explored in this chapter, is that children learn proper names by exploiting tacit knowledge of their semantic definition (e.g., Kripke 1980; Macnamara 1986; Macnamara and Reyes 1994), along with knowledge that labels used under certain conditions (related to this definition) should be interpreted as belonging to this class of expression. Possessing this knowledge, children would have a way both to establish appropriate links between individual proper names and their interpretations in the language they are acquiring, and to learn how these labels are expressed morphologically and syntactically in that language.

An important unaddressed issue concerns whether adults' use of proper names when speaking to children meshes with children's understanding of the semantics of these expressions, and with their understanding of the conditions—related to these semantics—under which speakers should use labels of this class. If children expect that proper names will be the words used to name (1) only one object each, (2) objects lacking proper names, (3) objects important as individuals (e.g., animate, human-possessed objects), and (4) objects already labeled by kind terms, then parents should tend to provide children with proper names under conditions that accord with these expectations. Furthermore, when parents introduce young children to words in situations that violate these conditions, they should flag these events as exceptional so as to minimize children's mapping errors.

For example, adults should strive to use a proper name in conjunction with only one object and attempt to signal as noteworthy those cases where the same proper name is used to label more than one individual. In such events, they should explain the usage directly, or they should take measures to modify the name in order to distinguish it from a previously learned proper name. For example, they might add a diminutive suffix to one (e.g., "John" and "Johnnie"), adjectives to both (e.g., "Big John" and "Little John"), or surnames to both (e.g., "John T." and "John S."). Parents should also attempt to preserve a rule of using only one name for each individual. They should single out for children those situations in which one object receives more than one proper name. In addition, parents should try to reserve proper names for objects that children expect to receive names (e.g., those that are animate or have animate properties, and are marked as possessed by people), and they should signal as exceptional the use of proper names for noncanonically namable kinds of objects. For example, if there is a proper name for the family car, boat, or computer, then parents should offer a special explanation of this fact to their young children when they first tell them the name. Finally, parents should provide proper names for objects that children have already typed by kinds, probably those objects for which children already know a count noun for the substance kind. If parents introduce an unfamiliar object to their children, they should refrain from providing a proper name until after they have first introduced a count noun for it, in particular a substance count noun. Some evidence from studies of how parents teach words for objects suggests that parents do tend to provide substance count nouns rather than other types of word when they first introduce unfamiliar objects to their children (e.g., Callanan 1985; Hall 1994b).

At present, there are no data that bear directly on the important question of whether adults introduce proper names to young children in a way that matches children's assumptions about which labels they hear in speech should be interpreted as belonging to this class. However, Tracey Burns and I are currently planning some studies to try to answer it.

Another important issue for future work to address is the origin of children's understanding. If young children do have knowledge of the universal semantic definition of proper names, along with knowledge that labels used under certain conditions (related to this definition) should be interpreted as proper names, then where does it come from? The results of the demonstrations described in this chapter are consistent with the possibility that young children possess this understanding between the ages of 2 and 4 years, during the period of rapid vocabulary development that occurs in the preschool years. Yet the relatively advanced age (in terms of the time course of language acquisition) of the children in these studies precludes making strong claims about the origins of this knowledge. Further research with infants and young toddlers (i.e., those at least as young as the 17-month-olds in the study reported in Katz et al. 1974) may shed light on whether any or all of the knowledge also exists in children on the brink of learning language. Evidence of the presence of this understanding in very young children would bolster support for the view that children initially acquire these expressions (e.g., make mappings between them and their interpretations; learn their grammatical properties as a class) via an unlearned semantic competence.

References

Alford, R. D. (1987). *Naming and identity*. New Haven, CT: HRAF Press.

Barwise, J., and Perry, J. (1983). *Situations and attitudes*. Cambridge, MA: MIT Press.

Bloom, P. (1990). Syntactic distinctions in child language. *Journal of Child Language, 17,* 343–355.

Bloom, P. (1994). Syntax-semantics mappings as an explanation for some transitions in language development. In Y. Levy (Ed.), *Other children, other languages: Issues in the theory of language acquisition* (pp. 41–75). Hillsdale, NJ: Erlbaum.

Callanan, M. (1985). How parents label objects for young children: The role of input in the acquisition of category hierarchies. *Child Development, 56,* 508–523.

Clark, E. V. (1987). The principle of contrast: A constraint on language acquisition. In B. MacWhinney (Ed.), *Mechanisms of language acquisition: The 20th Annual Carnegie Symposium on Cognition* (pp. 1–34). Hillsdale, NJ: Erlbaum.

Frege, G. (1892). Über Sinn und Bedeutung. *Zeitschrift für Philosophie und Philosophische Kritik, 100,* 25–50.

Gelman, S. A., and Taylor, M. (1984). How two-year-old children interpret proper and common names for unfamiliar objects. *Child Development, 55,* 1535–1540.

Gordon, P. (1985). Evaluating the semantic categories hypothesis: The case of the count-mass distinction. *Cognition, 20,* 209–242.

Gupta, A. (1980). *The logic of common nouns.* New Haven, CT: Yale University Press.

Hall, D. G. (1991). Acquiring proper names for familiar and unfamiliar animate objects: Two-year-olds' word learning biases. *Child Development, 62,* 1442–1454.

Hall, D. G. (1993a). Basic-level individuals. *Cognition, 48,* 199–221.

Hall, D. G. (1993b). Constraints on the interpretation of proper names. In E. Clark (Ed.), *Proceedings of the Twenty-fifth Annual Child Language Research Forum* (pp. 118–126). New York: Cambridge University Press.

Hall, D. G. (1994a). How children learn common nouns and proper names. In J. Macnamara and G. Reyes (Eds.), *The logical foundations of cognition* (pp. 212–240). Oxford: Oxford University Press.

Hall, D. G. (1994b). How mothers teach basic-level and situation-restricted count nouns. *Journal of Child Language, 21,* 391–414.

Hall, D. G. (1994c). Semantic constraints on word learning: Proper names and adjectives. *Child Development, 65,* 1291–1309.

Hall, D. G. (1996). Preschoolers' default assumptions about word meaning: Proper names designate unique individuals. *Developmental Psychology, 32,* 177–186.

Hall, D. G., and Graham, S. A. (in press). Lexical form class information guides word-to-object mapping in preschoolers. *Child Development.*

Hall, D. G., and Moore, C. E. (1997). Red bluebirds and black greenflies: Preschoolers' understanding of the semantics of adjectives and count nouns. *Journal of Experimental Child Psychology 67,* 236–267.

Hall, D. G., Veltkamp, B., and Turkel, W. (1997). *Proper namable things.* Unpublished manuscript, Department of Psychology, University of British Columbia.

Hall, D. G., and Waxman, S. R. (1993). Assumptions about word meaning: Individuation and basic-level kinds. *Child Development, 64,* 1550–1570.

Hall, D. G., Waxman, S. R., and Hurwitz, W. M. (1993). How 2- and 4-year-old children interpret adjectives and count nouns. *Child Development, 64,* 1651–1664.

Hockett, C. (1966). The problem of universals in language. In J. Greenberg (Ed.), *Universals of language* (pp. 1–29). Cambridge, MA: MIT Press.

Katz, N., Baker, E., and Macnamara, J. (1974). What's in a name? A study of how children learn common and proper names. *Child Development, 45,* 469–473.

Kripke, S. (1980). *Naming and necessity*. Oxford: Blackwell.

Liittschwager, J., and Markman, E. (1993). *Young children's acquisition of proper versus common nouns*. Poster presented at the biennial meeting of the Society for Research in Child Development, New Orleans, LA.

Macnamara, J. (1982). *Names for things: A study of human learning*. Cambridge, MA: MIT Press.

Macnamara, J. (1986). *A border dispute: The place of logic in psychology*. Cambridge, MA: MIT Press.

Macnamara, J., and Reyes, G. E. (1994). Foundational issues in the learning of proper names, count nouns, and mass nouns. In J. Macnamara and G. E. Reyes (Eds.), *The logical foundations of cognition* (pp. 144–176). Oxford: Oxford University Press.

Markman, E. (1994). Constraints on word meaning in early language acquisition. *Lingua, 92*, 199–227.

Merriman, W. (1986). How children learn the reference of concrete nouns: A critique of current hypotheses. In S. A. Kuczaj and M. D. Barrett (Eds.), *The acquisition of word meaning* (pp. 1–38). New York: Springer-Verlag.

Nelson, K. (1973). Structure and strategy in learning to talk. *Monographs of the Society for Research in Child Development, 38*(1–2, Serial No. 149).

Pinker, S. (1984). *Language learnability and language development*. Cambridge, MA: Harvard University Press.

Pinker, S. (1994). *The language instinct*. New York: Morrow.

Russell, B. (1905). On denoting. *Mind, 14*, 479–493.

Searle, J. (1958). Proper names. *Mind, 67*, 161–173.

Sorrentino, C. (1997). *The role of mental state attribution on young children's interpretation of proper nouns*. Poster presented at the biennial meeting of the Society for Research in Child Development, Washington, DC.

Taylor, M., and Gelman, S. (1988). Adjectives and nouns: Children's strategies for learning new words. *Child Development, 59*, 411–419.

Valentine, T., Brennen, T., and Brédart, S. (1996). *The cognitive psychology of proper names*. New York: Routledge.

Wiggins, D. (1980). *Sameness and substance*. Cambridge, MA: Harvard University Press.

Woodward, A., and Markman, E. (in press). Early word learning. In W. Damon, D. Kuhn, and R. Siegler (Eds.), *Handbook of child psychology: Vol. 2. Cognition, perception, and language*. New York: Wiley.

Chapter 15

The Learning of First and Second Person Pronouns in English

Yuriko Oshima-Takane

When I came to McGill as a graduate student, John was writing his book *Names for Things*. John told me to read a draft of his chapter on pronouns *I* and *you* for my first presentation in his graduate seminar. Since then, I have been fascinated by the problem of indexicals, particularly personal pronouns. I decided to pursue the problem of how children learn English personal pronouns as my Ph.D. research. John gently guided me on how to analyze the problem and showed me the complexities of the problem that children must solve. Understanding the mind of children solving such a complex problem is most interesting and challenging. I am deeply grateful to John for opening my eyes to such an exciting area of study and for sending me off on an endless but fascinating inquiry of true understanding. This chapter is about what I have learned about children's learning of personal pronouns since I began my investigation with John. The basic theoretical framework presented here was developed as part of my Ph.D. research and has been the guide for empirical studies I have carried out since then. John helped me greatly with the philosophical literature and deepened my understanding of reference and meaning.

I begin in section 15.1 by describing the problems that confront children in learning first and second person pronouns in English, grammatically as well as semantically. Then I analyze the semantic aspects of personal pronouns based on Kaplan's theory of indexicals. In section 15.2, using Kaplan's theory as a foundation, I propose a psychological theory

Preparation of this chapter was supported by a grant from the Natural Sciences and Engineering Research Council of Canada. I thank Ray Jackendoff, Paul Bloom, Thomas Shultz, David Alexandre Nicolas, Dean Sharpe, Marina Takane, and Hiroko Nakano for very helpful comments on earlier drafts.

of how children learn the correct semantic rules from observation and of what kind of competence the task of learning pronouns presupposes on the part of children. In section 15.3, I contrast my proposal with others that have been made in the psycholinguistic literature and discuss why none of the latter are satisfactory. In sections 15.4 and 15.5, I present evidence in support of my theoretical analysis. Finally, in section 15.6, I briefly discuss what my investigation into the learning of personal pronouns tells us about early word learning in children.

15.1   What Has to Be Learned

Every language has a group of words called *indexicals*, whose interpretation depends on the context of utterance. Personal pronouns are one type of indexical: the actual person referred to by a personal pronoun changes with the conversational role (i.e., speaker, addressee, or nonparticipants in a conversation). This change poses a problem for children who are learning such pronouns. Another problem is that the model for the correct use of these pronouns is not directly given in speech addressed to the children. When a mother speaks to her child—say, Mary—she says *you* to refer to Mary and *I* to refer to herself. However, when Mary speaks, she must reverse the pronouns; she must say *I* to refer to herself and *you* to refer to her mother. The child must be able to understand that the person referred to by these pronouns depends on who is speaking and who is being spoken to. In fact, it is commonly observed that autistic children fail to make this reversal and that blind children are often delayed in acquiring personal pronouns, whereas normally developing children usually master the correct use of personal pronouns by age 3 (Andersen, Dunlea, and Kekelis 1984; Charney 1980a; Clark 1978). This chapter investigates how normally developing children come to understand the meaning of first and second person pronouns so early.

Proper names or count nouns as well as personal pronouns can be used to refer to individuals (Macnamara 1982, 1986). For example, a particular person can be referred to by the proper name *David*, the definite description *the man on the corner*, the function expression *father of Tom*, and personal pronouns such as *I*, *you*, or *he*. These different expressions all refer to the same individual, yet they are distinct semantically as well as grammatically. In this section, I will specify the competence that anyone must have in order to use personal pronouns.

15.1.1 Grammatical Aspects

The third person pronouns substitute for noun phrases or proper names, not for nouns (Lyons 1983; Macnamara 1982). First and second person pronouns, however, do not seem to substitute for noun phrases or proper names (Lyons 1980). English speakers normally use pronouns to refer to a person in the role of speaker or addressee, although the use of proper names or kinship terms is commonly observed in child-directed talk (Wills 1977; Durkin, Rutter, and Tucker 1982; Durkin et al. 1982; Oshima-Takane 1993; Oshima-Takane and Derat 1996). Unlike count nouns, pronouns do not normally take determiners (i.e., *a*, *the*), quantifiers (i.e., *some*, *many*, etc.), or adjectives. Personal pronouns have case distinctions such as *I*, *me*, and *my*, whereas neither count nouns nor proper names do. These grammatical differences may draw children's attention to the semantic differences between personal pronouns and proper names or count nouns when they learn personal pronouns (Bloom 1990; Katz, Baker, and Macnamara 1974).

15.1.2 Semantic Aspects

In order to understand the semantic aspects of the personal pronouns, let us begin by comparing the following two pairs of sentences:

Mother   Mommy is reading a book.
Child   Mommy is reading a book.

Mother   I am reading a book.
Child   I am reading a book.

The sentence "Mommy is reading a book" expresses the same proposition whether the mother or the child utters it. In order to judge whether the proposition expressed by this sentence is true or false, we only need to know whether or not the mother is reading a book when the sentence is uttered. On the other hand, the sentence "I am reading a book" expresses different propositions depending on whether the mother or the child utters it. Thus, in order to judge whether the proposition expressed by the sentence "I am reading a book" is true or false, we should know not only who is reading a book when the sentence is uttered but also who utters the sentence. This does not deny that the sentence "I am reading a book" has a fixed meaning. The sentence has the same meaning whether the mother or the child utters it, just as the sentence "Mommy is reading a book" does. But the proposition expressed by the sentence changes depending on whether the mother or the child utters it.

In order to adequately capture such characteristics of a sentence containing indexicals, Kaplan (1977, 1978, 1989) distinguishes two functions: content and character. The *content* is what is expressed by an expression in a particular context of use, whereas the *character* of the expression is a semantic rule that is used to determine the content of the expression in any given context of use. If you say, "I am eating lunch," and I say the same, the content is different, since in saying that sentence you are describing what you are doing, whereas I am describing what I am doing. If I wish to express the same content as you, I must say, "You are eating lunch" (when talking to you) or "He/She is eating lunch" (when talking to someone else).

By contrast, the character of an expression does not change with the context of use. Rather, it is used to determine the content in any given context of use. The character of *I*, for example, tells us that the content of *I* used by you is you (referent) and the content of *I* used by me is me (referent). It tells us that the word *I* refers to the person who uses it, whoever uses it. The character is set by linguistic convention and is shared by competent speakers of a linguistic community. The character comes close to what we normally express by the word *meaning*.

If the expression is an assertive sentence such as "I am reading a book" or "Mommy is reading a book," the content is a proposition. In Kaplan's framework, the process of understanding an assertive sentence used by someone and of judging whether it is true or false may be viewed as follows: To determine the content of an expression, we use knowledge about the character of the expression and knowledge about the context where the expression is used. We then use knowledge about the content thus picked out in order to judge whether the content of the expression is true or false.

Thus, when we hear the utterance "I am reading a book," if we know who utters it and we also know the character of *I*, we can determine the content of *I*: the content of *I* used by the mother is the mother and the content of *I* used by the child is the child. By contrast, the content of *Mommy* in the utterance "Mommy is reading a book" does not change whether the mother or the child utters it. However, this does not mean that the content of *Mommy* is context-free. If the boy next door says the same sentence, the content of *Mommy* would probably be his mother. In order to determine the content of *Mommy* on a particular occasion, we use knowledge about the context as well as knowledge about the character. The same thing is true of a proper name and of a count noun phrase like *the girl*. When we hear the utterance "Mary is coming soon," the character of the proper name *Mary* tells us that it refers to the individual named *Mary*, whoever utters it. The content of the proper name *Mary* must be the same individual at all times and in all places in which the individual exists and in all circumstances in which the individual might possibly exist. In this sense, a proper name is a rigid designator (Kripke 1980).[1] However, there is more than one Mary in the world and the character of the proper name is not sufficient to determine the content on a particular occasion. Knowledge of the context is also necessary. Count noun phrases like *the girl* or *the dog running over there* are called *definite descriptions*, and we use them to refer to a particular object of which the description is true. In order to determine the content of a definite description in a particular context of use, again knowledge of the context is necessary unless there is only one object in the world that fits the description. Hence, proper names and definite descriptions as well as personal pronouns are all dependent on the context of use. However, the way personal pronouns depend on the context is systematically different from the way proper names or definite descriptions do.

In order to capture such differences, we should break the context further into three features, following Barwise and Perry (1983). These features of the context, which are used in different ways in getting from the character of an expression to its content on a particular occasion of use, are *discourse situation, connections,* and *resource situations.*

A *discourse situation* is a situation in which an utterance occurs; "it involves who is speaking, when, and where, what words are being uttered, and to whom" (Barwise and Perry 1983, 121). If the mother says to her child, "I am reading a book," the utterance ("I am reading a book"), the speaker (the mother), the addressee (the child), the time of the utterance, and the location of the utterance are the elements of discourse situation. The role of the facts of discourse situations in fixing the content is usually referred to as *indexicality*, and the content of any indexical must be among the elements of the discourse situation.[2] Particular elements in the discourse situation that are of crucial relevance to the first and second person pronouns are the speaker and the addressee. On the other hand, the contents of proper names or definite descriptions are not necessarily among the elements of the discourse situation and do not change so systematically with the discourse situation. In order to determine the content of proper names or the contents of definite descriptions, we use the speaker's connections and resource situations.

We are related to various things in the world. For example, there are many Marys and many dogs in the world, but we know only some of the Marys and some of the dogs. In other words, we have connections to certain Marys and certain dogs in the world. When we use the proper name *Mary* or the definite description *the dog*, we refer to a particular Mary among the Marys we know (or perceive) or we refer to a particular dog among the dogs we know (or perceive). Connections that link an utterance to its content on a particular occasion of use are called the *speaker's connections* in the utterance. The addressee must find out these connections to get from the character of the utterance to its content on a particular occasion of use, and the speaker must believe that the addressee can recover them. For example, if a child says, "Mommy is reading a book," the mother would think that her child refers to her by *Mommy*, whereas if the boy next door says the same sentence, she would think that he refers to his mother, not to her. To determine the content of *Mommy* used by her child, therefore, the mother uses her child's connections, whereas to determine the content of *Mommy* used by the boy next door, she uses the boy's connections. The character of an expression simply gives us a general rule to refer to things to which we and other people are connected.

Although there are many different expressions that refer to the same thing, not all of them are available to the speaker and the addressee all the time. For example, when I tell a friend something about Mary, I can refer to her by her name, *Mary*. But if I cannot remember her name or if my friend does not know Mary, I cannot use *Mary* to refer to her. However, if my friend and I see Mary standing at the door, I can use the description *the girl standing at the door* to refer to Mary. In this case, I am using the fact that Mary is standing at the door to refer to Mary. This fact about Mary is called a *resource situation* that allows me to use the description *the girl standing at the door* as referring to Mary, and my own and my friend's perceptual connections to this resource situation allow me to successfully refer to Mary by that description. However, if I am talking to my friend over the telephone and my friend cannot see Mary standing at the door, I have to use different resources to refer to Mary. For example, if my friend knows Mary's father, Mr. Clark, I may use the description *Mr. Clark's daughter* to refer to Mary. Here I use the fact that Mary's father is Mr. Clark as a resource situation, and my connections to this resource situation and my friend's connection to Mr. Clark allow me to successfully refer to Mary by this description.

To summarize: Proper names and definite descriptions as well as personal pronouns all depend on the context of use, and all have their own character that is used to determine their content in each context of use. In order to determine the content of a personal pronoun, we use knowledge about a particular feature of the context, the discourse situation, whereas in order to determine the content of a proper name or a definite description, we use knowledge about other features of the context, connections and resource situations. Unlike the content of personal pronouns, the content of proper names and definite descriptions need not be present in the discourse situation, although it has been reported that when talking to a child, parents most often talk about things to which the child is perceptually connected (Macnamara 1972, 1982).

What does all this tell us about what has to be learned when a child learns the singular first and second person pronouns? It tells us that the child has to learn at least two things: (1) the character of each pronoun (i.e., the semantic rule that is used to determine the content of the pronoun on each occasion of use), and (2) the elements of discourse situations that are relevant to pronouns. The characters of the singular first and second person pronouns are given by the following rules (Barwise and Perry 1983; Kaplan 1977):

(I)   A first person pronoun, in each utterance, refers to the person who uses it.

(II) A second person pronoun, in each utterance, refers to the person who is addressed when it is used.

The elements of the discourse situation relevant to the first and the second person pronouns are the speaker and the addressee, respectively.

15.2   Learning: A Proposal for a Psychological Theory

Children learn most of their words from hearing other people using them in the course of normal conversation. The personal pronouns are no exception. Many normally developing children master the first and second person pronouns with few errors by the age of 3, without explicit teaching (Clark 1978; Macnamara 1982, 1986; Oshima-Takane 1985, 1988; Shipley and Shipley 1969; Strayer 1977). This suggests that children learn the meaning of personal pronouns from hearing the pronouns used in the speech of others. Following Kaplan's analysis of indexicals, I assume that each personal pronoun has a fixed meaning (character), but the referent (content) of the pronoun shifts depending on the context of use, that is, who is speaking and who is spoken to. Starting from this premise, I have proposed that the child's task of learning personal pronouns consists of the following two parts (Oshima-Takane 1985): (1) to correctly determine the content of pronouns used by others in each instance of use (i.e., to comprehend pronouns correctly), and (2) to induce the correct semantic rules—character—that would lead to the correct production of pronouns as well as correct comprehension. In this section, I will analyze what abilities each presupposes on the part of the child and propose a psychological theory of how children learn first and second person pronouns.

15.2.1 Determining the Content of Personal Pronouns

In order to determine the content of a personal pronoun used by others in a particular context, a competent speaker can use knowledge about its semantic rule as well as knowledge about the context of use. However, the child learning the personal pronouns does not know the semantic rules. In fact, this is precisely what the child has to learn. Therefore, the child must use other means to determine the content of a pronoun used by others. What abilities, then, does this task presuppose on the part of the child? In order to determine the content of a pronoun in each instance of use, the child must be able (1) to identify the pronoun forms in each utterance, and (2) to understand that the pronoun used by someone refers to a particular person in the discourse situation. Let us analyze these requirements more closely.

15.2.1.1 Identifying the Pronouns In order to identity the pronoun forms in the utterance, the child must somehow be able to segment the speech stream into words. Although there is evidence suggesting that children learning language are able to use prosodic cues to identify word boundaries (e.g., Wijnen, Krikhaar, and Den Os 1994), studies of parental speech to young children have shown that parents greatly help young children to segment the speech stream into words or phrases by singling out and repeating individual words or phrases (Snow 1976). Parents often isolate a proper name or a common noun and repeat it several times when they want their child to say it (Macnamara 1982). Vocative uses of proper names probably also help children to identify the proper names in utterances. English personal pronouns, however, are unlikely to be singled out in this way, and the child may have to segment out the pronoun forms embedded in utterances. Developmental psycholinguists have pointed out that some of the earliest uses of pronouns by children are part of a set phrase such as "I do it," and pronouns are not differentiated from other words in utterances (Charney 1980b; Clark 1978).

Although children may not segment out the pronoun forms in the utterances from the beginning, they must do so at a certain point in order to figure out the character of the pronouns. The data reported in the literature show that before beginning to use any personal pronouns, all normally developing children correctly use some nonpronominal terms for others such as *Mommy, Daddy, Jamie,* and some count nouns such as *doggie, car, ball* (Macnamara 1982; Nelson 1973). Further, some children correctly use their own names and even use two-word sentences like "Mommy sit" or "More milk." These data suggest that personal pronouns are not the first words they learn. It is possible, then, that they can use their knowledge of the words they have already acquired to segment out the personal pronoun forms. Interchangeable uses of proper names and pronouns by parents (e.g., "That's you. That's David") may also help a child identify the pronoun forms in utterances (Macnamara 1982, 1986; Oshima-Takane 1985; Strayer 1977).

There is abundant evidence that children use kinship terms such as *Mommy* and *Daddy* and some proper names for others before using any personal pronouns (Nelson 1973; Oshima-Takane 1985; Seki 1992; Smiley and Huttenlocher 1995). However, most children start to use their own names at about the same time they start to use a personal pronoun to refer to themselves. Some children call themselves by their own names before they start to use any personal pronouns; other children use personal pronouns to refer to themselves before they start to use their own names (Macnamara 1982; McNeill 1963; Oshima-Takane 1985; Schiff-Myers 1983; Strayer 1977). Comprehension and production data on proper names and personal pronouns that I collected for my Ph.D. research indicated that most of the children who used personal pronouns in reference to themselves but did not yet use their own names responded to their own names correctly in comprehension tests (Oshima-Takane 1985). Further, studies with Japanese children provide some evidence suggesting that children understand their own names correctly before they begin to use their names or any pronouns designating themselves. Uemura (1979), who observed 19 Japanese children from 1 month to 20 months of age in experimental as well as natural settings, reported that they understood their names used by others about two months before they started to use their names themselves. For example, from 15 months on, one child began responding differently to hearing her own name and others' names. Before 15 months, she said "Yes" or smiled when she heard others' names as well as her name. Starting at 15 months, she said "Yes" only when she heard her own name. At 18 months, she started to use her name, and at 19 months, she started to point to herself when she was called by her name. More recently, Seki (1992) found that about half of the 12- to 17-month-old children that she studied responded only to their own names when their caregiver at the daycare center called children's names, but only when their caregiver looked at them while calling the names. More than 80% of the children aged between 18 and 23 months did so even when their caregiver did not look at them while calling the names. Parent report data in a separate study by Seki indicated that 96% of the children between 18 and 23 months called themselves by their own names but none of them used first person pronouns to designate themselves.

Since many English-speaking children begin using personal pronouns at around 20 months, the data from Japanese children together with my English data suggest that children know their own name as well as others' names before they begin to use any personal pronouns and may use their knowledge about proper names to identify the pronoun forms in utterances.

15.2.1.2   Understanding That a Personal Pronoun Refers to a Person   In order to understand that a personal pronoun in an utterance refers to a particular person, the child must have understood what a personal pronoun designates when it is used, and, in particular, that what is designated by the pronoun is a person, since it is only persons who can talk and take speech roles.[3] This does not, however, mean that the child has the notion of referring or the notion of reference—the relation between words and objects to which they refer (Macnamara 1982, 1986). When they hear someone using a word, children must understand the speaker's intention and identify an object the word refers to (Macnamara 1982, 1986). Recent evidence shows that young children actively search for non-linguistic cues to the speaker's intention and use them to infer what the speaker intends to indicate with the utterance (Akhtar and Tomasello 1996; Baldwin 1991; Tomasello 1995). Further, parents often give young children nonlinguistic cues to their intention. For instance, parents often show their child an object they are referring to by holding or pointing to it (Clark 1978; Macnamara 1977, 1982). Although this practice helps the child to identify what parents are referring to, parents rarely point to people when they use personal pronouns (Wales 1979).

How, then, do children come to identify a person referred to by a pronoun? Macnamara (1986) argues that to identify the referent of a personal pronoun, the child must have access to the basic-level kind PERSON. Kinds supply a principle of individuation, a principle of identity, and a principle of application for what they are true of. In the case of the kind PERSON, the principle of individuation specifies what counts as an individual person. The principle of identity provides the criteria for deciding whether individuals considered at different points in time are the same person or different persons. The principle of application picks out an individual person from all other things that are not a person. Macnamara emphasizes that access to the kind PERSON is particularly important because it is a person that is the referent of a personal pronoun, not just a person's face, nose, or visible surface. The ability to recognize an individual as a member of the kind PERSON is presupposed.

Application of the kind PERSON to an individual presupposes that the child is able to pick out a person from all other animate and inanimate objects and to assign the person as a member of the kind. Thus, having access to the kind PERSON helps the child figure out that a pronoun picks out a person. In fact, if the child were not able to recognize a person as distinct from all other animate and inanimate objects, the child would never be able to correctly determine what a personal pronoun refers to. Recent evidence suggests that children can make global kind distinctions (e.g., animal/artifact, vehicle/animal) and basic-level kind distinctions (e.g., bottle/ball, cup/book) before they talk (Mandler, Bauer, and McDonough 1991; Xu and Carey 1996). But how do children know that, when they hear a pronoun used by others, it refers to an entire person, not a body part such as a nose or an object other than a person such as a chair? This is what children must discover by observing how other people use pronouns. As just noted, children are sensitive to the speaker's intention and actively search for cues to understanding what the speaker is expressing with an utterance. Linguistic and nonlinguistic contexts in which the pronouns are used may help them discover the referents. Further, parents' interchangeable use of personal pronouns and proper names should help them discover that a pronoun refers to a person, not a body part or an object other than a person (Macnamara 1986; Oshima-Takane 1985). For example, if a child already knows the word *Mommy* to refer to his mother, who is a member of the kind PERSON, and if the child hears his mother saying, "Give it to me. Give it to Mommy (while extending her hand toward the child)," the child will be more likely to take *me* as referring to his mother, rather than referring to a body part such as her hand.

15.2.2   Inducing the Correct Semantic Rules

In order to induce the correct semantic rules, children must not only determine the referent of the pronouns used by others but also discover the relationship between the pronoun and the speech role of the person it designates. As noted, parents often use personal pronouns and proper names interchangeably when they talk to their child, and this practice may help the child understand what pronouns refer to. However, this practice does not necessarily help the child figure out the correct use of the pronouns. This is because when children use pronouns, they must reverse what they hear. Even if a child correctly determines the content of the pronouns used by others, several generalizations about the semantic rules for pronouns are logically possible. Children may think that first person pronouns are used to refer to another person with whom they talk, or that first person pronouns are used to refer to others who are speaking but cannot be used to refer to themselves even when they are speaking, or that first and second person pronouns refer to either participant in a conversation (i.e., the speaker or the addressee) or indeed to anybody. Children must discover the correct relationships between the pronouns and the speech roles from such variously interpretable data and induce the semantic rules.

What abilities does this task presuppose on the part of the child? Obviously, the child must be able to identify at least two elements of the discourse situation: who the speaker is and who the addressee is. This presupposes that the child is able to distinguish speaker from addressee and also able to distinguish participants from nonparticipants in a conversation. There is little evidence about when children come to identify speaker, addressee, and nonaddressee as such. Several developmental psycholinguists claim that children first distinguish the speaker from others, and then distinguish the addressee from nonaddressees (Brener 1983; Strayer 1977). However, this order of differentiation of speech roles is based on the observation that children initially come to use first person pronouns correctly, then second person pronouns, and finally third person pronouns. Thus, it is not clear *when* such differentiations occur. To determine whether children identify the speaker, the addressee, and the nonaddressee before they learn personal pronouns, an approach will be needed that directly examines their knowledge of speech roles.

In a series of experiments that examined children's interpretation of nonlinguistic signs as a clue to the speaker's intention, Macnamara (1977) showed that children between 14 and 20 months of age were more responsive and gave more correct responses to instructions when the tester was looking at them than when the tester was looking at their mother, whereas children between 11 and 14 months of age did not show such a differentiation. Since the tester did not give instructions until the child returned his or her look or the child looked at the mother, inattentiveness does not seem to explain the differences. Rather, the data suggest that 14- to 20-month-old children can interpret the speaker's eye contact with them as a sign that the speaker is talking to them. This, in turn, suggests that children can identify who the speaker is since they cannot use the speaker's eye contact as a sign without knowing who the speaker is.

Children begin to use personal pronouns between the ages of 18 and 24 months (Charney 1980b; Clark 1978; Macnamara 1982; Oshima-Takane 1985). The above results suggest that children about to learn personal pronouns have some knowledge about speech roles. Although 14- to 20-month-old children may not be able to use the speaker's eye contact as a cue in determining the addressee when they are not addressed, they can at least use the speaker's eye contact to determine whether they are being addressed or not. That is, the children can at least identify another person as speaker, themselves as addressee, and themselves as nonaddressee.

Whether children can induce the correct semantic rules for first and second person pronouns depends on whether the input they receive includes the following situations: ones in which they can recognize that the same pronoun used in different discourse situations refers to different persons, and ones in which they can recognize that different pronouns refer to the same person. The first type of situation is particularly important for distinguishing personal pronouns from proper names. This is because children can avoid interpreting a pronoun as a proper name (e.g., *you* as another name for the child) if they recognize that the referent of the pronoun is not limited to a specific individual. The second type of situation plays an important part in learning the distinctive meanings of different pronouns (i.e., first, second, and third person pronouns). Overheard speech is an input that is necessary for inducing the correct semantic rules of first and second person pronouns because it often provides children with these two situations, whereas child-directed speech does not

(Oshima-Takane 1985, 1988, 1992). For instance, in overheard speech children often have an opportunity to hear the pronoun *you* referring to a person other than themselves, and to hear different pronouns, *me* and *you*, referring to the same person. Furthermore, children can witness that the referent of *me* and *you* shifts systematically depending on who is speaking and who is addressed. In child-directed speech, on the other hand, they observe that *you* is always used to refer to themselves and *me* is always used to refer to the person talking to them. Thus, children who do not have enough opportunities to hear pronouns in overheard speech or fail to notice them are likely to make incorrect generalizations about the meaning of pronouns and to show errors in using them.

To recognize that the same pronoun used on different occasions refers to the same person and that different pronouns used on different occasions refer to the same person presupposes that children can trace their own identity and that of others over time. In fact, such identity is implicated in the use of many referring expressions, including personal pronouns (Gupta 1980; Hall 1994; Hall and Waxman 1993; La Palme Reyes, Macnamara, and Reyes 1994; Macnamara 1986; Macnamara and Reyes 1994; Oshima-Takane 1985). Suppose a child hears her mother saying *you* to refer to her on one occasion and her father saying *you* to refer to her on another occasion. In order to understand that the mother's use of *you* and the father's use of *you* both refer to the same person (the child), the child must be able to identify herself as herself over time. Similarly, in order to understand that the mother's use of *me* and the father's use of *you* both refer to the same person (the mother), the child must be able to identify the mother as the same person over time. This does not mean, however, that mistakes cannot happen, as when an adult or a child fails to identify a person when the person looks like someone else or the person's appearance has changed dramatically.

Macnamara (1986) argues that as in the case of proper names (for persons), access to the kind PERSON is necessary for learning personal pronouns, since it not only helps the learner understand that the referent of a personal pronoun is a whole person but also helps the learner handle the identity of the person over time. This means that when children learn personal pronouns or proper names, the kind PERSON must be available to them and can be used to trace the identity of members of that kind. It is likely that this knowledge is implicit in children who are learning pronouns; that is, they can recognize an individual as a member of the kind PERSON but do not know the count noun *person*. Macnamara noted that his son, Kieran, did not use the count noun *person*, which denotes the kind PERSON, until long after he used many proper names for persons and personal pronouns (Macnamara 1986). Consistent with this observation, examinations of children's early vocabularies indicate that the count noun *person* is not among the first 50 words (Nelson 1973; Oshima-Takane 1985). It is possible that children correctly interpret *person* used by others even though they do not produce it, although, as far as I am aware, no systematic investigation has attempted to determine when children come to understand this word. In any event, we have some evidence indicating that children correctly use others' names and also correctly understand or use their own names before they start to use any personal pronouns. Because children cannot understand or use others' names and their own names without identifying the persons named over time, the proper name data suggest that children can trace both their own identity and other people's by the time they start to use personal pronouns.

Some researchers (see, e.g., Smiley and Huttenlocher 1995) have suggested that children may initially fail to include themselves in the kind PERSON because they have limited access to "physical appearance of the whole self (except in the mirror)" (p. 41). This is certainly possible, but physical appearance is not the only information children use when categorizing objects into different kinds (Baldwin, Markman, and Melartin 1993; Xu and Carey 1996). Perhaps children categorize themselves in the same kind as their parents but not in the same kind as dogs and cats because they notice that they behave like their parents but unlike dogs and cats. The point is that children must be able to recognize themselves as members of the kind PERSON by the time they master personal pronouns, even though they may initially fail to do so. As Macnamara (1986) has argued, unless children know that they are also persons, it will be difficult for them to realize that they can use first person pronouns to refer to themselves.

15.2.3 Summary
The above analysis shows that the learning of first and second person pronouns presupposes that children have the following abilities:

• To identify the speaker, the addressee, and the nonaddressee in a discourse situation;
• To understand the speaker's intention;

- To segment out the pronoun forms in the utterance;
- To access the kind PERSON.

Although it is not known exactly when and how each prerequisite becomes available to children, the above analysis suggests that at least some of them are available from the time children begin to learn pronouns; thus, they can use them in determining the referents of pronouns and in inducing the semantic rules. All four prerequisites are necessary to determine the referent of a pronoun used by others; the first is particularly necessary to discover the relations between pronouns and speech roles. Of course, these prerequisites are necessary but not sufficient for correctly determining the content of a pronoun used by others and for inducing the correct semantic rules. They may help children reduce the number of logically possible hypotheses, but they do not tell them which one is correct.

15.3   Comparing the Present Proposal with Other Theories

The crucial requirement for understanding and using first and second person pronouns—what one needs beyond what is needed for dealing with other referring expressions such as proper names and definite descriptions—is noticing the regularities in their shifting referents. I have proposed that overheard speech provides situations important for discovering the systematic relationships between pronouns and speech roles (Oshima-Takane 1985, 1988). This proposal has challenged a prevailing view in the Western literature on child language, because it attributes to children the ability of analyzing overheard speech. Much of Western child language research has emphasized the importance of specially adapted speech that mothers use in child-directed talk. Overheard speech is not considered an important source of input from which children learn language, because utterances not addressed to children are generally longer and more complex than those addressed to them (see Oshima-Takane, Goodz, and Derevensky 1996 for more detailed discussion on this issue). My argument is this: If we assume that, without explicit teaching, children are able to understand that the same personal pronouns (in particular, second person pronouns) can be used to refer to different persons, and that different personal pronouns (i.e., first person and second person pronouns) can be used to refer to the same person, then we must also assume that children are able to analyze overheard speech (nonaddressed speech) as well as child-directed speech (addressed speech). If children do not attend to nonaddressed speech, as the prevailing view suggests, then we must assume that children are "biased" to make such generalizations solely on the basis of addressed speech (Oshima-Takane 1985, 1988).

My proposal about how children learn English first and second person pronouns differs from previous proposals in several important ways. In this section, I will contrast my proposal with others in the psycholinguistic literature (Charney 1980a,b; Chiat 1981, 1986; Clark 1978; Oshima-Takane 1985, 1988, 1992; Schiff-Myers 1983; Shipley and Shipley 1969; Strayer 1977) and discuss why none of the latter are satisfactory.

Interesting variations are observed in pronoun acquisition: most normally developing children acquire first and second person pronouns with few production errors, whereas a few persistently make such errors. Indeed, previous theories have focused either on children's pronominal errors or on their lack of pronominal errors. Clark (1978) has noted that there are two different routes for acquiring first and second person pronouns. One is that children learn these pronouns relative to the speech roles from the outset, and they therefore make few production errors. The other is that children initially entertain a proper name interpretation such as *you* = child and *me* = adult, and they therefore make persistent pronominal errors. However, Clark does not explain why some children make persistent errors, whereas many children do not. My proposal explains the observed variations using the same mechanism. Children who attend to shifting reference of personal pronouns in overheard speech would discover the relationship between pronouns and speech roles and would acquire the pronouns with few production errors. Children who do not have enough opportunities to hear overheard speech would not discover the relationship between the pronouns and speech roles and would be more likely to entertain the incorrect, reversed semantic rules; as a result, they would make persistent pronominal errors (Oshima-Takane 1985, 1988).

None of the existing theories has seriously considered the distinction between referent (content) and meaning (character). Consequently, they have failed to recognize the importance of the kind PERSON in learning personal pronouns. Most theories assume that children make few pronominal errors because they map a personal pronoun directly onto a speech role rather than onto the person taking the particular speech role. For instance, Shipley and Shipley (1969) argue that most children make few errors in production because they immediately comprehend pronouns as being relative to the speaker and the addressee (p. 113). Chiat (1981)

states that "the relative infrequency of pronoun reversals ... suggests that
the concepts of speaker and addressee are so salient for most children that
they select these, rather than the particular individuals to which they refer,
as the content underlying 1st and 2nd person pronoun forms" (p. 85).
However, it would be dangerous to draw such a conclusion from studies
of spontaneous speech alone, as these authors have, because children
can avoid making pronominal errors in production by simply replacing
pronouns with proper names (Oshima-Takane and Oram 1991). Furthermore, these theories do not explain why some children do show pronominal errors. According to my proposal, these children are able to identify
the referent of the pronouns used in the addressee speech correctly but
induce the incorrect semantic rules.

Charney (1980b) proposes a somewhat different view of why many
children do not make pronominal errors, but her account suffers from a
more serious problem. She argues that many children make few pronominal errors because they do not learn pronouns as referring to a person.
Rather, they first learn pronouns relative to their own speech roles. That
is, children initially learn first person pronouns as referring to themselves
in the role of speaker and second person pronouns as referring to themselves in the role of addressee. Only later do children recognize that first
person pronouns refer to the speaker and that second person pronouns
refer to the addressee. In this way, Charney suggests, many children can
avoid pronominal errors without discovering the correct semantic rules.
Charney's proposal, then, assumes that children come to use first person
pronouns correctly without understanding these pronouns used by others.
This assumption is logically impossible, because, as Chiat (1981) also
points out, if children use first person pronouns correctly without errors,
they must know that first person pronouns can refer to others as well as
themselves. Children must be able to recognize that others use a first
person pronoun as referring to themselves before or no later than they
correctly use the same first person pronoun as referring to themselves.
However, Charney claims that her proposal is based on the observed
developmental discrepancy between comprehension and production
(Charney 1980b; Strayer 1977). That is, some children correctly use first
person pronouns to refer to themselves without understanding them when
used by others, whereas children understand second person pronouns
referring to themselves, though they do not use them. Careful examination of Charney's data suggests that the children classified as correctly
using first person pronouns without comprehending them failed the com-

prehension test, not because they understood first person pronouns as referring to themselves as speaker, but because they produced them as a part of rote phrases such as "I got it" in which *I* does not have any self-reference at all (Chiat 1981, 1986; Oshima-Takane 1985). A major problem with Charney's claim lies in the assumption that children do not comprehend personal pronouns simply because they do not pass controlled comprehension tests. The literature indicates that compared with spontaneous speech studies, such controlled comprehension studies tend to underestimate children's linguistic competence, and the age estimates for particular kinds of linguistic competence change according to procedures employed to test them (Brown 1973). Charney's proposal has ignored these difficulties with comprehension tests. There seem to be no empirical grounds for claiming that children can use a first person pronoun correctly without knowing that the same pronoun can refer to another person in the speech of others (see Oshima-Takane 1985, 1988 for more detailed discussions on this issue).

Finally, several investigators have suggested that for children to understand the shifting reference of first and second person pronouns, they must be able to take the speaker's point of view (Andersen, Dunlea, and Kekelis 1984; Charney 1980a; de Villiers and de Villiers 1974; Loveland 1984; Tager-Flusberg 1989). For instance, Loveland (1984) proposes that understanding spatial viewpoints is a cognitive prerequisite to understanding the speaker's point of view, which, in turn, is a prerequisite to the correct use of personal pronouns. However, the evidence for a causal link between understanding of spatial viewpoints and acquisition of these pronouns is not conclusive (Girouard, Ricard, and Decarie 1995; Issler 1993; Loveland 1984; see Oshima-Takane, Takane, and Shultz 1996 for further discussion on this issue). Others, especially those focusing on autistic children's pronominal errors, take a similar view. For instance, Charney (1980a) and Tager-Flusberg (1989) attribute autistic children's difficulty in learning personal pronouns to their inability to take others' perspective. It should be noted that although pronominal errors are often observed in autistic children, some normally developing children also show persistent pronominal errors. Further, there is some evidence that at about 9 months of age, long before they begin to learn personal pronouns, normally developing children show behaviors suggesting that they can understand another's perspective (Baron-Cohen and Ring 1994; Tomasello 1995). Macnamara has remarked that "infants learn their language by first determining, independent of language, the meaning which a speaker intends to convey to them, and by then working out the relationship between the meaning and the language" (Macnamara 1972, 1; see also Macnamara 1982). In fact, unless children have the capacity to grasp the intention of other speakers, they cannot determine the referent of any words they hear (Akhtar and Tomasello 1996; Baldwin 1991). As discussed earlier, the major problems with first and second person pronouns are not only that the referent of the pronouns shifts with the speaker but also that the model for correct usage is not provided in speech addressed to children. Thus, even if children could correctly identify the person that a pronoun used by someone else referred to, they might be unable to produce the pronoun correctly. Understanding the speaker's intention is not sufficient for learning the semantic rules underlying the correct use of these pronouns. The present proposal stresses that observing shifting reference of the pronouns in overheard speech is necessary.

15.4   Empirical Evidence

In this section, I will present evidence in support of the proposal that children first determine the referent of a pronoun used by others and then induce the semantic rules. In particular, I will show that in learning personal pronouns, children do not map pronouns directly onto speech roles from the outset. Instead, they first determine the person a pronoun refers to in the speech of others and then make generalizations about the semantic rules. I will also present empirical findings in support of the claim that observing shifting reference of first and second person pronouns in overheard speech is necessary for inducing the correct semantic rules for these pronouns.

According to my analysis, children who do not have enough opportunities to observe shifting reference of personal pronouns in overheard speech should entertain a proper name interpretation at least for second person pronouns and use second person pronouns to refer to themselves. However, some researchers have questioned whether children who make pronominal errors in fact treat pronouns as proper names (Chiat 1981; Macnamara 1982). For instance, Chiat (1981) has argued that if children entertain a proper name interpretation, they should use a pronoun referring to a particular person consistently and therefore should make consistent pronominal errors. Nonetheless, the data reported in the literature suggest that their pronominal errors are inconsistent.

A major difficulty in determining whether children make pronominal errors because of an incorrect semantic representation such as a proper name interpretation is that normally developing children rarely make pronominal errors (Charney 1980b; Chiat 1981; Shipley and Shipley 1969). In fact, I might have reached a conclusion similar to Chiat's, had I not come across two normally developing children who went through periods of making consistent pronominal errors (Oshima-Takane 1985). One child was a boy named Donald. At the age of 18 months, he began using the second person pronoun *you* to refer to himself (e.g., "Daddy play with you") and the first person pronoun *me* to refer to his mother (e.g., "Give it to me"). His errors persisted for about 4 months. The other child, a boy named David, began making consistent errors with both first and second person pronouns at around 23 months. His errors persisted for about 10 months. Both children were firstborns, and each was the only child in his family. Their comprehension and production data indicated that they entertained a proper name interpretation for second person pronouns and used them interchangeably with their proper names in self-reference. For first person pronouns, evidence for the proper name interpretation was not as clear-cut as that for second person pronouns. For instance, David's comprehension data indicated that he initially interpreted first person pronouns to refer only to his mother; then to any other person; and then to any other person who was speaking. At the same time that David interpreted first person pronouns as referring only to his mother in the comprehension task, he was using them to refer to any person other than himself. The rapid shift from his initial misinterpretation of first person pronouns as referring to his mother to his later misinterpretation of first person pronouns as referring to any speaker other than himself and the fact that he held the latter misinterpretation for a longer period of time has led me to the following hypothesis: David initially assumed that first person pronouns referred only to his mother (i.e., proper name interpretation), probably because his mother was the person who used first person pronouns in self-reference most frequently when talking to him. He soon noticed other persons besides his mother using first person pronouns in self-reference, and began using first person pronouns to refer to them. However, it took him a long time to realize that first person pronouns could refer to any speaker including himself and that second person pronouns could refer to any addressee other than himself. All this suggests that David did not have any problem with determining the referent of first and second person pronouns in child-directed speech. His problem was that he had induced the incorrect semantic rules, which were based solely on the information provided in child-directed speech (see Oshima-Takane 1985, 1992 for more detailed discussions).

A subsequent longitudinal study of 10 girls (Oshima-Takane and Oram 1991) provides further evidence that children determine the referent of pronouns used by others before they learn the relationship between pronouns and speech roles. Children's comprehension and production data were collected at three different ages: 21, 24, and 30 months. Comprehension was tested both when the child was an addressed listener and when she was a nonaddressed listener. Spontaneous production data were collected by videotaping spontaneous speech in a 50-minute free play situation. Analyses of spontaneous language showed that children made few production errors in the course of acquisition. However, at the earlier stages (21 and 24 months), in nonaddressed listener trials half of the children exhibited systematic comprehension errors indicating that they thought that the pronoun *you* referred to themselves. No child showed systematic comprehension errors for *me*. These results suggest that even though children make few production errors, they do not necessarily understand the correct meaning of the pronouns. It appeared that children made few production errors because they did not use pronouns until they understood the correct meaning; they used proper names instead of pronouns. Since the children who showed systematic comprehension errors comprehended *you* correctly when they were addressed, they did not have any problem with determining the referent of *you* in speech addressed to them. Rather, they showed systematic errors because they induced the incorrect semantic rule based on child-directed speech only. These findings suggest that in learning personal pronouns, children do not immediately relate pronouns to speech roles from the outset. Rather, the data seem to support the proposal that children first determine the referents of pronouns used by others and then make generalizations about the meanings of the pronouns. Observational studies with hearing-impaired children and an experimental study with autistic children have also provided evidence supporting this proposal (Cole, Oshima-Takane, and Yaremko 1994; Oshima-Takane and Benaroya 1989; Oshima-Takane, Cole, and Yaremko 1993).

Now let us examine empirical evidence concerning another aspect of the present proposal, namely, that observing shifting reference of personal pronouns is necessary for inducing the correct semantic rules for first and second person pronouns. It was hypothesized that children induce the correct semantic rules by observing shifting reference of pronouns used in overheard speech, whereas they induce incorrect semantic rules by observing pronouns in child-directed speech. To test this hypothesis, I conducted a teaching experiment with 19-month-olds who were about to learn personal pronouns (Oshima-Takane 1985, 1988). In this experiment, I asked parents to play two pronoun games (the me-me game and the me-you game) with their child to model the pronouns *me* and *you* twice a week for six weeks under two different experimental conditions. In the addressee condition, the parents modeled the pronouns in turn while looking at the child. The mother pointed to herself and said *me*, or pointed to the child and said *you*. The father did the same thing, saying *me* when pointing to himself or saying *you* when pointing to the child. In the nonaddressee condition, the parents modeled the pronouns while looking at each other in half of the session and at the child in the other half. That is, while looking at the father, the mother said *me* while pointing to herself or said *you* while pointing to the father. The father then did the same thing. When the mother addressed the child, she looked at the child and said *me* while pointing to herself or said *you* while pointing to the child. In both conditions, the child was expected to imitate the parents' use of the pronouns and their pointing gestures. The results were consistent with my proposal. The nonaddressee condition facilitated the correct imitation pattern (i.e., without errors, the child said *me* while pointing to himself or herself and/or said *you* while pointing to the person he or she was looking at). The addressee condition, on the other hand, often led to the incorrect imitation pattern (i.e., at least once, the child said *me* while pointing to the person he or she was looking at and/or said *you* while pointing to himself or herself). However, only a few children imitated incorrectly all the time, and there was no significant condition effect. The most interesting finding was that not a single child in the addressee condition showed the correct imitation pattern; only children in the nonaddressee condition did. The finding suggests that in learning the correct meaning of personal pronouns, children need to observe pronouns occurring in overheard speech. Further, it suggests that even children under 2 years of age attend to and can extract information from speech addressed to another person.

A subsequent observational study has provided naturalistic evidence consistent with this experimental finding (Oshima-Takane, Goodz, and Derevensky 1996). The study demonstrated that secondborn children produced correct pronouns earlier than firstborns, even though the two groups of children did not differ on other language measures such as mean length of utterance and vocabulary size. Our argument is that secondborn children acquire the correct usage of pronouns earlier than firstborn children because they have relatively more opportunities to hear pronouns used in overheard speech, that is, in conversation between their parents and their older siblings. A correlational analysis of secondborn children's input and pronoun development (Oshima-Takane 1997) provides more direct evidence for the importance of overheard speech in pronoun acquisition. The more frequently the secondborns heard first person pronouns in overheard speech, the earlier they mastered the use of these pronouns. Furthermore, the fewer unconventional nominal references (e.g., use of *Mommy* or the older sibling's name instead of first and second person pronouns) the mothers or older siblings used in overheard speech, the earlier the child mastered the use of second person pronouns.

In sum, the evidence reviewed so far is consistent with the proposal that children first determine the referents of the pronouns used by others and then induce semantic rules. Experimental and observational studies provide converging evidence that, in inducing the correct semantic rules, children benefit from observing shifting reference of pronouns in overheard speech. Furthermore, observational studies have shown that some children make pronominal errors in production because they hold incorrect semantic representations, and these mirror the way first and second person pronouns are used in child-directed speech: *me* refers to any other person and *you* refers to themselves. Another important finding is that although a proper name interpretation for second person pronouns appears to be common among children at an earlier stage, many of them do not show production errors because they produce proper names instead when referring to themselves as speaker and to others as addressee. Nonetheless, the evidence that children induce the incorrect, reversed rules (i.e., *me* means any other person and *you* means themselves) by observing pronouns in child-directed speech is limited. This is because in the teaching experiment, there were more children in the addressee condition who showed an inconsistent error pattern than those who showed a consistent error pattern. Further, the number of children in the addressee condition who showed the consistent error pattern was not significantly greater than the number of children who showed this pattern in the non-addressee condition. One problem with the teaching experiment is that children who observed pronoun models in the addressee condition could observe the same pronouns used in overheard speech outside the experiment. Therefore, there is no guarantee that their imitative behaviors were based solely on the information provided in the addressee condition. Some of them might have been influenced by information provided in overheard speech and thus might have begun showing the correct imitative behavior, which would result in the inconsistent incorrect imitation pattern.

15.5 Computer Modeling

For ethical reasons, we cannot manipulate the linguistic input outside the teaching experiment in such a way that children in the addressee condition are not exposed to any overheard speech. Further, even though we analyze the children's task in order to specify the prior knowledge or abilities that they must have, we cannot directly test the effects of the hypothesized prior knowledge or abilities in empirical studies. Computer modeling may provide a way to complement such limitations associated with human empirical studies. One advantage of computer modeling is that we can test hypothetical learning mechanisms by setting up ideal environmental conditions that would be ethically impossible with human children. In this section, I present evidence obtained from computer modeling studies that I have been conducting with my collaborators (Oshima-Takane, Takane, and Shultz 1995, 1996; Shultz, Buckingham, and Oshima-Takane 1994). In these studies, we have concentrated on the second part of children's task in learning pronouns: how children induce the semantic rules of first and second person pronouns after determining the content of a pronoun in the speech of others. In particular, the studies were designed to obtain more clear-cut evidence that children induce the incorrect, reversed rules by observing pronouns used in addressed speech only, whereas they induce the correct rules by observing pronouns used in nonaddressed speech. In addition, we examined the role of knowing the kind PERSON in this induction process.

We used the cascade correlation (CC) learning algorithm (Fahlman and Lebiere 1990), with which networks can grow dynamically to adapt to more complicated problems. The algorithm starts with a network without hidden units. It first tries to improve its performance within a given network topology by adjusting the connection weights. When it can no longer improve its performance by merely adjusting the weights, it changes the network topology by adding a hidden unit that is good at detecting the current error. It then readjusts the connection weights going into the output units. This cycle is repeated until all output activations are within score-threshold of their targets for all training patterns. The topological changes in the network define distinct developmental stages in learning.

We used the CC learning algorithm because it can represent "rules" that connect inputs to outputs by learning regularities present in the training patterns. In the case of learning first and second person pronouns, the rules involve an interaction between two variables: the speech roles of the persons in the discourse situation and the intended referents of the pronouns, because the person referred to by a pronoun shifts depending on who is speaking or who is spoken to. The CC learning algorithm is particularly good at capturing interaction effects among input variables such as these without being told which interactions are important.

All modeling experiments described in this section involve two training phases to simulate how children learn to produce the two pronoun forms *me* and *you* by listening to other persons producing them. In phase I training, networks learn other-speaking patterns. In phase II training, networks learn child-speaking patterns that are added to phase I training patterns. Phase I training can be seen as the period during which children hear pronouns used by others but have not yet produced any pronouns, and phase II training as the period during which they not only hear the pronouns but also start producing them. The initial CC network used in our simulations had input units representing speaker, addressee, and referent, and output units representing the pronoun. In each training pattern (i.e., each instance of use), semantic cues (i.e., discourse as well as referent information) relevant to the pronoun produced were given: the speaker unit indicated who the speaker was, the addressee unit indicated who the addressee was, and the referent unit indicated who the speaker intended to refer to.

In the first set of simulations (Shultz, Buckingham, and Oshima-Takane 1994), networks learned other-speaking patterns with only the mother and the father using the pronouns in phase I training before they learned child-speaking patterns in phase II training, but information concerning the kind PERSON was not implemented as prior knowledge. We used binary distributed coding to represent mother (01), father (10), and child (11) as distinct individuals but not as members of the same kind. Two output units were used to code *me* ($+.5\ -.5$) and *you* ($-.5\ +.5$). We predicted that if the notion of the kind PERSON is not crucial for inducing the correct semantic rules, networks trained with addressee patterns (i.e., patterns in which the child was always addressed) during phase I training would learn the incorrect, reversed rules by the end of this training and would need phase II training to master the correct child-speaking patterns. By contrast, networks trained entirely with non-addressee patterns (i.e., patterns in which the child never was addressed) during phase I training would learn the correct rules and would produce the correct child-speaking patterns without phase II training. However, if the notion of the kind PERSON plays an important role in this induction process, as assumed in the present proposal, then even networks trained with nonaddressee patterns would not induce the fully correct semantic rules. They would need at least some phase II training to produce the correct child-speaking patterns. The results support the latter prediction. None of the networks trained with nonaddressee patterns in the first set of simulations could learn to produce the correct child-speaking patterns without requiring explicit error-correcting feedback (phase II training), although they corrected errors quickly. On the other hand, the networks trained with addressee patterns learned the incorrect, reversed rules and needed extensive phase II training to correct their errors.

The second set of simulations was designed to test whether adding prior knowledge of the kind PERSON, the information that the child (self) is a member of the same kind as mother and father (other), would facilitate the induction of the correct semantic rules without error-correcting feedback (Oshima-Takane, Takane, and Shultz 1995, 1996). We used analog coding to implement prior knowledge about PERSON. That is, the child was coded as 0, the mother was coded as $+2$, and the father was coded as -2. One output unit was used to code *me* $(+.5)$ and *you* $(-.5)$. The analog coding allows us to represent members and the class to which they belong by assigning a number to the members on the same unit.[4] Further, the distinction between self (child) and others can be derived from the regularities of pronoun use in the training patterns. With the previous binary distributed coding, on the other hand, the networks treat each person as a distinct object with no relation to other objects in the training patterns. In the second set of simulations, we also investigated whether experiencing many examples involving various persons was another important factor facilitating induction of the correct semantic rules. To do this, we added two other persons, coded as $+1$ and -1, respectively. We compared the conditions in which the networks heard only two other persons using pronouns (3-person conditions) with those in which they heard four other persons using pronouns (5-person conditions). Children learning personal pronouns normally hear persons other than parents using pronouns (e.g., older siblings, grandparents, baby-sitters) even though their parents' utterances are the major source of input they hear. Thus, we thought it reasonable to assume that overhearing pronouns used by more than two persons may help children to realize that a pronoun refers not only to a specific person who has interacted with them but also to any person, depending on that person's speech role.

As predicted, when prior knowledge about the kind PERSON was implemented with the analog coding, the CC networks were able to produce the correct child-speaking patterns without any error-correcting feedback if they heard pronouns used by a variety of speakers in non-addressed speech. The nonaddressee-trained networks in the 3-person conditions showed better generalizations than the addressee-trained networks. However, they needed some phase II training to master the child-speaking patterns. On the other hand, all of the nonaddressee-trained networks in the 5-person conditions showed perfect generalization to the child-speaking patterns without any error-correcting feedback, just like human children. Analysis of the knowledge representation of these networks indicated that generalization to untrained, other-speaking patterns was very good. By contrast, the networks trained with addressee patterns learned the incorrect, reversed rules and needed extensive phase II training to correct errors.

The child's natural language environment involves some mixture of addressed and nonaddressed speech. For instance, a firstborn child with no sibling may hear mostly addressed speech while one parent is away at work and some nonaddressed speech when that parent returns. A second-born child, on the other hand, may hear more nonaddressed speech (e.g., conversations between the at-home parent and older sibling while the other parent is at work). To simulate variations in children's natural language environment, another 5-person simulation experiment with different mixtures of addressee and nonaddressee materials included in phase I training was conducted. Interestingly, networks that were given non-addressee patterns 20% of the time or more showed perfect generalization to child-speaking patterns without any phase II training, just like the pure nonaddressee networks that are given nonaddressee patterns only. On the other hand, networks that were given nonaddressee patterns 10% of the time needed some phase II training to master the child-speaking patterns, just like the pure addressee networks that were given addressee patterns only. Network analysis revealed that without nonaddressed speech, networks would learn incorrect, reversed rules and make consistent reversal errors. A subsequent remedial experiment using the pure addressee networks with three different mixtures of addressee and nonaddressee materials provided evidence that opportunities to hear shifting reference of pronouns in nonaddressed speech facilitate the unlearning of incorrect semantic rules. Further, the results indicated that if the incorrect, reversed rules are learned solely from addressed speech, substantially more such opportunities are needed to unlearn the incorrect rules (see Oshima-Takane, Takane, and Shultz 1996 for more detailed information).

If children learning personal pronouns fail to include themselves in the kind PERSON, it will be difficult for them to realize that they, too, can use first person pronouns to refer to themselves (Macnamara 1986). We tested this with another modeling experiment in which the distinction between self (child) and other was explicitly coded but individuals were not coded as members of the same kind. The result supported our prediction. Generalization tests immediately after nonaddressee training revealed that none of the networks produced the first person pronoun *me* in reference to the child (self), although some did produce the second person pronoun *you* in reference to a person other than the child. In order to induce the correct semantic rules without error-correcting feedback, children need to have knowledge of the kind PERSON, in which both self and other are included (Oshima-Takane, Takane, and Shultz 1995, 1996; Shultz et al., 1995).

In sum, evidence from the computer modeling studies clearly shows that addressed speech is a source of incorrect, reversed semantic rules and that nonaddressed speech is a necessary ingredient for inducing the correct rules. Knowing the kind PERSON and being exposed to many examples involving various persons as the referents of the pronouns are also important factors for inducing the correct semantic rules without production errors.

15.6 Concluding Remarks

Following Kaplan's (1977, 1978, 1989) analysis of indexicals, I have assumed that a personal pronoun has a fixed meaning (character), although its referent (content) systematically shifts depending on the discourse situation. On the basis of the semantic rules for first and second person pronouns defined by Kaplan, I have proposed a psychological theory of how children learn the semantic rules as they observe other people use such pronouns. That is, children first determine the person referred to by a pronoun in each instance of use and then make generalizations about the semantic rules for first and second person pronouns. In order to induce the correct semantic rules, children must observe shifting reference of pronouns in overheard speech. Child-directed speech is a source of pronominal reversal errors; children who do not have enough opportunities to observe shifting pronominal reference in overheard speech induce the incorrect, reversed rules.

The empirical studies together with the computer modeling studies provide converging evidence in support of this proposal. The data indicate that children determine which person a pronoun used by others refers to in each context of use before they discover the relationship between the pronouns and speech roles. There is no indication that children map pronouns directly onto speech roles. Further, the empirical studies demonstrate that children even younger than 2 can extract information given in overheard speech to induce the correct semantic rules for first and second person pronouns. The computer modeling studies also provide clear-cut evidence that children induce the incorrect, reversed rules by observing pronouns used in addressed speech only, whereas they induce the correct rules by observing pronouns used in nonaddressed speech. In addition, the studies demonstrate that knowing the kind PERSON and being exposed to many examples involving various persons as the referents of the pronouns are important in this induction process.

In this chapter, I have not dealt with the problem of how children determine the content of pronouns in the speech of others. However, this does not mean that I assume that children have no problem in determining the content of the pronouns used by others. As discussed in section 15.1, there are several problems children must solve in order to correctly determine the content of pronouns used by others, and none of these problems is as simple as it looks. I have assumed that children use their prior knowledge of proper names (their own name and others' names) and of the kind PERSON in determining the content of personal pronouns used by others. Prior knowledge of proper names is important in several respects for determining the content of pronouns used by others. First, if children know their own and other people's names, we can assume that they are able to trace their own identity as well as that of others over time before they learn personal pronouns. Second, we can assume that the interchangeable use of proper names and personal pronouns by parents helps children identify both the pronoun forms in utterances and the referents of the pronouns. Knowing the kind PERSON is important because children's ability to recognize themselves and others as members of the same kind PERSON is essential for understanding that personal pronouns refer to a person.

This does not mean, however, that with access to their prior knowledge of proper names and the kind PERSON, children have no problem in determining the content of pronouns used by others. For instance, one mother, who participated in the teaching experiment described above, told me that her son appeared to think that *me* referred to a neck, probably because she and the father pointed toward their neck when they played the me-me game (Oshima-Takane 1985). Since this boy had already called himself by his name and his parents by *Daddy* and *Mommy*, his problem was not that he did not know any word that designated him or his parents as a whole person. Instead, he did not yet seem to have discovered that the particular word *me* refers to a whole person, not just a person's neck. Interestingly, this boy seemed to solve this problem the day after the final session of the me-me game. His mother's diary stated that when she went to her son's bedroom in the morning, he began pointing to himself and said, "Joe, me" several times with a confident look. This was the first time he used the pronoun *me* with his name, *Joe*. The mother interpreted this event as indicating that her son discovered that when he uttered *me*, it picked out himself as an entire person, just like his name. Since parents used *me* only in the me-me game and did not use names along with *me* at all, the boy must have discovered the coreferential relationship between names and the pronoun *me* used by adults outside the teaching experiment. In normal conversations, unlike the teaching experiment, the boy could hear pronouns used in sentences; thus, syntactic cues, too, might have helped him reject the body part interpretation. Further, the experience of observing his mother and father playing the me-me game with each other (i.e., in the nonaddressee condition) might have helped him to discover that *me* refers to the person who utters it. Perhaps his implicit assumption that he is of the same kind PERSON as his parents might have led him to use *me* to refer to himself without hesitation. Unless children actively search for cues to the speaker's intention, as this boy did, they will never be able to arrive at the correct interpretation.

The present approach does not assume any fast mapping mechanisms specific to word learning as do the special lexical constraints approaches popular in psychology (e.g., the object-kind bias or the mutual exclusivity assumption—Markman 1989; Merriman and Bowman 1989). Findings from the studies described here suggest that the learning of personal pronouns is gradual and cannot be explained by these fast mapping mechanisms. It could be that the constraints and biases posited to be specific to word learning are not yet fully developed during the early stage of pronoun learning. Or these constraints may be operating only for certain types of word learning. Logical analysis of children's task in learning words other than personal pronouns and detailed empirical studies of their solutions to the task such as those discussed here will elucidate the early language-learning process and will provide further insights into the ability children bring to language learning.

Notes

1. Note that other referring expressions such as indexicals and definite descriptions refer rigidly (i.e., the referent is taken as fixed for all possible circumstances), once the referent is determined. Kaplan uses *directly referential* for these referring expressions (see Kaplan 1989).

2. In the case of the direct-quotational use of indexicals, as in "Teddy Bear said, 'I'm sleepy,'" the person who reports what Teddy Bear said does not use the words in quotation marks but mentions them. Thus, the discourse situation of the expression being quoted is the one Teddy Bear was in when he uttered it.

3. This does not mean that we cannot use a personal pronoun to refer to a thing other than a person. In fact, people often talk to a dog or a cat or even an inanimate object using personal pronouns. However, it is considered that animals and inanimate objects in such cases are personified, and second person pronouns are used to refer to them.

4. The number assigned to each person is on a nominal scale, and it simply identifies the members with respect to the property in question. With this coding, networks represent the members (tokens) and the kind (type) to which they belong and trace their identity over time. It should be noted, however, that networks do not know what each number indicates and what the property in question is.

References

Akhtar, N., and Tomasello, M. (1996). Two-year-olds learn words for absent objects and actions. *British Journal of Developmental Psychology, 14,* 79–93.

Andersen, E. A., Dunlea, A., and Kekelis, L. S. (1984). Blind children's language: Resolving some differences. *Journal of Child Language, 11,* 645–664.

Baldwin, D. A. (1991). Infants' contribution to the achievement of joint reference. *Child Development, 62,* 875–890.

Baldwin, D. A., Markman, E. M., and Melartin, R. L. (1993). Infants' ability to draw inferences about nonobvious object properties: Evidence from exploratory play. *Child Development, 64,* 711–728.

Baron-Cohen, S., and Ring, H. (1994). A model of the mindreading system: Neuropsychological and neurobiological perspectives. In C. Lewis and P. Mitchell (Eds.), *Children's early understanding of mind: Origins and development* (pp. 183–207). Hillsdale, NJ: Erlbaum.

Barwise, J., and Perry, J. (1983). *Situations and attitudes.* Cambridge, MA: MIT Press.

Bloom, P. (1990). Syntactic distinctions in child language. *Journal of Child Language, 17,* 343–355.

Brener, R. (1983). Learning the deictic meaning of third person pronouns. *Journal of Psycholinguistic Research, 16,* 330–352.

Brown, R. (1973). *A first language: The early stages.* Cambridge, MA: Harvard University Press.

Charney, R. (1980a). Pronoun errors in autistic children: Support for a social explanation. *British Journal of Disorders of Communication, 15,* 39–43.

Charney, R. (1980b). Speech roles and the development of personal pronouns. *Journal of Child Language, 7,* 509–528.

Chiat, S. (1981). Context-specificity and generalization in the acquisition of pronominal distinctions. *Journal of Child Language, 8,* 75–91.

Chiat, S. (1986). Personal pronouns. In P. Fletcher and M. Garman (Eds.), *Language acquisition: Studies in first language development* (2nd ed., 339–355). Cambridge: Cambridge University Press.

Clark, E. V. (1978). From gesture to word: On the natural history of deixis in language acquisition. In J. S. Bruner and A. Garton (Eds.), *Human growth and development: Wolfson College Lectures* (pp. 85–121). Oxford: Oxford University Press.

Cole, E., Oshima-Takane, Y., and Yaremko, R. (1994). Case studies of pronoun development in two hearing-impaired children: Normal, delayed, or deviant? *European Journal of Disorders of Communication, 29,* 113–129.

de Villiers, P. A., and de Villiers, J. G. (1974). On this, that, and the other: Nonegocentrism in very young children. *Journal of Experimental Child Psychology, 18,* 438–447.

Durkin, K., Rutter, D. R., Room, S., and Grounds, P. (1982). Proper name usage in maternal speech: A longitudinal study. In C. E. Johnson and C. L. Thew (Eds.), *Proceedings of the Second International Congress for the Study of Child Language* (pp. 405–412). Washington, DC: University Press of America.

Durkin, K., Rutter, D. R., and Tucker, H. (1982). Social interaction and language acquisition: Motherese help you. *First Language, 3,* 107–120.

Fahlman, S. E., and Lebiere, C. (1990). The cascade correlation learning architecture. In D. S. Touretzky (Ed.), *Advances in neural information processing systems 2* (pp. 524–532). San Mateo, CA: Morgan Kaufmann.

Girouard, P. C., Ricard, M., and Decarie, T. G. (1995). *Perspective-taking skills and the acquisition of pronouns.* Paper presented at the biennial meeting of the Society for Research in Child Development, Indianapolis, April.

Gupta, A. (1980). *The logic of common nouns.* New Haven, CT: Yale University Press.

Hall, D. G. (1994). How children learn common nouns and proper names. In J. Macnamara and G. E. Reyes (Eds.), *The logical foundations of cognition* (pp. 212–240). New York: Oxford University Press.

Hall, D. G., and Waxman, S. R. (1993). Assumptions about word meaning: Individuation and basic-level kinds. *Child Development, 64,* 1550–1570.

Issler, D. (1993). *Comprehension of spatial points of view and acquisition of personal pronouns in Brazilian Portuguese.* Unpublished master's thesis, Pontifical Catholic University of Rio Grande do Sul, Brazil.

Kaplan, D. (1977). *Demonstratives.* Paper read at a symposium on demonstratives at the March 1977 meetings of the Pacific Division of the American Philosophical Association.

Kaplan, D. (1978). On the logic of demonstratives. *Journal of Philosophical Logic, 8,* 81–98.

Kaplan, D. (1989). Demonstratives: An essay on the semantics, logic, metaphysics, and epistemology of demonstratives and other indexicals. In J. Almog, J. Perry, and H. Wettstein (Eds.), *Themes from Kaplan* (pp. 481–614). New York: Oxford University Press.

Katz, N., Baker, E., and Macnamara, J. (1974). What's in a name? A study of how children learn common and proper names. *Child Development, 45,* 469–473.

Kripke, S. (1982). *Naming and necessity.* Oxford: Blackwell.

La Palme Reyes, M., Macnamara, J., and Reyes, G. (1994). Reference, kinds and predicates. In J. Macnamara and G. E. Reyes (Eds.), *The logical foundations of cognition* (pp. 91–143). New York: Oxford University Press.

Loveland, K. A. (1984). Learning about points of view: Spatial perspective and the acquisition of 'I/you'. *Journal of Child Language, 11,* 535–556.

Lyons, J. (1983). Deixis and modality. *Sophia Linguistica, 12,* 77–117. Tokyo: Sophia University.

Macnamara, J. (1972). The cognitive basis of language learning in infants. *Psychological Review, 79,* 1–13.

Macnamara, J. (1977). From sign to language. In J. Macnamara (Ed.), *Language learning and thought* (pp. 11–35). New York: Academic Press.

Macnamara, J. (1982). *Names for things: A study of human learning.* Cambridge, MA: MIT Press.

Macnamara, J. (1986). *A border dispute: The place of logic in psychology.* Cambridge, MA: MIT Press.

Macnamara, J., and Reyes, G. E. (1994). Foundational issues in the learning of proper names, count nouns and mass nouns. In J. Macnamara and G. E. Reyes (Eds.), *The logical foundations of cognition* (pp. 144–176). New York: Oxford University Press.

Mandler, J. M., Bauer, P. J., and McDonough, L. (1991). Separating the sheep from the goats: Differentiating global categories. *Cognitive Psychology, 23,* 263–298.

Markman, E. M. (1989). *Categorization and naming in children.* Cambridge, MA: MIT Press.

McNeill, D. (1963). *The psychology of* you *and* I: *A case history of a small language system.* Paper presented at the annual convention of the American Psychological Association.

Merriman, W., and Bowman, L. (1989). The mutual exclusivity bias in children's word learning. *Monographs of the Society for Research in Child Development, 54*(3–4, Serial No. 220).

Nelson, K. (1973). Structure and strategy in learning to talk. *Monographs of the Society for Research in Child Development, 38*(1–2, Serial No. 149).

Oshima-Takane, Y. (1985). *Learning of pronouns.* Unpublished doctoral dissertation, McGill University.

Oshima-Takane, Y. (1988). Children learn from speech not addressed to them: The case of personal pronouns. *Journal of Child Language, 15,* 94–108.

Oshima-Takane, Y. (1992). Analysis of pronominal errors: A case study. *Journal of Child Language, 19,* 111–131.

Oshima-Takane, Y. (1993). *Why do children make nominal reference?* Poster presented at the biennial meeting of the Society for Research in Child Development, New Orleans, March.

Oshima-Takane, Y. (1997). *Effects of overheard speech on pronoun development in secondborn children.* Paper presented at the biennial meeting of the Society for Research in Child Development, Washington, DC, April.

Oshima-Takane, Y., and Benaroya, S. (1989). An alternative view of pronominal errors in autistic children. *Journal of Autism and Developmental Disorders, 19,* 73–89.

Oshima-Takane, Y., Cole, E., and Yaremko, R. (1993). Semantic pronominal confusion in a hearing-impaired child: A case study. *First Language, 13,* 149–168.

Oshima-Takane, Y., and Derat, L. (1996). Nominal and pronominal references in maternal speech during the later stage of language acquisition: A longitudinal study. *First Language, 16,* 319–338.

Oshima-Takane, Y., Goodz, E., and Derevensky, J. L. (1996). Birth order effects on early language development: Do secondborn children learn from overheard speech? *Child Development, 67,* 621–643.

Oshima-Takane, Y., and Oram, J. (1991). *Acquisition of personal pronouns: What do comprehension data tell us?* Poster presented at the Biennial Meeting of the

International Society for the Study of Behavioural Development, Minneapolis, July.

Oshima-Takane, Y., Takane, Y., and Shultz, T. R. (1995). *Learning of personal pronouns: Network model and analysis* (Tech. Rep. No. 2095). Montreal: McGill University.

Oshima-Takane, Y., Takane, Y., and Shultz, T. R. (1996). Learning of first and second person pronouns in English: Network model and analysis. Unpublished paper, McGill University.

Schiff-Myers, N. (1983). From pronoun reversals to correct pronoun usage: A case study of a normally developing child. *Journal of Speech and Hearing Disorders, 48*, 385–394.

Seki, M. (1992). *Acquisition of the first person terms in infants: A comparison between normally developing children and mentally retarded children.* Unpublished master's thesis, Tsukuba University.

Shipley, E. F., and Shipley, T. E. (1969). Quaker children's use of thee: A relational analysis. *Journal of Verbal Learning and Verbal Behavior, 8*, 112–117.

Shultz, T. R., Buckingham, D., and Oshima-Takane, Y. (1994). A connectionist model of the learning of personal pronouns in English. In S. J. Hanson, T. Petsche, M. Kearns, and R. L. Rivest (Eds.), *Computational learning theory and natural learning systems: Vol. 2. Intersection between theory and experiment* (pp. 347–362). Cambridge, MA: MIT Press.

Shultz, T. R., Schmidt, W. C., Buckingham, D., and Mareschal, D. (1995). Modeling cognitive development with a generative connectionist algorithm. In T. J. Simon and G. S. Halford (Eds.), *Developing cognitive competence: New approaches to process modeling* (pp. 205–261). Hillsdale, NJ: Erlbaum.

Smiley, P., and Huttenlocher, J. (1995). Conceptual development and the child's early words for events, objects, and persons. In M. Tomasello and W. Merriman (Eds.), *Beyond names for things: Young children's acquisition of verbs* (pp. 21–61). Hillsdale, NJ: Erlbaum.

Snow, C. E. (1976). Mother's speech. In W. von Raddle-Engel and Y. Lebrun (Eds.), *Baby talk and infant speech* (pp. 263–264). Amsterdam: Swets and Zeitlinger.

Strayer, J. (1977). *The development of personal references in the language of two-year-olds.* Unpublished doctoral dissertation, Simon Fraser University.

Tager-Flusberg, H. (1989). *An analysis of discourse ability and internal state lexicons in a longitudinal study of autistic children.* Paper presented at the biennial meeting of the Society for Research in Child Development, Kansas City.

Tomasello, M. (1995). On the interpersonal origins of self-concept. In U. Neisser (Ed.), *The perceived self* (pp. 174–184). New York: Cambridge University Press.

Uemura, M. (1979). Development of ego in infancy. *Shinrigaku Hyoron, 22*, 28–44.

Wales, R. (1979). Deixis. In P. Fletcher and M. Garman (Eds.), *Language acquisition* (pp. 401–428). New York: Cambridge University Press.

Wijnen, F., Krikhaar, E., and Den Os, E. (1994). The (non) realization of unstressed elements in children's utterances: Evidence for a rhythmic constraint. *Journal of Child Language, 21,* 59–83.

Wills, D. D. (1977). Participant deixis in English and baby talk. In C. Snow and C. Ferguson (Eds.), *Talking to children* (pp. 271–295). Cambridge: Cambridge University Press.

Xu, F., and Carey, S. (1996). Infants' metaphysics: The case of numerical identity. *Cognitive Psychology, 30,* 111–153.

Chapter 16

Kinship and Mathematical Categories

F. William Lawvere

Those concepts that are historically stable tend to be those that in some way reflect reality, and in turn tend to be those that are teachable. "Mathematical" should mean in particular "teachable," and the modern mathematical theory of flexible categories can indeed be used to sharpen the teachability of basic concepts. A concept that has enjoyed some historical stability for 40,000 years is the one involving that structure of a society that arises from the biological process of reproduction and its reflection in the collective consciousness as ideas of genealogy and kinship. Sophisticated methods for teaching this concept were devised long ago, making possible regulation of the process itself. A more accurate model of kinship than heretofore possible can be sharpened with the help of the modern theory of flexible mathematical categories; at the same time, established cultural acquaintance with the concept helps to illuminate several aspects of the general theory, which I will therefore try to explain concurrently.

Abstracting the genealogical aspect of a given society yields a mathematical structure within which aunts, cousins, and so on can be precisely defined. Other objects, in the same category of such structures, that seem very different from actual societies, are nonetheless shown to be important tools in a society's conceptualizing about itself, so that for example gender and moiety become labeling morphisms within that category. Topological operations, such as contracting a connected subspace to a point, are shown to permit rationally neglecting the remote past. But such operations also lead to the qualitative transformation of a topos of pure particular Becoming into a topos of pure general Being; the latter two kinds of mathematical toposes are distinguished from each other by precise conditions. The mythology of a primal couple is thus shown to be a naturally arising didactic tool. The logic of genealogy is not at all 2-

valued or Boolean, because the truth-value space naturally associated with the ancestor concept has a rich lattice structure.

As John Macnamara emphasized, an explicit mathematical framework is required for progress in the science of cognition, much as multidimensional differential calculus has been required for 300 years as a framework for progress in such sciences as thermomechanics and electromagnetics. I hope that the examples considered here will contribute to constructing the sort of general framework John had in mind.

Although a framework for thinking about thinking would be called "logic" by some ancient definitions, in this century logic has come to have a much more restrictive connotation that emphasizes statements as such, rather than the objects to which the statements refer; this restrictive connotation treats systems of statements almost exclusively in terms of presentations (via primitives and axioms) of such systems, thus obscuring the objective aspects of abstract generals that are invariant under change of presentation. About 100 years ago the necessary objective support for this subjective logic began to be relegated to a rigidified set theory that shares with mereology the false presupposition that given any two sets, it is meaningful to ask whether one is included in the other or not. Although the combination of narrow logic and rigidified set theory is often said to be the framework for a "foundation of mathematics," it has in fact never served as a foundation in practice; for example, the inclusion question is posed in practice only between *subsets* of a given set, such as the set of real numbers or the set of real functions on a given domain. There are many different explicit transformations between different domains, but the presumption that there is a preferred one leads to fruitless complications.

The development of multidimensional differential calculus led in particular to functional analysis, algebraic geometry, and algebraic topology, that is, to subjects whose interrelationships and internal qualitative leaps are difficult to account for by the narrow and rigidified "foundations." This forced the development of a newer, more adequate framework (which of course takes full account of the positive results of previous attempts) 50 years ago, and 20 years later the resulting notions of category, functor, natural transformation, adjoint functor, and so on had become the standard explicit framework for algebraic topology and algebraic geometry, a framework that is even indispensable for the communication of many concepts. Then, inspired by developments in mechanics and algebraic geometry, it was shown how a broader logic and a less rigid notion of set are naturally incorporated in the categorical framework.

Toposes are categories of sets that have specified internal cohesion and variation and whose transformations are continuous or equivariant. The infinite variety of toposes now studied arises not in order to justify some constructivist or other philosophical prejudice, but in order to make usefully explicit the modes of cohesion and variation that are operative in multidimensional differential calculus. The internal logic of toposes turned out to be that which had been presented earlier by Heyting. Heyting logic (and co-Heyting logic) describes inclusions and transformations of subsets of such sets in a way that takes account of the internal cohesion and variation, refining the fragmented and static picture that the still earlier approximation by Boolean logic provides.

I will explore here two examples showing how the categorical insight can be used to make more explicitly calculable, not only the more overtly spatial and quantitative notions, but also other recurring general concepts that human consciousness has perfected over millennia for aiding in the accurate reflection of the world and in the planning of action. The two examples are kinship, in particular, and the becoming of parts versus the becoming of wholes, in general. Since the narrowing of Logic 100 years ago, it has been customary to describe kinships in terms of abstract "relations"; however, if we make the theory slightly less abstract, the category of examples gains considerably in concreteness and in power to represent concepts that naturally arise. Becoming has long been studied by resolving it into two aspects, time and states, with a map of time into the states; but when we consider the becoming of a whole "body" together with that of its parts (e.g., the development of collective consciousness or the motion of the solar system), there are several "conflicting" aspects that we need to manage: the collective state "is" nothing but the ensemble of the states of the parts, yet the constitutive law determining what the state (even of a part) "becomes" may depend on the state of all; the time of the whole may be taken as a prescribed synchronization of the times of each part, yet the news of the collective becoming may reach different parts with differing delays. A general philosophical idea is that the cohesiveness of being is both the basis in which these conflicts take place and also partly the result of the becoming (Hegel: "Wesen ist gewesen"—that is, the essence of what there is now is the product of the process it has gone through). I will try to show more precisely how the being of kinship in a given historical epoch relates to the becoming of reproduction and of intermarriage between clans, even when this kinship and reproduction are considered purely abstractly, neglecting their natural and societal setting.

16.1   A Concrete Category Abstracting the Notion of Reproduction

I want to consider general notions of kinship system, as suggested by known particular examples. The following fundamental notion was elaborated in collaboration with Steve Schanuel (Lawvere and Schanuel 1997).

An analysis of kinship can begin with the following biological observation:

(T_1) Each individual has exactly one mother and exactly one father, who are also individuals.

As a first approximation, we can explore the ramifications of this idea, taken in itself, as an abstract theory T_1. Though we may have thought originally of "individual" as meaning a member of a particular tribe, there is in fact in a "theory" no information at all about what individuals are; the mathematical concrete corresponding to the stated abstract theory T_1 is the category whose objects are sets, consisting of abstract elements, but structured by two specified self-mappings m and f. Such a structured set can be considered as a "society." We can immediately define such concepts as "a and b are siblings" by the equations $am = bm$ and $af = bf$, or "b's maternal grandfather is also c's paternal grandfather" by the equation $bmf = cff$. (In the Danish language 'morfar' means mother's father, 'farfar' means father's father, similarly 'farmor' and 'mormor'; and young children commonly address their grandparents using those four compound words.) There is a great variety of such systems, most of which seem at first glance to be ineligible, even mathematically, for more than this verbal relation to the kinship concepts; for example, I cannot be my own maternal grandfather. However, if we take the theory and the category seriously, we will find that some of these strange objects are actually useful for the understanding of kinship.

As is usual with the concrete realizations of any given abstract theory, these form a category in the mathematical sense that there is a notion of structure-preserving morphism $X \xrightarrow{\phi} Y$ between any two examples: in this case the requirement on ϕ is that $\phi(xm) = \phi(x)m$ and $\phi(xf) = \phi(x)f$ for all x in X. (It is convenient to write morphisms on the left, but structural maps on the right of the elements; in the two equations required, the occurrences of m and f on the right sides of the equality refer to the structure in the codomain Y of the morphism.) There are typically many morphisms from given domain X to given codomain Y. If $X \xrightarrow{\phi} Y \xrightarrow{\psi} Z$

are morphisms, there is a well-determined composite morphism $X \xrightarrow{\psi\phi} Z$, and for each object X, there is always the identity morphism from X to itself. Two objects X_1 and X_2 are isomorphic in their category if there exists a pair of morphisms $X_1 \to X_2 \to X_1$ with both composites equal to the respective identity morphisms. Most morphisms are not isomorphisms, and they indeed do not even satisfy the requirement of "injectivity," which just means that the cancellation law, $\phi x_1 = \phi x_2$ implies $x_1 = x_2$, holds for ϕ. If a morphism ξ is in fact injective, it is also called "a sub-object of its codomain, which taken in itself is the domain." (Contrary to some rigidified versions of set theory, a given object may occur as the domain of many different subobjects of another given object. A subobject may be thought of as a specified way of "including" its domain into its codomain.) An element y is said to "belong to" a subobject ξ (notation: $y \ \varepsilon \ \xi$) if there is x for which $y = \xi x$; this x will be unambiguous because of the injectivity requirement on ξ. Here by an element of X is often meant any morphism $T \to X$; such elements are also referred to as figures in X of shape T, but often we also restrict the word 'element' to mean 'figure of a sufficient few preferred shapes'. Sometimes we have between two subobjects an actual inclusion map $\xi_1 \subseteq \xi_2$ *as* subsets of Y (i.e., $X_1 \xrightarrow{\alpha} X_2$ for which $\xi_1 = \xi_2 \alpha$). It is these inclusions that the propositional logic of Y is about.

16.2 Genealogical Truth, Seen Topos-Theoretically

The category sketched above, that is, the mathematically concrete corre-spondent of the abstract theory T_1 of m and f, is in fact a "topos." That means, among other properties, that there is a "truth-value" object Ω that "classifies," via characteristic morphisms, all the subobjects of any given object. In the simpler topos of abstract (unstructured) sets, the set 2, whose elements are "true" and "false," plays that role; for if $X \xrightarrow{\xi} Y$ is any injective mapping of abstract sets, there is a unique mapping $Y \xrightarrow{\phi} 2$ such that for any element y of Y, $\phi y =$ true if and only if y belongs to the subset ξ; and if two maps ϕ_1, ϕ_2 from Y to 2 satisfy ϕ_1 entails ϕ_2 in the Boolean algebra of 2, then the corresponding subsets enjoy a unique inclusion map $\xi_1 \subseteq \xi_2$ as subsets of Y (i.e., $X_1 \xrightarrow{\alpha} X_2$ for which $\xi_1 = \xi_2 \alpha$). However, in our topos, 2 must be replaced by a bigger object of truth-values in order to have those features for all systems Y and for all sub-systems X, ξ, as explained below.

In our topos of all T_1-societies, there is a particular object I, which as an abstract set consists of all finite strings of the two symbols m and f, with the obvious right-action that increases length by 1, giving its cohesiveness and variation; in particular, the empty string 1_I is the generic individual, all of whose ancestors are *distinct*. A concrete individual in a society X is any morphism $I \to X$; in particular, the infinitely many endomorphisms $I \xrightarrow{w} I$ are easily seen to be in one-to-one correspondence with the strings in I. Composing with the two endomorphisms m and f, which correspond to the two strings of length 1, completely describes, in the context of the whole category, everything we need to know about the particular internal structure of X: the actions xm, xf are realized as special cases of the composition of morphisms. The condition that every morphism $X \xrightarrow{\phi} Y$ in the topos must satisfy is then seen to be just a special case of the associative law of composition, namely, the special case in which the first of the three morphisms being composed is an endomorphism of I. The facts stated in this paragraph constitute the special case of the Cayley-Yoneda lemma, applied to the small category W that has one object, whose endomorphisms are the strings in two letters, composed by juxtaposition; a category with one object only is often referred to as a *monoid*.

With loss in precision we can say that x' is an ancestor of x in case there exists some endomorphism w of I for which $x' = xw$. In the particular society X, the w may not be unique; for example, $xmff = xfmf$ might hold. But the precision is retained in the category W/X, discretely fibered over W, which is essentially the usual genealogical diagram of X. The correlation of the reproductive process in X with past solar time could be given by an additional age functor from this fibered category to a fixed ordered set; a construction of Grothendieck (1983) would permit internalizing such a chronology too in T_1's topos.

Now we can explain the truth-value system. The subsets of I in the sense of our topos are essentially just sets A of strings that, however, are not arbitrary but subject to the two conditions that if $I \xrightarrow{w} A$ is a member of A, then also wm and wf must be members of A. Thus, A can be thought of as all my ancestors before a certain stage, the antiquity of that stage depending however on the branch of the family. These As constitute the truth-values! To justify that claim, we must first define the action of m and f on As; this is what is often thought of as "division":

$A : m = \{w \; \varepsilon \; W : mw \; \varepsilon \; A\}$,

$A : f = \{w \; \varepsilon \; W : fw \; \varepsilon \; A\}$.

It is easily verified that these two are again subobjects of I if A is. Note that $A : f$ consists of all my father's ancestors who were in A. The truth-value true is $A = W$, the whole set of strings, and union and intersection $A \cup B$, $A \cap B$ are the basic propositional operations *or*, *and* on truth-values. The operation *not A* of negation does not satisfy all the Boolean laws, since it must again yield a subobject of *I*:

not A = $\{w \ \varepsilon \ W$: for all $v \ \varepsilon \ W, wv$ does not belong to $A\}$

is the set of all my ancestors none of whose ancestors were in A, so (A *or not A*) is usually much smaller than true. Why does the object Ω thus defined serve as the unique notion of truth-value set for the whole topos? Consider any subset $X \overset{\xi}{\to} Y$ in the sense of the topos; then there is a unique morphism $Y \overset{\phi}{\to} \Omega$ such that for all individuals $I \overset{y}{\to} Y$ in Y,

$y \ \varepsilon \ \xi$ if and only if $\phi(y) =$ true.

The value of ϕ on any element y is forced to be

$\phi(y) = \{w \ \varepsilon \ W : yw \ \varepsilon \ \xi\}$.

This is the measured answer to the question "Precisely how Irish is y?"

16.3   How to Rationally Neglect the Remote Past

Every X is a disjoint union of minimal components that have no mutual interaction; if we parameterize this set of components by a set $\Pi_0(X)$ and give the latter the trivial (identity) action of m, f, then there is an obvious morphism $X \to \Pi_0(X)$. If $\Pi_0(X) = 1$, a one-point set, we say X is connected; that does not necessarily mean that any two individuals in X have some common ancestor, because more generally connecting can be verified through cousins of cousins of cousins, and so on.

An important construction borrowed from algebraic topology is the following:

Given a subobject $A \hookrightarrow X$, we can form the "pushout" $X \bmod A$ that fits into a commutative rectangular diagram involving a collapsing morphism $X \to X \bmod A$ and an inclusion $\Pi_0(A) \hookrightarrow X \bmod A$ as well as the canonical $A \to \Pi_0(A)$ and satisfies the universal property that, if we are given any morphism $X \overset{\psi}{\to} Y$ whose restriction to A depends only on $\Pi_0(A)$, then there is a unique morphism $X \bmod A \overset{\psi_0}{\to} Y$ for which ψ is the composite, ψ_0 following $X \to X \bmod A$, and which also agrees on $\Pi_0(A)$ with that restriction.

This $X \bmod A$ is a very natural thing to consider because practical genealogical calculations cannot cope with an infinite past. For example, the Habsburg X are mainly active over the past 1,000 years and the Orsini over the past 2,000 years. But this collapsing of the remote ancestors A to $\Pi_0(A)$ introduces an interesting idealization; for simplicity we consider the case where A is connected, $\Pi_0 A = 1$. Then the construction has given rise to a morphism $1 \to X \, mod \, A$ that is the residuum of A. But what is a "point" (= figure of shape 1) in a topos like ours? Since m and f act as identity in 1, a point (e.g., the point of $X \, mod \, A$ that has arisen) is a special sort of individual x that is its own mother and father:

$xm = x = xf$.

This idea of a superindividual is of course merely a convenience in genealogical bookkeeping.

16.4 Deepening the Theory to Make Gender Explicit

A reasonable gender structure is not definable in the abstract theory T_1 above, since there is no requirement that the values of the operator m be disjoint from the values of the operator f and also no way of determining the gender of infertile individuals. So as usual we refine our theory to a richer one:

(T_2) In addition to T_1, every individual has a definite gender, every
         individual's mother is female, and every individual's father is male.

The corresponding category of all concrete applications of T_2 will also be a topos and in fact have a direct relation to the topos of T_1. Namely, in the first topos there is a particular object G with only two individuals called *male* and *female* and where the two structural operations act as the constant maps. Our refined topos has objects that may be described as pairs X, γ where $X \overset{\gamma}{\to} G$ is a morphism in the first topos and has as morphisms all triangular diagrams $[X \overset{\gamma}{\to} G, X \overset{\phi}{\to} Y, Y \overset{\delta}{\to} G]$ in the first topos for which $\delta\phi = \gamma$; the codomain of this triangle is defined to be the pair Y, δ. The conditions

$\gamma(xm) = (\gamma x)m$

and

$\gamma(xf) = (\gamma x)f$

that morphisms must satisfy state in this case that γ is a compatible gender-labeling, and the further condition on a triangular diagram means that morphisms in our refined topos moreover preserve gender. That applies in particular to the individuals in X that happen to be (in our purely reproductive sense) spinsters or bachelors. This topos has two generic individuals, because labeling maps $I \to G$ can map 1_I either to m or to f. The terminal object of this new topos is actually 1_G so that a point in the new sense is really the "locus of a point moving virtually between m and f"; more exactly, a morphism $1_G \to Y$ in this topos amounts to an Eve/Adam pair for which

$$ef = af = a \quad \& \quad em = am = e.$$

If we construct the pushout along $A \to \Pi_0 A$ of a subobject $A \hookrightarrow X$ in the sense of this topos, we get in particular $\Pi_0 A \hookrightarrow X/A$, which specifies a different Eve/Adam pair for each of the mutually oblivious subsocieties among the specified ancestors.

16.5 Moieties

A still further refinement makes precise the idea of a society equipped with a strategy for incest avoidance. The simplest idea T_3 of such is that of (matrilineal) moiety labeling, which can be explained in terms of another two-individual application C of T_1. The two "individuals" are called Bear and Wolf in Lawvere and Schanuel 1997. The idea is that the moiety of any individual x is the same as that of x's mother and distinct from that of x's father. Thus, on the two individuals in C, m acts as the identity, whereas $f^2 = \text{id}$ but $f \neq \text{id}$. Any T_1-respecting morphism $X \to C$ is a labeling with the expected properties, and commuting triangles over C constitute the morphisms of a further topos that should be investigated. However, I will denote by T_3 the richer abstract theory whose applications are all the T_1-applications X equipped with a labeling morphism $X \to G \times C$. Thus, in T_3's topos there are four generic individuals I (one for each pair in $G \times C$), morphisms from which are concrete individuals of either gender and of either Bear or Wolf moiety.

16.6 Congealing Becoming into Being

According to the criteria proposed in Lawvere 1991, the three toposes thus far introduced represent particular forms of pure becoming, because they satisfy the condition that every object X receives a surjective morphism from another one E that has the special property

$$z_1 w = z_2 w \quad \text{implies} \quad z_1 = z_2$$

for any given w in W and any two individuals z_1, z_2 in E. This "separable covering" E of X is achieved through refining each individual (if necessary) into several individuals with formally distinct genealogies (e.g., $xmf \neq yf$ in E even if $y = xm$ in X). However, by restricting to certain subcategories consisting only of objects that contain something roughly like the Eve/Adam pair, we obtain toposes that have instead the qualitative character of pure being; for example, the Habsburg era had a certain quality of being (and was the basis for a lot of motion).

More precisely, let us consider various theories corresponding to monoid homomorphisms

$$W \xrightarrow{p} M$$

that are epimorphic. Epimorphic homomorphisms may be surjective (induced by a congruence on W), or may adjoin at most new operator symbols that are two-sided inverses of operator symbols coming from W, or may involve a combination of these two kinds of "simplifications" of W. Such a homomorphism gives rise to a well-defined subcategory of T_1's topos, namely, the one consisting of all those systems X satisfying the congruence or invertibility conditions that become true in M. (For analogous subcategories of the other two toposes, we would need to consider epimorphic functors

$$W/G \xrightarrow{p} D$$

and

$$W/G \times C \xrightarrow{p} E$$

to small categories D or E of two (respectively four) objects.) The resulting subcategories, although toposes, are not subtoposes but "quotient toposes." Here a quotient morphism of toposes, compressing a bigger situation into a smaller situation, involves a full and faithful inverse functor p^* (the obvious inclusion in our example) and two forward functors $p_!$ and p_* that are respectively left and right adjoint to p^* in the sense that there are natural one-to-one correspondences

$$\frac{p_! X \to Y}{X \to p^* Y} \qquad \frac{Z \to p_* X}{p^* Z \to X}$$

between morphisms, for all sets X defined over the big situation and all Y, Z defined over the smaller one. Note that the notion of morphism is the same in both situations; that is what it means to be full and faithful.

These adjointnesses are the refined objective version of relations whose subjective reflections are the rules of inference for existential quantification $p_!$, resp. universal quantification p_* of predicates relative to a substitution operation p^* (indeed, p^* preserves coproducts and products of objects, as is subjectively reflected in the fact that a substitution preserves disjunction and conjunction of predicates; it may fail to preserve the analogous negations however, for example in the case of continuous predicates in topology). Specifically, $p_* X$ extracts those individuals from X whose genealogy happens to conform to the requirements specified in M, whereas $p_! X$ applies to all individuals in X, the minimal forcing required to merge them into a new object that conforms to M.

These facts will be used below in investigating elementary examples of quotient toposes, in particular, some of those that seem to congeal becoming into being.

To distinguish a topos of general pure being, I proposed in Lawvere 1986 and 1991 the two criteria that $\Pi_0(X \times Y) = \Pi_0(X) \times \Pi_0(Y)$ and that every object is the domain of a subobject of some connected object. The first of these means that any pair consisting of a component of X and a component of Y comes from a unique single component of the Cartesian product $X \times Y$; in particular, the product of connected objects should be again connected (since $1 \times 1 = 1$), which is rarely true in a topos of particular becoming. That condition will be important for the qualitative, homotopical classification of the objects, but I will not discuss it further here.

The second criterion mentioned above, that every object can be embedded as a subobject of some connected object, has the flavor "We are all related," but is much stronger than merely requiring that a particular object be connected; for example, the disjoint sum of two connected objects, which is always disconnected, should be embeddable in a connected object.

It follows from a remark of Grothendieck (1983) that both proposed criteria will be satisfied by a topos of M-actions if the generic individual I ($= M$ acting on itself) has at least two distinct points $1 \rightrightarrows I$. The distinctness must be in a strong sense that will be automatic in our example where 1 has only two subobjects; it is also crucial that the generic individual I itself be connected. Part of the reason why this special condition of Grothendieck implies the two general criteria can be understood in the following terms: it is not that becoming is absent in a topos of general being; rather, it is expressed in a different way. An object X may be a space of locations or states in the tradition of Aristotle; that is, X is an arena in which becoming can take place. In particular, some such spaces T can measure time intervals and hence a particular motion in X during T may give rise to a morphism $T \xrightarrow{\mu} X$ describing the result of the becoming process; that is, if T is connected, if we can distinguish two instants $1 \rightrightarrows T$ called t_0, t_1 and if $\mu t_k = x_k$ for $k = 0, 1$, then we can say that x_0 became x_1 during the process μ; this is the common practice in mathematical engineering (at least for certain categories within which it has, in effect, become customary to work in the past 300 years). But then if we consider t_1 as a subobject of T, its characteristic map from T to the truth-value space will be a process along which false becomes true; this in turn implies that the truth-value space is itself connected since T is, and because of the propositional structure of truth-values, it follows that indeed the hyper-space, whose points parameterize the subspaces of X, is connected too. On the other hand, in any topos any object X is embedded as a subobject of its hyperspace via the "singleton" map. Taking $T = I$, it follows that in the cases under discussion every object can be embedded in an object that is not only connected, but moreover has no holes or other homotopical irregularities. Note that now each individual $I \xrightarrow{x} X$ involves also a process in his or her society. There are many such situations, but what can such a process mean?

As a simple example, suppose that we want a category of models of societies in which genealogical records go back to grandparents. Thus, we consider the homomorphism $W \xrightarrow{p} M$ onto a seven-element monoid in which

$$m^3 = mfm = m^2$$

and

$$mf^2 = m^2 f = mf$$

hold, together with similar equations with f and m interchanged. Drawing the obvious genealogical diagram, we see that the generic individual I in the topos of M actions has parents that represent the first intermarriage between two distinct lines, and that I's grandparents are the "Eves and Adams" of those two distinct lines. Indeed, this object I permits a unique gender structuring and so we may pass instead into the topos whose theory is M/G, finding there that each of the two generic individuals I_G has two distinct points $1_G \rightrightarrows I_G$. The "process" involved in an individual boy $I_G \xrightarrow{x} X$ in a society X in this topos is that whereby his father's line united with his mother's.

16.7   Finer Analysis of the Coarser Theories

Given any object L in a topos, one can form a new topos of objects further structured by a given labeling morphism to L. However, it is worthy of note that in our examples, one $L = G$ (leading to T_2) and the other one $L = G \times C$ (leading to T_3), these labeling objects belong to a much restricted subcategory (quotient topos) within the topos of all T_1-objects. Although the T_1 topos, consisting of all right actions of the free monoid W on two symbols, is too vast to hope for a complete survey of its objects (as is borne out by theorems of Vera Trnková stating that any category can be embedded as a full subcategory of it; see Pultr and Trnková 1980), by contrast these smaller toposes are more tractable.

Consider first the case G of gender in itself. It belongs to the subcategory corresponding to $W \to W_3$, the three-element monoid in which $xf = f$, $xm = m$ for all three $x = 1, f, m$. If we restrict attention to the right actions of W_3 only, we see that the generic individual I in the sense of that topos has only one nontrivial subobject, which is G itself. Therefore, the truth-value space Ω_3 for that topos (in contrast to the infinite Ω for W) has only three elements also. The most general "society" X is a sum of a number of noninteracting nuclear families, some with two parents and some with a single parent, and a society is determined up to isomorphism by the double coefficient array that counts families of all possible sizes of these two kinds. Cartesian products are easily computed.

Second, consider the simple moiety-labeler C in itself; it belongs to the quotient topos determined by $W \to W_2$, the two-element group generated by f with $f^2 = 1$, where we moreover interpret m as 1. Here C is itself the generic individual and has no nontrivial subobjects, so that Ω_2 is the two-element Boolean algebra. All right W_2-actions are of the form $X = a + bC$, where a is the number of individuals fixed, and b half the number moved, by f. These objects are multiplied by the rule $C^2 = 2C$.

Third, we can include both G and C in a single subcategory as follows: the infinite free monoid W maps surjectively to each of W_3 and W_2; therefore, it maps to the six-element product monoid $W_3 \times W_2$, but not surjectively since the image W_5 is a five-element submonoid (the missed element is the only nonidentity invertible element in the product monoid). The category of right W_5-sets can be probed with the help of its generic individual I, which again (surprisingly) has only three subobjects so that Ω_5 has again three truth-value-individuals. In I (i.e., W_5) there are besides me my four distinct grandparents, the T_1-structure coming from the fact that my parents are identical with my maternal grandparents in this theory. The unique nontrivial subobject of I is precisely $G \times C$, the label object for our central noncollapsed theory T_3; it is generated by any single one of its four elements. I leave it to the reader to determine a structural description of all right W_5-actions, with or without $G \times C$ labelings.

16.8 Possible Further Elaborations

To the T_2 topos (whose abstract general is the two-object category W/G) we can apply separately our concrete construction idealizing remote ancestors and also our refinement of the abstract general by moiety-labeling. However, it does not seem consistent to apply both of these simultaneously, owing to the simple group-theoretic nature of our C. A reasonable conjecture is that tribal elders in some part of the world have devised a more subtle abstract general C' that relaxes the incest avoidance for the idealized remote ancestors, thus permitting a smoothly functioning genealogical system enjoying both kinds of advantages.

Some more general examples of simplifying abstractions include that based on a homomorphism $W \xrightarrow{p} M_n$ that makes every string of length greater than n (where, e.g., $n = 17$) congruent to a well-defined associated string of length n. An interesting construction to consider is the application of the pushout construction to an arbitrary T_1-object X, not with respect to some arbitrarily chosen remoteness of ancestry A, but with respect to the canonical morphism $p^* p_* X \to X$.

The need for Eve and Adam arises from the central role of self-maps as structure in the above theories and might be alleviated by considering instead a two-object category as the fundamental abstract general, although possibly at the expense of too great a multiplicity of interpretations. This category simply consists of three parallel arrows, as described in Lawvere 1989. A concrete application of this theory T_0 involves two sets (rather than one) and three internal structural maps

$$X_{now} \to X_{up \ to \ now}$$

called m, f, and s, where s specifies, for each contemporary individual, the place of his or her "self" in genealogical history. There is a natural notion of morphism between two such objects (involving two set-maps subject to three equations) yielding again a topos, whose truth-value object is finite and illuminating to work out. T_0's topos has T_1's topos as a quotient, because forcing the structural map s to become invertible yields a small category equivalent to the monoid W. If s is not inverted, iteration of m and f is a more complicated partial affair: in case xm has the property that there is a contemporary mother y for which $ys = xm$, then yf is a maternal grandfather of x; but there may not be such a y, and on the other hand, mathematical experience counsels against excluding in general the possibility of several such y for a given x. If we do invert s, we make explicit that which, in a larger sense, is the theme of this book, the continuing role of each past individual in our cognition at present.

References

Grothendieck, A. (1983). *Pursuing stacks.* Unpublished manuscript, University of Montpellier, France.

Lawvere, F. W. (1986). Taking categories seriously. *Revista Colombiana de Matemáticas, 20,* 147–178.

Lawvere, F. W. (1989). Qualitative distinctions between some toposes of generalized graphs. In J. Gray and A. Scedrov (Eds.), *Logic, categories, and computer science* (Contemporary Mathematics 92, pp. 261–299). Providence, RI: American Mathematical Society.

Lawvere, F. W. (1991). Some thoughts on the future of category theory. In A. Carboni, M. C. Pedicchio, and G. Rosolini (Eds.), *Category theory* (Lecture Notes in Mathematics 1488, pp. 1–13). Heidelberg: Springer-Verlag.

Lawvere, F. W., and Schanuel, S. (1997). *Conceptual mathematics.* Cambridge: Cambridge University Press.

Macnamara, J., and Reyes, G. E. (1994). *The logical foundations of cognition.* Oxford: Oxford University Press.

Pultr, A., and Trnková, V. (1980). *Combinatorial, algebraic, and topological representations of groups, semigroups, and categories.* Amsterdam: North-Holland.

Chapter 17

Count Nouns, Mass Nouns, and Their Transformations: A Unified Category-Theoretic Semantics

Marie La Palme Reyes, John Macnamara, Gonzalo E. Reyes, and Houman Zolfaghari

17.1 Introduction

17.1.1 Prototypical Count Nouns and Mass Nouns

All natural languages seem to distinguish at the semantic level between count nouns (CNs) and mass nouns (MNs). Some natural languages, like English, mark the distinction at the syntactic level. Prototypical of CNs is 'dog' and of MNs is 'matter' (in the sense of physical stuff, not in the sense of concern or affair). One syntactic difference is that usually CNs take the plural ('dogs') whereas MNs do not. Other syntactic distinctions

This chapter has been "in the making" for a number of years, and it would be difficult to thank all the people and institutions that have given us criticism, advice, and encouragement. In spite of this, we would like to single out the following: John Macnamara and Gonzalo E. Reyes gratefully acknowledge the support of individual grants from Canada's Natural Sciences and Engineering Research Council (NSERC) and of a collaborative grant from Quebec's Fonds pour la formation de chercheurs et l'aide à la recherche (FCAR). Marie La Palme Reyes is grateful for the support of a Social Sciences and Humanities Research Council of Canada (SSHRC) postdoctoral fellowship during the early years of research, as well as support from Macnamara's NSERC grant and the FCAR grant to Macnamara and Reyes during the later years. Houman Zolfaghari was partly supported from the NSERC grants of Macnamara and Reyes. Gonzalo E. Reyes would like to acknowledge an invitation from the Departments of Mathematics and Philosophy of the Université Catholique de Louvain-la-Neuve, where parts of this chapter were presented. Brendan Gillon and Jeff Pelletier helped us to find our way through the mass of papers on mass nouns and count nouns, and we are grateful to them. Joyce Macnamara was kind enough to improve our text and discuss intuitions relating to many linguistic examples. Finally, we would like to acknowledge valuable conversations with Anders Kock, Mihály Makkai, and Richard Squire on the subject of this chapter.

relate to determiners and quantifiers. One can say 'a dog', 'another dog', 'many dogs', 'two dogs'; one cannot correctly say *'a matter', *'another matter', *'many matter', *'two matter'. It seems that the distinction in English grammar was first described by Jespersen (1924, 198).

Languages differ in morphology, agreement rules, and phrase structure, so one does not expect to find in every natural language a count/mass distinction with the same linguistic correlates as in English. Although many European languages are like English in this connection, not all are. Irish and Latin, for example, lack the indefinite article, and so one cannot distinguish CNs from MNs in those languages by the possibility or impossibility of adding the indefinite article to the noun. Japanese has neither definite nor indefinite articles and lacks a uniform way to build plurals. Yet Japanese requires classifiers to license the application of certain quantifiers such as numerals to nouns. Thus, in order to apply the numeral 'ni' ('two') to the noun 'inu' ('dog'), the classifier 'hiki' is required to form the expression 'Inu-ga ni-hiki iru' ('There are two dogs'). This classifier is required also for words denoting fishes and insects, although not for words denoting birds, for which the classifier 'wa' is required. On the other hand, with almost any count noun denoting inanimate entities the classifier 'tsu' is required, as in the expression 'Ringo-o yo-tsu tabeta' ('I ate four apples'). This classifier cannot be used with mass nouns. With mass nouns such as 'mizu' ('water'), a different classifier 'hai' or 'bai' is required to form expressions such as 'Mizu-o san-bai (hai) nonda' ('I drank three glasses of water'). This classifier cannot be used with count nouns or with other mass nouns such as 'nendo' ('clay'). Thus, the correct use of some classifiers seems to require a count/mass (as well as an animate/inanimate) distinction at the level of nouns. (We owe the details about Japanese to Yuriko Oshima-Takane.)

Incidentally, if we inquire what guides linguists to the decision that there are common nouns in languages other than English, the answer cannot simply be grammar. As just illustrated, grammar varies greatly from language to language. Something other than grammar must be contributing to the decision. We submit that the type of reference for prototypical words plays a major role. We think that across variations in grammar there is a semantic uniformity in the interpretation of at least such prototypical count nouns as 'dog' as well as in the interpretation of such prototypical mass nouns as 'matter' and that this semantic uniformity is a good guide to the relevant grammatical facts in each language. We propose to exploit the semantic uniformity as far as possible.

This should not be taken as an assumption that the perceptual experience of a noun's extension determines whether a noun applied to it is count or mass. It clearly does not. The very same perceptual experience that licenses the application of the MN 'gravel' licenses that of the CN 'pebble'. Moreover, languages vary in what they choose to present in the first instance as mass and what as count. French speakers, for example, apply the CN 'meuble' where English speakers would normally apply the MN 'furniture'. Notice that 'furniture' does supply natural units, or as we say articles of furniture (chairs, tables, lamps, etc.). The importance of the prototypical examples also shows up in work on child language learning. Young children tend to take a new word taught them for a stuff that is like sand in its consistency as a MN, and a word for unfamiliar creatures reminiscent of animals as a CN (see especially McPherson 1991; Soja, Carey, and Spelke 1991).

Pelletier and Schubert (1989) document the difficulty in deciding what precisely falls under the classifications mass or count: nouns and noun phrases, adjectives and adjectival phrases, verbs and verb phrases, or adverbs and adverbial phrases? Even if one could settle on the relevant syntactic category or categories, there is still the issue of what precisely in those categories is mass or count: the expressions themselves, their senses, or their occurrences? All this in addition to the problem of how to decide whether something, whatever that something is, is mass rather than count. But notice that to start work on these questions assumes that we understand the count/mass distinction. On the basis of the prototypical examples discussed above, we take the view that this distinction applies to nouns, whether or not it applies to other grammatical categories. Our work is concerned only with the count/mass distinction for nouns, whose solution is presupposed in formulating some of the previous questions. Despite their obvious interest, those questions we do not propose to tackle.

17.1.2 Cumulative and Distributive Reference

The usual way of distinguishing MNs from CNs is by specifying semantic properties that MNs have but CNs lack.

Two or more dogs do not together constitute a larger dog, whereas two or more quantities of matter together constitute a larger quantity of matter. It is customary, following Quine (1960, 91), to refer to this property of the extension of MNs as *cumulative reference*. Likewise, a (proper) part of a dog is not a smaller dog, whereas a part of matter is matter in the sense that a part of a portion of matter is a smaller portion of matter.

Many writers refer to this semantic property of MNs as *homogeneous* (or *distributed* or *divided* or *divisive*) *reference*. All the authors that we have consulted accept the cumulative reference (as we do), but the property of divisiveness of reference divides them!

What is our position in this debate? Our position can be best formulated by paraphrasing the great Mexican comic Mario Moreno, Cantinflas: "We are neither for nor against, but quite the opposite." In fact, if in accordance with the test of cumulative reference we interpret a MN as a sup-lattice M (i.e., a poset such that every subset has a least upper bound), then it makes no sense to ask whether *a part* of an element of M is again an element of M. What could be a part over and above the elements of M? We believe that this discussion presupposes (perhaps inadvertently) a universal substance, a sup-lattice containing every interpretation of a MN as a sub sup-lattice. With such a substance it makes sense to ask whether every element of the universal substance, which is a part of an element of M, is an element of M. We reject the notion of a universal substance, however, and so we are led to reject the whole debate as meaningless. This rejection, however, seems to go too far. Take for instance the MN 'footwear'. It applies to a shoe and to any collection of shoes, but does not apply to a proper *part* of a shoe. A shoe's heel is certainly not footwear, and a leg of a table is not furniture. Thus, there is a truth of the matter whether a *part* of a shoe is a shoe and a part of a table is a table. All of this seems perfectly meaningful, and such knowledge is assumed in the everyday use of the language. Indeed, later we will introduce a notion of substance relative to a system of interpretations of nouns (like 'heel' and 'leg'), and these questions will in fact become meaningful. The answer will depend of course on the system of interpretations considered.

Notice that a related although different question may be formulated meaningfully without invoking a universal substance: is the sup-lattice M atomless? The reason is that the notion of an atom (or primitive element) is definable in any sup-lattice. We believe that these two questions (whether the part of an element of M is again an element of M and whether M is atomless) have sometimes been confounded, and this has obscured the fact that the first can be formulated only if a universal notion of substance is assumed. At any rate, under the assumption of a universal substance, divisiveness of reference implies that the extensions of MNs are atomless. This is the only issue that we will address at this point.

Several authors (see, e.g., Roeper 1983; Lonning 1987; Bunt 1985) have erected divisiveness of reference into a characteristic of MNs. Bunt

(1985, 45–46), for example, allows that in the actual physical extensions of many MNs there are minimal parts, but dismisses the fact as linguistically irrelevant. Quine (1960), Parsons (1970), Gillon (1992), and others reject this claim for the reason that we formulate as follows. It may well be that for many centuries users of the English word 'water' have not realized that there are minimal portions of water—namely, molecules—whose parts are not water. (Notice how both questions, already discussed, are here confounded.) The effective use of the word does not depend on knowledge of that scientific fact. This seems to have led some writers to the conclusion that the facts of the matter have no bearing on the extensions of common nouns. But extension is extension, independent of our knowledge. There is a truth of the matter that there are minimal parts in extensions of some MNs at least: witness the examples of 'footwear' and 'furniture' already discussed. Thus, we do not see reasons to set limitations a priori to extensions of MNs. Furthermore, excluding atomic extensions would rule out the possibility of considering plurals as MNs. Not only is there linguistic evidence to consider plurals as MNs, discussed by Carlson and Link (see below), but we will see that the plural construction may be viewed as a basic link between CNs and MNs. The fruitfulness of this approach will be apparent in the chapter.

17.1.3 Categories of Nouns and Their Interpretations

One of the main novelties of our approach is our taking into account the connections between MNs, the connections between CNs, and the ways in which MNs can be transformed into CNs and vice versa. For instance, there is a connection between the MN 'iron' and the MN 'metal' described in colloquial language by the sentence 'Iron is metal', analogous to that between 'a dog' and 'an animal' that we studied in La Palme Reyes, Macnamara, and Reyes 1994a. Furthermore, there must be some way of connecting the MN 'metal' and the CN 'a metal' to validate some arguments involving both expressions. This net of connections may be organized in an objective way by means of a system of categories and functors: the nominal theory. This system includes the category $\mathscr{CN}$ whose objects are CNs and whose morphisms are axioms of the form 'a dog is a mammal', 'a mammal is an animal', which may be thought of as a system of identifications. By composing those axioms, we obtain the new identification 'a dog is an animal'. In a similar vein, the nominal theory includes the category $\mathscr{MN}$ of MNs such as 'iron' and 'metal', whose morphisms are axioms such as 'iron is metal'. The transformations mentioned before between CNs and MNs are described by functors. One example is the plural formation that takes the CN 'dog' into 'dogs'. Since the extension of this term obviously has the property of cumulative reference, we categorize 'dogs' as a MN. Carlson (1977) and then Link (1983) called attention to the affinity between plurals and MNs. In fact, this affinity even extends to the syntax of both expressions. As an example, just like MNs, plural CNs do not take the plural. Also on a par with MNs, such combinations as *'a dogs' and *'another dogs' are ungrammatical.

We interpret the nominal theory as follows: CNs are interpreted as sets (or kinds). Morphisms between CNs are interpreted as set-theoretical maps. Such maps we call *underlying*. MNs are interpreted as sup-lattices (to be defined precisely later) and morphisms as sup-preserving maps. Functors of the nominal theory are interpreted as functors of the corresponding interpretations. For instance, formation of the plural is interpreted as the power set functor between the interpretations of $\mathscr{C}\mathscr{N}$ and those of $\mathscr{M}\mathscr{N}$, that is, between the category of sets, *Sets*, and the category of sup-lattices, *Sl*.

17.1.4   Grammatical Transformations and Syllogisms

The nominal theory and its interpretation will be used in this chapter for a single goal: to discuss the validity of a sample of eight syllogisms discussed by Pelletier and Schubert (1989), involving CNs, MNs, and predicables. To achieve this purpose, we need to build semantic counterparts to grammatical transformations of CNs into MNs, MNs into predicables, and so on, extending our previous work (La Palme Reyes, Macnamara, and Reyes 1994a). As an example, consider the syllogism

Claret is a wine, wine is a liquid, so claret is liquid.

In the first premise, 'claret' is a NP (noun phrase) and 'is a wine' a VP (verb phrase); in the second, 'wine' is a NP and 'is a liquid' a VP. In the conclusion, 'claret' is a NP (as in the first premise) and 'is liquid' is a VP. The NPs in this example are, however, like PNs (proper names) or descriptions. Crosslinguistic evidence suggests that 'claret' is not a PN. In fact, in French, one uses the expression 'le bordeaux', and French does not allow the definite article in front of a PN. This suggests categorizing 'claret' as a descriptive noun phrase (DNP), that is, as a NP whose interpretation is a member of a kind. As in La Palme Reyes, Macnamara, and Reyes 1994a, we consider 'is a wine' as a predicable derived from the term 'wine' (a CN, as indicated by the occurrence of 'a'). The second premise can be analyzed in a similar way. On the other hand, we will assume that 'is liquid' in the conclusion is a predicable derived from the term 'liquid' (a MN, as indicated by the absence of 'a').

At the level of interpretation, these grammatical transformations (or derivations) will take us into computations of colimits of interpretations in our categories to define notions of relative entity, relative substance, and so on.

17.1.5   Category Theory versus Set Theory

A final word about the use of category theory (rather than set theory) in this chapter. (For a more thorough discussion, see Magnan and Reyes 1994.) A first observation concerns generality: sets themselves constitute a particular category. The use of category theory allows us to formulate semantics that are free of the particular determinations imposed by a too rigid adherence to set theory. From this point of view, we would like to emphasize that the semantics introduced here is one among several possible ones.

A second observation concerns abstractness. Contrary to widespread belief, set-theoretic semantics are more abstract than category-theoretic ones. This is easily understood when we compare usual set-theoretic semantics of CNs and MNs with our category-theoretic semantics. As we pointed out, one of the main novelties of our approach is to take as the basic ingredients of our semantics the connections between dogs and animals, iron and metal, wines and wine, and so on. These connections guided the choice of the categories used to interpret CNs and MNs.

To give an example, any sup-lattice is also an inf-lattice; thus, from a set-theoretical point of view, it makes no difference whether one works with sup-lattices or inf-lattices. On the other hand, morphisms of sup-lattices are quite different from morphisms of inf-lattices. The following example shows that underlying relations do not preserve $\wedge$ in general: take a person who has traveled twice, say, and consider the underlying map at the level of sets of persons (which are sup-lattices as well as inf-lattices),

$$2^{PASSENGER} \xrightarrow{u} 2^{PERSON},$$

which associates with a set of passengers the underlying set of persons. Clearly, u preserves $\bigvee$ (arbitrary unions in this case). On the other hand, u does not preserve binary $\wedge$: Let p_1, p_2 be the two passengers whose underlying person is John. Then $\{p_1\} \wedge \{p_2\} = \varnothing$ and hence $u(\{p_1\} \wedge$

$\{p_2\}) = \varnothing$. But $u\{p_1\} \wedge u\{p_2\} = \{John\}$. Other examples of this kind can be given to justify our choice of categories.

From this point of view, the trouble with set-theoretical semantics is simply this: they are too abstract, since they abstract away these fundamental relations, which are therefore not properly represented (in these semantics). As a consequence, set-theoretical constructions are not constrained in a natural way: there are just too many, and when a choice is required, extraneous principles, usually of a pragmatic nature, are brought in to decide the issue. On the other hand, categorical constructions are highly constrained through the use of universal properties: among all possible constructions, one is distinguished as satisfying a universal property. Because of this feature, it has been argued that the theory of categories constitutes a theory of concrete universals, set theory being rather a theory of abstract universals (Ellerman 1988). This explains the ubiquity of universal constructions in this chapter. In a more speculative way, we are tempted to believe that universal constructions may capture what is universal in the human mind, including what is fundamental in human language.

17.2   The Nominal Theory

We now describe the *nominal theory*. This theory describes in an objective way the count nouns (CNs), the mass nouns (MNs), and their transformations by means of a system of categories and functors

$$\mathscr{CN} \atop p \left\downarrow \uparrow\right. u \atop \mathscr{MN}$$

satisfying the following relation: $p \dashv u$, namely, p is left adjoint to u. We will illustrate this relation below. We think of p as 'plural of' and of u as 'a portion of', 'a number of', 'a set of', and so on, since there is no unified way (and sometimes simply no way) of expressing u at the surface level. The adjointness relation states the equivalence between an axiom of the form $p(\boxed{\text{a portion of meat}}) \overset{are}{\to} \boxed{\text{food}}$ in $\mathscr{MN}$ ('portions of meat are food') and the axiom $\boxed{\text{a portion of meat}} \overset{is}{\to} u(\boxed{\text{food}})$ in $\mathscr{CN}$ ('a portion of meat is a portion of food'). This is clear enough. Sometimes, however, we lack lexical items to express u, as in the equivalence (also obtained from the adjunction) between $p(\boxed{\text{a dog}}) \overset{are}{\to} \boxed{\text{animals}}$ in $\mathscr{MN}$ ('dogs are animals') and the axiom $\boxed{\text{a dog}} \xrightarrow{is} u(\boxed{\text{animals}})$ in $\mathscr{CN}$ (which could be expressed rather clumsily as 'a dog is a number of animals', with the understanding that this number could be one). Axioms in this relation are said to be *transposes* of each other.

Notice that under this adjunction, $pu(\boxed{\text{meat}}) \xrightarrow{are} \boxed{\text{meat}}$ ('portions of meat are meat') is an axiom of $\mathscr{MN}$, since its transpose $u(\boxed{\text{meat}}) \xrightarrow{} u(\boxed{\text{meat}})$ ('a portion of meat is a portion of meat') is an axiom of $\mathscr{CN}$, indeed an identity axiom. Axioms obtained in this way are called *co-units* of the adjunction. Similarly, $\boxed{\text{a dog}} \xrightarrow{is} up(\boxed{\text{a dog}})$ ('a dog is a number of dogs') is an axiom of $\mathscr{CN}$, since its transpose $p(\boxed{\text{a dog}}) \xrightarrow{are} p(\boxed{\text{a dog}})$ ('dogs are dogs') is an identity axiom of $\mathscr{MN}$. Axioms obtained in this way are called *units* of the adjunction.

This way of conceptualizing the plural formation seems compatible with that of Jackendoff (1991). The main difference between the two approaches is that we organize nouns into categories ($\mathscr{CN}$ and $\mathscr{MN}$) and so we can consider plural formation as a functor between them, whereas Jackendoff divides nouns into sets: 'individuals' ('*a dog*'), 'groups' ('*a committee*'), 'substances' ('*water*'), and 'aggregates' ('*buses*', '*cattle*'). Plural formation in his theory is a map (between some of these sets) that sends, for instance, 'a dog' into 'dogs' and 'a committee' into 'committees'. This is precisely the way our functor acts on objects of the category $\mathscr{CN}$. A further difference concerns his division of nouns. It may be possible to introduce these further divisions in our approach, a question we have not investigated. We plan to return to this question in a forthcoming paper.

Each category of the nominal theory may be considered as a system of identifications that replaces the '=' of a single sorted theory. These categories seem to be posetal in the sense that there is at most one arrow between two objects, but we will not require them to be so.

$\mathscr{CN}$ is the category whose objects are "genuine" CNs such as $\boxed{\text{a dog}}$, $\boxed{\text{a mammal}}$, $\boxed{\text{an animal}}$ and whose morphisms are axioms of identification of the form

$$\boxed{\text{a dog}} \xrightarrow{is} \boxed{\text{a mammal}},$$

$$\boxed{\text{a mammal}} \xrightarrow{is} \boxed{\text{an animal}}.$$

The identity morphisms are particular axioms of the form

$$\boxed{\text{a dog}} \xrightarrow{is} \boxed{\text{a dog}},$$

and composition is given by modus ponens. For instance, from

$$\boxed{\text{a dog}} \xrightarrow{\text{is}} \boxed{\text{a mammal}}$$

and

$$\boxed{\text{a mammal}} \xrightarrow{\text{is}} \boxed{\text{an animal}},$$

we obtain

$$\boxed{\text{a dog}} \xrightarrow{\text{is}} \boxed{\text{an animal}}.$$

Similarly, $\mathcal{MN}$ is the category whose objects are MNs such as $\boxed{\text{water}}$, $\boxed{\text{iron}}$, $\boxed{\text{veal}}$, $\boxed{\text{meat}}$, $\boxed{\text{food}}$ and whose morphisms are of the form

$$\boxed{\text{veal}} \xrightarrow{\text{is}} \boxed{\text{meat}},$$

$$\boxed{\text{meat}} \xrightarrow{\text{is}} \boxed{\text{food}}.$$

Identity morphisms and composition of morphisms are as above.

The maps p and u are assumed to be functorial. The functoriality of p amounts to saying that from

$$\boxed{\text{an A}} \xrightarrow{\text{is}} \boxed{\text{a B}},$$

we may conclude that

$$\boxed{\text{As}} \xrightarrow{\text{are}} \boxed{\text{Bs}}.$$

As an example, from

$$\boxed{\text{a portion of meat}} \xrightarrow{\text{is}} \boxed{\text{a portion of food}},$$

we may conclude that

$$\boxed{\text{portions of meat}} \xrightarrow{\text{are}} \boxed{\text{portions of food}}.$$

The functoriality of u says that from

$$\boxed{\text{M}} \xrightarrow{\text{is}} \boxed{\text{N}},$$

we obtain

$$\boxed{\text{a portion of M}} \xrightarrow{\text{is}} \boxed{\text{a portion of N}}.$$

In particular, from

$$\boxed{\text{veal}} \xrightarrow{\text{is}} \boxed{\text{meat}},$$

we obtain

$$\boxed{\text{a portion of veal}} \xrightarrow{\text{is}} \boxed{\text{a portion of meat}},$$

which agrees with intuition.

Notice that there is a link between, say, $\boxed{\text{meat}}$ and $\boxed{\text{portions of meat}}$. These links are precisely what the functors of the nominal theory are supposed to describe. For instance, from $p \dashv u$ it follows that

$$pu\,\boxed{\text{meat}} \xrightarrow{\text{are}} \boxed{\text{meat}}$$

is an instance of the co-unit of the adjunction and hence a morphism of the nominal theory. Recalling that $pu\,\boxed{\text{meat}} = \boxed{\text{portions of meat}}$, this morphism says that 'portions of meat are meat'.

A very interesting feature of the count/mass categorization of nouns is its nonexclusive character. In fact, some nouns such as 'wine' belong to both categories. Thus, we may say 'Claret is a wine' and 'More wine was served after the dessert'. In the first sentence, 'wine' appears as a CN, whereas in the second, it appears as a MN. At the level of the nominal theory, this means that we have two objects:

$$\boxed{\text{a wine}} \in \mathscr{CN} \quad \text{and} \quad \boxed{\text{wine}} \in \mathscr{MN}.$$

But surely there must be a connection between them. We represent the connection by a morphism of $\mathscr{CN}$:

$$\boxed{\text{a wine}} \xrightarrow{\text{is}} u\,\boxed{\text{wine}}.$$

Equivalently, since p is left adjoint to u, the connection may be expressed by a morphism of $\mathscr{MN}$:

$$\boxed{\text{wines}} \xrightarrow{\text{are}} \boxed{\text{wine}}.$$

These morphisms express that 'a wine is wine' and 'wines are wine', respectively (these assertions are indeed obviously equivalent). In section 3 we will interpret the first as a morphism of the category of sets. The second, on the other hand, we will interpret as a morphism of the category of sup-lattices, its transpose. Notice that the morphism $\boxed{\text{a wine}} \overset{is}{\to} u\,\boxed{\text{wine}}$ is quite different from $\boxed{\text{a wine}} \overset{is}{\to} \boxed{\text{a wine}}$, a morphism of $\mathscr{CN}$ that expresses that 'a wine is a wine' and that will be interpreted as an identity map in the category of sets.

The case of wine is not an isolated one. Another example is 'metal'. Thus, we can say 'Iron is a metal', but also 'Iron is metal'. Once again, the connection between the two occurrences of 'metal' is expressed in the nominal theory by a morphism in $\mathscr{CN}$:

$$\boxed{\text{a metal}} \overset{is}{\longrightarrow} u\,\boxed{\text{metal}}.$$

Equivalently, we may express the connection by a morphism in $\mathscr{MN}$:

$$\boxed{\text{metals}} \overset{are}{\longrightarrow} \boxed{\text{metal}}.$$

Note that in addition to the previously mentioned endofunctor $pu : \mathscr{MN} \to \mathscr{MN}$, which may be read as 'portions of' or 'numbers of', $up : \mathscr{CN} \to \mathscr{CN}$ is an endofunctor that may be read as 'a set of' (or 'a number of'), whose interpretation will be the power set operation.

REMARK 1   It is interesting to observe that the functor p is not full in general. This means that there might be morphisms $p(\boxed{\text{an A}}) \overset{are}{\to} p(\boxed{\text{a B}})$ in $\mathscr{MN}$ that do not come from any morphism $\boxed{\text{an A}} \overset{is}{\to} \boxed{\text{a B}}$ of $\mathscr{CN}$. In more logical terms: the sentences 'A's are B's' and 'An A is a B' are not equivalent in general (although the second implies the first). This fact seems to contradict a widespread belief. As an example, consider 'Living room sets are items of furniture' and 'A living room set is an item of furniture'. The first is true; the second is false.

17.3   Interpretations of the Nominal Theory

Our goal in this section is to define the notion of an interpretation of the nominal theory. As we explained in section 17.1.3, CNs are interpreted as sets and MNs as sup-lattices. Notice, however, that sets and sup-lattices constitute categories. Indeed, the category of sets, *Sets*, has sets as objects and set-theoretical functions as morphisms. Composition is the ordinary notion of composition between functions. The category of sup-lattices, *Sl*, has sup-lattices as objects and sup-preserving functions as morphisms. More precisely, an *object* of *Sl* is a triple $(M, \leq, \bigvee)$ where $(M, \leq)$ is a poset and $\bigvee : 2^M \to M$ associates with every subset of M its supremum. Thus, $\bigvee A \leq m$ iff $\forall m' \in A \; m' \leq m$. A *morphism* of *Sl*

$$f : (M, \leq, \bigvee) \rightarrow (N, \leq, \bigvee)$$

is a set-theoretical map between $f : M \rightarrow N$ that preserves suprema in the sense that $f(\bigvee A) = \bigvee \exists_f(A)$, where $\exists_f(A) = \{y \in N : \exists x \in A(y = f(x))\}$, that is, the image of A under the function f. Once again, composition is the usual composition between functions.

REMARK 2   In La Palme Reyes, Macnamara, and Reyes 1994b, interpretations of CNs are *kinds*, namely, sets with a relation of constituency, associating with each member the set of situations of which that member is a constituent. This allows us to study predicables like 'sick' or 'run' that may hold of a member of a kind at a given situation but fail to hold at another. To simplify the presentation, we will leave situations out of the picture and interpret CNs as sets and MNs as sup-lattices. Furthermore, these simplified notions will suffice for the limited aim of this chapter.

There is a connection between these categories that may be described by means of two functors

Set

$P \Big\Updownarrow U$

Sl

such that $P \dashv U$. P is the (covariant) power set functor and U is the forgetful functor. More precisely, P is the functor that associates with a set X the sup-lattice PX of the subsets of X, and with a function $f : X \rightarrow Y$ the function $\exists_f : PX \rightarrow PY$ defined above. This is clearly a *Sl*-morphism.

On the other hand, U is the functor that associates with a sup-lattice $(M, \leq, \bigvee)$ the set M and with the morphism $f : (M, \leq, \bigvee) \rightarrow (N, \leq, \bigvee)$ the function f itself.

We will usually denote by '$O(A)$', '$O(B)$', '$O(C)$', ... the objects of *Sl* and write '$|O(A)|$' instead of '$U(O(A))$'.

An *interpretation* of the nominal theory in the system of categories just described is given by two functors (both denoted by I) making the following diagram commutative

$$\mathscr{CN} \xrightarrow{\;I\;} Set$$
$$p \Big\Updownarrow u \qquad\qquad P \Big\Updownarrow U$$
$$\mathscr{MN} \xrightarrow{\;I\;} Sl$$

in the obvious sense; for instance, $PI = Ip$, and so on.

This means that the objects and the morphisms of $\mathcal{CN}$ are interpreted as sets and morphisms between these sets, the objects and the morphisms of $\mathcal{MN}$ as objects and morphisms of Sl. Furthermore, the interpretations should "behave well" with respect to functors of the nominal category. Thus, for instance, $PI = Ip$ means that if the interpretation of $\boxed{\text{a dog}}$ is the set of dogs, then the interpretation of $\boxed{\text{dogs}}$ should be the set of sets of dogs, and so on. (It is worthwhile to notice that axioms in the nominal theory are interpreted not as truth-values but as maps.)

Functoriality of $I : \mathcal{CN} \rightarrow Sets$ means that the interpretation of 'is' in the axiom

$$\boxed{\text{a dog}} \xrightarrow{\;is\;} \boxed{\text{an animal}}$$

is a morphism of sets—intuitively the one that assigns to a dog its underlying animal. Furthermore, the interpretation of 'is' in the axiom

$$\boxed{\text{a dog}} \xrightarrow{\;is\;} \boxed{\text{a dog}}$$

is the identity map; and so on.

REMARK 3 Lawvere (1992) has suggested identifying categories of space with distributive categories and categories of quantity with linear categories. In the appendix we will show that the target category of the interpretations of CNs, $Sets$, constitutes a category of space whereas the target category of the interpretations of MNs, Sl, constitutes a category of quantity. We feel that any determination of the interpretations of CNs and MNs should have these properties. Ours is just one such determination, chosen mainly for simplicity.

17.4 Syllogisms and Their Validity

17.4.1 Some Types of Syllogisms
After defining the notion of interpretation we may study validity of all kinds of reasoning involving CNs, MNs, DNPs, and predicables, as is usually done in logic. Lacking a systematic way of generating these kinds of reasoning, we will limit ourselves mainly to a few syllogisms that have been studied in the literature (Pelletier and Schubert 1989). The notion of validity for syllogisms is the usual Tarski's notion of truth, defined by recursion on complexity of formulas.

(a) Syllogisms involving CNs, PNs, and predicables. These are the usual Aristotelian syllogisms such as

All Greeks are men, all men are mortal, so all Greeks are mortal.

In La Palme Reyes, Macnamara, and Reyes 1994a, we noticed two problems connected with such syllogisms: one due to the change of grammatical role of some of the terms (e.g., 'men' appears as part of a predicable in the first premise and as a CN in referring position, subject of the sentence, in the second); the other due to the change of sorting of predicables (e.g., 'mortal' is sorted by the CN 'men' in the second premise and by the CN 'Greek' in the conclusion).

These problems were dealt with in the work cited, and we will say nothing more about them here beyond remarking that the main idea was to use the colimit of a system of kinds to construct a coincidence relation that in turn provides a semantical counterpart to the transformation of a CN into a predicable. We will extend these notions here to systems of sup-lattices giving semantical counterparts to the transformations of MNs into predicables, essential for the validity of the syllogisms.

(b) Syllogisms involving MNs, DNPs, and predicables. An example of these is

Claret is beer, beer is alcoholic, so claret is alcoholic.

Notice that here we have problems similar to those found in the Aristotelian syllogisms: 'is beer' is a VP (or predicable) in the first premise and a NP—in fact, a DNP—in the second. A further problem concerns the sort of the predicable 'alcoholic': it seems to be sorted by 'beer' in the second premise but by 'claret' in the conclusion. However, 'claret' is categorized only as a MN in the nominal theory. If this is so, should we allow MNs as well as CNs to sort predicables?

Another example of such a syllogism is

Claret is a beer, beer is a liquid, so claret is liquid.

In this syllogism a new difficulty presents itself. In fact, 'liquid' appears as a predicable derived from the CN 'liquid' in the second premise (as witnessed by the particle 'a'), but as a predicable derived from the MN 'liquid' in the conclusion.

We must give a semantical account of these transformations if we ever hope to test the validity of this type of syllogism.

The way to tackle these problems is parallel to that employed with the Aristotelian syllogisms and depends on a notion of coincidence that allows us to transform a MN into a predicable, for instance, from 'beer' to 'to be beer'. We will deal with these questions in section 17.4.4.

REMARK 4   (1) We have given as examples syllogisms whose premises are not necessarily true to avoid falling into the trap of believing that they should be taken as axioms of the nominal theory, thereby limiting the validity of syllogisms to a very restricted class. (2) We have given what we believe to be a "literal" reading of the syllogisms. This does not seem to be the only possible reading. In fact, we could also read the first premise as 'claret is a kind of beer'. It is important to keep this in mind when testing the validity of syllogisms.

17.4.2   Coincidence Relations and Predicates

In the appendix we will construct notions of entity (a set E) and substance (a sup-lattice $O(S)$), relative to an interpretation, with a map $\theta : E \rightarrow O(S)$ and underlying maps $can_X : X \rightarrow E$ from each set X that interprets a CN and underlying sup-lattice maps $can_{O(A)} : O(A) \rightarrow O(S)$ from each sup-lattice $O(A)$ that interprets a MN.

In turn, these notions will allow us to define two coincidence relations between members of kinds. Both of these notions are reflexive, symmetric, and transitive. According to the first, a and b are E-coincident if they have the same underlying entity. As an example, a dog is E-coincident with its underlying animal. According to the second, a and b are $O(S)$-coincident if they have the same underlying substance. As an example, a portion of iron is $O(S)$-coincident with its underlying portion of metal. Because of the existence of the map $E \rightarrow O(S)$, E-coincidence implies $O(S)$-coincidence. Thus, a dog and its underlying animal have the same underlying substance.

In terms of these notions, we will define the semantical counterpart of the grammatical transformations between CNs, MNs, and predicables in section 17.4.4.

17.4.3   Grammatical Analysis

Following Pelletier and Schubert (1989), we will limit ourselves to the following list of eight syllogisms and compare our results with theirs.

1. Claret is a wine, wine is a liquid, so claret is a liquid.
2. Claret is a wine, wine is a liquid, so claret is liquid.
3. Claret is a wine, wine is liquid, so claret is liquid.
4. Claret is a wine, wine is liquid, so claret is a liquid.
5. Claret is wine, wine is a liquid, so claret is a liquid.

6. Claret is wine, wine is a liquid, so claret is liquid.
7. Claret is wine, wine is liquid, so claret is a liquid.
8. Claret is wine, wine is liquid, so claret is liquid.

Before testing the validity of these syllogisms, we need to assign grammatical roles to their terms. As noted in remark 4, we will make our reading of them as literal as possible.

First, a general remark to motivate the analysis. Syllogisms are grounded in the nominal theory, in the sense that terms other than predicables belong to the nominal theory and are thus categorized as either a CN or a MN. (Some terms may appear in more than one category.)

We will assume that the nominal theory categorizes 'claret' as a MN ($\boxed{\text{claret}}$), but 'wine' and 'liquid' as both CNs ($\boxed{\text{a wine}}$, $\boxed{\text{a liquid}}$) and MNs ($\boxed{\text{wine}}$, $\boxed{\text{liquid}}$).

Let us consider the second syllogism. The first premise, 'claret is a wine', is analyzed grammatically as NP + VP. In turn, NP is analyzed as DNP (descriptive noun phrase) with lexical item $\boxed{\text{claret}}$. On the other hand, VP is analyzed as V + NP with lexical items 'is' and $\boxed{\text{a wine}}$. Following proposals in La Palme Reyes, Macnamara, and Reyes 1994a, the VP 'is a wine' is deduced from the CN 'wine'. The second premise, 'wine is a liquid', is analyzed similarly. On the other hand, the conclusion, 'claret is liquid', will be analyzed as DNP + VP, where 'is liquid' is derived from the MN 'liquid'.

17.4.4 Interpretation and Validity

As we said in section 17.3, a CN is interpreted as a kind (or set in this chapter), a MN as a sup-lattice, a DNP as a member of a kind, and a VP as a predicate.

Coming back to the second syllogism, the lexical item $\boxed{\text{claret}}$ in $\mathcal{MN}$, analyzed as a DNP, should be interpreted as a member of a kind. But what member of what kind? We propose to interpret it as the largest element $1_{O(C)}$ of the sup-lattice $O(C)$ that interprets (the MN) $\boxed{\text{claret}}$ — namely, as the largest portion of claret, in the kind $|O(C)|$. The predicable 'is a wine' is interpreted as the predicate of being E-coincident with a particular wine. Thus, 'claret is a wine' is true iff $1_{O(C)}$ E-coincides with some $w \in W$, where W is the kind of wines. Similarly, 'wine is a liquid' is true iff $1_{O(W)}$ E-coincides with some $l \in L$. where L is the kind of liquids. On the other hand, the conclusion, 'claret is liquid', is true iff $1_{O(C)}$ has the property of being liquid. We consider this property as sorted by the CN 'a portion of claret'. Thus, the predicate *IS LIQUID* sorted by $u(\boxed{\text{claret}})$ is a function $I(u(\boxed{\text{claret}})) = |I(\boxed{\text{claret}})| \to \{\text{True, False}\}$. This means that $1_{O(C)}O(S)$-coincides with a portion $\lambda \in O(L)$, where $O(L)$ is the sup-lattice of portions of liquid, which is the interpretation of the MN 'liquid'. To derive the conclusion, recall that we have a morphism 'wines are wine' in the nominal theory. This morphism is interpreted as a map $f : W \to O(W)$, which to w associates $f(w)$, a portion of wine in $O(W)$. Similarly, the morphism 'liquids are liquid' is interpreted as a map $g : L \to O(L)$.

Since E-coincidence implies $O(S)$-coincidence, from the premises we may conclude

(1) $1_{O(C)}$ is $O(S)$-coincident with $f(w)$;

(2) $1_{O(W)}$ is $O(S)$-coincident with $g(l)$.

By definition of $1_{O(W)}$, $f(w) \le 1_{O(W)}$, and this implies the corresponding inequality between the underlying substances,

(3) $can_{O(W)}(f(w)) \le can_{O(W)}(1_{O(W)})$,

since $can_{O(W)}$ is a sup-lattice map.

From (1), (2), and (3) we conclude easily that

(4) $can_{O(C)}(1_{O(C)}) \le can_{O(L)}(g(l))$.

To go further, we need another postulate. We shall assume that 'an $O(S)$-portion of liquid is liquid' in the precise sense that $can_{O(L)} : O(L) \to O(S)$ is *downward surjective*: if $s \le can_{O(L)}(\lambda)$, then there is $\lambda' \le \lambda$ such that $s = can_{O(L)}(\lambda')$. If this property is satisfied, we will say that $O(L)$ *is homogeneous* (or *distributed* or *divisive* or *divided*).

Putting all of this together, we have

PROPOSITION 1   If the interpretation $O(L)$ of 'liquid' is homogeneous, then the second syllogism is valid.

On the other hand, the first syllogism is not valid, even if $O(L)$ is homogeneous: 'an $O(S)$-portion of a liquid, although liquid, need not be *a* liquid'. In fact, proceeding in this way, we can prove the following:

THEOREM 1   If the interpretation $O(L)$ of 'liquid' is homogeneous, then the syllogisms 2, 3, 6, and 8 are valid, and the syllogisms 1, 4, 5, and 7 are not valid.

REMARK 5   Our conclusions put us at odds with Pelletier and Schubert (1989). Indeed, these authors consider the first syllogism as valid. However, we agree on the validity (and nonvalidity) of the remaining ones. The disagreement comes about from the different interpretations assigned to the CN 'a wine'. Unlike us, Pelletier and Schubert interpret it as 'a kind of wine' and they prove validity from the postulate that 'kinds of kinds are kinds'. Two remarks are in order. First, their interpretation is higher-order, since they quantify over 'kinds of wine'. Second, we do not believe that this rather vague notion allows us to found a logical theory. In particular, the postulate of transitivity is not evident to us.

Appendix

In this appendix, we formulate and prove some mathematical statements used in the main text.

A.1 (Co)cones and (Co)limits in a Category

Given a functor $F : \mathscr{I} \to \mathscr{A}$, a *cocone* for F consists of an object $A \in \mathscr{A}$ and a family $\{F(i) \xrightarrow{f_i} A\}_i$ of morphisms of $\mathscr{A}$ such that for every arrow $i \xrightarrow{\alpha} j \in \mathscr{I}$ the diagram

$$
\begin{array}{l}
F(i) \\
\quad \big\downarrow F(\alpha) \qquad \xrightarrow{f_i} A \\
F(j) \qquad \nearrow f_j
\end{array}
$$

commutes. This cocone will be denoted $(A, \{f_i\}_i)$. Cocones for F constitute a category by defining a morphism

$$\Phi : (A, \{f_i\}_i) \to (B, \{g_i\}_i)$$

to be a morphism of $\mathscr{A}, \Phi : A \to B$, such that $\Phi \circ f_i = g_i$ for all $i \in \mathscr{I}$.

We define the *colimit of F, colim F*, to be the initial cocone of this category. By spelling this out, *colim F* is a family $\{F(i) \xrightarrow{f_i} A\}_i$ of morphisms of $\mathscr{A}$ such that

1. For every arrow $i \xrightarrow{\alpha} j \in \mathscr{I}$ the diagram

commutes.

2. (Universal Property) Whenever $\{F(i) \xrightarrow{g_i} B\}_i$ is a family of maps such that for every $i \xrightarrow{\alpha} j \in \mathscr{I}$ the diagram

commutes, there is a unique morphism $\theta : A \to B \in \mathscr{A}$ such that $\theta f_i = g_i$ for all i:

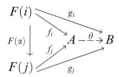

We say that the category $\mathscr{A}$ is *cocomplete* if every functor $F : \mathscr{I} \to \mathscr{A}$, $\mathscr{I}$ being a small category, has a colimit.

REMARK 6 (1) Since terminal objects are unique up to unique iso-morphism, we are justified in talking about "the" colimit of a functor. (2) Dually, we can define *cones* and *limits* in a category by considering $\mathscr{A}^{op}$, rather than $\mathscr{A}$. We say that $\mathscr{A}$ is *complete* if every functor $F : \mathscr{I} \to \mathscr{A}$, $\mathscr{I}$ being a small category, has a limit.

A.2 Exactness Properties of *Sets* and *Sl*

THEOREM 2   The category of sets, Sets, is complete, cocomplete, and dis-tributive in the strong sense that coproducts commute with pull-backs. Furthermore, surjections are stable.

Proof   All of this is well known (see, e.g., Mac Lane 1971).

As an example of colimits, let $\mathscr{I} = \mathscr{CN}$ and $F = I : \mathscr{CN} \to$ *Sets* be an interpretation of the category of CNs. The colimit of I may be described as follows:

1. Take the disjoint union $E_0 = \bigsqcup_i I(i)$. Thus, an element of E_0 is a couple (i, a) where $a \in I(i)$.
2. Take the smallest equivalence relation $\equiv$ on E_0 generated by the pairs $((i, a), (j, b))$ where there is $\alpha : i \to j \in \mathscr{CN}$ such that $I(i)(a) = b$.
3. Define $E = E_0/\equiv$ and maps, for each i,

$$I(i) \xrightarrow{u_i} E_0 \xrightarrow{[\,]} E,$$

as follows: $a \mapsto (i, a) \mapsto [(i, a)]$ where $[(i, a)]$ is the equivalence class of (i, a) under the relation $\equiv$.

Then $(I(i) \overset{[\ ]\circ u_i}{\longrightarrow} E)_i$ is the colimit of I.

To explain this construction in one example, assume that

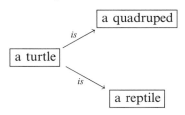

is a diagram in $\mathscr{CN}$ that expresses that 'a turtle is a quadruped' and 'a turtle is a reptile'. In E_0 we have couples like ($\boxed{\text{a quadruped}}$, q), ($\boxed{\text{a turtle}}$, t), and ($\boxed{\text{a reptile}}$, r), where $q \in I(\boxed{\text{a quadruped}})$, $t \in I(\boxed{\text{a turtle}})$, and $r \in I(\boxed{\text{a reptile}})$, respectively. Assume that q is the quadruped underlying the turtle t and r the reptile underlying t. Then ($\boxed{\text{a quadruped}}$, q), ($\boxed{\text{a turtle}}$, t), and ($\boxed{\text{a reptile}}$, r) are among the pairs generating $\equiv$. On the other hand, (($\boxed{\text{a quadruped}}$, q), ($\boxed{\text{a reptile}}$, r)), although not a generating pair, is in $\equiv$.

THEOREM 3   The category Sl is complete, cocomplete, and linear.

Proof This is again well known (see, e.g., Joyal and Tierney 1984). Recall that a category is linear if it has the following properties:

1. $\mathscr{C}$ has finite products and coproducts (including terminal and initial objects: 1 and 0, respectively).
2. The unique morphism $0 \to 1$ is an isomorphism with inverse $1 \to 0$.
3. The canonical morphism $A + B \to A \times B$ obtained from the morphisms

$$(1_A, 0_{AB}) : A \to A \times B$$

and

$$(0_{BA}, 1_B) : B \to A \times B$$

is an isomorphism, where 0_{AB} is the composite of $A \to 1$, $1 \to 0$, and $0 \to B$.

We proceed as in Joyal and Tierney 1984. In this category $1 = 0 = (\{*\}, \leq, \bigvee)$.

Products are diagrams

$$(M, \leq_M, \bigvee)$$

$$\overset{\pi_M}{\nearrow}$$

$$(M \times N, \leq, \bigvee)$$

$$\overset{\pi_N}{\searrow}$$

$$(N, \leq_N, \bigvee)$$

where $\leq$ is defined pointwise:

$$\bigvee_i (x_i, y_i) = (\bigvee_i x_i, \bigvee_i y_i), \pi_M(x, y) = x, \pi_N(x, y) = y.$$

Coproducts are diagrams

$$(M, \leq_M, \bigvee)$$

$$\overset{i_M}{\searrow}$$

$$(M \times N, \leq, \bigvee)$$

$$\overset{i_N}{\nearrow}$$

$$(N, \leq_N, \bigvee)$$

where $i_M(x) = (x, 0)$ and $i_N(y) = (0, y)$.

Equalizers are diagrams

$$(E, \leq_E, \bigvee) \overset{e}{\hookrightarrow} (M, \leq_M, \bigvee) \underset{g}{\overset{f}{\rightrightarrows}} (N, \leq_N, \bigvee)$$

such that

$$E \overset{e}{\hookrightarrow} M \underset{g}{\overset{f}{\rightrightarrows}} N$$

is an equalizer in *Sets*, $\leq = (e \times e)^{-1}(\leq_M)$.

Coequalizers are diagrams

$$(M, \leq_M, \bigvee) \underset{g}{\overset{f}{\rightrightarrows}} (N, \leq_N, \bigvee) \overset{q}{\rightarrow} (Q, \leq, \bigvee)$$

where

$$Q = \{z \in N : \forall x \in M(f(x) \leq z \leftrightarrow g(x) \leq z)\} \overset{i}{\hookrightarrow} N$$

and $q \dashv i$. (See Joyal and Tierney 1984 for this characterization.)

The universal property of the coequalizer is easy and left to the reader.

As an example of colimit (substance) in *Sl*, assume that $\mathscr{I}$ is the category

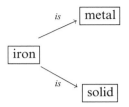

where identities have been omitted. Let $I : \mathscr{I} \to Sl$ be a functor. We will compute $O(S) = colimI$, following the description of colimits in terms of coequalizers (see Mac Lane 1971), as the coequalizer

$$I(\boxed{\text{iron}}) \overset{f}{\underset{g}{\rightrightarrows}} I(\boxed{\text{metal}}) \times I(\boxed{\text{solid}}) \overset{q}{\to} O(S),$$

where $f(a) = (u(a), 0)$ and $g(a) = (0, v(a))$ and $I(\boxed{\text{iron}}) \overset{u}{\to} I(\boxed{\text{metal}})$, $I(\boxed{\text{iron}}) \overset{v}{\to} I(\boxed{\text{solid}})$ are the interpretations of 'is' in $\mathscr{MN}$.

But $O(S)$ is then obtained by dividing out the coproduct

$$I(\boxed{\text{metal}}) \times I(\boxed{\text{solid}})$$

by the smallest sup-lattice congruence relation $\equiv$ such that

$$\forall a \in I(\boxed{\text{iron}})(u(a), 0) \equiv (0, v(a)).$$

As described in the preceding theorem,

$$O(S) = \{(b, c) \in I(\boxed{\text{metal}}) \times I(\boxed{\text{solid}}) :$$
$$\forall a \in I(\boxed{\text{iron}})(u(a) \leq b \leftrightarrow v(a) \leq c)\}$$

and $q(b, c) =$ the smallest $(b', c') \in O(S)$ such that $b \leq b'$ and $c \leq c'$.

The connection between *Sets* and *Sl* is given by the couple of functors P and U. These functors are of a special kind:

THEOREM 4   The functor P is left adjoint to U. (In symbols: $P \dashv U$.)

Proof   This is well known (see, e.g., Mac Lane 1971). The theorem says that there is a natural bijection between $Sl(PX, M)$, the set of sup-preserving maps from PX to M, and $Set(X, UM)$, the set of maps between X and the underlying set of M. This is a consequence of the following universal property of the singleton map $X \overset{\{\}}{\to} UPX$: for every set map $f : X \to U(M)$ there is a unique sup-preserving map $\tilde{f} : PX \to M$ such that $U(\tilde{f}) \circ \{ \} = f$. The proof of this assertion is rather immediate: the definition of the sup-preserving $\tilde{f}$ is forced to be

$$\tilde{f}(A) = \bigvee_{a \in A} f(a)$$

since $\tilde{f}$ must preserve $\bigvee$'s and $A = \bigcup_{a \in A}\{a\}$. (Of course one must prove that the map, so defined, is sup-preserving.)

This connection is reflected in a connection between entity and substance:

THEOREM 5   There is a unique map $\theta : E \to O(S)$ such that for each i the diagram

$$
\begin{array}{ccc}
I(i) & \xrightarrow{\{\}} & |PI(i)| = |Ip(i)| \\
\end{array}
$$

with $can_{I(i)}$ and $|can_{Ip(i)}|$ to $E \xrightarrow{\ \theta\ } |O(S)|$

is commutative.

Proof According to the definition of $E = colimI$, it is enough to show the commutativity of

$$
\begin{array}{ccc}
I(i) & \xrightarrow{\{\}} & |PI(i)| \\
\downarrow{I(\alpha)} & & \searrow^{|can_{Ip(i)}|} \\
& & |O(S)| \\
I(j) & \xrightarrow[\{\}]{} & |PI(j)| \nearrow_{|can_{Ip(j)}|}
\end{array}
$$

for all $i \xrightarrow{\alpha} j \in \mathscr{CN}$. But the diagram may be decomposed into a diagram in *Sets* and another in *Sl*:

$$
\begin{array}{ccc}
I(i) & \xrightarrow{\{\}} & |PI(i)| \\
\downarrow{I(\alpha)} & & \downarrow{|\exists_{I(\alpha)}|} \\
I(j) & \xrightarrow[\{\}]{} & |PI(j)|
\end{array}
$$

$$
\begin{array}{ccc}
PI(i) = Ip(i) & & \\
\downarrow{\exists_{I(\alpha)} = Ip(\alpha)} & \searrow^{can_{Ip(i)}} & \\
& & O(S) \\
PI(j) = Ip(j) & \nearrow_{can_{Ip(j)}} &
\end{array}
$$

The first commutes trivially: $\exists_{I(\alpha)}\{a\} = \{I(\alpha)(a)\}$. The second commutes by definition of $O(S)$. By property (2) of the definition of $E = colimI$, there is a unique $E \xrightarrow{\theta} |O(S)|$ such that $\theta \circ can_{I(i)} = |can_{Ip(i)}| \circ \{ \ \}$, which is the conclusion of the theorem.

References

Bunt, H. C. (1985). *Mass terms and model-theoretic semantics*. Cambridge: Cambridge University Press.

Carlson, G. (1977). A unified account of the English bare plural. *Linguistics and Philosophy, 1*, 413–457.

Ellerman, D. P. (1988). Category theory and concrete universals. *Erkenntnis, 28*, 409–429.

Gillon, B. S. (1992). Towards a common semantics for English count and mass nouns. *Linguistics and Philosophy, 15*, 597–639.

Jackendoff, R. (1991). Parts and boundaries. *Cognition, 41*, 9–45.

Jespersen, O. (1924). *The philosophy of grammar*. London: Allen and Unwin.

Joyal, A., and Tierney, M. (1984). *An extension of the Galois theory of Grothendieck* (Memoirs of the A.M.S., 309). Providence, RI: American Mathematical Society.

La Palme Reyes, M., Macnamara, J., and Reyes G. E. (1994a). Functoriality and grammatical role in syllogisms. *Notre Dame Journal of Formal Logic, 35*, 41–66.

La Palme Reyes, M., Macnamara, J., and Reyes, G. E. (1994b). Reference, kinds and predicates. In J. Macnamara and G. E. Reyes (Eds.), *The logical foundations of cognition* (pp. 91–143). Oxford: Oxford University Press.

La Palme Reyes, M., and Reyes, G. E. (to appear). *Generic figures and their glueings: A constructive approach to functor categories*.

Lawvere, F. W. (1992). Categories of space and of quantity. In J. Echeverría, A. Ibarra, and T. Mormann (Eds.), *The space of mathematics* (pp. 14–30). Berlin: de Gruyter.

Lawvere, F. W., and Schanuel, S. (1997). *Conceptual mathematics*. Cambridge: Cambridge University Press.

Link, G. (1983). The logical analysis of plurals and mass terms: A lattice-theoretic approach. In R. Bäuerle, C. Schwarze, and A. von Stechow (Eds.), *Meaning, use and interpretation of language* (pp. 302–323). Berlin: de Gruyter.

Lonning, J. T. (1987). Mass terms and quantification. *Linguistics and Philosophy, 10*, 1–52.

Mac Lane, S. (1971). *Categories for the working mathematician*. New York: Springer-Verlag.

Magnan, F., and Reyes, G. E. (1994). Category theory as a conceptual tool in the study of cognition. In J. Macnamara and G. E. Reyes (Eds.), *The logical foundations of cognition* (pp. 57–90). Oxford: Oxford University Press.

McPherson, L. M. P. (1991). A little goes a long way: Evidence for a perceptual basis of learning for the noun categories count and mass. *Journal of Child Language, 18*, 315–338.

Parsons, T. (1970). An analysis of mass and amount terms. *Foundations of Language, 6,* 363–388.

Pelletier, F. J., and Schubert, L. K. (1989). Mass expressions. In D. Gabbay and F. Guenthner (Eds.), *Handbook of philosophical logic* (vol. 4, pp. 327–407). Dordrecht: Reidel.

Quine, W. V. O. (1960). *Word and object.* Cambridge, MA: MIT Press.

Roeper, P. (1983). Semantics for mass terms with quantifiers. *Noûs, 17,* 251–265.

Soja, N. N., Carey, S., and Spelke, E. S. (1991). Ontological categories guide young children's inductions of word meaning: Object terms and substance terms. *Cognition, 38,* 179–211.

Index

Absolute theory
and discourse error, 27
Absolute theory of meaning, 18–24
Absolute truth-value
assessment of, 30
Abstraction
and superordinate concepts, 135–139
Abstractness
and the nominal theory, 433
Accidental properties, 129
Accommodation, xv
Acquired sense
and conceptual sedimentation, 178
Acquisition, xii. *See also* Acquisition
theory
boundedness, 325
and categorization, 297
and changes in irregular verbs, 243
in computation associator, 239
and continuity thesis, 313
of disappearance concept, 113
of essentiality, 142n9
and innateness, 263
and mapping, 289
of names of things, 131–135
past tense formation, 234–237
past tense verbs, 223
presemantic stage, 285–306
proper names, 337–370
proper nouns, 311
Acquisition theory, 110. *See also*
Acquisition
and truth/falsity judgment, 112
Action argument
constraints upon, 73
Active/passive statements, 198
and concept sedimentation, 203
Actor and Action
in rights and obligations, 72, 75–77
Addressee/speaker distinctions, 388

computer pronoun study, 399
and pronoun acquisition, 384, 394, 395,
402
and pronoun acquisition errors, 392
Adjectives
and child proper name use, 342
and proper names, 339, 351
Adult lexicon
and child acquisition, 314
Adult models. *See also* Parent teaching
and child verb learning, 243
and proper name acquisition, 368
Aesthetics
and semiosis, 151
"Aiming" notion
as first intention, 175
Akrasia, 100
Aletheia, 172
Algebra
and number theory, 186
Algebraic geometry, 412
Algebraic topology, 412
Alternatives
characteristics of, 102
in deliberation, 97
Altruism
in non-humans, 91
reciprocal, 86
Ambiguity
infant studies of, 320
and "up," 23
American Sign Language
and presyntactic learning, 289
Animals
and rights, 71
Animate objects
and proper name acquisition, 357–362
Antirealism
and realism, 33–37
Apex norm, 89

Aphasia
  mental representations in, 275
Appeal to authority
  and indexical view, 25
Application
  and pronoun acquisition, 383
Apraxia
  and specific language impairment, 266
Arbitrariness
  in decision making, 101
Argument structure
  of rights and obligations, 70–74
Aristotelian cause, 121–124
Aristotelian conception, 130–131
Aristotelian conception of things, 124–127
Aristotelian essences, 127–130
Aristotelian logic
  and naming of things, 119–141
Aristotelian syllogisms, 441
Aristotle, 97, 111, 113, 121
  number theory, 181
  theory of predication, 193
Arithmetic
  classical categories in, 249
Arithmetical theory of numbers, 181
Articles
  in European languages, 428
  and proper names, 339
Artifacts
  and proper name acquisition, 358–362
Assertions
  and child knowledge, 110
Assessment, 30
Assimilation, xv
Attention
  and sense of intention, 163
Attention disengagement, 332n2
Attitudes and beliefs
  contrasted with rights and obligations, 78
Aural cues
  and infant sound quantification, 296
Authenticity
  and ostension, 63–64
Authority
  forms, 94n13
  and indexical view, 25
  limitations, 88
  and rights and obligations, 75
  and rights and obligations theory, 87–89
Autism
  and pronoun acquisition, 394
  and referential acquisition, 374

Babylonian numeral system, 183
"Baptism"
  and acquisition of names, 132
Basic level category, 247

Basic-level object, 121
Becoming of parts, 413
Becoming of wholes, 413
Behaviorism
  and semiotic, 153
Being
  and Aristotelian predication theory, 195
  collections of, 181, 183, 203
  and conceptual sedimentation, 178
  and first/second intentions, 174–177
  and monad theory, 182
  as object of intention, 163
  and original concepts, 181
  theory generation regarding, 204
  unconcealment of, 161–207
  use of, 207n2
Belief content
  and expression, 26
Beliefs and attitudes
  contrasted with rights and obligations, 78
Benaceraff, P., 44, 45, 48, 57, 65
Beneficiary
  and Authority concept, 88
  and rights and obligations theory, 80, 82
Bias
  and decision making, 102
Binary relation
  and ratio theory, 191
Biological taxonomy
  and family resemblance categories, 251
Biology
  and language, 263
Blake, W., 60
Blindness
  and referential acquisition, 374
Blocking Principle
  and past tense formation, 229
Bloom, P., 285–305
Book of the Abacus, 184
Bootstrapping issue, 285–306. See also
  Prelinguistic representation; Presyntactic
  stage
Bouleusis, 97
Boundedness
  acquisition, 325
  and noun phrase distinctions, 297
Brain architecture
  nonassociative, 241
Brain development
  and specific language impairment, 265
Brain function
  indeterministic nature of, 104
Brentano, 173
Britain
  as nation-state, 2
Buridan's ass example, 101

Cantorian set theory, 44
Carey, S., 311–332
Cascade correlation learning algorithm
  for pronoun acquisition study, 397
Categorical logic, 43
Categories, 135–139. *See also* Classical
    categories; Conceptual categories
  cognitive purpose of, 246
  mathematical, 411
Categorization, 241, 312. *See also* Physical
    objects, individuation studies
  and cognition, 254, 295
  cognitive process, 255
  cognitive purpose, 246
  early acquisition, 289
  of mass/count nouns, 431
  and presemantics, 285, 286
  and proper name acquisition, 344
  studies, 222–224
Category-theoretical semantics, 427–450
Category theory, 44
  classical, 249
  vs. set theory, 433, 435
Catholicism
  and Irish nationality, 6, 7
Cauchy sequences, 185
Causal chains, 166
Causal determinism, 103
Causality, 106
  and explanation reasons, 103
Causal theory of reference, 59
Cause
  Aristotelian, 121–124
Certainty
  and logic systems, 109
Chains
  causal, 166
Character and content
  and pronoun semantics, 376
Cheater detection
  and cognitive bias, 86
Child-directed speech
  and pronoun acquisition, 402
Child knowledge
  and Macnamara's work, 67, 110
  and truth judgment, 112
Child language learning
  and continuity thesis, 313
  and count/mass syntax, 429
  and distributional properties theory, 286–288
  and essentialist thinking, 256
  and family resemblance categories, 223
  first words, 381
  and naming of things, 127, 131–135, 311

and past tense formation, 234–237
and past tense over-regularization, 239
personal pronouns, 373
presemantic stage, 285–306
pronouns, 379, 402
and proper name acquisition, 346
proper names, 337–370
and rights and obligations, 90
and role of memory, 242
syntactic first words, 290
Child speech
  proper names in, 342
Choice making, 99
Choice sets
  in deliberation, 97
  and determinism, 105
  formation of, 102
Church of England, 8
Civic nationalism, 2, 9n1
Classical categories, 221, 249. *See also*
    Categories
  and family resemblance categories, 254
  and idealization, 248
  and innateness, 234
  judges of, 223
  and linguistic rules, 229
  and proposition formation, 236
  and regular verbs, 233
Classifiers
  in Japanese language, 428
Class-inclusion
  and copula use, 197
Clusters of properties, 251. *See also*
    Properties
Cognition, 90. *See also* Spatial cognition
  and categorization, 254, 295
  conceptual categories, 221–257
  and essential properties of things, 131
  evolution of, 68
  and family resemblance categories, 229
  first year, 318
  and formal systems, 246–251
  infant, xiv
  and logical schema, 109
  and mathematical categories, 412
  nonlinguistic, 305
  thinking and reasoning, 67
Cognitive bias
  and cheater detection, 86
Cognitive deliberation, 97
Collections of beings
  and numbers, 181, 183
  and number theory sedimentation, 203
Common names. *See* Sortals

Common nouns. *See also* Proper names; Proper nouns; Sortals
  presyntactic acquisition, 380
  presyntactic acquisition of, 298
Communication
  nonhuman, 113
  theory of, 147
Comprehension
  and production, 363
  and pronoun acquisition, 390
Computational architecture
  and connectionist models, 240
  and pattern associators, 237
Computer modeling
  pronoun acquisition, 397–401
Concealment
  through second intentions, 177
Conceptions
  Aristotelian, 130–131
  and intentions, 176, 315
  in scientific theory, 161–207
Concepts
  and categorization, 312
  as family resemblance categories, 222
  and mathematical categories, 411
  nature of, 221–257
Concept sedimentation, 177–181, 202–204
Conceptual categories, 241
  and clusters of properties, 251
  cognitive purpose of, 246
  and legal/judicial systems, 256
Conceptual disengagement, 26–29
Conceptualization
  first year, 318
Conceptualization of things
  Aristotelian, 124–127
  and perception, 119
Conceptual-role approach to meaning, 18
Conceptual structure
  evidence for, 69
  and rights and obligations, 68
Conditioned behavior
  and semiotic linguistic theory, 154
Connectionist theory, 156, 240, 287
Connections
  as pronoun feature, 377, 378
Consequential regions, 248
Content
  effective, 39n18
  and meaning, 18
  and meaning through frames, 30
  personal pronouns, 380
Content and character
  and pronoun semantics, 376
Context
  compared to frames, 31

  and pronoun acquisition, 383
  and understanding, 32
Context features
  pronouns, 377
Continuity thesis, 313–315, 323
Contractual rights
  and social organization, 68
Conventions
  and pragmatism, 149
Convergence process
  and conceptual categories, 253
Copula
  and Aristotelian predication theory, 195
  interpretations of, 213n20
  and proper noun acquisition, 312
  and relation to being, 197
Coreference
  and presyntactic learning, 288
Corporations
  and rights and obligations, 71
Correspondence of being, 167
Correspondence rules
  and conceptual structure, 69
Counterpart function
  and change in number theory, 189
  and number theory, 183
Counting theory
  and modern concept of number, 181–189
Count/mass syntax, 295. *See also* Count nouns
  earliest command of, 287
  earliest stage of, 134
  early acquisition, 289
  French, 429
  and noun phrase acquisition, 306n3
  and semantics, 286
  and sortals, 312
  transformations of, 427–450
Count nouns. *See also* Count/mass syntax
  and conceptualization of things, 125–127
  and determiners, 375
  and number theory, 188
  and pronoun acquisition, 387
  and proper name acquisition, 343, 362–366
  role of, 374
  types of, 366
Creolization
  and presyntactic learning, 289
Cultural learning
  and rights and obligations concept, 90
Culture
  and language, 1
  and national identity, 5
  and noncompliance, 81
Cumulative reference
  and count/mass distinctions, 429

Customs
  and noncompliance, 81

Darwin, 263, 237
Davis, S., 147–158
Decisional paralysis, 101
Decision making, 99
  arbitrariness in, 101
  bias, 102
Declarative sentences
  and Aristotelian predication theory, 194
  and intention theory, 172
  and unconcealment, 205
Decomposition
  of idioms, 300
  of noun phrase, 298
Dedekind cuts, 185
Deep structure, 204
Deictic pronouns
  acquisition, 304
Deliberation, 97–107
Delimitation, 182
Demonstratives
  acquisition, 315
Denial concept
  acquisition, 113
Denominations
  and early number theory, 190
Denotation, 153
Denotation theory, 56
Deontic concepts. *See also* Deontic logic
  emergence, 91
  innateness, 90
Deontic logic, 71, 73. *See also* Deontic
    concepts
  and rights and obligations, 78
Depression
  and specific language impairment, 266
Descartes, 189, 197
Descartian models
  and logical positivism, 148
Descriptive noun phrase
  and transformation theory, 432
Designatum, 153
Determiners
  and count nouns, 375
  presyntactic acquisition, 298
  and presyntactic learning, 293
Determinism
  causal, 103
  choice sets, 105
Developmental language disorder. *See*
    Specific language impairment
Development theory, 111
Dialect formation, 244
Differential calculus, 412

Disappearance concept
  acquisition, 113
Discourse
  and essential properties of things, 131
  fictional/theoretical, 36
  and indexicals, 27
  and realism/antirealism debate, 33
  truth and falsity in, 111
  and unity of thought, 35
Discourse situation
  as pronoun feature, 377
Discovery
  and first intention, 177
Discrete functions, 138
Disengagement
  attention, 332n2
  conceptual, 26–29
Distributed reference. *See* Distributive
    reference
Distributional properties
  and presyntactic learning, 286–288
  and proper names learning, 347
Distributive reference, 314
  and count/mass distinctions, 430
"Divergence"
  and verb learning, 244
Divided reference. *See* Distributive
    reference; Individuation
Divisive reference. *See* Distributive
    reference
DNP. *See* Descriptive noun phrase
Dunamis, 172
Dyslexia
  and specific language impairment, 266

Eccentricity
  and error theory, 28
Economic nationalism
  in Ireland, 8
Effective contents, 39n18
Effective truth-value
  assessment of, 30
Efficient cause, 121
Eliminativism
  refutation of, 164–165
Empiricism
  and logical positivism, 148
Ends
  and deliberation, 97
Engagement with world discourse
  and realism/antirealism debate, 33
English language
  count/mass syntax, 427
  and Irish identity, 1
  and Irish nationality, 6, 12n9
  overt subject requirement in, 300

English language (cont.)
  past tense and categorization, 225
  pluralization in, 428
Entia realis, 174
Enti rationis, 174
Entities
  as objects, 142n5
  spatiotemporal, 120
Epistemological categories, 241
Epistemology
  and contemporary thought, 36
  and semiosis, 151
Equivalence
  and use of *for*, 84–85
Erkenntnis, 151
Error theory, 23, 28
  and pronoun acquisition, 389, 392
Essence of things. *See also* Entities; Nature
    of things
  Aristotelian, 121
Essences
  Aristotelian representation of, 127–131
Essentialist thinking, 255
Essential properties of things, 131
Ethical statements
  and error theories, 23
Ethnicity as state, 3
Euclid
  monad theory, 183
Euclidean models
  and logical positivism, 148
European languages
  count/mass syntax in, 428
Eustachius, 175
Evaluation
  process of, 98
Evolution, 251
Exchange notion
  linguistic expression of, 84–87
Existence of things, 60–62
Existential predicates
  and child knowledge, 110
Explanation reasons, 97–107
  life of, 100
Expletives
  categorization by child learner, 300
Extensional thinking, 197
Externalist perspective, 163
External world
  and conceptual structure mapping, 69
Eye contact
  and pronoun acquisition, 385

Fad theories, 206
False/true distinctions. *See under* True/false
Family history
  and specific language impairment, 264

Family resemblance categories, 221, 254
  and clusters of properties, 251
  and cognition, 229
  and Darwinian survival, 237
  and effect of memory, 236
  evidence against, 223
  evidence for, 222
  and memory, 242
  past tense formation by children, 235
  and pattern associators, 238
Fetal brain development
  and specific language impairment, 265
Fibonacci, Leonardo, 184
Fictional discourse, 36
Final cause, 121
Firstborns
  and computer pronoun study, 400
  and pronoun acquisition, 395
First intentions
  and number theory, 202, 203
  Renaissance sense of, 174
  and second intentions, 174–177
  and theoretical work, 206
First person pronouns. *See also* Pronoun
    acquisition; Pronouns
  acquisition, 373, 396
  character, 379
  learning in English, 373–404
Folk biology
  classical categories in, 249
Folk physiology
  classical categories in, 249
Folk science
  and formal systems, 249
Folk theory of mind
  and cognitive bias, 86
Force-dynamic expressions
  and rights and obligations predication, 76
Form
  as aspect of the object, 122
Formal cause, 121
  as matter of the object, 123
Formalist expression, 93n6
Formalist mathematicians, 188
Formal rules, 241
Formal systems
  and cognition, 246–251
  and regularities, 248
For use
  and equivalence, 84–85
Fractions
  as numbers, 184
Fragmentation
  and contemporary thought, 36
Frames, 29–33
  and context, 31
  and realist/antirealist synthesis, 34

Frege, G., 43, 51, 109, 110, 198
Fregean theory, 43, 46, 51
Frege-Tarski tradition, 69
French language
  count/mass syntax in, 429
  and impaired tense marking, 271
Frequency effects
  and specific language impairment, 274
Functional analysis, 412
Functions
  discrete/nondiscrete, 138
Functors, 57–58

Gaelic. *See* Irish language
  and Irish nationality, 6
Gender
  and genealogical categories, 418
  and topos formation, 423
Genealogical categories, 415
  and gender, 418
Genealogy
  and mathematical categories, 411
Generalization notion, 136–137
General rights, 79
"Genetic analysis," 178
Genetics
  and specific language impairment, 264, 280
    (*see also* Neurology)
Geography
  and nationality, 3
Geometry
  classical categories in, 249
  and Macnamara theory of morality, xv
  and number theory, 186
German language
  past tense characteristics, 240
Germany
  as ethnic nation, 4, 9n4
Goal generation, 165
Gopnik, M., 263–280
Grammar
  acquisition, xiii
  and innateness, 115
  linguistic variations in, 428
  and presyntactic learning, 285–305
  and pronoun acquisition, 375
  and proper names, 339
  and specific language impairment, 263–280
Grammaticality judgment
  and specific language impairment, 269
"Grammatical" subject, 203
Greek
  geometry ratios in, 186
  and impaired tense marking, 271
  number theory, 181–189, 210n9
  ratio theory, 189

Group theory, 56
Gupta, A., 15–37

Habit
  and linguistic utterance, 154
Habituation studies
  and sortal acquisition, 318
Hall, G., 337–370
Hearing impairment
  and pronoun acquisition, 394
"Hedges"
  and family resemblance categories,
    223
Heyting logic, 413
Hierarchy
  and obligations, 87
Hindu-Arabic number theory, 184
Home signs
  and presyntactic learning, 289
Homogeneity issue
  of semantical theory, 64–65
Homogeneous reference. *See* Distributive
    reference
Homophony
  and child acquisition, 305n1
  and past tense formation, 230
Human concepts
  nature of, 221–257
Human knowledge
  and logical positivism, 150
Human languages
  theory of, 147
Human reasoning
  role of logic in, 110
Human rights, 68
  acknowledgment of, 94n14
Husserl, E., 178, 180, 188

Idealism
  human capacity for, xv
Idealization
  and conceptual categories, 248, 255
Ideal Mathematician, 50
"Ideal" relation, 191–192
Identification
  and pronoun acquisition, 383, 385
Identity. *See also* Transitivity of identity
  and proper noun acquisition, 312
Idioms
  decomposition of, 300
"I" discourse, 32
I.M. *See* Ideal Mathematician
Immutability of concepts, 179
Impaired grammars, 263–280
Importance of object
  and proper name acquisition, 357–362

Indefinite articles
in European languages, 428
Indeterminacy and "up," 23
Indexicality
and acquisition of names, 132
Indexicals, 374
acquisition, 373
and discourse error, 27
"up," 23, 24–25
Individual
and rights and obligations concept, 89
and scientific inquiry, 149
Individuation, 294, 297, 311
acquisition, 289, 322
and kind PERSON, 383
and proper names, 341, 349
and sortals, 318
Infants
cognition, xiv, 315
language, xiii, 263
Infant studies
ambiguity, 320
habituation, 318
memory, 320
spatiotemporal, 320
Inference
and cognitive categorization, 247
and conceptual categories, 249
Inference rules
and reciprocity, 83
and rights and obligations theory, 89
Inflection marking
and specific language impairment, 272
Innateness, 263
and classical categories, 234
of grammar and logic, 115
and logical competence, 110
Macnamara on, 111
and nonassociative learning, 241
and past tense formation, 234
and presyntactic learning, 290
and proper name acquisition, 338, 348, 370
and rights and obligations cognition, 90
and sortal acquisition, 315
Inner perception
and inner observation, 173
and the study of intention, 172–174
In personam rights, 79
In rem rights, 79
Intensional thinking, 197
Intention
sense of, 163
Intentionality, 209n5
and causal explanation, 106
and infant learning, 315
and meaning acquisition, 392

and pronoun acquisition, 387
Intentional objects
and semantic theory, 170–172
Intentions, 162–163
claims about nonexistence, 163–170
and conceptions, 315
first/second, 174–177
notion of, 207n3
in scientific theory, 161–207
Intention theory. *See* First intentions;
Second intentions
Internal language
truth and falsity in, 111
International Pragmatics Association, 148
Interpretant
in semiotic, 153
Interpreter
in semiotic, 153
Intuition
and conceptual categorization, 256
and formal systems, 249
and language, 179
IQ, performance, 266
Ireland
and Catholicism, 6, 7
constitution, 9n3
and ethnicity, 4, 5
nationalism, 8
and religion, 8
territory of, 3
Irish language, 1
count/mass syntax in, 428
and Irish identity, 1
Irrationality
and decision making, 100
Irrational numbers, 184
and "numbers as continuous" theory, 186
Irregular verbs. *See also* Regular verbs;
Verbs
as family resemblance categories, 228
and memory, 237
origins, 242
past tense formation by children, 234
past tense subclasses, 225
and pattern associators, 238
psychology of, 234–237
real-world origin of, 251
trans-generational changes in, 243

Jackendoff, R., 67–92
Japanese language
count/mass syntax in, 428
and impaired tense marking, 271

Kaluli language
and proper name acquisition, 304

and word learning, 302
Kaplan's theory, 373
Kearney, R., xviii, 1–8
Kind. *See also* Kind PERSON
  and child acquisition, 311
  and child knowledge, 110, 383
  infant studies of, 318, 321
  and proper name acquisition, 362–367
  and proper names, 341
  and properties of objects studies, 324
  and sortals, 311–332
Kind PERSON, 342, 383, 386
  and computer pronoun study, 398
  and pronoun acquisition, 389, 401, 402–403
Kinship. *See also* Genealogical categories
  and classical categories, 250
  and mathematical categories, 411–425
Kipke Putnam theory, 312
Knowledge
  and Macnamara's work, 67

Labeling
  and proper name acquisition, 344
  and word learning, 302
Lakoff and Johnson methodology, 77
"Lamp" example, 21
Language and nationalism, 1–9
Language disorder. *See* Specific language impairment
Language of mathematical practice, 49
Language of mathematics, 44
Language of science
  and philosophical inquiry, 150
Language of set theory, 49
Language of thought, 166
Latin
  count/mass syntax in, 428
Law
  classical categories in, 250
  and noncompliance, 81
Laws of form/function
  and categorization, 248
Lawvere, F. W., 411–425
Laxing, 225, 236
Layers of sense, 178
Learning. *See* Child language learning
Legal/judicial systems
  and conceptual categorization, 256
  roots, 83
Legal rights, 68
Legal thought
  and rights and obligations, 71
Leibniz, G., 191
Leonardo of Pisa, 184
Lexical categorization, 297

Lexical learning, 293
Lexical noun phrase, 340
Linguistic rules
  as classical categories, 229
  and specific language impairment, 268
Linguistics
  domains of, 147
  and semiosis, 151
  and semiotic, 154
  universals, 288
Linguistic semantics
  and conceptual structure, 68
  and spatial cognition, 69
Linguistic structures
  and behaviorism, 154
  interconnectedness, 26–27
  and native speaker competence, 110
Logic
  Aristotelian, 119–141
  changing scope of, 412
  classical categories in, 249
  in cognitive psychology, 109–116
  deontic, 71
  and infants, xiv
  and mathematics, 152
  and predication theory, 197
  of rights and obligations, 67–92
  and semiosis, 151
  and structures, 54–56
Logical competence
  implicit knowledge of, 110
Logical positivism
  growth of, 151
  roots of, 148
  and traditional philosophical inquiry, 149
  and verificationist theory, 156
Logical schema, 109
"Logical" subject, 203

Macnamara, J., 427–450
Macnamara, John, xi, xvi, 89, 101, 109–116, 119, 121, 134, 147, 161, 167, 170–172, 206, 221, 285, 290, 294, 311, 317, 326, 341, 343, 350, 363, 373, 383, 385, 386, 401, 412
Makkai, M., 43–65
Mapping
  of conceptual structure, 69
  of presyntactic nominals, 294–306
  of syntactical categories, 286–289
Markers
  and novel word introduction, 132–133
Mass/count nouns
  connections of, 431
Mass nouns. *See* Count/mass syntax
Material, 121

Material cause, 121
Materialism
and predication theory, 196
Mathematical categories
and cognition, 412
and kinship, 411–425
Mathematical formulation
and unconcealment, 206
Mathematical intuitions
and formal systems, 249
Mathematical laws
and regularities, 248
Mathematical logic
and syntax, 152
Mathematical practice
language of, 49
Mathematical statements
and error theories, 23
Mathematics
and conceptual sedimentation, 180
and logical positivism, 148
and number theory, 185
and semantical theory, 63
and semiosis, 151
structuralism foundation of, 43–65
Matter, 121
and entities, 120
and structure of things, 122
May and *must*
and rights and obligations expression, 70
McCall, S., 97–107
McPherson, L., 161–207
Meaning
acquisition, xii, 314, 392
and content in frames, 30
linguistic approaches, 19
and Macnamara's work, 67, 312
and misconception, 15–37
and pronoun semantics, 376
true/false approaches, 19
Meaningfulness
and logic of structures, 55
and Peano systems, 54
Means
and deliberation, 97
Members of a kind. *See also* Kind; Kind
PERSON
Aristotelian, 129
and categorization, 224
graded, 227
Memorization
and family resemblance categories, 242
and irregular verbs, 237
in Old/Middle English, 245
and specific language impairment, 268,
273, 279
and verb evolution, 244

Memory
and family resemblance categories, 242
role of, 242
and sortal acquisition, 321
Mental architecture
nonassociative, 241
Mentalese, 166
Mental representations, 165–166. *See also*
Representations
and formal systems, 246–251
and number theory, 203
and psychosemantics, 209n5
and semantics, 209n6
and specific language impairment, 268,
275, 278
Metalanguage
evolution, 115
Metaphoric rights and obligations, 77, 90
Metaphysics
and logical positivism, 150
"Metascience," 150, 151
Methodological solipsism, 162
Middle Ages
number theory in, 185
Middle English
verb changes in, 245
Middle-voice
and Aristotelian predication theory,
194
Migrant nation, 4
Mill, J. S., 109
Mind
concept of, 213n22
current discourse on, 110
"Miracle"
and realism discourse, 34
Misconception
and contemporary thought, 36
and meaning, 15–37
Modal expression
as part of semiotic, 152
Modern science
and theory generation, 149
Moiety labeling, 419
Monad, 210n11
Euclidean, 183
in number theory, 181
Moral obligations, 68. *See also* Deontic
logic
and noncompliance, 81
Moral reasoning, 67
Morphemes
and presyntactic learning, 287
Morphemic structure
and behaviorism, 154
changes in, 245
and theory of signs, 157

Morphology
  presyntactic acquisition, 299
  and proper names, 339
  and specific language impairment, 271, 279
Morris, C., 148, 149, 151, 152, 153, 155, 157
Mozart, W. A., 65n1

Names, 119–141. *See also* Naming of
    things; Proper names; Sortals
  and pronoun acquisition, 387
Naming of self, 381
Naming of things, 59, 110
  acquisition, xiii, 127, 131–135, 299, 311
  adult models for, 369
Nation
  characteristics, 2–5
Nationalism, 2, 9n1, 9n4
  contemporary, 11n8
  economic, 8
  and Ireland, 6
  and language, 1–9
  long-distance, 11n8
  and religion, 12n10
  and territory, 3, 9n2
Nationality
  and 20th-century pluralism, 10n7
Native speaker competence
  linguistic structures, 110
"Natural" authority, 89
Natural language
  count/mass syntax in, 427
  theory of, 147
Natural modes, 248
Natural numbers
  theories of, 181–189
Natural selection, 251
Nature of numbers, 50
Nature of things, 56–65
  Aristotelian, 121–124
Necessity
  and logic systems, 109
Negation
  acquisition, 113
  concept, 112
  and truth, 109–116
Negation and falsity
  child acquisition, 113
Negative numbers
  and "numbers as continuous" theory, 187
Negotiation
  and cognitive bias, 85–86
Neonates. *See* Infants; Infant studies
Neurology
  and specific language impairment, 265
Neurophysiologic function
  and probabilistic theory, 104

Neuropsychology
  and specific language impairment, 266
Newtonian science
  and probabilistic theory, 104
Nominalist philosophy, 38n12
Nominalist theory
  of predication, 196
Nominal properties
  and presyntactic learning, 291
Nominals
  acquisition, 294–306
Nominal theory
  and count/mass syntax, 434–440
  count/mass syntax, 431
Nonaddressed speech, 388. *See also*
    Addressee/speaker distinctions
  and pronoun acquisition, 394, 395
Nonassociative learning
  and innateness, 241
Noncompliance
  and social/legal/contractual rights, 80–83
Nondiscrete functions, 138
Nonessential properties, 128. *See also*
    Properties of objects
Nonexistence
  and intentions, 163–170
Nonhuman altruism, 91
Nonhuman communication
  absence of negation in, 113
Nonintentionality, 106
Nonsemantic learning system, 286
Nonunits
  learner construction of, 135
Notation
  and number theory, 183, 185
Notion of reference. *See* Referential
    acquisition
Notions of meaning
  true/false, 18
Noun phrase. *See also* Acquisition
  as child's linguistic entry, 293–304
  decomposition, 298
  from labeling model, 303
  and proper names, 341
Nouns
  acquisition, 311
  categories of, 431
  as child's linguistic entry, 291
  roots of verbs, 231
Novel words
  and markers, 132–133
  and proper name acquisition, 360–362
  and specific language impairment, 274
NP. *See* Noun phrase
Numbers. *See also* Number theory
  as continuum, 211n14

Numbers (cont.)
  and count nouns, 188
  as imagination, 186
  infant studies, 322
  nature of, 50
  philosophy of, 44
  and physical object studies, 325
  ratio interpretation as, 189
  real, 185
  and sense depletion, 180
  as sets, 45–48
  as symbols, 184
Number theory. *See also* Numbers
  Aristotelian, 181
  Babylonian, 183
  continuous, 184–186, 187
  denominations, 190
  Greek, 181, 210n9
  Hindu-Arabic, 184
  modern, 188
  Roman, 183
Numeral
  and number theory, 187

Object. *See* Physical object
Objective entities
  and rights and obligations, 78
Objectivity
  and decision making, 102
Obligations. *See also* Rights and obligations
  and hierarchy, 87
  in nonhumans, 91
Observation
  and theory generation, 148
Old English strong classes
  verb changes in, 244
Olson, D., 109–116
Oneness
  and monad theory, 182
Ontological categories, 241
Operators and propositions, 71
Original meaning, 179
Oshima-Takane, Y., 373–404
Ostension, 382
  and proper noun acquisition, 311
  and semantic theory, 63
  and sortals, 312
  and word learning, 302
Overheard speech. *See also* Addressee/
    speaker distinctions
  and pronoun acquisition, 385, 388, 395
Over-regularization, 243
  and AI past tense formation, 239
Overt subject requirement, 300
Ownership
  and social organization, 68

Paradox
  as part of semiotic, 152
Parallel distributed processing (PDP),
    237
Parent teaching, 380, 382. *See also* Adult
    models
Partial conception, 176
Particular rights, 79
Passive rights, 72
  of beneficiaries, 83
  and deontic logic, 73
Passive statements
  and concept sedimentation, 203
Passive voice
  origin of, 199
Past tense. *See also* Verbs
  and familiarity of stem, 232
  formation by children, 234
  German, 240
  and homophony, 230
  irregular verbs, 225–229
  origins of rules, 242
  and "out" plus proper names, 231
  and over-regularization, 239
  regular verbs, 229–233
  specialized and idiomatic, 228
  transgenerational changes in, 244
Pattern associators
  in computation architecture, 237
Peano systems
  properties of, 51–56
Perception
  and conceptualization, 119
Performance IQ
  and specific language impairment, 266
Personal pronoun. *See* Pronoun
Persons
  as argument of operators, 71
Perspectivalism, 148
Pet status
  and proper name acquisition, 361
"Phase" count nouns, 366
Philosophy, xii
  of linguistics, 147
  and logical positivism, 150
  of mathematics, 44
Phonology
  changes in, 245
  and impaired tense marking, 271
  and past tense formation, 226, 230
  and presyntactic acquisition, 298
  and presyntactic learning, 287
Physical objects, 121. *See also* Properties of
    objects
  and count nouns, 125
  definition, 137

individuation studies, 318–323
  and proper names acquisition, 352–357
nature of, 45
and proper name acquisition, 357–362
representation, 140
representation and individuation, 295
representation and noun phrase, 297
representation and sortal acquisition, 318
as sortal, 326
and sortal acquisition, 330
Piaget, J., xiv, 90, 91, 112, 113
Pinker, S., 221–257
Platonic philosophy, 38n12
Platonist theory
  and existence of things, 63
  and set theory, 47
Pluralization, 435
  and count/mass syntax, 427, 432
  and universal quantification, 130
Plurals
  as mass nouns, 431
PN. See Proper noun
Point of view
  and pronoun acquisition, 391
Points in a game
  as objective entity, 78
Political structure
  classical categories in, 250
Politics of language, 1–8
Positivism. See Logical positivism
Practical deliberation, 97
Pragmatics
  basis of, 148
  domain of, 147, 157
  and the language of science, 152
  and novel word introduction, 133
  as part of semiotic, 153
Pragmatism
  and conventions, 149
Prasada, S., 119–140
Predicate
  early theory of, 193–202
  as mathematical term, 199–201
  role, 301
  as symbolic logic term, 202
Predication
  Aristotelian theory of, 193–202
  modern linguistic theory, 201
  with rights and obligations, 75–77
  and sense depletion, 180
Prelinguistic representation, 316–317. See
  also Child language learning;
  Presyntactic stage; Representation
Presemantic stage, 285–306
Presyntactic stage
  acquisition, 285–305
  and American Sign Language, 289

and common nouns, 298
and coreference, 288
and creolization, 289
and determiners, 298
and distributional properties, 286–288
and home signs, 289
and innateness, 290
and linguistic universals, 288
and morphemes, 287
and morphology, 299
and naming of things, 299
and nominal properties, 291
and nominals mapping, 294–306
and phonology, 287, 298
and pronouns, 298
and proper nouns, 298, 380
and prosody, 287, 293
and quantification, 296
and question formation, 288
representation in, 316–317
and SVO order, 288
Prince, A., 221–257
Principle of application. See Application
Principle of change and rest, 122
Principle of growth and maintenance
  Aristotelian, 122–123
Principle of identity. See Identification
Principle of Induction, 52
Principle of Iteration, 52
Probabilistic theory, 103–106
Procedures
  and pragmatism, 149
Production
  and comprehension, 363
Prohairesis, 99
Promises and fulfillment
  and rights and obligations theory, 87
  and social organization, 68
Pronoun acquisition, 373–404. See also
  Pronouns
  and application, 383
  and autism, 394
  and child-directed speech, 402
  computer models, 397–401
  and consistency of error, 392
  errors in, 389
  and eye contact, 385
Pronouns. See also Pronoun acquisition;
  Second person pronouns
  earliest use, 381, 385
  features of context, 377
  grammatical aspects, 375
  learning in English, 373–404
  as presyntactic noun phrase, 298
  and proper names, 341
  semantic aspects, 375–379
  in speech stream, 380

Proper fractions
  as numbers, 184
Proper names. *See also* Proper nouns
  acquisition and noun phrase analysis, 303
  acquisition and truth/falsity judgment, 112
  and artifacts, 358–362
  child's understanding of, 344
  cultural differences, 337
  distributional properties, 347
  and kind PERSON, 386
  Macnamara theory, 171–172
  and pronoun acquisition, 396, 402
  and pronoun distinction, 392
  qualities, 348
  role, 374
  and semantics, 337–370
  universality, 337
  use and child knowledge, 110
  use and innateness theory, 115
Proper nouns. *See also* Proper names
  acquisition, 311
  and context, 379
  presyntactic acquisition, 380
  as presyntactic noun phrase, 298
Properties
  and cognitive categorization, 247
  and proper name acquisition, 345
  and proper noun acquisition, 312
Properties of objects. *See also* Physical
    objects
  accidental, 129
  Aristotelian, 122
  essential, 128
  and family resemblance categories, 253
  and sortal acquisition, 323
Propositional attitude, 162
Propositions, 38n13
  and classical categories, 236
  implicit knowledge of, 110
  and operators, 71
Prosody
  and presyntactic learning, 287, 293
  and pronoun acquisition, 380
Protestantism
  and Irish nationalism, 7
Proto-Indo-European classes, 244
Prototype, 221
  in categories, 222
Prototypicality
  and count/mass syntax, 428
  and past tense formation, 227
Psychological essentialism, 128
Psychologism, 109
Psychology, xii
  and semiosis, 151
  and the study of intention, 173

Psychosemantics, 209n5
Punishment
  in nonhumans, 91
  and rights and obligations theory, 81–83

Quantification
  and number theory, 186
  and presyntactic learning, 296
  universal, 130
Quantum mechanics
  and probabilistic theory, 103
Quechua
  characteristics of, 294
"Queerness"
  and antirealism discourse, 34
Question formation
  and presyntactic learning, 288

Racial identity
  and language, 1
"Railroad dilemma," 101, 107n3
Ratio
  new interpretation of, 189–193
  as rational numbers, 184
Rationalism
  and logical positivism, 148
Rationality
  and decision-making, 100, 102
Rational numbers, 184. *See also* Numbers
  ratios as, 189
Realism
  and antirealism, 33–37
Reality. *See also* Physical objects; Properties
    of objects
  and conceptual structure mapping, 69
  and language, 45–50
Real numbers, 185
Real-world "baptism"
  and acquisition of names, 132
Reason
  and Macnamara's work, 67
Reasoning
  role of logic in, 110
Reasons, 97–107
Reassertion
  and indexical view, 25
Reciprocal altruism, 86
  in nonhumans, 91
Reciprocity
  and rights and obligations, 83
Reference
  causal theory of, 59
Referential acquisition, 300, 312, 315,
    382
  blindness, 374
Reflective consciousness, 116

Reflex
  as second intention, 176
Regularities
  and mathematical laws, 248
Regular verbs. *See also* Irregular verbs;
    Verbs
  as classical category, 233
  origins, 242
  past tense formation, 229–233
  past tense formation by children, 234
  and pattern associators, 238
  properties, 229
  psychology, 234–237
  and rule universality, 242
Rejection concept
  acquisition, 113
Relation concept
  and sense depletion, 180
Relations
  domain and range, 191
  mathematicians' language for, 190
Relations (ratio), 189–193
Relativistic theory of meaning, 18, 24–26
  and discourse error, 27
Religion
  and deontic concepts, 93n10
  and Irish nationality, 6
  and nationality, 12n10
Renaissance
  and first intentions, 174
  number theory in, 185
Renaissance Scholastics, 174–176
Representational approach to meaning, 18
Representational discourse
  and realism/antirealism debate, 33
Representational objects, 59
Representational semantics, 22–26
Representations. *See also* Mental
    representations
  and categories, 137–138
  implicit knowledge of, 110
  and language pathologies, 275
  in scientific theory, 166–167
  and sortal concepts, 316
  and specific language impairment, 268
  unlearned, 213n21
Reproduction
  category abstraction of, 414
Resource situations
  as pronoun feature, 377, 378
Restitution, 86
Retaliation
  and noncompliance, 82–83
Retribution, 86
Reyes, G., 427–450
Reyes, M., 427–450

Rhetoric
  and semiosis, 151
Rights and obligations, 67–92
  as conceptual entities, 77–78
  and cultural learning, 90
  and deontic logic, 71
  existential nature, 78–80
  expressions, 70
  ontology, 77–78
  possibilities, 74–77
  and temporality, 79
  universality, 68, 78–80, 92n1
Roman number theory, 183
Roots of words, 231
  and specific language impairment, 272
Rules
  formal, 241
  implicit knowledge, 110, 237
  for language community, 242
  and pragmatism, 149
Rules of grammar
  and specific language impairment, 268
Rules of nature
  and categorization, 248
Rumelhart McClelland (RM) model, 237

Sameness concept, 326
Scholastics philosophers, 174–176
Science
  elements of, 149
  and intentions, 165
  laws and regularities, 248
  and logical positivism, 148, 150
  and sedimentation, 203
  and theory generation, 149
  unity of, 147–158
"Science of science," 150, 151
Secondborns
  and computer pronoun study, 400
  and pronoun acquisition, 395
Second intentions
  and first intentions, 174–177
  Scholastic definition, 175
Second language learning
  grammar in, 288
Second person pronouns
  acquisition, 396
  character of, 379
  learning in English, 373–404
Sedimentation of significance, 180
Sedimentation of theory, 202–204
Self-intelligibility, 179
Self-naming, 381, 403
Sellars-Brandom semantics, 37n4
Semantic competence
  unlearned, 370

Semantic learning
  as child's linguistic entry, 291
Semantics
  and bootstrapping problem, 285–305
  and count/mass transformations, 427–450
  domain of, 147
  and the language of science, 152
  and pronoun acquisition, 375, 383, 390
  of pronoun acquisition, 396
  and proper names, 337–370, 340
  and proper names acquisition, 367
  and semiotic, 153
Semantic theory, 58
  and intentional objects, 170–172
Semiology, 158n1
Semiosis, 151
  and epistemology, 151
  theory faults in, 157
Semiotic
  and behaviorism, 153
  place of, 154
  range of, 156
Semiotic theory, 148
  and unity of science, 151
Sense depletion, 177–181
  and "taken-for-grantedness," 179
Sense-depletion, 202–204
Sentences
  and misconceptions, 15–37
  as part of semiotic, 152
  theory of, 170–172
Sentential connectives
  and child knowledge, 110
Set of ordered pairs
  and ratio theory, 191
Set theory, 44, 45–47
  language of, 49
  and logic, 412
  and ratio interpretation, 192
  vs. category theory, 433, 435
Significance
  sense depletion through language, 180
Signification, 165
Significatum, 153
Signs
  and conceptual sedimentation, 178–179
  theory of, 147, 155
Sinfonia Concertante, 65n1
Sinn Fein, 8
Skepticism
  and contemporary thought, 36
Social cognition, 90
  and rights and obligations theory, 70
Social hierarchy
  and obligations, 87
Social institutions

  and scientific inquiry, 149
  universality of, 250
Social/legal/contractual rights
  and noncompliance, 80–83
Social organization
  and conceptual categories, 250
  and rights and obligations, 68
Social relations
  and rights and obligations theory, 70
Social rights, 68
Social sciences
  and semiosis, 151
Social status, 68
Sociology of knowledge
  and semiosis, 151
Software
  as representational object, 62
Sortals
  acquisition, 311–332
  and child knowledge, 110
  prelinguistic representation, 316
  and proper noun acquisition, 311
  relationships among, 328
Sound quantification
  in infants, 296
Spatial cognition, 69
  domain, 69
  and pronoun acquisition, 391
Spatial rotation difficulty
  and specific language impairment, 266
Spatiotemporal concept
  distinctions, 120
  domain, 69
  and sortal acquisition, 319, 323
Speaker/addressee distinctions
  computer pronoun study, 399
  and pronoun acquisition, 384, 394, 395
  pronoun acquisition, 402
  pronoun acquisition errors, 392
Specificity
  and categorization, 247
  and dyslexia, 266
Specific language impairment
  and apraxia, 266
  and brain development, 265
  and depression, 266
  family history, 2264
  grammar in, 288
  and grammar origins, 263–280
Speech. See also Addressee/speaker
    distinctions; Spoken word
  overheard
    and pronoun acquisition, 385
  rules governing community, 242
  spontaneous and acquisition theory,
    299

Speech role
and pronoun acquisition, 384, 389, 395, 402
and proper names acquisition, 347
Speech stream
and pronoun acquisition, 380
Spelke-object, 327
Spoken word. *See also* Speech
and original "significance," 180
"Standard" up discourse, 15–37
State
as nation, 2
Status
and social organization, 68
Stem of verb
and past tense formation, 230
Stevin, S., 185, 189
Stimulus patterns
and morphemic structure, 155
Straits Salish
characteristics of, 293
"Stretching" notion
as first intention, 175
Strong classes, 244
attrition, 245
morphological changes, 245
phonological changes, 245
Structuralism
in mathematics, 43–65
Structural language, 44–45
Structure of objects
and form, 122
implicit knowledge of, 110
Structures
and logic, 54–56
and Peano systems, 50–54
Stuff
names for, 119–140
Suárez, 175
Subject-predicate relationship
Aristotelian, 193
Sublexical knowledge, 268
"Substance" count nouns
and proper name acquisition, 366
Substantial form, 123
Super-antithesis dialectic, 40
Superordinate concepts, 135–139
Superordinate representation, 139
Superordination
and child learning, 223
Sup-lattice theory
and count/mass distinctions, 430
SVO order
and presyntactic learning, 288
Syllogism
Aristotelian, 441

Syllogisms
and the nominal theory, 432
validity of, 440
Symbol-grounding problem, 166
Symbolic fallacy, 166
Symbolic logic, 197
Synonymy, 152
Syntax. *See also* Count/mass syntax
and count/mass theory, 429
domain of, 147
earliest acquisition, 285
and the language of science, 152
and proper names, 339
System of signs
and sedimentation of concept, 178

"Table" argument, 120–141
"Take account" notion
in semiotic, 153, 155
"Taken-for-grantedness," 179
Tarski's notion of truth, 55, 440
Taxonomy
and family resemblance categories, 251
Temporality
and genealogical categories, 417
Tense
formation in normals, 269
formation in specific language impairment, 268
irregular past formation, 225–229
and rights and obligations, 72
Territorial nationalism, 9n2
Territory
and nation status, 3
The Chimney Sweeper poem
as representational object, 60–64
Theoretical discourse, 36
Theorizing
and first/second intentions, 176–177
Theory
definition of, 162
generation and logical positivism, 148
generation and sedimentation, 202–204
of signs, 147, 151, 155
Theta Criterion, 301
Things, names for, 119–141
Thinking. *See* Cognition
Thomas of Bradwardine, 190
Tokening, 166
Toposes, 43, 411, 413
Totalities
mathematical, 44
Transformations
mass/count syntax, 431
and passive sentences, 43
Transitivity of identity, 327, 329, 385

True/false
  deliberation, 97
  distinctions, 195
  notion of meaning, 18
Truth
  acquisition of judgment, 114
  judgment and child knowledge, 112
  judgment and innate ability, 111
  as metalanguage property, 115
  and negation, 109–116, 111
  predicates and child knowledge, 110
Truth-value
  and community discourse, 27
  and frames, 30
Twins
  and specific language impairment, 264

Ulster Protestants
  and Irish nationalism, 7
Unconcealment, 161–207
  and Aristotelian predication theory, 194–195
Underlying maps
  and mass/count syntax, 432
Understanding
  and frames, 32
Unique Entry Principle
  and past tense formation, 229
United Irish rebellion, 6
Units
  learner construction, 135
Unity of science movement, 147–158
  and logical positivism, 150
Unity of thought, 35
Universal Grammar
  and syntactic first words, 291
Universal quantification, 130
Universal substance
  and count/mass distinctions, 430
Unlearned representations, 213n21
Unwarranted/warranted distinctions, 19
"Up" discourse, 15–37
  ambiguity of, 23
  and realist/antirealist synthesis, 34

Value
  and Action arguments, 73
Value equivalence
  and exchange situations, 85
Value of money
  as objective entity, 78
Verb phrase
  of an obligation, 72
  early acquisition, 289
  of a right, 72
  and rights and obligations, 71

Verbs. See also Irregular verbs; Past tense;
    Regular verbs; Verb phrase
  acquisition, 301
  evolutions in, 243
  irregular past tense, 225–229
  origins of past tense formation rules, 242
  past tense formation by children, 234
  psychology of, 234–237
  regular, 232
  roots of, 231
  specialized and idiomatic, 228
Verificationist theory, 156
"Vishnu" example, 21
Volk concept, 3
Vowel laxing, 236
Vowels
  laxing, 225
  pronunciation, 245

Wallis, J., 186, 189
Warrant
  absolute notion of, 37n5
Warranted/unwarranted distinctions, 19
"What is it" argument, 119–141
Whole-word processing
  and specific language impairment, 278
Whorf, B. L., 1
"Wood" argument, 120–141
Word frequency
  and past tense formation, 240
Word learning
  earliest stage, 381
  mechanisms of, 302–304
  and pronoun acquisition, 404
  and sortal acquisition, 329, 331
Word meanings
  and semantic bootstrapping theory, 292
Written word
  and original "significance," 180

Xu, F., 311–332

Zabarella, J., 174
Zodiac discourse
  and conceptual disengagement, 29
Zolfaghari, H., 427–450